SECOND EDI

Alcohol, Other Drugs, and Behavior

To Tomy,
who withheld not from his heart any joy

SECOND EDITION

Alcohol, Other Drugs, and Behavior

Psychological Research Perspectives

JOHN JUNG

California State University, Long Beach

SAGE

Los Angeles | London | New Delhi
Singapore | Washington DC

For information:

SAGE Publications, Inc.
2455 Teller Road
Thousand Oaks, California 91320
E-mail: order@sagepub.com

SAGE Publications India Pvt. Ltd.
B 1/I 1 Mohan Cooperative Industrial Area
Mathura Road, New Delhi 110 044
India

SAGE Publications Ltd.
1 Oliver's Yard
55 City Road
London EC1Y 1SP
United Kingdom

SAGE Publications Asia-Pacific Pte. Ltd.
33 Pekin Street #02-01
Far East Square
Singapore 048763

Printed in the United States of America.

Library of Congress Cataloging-in-Publication Data

Jung, John, 1937–
Alcohol, other drugs, and behavior : psychological research perspectives / John Jung. — 2nd. ed.
    p. cm.
Includes bibliographical references and index.
ISBN 978-1-4129-6764-8 (pbk.)
    1. Alcoholism—Psychological aspects. 2. Drug abuse—Psychological aspects. I. Title.

RC565.J856 2009
616.86—dc22   2008054582

This book is printed on acid-free paper.

09   10   11   12   13   10   9   8   7   6   5   4   3   2   1

Acquisitions Editor:	Erik Evans
Associate Editor:	Lindsay Dutro
Editorial Assistant:	Sarita Sarak
Production Editor:	Brittany Bauhaus
Copy Editor:	Melinda Masson
Typesetter:	C&M Digitals (P) Ltd.
Proofreader:	Victoria Reed-Castro
Indexer:	Diggs Publication Services, Inc.
Cover Designer:	Gail Buschman
Marketing Manager:	Stephanie Adams

Brief Contents

Detailed Contents

3   Alcohol and Other Drugs: Use, Abuse, and Dependence   57

4   The Extent of Alcohol and Other Drug Use   81

5 Neurobiology of Alcohol and Other Drug Use

Preface

Understanding the use—and often misuse—of alcohol and other drugs is a challenging and continuing task that is critically important because of the substantial impact that substance abuse and dependence have on the psychological states and behaviors of millions of afflicted persons and those affected by them. Identifying the causes and effects of alcohol and other drug use, developing effective interventions and treatments for problematic use, and planning social policy to regulate the availability and consumption of alcohol and other drugs require research across many disciplines including psychology, neuroscience, sociology, anthropology, and public health, among the major fields.

This need for interdisciplinary investigation has hampered the growth of alcohol and other drug studies because university departments or units typically focus on a single discipline and do not even offer courses or majors on alcohol and other drugs. This neglect is particularly disturbing as major psychological problems such as mood disorders, aggression, stress, poor achievement at work and in school, and problems related to physical health and illness, to name a few, are investigated without little awareness of—or attention to—the significant role played by alcohol and other drug use. Many of the problems studied by clinical, social, industrial, and personality and other psychologists turn out to be either "causes" or "effects"—or both—of abuse of alcohol and other drugs.

Concern about this situation led to the first edition of *Alcohol, Other Drugs, and Behavior,* to provide a resource for instructors of courses in the field that presented theory and research from different disciplines examining important psychological aspects of substance use and abuse including epidemiological, neurobiological, genetic, developmental, personality, social, and clinical research.

The approach and emphasis in this revision are the same as in the first edition. An overview of the psychological aspects of alcohol and other major drugs presents central concepts, reviews representative research findings, and provides critical evaluation of the evidence. The focus is on alcohol and, to some extent, other licit drugs such as nicotine and caffeine. *Alcohol, Other Drugs, and Behavior* provides a selective and detailed presentation of recent important studies on key topics selected to illustrate important issues, concepts, and theories rather than to provide exhaustive coverage of topics.

Attention is first directed toward research on the much larger population of users of these substances who apparently do not have substance-use-related problems, although they may develop them eventually. The majority of adults use alcohol to varying degrees, with no apparent problems. Similarly, although there is evidence that they incur harmful health consequences, most smokers manage to function ably in their daily activities. And, while the number of illicit drug users is more difficult to obtain for obvious reasons, it is apparent that a sizeable minority of the population uses different illicit drugs in ways that do not create problems for the users or others. Research and theory about why people begin to use alcohol and other drugs are important in their own right and are valuable in understanding the development of problematic use of alcohol and other drugs. The last third of the book focuses on the causes and correlates of substance abuse and dependence as well as methods of recovery from and the treatment and prevention of these problems.

The sequence of topics in the revision departs slightly from that of the first edition. The overview of major theories has been expanded and moved to Chapter 2 to quickly give students a big picture of the diversity of conceptual approaches before discussing definitions, epidemiological evidence, neurobiology, and heredity-environment issues in Chapters 3–6. To provide better continuity, the location of Chapters 7, 8, and 9 on basic or general psychological processes such as cognition, mood, aggression, sensory motor behavior, and family interactions has switched from the first edition with Chapters 10, 11, and 12 that examine individual differences related to age, gender, and minority groups including coverage of alcohol issues related to both racial/ethnic and sexual minority groups. The remaining Chapters 13–16 maintain the organization of the first edition and update the coverage of recovery, treatment, relapse, and social policy.

Major additions in the revision include more coverage of the extent and correlates of use of licit drugs such as nicotine and caffeine, the extent and correlates of simultaneous and concurrent polydrug use, and comorbidity of substance use disorders and psychiatric disorders. There is expanded coverage on correlates of subtypes of alcohol abuse and dependency. Finally, more attention is directed toward longitudinal analyses, which offer more insight into psychological processes than the prevalent cross-sectional studies. One example is research on the causes and correlates of different developmental or age trajectories of alcohol use and abuse. A second example is the use of event-specific correlations or intra-individual data instead of the dominant reliance on aggregated or group average data to determine outcomes of substance use.

An important goal of the first edition that is retained is to challenge students to become "educated" consumers, rather than passive or uncritical recipients, of research information. Although most students will never conduct scientific research on alcohol and other drugs themselves, they need and benefit from some knowledge of the strengths and weaknesses of different research methods used to obtain evidence so they can evaluate research findings. For example, much psychological research in the field of alcohol and other drugs is correlational, describing patterns of relationships among substance use patterns, situational contexts, outcomes, and demographic and psychological characteristics of users. As valuable as such evidence is, it leads to many unwarranted conclusions about causality. In this book, students are urged to consider and formulate alternative explanations for research findings and to propose and design new research that can help rule out alternative explanations.

Alcohol, Other Drugs, and Behavior can be used as either a primary or a supplementary text for upper-division and graduate-level college courses in several disciplines, including basic and applied social sciences such as psychology and sociology, educational psychology, applied human services such as social work and criminal justice, applied health-related fields such as nursing, health science, and physical therapy—and, of course, alcohol and other drug counseling. Students in professional fields such as law and medicine where critical evaluation about research on the psychological aspects of alcohol and other drug use is valuable will find the book worthwhile.

ACKNOWLEDGMENTS

I thank the students in my Psychology of Alcohol and Other Drugs classes over the past decade for providing encouragement and invaluable "field-testing" of the materials that formed the basis for this revised edition. I am indebted to the advice and encouragement of many individuals who have helped improve this book immensely. Douglas Parker and Betty Deckard, my colleagues at California State University–Long Beach, read portions and offered many helpful suggestions and valid evaluations that helped me improve the presentation.

Finally, I want to acknowledge the outstanding support that SAGE Publications, Inc., offered. Jim Brace-Thompson was enthusiastic about the rationale for the first edition, recognizing the value of a psychological perspective and the emphasis on the strengths and weaknesses of evidence obtained by different research methods, which set it apart from the traditional model of textbooks in this field. His successor, Erik Evans, has continued to support this approach in the revision. SAGE lived up to its name by providing wise editorial advice and judgment from Lindsay Dutro and Brittany Bauhaus that guided me through some of the difficult choice points every author faces during the many stages of writing a textbook.

The author and SAGE gratefully acknowledge the contributions of the following reviewers:

Gregory A. Blevins, *Governors State University, Addiction Studies*

Marsha Dopheide, *Monmouth College*

Cheryl Hardy, *Columbia College*

Stanley Jackson, *Westfield State College*

Craig Nagoshi, *Arizona State University, Department of Psychology*

Dr. Maryse Nazon, *Chicago State University and University of Phoenix, Chicagoland Campuses*

Diane Sevening, *University of South Dakota, School of Medicine/Division of Health Sciences, Alcohol/Drug Studies*

Roger Shipley, *Texas Woman's University, Department of Health Studies*

C. Robin Timmons, *Drew University*

James C. Woodson, *University of Tampa*

Psychology of Alcohol and Other Drugs

Here's to alcohol: the cause of, and solution to, all of life's problems.

—Homer Simpson

Booze, pot, dope, coffin nails, horse, crack, bennies, reds, coke, speed, ice, Ecstasy, speedball, junk—the list of colorful names for psychoactive drugs is a long one that continues to grow. Throughout recorded history in most societies, people have discovered and used substances capable of altering normal experiences and consciousness. Most of these substances have come from natural sources such as plants, seeds, mushrooms, yeast, and grains, but in modern times synthetic products such as heroin and amphetamines have been added to the list. For a variety of reasons ranging from curiosity to boredom to stress, people are motivated to seek variations in mood, going from high to low as well as from low to high activation. Psychoactive drugs are a potent means of producing these mood states. In addition, many of them, including alcohol, nicotine, hallucinogens, opioids, and marijuana, have been used for medicinal and healing purposes.

Alcohol, tobacco, marijuana, cocaine, heroin, amphetamines, hallucinogens, crack—the list of psychoactive drugs used by humans throughout history is, as already noted, rather extensive. In the present book, we will consider all chemical substances as drugs if they are voluntarily consumed for social and recreational purposes to alter mood and conscious states as opposed to being used medicinally to treat, for example, physical and psychological disorders.

Using this definition, alcohol would be classified as a "drug," contrary to a longstanding distinction between alcohol *and* drugs held by the public as well as many professionals working in the field of addictions. This separation of alcohol and other drugs into their own domains appears at the highest levels of the federal government, as reflected by the creation in the early 1970s of separate governmental agencies to deal with funding for treatment and prevention research on alcohol (National Institute on Alcohol Abuse and Alcoholism) and drugs (National Institute on Drug Abuse). This separation of alcohol from other drugs has perpetuated the failure of many research, treatment, and prevention activities to acknowledge the reality that many users of psychoactive drugs started with—and usually continue—the use of alcohol. A more accurate understanding of substance use needs to recognize the central role that use of alcohol plays in the development of the use of other drugs.

FOCUS AND GOALS OF THIS BOOK

This book will examine the major legal psychoactive drugs of current concern to society due to their widespread use and/or because of the potential harm to the users and to society that may occur from excessive use. Considerably more coverage will be devoted to alcohol because for most American adults it is the psychoactive drug of choice, consumed by more people, in larger volume and on more frequent occasions, than any other drug. Our society approves of—and even expects and encourages—drinking in many situations.

Many prescription and over-the-counter drugs such as sedatives, tranquilizers, stimulants, and analgesics developed and intended for medical treatment unfortunately are also abused for nonmedical purposes. These drugs include barbiturates (e.g., Mebaral® and Nembutal®) used to treat anxiety, tension, and sleep disorders; benzodiazepines (e.g., Valium®, Librium®, and Xanax®) prescribed to treat anxiety, acute stress reactions, and panic attacks; stimulants (e.g., Dexedrine® and Ritalin®) used to treat depression, attention deficit hyperactivity disorder, and narcolepsy; and opioids (e.g., OxyContin®, Darvon®, Vicodin®, and Demerol®) prescribed to alleviate pain.

Although these are legal drugs for medical purposes, their increasing use to produce psychoactive rather than therapeutic outcomes represents a serious problem for society because of the risk of addiction to these substances and the dangers when their use is combined with use of alcohol. In 2006, 16.2 million Americans age 12 and older had taken a prescription pain reliever, tranquilizer, stimulant, or sedative for nonmedical purposes at least once in the past year (Substance Abuse and Mental Health Services Administration [SAMHSA], 2007). However, research on the misuse of these drugs is beyond the scope of this book, which focuses on alcohol and other drugs that were developed primarily for psychoactive effects.

Alcohol is more thoroughly researched than other drugs, a result in large part of the significant population of drinkers. Another justification for a focus on alcohol is that, like tobacco, it is widely assumed to be a **gateway drug**, which may lead to subsequent as well as concurrent use of illicit drugs. In contrast, relatively less research on illicit drugs is available due to the difficulty of identifying and recruiting large and representative samples of illicit drug users. Most of the research on illicit drug use comes from treatment samples, which may not be generalizable to other users. Unlike legal drugs on which controlled studies are available, there are major ethical and legal barriers to conducting experiments with illicit drugs so that findings from these studies are limited to correlational data, which do not permit firm causal conclusions.

A secondary goal is to show some of the similarities and differences among these drugs in their origins and their effects. The norms of use patterns will be compared across major demographic factors such as age, sex, and social class and/or ethnicity. By comparing different major drugs, we hope to identify some common factors underlying the causes and effects of drug use. Issues, methods, and theories of treatment of drug abuse and dependency will be examined.

A Psychological Emphasis

A psychology of alcohol and drugs needs no more justification than we require for the study of any other behavior whether it be watching movies, reading books, attending church, gambling, or working. People use alcohol and other drugs, and it is important to identify and understand the factors that influence such behaviors, especially since alcohol and other drug abuse and dependency develop for some users, with destructive and harmful consequences for them and others around them. This book will examine the central role of psychological causes, correlates, and effects of alcohol and other drug use and abuse. Understanding how adverse outcomes develop and how to treat them calls for a psychological approach. Furthermore, a psychology of alcohol and drug use is essential for designing effective methods for intervention and prevention of drug problems.

Psychology Precedes Pharmacology

Multiple factors are involved in alcohol and other drug use. First, the substance must be physically available. A complex process involving cultural, historical, legal, political, and economic factors determines the extent to which a drug is available in a particular society at a given time.

As we grow up, we form many beliefs and attitudes about alcohol and other drugs. We learn that these substances can exert powerful changes on our conscious states, behaviors, and experiences. Such beliefs may increase the desire to use drugs for some people. Without these psychological factors first leading to drug use, the potential pharmacological effects that drugs can produce on the nervous system to affect behavior and experience cannot occur. Subsequently, these pharmacological processes exert a reciprocal influence on the psychological processes and behavior of the user.

And although alcohol and other drugs may be readily available, not everyone will be attracted to them. Those more concerned about the risks and dangers of drugs than enticed by their possible benefits will be less likely to use them. Psychological beliefs and attitudes again are a critical determinant, in this case preventing the use of drugs. Without certain beliefs, motives, and personality characteristics, a person will not use a particular drug even if the opportunity is present. Understanding why people seek drugs, why they may not seek treatment, and why relapse is so common are important tasks of a psychology of drugs. Thus, psychology may help in developing methods for prevention of drug use by identifying what motivates users to engage in drug use as well as what deters nonusers.

A psychology of drugs is also useful for developing methods to convince users to want to reduce or stop their use of drugs. Thus, quitting—or at least the attempt to quit—may work best when it is perceived to be a choice rather than a mandate. But fear of failure may prevent some from even making the attempt. Such efforts may be more likely if positive consequences or alternatives are offered. These psychological considerations may be needed to design effective methods for improving success in quitting. Psychology can help reduce these setbacks by identifying the conditions, such as psychological state and social and physical environment, that are associated with relapse.

HISTORY OF DRUGS IN AMERICA

An overview of the history and background of major psychoactive drugs currently used in the United States is essential for understanding contemporary alcohol and other drug issues and problems. Prior to about 1900, although many states passed drug control legislation, there were no federal laws against any psychoactive drugs in the United States, and such drugs were widely available and consumed. How this situation changed and what determined which drugs were regarded as more dangerous than others and thus warranted penalties for possession and use is an intriguing tale of politics, prejudice, and propaganda more than one informed by persuasive scientific evidence.

Alcohol consumption prior to the 20th century was quite extensive, and heavy levels of use were commonplace. The immigrants who settled the American colonies in the late 17th century came from European countries with long histories of alcohol use, and they continued their drinking-related cultural traditions and practices after they settled. In colonial America, drinking was a widespread, generally tolerated, and accepted activity. Alcohol was not only widely available as a beverage but also served as a home remedy for many medicinal purposes. Drunkenness was commonplace, but it was not considered a social problem for the society of that era (Gusfield, 1963). However, from the early 1700s to the mid-1800s, drunkenness and alcohol problems increased, generating greater societal disruption as the nation changed from an agrarian economy to an urban industrial society.

The widespread social problems such as poverty, crime, and disorderly public conduct created by excessive use of alcohol led to reform movements by religious groups such as the Quakers and many Protestant denominations. Organized efforts against alcohol were formed, including the American Temperance Society in 1833. As the movement gathered strength, by the late 1800s calls for **temperance** yielded to efforts to eliminate alcohol entirely as organizations such as the Woman's Christian Temperance Union (WCTU) and the Anti-Saloon League led the fight against the evils of alcohol, tobacco, and other drugs (Gusfield, 1963).

Tobacco was, in contrast, completely unfamiliar to Christopher Columbus in 1492. However, the Native Americans who met him had been chewing and smoking tobacco in pipes for a long while. By the time the American colonies were settled a little over a century later, smoking tobacco was also an established and acceptable drug for the early European immigrants.

Morphine was widely used during the Civil War on the battlefield as an anesthetic for the wounded and dying. Unfortunately, many who survived their battle wounds with the aid of morphine later succumbed to morphine addiction. Interestingly, cocaine injections were initially used to treat morphine withdrawal before it came to be recognized that cocaine itself was an addictive substance. The widely used patent medicines, supposedly cure-alls for "whatever ails you," contained alcohol and cocaine. They became drugs of abuse, especially by women.

American cities suffered increasingly from child labor, excessive drug use, crime, and violence, leading social reformers to launch vigorous moral reform campaigns. Many of the poor urban living conditions stemmed from or were exacerbated by alcohol and other drug abuse, but economic oppression, prejudice, and social injustice were also contributory factors. In addition, some substance abuse may have been the effect, rather than the cause, of poverty and oppression. Nonetheless, political and social pressures encouraged a focus on drugs as the major culprit of society's ills, and the social reformers helped make many of them illegal in the early part of this century.

In contrast to the 19th century when drugs were unregulated for the most part, state and federal legislation to control drugs increased in the 20th century. Thomas Szasz (1985), a prominent psychiatrist and critic of many social policies restricting choice, contended that drugs served as a convenient scapegoat for the social ills of urban life. He observed that a double standard was used in setting drug policy and suggested that because alcohol and tobacco are so well ingrained in Christian and English-speaking cultures, we regard them as good while drugs such as opium and marijuana, which originated in foreign countries, are viewed as bad. Thus, consider the different labels and terms used in connection with legal and illegal drugs: "People who sell liquor are retail merchants, not 'pushers'; and people who buy liquor are citizens, not 'dope fiends.'" The same goes for tobacco, coffee, and tea (Szasz, 1985, pp. 52–53).

Table 1.1 identifies some major developments in drug legislation and other aspects of drug control in America over the course of the 20th century. One of the earliest drugs to be controlled in America was opium, banned in San Francisco in 1875. At the federal level, the Pure Food and Drug Act was passed in 1906 due to increasing concern about impurities from opioid drugs in foods and patent medicines. It did not make drugs illegal but required labels to specify the contents.

In 1914, the **Harrison Narcotic Act** was passed as part of an international effort to reduce the widespread and increasing use of opiate drugs as well as cocaine (Musto, 1987). This law did not make these drugs illegal but required that heroin and morphine be prescribed by a physician. During this era, the federal government was prevented from passing national laws by the doctrine that the states held the rights to make these laws for themselves. The federal government adroitly circumvented this problem by exercising its powers to raise tax revenues and placing a tax on opiates.

The restrictions against opium may have been a statement against the Chinese as much as the drug (Gusfield, 1963). The opium tax was directed toward the Chinese in America, the heaviest users of opium. In the late 1800s, Chinese immigrants were regarded as the "yellow peril" because they provided a large, industrious, and cheap source of labor against which the White population could not compete. Public attitudes were extremely hostile

TABLE 1.1   Historical timeline of national events, concerns, and federal drug control legislation.

Year	National Events and Concerns	Federal Drug Control Legislation
1900s	◆ Temperance Movement	Pure Food and Drug Act (1906) led to decline of patent medicines
1910s	◆ World War I	Harrison Narcotic Act (1914) taxed and regulated distribution and sale of narcotics
1920s	◆ Attitudes of nationalism and nativism and fear of anarchy and communism were tied to regulation of alcohol and drugs	Volstead Act (1920): national alcohol prohibition
1930s	◆ Onset of Depression Prohibition repealed (1933)	Federal Bureau of Narcotics established (1930) Marijuana Tax Act (1937)
1940s	◆ Drug interest dwindled due to concerns with events in Europe World War II (1941–1945) By the end of World War II, the public considered drugs to have no major societal impact	
1950s	◆ Korean War Tolerance of drugs associated with unpatriotic attitudes in early 1950s	Boggs Act (1951): harsher penalties for narcotics and marijuana offenses Narcotic Control Act (1956) increased penalties for narcotics and marijuana offenses
1960s	◆ Treatment, rehabilitation efforts rose Psychedelics (e.g., LSD) appeared; marijuana use rose; amphetamines and barbiturates became street drugs; rise in heroin use led to methadone maintenance programs Vietnam War	Mental Retardation Facilities and Community Mental Health Centers Construction Act (1963): federal support for local treatment of addiction classified as mental illness Surgeon General's report on smoking (1964) Drug Abuse Control Amendments (1965) Bureau of Drug Abuse Control (1966) Bureau of Narcotics and Dangerous Drugs (1968)
1970s	◆ Rise in cocaine use	Controlled Substances Act (1970) Drug Abuse Office and Treatment Act (1972) Drug Enforcement Administration (1973)
1980s	◆ Crack arrived in inner cities AIDS problem arose	Comprehensive Crime Control Act (1984) Anti-Drug Abuse Act created Office for Substance Abuse Prevention (1986) and Office of National Drug Control Policy (1988)

Year	National Events and Concerns	Federal Drug Control Legislation
1990s	◆ Cigarettes recognized as addictive	Crime Control Act (1990)
	Tougher drug control and legislation	Food and Drug Administration (FDA) rules cigarettes to be "drug delivery devices" (1995)
2000s	◆ Increased methamphetamine abuse	U.S. Supreme Court rules FDA has no authority to regulate cigarettes as drugs (2000)
		Anabolic Steroid Control Act of 2004
		Combat Methamphetamine Epidemic Act of 2005

Source: Adapted from *Drugs, Crime, and the Justice System: A National Report From the Bureau of Justice Statistics (NCJ-133652),* by the Bureau of Justice Statistics, 1992, Washington, DC: U.S. Government Printing Office.

toward this easily identifiable ethnic group, with its differences in cultural customs and physical appearance. Similarly, some of the opposition to cocaine was related to prejudices toward Blacks in the South during the Reconstruction period after the Civil War. Unsubstantiated beliefs that cocaine-using Blacks might become violent toward Whites aroused fear. Restrictions imposed in the 1930s against marijuana were similarly tied to violence and crimes committed by immigrant Mexican workers under the influence of marijuana in the Southwest, a perception for which there was flimsy evidence (Musto, 1987). Despite these attempts to control these drugs, after World War I, the use of opioids and cocaine expanded rapidly in the United States. Physicians were still able to prescribe narcotics to patients, but this practice soon was halted as law enforcement agencies began to arrest physicians and druggists for use of opiates even for medical purposes.

The temperance movement, led by such groups as the WCTU, waged vigorous moral crusades against the harms of alcohol to society. Alcohol was made illegal in 1920 with the Volstead Act although Prohibition was repealed in 1933 and considered a failure as a means of controlling alcohol use (Musto, 1987). Many who voted in favor of Prohibition were actually unopposed to drinking. Their vote was a means of attacking the powerful saloons and the alcohol industry. Drinking continued illegally with so many people violating the law that it was unworkable, creating other problems such as crime and corruption associated with the underground manufacture and sale of alcohol.

In the 1920s, several federal agencies were established to control narcotics, culminating with the formation of the Federal Bureau of Narcotics in 1930. Its commissioner, Harry Anslinger, was given strong authority over drug interdiction and law enforcement with the goal of stemming the widespread and increasing narcotics problem. The term *narcotic* (meaning "sleep inducing") was later dropped since it is inaccurate. Nonetheless, people still refer to "hard drugs," both depressants and stimulants alike, as "**narcotics**." Also during this period, there was recognition of a need for treatment of drug addicts, and hospitals were started in some federal prisons in the mid-1930s.

It might be only coincidental that as alcohol was made less available during Prohibition, Americans increased their use of marijuana. Possibly, when a widely used drug declines in availability and/or acceptance, other drugs increase in popularity to fill the void. Thus, after alcohol was outlawed, immigrant Mexican laborers introduced marijuana during the 1920s to the southwestern United States (Musto, 1987). They smoked joints made with leaves from one variety of marijuana plant, *Cannabis indica*.

However, by 1933 the promise of Prohibition failed, and the nation was ready to repeal it. With the return of alcohol, law enforcement officials increasingly depicted marijuana as evil and harmful. Incorrectly classified as a narcotic, it was portrayed to the public as "the killer drug," as newspapers linked its use to violence and crime. Its harmful effects were promoted in propaganda films of the era such as *Reefer Madness*. This hysterical atmosphere led to the Marihuana Tax Act, passed in 1937, which placed controls on marijuana use by imposing a tax on its sale or purchase.

By the mid-1930s, a grassroots movement for helping alcoholics eventually led to the formation of **Alcoholics Anonymous (AA)**, a mutual support and recovery group that grew worldwide (White, 1998) and will be discussed in more detail in Chapter 14. Similar organizations, including Narcotics Anonymous (NA) and Cocaine Anonymous (CA), soon developed and employed a similar program for recovery from other drugs.

One of the leading alcohol researchers of his time (Jellinek, 1960) proposed the **disease conception of alcoholism**, which was based in part on surveys of AA members and observations at AA meetings. The disease conception of alcoholism was an advance because it offered an alternative to the prevailing moral model that held that alcoholics drink because they lack willpower. The disease model called for a nonjudgmental response and compassionate treatment of alcoholics just as patients with medical diseases receive. Alcoholics were seen as unable to control the disease and in need of expert medical attention. A central tenet of Jellinek's model was that the disease involves a **loss of control** over drinking. Once drinking starts, the alcoholic is unable to stop. Instead of condemning the alcoholic, this view had a major influence on improving the way society viewed **alcoholism** as well as other drug dependencies that continues to this day. Alcoholism was now seen as a treatable problem rather than a hopeless condition.

Drugs designed originally for medical purposes, such as barbiturates and amphetamines, began being widely dispensed by physicians. Before long, these drugs, some of which could readily be made at home, were being abused for nonmedical purposes and became part of the growing drug problem.

During World War II, drug problems declined, perhaps due to the priorities of the war effort and concerns with national defense. The end of this conflict saw a resumption of illicit drug use, leading the federal government to pass stiffer penalties and mandatory jail sentences for offenders during the 1950s. Heroin use, dormant since the Harrison Narcotic Act in 1914, started to increase mainly in lower socioeconomic areas. Prices started to rise as well, leading dealers to adulterate the drug by mixing in fillers to meet the demand and increase profits.

During the 1960s, social activism in civil rights and other empowerment movements led to major social changes. This activism involved many young people and was accompanied by widespread use of many drugs, including marijuana and hallucinogens popularized by the experiences described by Timothy Leary, a Harvard professor who was a pioneer in the experimental use of LSD-25. Due to the influence of "hippies" and "flower children" during this era, alternative lifestyles flourished, including experimentation with drugs.

At the same time, changes in social attitudes, social policy, and drug legislation occurred with a de-emphasis on a law enforcement "lock them up and throw away the key" philosophy toward drug offenders to a focus on treatment and rehabilitation of drug abusers. In 1962, the Supreme Court viewed addiction as a disease, not a criminal activity in itself. The Mental Retardation Facilities and Community Health Centers Construction Act of 1963 facilitated rehabilitation of drug abusers. The Narcotic Addict Rehabilitation Act of 1966 regarded opioid abuse as a disease. The disease conception encouraged a medical treatment rather than an incarceration approach to drugs.

The heroin problem increased throughout the 1960s. The almost pure supply of inexpensive heroin in Southeast Asia led to a high rate of heroin use by American military personnel during the Vietnam War. As this war wound down, the threat of so many young American military personnel coming back from Vietnam with heroin addiction was a real concern. The danger turned out to be less serious than originally expected as most of the opiate users in Vietnam were able to quit once they returned to their own communities in the United States (Musto, 1987).

One explanation is that the resumption of their former lives reduced their psychological need to use heroin, but it is also possible that the unavailability of pure or high-grade heroin in the United States was a factor. Heroin use became perceived as a problem primarily of the urban poor living in the inner city. The dangers of heroin use were compounded with the advent of AIDS in the 1980s. Heroin users were at high risk for HIV infection from the shared needles used for their injections.

President Richard Nixon launched a "war on drugs" in 1971 and passed significant legislation changing how drug possession, sale, and use were handled in the United States. Law enforcement through the Drug Enforcement Administration (DEA), the successor in 1973 to the Federal Bureau of Narcotics, became the approach for controlling substances, replacing the excise tax method of earlier eras (Musto, 1987). Drug interdiction to cut off the supply of heroin from Turkey became a priority. Greater efforts were made to provide treatment facilities as well.

The Comprehensive Drug Abuse Prevention and Control Act of 1970 (Public Law 91-513) was a landmark piece of federal drug legislation that overturned or replaced the existing laws. It authorized the creation of two separate federal agencies for the development of research, prevention, and treatment programs: the National Institute on Alcohol Abuse and Alcoholism (NIAAA) in 1971 to address alcohol issues and the National Institute on Drug Abuse (NIDA) in 1973 to deal with illicit drug problems.

A new approach for classifying drugs, or a **schedule of drugs**, was implemented. Instead of banning classes of drugs and setting penalties for their use based on their chemical structure and pharmacological effect, the **Controlled Substances Act** passed by Congress in 1970 classified all drugs except nicotine and alcohol by two functional criteria: the drug's medical use and the drug's potential for abuse. Using only those two criteria, all drugs were placed in one of five categories, each with different penalties based on its relative benefits and potential for harm.

As shown in Table 1.2, Schedule I drugs are those such as **marijuana** (cannabis) and **hashish** that have little or no medical use but a high potential for abuse. Campaigns exist to legalize the medical use of marijuana, but it is not yet widely accepted. Schedule II drugs

TABLE 1.2 Schedule of drugs based on effects, medical use, and abuse potential.				
Drugs are scheduled under federal law according to their effects, medical use, and potential for abuse.				
DEA Schedule	**Abuse Potential**	**Examples of Drugs Covered**	**Some of the Effects**	**Medical Use**
I	Highest	Heroin, LSD, hashish, marijuana, methaqualone, designer drugs	Unpredictable effects, severe psychological or physical dependence, death	No accepted use; some are legal for limited research use only
II	High	Morphine, PCP, codeine, cocaine, methadone, Demerol®, Benzedrine®, Dexedrine®	May lead to severe psychological or physical dependence	Accepted use with restrictions
III	Medium	Codeine with aspirin or Tylenol®, some amphetamines, anabolic steroids	May lead to moderate or low physical or high psychological dependence	Accepted use
IV	Low	Darvon®, Talwin®, phenobarbital, Equanil®, Miltown®, Librium®, diazepam	May lead to limited physical or psychological dependence	Accepted use
V	Lowest	Over-the-counter or prescription compounds with codeine, Lomotil®, Robitussin A-C®	May lead to limited physical or psychological dependence	Accepted use

Source: Adapted from the Controlled Substances Act, by the Drug Enforcement Administration, 1989, Washington, DC: U.S. Department of Justice.

have some medical use but also a high potential for abuse, such as barbiturates, cocaine, and amphetamines. Schedule III drugs have medical use and a high potential for abuse and include morphine and codeine, which is found in prescription cough medicine and is highly addictive. Schedule IV drugs such as sedative-hypnotics and minor tranquilizers have therapeutic value but less risk of abuse and dependency than Schedule III drugs. Finally, Schedule V drugs such as antibiotics have high medical use but little potential for abuse and often do not require a prescription.

In the 1960s, as mounting research called into question the seriousness of the harm produced by marijuana, its use began increasing, especially among college students and lower socioeconomic groups. By 1969, due to the widespread use and growing public sentiment, the government lowered the penalties for marijuana below the level associated with other Schedule I drugs.

A shift in attitudes toward more tolerant positions occurred, as exemplified by the recommendation in 1973 by the National Commission on Marijuana and Drug Abuse that marijuana possession for personal use be "decriminalized." The commission's view was partly based on its conclusions that alcohol and tobacco presented more serious problems. However, concern over the sharp increase in marijuana use, especially among high school students by the 1970s, prompted President Nixon to reject the commission report and its recommendations.

Federal drug policies were more relaxed under Nixon's successor, President Gerald Ford. He used a containment approach to drugs aimed to limit damage in contrast to Nixon's all-out-war approach. A peak in marijuana use occurred in 1973, and a continuing decline was seen until it began regaining popularity in the 1990s. Before long, however, new problems began to surface. Cocaine use, which had peaked in the 1920s, began to increase again in the late 1960s, especially among the affluent and upwardly mobile, fueled by supplies from Colombian drug cartels. Initially viewed as a drug with few dangers, its popularity reached a peak in 1982 before declining (Gfroerer & Brodsky, 1992), according to retrospective data from the National Household Survey on Drug Abuse between 1962 and 1989. A new upsurge in cocaine use occurred during the late 1980s before subsiding in the 1990s, spreading to the streets and to underclass users as well. **Crack cocaine**, a more potent smokeable form of the drug, arrived on the scene in 1985 and caused great concern, especially in the inner cities. Heroin also made a comeback in the mid-1970s as new sources of less expensive heroin from Mexico replaced the curtailed supplies from Turkey.

President Jimmy Carter supported efforts to decriminalize marijuana use in the late 1970s, but these and other attempts to decriminalize possession of less than an ounce of marijuana did not succeed. The politics of drug policy shifted back under the administration of President Ronald Reagan starting in the early 1980s. He renewed Nixon's strong antidrug campaigns with crusades against illicit drugs such as cocaine, heroin, and marijuana. In Nancy Reagan's terms, the solution was to "just say no." The Anti-Drug Abuse Act of 1986 allowed for almost $4 billion, primarily for law enforcement, toward a renewed war on drugs. Stiffer penalties were imposed for illegal drug use and trafficking, with mandatory minimum jail time imposed for drug offenses.

Drug use continued to increase, leading to more arrests as a zero-tolerance attitude was promoted by a law-and-order administration. In contrast, increased beliefs that drug addiction was a disease rather than a crime led to campaigns for drug treatment rather than incarceration. More and more businesses, realizing that drug-abusing employees were costly in terms of absenteeism, lower productivity, and workplace accidents, had the incentive to provide drug treatment coverage to employees as part of their benefits. In the 1980s, the private sector aggressively promoted inpatient treatment programs and created an addiction treatment industry that grew rapidly.

But by the late 1980s, faced with rapidly increasing costs and rising demand for treatment of alcohol and drug abuse and dependency, employers that paid health care providers for treatment moved to contain costs by instituting managed care (Institute of Medicine [IOM], 1990). The outpatient treatment industry was no longer viable. Insurance providers required preutilization approval for access to services from health maintenance organizations (HMOs) and preferred provider organizations (PPOs). This approach is governed more by efficiency and costs than by considerations of therapeutic effectiveness. Managed care led to reduced access to inpatient care and increased reliance on less expensive outpatient services and briefer therapy (Steenrod, Brisson, McCarty, & Hodgkin, 2001).

Under the first President George Bush, the Anti-Drug Abuse Act of 1988 established the White House Office of National Drug Control Policy (ONDCP), which was charged with formulating policies, priorities, and objectives for national drug control. Its aim was to reduce illicit drug use, manufacturing, and trafficking; drug-related crime and violence; and drug-related health consequences.

Toward the end of the 20th century, the war on drugs faced new challenges. Pressures to decriminalize marijuana and to allow medical marijuana for terminally ill patients increased. Other drugs of abuse developed. Increased abuse of anabolic steroids received more attention as world-class athletes were discovered to be using them to increase muscle strength. A bill, H.R. 4658, the Anabolic Steroid Control Act of 1990, added these substances to Schedule III of the Controlled Substances Act. The growing problem of methamphetamine abuse, aided by the ease of clandestine home production using over-the-counter cough medicines, led to the Combat Methamphetamine Epidemic Act of 2005 as a subsection of the Patriot Act. It restricted the amount of ephedrine and pseudoephedrine one could purchase in a specified time period and required that these products be stored securely.

This brief overview of American drug policies shows how directions can shift back and forth over history depending on the political climate. History seems to have repeated itself, with the strong fears of cocaine triggering a broad antidrug atmosphere as they did during the early 1900s (Musto, 1987). The history of drug attitudes and policies from the early years of the nation to the present involves a struggle among three types of values: libertarian, medical, and criminal (IOM, 1990). During the colonial period, a laissez-faire individual-freedom approach seemed adequate. Government involvement with drugs was mainly to impose taxes. As industrialization developed and the nation grew more urbanized, however, the dangers of excessive drug use became recognized as a growing social problem, and medical approaches to treating drug problems developed. The third approach, criminalization, more prevalent in the 20th century, emphasized punishment of drug users and legal restriction of availability and consumption of drugs.

ORIGINS OF LICIT DRUGS

Depressants

Alcohol

Most civilizations throughout recorded history have used alcoholic beverages like beer and wine, derived from the fermentation of grains and grapes, respectively. They have been used in rituals and ceremonies as well as for healing purposes since ancient times. The ancient

Egyptians honored a god, Osiris, who cultivated the vine and created wine and beer. Hippocrates, the Greek father of medicine, is known to have recommended wine for its therapeutic properties. The Greeks paid homage to wine through Dionysus (known to the Romans as Bacchus), the god of wine, with celebrations and festivities. Fermented rice wines were known in the Far East as well as in ancient China and India.

In the 10th century, the Arabians developed the practice of distillation, a process by which the alcohol from fermented beverages is extracted by being boiled until it vaporizes. Then, the alcohol is recaptured after condensation to create more potent beverages with higher concentrations of alcohol.

All alcoholic beverages contain the same active ingredient, ethyl alcohol or **ethanol**. The percentage of ethanol in the total volume ranges from low levels of around 3%–4% in beer and 12%–14% in wines to higher levels of 45%–50% in distilled spirits such as liquor (Maisto, Galizio, & Conners, 1995).

Alcoholic beverages are consumed for many different reasons, including celebrations, social conviviality, coping with negative emotions, and feelings of intoxication. Sometimes alcohol is consumed to disinhibit or release suppressed feelings, and sometimes it is used to calm or reduce tension and anxiety. The effects can vary with the dose consumed, with low levels generally releasing inhibitions and higher levels often producing drowsiness, lack of concentration, and lack of coordination.

Today, alcohol, in its various beverage types, has annual sales of billions of dollars in the United States. After the end of Prohibition in 1933, the rate of alcohol consumption grew rapidly, although there has been a slight decline in the sale of distilled liquor in the past decade. Drinking is widely promoted and advertised. Although societal attitudes toward drunkenness have become more negative, drinking is generally accepted in our society.

Stimulants

Nicotine

Tobacco is America's homegrown drug. It had already been used for a long time by Native Americans when Columbus arrived in 1492. **Nicotine**, a potent but highly toxic central nervous system stimulant, comes from the dried tobacco plant, *Nicotiana tabacum*, which is native to North America (McKim, 2007).

About 8 mg of nicotine exists in a cigarette, but the amount delivered to the smoker ranges from 0.1 to 0.9 mg depending on specific brands. Cigarettes involve more than nicotine, containing over 2,500 different compounds, with cigarette smoke involving over 4,000 compounds. In addition, as there are no legal restrictions on additives to cigarettes, wide variations exist in what manufacturers add to their products, including sugar, preservatives, and taste improvers.

When first introduced to Europe, tobacco was used for various medicinal purposes. It later became a major source of revenue for the American colonies in trade with England, and tobacco use became widespread, so much so that King James I came to ban smoking. During the early 1700s, tobacco use continued in England but in the form of snuff. Users held a pinch of powdered tobacco near the nose for sniffing, usually until a sneeze was induced, a method that never was popular in the United States where smokeless or chewing tobacco developed as an alternative to smoking. As a stimulant, nicotine increases alertness and concentration by activating the central nervous system, but it also can paradoxically facilitate relaxation on other occasions, as its effects are biphasic and reverse direction at higher doses.

By the mid-1800s, temperance organizations in America were already condemning the moral and health hazards of smoking as its addictive propensities were recognized. But the development in 1881 of a machine that could manufacture cigarettes rapidly and substantially increased the availability and use of cigarettes. Advertising and promotion, which even had doctors testifying to the relaxing benefits of smoking, aided its growth as a major industry. As in the case of alcohol, smoking survived these early attempts to restrict its use. It was not until the 1960s, with increased awareness and scientific evidence about the health risks of smoking, that growing regulation of many aspects of cigarette sales and use in public settings gained widespread popular support.

Caffeine

The methylxanthines include stimulants such as caffeine, typically consumed in coffee, tea, cocoa, and carbonated soft drinks (McKim, 2007). Beans of the coffee bush in Ethiopia date back more than a thousand years. Coffee was thought to have medicinal value, but it seems to increase alertness and energy. It became highly popular in England when coffeehouses proliferated there in the 1600s to such an extent that in 1674 some women published a petition against coffee in which they protested the waste of time and money by men for a "little base, black, thick, nasty bitter stinking, nauseous Puddle water . . ." (*The women's petition against coffee*, 1674, ¶ 6).

Although methylxanthines, which stimulate the central nervous system, are widely consumed, they are not commonly viewed as "drugs." An estimated 80%–90% of American adults consume caffeine in some form daily with a mean daily level of over 200 mg, and many children consume it in soft drinks. Large doses may cause insomnia, jitteriness, and tension. Discontinued use may be associated with headaches, fatigue, and lowered alertness.

Use of these beverages does not interfere with holding a job, produce intoxication, or cause automobile accidents. In fact, coffee is commonly regarded as a stimulant, one that may improve alertness, cognitive processes, and work productivity. Coffee drinking is also closely tied to social gatherings, meals, and work breaks. Perhaps there are no laws or penalties associated with its use because it does not produce the major social problems associated with alcohol. Unlike nicotine, health concerns about caffeine have not yet produced legislation restricting its use. The coffee industry has responded to concerns about insomnia, headaches, and stomachaches by successfully promoting decaffeinated alternatives for consumers.

ORIGINS OF ILLICIT DRUGS

Opioids

Opium

Opium comes from the resin of poppy flowers found in the Middle East. As a central nervous system depressant, opium sedates and dulls responsiveness. Pain is deadened, coughing is suppressed, mental alertness is reduced, and drowsiness is induced (McKim, 2007).

From early Egyptian and Greek accounts, opium was widely used for a variety of medical problems, primarily for its analgesic, or pain-killing, capacity. Islamic cultures utilized opium as well and spread its use to India and China where it began to be smoked, leading to widespread opium addiction. Eventually the Chinese government banned opium, but the British persisted in trading opium to the Chinese to pay for their tea, which was highly popular in Britain. Finally, the opium wars were waged between the two nations in the mid-1800s with the victorious British acquiring the rights to Hong Kong in 1842, which they held until 1997.

The British, however, did not avoid their own addiction problems with opium. Leading 19th-century English poets such as Elizabeth Barrett Browning and Samuel Taylor Coleridge who fell under its spell romanticized the drug by associating it with creative powers. The use of opium in England expanded after Thomas De Quincey published a literary account in 1821, *Confessions of an English Opium Eater*, in praise of the dreamlike states experienced from his drinking laudanum, a mixture of opium with alcohol (Hart, Ray, & Ksir, 2006).

Morphine

In Germany, the active ingredient in opium was identified in 1803 and named morphine. It is about 10 times as potent as opium itself. That fact, coupled with the development of the hypodermic needle in 1853, which allowed for faster delivery of the drug, made it a powerful medical resource. As an analgesic, it found immediate and widespread application during several major wars of the mid-19th century; during the American Civil War, for example, morphine addiction became known as the "army disease" because of the high rates of such addiction among wounded soldiers (McKim, 2007).

Heroin

A synthetic compound, **heroin**, was developed in 1874 in Germany based on morphine. Originally thought to be free from addictive propensities, it came to be recognized as a dangerous drug, with about three times the potency of morphine. Heroin users typically inject the drug directly into their veins with hypodermic needles to produce a stronger effect from the faster delivery of the drug to the brain (Beck & Bargman, 1993). On the street, it is typically found as a white or brown powder and commonly called "smack," "H," "skag," and "junk."

Methadone

Another synthetic drug, methadone, has properties similar to heroin but is less potent, slower acting, and available in tablet form for daily oral use. Due to these features, methadone has less potential for creating addiction or dependency (Hart et al., 2006). Methadone has been used since the 1970s to help heroin abusers deal with their withdrawal reactions when they try to stop using heroin. This method of using one drug to treat another drug is controversial but was widely used in England until abuses in the control of access to the drug became common in the 1960s.

Stimulants

Cocaine

Coca shrubs found in the Andes mountains of Peru are the source of **cocaine**, a potent stimulant extracted from their leaves. Cocaine use leads to short but immediate bursts of energy, strength, and pleasure (McKim, 2007). Its discovery dates back to before the Incas, who chewed its leaves during ceremonies and religious activities until their Spanish conquerors banned its use in the 1500s. It was not until the 1800s that the drug became widely used in Europe for its energizing and stimulating effects on well-being. Extraction of the active ingredient from the leaves provided a more potent form, one that could be sniffed or injected intravenously. Cocaine became widely used in patent medicines that could be obtained without prescription.

This alkaloid is made into a paste by being heated with hydrochloric acid to produce cocaine hydrochloride (Maisto et al., 1995). Cocaine is approximately only 80%–90% pure because of manufacturing impurities. Drug dealers often "cut" their supply by using cheaper substances such as talcum powder, amphetamines, and other fillers until street cocaine is less than 50% pure (Hart et al., 2006).

Cocaine can be snorted through the nasal passages, intravenously injected, or taken by mouth. It gradually loses its potency so that the frequency and dosage must be increased to maintain the pleasurable feelings. Higher doses can be directly inhaled by snorting cocaine powder through nasal passages, injecting it in veins, or smoking it to produce greater stimulation than is possible from the low levels obtained from chewing the leaves. However, high doses may also lead to paranoialike responses, irritability, and hallucinations.

By boiling cocaine in a mixture of strong alkali and explosive solvents, "pure" cocaine is "freed' from many of the impurities. Cocaine without its water-soluble component, or "base," is called freebase. Since it is not water soluble, freebase must be vaporized and inhaled to be absorbed by the body.

Crack Cocaine

Another form of cocaine, crack, developed in the mid-1980s, is more concentrated since the water base of cocaine hydrochloride is boiled out by being heated with a baking soda solution and does not require dangerous explosive solvents. The product is a crystal or rock, a more concentrated form of the drug that is more dangerous since it can be smoked, producing a stronger effect than cocaine powder, which is used intranasally (Maisto et al., 1995).

Amphetamines

About the same time that use of cocaine declined in the 1920s, another group of stimulants with similar effects, **amphetamines**, became popular. These synthetic drugs were developed for medicinal purposes such as the treatment of asthma and colds or the induction of weight loss through appetite suppression (McKim, 2007). Their chemical structure is similar to that of ephedrine, the active ingredient in an ancient Chinese herb, *ma huang,* which stimulates the sympathetic nervous system. From the 1930s through the early 1960s, amphetamines were routinely prescribed for treating a variety of clinical problems, including childhood hyperactivity, obesity, depression, and narcolepsy, a sleep disorder.

However, the recreational use of amphetamines soon increased, especially since home-made versions can be made illegally. Amphetamines, as drugs of abuse, were commonly referred to by colorful street names such as "speed," "uppers," "dexies," and "bennies." Amphetamines began to be used illegally for the heightened experiences they produce. Intravenous injection produces stronger effects than does taking them in capsule form, but this method increases the likelihood of dependence on the drugs (Maisto et al., 1995).

Methamphetamine

Before long, stronger variants of amphetamines were developed. Methamphetamine, or "meth," the most potent form, is readily available with or without a prescription, and its effectiveness lasts several times longer than that of amphetamines. Users smoke, swallow, snort, or inject the drug.

A stronger, smokeable form of methamphetamine comes in a crystal rock and is commonly called "crank," "crystal," or "ice" because of its resemblance. The effects of ice resemble those of cocaine but are longer lasting, with highs that last from 2 to 24 hours. Following use, a crash or depression may occur and can last as long as 3 days, during which erratic, violent behavior may occur (Hart et al., 2006).

Until the late 1980s, the illicit use and manufacture of methamphetamine was concentrated in California, but increased use has since occurred, especially in the Midwest (Anglin, Burke, Perrochet, Stamper, & Dawud-Noursi, 2000). Homemade methamphetamine is easily "cooked up" using pseudoephedrine or ephedrine, the active ingredients in over-the-counter cold medicines.

MDMA

A synthetic or "designer" drug receiving much publicity in recent years, MDMA (methylene-dioxymethamphetamine) acts simultaneously as a stimulant and a hallucinogen. "**Ecstasy**," its glamorous street name, is derived from both methamphetamine and amphetamine. Also called the "love drug," it is often used during "raves," all-night underground dance parties with techno music that involve extensive drug use. Ecstasy stimulates the central nervous system so that users experience hallucinogenic effects such as time and perceptual distortion and enhanced energy. Using Ecstasy at raves increases the risk of exhaustion and dehydration, and there have been reported cases of fatalities from heat stroke.

Barbiturates

Barbiturates, a class of synthetic drug used to relieve anxiety and facilitate sleep, were developed in Germany in 1864. Introduced into the United States around the early 1900s for medical purposes, they come in many different types that vary in duration of action. Phenobarbital is a long-acting form, which might calm but not induce sleep, whereas a shorter-acting form such as secobarbital would bring about sleep (Maisto et al., 1995). Unfortunately, the faster-acting forms are capable of inducing euphoria and became widely abused street drugs during the 1950s. Clinical use involves the dangers of eventual rebound effects, including impaired sleep, as well as carries the potential for fatal over-doses (McKim, 2007).

Benzodiazepines

Synthetic antianxiety drugs called benzodiazepines became available in the 1960s and are much safer than barbiturates, which fell into medical disfavor. The best known examples, chlordiazepoxide (Librium®) promoted in 1960 and diazepam (Valium®) introduced in 1963, were widely prescribed. Librium®, with a long duration and slow onset, was relatively safe, but Valium®, with a more rapid onset, had greater risk of users developing dependence (Maisto et al., 1995).

One benzodiazepine, flunitrazepam, which started to receive much attention in the 1990s, is commonly called "roofies." Marketed as **Rohypnol**®, it is available only by pre-scription for the short-term treatment of insomnia, as a sedative hypnotic, and as a preanes-thetic medication. It is not manufactured or approved for medical use in the United States but is smuggled into the country because of its low cost and growing popularity among young people. The drug is often taken with alcohol or after cocaine ingestion, possibly to reduce the discomfort experienced after coming down from highs produced by cocaine. The drug has received much notoriety and been dubbed the "date-rape drug" because of cases in which men have provided beverages secretly spiked with this colorless, odorless drug to women to render them incapable of resisting sexual advances. Victims may experience anterograde amnesia, a state in which they cannot remember experiences while under the effects of the drug. It may lead to reduced blood pressure, drowsiness, visual disturbances, dizziness, confusion, gastrointestinal disturbances, and urinary retention. Some users experience an increase in excitability or aggressive behavior, although the drug is classified as a depressant. The Drug-Induced Rape Prevention and Punishment Act of 1996 was enacted to combat this misuse.

In the 1990s, increased abuse of GHB (gamma hydroxybutyrate), a central nervous system depressant known on the street as "liquid Ecstasy," "easy lay," "vita-G," and "Georgia home boy," occurred mainly among body builders for fat reduction and muscle building.

Sedative-Hypnotics

Cannabis

Marijuana is extracted from the dried flowers and leaves of hemp, *Cannabis sativa,* a plant found in about 2800 BC in ancient China, where it was used for medicinal as well as recreational purposes. From China, it spread to many parts of the world, but it was not until the 19th century that marijuana was introduced to Europe (Maisto et al., 1995). The plant also provided hemp, which was important as a source of rope for sailing ships but is no longer a major need in modern ships. The American colonists used the plant for its fiber and also found medicinal applications, but there were no social problems associated with its use during colo-nial days. During the 1920s, it received a bad reputation because its use by immigrant Mexican laborers in the Southwest was perceived to be associated with violence and crime (Musto, 1987).

Marijuana, colloquially referred to as "grass," "weed," and "pot," is usually smoked in cigarettes ("joints") or in pipes. Users seek the drug for its relaxing and euphoric effects at low levels. Perceptions of time and space can be altered, as with hallucinogens, but high doses can produce hallucinations, panic, and anxiety. The primary active ingredient in marijuana is delta-9-tetrahydrocannabinol (Δ-9 THC), one of 60 cannabinoids found in the plant. Hashish, a related and much stronger drug, is made from the resin of the hemp plant (Maisto et al., 1995).

Hallucinogens

There are many drugs classified as **hallucinogens**, even though it is not clear what constitutes a "hallucination," the altered experience associated with use of these drugs. The best known example is lysergic acid diethylamide, more commonly known as LSD-25. This synthetic drug became popular during the drug atmosphere and hippie lifestyle of the 1960s, especially due to the publicity created by its chief proponent, Timothy Leary, a Harvard University professor who championed its use as a means of self-discovery and attainment of personal insight and growth (McKim, 2007).

LSD-25 comes in different forms that can be swallowed, as sugar cubes, as capsules, or in blotters. A variety of reactions to psychedelic drugs such as LSD-25 can occur, ranging from aesthetic and mystical journeys to frightening and anxiety-producing "bad trips." LSD-25 is made from alkaloids extracted from the ergot molds found on grains. When breads made from infected grains were eaten during famines in medieval France, violent illnesses involving burning sensations, convulsions, and thought disturbances occurred that have been likened to the psychoactive effects of LSD-25.

Mescaline is another hallucinogen that produces effects similar to those of LSD-25. It is derived from the peyote cactus of the Southwest that the Aztecs used in ceremonies for centuries. Sacramental use of mescaline in rituals is legal in the Native American Church. Psilocybin, a hallucinogen less potent than LSD-25, is obtained from some species of North American mushrooms long regarded as sacred by Aztecs in Mexico and Central America.

A synthetic drug, phencyclidine, commonly called PCP, is of recent origin. It was developed as an anesthetic for medical purposes but became a street drug that was popular during the 1970s because of its ability to create trancelike states. PCP gained notoriety because it was often used to lace marijuana cigarettes given to unsuspecting smokers, which reputedly led them into violent and criminal behaviors.

Anabolic Steroids

The term *steroids* refers to a class of drugs (Hart et al., 2006) available legally only by prescription to treat conditions that occur when the body produces abnormally low amounts of testosterone, such as delayed puberty and some types of impotence. Steroids are also prescribed to treat body wasting in patients with AIDS and other diseases that result in loss of lean muscle mass (McKim, 2007).

For decades, competitive athletes and others have secretly used anabolic steroids to enhance physical performance and improve physical appearance. Much attention is directed toward this form of "cheating," but one survey on the Internet of male users found most were not athletes (Cohen, Collins, Darkes, & Gwartney, 2007) and that the primary motivations of steroid use are to increase skeletal muscle mass, strength, and physical attractiveness. Anabolic steroids, whether taken orally or injected, are typically used in cycles of weeks or months (referred to as "cycling") rather than continuously—that is, abusers take multiple doses of steroids over a period, stop for a period, and resume. Anabolic steroid abuse, however, can lead to serious health problems, some irreversible.

SOME CENTRAL QUESTIONS

In view of the widespread and significant harmful potential impact of drugs, both licit and illicit, on human behavior, the study of the causes and effects of alcohol and drug consumption is an important undertaking. Following is a preview of some of the broad issues and questions about the psychology of alcohol and drugs that will be raised in the rest of this book.

Why Do People Use Alcohol and Other Drugs?

Theories about the psychology of alcohol and drug use—those held by laypersons as well as those formulated by researchers—are examined in Chapter 2. Use norms and values differ widely across subpopulations and fluctuate over time within a given society. These social norms and values associated with the use of different drugs will be examined first since they provide a general context in which individual motives operate.

Different moods and motives precede and accompany the use of psychoactive substances. For example, people who drink alcohol, smoke cigarettes, or take illicit drugs do so when they feel sad, depressed, or lonely. But they also drink, smoke, or "do drugs" when they feel happy, elated, and sociable. Psychoactive drugs are typically used in group settings, but they are also used when people are alone. Social pressure to conform to norms may lead some individuals to engage in drug use to avoid appearing "unsociable." Social factors such as family and parental drug attitudes and behavior influence an individual's drug use. After gaining experience using a drug, some may continue to use while others may decide to stop using for many different reasons. Personality is a factor in whether or not an individual takes drugs, as well as their effects. Following the use of alcohol and other drugs, some people become aggressive and hostile, others show avoidance or detachment, and still others seem more relaxed and friendly.

Some drugs are illegal in a given society, although the status of a specific drug may change over time. Most people will avoid the use of drugs when they are illegal mainly because they are afraid of punishment such as fines and imprisonment. Others may avoid them because they fear their addictive reputation. Yet for others the illegal status or addictive properties of drugs may enhance their attraction. Being illegal, they are often expensive and also difficult to obtain readily. Despite these barriers, some may use drugs such as morphine or heroin to relieve pain. Other illicit drugs such as cocaine and amphetamines may be used to produce heightened sensations and stimulation.

How Is Alcohol and Other Drug Use Defined and Measured?

Before we can answer many questions about alcohol and other drug use, we must reach some agreement on the units of measurement in describing use. Chapter 3 deals with the conceptual and methodological issues involved in defining and measuring substance use. How is *use* distinguished from *abuse* or from *dependence?* What criteria distinguish abuse from dependence?

How Many Alcohol and Other Drug Users Are There?

Chapter 4 focuses on survey findings from general household populations that can identify nonusers and users, as shown in Figure 1.1. These surveys determine the relationship of demographic characteristics to the amounts and frequencies of use of different types of drugs for specific lengths of time.

Figure 1.1 also shows that, among users, a sizable minority has developed or will eventually develop major difficulties associated with use that often lead to adverse consequences, including loss of friends, family, jobs, and self-respect. These users may become dependent on these substances and possibly move on to more dangerous drugs.

Among those with such problems, some will become part of a clinical population (see Figure 1.1). They will seek—or be required to accept—some type of substance abuse treatment. In later chapters, we will see that this clinical population differs in many characteristics from the general population, and it is important not to assume that generalizations based on one population necessarily apply to the other. Additionally, there are those who might benefit from treatment but who do not seek or find it. The closing part of Chapter 4 presents evidence on the rates of substance-related abuse and dependency and associated problems.

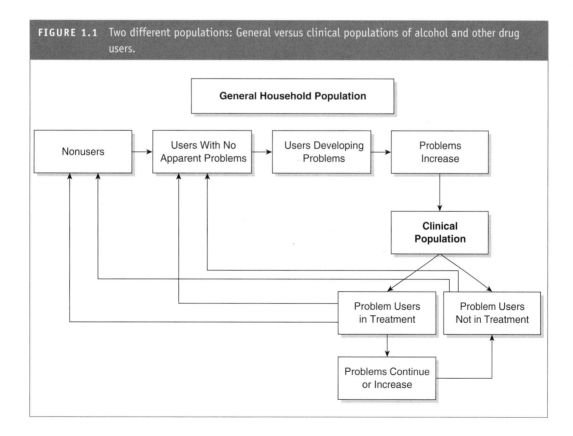

FIGURE 1.1 Two different populations: General versus clinical populations of alcohol and other drug users.

How Do Alcohol and Other Drugs Affect the Body?

A basic understanding of the psychopharmacology and neurobiology of drugs is presented in Chapter 5. Alcohol and other drugs, to have any effect, must reach the brain centers that control our behavior. Depending on how they enter the body, many factors, including characteristics of the drug and of the user, affect the speed with which they circulate through the body and reach the brain and the rate and means by which they are removed from the body.

Alcohol and drugs affect neurophysiological processes that are the underlying basis of our affective feelings, moods, and emotions as well as our cognitive and motivational processes. Information about these processes is essential for the study of how drugs achieve their effects and helps explain why drugs are used.

What Is the Relative Role of Heredity and Environment?

Considerable debate occurs over the roles of heredity and environment in the development of alcohol and drug use. Chapter 6 examines evidence on the relative influence of genetic and environmental factors as well as their joint or interactive effects on drug use and consequences. Findings from this research have implications for developing strategies that may hold the best chances for successful intervention, treatment, and prevention of alcohol and drug problems.

What Are Major Psychological Effects of Alcohol and Other Drugs?

The next three chapters look at how alcohol and other drugs affect basic psychological processes such as mood, cognition, emotion, motivation, and sensory motor skills (Chapter 7); aggression, violence, and sexual behavior (Chapter 8); and family processes and social interaction (Chapter 9). These effects can also be viewed as determinants of subsequent drug use, acting to either sustain, increase, or reduce it.

What Individual Differences Exist in Alcohol and Other Drug Use?

The next three chapters examine theories about factors responsible for the relationship of important individual differences to alcohol and other drug use patterns as described in Chapter 4, specifically age (Chapter 10), gender (Chapter 11), and race/ethnic background (Chapter 12).

How Can Alcohol and Other Drug Use Disorders Be Treated?

Abuse of many drugs is a major threat to well-being, creating serious physical and mental health problems. Chapters 13–15 deal with recovery and treatment methods and issues. How effectively can individuals stop drinking, smoking, or using drugs on their own? How successful are mutual help groups such as AA in promoting recovery? How effective are different professional treatment methods for dealing with alcohol and drug dependence? Why do relapses occur in many cases, and how can they be prevented?

How Can Alcohol and Other Drug Use Disorders and Related Problems Be Prevented?

Chapter 16 describes psychological approaches to the primary prevention of alcohol and other drug abuse. What types of social policy and control of drug availability and consumption are effective in ameliorating the harmful effects of drugs in our society? How effective are education, taxation, and legislation in controlling drug use to acceptable levels and preventing and reducing harmful consequences?

For each of these broad questions and issues, there have been numerous approaches, theories, and explanations involving physiological, psychological, and sociological factors. In all likelihood, multiple factors act concurrently, sometimes with counteracting influences, to produce the observed differences in drug use behavior, its consequences, and the degree of success in treatment, recovery, and prevention. Theories that focus on single causes will probably not prove as successful as explanations that consider the interplay of multiple determinants ranging from the physiological to the psychological to the sociological.

Summary

Throughout history, humans have used a variety of psychoactive drugs, including depressants, opiates, stimulants, and hallucinogens. In this chapter, a review of the nature and origins of major psychoactive drugs was presented, with emphasis on the history of use in the United States. Political factors, economic conditions, religious movements, social activism, social policy, drug legislation, and urbanization have all influenced the extent and conditions of both licit and illicit drug use.

Alcohol is the drug most widely used by most American adults and in many cases may lead eventually to illicit drugs. We will use research, concepts, and theories developed from the study of alcohol use as a basis for comparison when examining conceptions and evidence about less frequently studied drugs. Use of this strategy is not to deny the seriousness of involvement with use of other drugs, especially those that are illegal. Many who drink alcohol without any reservations would never think of experimenting with illegal drugs. Use of alcohol is generally tolerated by all but the most moralistic members of society. Understanding the psychological causes, correlates, and effects of alcohol use may contribute to the study and analysis of illicit drug use.

Major questions about alcohol and other drugs for research investigation include the following: Who uses alcohol and other drugs, and in what patterns? What are the effects of these drugs on the body, behavior, and psychological processes? What motivates the use of alcohol and other drugs? What is the relative role of heredity and environment on drug use and its consequences? How do individual differences affect use? Which users develop use-related problems, and how can individuals afflicted with drug abuse, dependency, and use-related problems be treated? How can these problems be prevented in future generations?

Stimulus/Response

1. It is instructive to compare the history of social policies that regulate the use of alcohol and various drugs in the United States with those of other societies to get a broader perspective. For example, examine the history of drug policy on heroin in the United Kingdom versus in the United States. Or compare the drug policies on marijuana in the Netherlands with those in the United States. Based on your own views of human behavior, which drug policies in different countries do you think would be most effective or ineffective? Explain your rationale. Do you think adoption of policies from one country would work the same way in another country? Why or why not?

2. Attempts to prohibit alcohol in the United States as well as in many other countries have generally failed. What do you think are major reasons for this lack of success? What alternative approaches to reducing the problems of alcohol can you suggest that might be better accepted?

3. The U.S. social cost of alcohol abuse in 2000 was nearly $160 billion, according to a 1992 report from a federal agency (Office of National Drug Control Policy, 2001). How do you think this determination of the economic costs of alcohol abuse to society is calculated? What categories of outcomes do you think should be considered a "cost to society"? What problems do you see with the criteria used to define the costs of drugs to society? Do you think alcohol and drugs have any psychological benefits to society? What do you think are some of the economics benefits of alcohol and drug use to society? How would one quantify the benefits of alcohol and drug use?

4. Most alcohol and other drug research examines only the negative effects and consequences of their use. Do you feel this imbalance reflects the reality that the negatives exceed the positives, or do you think it reflects a bias of researchers? If you think there is this bias, what reasons can you offer to explain its existence?

5. Many assume that licit drugs are less harmful than illicit drugs to most individuals. However, because there are so many more users of licit than illicit drugs, the aggregate harm in the nation as a whole is much higher from the use of licit drugs. Do you think society should spend more effort on preventing and treating problems stemming from alcohol and cigarette addiction or in preventing the use of illicit drugs?

Theories of Alcohol and Other Drug Use

A "Layperson" Theory
Psychological Theories
Mediators, Moderators, and Direct Causes
Theories of Smoking

Theory of Caffeine Use
Illicit Drug Theory
Summary
Stimulus/Response

There is nothing as practical as a good theory.

—Kurt Lewin

Why do people consume alcohol and other psychoactive drugs? This is a complex question, and the answer will differ across individuals, circumstances, and specific drugs. Theories involving factors as diverse as curiosity, taste, physical sensations, rebellion, peer pressure, social reward, and coping with stress and anxiety, among others, have been proposed as explanations for initial as well as continued use. Psychological theories are abstract formulations developed to organize or explain the relationships among different variables that affect some behavior of interest, as Figure 2.1 suggests. Formal theories about why people use alcohol and other drugs tend to focus on specific or limited aspects of these behaviors. To be useful, theories must generate predictions that can be tested with new observations, which either support or call into question the theory's validity. If most predictions are upheld, only minor revisions or additions may then be made to the theory, but if too many contradictory findings occur, other theories may need to be developed to better explain the overall evidence.

However, one can easily get lost in the forest of theoretical formulations or be overwhelmed by tons of detailed data collected to test them. Therefore, prior to examining some major theories of alcohol and other drug use, it may be helpful to first consider what a layperson's view of the origins and maintenance of alcohol and other drug use might look like. Such

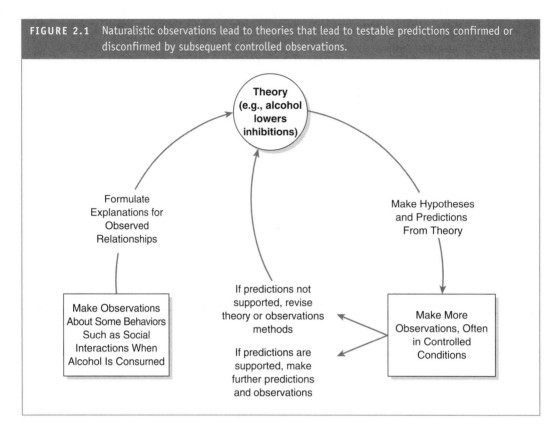

FIGURE 2.1   Naturalistic observations lead to theories that lead to testable predictions confirmed or disconfirmed by subsequent controlled observations.

a broad overview of the nature of alcohol and other drug use will help identify the major characteristics of alcohol and other drug use that psychological theories must account for.

A "LAYPERSON" THEORY

The use of any drug, licit or illicit, does not just happen. Drug taking occurs in a context of social, cultural, and historical factors that set boundaries and limits for how, where, when, and the quantity and frequency with which drugs are used. Beginning use levels of alcohol and other drugs may be low as the uninitiated to these substances generally find they are unpleasant in taste. But over time, the user, especially of licit drugs, "acquires the taste." In addition, increased social acceptance and/or social pressure motivate drinking alcohol, smoking cigarettes, and drinking coffee.

As depicted in Figure 2.2, sociocultural factors such as societal conditions, cultural values, and drug-specific beliefs, attitudes, and practices provide a stage on which other more immediate factors operate to determine individual use of alcohol and other drugs. How and when we acquire our beliefs, attitudes, and expectations about alcohol and drugs as we grow up is important for understanding our use of these substances.

FIGURE 2.2   Multiple factors lead to the initiation and subsequent levels of alcohol use, cessation, and resumption.

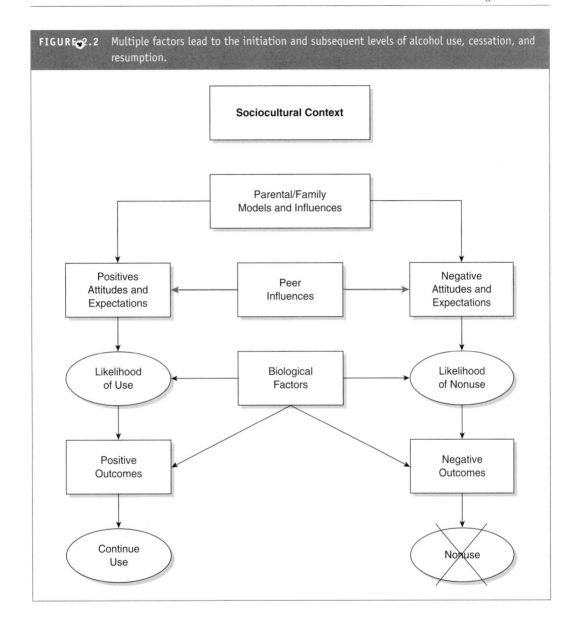

Children, long before they first use any psychoactive drugs, have countless opportunities to observe adults, often parents and relatives, using various drugs. They observe the use of legal substances such as alcohol and cigarettes in many contexts stemming from varied motives and with different consequences. In addition, they view media portrayals of alcohol and other drug use in movies and on television. While less likely to directly observe the use of illicit drugs, they still form conceptions about the psychological and behavioral effects of such drugs from media. Thus, prior to their first use of any psychoactive drug, children will have already formed expectations and conceptions, right or wrong, about many of the effects and consequences of using these drugs.

Children also observe that many adults consume alcohol, cigarettes, and coffee in positive contexts—for example, during work or study breaks or in settings where friends gather to relax and socialize. They also may notice that people do not take popular drugs separately but frequently use two or more substances such as alcohol, cigarettes, and coffee on the same occasion and often in conjunction with food. Wide use of alcohol and, to a lesser extent, cigarettes occurs on many happy occasions such as parties and celebrations.

Prior to ever using drugs themselves, children also observe the darker side of drug use. They witness people who consume too much of a drug behave in ways that create problems for themselves and for others around them. Opposite effects may occur as drug use may render the user boisterous or sullen, aggressive or compliant, and hostile or overfriendly. Excessive use can produce intoxicated states that lead to impaired physical coordination, alertness, cognitive function, and emotional control, as well as interpersonal problems.

Despite their observations of how people behave during and after drug use, children are generally not deterred from wanting the future opportunity to use drugs themselves. The positive images that society has led them to associate with drug use entice them. They discount or ignore the many negative images related to drugs that they also have encountered. They believe that they, unlike some others, will be able to control their own drug use and thus enjoy the pleasures but avoid the painful consequences.

Children realize they are expected to wait until adulthood to drink or smoke. But they observe that some peers begin to use alcohol and tobacco before they attain the legal age. Some adolescents may regard these peers as "cool" or sophisticated because they seem grown-up. Initiation into licit drug use represents a rite of passage from childhood into adult status in many societies. Once the legal age is attained, use of alcohol is no longer disapproved but actually expected, as with abstainers who receive social pressure to drink.

Licit Versus Illicit Drugs

The distinction between licit and illicit drug use is important as theories about major licit drugs such as alcohol, nicotine, and caffeine may be incomplete for understanding illicit drugs such as cocaine, marijuana, and heroin. Although the pharmacological effects of many illicit drugs may be similar to those of some licit drugs insofar as altering mood states and behavior, the social consequences of using each drug are markedly different. The use of legal drugs in moderate amounts is acceptable—even expected—for adults, although cigarette smoking is no longer tolerated and promoted as it was a generation ago. In contrast, illegal drug use is generally condemned and can lead to major fines and imprisonment.

Legal drugs are often consumed publicly by a wide cross section of the adult population. If we use an iceberg to represent the size of the user population, most of the iceberg is above the surface and visible for legal drugs. But for illegal drugs, we see only the "tip of the iceberg," and the size of the unseen portion is unknown because illicit drugs are used by a small segment of the population. Due to the hidden nature of illicit drug use, less evidence is available about the extent to which such use leads to problems among all users. Aside from any health risks from a specific drug, using an illicit drug carries with it the risk of heavy penalties such as fines or imprisonment, which are absent or minimal for licit drugs.

Most people who use licit drugs will not cross the line into illicit drug use, but virtually all illicit drug users have experienced—and continue to use—licit drugs. Theories of illicit drug use must explain why some individuals assume this additional risk and how this risk might affect outcomes of use.

In view of the social importance attached to licit drug use, it is not surprising some combination of curiosity, rebellion against authority, and peer influence might tempt some youth to try the forbidden fruit. Even though all adolescents are well aware of the substantial physical, psychological, and social risks involved with the use of many drugs before they have ever used them, the promise of rewarding and exciting experiences counters the threat of adverse physical, social, and (in some cases) legal consequences associated with the use of alcohol and other drugs.

Beliefs that getting "high," "drunk," "bombed," or "smashed" from drugs can help one forget his or her problems, feel more attractive, be witty, be sophisticated, be humorous, and have self-confidence entice those with feelings of insecurity and inadequacy to take these drugs. For many adolescents, the attractive promise of such rewarding experiences from experimenting with alcohol and other drugs will exceed the fear of physical, social, and (in some cases) legal costs. Despite the fact that underage use, even with licit drugs, can lead to harsh punishment, powerful psychological and social factors will lead some youth to initiate use of alcohol and other drugs before they reach the age for legal use.

For some adolescents, the initial foray into drinking, smoking, and using other drugs may be short lived. Once the curiosity is satisfied, they may not find the rewards of drugs fulfilling. Drugs not only taste bad but also may fail to produce the expected positive psychological or physical transformations. The initial use of many drugs, including alcohol, nicotine, and marijuana, often produces nausea and vomiting as well as embarrassment. More often than not, users suffer a letdown if their first experiences are negative or, at best, neutral. As one cocaine user lamented, "And all I felt was something going up my nose that had a slight bite to it and no noticeable change in my functions or anything" (Waldorf, Reinarman, & Murphy, 1991, p. 18). Some may quit entirely, others may use intermittently without any apparent problems, and still others may develop personal and interpersonal problems from their drug use.

Nonetheless, with persistence and social encouragement or pressure, many will continue to use until they develop a physical tolerance to drugs. Many will find that some level of drug use confers benefits that outweigh any immediate costs. It makes them part of the gang, helps them lose their inhibitions, and helps them have more fun. Alcohol and other drug use can even provide an excuse for rudeness, ineptitude, and inappropriate sexual boldness that others will tolerate.

It is apparent to children that even with continued use many individuals derive considerable pleasure and enjoyment from drinking alcoholic beverages, drinking coffee, and smoking tobacco products without adverse social, psychological, or physical impairment. Licit drugs are commonly used during social gatherings at parties and celebrations, at home and in the workplace. Although researchers seem to ignore these "benefits" and focus on the harms of drug use, the reverse is true for alcohol and cigarette industries that portray the "joys" of drug use in marketing and advertising and downplay the adverse effects except in small-print disclaimers. Children also observe that a small but sizable percentage of users of alcohol develop significant problems for themselves and others. And while smoking and drinking coffee do not produce interpersonal harm anywhere close to the extent alcohol is capable of, all three substances may contribute to harmful health consequences in the long run.

PSYCHOLOGICAL THEORIES

Now that we have considered the psychological and social context for licit drug use from a layperson's perspective, we will describe major psychological theories of alcohol and other drug use as well as discuss the research evidence to evaluate their validity. These theories focus variously on physiological, affective, cognitive, and social psychological factors. There are some common factors underlying the initiation into use of alcohol, cigarettes, and coffee, and we will focus on these similarities, although the details of a complete theory for each drug will differ.

Theories that focus on the role of pharmacological properties of drugs ignore the role of psychological variables such as the social and physical setting where a drug is used, personality and **temperament** differences, and the prevailing mood and motivation leading to drug use. Conversely, theories concerned with social and psychological factors discount pharmacological effects on neurophysiological processes that underlie the subjective experiences and behavioral consequences of drugs.

Psychological theories are needed to understand what leads to initial drug use. After use begins, theories about pharmacological and neurophysiological processes become of increased value in explaining continued drug use, especially when it develops into drug abuse and dependence. Dependence may develop after long-term habitual drug use in which the user may no longer have conscious or volitional control over drug use that initially involved choice.

Both types of theories are needed. They should be viewed as complementary rather than competing rivals. It may be useful to think of different types of theory as focusing on different aspects of drug use as well as on drug use during different points over time. No single theory can provide a complete understanding.

Social Learning Theory

Social learning theory (Bandura, 1977) emphasizes expectancies formed about the effects of alcohol and other drugs through observation. First, we learn social norms regarding when, where, and how others use different drugs. We observe what situations permit which amounts of drug use. We see what kinds of effects typically occur with different use patterns. In addition, we learn what effects to expect on our behavior and experience if we use these drugs ourselves. Drugs do not have automatic, universal effects; the user must recognize what the effects of drug use are. Thus, marijuana users have to "learn" how to identify or label the effects of the drug on them during their initial use (Becker, 1963).

Original expectations may be revised in line with each individual's actual experience, as determined by factors as varied as sensitivity and tolerance to a specific drug, the amount consumed, and the conditions or context of use. In one study of cocaine use, a user recalled the effects of his first experience:

> I was looking for bells to ring and stuff. I mean you hear so much about cocaine—cocaine this, cocaine that—so, you know, being ignorant of [what] its effects were, I thought that well, shit, it'd have to be something really spectacular. (Waldorf et al., 1991, p. 18)

In addition to holding these expectancies about drug use, social learning theory also proposes that we form beliefs about **self-efficacy** in our use of drugs, or the extent to which we feel competent to cope with or control our drug use. This subjective evaluation can be determined by factors such as the past history of success and failure in specific situations and the reactions of others to our behavior. Affective or mood states can distort this perception, with self-efficacy being enhanced by positive affect but lowered by negative affect.

Social learning theory also recognizes interactions between cognitive and affective states. If we believe that alcohol or drugs can reduce negative affect, we might try to "drink our troubles away" when we are depressed or anxious. Or at a party, where we hope to experience positive affect, if our expectations are that drinking, smoking, or doing drugs will lower our inhibitions and create positive affective states, we will be more likely to engage in these activities.

The relationship of coping skills to drug use is also considered by social learning theory. Individuals who have adequate coping skills and high self-esteem are able to drink at socially acceptable levels and to develop friendships with others who avoid **alcohol abuse**. In contrast, those who will probably develop into problem drinkers and alcoholics are those with poor coping skills in general for dealing with life's problems. Consequently, they may turn to alcohol and drugs as means to reduce tension, escape from problems, and feel better. But such excessive use of drugs will only serve to isolate them from those with drug use levels acceptable in society. Eventually, they will affiliate increasingly with similar drug abusers, and they will mutually reinforce this lifestyle so that a reciprocal influence exists among members of this group.

Beliefs and Expectancies

The Alcohol Expectancy Questionnaire (AEQ; Brown, Goldman, Inn, & Anderson, 1980) is a widely used survey for measuring individuals' explicit expectancies about the effects of alcohol. The expectancies held by a sample of college students fell into six categories, each of which is listed below with a corresponding sample item:

1. Global positive transforming effect ("Alcohol seems like magic.")

2. Social/physical pleasure ("Alcohol makes me feel good.")

3. Sexual enhancement ("I often feel sexier after I've had a few drinks.")

4. Arousal/power/aggression ("If I'm feeling restricted in any way, a few drinks make me feel better.")

5. Increased social assertiveness ("A few drinks make it easier to talk to people.")

6. Relaxation/tension reduction ("I am not as tense if I am drinking.")

The AEQ scale does not ask about the expected effects of different dose levels, a factor that should have an influence. It is likely that respondents based their ratings on their typical drinking levels. Furthermore, the scale measures only generalized expectancies since the specific situation or context of drinking is not specified on the instrument.

Expectancy in Relation to Drinking

Long before their initial use of a drug, children form expectancies of its effects from direct observation, media portrayal, and other sources. These expectancies, by suggestion, may lead to effects similar to those produced by actual drug use. In some cases, however, the expectancies are wrong. Original expectancies will be either confirmed or, if they are disconfirmed after drugs are consumed, revised.

The expectancy that drinking alcohol leads to social facilitation and actual drinking experience influenced each other in a reciprocal fashion for adolescents over a 2-year period during which many first began to drink (Smith, Goldman, Greenbaum, & Christiansen, 1995). Higher expectancy of social facilitation from alcohol was related to higher subsequent drinking levels. In addition, the higher the drinking levels, the greater the expectancy for subsequent social facilitation. The initial social expectancies of nondrinkers predicted individual differences in the rate of alcohol use increases over the 2 years.

Using data from 2,875 respondents in the National Alcohol Survey, a probability household sample in the United States, one study (Leigh & Stacy, 2004) assessed the relationship of expectancies about alcohol to different aspects of alcohol use for six groups of respondents as classified by age, from 12 across the life span. Positive expectancies more often led to drinking than did negative expectancies among respondents under 35, while the opposite was found for most respondents over 35 years.

Expectancies for Other Drugs

Expectancies similar to those for alcohol exist for other drugs. Self-reports from 704 college students were used (Schafer & Brown, 1991) to develop the Marijuana Effects Expectancy Questionnaire and the Cocaine Effects Expectancy Questionnaire.

As Table 2.1 shows, two of the anticipated effects of marijuana were generally negative (cognitive/behavioral impairment and global negative effects), and three of the factors were positive (relaxation/tension reduction, social/sexual facilitation, and perceptual and cognitive enhancement).

The positive effect expectancies for cocaine were similar to those for alcohol and marijuana (global positive effects and relaxation and tension reduction). In addition, there were two negative expectancies (global negative effects and anxiety), properties that are indeed likely for stimulants like cocaine. A higher frequency of use of marijuana or cocaine

TABLE 2.1   Summary of expectations for alcohol, marijuana, and cocaine use.

Six Alcohol Expectancies	Six Marijuana Expectancies	Five Cocaine Expectancies
1. Global positive transforming effect	1. Cognitive and behavioral impairment	1. Global positive effects
2. Social/physical pleasure	2. Relaxation and tension reduction	2. Global negative effects
3. Sexual enhancement	3. Social and sexual facilitation	3. Generalized arousal
4. Arousal/power/aggression	4. Perceptual and cognitive enhancement	4. Anxiety
5. Increased social assertiveness	5. Global negative effects	5. Relaxation and tension reduction
6. Relaxation/tension reduction	6. Craving and physical effects	

was associated with a greater expectation of positive drug effects, whereas nonuse of both drugs was related to expectations of stronger negative drug consequences for both men and women.

Self-reported global positive scores for initial use of marijuana were correlated with latency to next use and with lifetime use of the drug by college students, suggesting that the potential for marijuana abuse is related to the magnitude of the drug's initial positive effect (Davidson & Schenk, 1994). Global negative scores for initial use did not correlate with either measure of future use.

Expectancies for cigarette smoking were assessed with a 50-item Smoking Consequences Questionnaire (Brandon & Baker, 1991). This measure identified four factors: negative consequences (e.g., health risks), positive reinforcement/sensory satisfaction (e.g., taste, relaxation), negative reinforcement/negative affect reduction (e.g., reduction of sadness and anxiety), and appetite/weight control.

A study of the relationship of these expectancies to smoking (Cohen, McCarthy, Brown, & Myers, 2002) used three interviews over 4 years with 121 young men and women smokers recruited from treatment centers and the community. It was hypothesized that individuals prone to experiencing higher negative affective states would be more likely to detect benefits from smoking and hence have greater expectancies of positive smoking outcomes. In addition, because they experience high negative affect, they may have gained more relief of these states from smoking. The prediction that those with higher negative affect would smoke more over this period was upheld.

Negative Expectancies

One limitation of the AEQ is that it examines only positive expectancies. Negative expectancies about the effects of alcohol should also be tested as predictors of alcohol use (McMahon & Jones, 1994). Some negative expectations may have weaker effects because they involve distal or delayed consequences—for example, hangovers that may not occur until the morning after drinking. Heavier drinkers expected less impairment but more nastiness and disinhibition from drinking than did lighter drinkers (Leigh, 1987).

Heavy Versus Light Drinkers

Drinkers who differ in their typical dose have different expectancies because they differ in the conditions that prompt them to engage in their drinking episodes and in the consequences of their drinking (Southwick & Steele, 1987). The typical light drinker is in a positive mood when a drug use episode starts. The drinking might take place at a party or celebration where a festive mood prevails and the alcohol is intended to enhance the prevailing good time. This mood coupled with alcohol's initial ability to enhance mood accentuates positive affect. After drinking ends, negative affect occurs, but it is offset by the positive affect experienced earlier while drinking, so there is a gradual decline to a state of neutral feeling or a mildly negative state. In short, a restoration of balanced emotions occurs.

In contrast, heavy drinkers more often drink when they are already in a negative mood. Depressed, lonely, or angry, they may seek drug use to improve their mood. In Phase 1, alcohol may work to counter the negative mood they start out with. A few extrastrong drinks gulped down quickly may give a momentary positive lift. However, in Phase 2, after drinking ends and the effects wear off, negative feelings and fatigue arise. These conditions are apt to prompt drinking episodes in the near future, which repeat the cycle just described with increasing frequency and severity.

Positive alcohol expectancies and lower self-efficacy were related to coping with avoidant, emotion-focused strategies and higher alcohol consumption in a sample of college students (Evans & Dunn, 1995), as well as in a sample of individuals diagnosed with drinking problems (Blume, Lostutter, Schmaling, & Marlatt, 2003). Heavier drinkers, not surprisingly, may believe adverse drinking effects are less likely than may lighter drinkers. In part, this leniency could be a self-serving rationalization for their behavior, but it might be that heavier drinkers have adapted to heavy use and actually experience less negative impact from their drinking.

In summary, correlations among peers' use of alcohol and drugs suggest that adolescents imitate the drug use of peer models. Consistent with social learning theory, adolescents' own drug use gets reinforced socially by fitting in with the use levels of peers. However, social learning theory does not account for why some adolescents choose one type of role model while others choose different ones.

Theories emphasizing cognitive factors also do not adequately distinguish between causes and effects of adolescent drug attitudes/behaviors. Because most expectancy studies are cross sectional in design, they are inconclusive as to questions of causality. Thus, it is possible that the expectancies are the effect, not the cause, of drug use. Longitudinal studies in which the expectancies are first measured and then correlated with later drug use help answer this question. Findings in one such study (Bauman, Fisher, Bryan, & Chenoweth, 1985) support the view that expectancies and alcohol use are related in a complex reciprocal manner, with initial expectancies determining alcohol use and drinking outcomes, then modifying those expectancies, and so on.

Finally, cognitive theories typically use measures of generalized expectancies, but the specific context or situation in which drug use takes place can influence expectancies.

For example, in one study (Wall, McKee, & Hinson, 2000), college students experienced with drinking were randomly assigned to four different combinations of two settings (an on-campus bar vs. a laboratory) and two sets of instructions about a hypothetical intoxication level ("just enough to begin to feel intoxicated" vs. "too much to drink"). Individuals exposed to the on-campus bar expected greater alcohol-related stimulation/perceived dominance and pleasurable disinhibition than did those tested in the laboratory setting.

Implicit Cognitions

Implicit cognitions or associations formed between alcohol use and cues may exert subtle influences on subsequent drinking (Wiers & Stacy, 2006). Past drinking experiences involve many interrelated associations, and these networks of memories affect expectancies. Another view involves classical conditioning in which various stimuli such as sights, sounds, and smells related to past use of a drug can come to activate thoughts of and urges for its renewed use. In Pavlov's (1927) famous experiments, dogs who heard a previously neutral tone presented a fraction of a second before they received food powder soon gained the capacity to elicit salivation on later occasions even when no food was present. Similarly, users acquire associations between different stimuli related to consumption of alcohol and other drugs. However, unlike expectancies, which are conscious factors, classical conditioning associations are implicit and beyond the user's awareness and control.

Whereas self-reports of expectancies on surveys like the AEQ might sometimes be inaccurate and reflect socially expected or desired responses, respondents are not conscious of their implicit cognitions, which hence may be more valid. Several laboratory methods are used to study implicit cognition such as word association, semantic priming, and reaction time. For example, on a word association task, drinkers in comparison to low- or nondrinking controls are more likely to think of alcohol-related words when presented with words like *beer* or *wine*.

In semantic priming experiments, alcohol-related images or words are presented prior to a task involving an opportunity to consume alcohol in an alleged "taste rating" task. In comparison to non-alcohol-related stimuli, when presented with the alcohol cues, more drinking will occur for heavy drinkers but not for light drinkers or nondrinkers.

On a reaction time (RT) task, stronger expectancies should elicit faster responses. A widely used task is sentence verification. For example, a sentence stem such as "Alcohol makes me _____" is followed by a specific effect such as "relaxed" or "excited." The task involves many sentences of this format to which participants must respond as quickly as possible whether each statement is true or false for them. RT is an index of the strength of the underlying association between beliefs and behaviors.

Furthermore, because the RT task is typically administered in a laboratory setting resembling a bar, it should provide better access to memories that reflect alcohol expectancies, unlike survey measures that are generally made in a classroom setting. This type of task has been used to evaluate the accessibility of both alcohol and smoking expectancies in past studies (Palfai, Monti, Colby, & Rohsenow, 1997).

Using this approach, one study (Aarons, Goldman, Greenbaum, & Coovert, 2003) developed models of alcohol expectancies based on responses of 927 male and female college students on a computerized RT sentence verification task, measures of alcohol use and effects, and the Drinking Styles Questionnaire.

Several models have been proposed that identify more complex dimensions of expectancies using a technique known as multidimensional scaling that allows each item to be represented on more than one dimension. New dimensions of alcohol expectancies such as arousal–sedation and positive–negative effects have been proposed. These models have been validated on a separate sample and finally correlated to drinking behavior.

Models with arousing and positive effects of alcohol as single dimensions do not differ in predicting drinking patterns. However, both dimensions are more strongly related to drinking patterns than are alcohol expectancies of sedating effects or negative effects.

Implicit associations between cues and alcohol can predict future drinking levels (Wiers et al., 2002). Some indirect evidence that implicit cues might influence drinking comes from studies that found adolescents with strong alcohol associations to alcohol-related words tended to have drank more recently, in larger quantity, and more frequently over the past 30 days. Among nondrinkers, those with more positive expectancies also showed greater intentions for future drinking. A 12-month follow-up of a subsample showed similar relationships between positive alcohol expectancies and the same indices of drinking for the drinkers. Nondrinkers of a year earlier who had higher positive expectancies were more likely to have initiated drinking (Krank, Wall, Stewart, Wiers, & Goldman, 2005).

Another study illustrating the power of implicit cognitions (Friedman, McCarthy, Bartholow, & Hicks, 2007) found that individuals with high expectancies that alcohol reduces tension were more willing to meet with an opposite-gender stranger in an anxiety-producing context after being exposed to alcohol-related words than to nonalcoholic beverage-related words. In a second study, individuals with stronger expectancies that alcohol releases aggression showed greater hostility toward a target person following provocation by that person if they had received near-subliminal exposure to alcohol-related as opposed to non-alcohol-related words.

These demonstrations of the link between implicit associations and subsequent drinking provide evidence for a possibly important mechanism involved in addictive behaviors. Those cues that, by definition, are implicit may disrupt attempts of drinkers to abstain or control their consumption because it is difficult to be aware of their influence.

Social Influence Theories

Peer Cluster Theory

Are one's peers the cause of drug use or vice versa? The **peer cluster theory** (Oetting & Beauvais, 1987; Oetting & Donnermeyer, 1998) considers the central role of peers as socializing influences on deviant behaviors such as drug use. Peer clusters can transmit either prosocial or deviant norms, but the major source of deviant norms is usually peer clusters, especially when family-child bonds are weak. Personal characteristics such as low self-confidence or poor school performance may lead to increased association with peers who engage in deviant behaviors, including drug use. A study (Swaim, Bates, & Chavez, 1998) of 910 Mexican American and White non-Hispanic school dropouts supported a model based on peer cluster theory. Association with drug-using peers was the best direct predictor of school dropouts among the drug users.

Personality problems such as oppositional disorder, conduct disorder, attention deficit disorder, and **antisocial personality disorder** are more likely to interfere with primary socialization and increase chances of affiliation with peers with drug problems (Oetting, Deffenbacher, & Donnermeyer, 1998). Other factors that favor choice of peers who engage in drug use include physical and social characteristics of the local neighborhood or community, poverty, and neighborhood deviance (Oetting, Donnermeyer, & Deffenbacher, 1998).

Peer Selection Theory

A different explanation for the same evidence, **peer selection theory**, however, proposes that adolescents who already use drugs seek out or prefer the company of other adolescents who share their drug involvement. Those who disdain drugs will tend to choose as friends those who also reject drugs. Thus, it is not so much that drug-using peers exert social influence to determine the drug use of other group members as it is that "birds of a feather" tend to flock together. Adolescents who are already involved with drugs seek out the company of those similarly engaged.

A longitudinal study involving assessments over four time points (Urberg, Luo, Pilgrim, & Degirmencioglu, 2003) assessed adolescents' initial selection of cigarette- and alcohol-using peers and the extent to which such peers affected their drug use. In line with peer selection, those adolescents who did not value school achievement or spending time with parents were more apt than others to later choose friends who smoked cigarettes more than they did. Among friends, there was little peer influence on later drug use. Only high peer acceptance and high friendship quality showed correlations with substance use similarity among friends.

Family Interaction Theory

The **family interaction theory** (Brook, Brook, Gordon, Whiteman, & Cohen, 1990) proposes that adolescents who have affectionate parents, a good attachment to them, and conventional values experiment less with substance use and have fewer associations with peers who use alcohol and drugs. Adolescents with warm ties to their families risk jeopardizing these relationships if they use drugs excessively. Maternal control and maternal psychological adjustment minimizes the involvement of adolescents with drug use.

Support for the theory was obtained in a two-stage study (Brook, Cohen, & Jaeger, 1998) that interviewed mothers and 210 younger adolescents (ages 12–14) and 199 older adolescents (ages 15–18) twice over a 3-year period. Adolescent unconventionality was a determinant for both initial and increased levels of drug use for both age groups, but intrapsychic distress was a stronger factor for initial use among younger adolescents. Lack of maternal attachment and poor control techniques were associated with initial levels of drug use for both age groups. However, the mother-child relationship and models of the mother's unconventionality had a greater impact on increased drug involvement for the older than for the younger group.

Social Development Model

Weak bonds to parents, teachers, family, and conventional role models contribute to drug use in the **social development model** (Hawkins & Weis, 1985). Poor home and school reinforcements may be linked to a lack of academic and interpersonal skills. Adolescents with poor family life might find alcohol and other drugs a means of coping with the family and parental conflict they face at home. Thus, nonconforming, rebellious, and alienated youth are more likely to use alcohol and drugs. Poor social development may lead to early initiation of alcohol and drug use, as was found in a **prospective study** of 808 (412 male) schoolchildren studied from age 10 to 11 and again from age 17 to 18 (Hawkins et al., 1997). The younger a child was when drinking began, the more he or she misused alcohol at age 17–18. Early initiation into drinking was a better predictor of subsequent alcohol problems than were parent drinking, proactive parenting, school bonding, peer alcohol initiation, perceived harmfulness of alcohol use, and ethnicity.

Intrapersonal Theories

In addition to attitudes and behavior related to specific drugs, general intrapersonal factors may influence individual differences in drug use. Self-esteem, social interaction skills, and coping skills play important roles in determining the extent to which drug abuse occurs.

For example, adolescents with poor academic achievement or values may drink to cope with the negative feelings associated with this failure. Those with low commitment or success academically will be more likely to affiliate with other low-achieving peers who find frequent and heavy drinking to be a rewarding source of escape from their frustration in school. In contrast, academically successful students are less likely to drink as much because it interferes with cognitive function and memory. Increased drinking, for whatever benefit they expect, will be at the expense of their academic achievement, a primary source of their self-esteem.

Tension Reduction

A widely held view of the reason people engage in some types of drug use is to relieve stress and anxiety. When tension is unpleasantly high, people may drink or smoke, expecting that the drug use will lower the tension. If this expectation is upheld, their tendency to resort to these drugs in the future to cope with tension may increase.

According to an influential early behaviorist, Clark Hull (1943), any response that leads to reduction of drive states such as hunger, thirst, or anxiety becomes reinforced. On future occasions when an individual is in a similar situation, his or her alcohol or drug use will be more likely to initiate the same response that was previously successful in lowering the drive state.

However, drinking might increase rather than lower tension in some situations. In the case of alcoholics in treatment who may or may not want to stop alcohol use, the therapists' reminding them of the adverse effects of drinking might increase the likelihood that their subsequent alcohol use would increase tension. In contrast, alcohol use might lower tension at a social gathering where most drinkers seek enjoyment.

Finally, alcohol may initially lead to tension reduction with positive affective feelings such as relief and pleasure. This positive state might continue as the blood alcohol level from a given dose increases over time or if additional drinks are consumed. Eventually, however, the tension reduction may reverse and start to increase along with negative affective feelings of discomfort and anxiety. Thus, drug use can produce both positive and negative affective states, with the dose level and temporal factors being important determinants of the outcome.

These self-reported **biphasic effects**, however, may not closely correspond to the objective or physical effects. Self-reports of physical activity levels over 4 consecutive days during which 30 young men and women had one drink in a counterbalanced sequence (a placebo followed by 0.4, 0.6, and 0.8 g/kg doses of 95% alcohol) showed that all alcohol doses increased physical activity that lasted across both ascending and descending limbs (Addicott, Marsh-Richard, Mathias, & Dougherty, 2007). Following the 0.6 g/kg dose, both physical activity and self-reported stimulation increased during the ascending limb. Other analyses indicated that alcohol consumption also increased sedation for the 0.6 and 0.8 g/kg doses. Self-reported stimulation and sedation and objectively measured physical activity assess different aspects of the effects of alcohol, and it may be necessary to include all of them to identify the impact of alcohol on behavior.

Stress and tension may actually cause some forms of drug use. Stress might motivate drug use if people believe drug use reduces tension, even if it does not directly do so. One model of alcohol use (Cooper, Frone, Russell, & Mudar, 1995) posits there are two basic motives: to cope with negative emotions and to enhance positive or pleasurable emotions.

A study (Cooper, Russell, Skinner, Frone, & Mudar, 1992) of the stress-alcohol relationship in a random sample of 1,316 Black and White drinkers found that coping styles and expectancies about drug use were important factors in this relationship for men. Both higher alcohol use and alcohol problems were related to stress among men who relied on avoidant forms of coping or held strong positive expectancies for alcohol's effects. In contrast, stressors were negatively related to alcohol use among men who were low in both avoidant coping and positive alcohol expectancies but unrelated among women to either avoidant coping or positive alcohol expectancies.

Use of alcohol and other drugs, of course, is not the only possible response available in many situations for relieving tension. If other responses such as exercise and recreational social activities are available that can lower the tension, drug use may not be necessary. Furthermore, tension reduction may not be the primary motive for drug use. In fact, when the tired worker comes home and has a drink or two, it probably creates physiological arousal but is paradoxically interpreted as a "relaxation" instead of as an excitation. Instead, feelings of power and control rather than tension reduction may be important reasons for drug use.

Situations where no alternatives for coping with tension exist may increase the chance that drugs will be used in hopes of producing a feeling of power. Ironically, excessive drug use may produce adverse consequences that eventually increase rather than lower tension. In contrast, if there are other alternatives for reducing tension, the likelihood of drug use may be lower.

Using alcohol to cope with stress may temporarily reduce feelings of anxiety and depression in individuals (Kassel, 1997; Sayette, 1999). Yet, if drinking becomes a major means of coping with stress, heavy and regular alcohol use may increase rather than decrease stress over many years of drinking (Brennan, Schutte, & Moos, 1999).

Stress Response Dampening Theory

Stress is a determinant of drug use but not a necessary or sufficient one. The **stress response dampening model** (Sher, 1987) focuses on the pharmacological effects of drug use. It is a pared-down version of the tension reduction hypothesis discussed earlier. Cognitive factors such as expectancies are not as important as psychophysiological factors. This model assumes there is a complex psychophysiological response to alcohol and other drugs, especially due to factors such as individual differences and social context. In one study (Sher, Bartholow, Peuser, Erickson, & Wood, 2007), 106 men consumed either an alcoholic beverage (0.7 g/kg) or a placebo before a stressful event was introduced in which they had to deliver a self-disclosing speech. Under the alcohol condition, self-reported anxiety and skin conductance levels—but not heart rate—were reduced in response to the stressor.

Drug use typically dampens or reduces stress, especially cardiovascular reactions, so drug consumption is reinforcing because it moderates the physical reaction to stress. The type of stressor, physical or psychological, is also a factor that determines the effect of drugs. Most people do not use drugs to reduce all types of stresses because they realize that it would only add to stress in some situations (e.g., drug use at the office). Instead, they may selectively use drugs for only those stressors that they believe will be alleviated by it.

Personality/Temperament Theories

Personality theories of alcohol and other drug use propose that some long-term or stable characteristics of individuals such as inborn temperament or acquired personality traits distinguish alcoholics from nonalcoholics. Users are a heterogeneous group, and the factors leading to use disorders differ widely across individuals as well as across different drugs. Nonetheless, people have a strong conviction that some set of personality traits differentiates those with drug use disorders from those without them. If such differences could be identified, it might be possible to design more effective methods of intervention, treatment, and prevention. Consequently, researchers have devoted much effort to the search for personality factors associated with use disorders for a variety of substances.

Psychoanalytic Approach

The **psychoanalytic approach** emphasizes unconscious motives for excessive use of alcohol and drugs. These motives may reflect the influence of intensely emotional experiences during infancy or early childhood. Early psychological theories of alcoholism had roots in psychoanalytic theory. This emphasis was perhaps due to the fact that many alcoholics sought therapy from psychoanalytically oriented psychiatrists (Cox, 1987). As with psychoanalytic views about many forms of psychopathology, these psychiatrists' explanations of alcoholism focused on unresolved early-childhood conflicts of an unconscious nature. Psychosexual development, as proposed by Sigmund Freud (1905/1989), involves a series of stages. Perhaps due to arrested development or fixation at the oral stage of development, a need for alcohol may develop as a means of achieving immediate oral gratification and pleasure. Freud saw alcoholics as immature, dependent, and unable to delay gratification. They drank, according to Freud, to produce immediate gratification or to achieve a feeling of power.

Society demands that males be independent to fulfill the masculine role, which involves aggressiveness. However, Freudian theory holds that if a male is fixated or blocked at the oral stage of development, a dilemma exists because unresolved dependency needs do not fit the male role. Drinking heavily enables men to fulfill aspects of the expected masculine role behavior. Although drinking also creates dependence on others, it is tolerated because the dependence can be attributed to the influence of alcohol.

The **power theory** of alcoholism (McClelland, Davis, Kalin, & Wanner, 1972) proposes a model of the motivation for drinking in general rather than one limited to the drinking of alcoholics. The independence and aggressiveness often seen in male drinkers are inter-preted as a direct manifestation of a drive for power rather than a reaction against depen-dency. Drinking enables men to engage in fantasies and feelings of power. Thus, lack of power leads to drinking. Studies of fantasies and imagery in projective test situations before and after the consumption of alcohol have provided a major line of evidence in support of the theory. As larger amounts of alcohol were consumed, the fantasies revealed greater degrees of personal power.

This approach to explaining the drinking of men has been extended to the analysis of drinking among women (Wilsnack, 1974). In contrast to the model proposed for men, this view proposes that drinking serves to reduce rather than elicit fantasies of power among women. Wilsnack (1974) depicted women as having more fantasies about engaging in traditionally feminine activities after drinking. Those women who developed alcoholism were assumed to be more likely to have anxieties about their womanliness. According to this view, alcohol-dependent women might turn to alcohol to help them cope with these feelings of inadequacy (Wilsnack, 1973).

One problem with psychoanalytic theories of drinking is that the formulations are difficult to test because they involve assumptions about early experiences about which there is usually no objective evidence. Unconscious processes are controversial because they are not readily amenable to investigation with objective methods. Also, as with the dependency and power formulations, the predictions are sometimes diametrically opposed.

Personality Typologies

Although criticized as simplistic, theories of personality often have involved identifying typologies or classifications of basic groups, such as introversion-extraversion, as if every-one could be categorized as one or the other type. Similarly, in the field of alcoholism, several classifications have been proposed.

Type 1 and Type 2

One typology, based on Swedish studies of adopted children from alcoholic families (Cloninger, 1987) distinguishes two forms of alcoholism. One form, termed **Type 1 alcoholism (milieu-limited)**, shown in Table 2.2, emerges at a later age, generally after age 25, and in a less severe form. It represented about 13% of the sample as studied by Cloninger. These drinkers did not engage in much aggressive behavior when drinking but did show problems with loss of control or psychological dependence on alcohol along with guilt and fear about this outcome.

TABLE 2.2   Comparison of Cloninger (1987) Type 1 and Type 2 alcoholics with Babor et al. (1992) Type A and Type B alcoholics.

Characteristic	Type 1 (Milieu-Limited)	Type 2 (Male-Limited)
Usual Age of Onset	After 25	Before 25
Inability to Abstain	Less Likely	More Likely
Fighting and Arrests When Drinking	Less Likely	More Likely
Loss of Control	Less Likely	More Likely
Fear and Guilt Over Dependence	Less Likely	More Likely
	Type A	**Type B**
Usual Age of Onset	Later	Earlier
Alcohol Family History	Less Likely	More Likely
Alcohol-Related Problem	Less Likely	More Likely
Psychopathology	Less Likely	More Likely

A more severe form of alcoholism, typically developing before age 25, is defined as **Type 2 alcoholism (male-limited)**, as this type seemed absent among women in the Cloninger (1987) study. The biological fathers in the study tended to have severe alcoholism. Variations in the environment of these fathers as children did not affect the number of abusers. This type of alcoholism occurred in 4% of the sample. Most of the adoptees had moderate alcohol abuse, but such abuse often led to fighting and aggression without much psychological dependence or guilt. Although both types of alcoholism involve heritable factors, environmental conditions play an additional role with the milieu-limited type but not with the male-limited variety.

Three behavioral dimensions, novelty seeking, harm avoidance, and reward dependence, have been proposed as contributors to the different patterns and consequences of drinking displayed by the two types. Type 1 alcoholics are governed by inhibition. They do not seek novelty, avoid harm, and depend highly on social rewards. They have less severe alcoholism. In contrast, Type 2 individuals seek novelty, do not avoid potential harm, and have low reliance on social rewards; these characteristics may contribute to their likelihood of more severe and earlier problems related to alcohol.

A validation study (Yoshino, Kato, Takeuchi, Ono, & Kitamura, 1994) found partial support for the typology. Scores of 191 male Type 1 and Type 2 alcoholics were compared on the **Tridimensional Personality Questionnaire (TPQ)**, which measures novelty seeking (NS), harm avoidance (HA), and reward dependence (RD). Scores on the NS and RD scales were in line with the expected differences, but the HA score was not.

Type A and Type B

A typology similar to that of Type 1 and Type 2, based on samples of male and female alcoholics, distinguishes two types: A and B (Babor et al., 1992). The **Type A alcoholic** is similar to the Type 1 in taking longer to develop the disease and having less dependence on alcohol, fewer alcohol-related problems, and less psychopathology. The **Type B alcoholic**, in contrast, is similar to the Type 2, showing earlier onset of alcoholism, more childhood risk factors, a **family history** of the disease, and greater psychopathology. Babor et al.'s Type A/Type B distinction was used in a study of untreated community problem drinkers (Carpenter, Liu, & Hasin, 2006). A random sample of 876 participants who met eligibility criteria were interviewed by telephone. They completed a structured interview on alcohol and other health-related behaviors at baseline and at 1-year follow-up that identified subgroups of problem drinkers fitting the Type A/Type B distinction. At the 1-year follow-up, Type B drinkers with no history of alcoholism were approximately five times more likely to develop it than were Type A drinkers.

However, based on a review (Babor & Caetano, 2006) of findings from research aimed at measuring the validity of Cloninger's (1987) and Babor et al.'s (1992) taxonomy, it is premature to use either typology as there is no consensus about the nature or number of subtypes among individuals with substance use disorders, although some researchers suggest there are at least four useful subtypes (Hesselbrock & Hesselbrock, 2006). For example, a study (Windle & Scheidt, 2004) of an ethnically diverse sample of 802 male and female alcoholic inpatients at five treatment settings proposed four subtypes for both men and women. The chronic/antisocial personality (ASP) subtype, similar to Babor et al.'s Type B and Cloninger's Type 2, had the most severe pattern of drinking and antisocial behavior. The negative affect subtype, similar to the negative affect alcoholic identified by Zucker (1987), had the highest rate of childhood sexual abuse, attempted suicide, and childhood homelessness. The polydrug subtype had the highest rate of family criminality, high-risk sexual behavior, and intravenous drug use. Finally, the mild course subtype had the least severe alcohol impairment, the fewest childhood conduct problems, and the lowest level of family history of alcoholism.

Biologically Based Personality Theories

Vulnerability models (Johnson, Sher, & Rolf, 1991; Sher, Walitzer, Wood, & Brent, 1991) emphasize individual differences in temperament or biological sensitivity to stimulation as a basis for explaining individual differences in response to alcohol.

Enhanced Reinforcement Model

In the **enhanced reinforcement model**, innate dispositions of greater sensitivity to drugs increase the likelihood that alcohol and other drugs will function as reinforcers in reducing stress, especially for individuals who have not acquired good psychological coping skills. In addition, there may be lower sensitivity to intoxication, also attributed to biological differences. Drinking problems could develop because higher alcohol tolerance and lower sensitivity to intoxication allows these individuals to drink to higher levels before they obtain the desired reinforcing effects of alcohol.

Negative Affect Model

The **negative affect model** concentrates on unpleasant feelings that may lead to alcohol and drug use as a form of **self-medication**. Temperamental factors favoring depression or anxiety, combined with stressful life events as well as poor coping skills, facilitate the onset of drug abuse. A generalized vulnerability to drug dependence may exist. Although the neuropharmacological properties of different psychoactive drugs may affect the rate at which dependence develops, individuals who prefer one drug to others are not fundamentally different in any neurophysiological sense. It may be the cultural factors, social norms, and prevailing social policies governing the legal status of different drugs that ultimately determine which are used.

A Heuristic Integrative Model

One comprehensive model (Pihl, Peterson, & Finn, 1990a, 1990b) examines the interrelationship among inherited tendencies toward alcoholism, localized brain functions, childhood behavior problems, and alcohol abuse. It assumes that offspring of alcoholics, especially sons, may have deficits in cognitive functioning and attention that in turn place these children at higher risk for future alcohol abuse. First, these deficits impair the learning of conceptual rules, abstract categories, and rules of social behavior. Second, many of these children receive poor socialization about rules of social behavior because they often come from families with low socioeconomic status, hostility, and alcohol and drug abuse (Hinshaw, 1987). These children may be hyperactive and inattentive. They act out with conduct disorders at school. Later, they may find alcohol and other drugs reinforcing because they reduce anxiety and stress. Unfortunately, extended use of alcohol may further disrupt cognitive functions, leading to additional problem behaviors and creating a vicious cycle of more drinking and greater impairment.

This model is supported by a wide array of evidence from biochemical studies, investigations of the function of specific brain areas involved with organization and categorization, neuropsychological studies of information processing, and studies of childhood behavior problems such as hyperactivity. To test the model, Pihl et al. (1990a, 1990b) examined lab task performance of the young sons of male alcoholics because they have the highest risk of alcohol abuse. In laboratory experiments with tasks involving threats such as a signal followed in a few seconds by electric shock, the sons of alcoholics and a control group of sons of nonalcoholics received either a dose of alcohol or a placebo before being compared in their reactions to the task.

Psychophysiological measures such as heart rate, evoked potentials, and electroencephalogram (EEG) waves were recorded when subjects worked on lab tasks. Results showed that sons of male alcoholics are hyperactive when sober but, after consuming alcohol, achieve a calmer state (Finn & Pihl, 1987). In contrast, sons of nonalcoholics are less active when sober but more reactive on intoxication.

Overall, the model ties together many differences observed between sons of male alcoholics and controls in behavioral, neurophysiological, and biochemical reactions to alcohol challenge tests. It provides a useful framework for developing and testing hypotheses about the bases for differences in response to alcohol.

That these predispositions are stronger among men may reflect the additional role of the different social norms and attitudes about drinking for men and women. Because women traditionally have not been encouraged to drink at a level comparable to that for men, any biologically based temperamental characteristics that might increase the risk of excessive drinking among women may be countered by these sex role expectations in our society that act as a protective mechanism for women.

In summary, neuropsychological differences can be viewed as predisposing factors. Biological factors determine initial vulnerability to alcohol and other drug dependence. Biologically based differences in temperament for stimulation and risk taking combine with tendencies acquired from early environmental influences such as expectancies about effects of specific drugs, observed alcohol and drug use by parents, school performance, adequacy of coping skills, and peer influences. Together, all of these factors determine the likelihood of drug use.

MEDIATORS, MODERATORS, AND DIRECT CAUSES

Personality can be related to alcohol and other drug use in several ways: as a cause or **mediator (mediator variable)**, as a **moderator (moderator variable)**, or as a **direct cause**. Sometimes, researchers interpret findings as evidence of one of these relationships without ruling out the other possibilities.

Mediators

Underlying causes of dependency can involve physiological, psychological, or cultural factors. The top section of Figure 2.3 illustrates the situation where some personality variables mediate or increase the likelihood of alcohol use disorders. The greater the extent to which these variables are present for an individual, the more likely that person will be to develop problems. Some of these variables, such as genetic tendencies, may exist well before actual use of alcohol or other drugs begins. But other factors, such as certain life stressors (e.g., divorce or retirement), may not appear until later in life. In both cases, they are viewed as antecedent to, or leading to, alcohol use disorders.

Some biological characteristics may heighten the likelihood of alcohol problems, at least for males (Tarter, Alterman, & Edwards, 1985). Temperamental factors such as activity level (high), attention span (short), and sociability (high) have been found to be associated with a greater likelihood of alcohol problems among males. Emotionality, high activity, and impaired behavioral self-regulation can put individuals at higher risk for drug abuse (Tarter & Edwards, 1988). A neuropsychological model of differences in biological vulnerability (Tarter, Moss, & Laird, 1990) proposes that alcohol may be inherently more reinforcing for individuals with certain biologically based temperaments that affect their sensitivity to alcohol and other drugs.

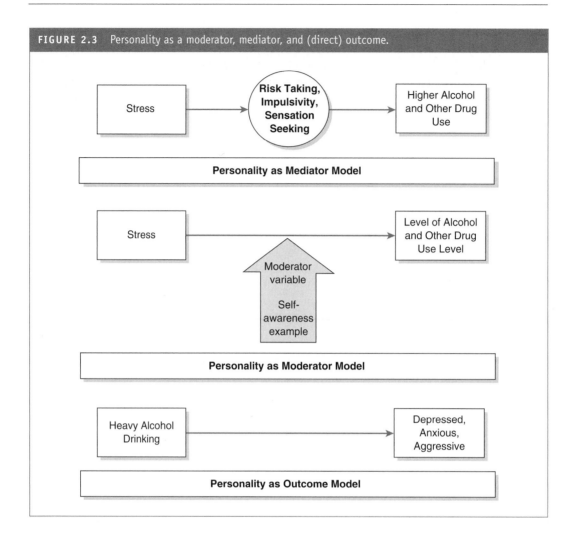

FIGURE 2.3 Personality as a moderator, mediator, and (direct) outcome.

In the face of stress, such undercontrolled individuals may be more likely to engage in activities that increase drinking or to have adverse physical and social consequences when they do drink. As Figure 2.4 shows, a vicious cycle may start in which these tendencies may lead to more punishment, although the punishment may not be highly effective. Frequent and heavy drinking may generate lowered self-esteem, negative reactions from others, and physical and social debilitation, leading to anxiety, depression, and other negative emotions. Work and school performance will be impaired. When alcohol is not available, the physical withdrawal symptoms experienced may create added anxiety and tension. Unfortunately, the solution typically adopted by the alcohol dependent to deal with these overpowering negative effects is to drink even more alcohol, hoping to escape the harsh reality.

FIGURE 2.4   A model of how initial personality dispositions affect initial drinking levels. In turn, initial drinking can lead to positive or negative affect, each of which has different long-term consequences. If drinking leads to positive affect, it may lead to the loss of other sources of positive reinforcement, and drinking may become more pronounced. As many alcohol-related problems develop, there is further—and increased—drinking.

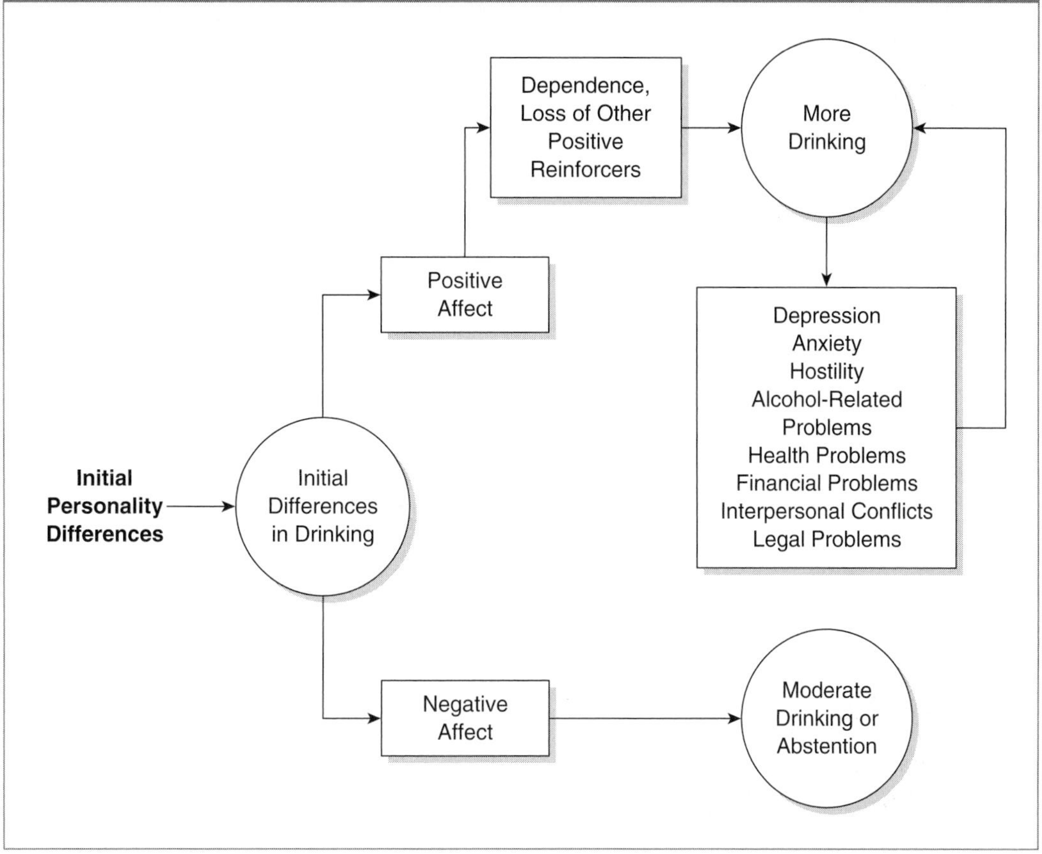

Moderators

Can some personality traits that lead some individuals into harm's way with drugs also serve to protect other individuals from exposure to conditions that tend to lead to alcohol and other drug use problems? When the effect of a particular variable is not universal but instead depends on the level of another variable, such as a personality trait, that trait is referred to as a moderator variable (Baron & Kenny, 1986). The middle section of Figure 2.3 provides an example of how a personality variable, self-awareness, might function as a moderator of alcohol use disorders.

Self-Awareness

Self-awareness, the extent to which individuals are conscious of their own behaviors and feelings, has been found to lessen the harmful influence of a family history of alcoholism on drinking (Rogosch, Chassin, & Sher, 1990). This may be because individuals high in self-awareness react to alcohol cautiously because they come from families with a history of alcohol problems. By recognizing their higher risk, they may take preventive measures to reduce the chances that they will develop alcohol problems. In contrast, individuals with a similar family history of alcoholism but who are low in self-awareness are less vigilant and thus more likely to develop drinking problems.

In this example, the trait of self-awareness is a moderator variable of the effect of a family history (FH) of alcoholism. Individuals with high risk (FH+) background and low self-awareness are at risk of developing drinking problems under stress, whereas individuals with the same FH+ background but high self-awareness are less likely to have alcohol use disorders.

Direct Causes

As users become dependent on alcohol and other drugs, they may undergo changes in their outlook on life, as reflected by negative attitudes, hostility, depression, and so on. In other words, the bottom section of Figure 2.3 shows that certain personality characteristics may emerge after prolonged excessive use of alcohol and other drugs. In this situation, personality differences between drinkers with and without alcohol use disorders are the outcome or effect, rather than the cause, of higher drug use.

In addition, the reactions of others to an individual's drinking behavior may further modify the personality traits of the drug-dependent individual. For example, as an individual's drug use becomes heavier and more frequent, with its attendant loss of social status and financial, social, and psychological well-being, there will be adverse social consequences such as embarrassment, ostracism, and rejection. In turn, increased drinking may occur. Consequently, additional personality differences may begin to emerge to distinguish alcoholics from nonalcoholics—differences that are also consequences, rather than antecedents, of alcoholism.

Difficulties With Causal Interpretations

The role of personality in alcohol and other drug use is complicated. Characteristics of individuals that exist prior to their adoption of a pattern of drug use may be responsible for some of the behavioral correlates of heavy or frequent drug use. Thus, low motivation, aggression, and hostility, often seen as outcomes or effects of drug abuse, might in some cases actually be precursors or preexisting factors associated with subsequent drug abuse. They may or may not be causes, but they would not be effects. The term *factors* is often used to describe them because it is neutral with respect to causality or the existence of an **addictive personality**; it merely indicates that these variables are predictive of drug abuse.

The same interpretative problem arises in comparing users of legal versus illegal drugs. Suppose that prior to the initiation into drug use, those who end up using only legal drugs have different traits than do those who use both legal and illegal drugs. Because these correlates existed prior to the use of different classes of drugs, it would be difficult to conclude that the risk factors distinguishing these groups are the *effects* of using legal versus illegal drugs instead of the *causes* of the types of drugs chosen. Thus, higher risk takers and sensation seekers may be more likely to cross the line to use illegal drugs than may law-abiding users who stick with alcohol and tobacco or those who avoid all drugs.

An alternative possibility is that individuals who eventually develop alcohol or drug problems are actually not atypical in personality or very different in their predrinking years from those who use alcohol and some drugs without serious problems. Consider the case of drinking. Because our society encourages drinking within limits as acceptable behavior in many settings, most young people engage in "social drinking," or at least experimental use, to some extent. However, some individuals may eventually turn to excessive drinking, drug use, or both as a means of coping by escaping the harsh realities of their lives due to factors beyond their control. Adverse environmental conditions, including poverty, racial prejudice and discrimination, poor education, and low income or personal misfortunes such as **child abuse** or neglect and chronic poor physical health, all increase the risk of alcohol and other drug dependency.

Causal inferences are difficult to make because the connection between personality and drugs is not always direct. The relationship may be indirect in that some personality traits create one set of conditions that in turn promotes substance abuse and dependency. Thus, restlessness and inattentiveness in school may lead some individuals to frustration and eventually to low achievement. Failing to receive rewards in school may in turn lead them to truancy and eventually to dropping out of school. Turning to drugs may help these individuals cope with their alienation. In this scenario, personality factors do not directly lead to drug use, but individuals' personality characteristics contribute to outcomes that increase the likelihood that drugs will become a part of their lifestyles.

THEORIES OF SMOKING

> *Smoking is hateful to the nose, harmful to the brain, and dangerous to the lungs.*
>
> —King James I

People smoke cigarettes and other tobacco products for many different reasons. Smoking is more than the physical acts of lighting a cigarette, inhaling, and exhaling smoke. Many adolescents regard smoking as an action that declares their adult status. Smoking can be an expression of one's image. How the cigarette is held, how it is placed in the mouth, how it is smoked, and even how it is extinguished and discarded can convey various feelings ranging from sophistication and being "hip" to defiance and rebellion to resignation and defeat.

Smoking is often a social behavior, associated with parties, bars, and other social activities. Cigarettes have been widely marketed and consumed in America for many years. Major tobacco companies tout the pleasures of smoking in their advertising. During the 1940s, smoking was often portrayed in ways ranging from glamorous, sophisticated, and elegant to daring, adventuresome, and independent. Smoking was depicted as a way of coping with stress as well as an enjoyable form of relaxation whether alone or at social gatherings. One major cigarette manufacturer even used prestige suggestion by boasting that doctors, who obviously are experts, smoked its brand more than any other.

Although many aspects of theories about alcohol use are applicable to understanding smoking, some distinct aspects of smoking require additional mechanisms. Whereas alcohol use involves the oral intake of beverages, nicotine is generally obtained by smoking cigarettes. Alcohol in large doses produces intoxication with impairment of cognitive, affective, and motor functions, but such risks are negligible for drugs like nicotine and caffeine. Cigarette smoking occurs periodically throughout the day, every day, for those who smoke regularly, unlike the case for alcohol for most people. For example, most drinkers, except for highly dependent drinkers, do not drink every day but drink more on weekends. Their drinking does not occur evenly in the course of each day but more often with meals or in the evening. Furthermore, due to the rapid process by which inhaled tobacco smoke carries nicotine directly to the brain, the impact is much quicker than the effect of alcohol, which must be absorbed from the gastrointestinal tract into the blood-stream before it can reach the brain.

Psychological Theories of Smoking

Smoking Expectancies

Smoking expectancies generally show similar effects to those found for alcohol (Copeland, Brandon, & Quinn, 1995). Expectancies about the effects of a drug (Goldman, Brown, & Christiansen, 1987) can either promote or inhibit its use (Brown, 1993). Heavier smokers have more positive expectancies about the consequences of smoking than do lighter smokers or nonsmokers (Brandon & Baker, 1991).

Mood Moderation

Smoking relieves negative emotions or affective states like depression and anxiety (Brandon, 1994; Warburton, Revell, & Thompson, 1991). Tension reduction or relaxation is a frequent reason smokers give for using cigarettes. People smoke to deal with depression (Breslau, Kilbey, & Andreski, 1993). Thus, during breaks from work, employees smoke, presumably to relieve stress. And, although nothing might completely relax prisoners who are facing execution, it is a customary act of compassion to allow them to smoke a cigarette before they are executed. Similarly, wounded and dying soldiers on the battlefield are often allowed cigarettes for comfort.

Several studies have examined the relationship between cigarette smoking and stress over the course of a day (Parrott, 1995). After smoking, study participants' immediate feelings of anxiety or stress were lowered, but they increased with the time between cigarettes. Such mood cycles may help explain the repetitive nature of cigarette addiction. The lack of nicotine between cigarettes produces withdrawal reactions. Thus, smoking resumes after deprivation to alleviate such adverse states and "normalize" smokers' mood rather than to produce a beneficial mood.

Smoking also occurred in response to negative mood in a laboratory study (Perkins et al., 2008) in which smokers received a cigarette with 0.6 mg of nicotine or a denicotinized (0.05 mg) cigarette. Half of the smokers in each condition expected a nicotine cigarette, and half expected a denicotinized cigarette. A fifth group was a no-smoking control condition. When a negative mood was induced, smoking increased even among smokers receiving and expecting a denicotinized cigarette. Thus, psychological factors were more important than pharmacological ones in these smokers.

However, in another study, smoking by 304 heavy smokers in natural surroundings rather than under laboratory conditions showed little influence of stress on smoking (Shiffman et al., 2002). Smokers recorded each cigarette they smoked for 1 week using palm-top computers. Smoking urges, consumption of coffee and food, the presence of other smokers, and several activities had a stronger relationship to smoking than did negative or positive affect.

Smoking has an alerting function that leads to improvements in many areas, including motor performance (Perkins, Epstein, Sexton, Stiller, & Jacob, 1991) and vigilance or sustained attention (Warburton, 1989). The heightened alertness created by nicotine obtained from smoking may improve cognitive and mental functioning.

The belief that smoking helps produce or maintain weight loss by increasing **metabolism** and/or physical activity and suppressing appetite may be another motivator. One study (McKee, Nhean, Hinson, & Mase, 2006) illustrated how cigarette advertising can promote such beliefs. Dieting women who viewed slides depicting fashion models similar to those used in tobacco advertising held stronger beliefs that smoking aids appetite and weight control in comparison to dieters who viewed slides of nature scenes or to nondieters who viewed either type of slides.

Physical Sensations of Smoking

The importance of taste as a factor in smoking, highly promoted in cigarette ads, is probably more a myth than a reality. In one study (Jaffe & Glaros, 1986), smokers made taste comparisons among pairs of different cigarette brands. Their judgments fell along two taste dimensions, flat–sharp and high nicotine–low nicotine. While smokers could distinguish differences on these aspects among cigarettes, they generally were unable to recognize their own brand from the others. However, taste could be just one of many factors that contribute to overall smoking motivation.

The physical actions and rituals of lighting, handling, and even extinguishing cigarettes as well as the sensation of smoke inhalation through the mouth and nostrils may be additional factors. Smoke inhalation sensations were sufficient to reduce negative mood when the motor movements associated with the lighting and handling of cigarettes during smoking were controlled (Perkins et al., 2008).

Pharmacological Theory of Smoking

The **nicotine regulation model** (Jarvik, 1979) proposes that smokers use cigarettes in a pattern that attempts to maintain a preferred level of nicotine. The importance of nicotine level is illustrated by the observation that habitual smokers typically need a cigarette to begin the day because their nicotine level from the last cigarette before falling asleep has dropped to an uncomfortably low level overnight.

One experiment (Schachter, 1977) gave smokers cigarettes that looked identical but, unknown to them, varied in nicotine level. As expected, they inhaled more deeply when smoking low-nicotine than regular-strength cigarettes, as if they were adjusting for the lower nicotine.

Relationship of Pharmacological and Psychological Processes

The **multiple regulation model** (Leventhal & McCleary, 1980) acknowledges the role of nicotine regulation as a pharmacological factor underlying smoking, but it also includes a parallel psychological process in which smoking occurs in response to negative affect. This model assumes that psychological stressors are a major motivator of smoking. Cues associated with smoking become conditioned to the nicotine in the cigarettes and will trigger craving in the absence of smoking. Over time, smokers will attempt to regulate or maintain nicotine levels that make them feel comfortable.

Thus, psychological factors initially activate smoking, but nicotine level becomes the major determinant during later stages in the development of smoking. At the outset, social factors such as peers and media images are important motivators of adolescent smoking. When smoking reaches the point of dependence, nicotine has a stronger role through its physiological effects on arousal and affect regulation. By then, social factors have become secondary (Mayhew, Flay, & Mott, 2000).

Habitual smokers do not consciously smoke to regulate or achieve desired levels of nicotine so much as they strive to modulate emotional states associated with past smoking. These affective states originated as conditioned responses to nicotine levels and the bodily feelings generated when smoking occurred in the past. Subsequent smoking, of course, does actually affect nicotine levels, but the mind of the smoker is focused on achieving the emotional, not the pharmacological, states. For example, when smoking occurs, so does increased arousal from the nicotine, which becomes conditioned to the situation involving smoking. If smoking has occurred in a fearful or anxiety-producing situation, it becomes a conditioned response to these negative emotions. Similarly, if smoking has occurred in a joyful and positive situation, the activation from the nicotine would become conditioned to these positive emotions. Subsequently, when these emotions are aroused, they may trigger the urge to smoke. When experienced smokers are unable to smoke, they typically suffer unpleasant withdrawal reactions. This negative affect can become conditioned to those situations where smoking does not occur.

THEORY OF CAFFEINE USE

Caffeine is a psychoactive ingredient in coffee, which is commonly used to increase alertness and vigilance, improve cognitive function and memory, lower RT, and offset fatigue and drowsiness (Brice & Smith, 2002; Haskell, Kennedy, Wesnes, & Scholey, 2005/2006), although high levels can produce anxiety. Caffeine is widely available in other beverages such as tea and soft drinks, in chocolates, and in some foods that children as well as adults consume, but the present discussion focuses on coffee.

In addition to the psychological and behavioral effects that motivate the use of caffeine, it is important to recognize the social context. Drinking coffee may often be motivated by opportunities to socialize with coworkers and friends. Coffee breaks are socially motivated and not viewed as occasions to consume caffeine primarily for its physical effect.

Caffeine products, like those containing alcohol and nicotine, are licit drugs. All three are generally restricted to adult use, a factor that ironically induces use as a rite of passage for those under the legal age. Considered relatively benign, caffeine has led to little long-term public concern over health risks from its use. Coffee drinkers quickly develop tolerance, and only a small percentage of users experience mild withdrawal reactions from its discontinued use (Nehlig, 1999). Although some health risks are present, they are not as life threatening as lung cancer from smoking cigarettes or liver **cirrhosis** from drinking alcohol. However, caffeine use is associated with many psychiatric disorders such as depression, schizophrenia, eating disorders, attention deficit hyperactivity disorder (ADHD), and restless legs syndrome, but it is not clear if there is any causal relationship (Smith, Osborne, Mann, Jones, & White, 2004).

Sensation seeking may contribute to caffeine consumption. However, smoking, which is correlated with coffee consumption, complicates the interpretation. One study of 498 adults (Gurpegui et al., 2007) examined personality traits in relation to both caffeine intake and smoking after controlling for sex and age. Heavy caffeine consumption (>200 mg/day) was associated with novelty seeking even after controlling for the effect of smoking. In addition, both smoking and heavy smoking (>20 cigarettes/day) were related to novelty seeking after controlling for the effect of caffeine intake. Another study (Jones & Lejuez, 2005) compared 60 college students, either caffeine dependent and high consuming or caffeine nondependent and low consuming, on self-report and behavioral measures of sensation seeking, impulsivity, and risk taking. Only sensation seeking had a significant relationship to caffeine use. The combined findings suggest that coffee drinking—and smoking—reflect sensation-seeking tendencies.

ILLICIT DRUG THEORY

Social norms encourage most people to at least experiment with or dabble in the use of licit drugs, but this same factor would seemingly minimize the use of illicit drugs. Potential users might assume that because illicit drugs are banned they must be more dangerous and hence should be avoided. In addition, the fear of being caught and either fined or imprisoned is a strong disincentive for the use of illicit drugs. Nonetheless, a sizeable minority does take these risks, and it is important to identify factors that increase vulnerability to illicit drugs.

Problem Behavior Theory

An undercontrolled behavior style can lead to a set of adolescent problem behaviors involving deviance from social norms, only one of which is excessive use of alcohol and drugs. Problem behavior theory (Jessor & Jessor, 1977) holds that adolescents who experience problems such as deviant sexual activity or criminal behavior also participate in deviant alcohol and drug use.

Several categories of risk factors are postulated in the theory. Background or distal factors associated with increased risk of drug use include the extent to which adolescents are unattached to parents and too attached to peers who use drugs. Higher risk also exists if adolescents have alienation from conventional values, low self-esteem, and external locus of control. At an intermediate level, more drug use is also likely with adolescents who devalue academic achievement, have low academic expectations, seek independence from parents, and value involvement with drug-using peers. The most immediate or proximal factors associated with more risk of drug use are tolerance of deviant behaviors and beliefs that drug benefits outweigh their costs.

Regular drug users or those committed to an alcohol-and-drugs lifestyle have been found to be higher than nonusers or less frequent users on dimensions such as rebellion, lack of conformity to traditional values, and other socially deviant or illegal behaviors (Jessor & Jessor, 1975). Alienation and distance from family, early sexual activity, and low involvement in school are also associated with the lifestyle of alcohol and drug abusers. Problem behavior theory focuses on individual differences as the cause of problem drug use. However, these problems might be the effect of bad choices that lead to continued and often increased use of many drugs, licit or illicit. Such involvement will lead to problems in many areas, including physical, academic, social, and even legal matters.

Drug Use Vulnerability Model

A developmental model of vulnerability to drug use (Glantz, 1992) covers the major factors leading to the use of illicit drugs. This formulation proposes that **risk factors** such as parental drug abuse or depressed mood increase the likelihood that a child will develop drug abuse. First, if abuse occurs during pregnancy, impulsivity, attention deficits, and aggressiveness may be more likely. These infants, more difficult to handle, may not develop good attachment with their caregivers, jeopardizing the quality of subsequent interactions with their parents.

Parental drug abuse may lead to child abuse or neglect. Parents who use drugs may also serve as models for drug abuse. These factors may extend to school adjustment and could interfere with learning. Children who do poorly in school may drop out or develop behavior problems. By adolescence, alienation, self-derogation, hostility, low self-esteem, and depression may have developed. Use and abuse of drugs may be a form of coping with these problems to reduce negative feelings.

On the other hand, protective factors such as high self-esteem or coping skills would reduce this possibility for illicit drug use. The multiple risk and protective factors are not static components but evolve through interactions with environmental events over time.

Summary

Social learning theory emphasizes cognitive factors such as the expectancies one has about drug use as determinants of actual drug use. These expectancies exist for most people before their first actual use of a specific drug. Users learn from watching others, as well as from past experiences, what effects drug use can produce. They adjust their drug use according to their own needs and values. Expectations about the effects of psychoactive substances can affect the physiological responses to alcohol and other drugs just as emotional reactions can alter the cognitive processes occurring with their use. Motivation for initial use can come from many factors, including mass media, social models, peer influence, and poor family life.

Tension reduction theory assumes a direct, pharmacological influence of drug use such as relaxation whereas self-awareness theory assumes an indirect process in which drug use reduces self-awareness of distressful situations. Although users of some drugs may seek to reduce stress and self-awareness by drug use, sometimes the opposite effect may actually occur due to the impaired functioning and social criticism created by excessive drug use.

The stress response dampening theory focuses on the underlying physiological processes for drug use effects. Cardiovascular responses, in particular, and other physiologic stress reactions are dampened or reduced by drug use. Those for whom these effects occur are more likely to drink alcohol to cope when under stress. This model focuses on how the physiological responses to drug use reduce stress.

In the enhanced reinforcement model, dispositions of greater sensitivity to alcohol and other drugs increase the likelihood that they will function as reinforcers in reducing stress, especially for individuals without good psychological coping skills. The negative affect model concentrates on negative feelings that may lead to alcohol and drug use as a form of self-medication. Temperamental factors favoring depression or anxiety, combined with stressful life events as well as poor coping skills, facilitate the onset of drug abuse.

Psychodynamic theory emphasizes unconscious motives for excessive use of alcohol and drugs. These motives may reflect the influence of intensely emotional experiences during infancy or early childhood. Use of alcohol to achieve immediate oral gratification and pleasure may stem from arrested development or fixation at the oral stage of development.

Alcoholics have been observed to differ from nonalcoholics in many aspects of their personalities, suggesting the possibility that there is an "alcoholic personality." If these differences existed prior to the onset of alcoholism, they might be viewed as having a causal role in alcoholism, but if they appear only after alcohol abuse or dependence occurs, they are more likely effects of the drinking. Some personality theories propose typologies or classifications of basic groups such as introversion-extraversion. Similar classifications have been proposed for alcoholics, including milieu-limited alcoholism or Type 1, male-limited alcoholism or Type 2, and Type A and Type B alcoholic. This formulation emphasizes individual differences in temperament or biological sensitivity to stimulation.

Although many theories of alcoholism apply to smoking, it is necessary to develop smoking-specific theories as well. The pattern of cigarette use is markedly different from that of most other drugs; in addition, unlike alcohol, there is no loss of control or intoxication with excessive use. Smoking expectancy studies generally show similar effects to those found for alcohol. Heavier smokers have more positive expectancies about the consequences of smoking than do lighter smokers or nonsmokers. Smoking relieves negative emotions like depression and anxiety and can aid in coping with negative affective states. Tension reduction or relaxation is a frequent reason smokers give for using cigarettes. Smoking also provides pleasurable physical sensations and aids in weight regulation.

The multiple regulation model acknowledges the role of nicotine regulation as a pharmacological factor underlying smoking, but it also includes a parallel psychological process in which smoking occurs in response to negative affect. This model assumes that psychological stressors are a major motivator of smoking. Cues associated with smoking become conditioned to the nicotine in the cigarettes and can trigger craving in the absence of smoking. Over time, smokers attempt to regulate or maintain nicotine levels that make them feel comfortable.

Caffeine, like nicotine, is regarded as an alerting influence. It also is associated with work breaks and social encounters as a relaxing drug. Caffeine is a psychoactive substance used to increase alertness and wakefulness, improve cognitive function, and relieve fatigue. Although caffeine use is associated with many psychiatric disorders such as depression, schizophrenia, eating disorders, ADHD, and restless legs syndrome, it is not clear if there is any causal relationship. Considered benign, there has been little public concern over the health risks of caffeine.

Theories that deal with legal drugs are inadequate to fully explain the use of illicit drugs. A theory of illicit drugs needs to explain why users engage in such activities at the additional risk of imprisonment and other strong social disincentives. While there may be differences in biological vulnerability that increase the reinforcement received from illicit drugs, the potential user must first be sufficiently motivated to transgress societal norms and laws. A social psychological view of illicit drug use is that it is only one of several deviant behaviors engaged in by individuals who have become alienated from society. According to problem behavior theory, a general level of undercontrol by heavy alcohol users may set in motion a series of consequences that eventually produces many deviant behaviors.

Stimulus/Response

1. Do you find that your use of alcohol, tobacco, and coffee relieves stress in some situations but not in others? Can you identify some of the conditions associated with each type of outcome for the same drug usage?

2. Because most drugs are off-limits to minors, curiosity may play a major role in the initial use of a specific drug. What approaches might be used to satisfy or reduce this curiosity? If curiosity about a specific drug could be reduced safely, would it lower the risk of future problems with that drug?

3. One motivator for youth to drink or smoke may be to defy rules and prohibitions against their underage use. If minors were permitted to engage openly in drinking and smoking, do you think adult drinking and smoking problems would be reduced?

4. Many people say they drink alcohol, smoke, or drink coffee for positive benefits such as relaxation or to be sociable. To what extent is this recognized by theories of drinking, smoking, and drinking coffee discussed in this chapter?

Alcohol and Other Drugs

Use, Abuse, and Dependence

Defining Use	Criteria of Abuse and Dependence
Methods of Measuring Use	Assessment of *DSM-IV* Disorders
Use, Abuse, and Dependence	Summary
Major Conceptions of Alcohol Use Disorders	Stimulus/Response

An alcoholic is someone you don't like who drinks as much as you do.

—Dylan Thomas

One often hears depictions about alcohol and other drug use by others like "He's a heavy drinker," "She's a real boozer," "She smokes an awful lot," or "He takes pot sometimes." These descriptions of how much or how often someone uses a drug are vague and do not tell us very much. Compare Cheryl who drinks a glass of wine every evening at dinner, Brad who drinks about a six-pack of beer but only on weekends, and Scott who consumes three or four drinks of scotch and soda about three times a week. Which drinker is the heaviest drinker? Which drinker consumes the most alcohol during a typical week? Since the three individuals vary in their temporal pattern of drinking, the type of alcoholic beverage consumed, and the number of drinks per occasion, it is not easy to clearly see which drinker is the "heaviest drinker."

How does one define and measure alcohol and other drug use? "**Use**" is primarily a descriptive index, typically based on how often a substance is used and in what amounts. The extent of use is related to but is not perfectly correlated with the degree of problems such behavior creates for the user or for others. In the first portion of this chapter, we will describe the basic methods for defining and obtaining measures of drug use, without consideration of the physical, psychological, or behavioral effects of such use levels. Measuring the use of licit and illicit drugs involves different methods because of the great difficulty in obtaining information from a representative sample of illicit drug users.

In contrast, other constructs exist that refer to conditions generated by alcohol and other drug use that are troublesome for the users and for others. Alcohol and other drugs can lead to adverse consequences, or states referred to as **addiction**, **abuse**, and **dependence**. These conditions, which can occur even with low use levels, reflect the negative effects rather than the actual levels of use. In the second part of this chapter, we will examine the diagnostic criteria used in several major taxonomic classification systems to distinguish use, abuse, and dependence.

DEFINING USE

The use of any drug is multidimensional, and most measures capture only one or a few of these aspects. Thus far, these indices fall far short of capturing a clear picture of the nature of alcohol and other drug use. To illustrate some of the problems associated with describing the use of any drug, we will describe in detail the measurement of the use of alcohol, the psychoactive drug that has been studied more extensively than any other. Due to its wide use and because it is a legal drug that most adult users do not bother to conceal, we are able to obtain more precise information about its use than we usually can learn about the use of illicit substances, which are not as readily reported or observed.

Furthermore, the pharmacological ingredients and potency of alcoholic beverages, as with other legal drugs, are regulated and fairly standardized. In contrast, illicit drugs can vary widely in potency and purity from sample to sample. Since "packaging" of illegal drugs is not standard, users often do not know the dose level of drugs they are taking. Even with alcoholic beverages, however, it is not easy to determine the best way to measure the amount of intake, as we shall see.

For any occasion involving alcohol use, one can measure the type of beverage, the number of drinks consumed, and the duration of drinking. Over an extended period, the frequency of drinking episodes and the amount consumed on each episode will differ across drinking occasions as well as for different individuals. The pattern or topography of drinking, which involves the rate of drinking within an episode, also varies for different individuals. Moreover, different beverage types may be consumed differently as wine may tend to be sipped delicately while beer might be often gulped down.

Alcoholic beverages such as beer, wine, and liquor differ in many respects including alcohol content, taste, and price. Despite these differences, for most research on alcohol consumption, when researchers refer to a "drink" of alcohol, they usually regard one standard-sized drink of any of these beverages as equivalent in terms of alcohol. In fact, the concentration of alcohol in these different alcoholic beverages is not equivalent, with most beer containing about 3%–5% alcohol by volume, wine containing 12%–14%, and liquor containing 45%–50%. Because the liquid volume of a typical drink of each beverage type also varies, the amount of **absolute alcohol** is roughly equivalent in a 12-oz can or bottle of beer, a 5-oz glass of wine, and a mixed drink or cocktail containing 1.5 oz of liquor.

Defining Amount of Drinking

The total volume of alcoholic beverages an individual drinks over a given period such as a day, a week, or a month is a widely used convenient summary index of the total amount of alcohol consumed. This aggregate index affords convenient comparisons of the drinking of individuals who differ in their patterns of drinking. Thus, the total volume of alcohol consumed can be calculated for individuals with varied drinking habits. The total alcohol is about the same for Tom who drinks daily but has only one or two drinks of wine each time, Jeff who drinks beer occasionally in large quantities coupled with a few occasions involving a small amount of wine, and Brad who drinks liquor in large quantities but only on weekends.

A volume index of drinking such as a quantity-frequency (QF) score is derived from two more basic dimensions, frequency of consumption and quantity of consumption. For simplicity's sake, assume that people generally drink the same number of times in a period such as a week or a month and that when they drink they consume about the same number of drinks each time. By simply multiplying the frequency by the quantity consumed per drinking occasion, we obtain a measure that represents the total volume of consumption, known as a **quantity-frequency index**. However, using total volume as the index of drinking ignores the fact that different combinations of frequency and amount can produce a given total volume, as shown in Table 3.1.

The variables, quantity and frequency, can offset each other in one sense. Thus, a high frequency (30 days in 1 month) of drinking with a typical low quantity (1 drink) consumed per occasion yields an aggregate total of 30 drinks per month. Exactly the same total volume of consumption occurs for a drinker with a low frequency (three times a month) of drinking who typically drinks very high quantities (10 drinks) per occasion.

TABLE 3.1 It is possible for different combinations of quantity of drinks per occasion and frequency of drinking occasions that can produce widely different effects on behavior to yield the same QF score—in this example, 30.

Quantity of Drinks	Frequency of Drinking	Quantity-Frequency (QF) Score
1	30	30
2	15	30
3	10	30
5	6	30
6	5	30
10	3	30

Note: The same QF score of 30 can be produced by different combinations of quantity of drinks per occasion and frequency of drinking occasions.

These two extremely different patterns of drinking will undoubtedly have different effects as well as represent individuals with different characteristics and backgrounds. For the same total volume of alcohol, the drinker who engages in heavy drinking, albeit infrequently, is more likely than the one who drinks in smaller amounts spaced over more occasions to have problems caused by drinking such as physical harm, cognitive impairment, accidents, and disruption of social relationships.

The maximum consumption level refers to the highest quantity consumed on an occasion by an individual. This index might be more important than the frequency of consumption when seeking factors that are associated with immediate harmful consequences of drinking such as accidents or aggressive behavior. Frequent drinking, if it involves only low levels, does not necessarily entail serious physical or psychological harm to drinkers. On the other hand, drinking very high quantities, even if rarely done, is more likely to cause harm.

One index of drinking that would likely be associated with harm is the frequency of intoxication, referring to a subjective condition of disorientation and disinhibition often associated with higher quantities of consumption. Another index assumed to be risky is **heavy drinking**, arbitrarily defined in some major surveys as five or more drinks on one occasion five or more times in a month.

The extent of heavy drinking episodes will be missed by measures of "typical drinking." When drinkers are only asked for their typical quantity, they may not consider heavy or **binge drinking** occasions, especially if they are not typical. One study (Stahre, Naimi, Brewer, & Holt, 2006) used a QF measure of drinking that also asked about binge drinking. Calculations of average daily alcohol consumption that included binge drinking increased the relative prevalence of heavy drinking among all adults by 19%–42%, depending on how the number of drinks per binge was estimated. The prevalence estimates for heavy drinking were higher if the binge drinks were included in the calculation of average daily alcohol consumption.

Most epidemiological studies focus on the total volume of drinking over a period but need to include measures of other aspects of drinking (Rehm et al., 1996). The pattern of drinking reflects the social and psychological aspects of the occasion for an individual's drinking such as the social context or setting, the day of the week, the time of day, and the type of drinking companions. Drinking patterns as well as the volume of consumption can affect the social consequences of drinking.

Although some drinkers are consistent in drinking the same amounts and at regular intervals, many individuals have variable use patterns over time. The *graduated frequency (GF) method* does not assume that there is a "typical" quantity or frequency of use but asks how often the respondent drinks various quantities during a specific time period (Greenfield, 2000; Rehm, 2000). The GF method allows more complex patterns of drinking to be measured by including variability of drinking over time as a third dimension in addition to quantity and frequency.

Defining Tobacco Use

There are also difficulties in obtaining an adequate description of tobacco use. The total number of cigarettes smoked over a given time period is a crude index of smoking, which does not consider how cigarettes are smoked. First, the temporal patterns of smoking are ignored when looking only at total consumption. The patterns of cigarette use over the course of a day or week are more like those of caffeine consumption than those of alcohol and many other drugs. Whereas many drinkers restrict their use of alcohol to weekends, mostly in the evening, or in conjunction with meals, cigarettes and coffee tend to be consumed many times each day. Hence, whereas all but the most addicted drinkers are free of alcohol during part of the day, cigarette smokers are more likely to be under some degree of influence from nicotine throughout the waking hours. In part, these differences may reflect the lesser impairment of daily work activities by continuous use of cigarettes than by similar involvement with alcohol.

Another reason the number of cigarettes smoked is a poor index of the actual level of smoking is because there is more than one way a cigarette can be smoked. The extent to which each cigarette is smoked and the degree of inhalation of smoke can vary across smokers and even within the same smoker in different situations. For example, low-tar and low-nicotine cigarettes with filters were developed to combat the health threats from nicotine. However, these devices do not work as well as hoped to reduce the hazards of smoking because smokers of "lights" adjust or titrate nicotine intake levels by smoking more cigarettes; taking more puffs; increasing puff volume, puff depth, and duration of inhalation; and blocking vents on the filters by covering them with their fingers (Kozlowski, Pillitteri, & Sweeney, 1994). Ironically, these tactics to increase nicotine intake may expose smokers to greater health risks from the tars and carbon monoxide associated with the higher volume of smoke in their lungs.

If one used the common approach for measuring alcohol use, a QF smoking index could be computed by determining the typical number of cigarettes smoked each day and the number of days a person smokes during that period. It would have to be adjusted by the amount of nicotine and tar levels contained in different brands and whether the cigarettes were filtered or mentholated.

An aggregate measure of the total number of cigarettes smoked does not adequately reflect variations in the patterns in which individuals smoke their cigarettes. This index would fail to reveal whether that total represented a chain smoker (one who smokes evenly throughout the day) or one who does not smoke every day. Smokers also vary in the number of puffs per cigarette, the time between puffs, the depth of inhalation, and how much of the entire cigarette is smoked. These factors are important since they affect the amount of nicotine and combustion products such as tars that their lungs receive. As with aggregate indices for any drug, this measure would miss the patterning of use.

Defining Illegal Drug Use

Attempts to determine the frequency and amount of any illicit drug use may not yield valid self-reports, simply because of the illegal nature of such use. In addition to this problem, the quantity or strength of the dose might prove difficult to measure accurately due to the unregulated production of illegal drugs. For example, by the time cocaine reaches the street, drug dealers have adulterated and cut it with filler materials to increase the profits. For example, although morphine constitutes 10% by weight of opium, the samples used by drug abusers can vary from 2.6% to 9.9% (Kalant, 1997). Marijuana obtained from different sources may vary in potency or concentration of its psychoactive substance, **delta-9-THC**, depending on factors such as the subspecies of cannabis plant or the conditions under which it was grown. Cocaine and heroin, cut with fillers by drug dealers to increase their profits, range widely in purity. Without knowledge of the potency and purity of drugs used, it is impossible to accurately determine the dose effect of these drugs on behavior.

Unlike the case for alcohol and tobacco, the route of administration of many illicit drugs varies widely. Injecting or smoking the same quantity of heroin or cocaine, for example, allows for a much more rapid and complete intake of the psychoactive ingredients than does oral ingestion. However, this variable must be taken into consideration in addition to the amount consumed since the impact of a drug depends directly on how quickly it gets into the bloodstream to reach the brain.

METHODS OF MEASURING USE

Self-Report Measures

Drug research relies heavily on **self-reports** of past or current use that are typically obtained under conditions that protect anonymity. Since admission of the use of any drug can lead to undesired consequences, an underreporting bias may occur. Even if anonymity is offered, respondents may not trust such promises. For illegal drugs, this problem is obviously much greater.

In addition, retrospective self-reports of drug use are often flawed by inaccuracy of memory. An alternative procedure for legal drugs is to use a prospective self-report in which memory flaws might be minimized or even eliminated if respondents are motivated to monitor and record future use as it happens. However, such self-monitoring might alter the very behavior being recorded because individuals might have used more than they realize. Such feedback might change the use levels for some.

Whether retrospective or prospective, self-reports have been criticized as subjective and apt to be inaccurate or falsified in some contexts. Self-reports can sometimes be compared with collateral reports from a family member, spouse, or friend who can provide an independent report about the respondent's drug use that can be compared with the self-report (Midanik, Klatsky, & Armstrong, 1989). One bias is the tendency to accept the report of a collateral, or another person acquainted with the individual, as providing the more objective or accurate measure. For example, if self-reported drinking is lower than what the collateral reports, the drinker is viewed as being in **denial**. But if the self-reported drinking level is higher than what the collateral reports, it is dismissed as inaccurate.

This bias against self-report, where it is assumed to be the inferior method, may be unwarranted. Many collaterals make estimates based on their expectations about the drug use of the significant other and do not necessarily rely on direct observation, which may be infrequent. Indeed, their reports may sometimes be based heavily on the self-reports of the significant other, which can be inflated if the user is bragging to impress others or underestimated as when the user is motivated to hide his or her substance abuse.

One study (Searles, Perrine, Mundt, & Helzer, 1995) measured the validity of self-reports of drinking by providing respondents with pagers to obtain 24-hour surveillance of their real-world drinking for 112 consecutive days. The participants were a heavy drinking sample with over 40% consuming five or more drinks per occasion. Retrospective self-reports of heavy drinkers underreported their alcohol use as the beeper data revealed they engaged in higher use of alcohol than their questionnaire data suggested.

A telephone survey of 307 adults on two occasions separated by one month (Gruenewald & Johnson, 2006) examined the test-retest reliabilities of self-reported drinking. However, "unreliable" reports may not necessarily be inaccurate because some respondents with fluctuations in drinking between the two assessments may have given valid reports of "unstable" drinking, yielding low correlations over time. Respondents with stable drinking showed strong reliability of self-reports, which were higher than the reliability of self-reports of those with unstable drinking.

Physical Measures

Many drugs consumed remain in the blood until they are metabolized or excreted. Current alcohol concentrations can be obtained from readings of breath, blood samples, and urine samples. Other objective indices of the amount of alcohol consumption are biochemical measures of metabolic products of alcohol like enzymes such as gamma-glutamyltransferase (GGT), as well as physiological indices such as mean corpuscular volume (MCV).

For nicotine, urine measures of the major metabolite, cotinine, provide evidence of the extent of cigarette use. Urinanalysis can also detect metabolites of illegal drugs. Cocaine can be detected through the presence of benzoylecgonine, its primary metabolite, in urine for up to about 48 hours after its use. This is not a precise indicator, however, of the amount of use and is apt to overestimate actual use. Marijuana metabolites are more difficult to obtain since the majority is eliminated in feces rather than in urine.

However, biological indices are limited to measuring very recent usage and must be obtained within a short period following consumption. Moreover, these measures cannot determine the amount of a drug that was consumed or the duration involved. For example, a physical index may indicate that drinking occurred, but whether a given reading reflects a small amount recently consumed or a large amount consumed over a longer interval is indeterminate. Moreover, these measures are not tamperproof.

Indirect measures of consumption such as physical traces are not perfect and must be assessed along two important dimensions, **sensitivity** and **specificity**. Sensitivity is an index of the extent to which the measure can detect the consumption of a given drug. As Table 3.2 shows, a highly sensitive measure would infrequently miss detecting users. The specificity of an index refers to the extent that it does not make false positive identifications. If other drugs than a specific drug under investigation can produce similar results on the index, specificity of this measure will be low. When other substances also produce high readings on this measure, false positive cases will occur in which someone who did not use that specific drug will be mis-classified as having done so—and sometimes with serious legal consequences.

Thus, cigarette smoking produces cotinine, carbon monoxide, and thiocyanate (SCN), but these products are not specific to smoking as other behaviors can also leave these traces in the body. Dieting, as well as eating broccoli and cauliflower, can increase SCN levels.

TABLE 3.2 Specificity and sensitivity are two important characteristics of measures for detecting use of alcohol and other drugs.		
	High-Specificity Measure of Use of a Specific Drug	**Low-Specificity Measure of Use of a Specific Drug**
High-Sensitivity Measure of Using a Specific Drug	Detects higher percentage of positive cases and makes fewer false positive errors	Detects higher percentage of positive cases but also makes more false positive errors
Low-Sensitivity Measure of Using a Specific Drug	Detects lower percentage of positive cases but does not make many false positive errors	Detects lower percentage of positive cases and makes more false positive errors

Surveillance Measures

Another indirect source of evidence about legal drug consumption is **surveillance indicators of use** such as records associated with the sale of alcohol such as tax revenues. Such data merely document levels of possible total consumption but do not reveal patterns of use, heavy or light, or how the total consumption is distributed over different segments of the population. Nor do such data deal with how drug use is linked to problems such as poor health, accidents, or aggression. Obviously this approach would not be possible for illicit drugs since official sales figures and manufacturing records are not available as they are for alcohol and tobacco products.

Data on adverse consequences related to drug use such as traffic fatalities involving drugs, physical diseases such as cirrhosis of the liver, and admissions to drug treatment facilities provide indirect evidence about the harmful effects of drug use. Such information, however, is correlational and inconclusive about causality. Finally, although sometimes biased or incomplete, historical records and official statistics from government and industry sources can allow for insights into the nature of drug use in the historical past.

USE, ABUSE, AND DEPENDENCE

There are several distinct but often related aspects of alcohol and other drug use shown in Figure 3.1: *use* (especially if heavy), *abuse or use-related problems*, and *dependence*.

Use

Light infrequent use of alcohol and many other drugs is not a major concern in terms of adverse physical and psychological consequences. It is heavy or excessive use of drugs that creates social concern. *Heavy* is a rather subjective and relative term, referring to a style of drug use that leads to immediate as well as long-term impaired functioning in the user, conflicts with others around the user, and potential physical health risks for the user. The exact

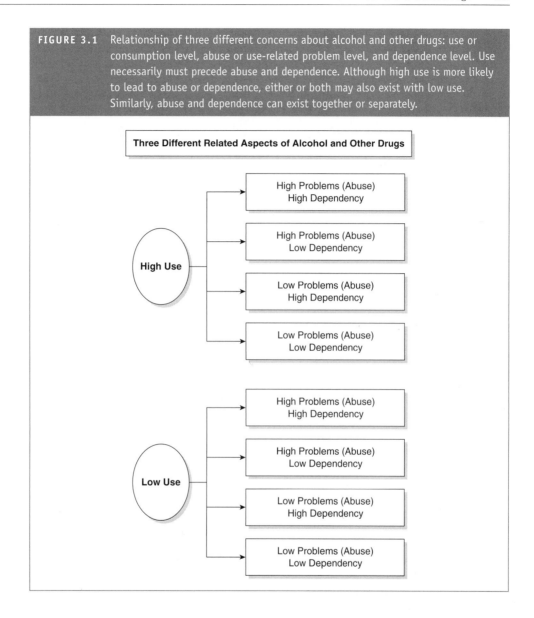

FIGURE 3.1   Relationship of three different concerns about alcohol and other drugs: use or consumption level, abuse or use-related problem level, and dependence level. Use necessarily must precede abuse and dependence. Although high use is more likely to lead to abuse or dependence, either or both may also exist with low use. Similarly, abuse and dependence can exist together or separately.

Three Different Related Aspects of Alcohol and Other Drugs

High Use

High Problems (Abuse)
High Dependency

High Problems (Abuse)
Low Dependency

Low Problems (Abuse)
High Dependency

Low Problems (Abuse)
Low Dependency

Low Use

High Problems (Abuse)
High Dependency

High Problems (Abuse)
Low Dependency

Low Problems (Abuse)
High Dependency

Low Problems (Abuse)
Low Dependency

number of drinks that produce impairment will be affected by other factors such as an individual's past experience with drinking and characteristics such as weight, gender, and genetic background. There is no consistent definition of heavy drinking. In many research surveys, as noted above, it is *arbitrarily* defined as having five or more drinks on one occasion at least five times in a single month. However, heavy use per se does not necessarily indicate that the alcohol abuser is "addicted" or has no voluntary control over his or her future use of alcohol.

Similarly, heavy use of other drugs may or may not constitute addiction to those drugs. Of course, such use might still be cause for alarm due to the risk of harm to oneself and to others. Thus, extensive cigarette smoking has considerable health risks such as coronary and lung disease even though it does not put one at risk for violence or automobile accidents as does heavy alcohol use.

Abuse or Use-Related Problems

A second concern about alcohol and other drug use focuses on abuse in which *use-related problems* occur: adverse consequences created during and after alcohol or other drug intake. Physical, psychological, and social problems related to the use of alcohol produce a considerable burden on society as well as on individuals. Heavier levels of use are more likely to be associated with more adverse psychological and social consequences as well as with eventual medical problems, but even light and occasional users who use alcohol and drugs excessively on a single occasion may also suffer harmful effects.

Dependence

Dependence is a formulation about substance use developed by psychiatrists and psychologists based on extensive clinical observation of drug users in treatment. Dependence refers to the condition in which the user no longer seems to be able to control consumption. Although it may often be accompanied by use-related problems such as physical, psychological, or interpersonal harm, the two aspects should not be confused with each other. Dependence involves the inability to stop recurrent use of substances such as alcohol or other drugs even though this behavior creates major problems for the user and others. Some but not all definitions of dependency include physical changes in reaction to the substance that lead to increased quantities of use (tolerance) or use to relieve the distress experienced in the absence of the substance (withdrawal) as components.

Dependence is essentially what is popularly called *addiction*, a term avoided by researchers because it has past moralistic and judgmental connotations. Moreover, today, "addiction" is too loosely defined and overused, serving as a metaphor for any excessive behaviors regardless of whether drugs are involved, as in "cell phone addiction" or "shopping addiction." Nonetheless, the terms *addiction*, *alcoholism*, and *dependence* refer to essentially the same condition (Kranzler & Li, 2008).

Although some users seem to be able to control their use for many years, it is clear that for others dependence takes control over their lives and disrupts their ability to function normally. This condition, which involves a compelling physiological or psychological need to use alcohol or drugs, is not a strict function of the amount or frequency of use. It is not limited to heavy and frequent users, as even some light or infrequent users may experience dependence. And, as noted above, it may or may not occur with abuse or harmful outcomes, per se.

Overview

A focus on any one of these three aspects of substance use—use, abuse or use-related problems, and dependence—without recognition of the other aspects yields an incomplete picture. Each aspect, as well as different combinations of the three, reflects unique conditions. Some individuals might have only one or two of these three problems. Thus, one person might use a substance and suffer use-related problems yet not show dependence. Another person might be dependent and have use-related problems despite a low use level. Still another person might use heavily and be dependent but not show much evidence of use-related problems. Finally, some users may engage in heavy use, have use-related problems, and be dependent.

How closely are these different aspects of substance use related? For example, is use level highly correlated with dependence? Are use-related problems associated strongly with use level? And how closely is dependence related to use-related problems?

A comparison (York, 1995) of alcoholics and social drinkers assessed drinking patterns from the start of regular drinking to the present. Drinkers who later became alcoholics began drinking at higher quantities and frequencies compared with social drinkers. Consumption in alcoholics rose rapidly and peaked near age 40. In contrast, intake of social drinkers remained relatively constant across subsequent drinking phases at about three to four drinks per drinking occasion, with a slight increase in the frequency of drinking over time.

Early onset of drinking is a predictor of illicit drug use and dependence (Hingson, Heeren, & Edwards, 2008). An analysis of data from 27,616 drinkers in the National Longitudinal Alcohol Epidemiologic Survey (NLAES) found that half of those who began drinking before age 14, compared with only one tenth of those who started drinking after age 20, used illicit drugs later in life. Those who began drinking before age 14 were three times more likely to become drug dependent than those who did not start drinking until after age 20.

MAJOR CONCEPTIONS OF ALCOHOL USE DISORDERS

Alcohol Dependence Syndrome

Currently, even though the term *alcoholism* is still more familiar and commonly used by the public, clinicians and researchers increasingly refer to it as *alcohol dependence*. This term originated with the **alcohol dependence syndrome (ADS)**, a formulation proposed by British researchers (Edwards & Gross, 1976). Instead of relying on the drinker's self-perception as the disease concept does, this approach defines dependence in terms of the physical and behavioral criteria listed below and described briefly in Figure 3.2.

The ADS formulation emphasizes a continuum of drinking rather than the dichotomy implied by the alcoholic/nonalcoholic distinction. The separation between physical and psychological dependence is blurred under this conception. **Impaired control** of drinking, rather than a loss of control, was postulated to emphasize that the phenomenon does not involve a dichotomy of control versus loss of control as the disease conception proposes.

The ADS is biaxial, involving two separate dimensions, alcohol dependence and alcohol-related problems. Dependence may or may not be associated with alcohol-related problems. Thus, a drinker who is alcohol dependent may be surprisingly free from physical, economic, or social problems from drinking. Also, a drinker who has sustained physical damage or adverse social consequences from heavy drinking may not necessarily be alcohol dependent.

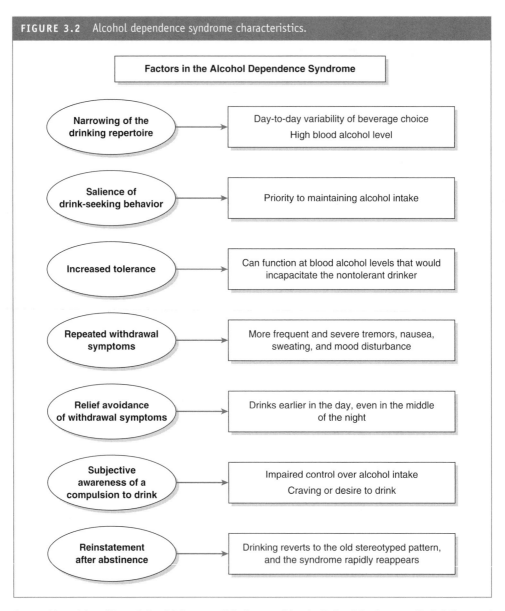

FIGURE 3.2   Alcohol dependence syndrome characteristics.

Factors in the Alcohol Dependence Syndrome

Narrowing of the drinking repertoire	Day-to-day variability of beverage choice High blood alcohol level
Salience of drink-seeking behavior	Priority to maintaining alcohol intake
Increased tolerance	Can function at blood alcohol levels that would incapacitate the nontolerant drinker
Repeated withdrawal symptoms	More frequent and severe tremors, nausea, sweating, and mood disturbance
Relief avoidance of withdrawal symptoms	Drinks earlier in the day, even in the middle of the night
Subjective awareness of a compulsion to drink	Impaired control over alcohol intake Craving or desire to drink
Reinstatement after abstinence	Drinking reverts to the old stereotyped pattern, and the syndrome rapidly reappears

Source: Adapted from "Seventh Special Report to U.S. Congress," by the National Institute on Alcohol Abuse and Alcoholism, 1990, Washington, DC: U.S. Government Printing Office.

The **World Health Organization** (1978) first included ADS in its 9th revision of the *International Classification of Diseases (ICD-9)*. Considered an improvement over the disease concept of alcoholism, ADS does not place as much focus on the physiological basis of alcohol problems. Instead, it recognizes psychological and sociological factors. The ADS formulation has been highly influential for more than 30 years, but its view that abuse and dependence are separate, rather than the ends of a single dimension, has been recently called into question (Li, Hewitt, & Grant, 2007).

CRITERIA OF ABUSE AND DEPENDENCE

Controversies and debates in the field have sometimes stemmed from variations in how alcohol and drug dependence was defined and diagnosed. Answers to questions about the causes of alcohol and drug dependency or the best methods for its treatment often depend on which definition is used. Jellinek's (1960) disease concept of alcoholism used by Alcoholics Anonymous requires alcoholics to label themselves as such. In contrast, major alternative conceptions such as the **Diagnostic and Statistical Manual of Mental Disorders** criteria in its several revisions (*DSM-III-R, DSM-IV, DSM-IV-TR*) and the *International Classification of Diseases*, now in its 10th version (*ICD-10*), have relied more on behavioral, social, and physical criteria for defining dependency.

Diagnostic and Statistical Manual Criteria

The American Psychiatric Association developed its own set of criteria for defining major psychological disorders, including substance use disorders, known as the *Diagnostic and Statistical Manual of Mental Disorders (DSM)*. Different versions of the *DSM* use the term *alcohol* in specific reference to alcohol but use *substance* to include other drugs as well. One widely used version, the *DSM-III-R* (American Psychiatric Association [APA], 1987), is still described here despite being outdated because it was used in many earlier studies that are still influential.

The *DSM-III-R* distinguishes between abuse and dependence. Abuse involves a maladaptive pattern during the past year of drug use or recurrent use in physically hazardous situations lasting at least one month or occurring repeatedly over a longer period, as noted in Table 3.3. A diagnosis of dependence requires the presence of *any* three of the nine criteria shown in Table 3.4, with symptoms involving at least two of these criteria occurring two or more times in the past year.

One study of the validity of the *DSM-III-R* definition of dependence used 99 patients with differing degrees of dependence severity (Andreatini, Galduroz, Ferri, & Oliveira De Souza Formigioni, 1994). Only some of the nine criteria ("markedly increased amounts of drinking," "unsuccessful efforts to cut down or control drinking," and "continued drinking despite major problems") occurred frequently across the spectrum of dependence severity. In contrast, other criteria appeared prominently only in the more severe cases ("a great deal of time devoted to obtaining alcohol," "important activities given up," and "drinking to relieve withdrawal"). Thus, the nine criteria are *not* equal in importance even though they are treated as if they are when making diagnoses.

In the *DSM-IV*, published in 1994, the distinction between abuse and dependence is further refined. The *DSM-IV-TR* (APA, 2000) is an update of the *DSM-IV* text, which reflects research up to 1992. The revisions are confined to the descriptive text and do not involve changes in criteria or diagnostic categories.

TABLE 3.3 Comparisons of criteria for substance abuse under the *DSM-III-R, DSM-IV,* and *ICD-10.*

DSM-III-R, DSM-IV, and *ICD-10* Diagnostic Criteria for
Alcohol Abuse/Harmful Use of Alcohol*

DSM-III-R Alcohol Abuse

  A. A maladaptive pattern of alcohol use indicated by at least one of the following:

    (1) Continued use despite knowledge of having a persistent or recurrent social, occupational, psychological, or physical problem that is caused or exacerbated by use of alcohol

    (2) Drinking in situations in which use is physically hazardous

  B. Some symptoms of the disturbance have persisted for at least one month or have occurred repeatedly over a period of time.

  C. Never met the criteria for alcohol dependence.

DSM-IV Alcohol Abuse

  A. A maladaptive pattern of alcohol use leading to clinically significant impairment or distress, as manifested by one (or more) of the following occurring within a 12-month period:

    (1) Recurrent drinking resulting in a failure to fulfill major role obligations at work, school, or home

    (2) Recurrent drinking in situations in which it is physically hazardous

    (3) Recurrent alcohol-related legal problems

    (4) Continued alcohol use despite having persistent or recurrent social or interpersonal problems caused by or exacerbated by the effects of alcohol

  B. The symptoms have never met the criteria for alcohol dependence.

ICD-10 Harmful Use of Alcohol

  A. A pattern of alcohol use that is causing damage to health. The damage may be physical or mental. The diagnosis requires that actual damage should have been caused to the mental or physical health of the user.

  B. No concurrent diagnosis of the alcohol dependence syndrome.

Source: Alcohol Alert No. 30. PH 359 October. Rockville, MD: National Institute of Alcoholism and Alcohol Abuse, 1995.

*The *DSM-III-R, DSM-IV,* and *ICD-10* refer to substance abuse and harmful use. These criteria have been adapted to focus solely on alcohol.

In both versions of the *DSM-IV,* abuse requires a maladaptive pattern of drug use, showing at least one of the four criteria listed in Table 3.3, provided that the individual being diagnosed has never previously met the criteria for dependence for that substance. To be classified as dependent by the *DSM-IV,* a drug user must meet three or more of the seven criteria listed in Table 3.4 in the same 12-month period. The criteria involve adverse physical consequences of drinking as well as social and behavioral impairments. However, they do not include any direct indicators of alcohol use such as the frequency or quantity and refer only to a *maladaptive pattern of use.*

TABLE 3.4   Comparisons of criteria for substance dependency under the *DSM-III-R, DSM-IV,* and *ICD-10.*

DSM-III-R, DSM-IV, and *ICD-10* Diagnostic Criteria for Alcohol Dependence*

	DSM-III-R	*DSM-IV*	*ICD-10*
SYMPTOMS	A. At least three of the following:	A. A maladaptive pattern of alcohol use, leading to clinically significant impairment or distress as manifested by three or more of the following occurring at any time in the same 12-month period:	A. Three or more of the following have been experienced or exhibited at some time during the previous year:
TOLERANCE	(1) Marked tolerance—need for markedly increased amounts of alcohol (i.e., at least a 50% increase in order to achieve intoxication or diminished effect with the same amount of alcohol)	(1) Need for markedly increased amounts of alcohol to achieve intoxication or desired effect—or markedly diminished effect— with continued use of the same amount of alcohol	(1) Evidence of tolerance, such that increased doses are required in order to achieve effects originally produced by lower doses
WITHDRAWAL	(2) Characteristic withdrawal symptoms for alcohol (3) Alcohol often taken to relieve or avoid alcohol withdrawal syndrome	(2) The characteristic withdrawal syndrome for alcohol, or alcohol (or a closely related substance) is taken to relieve or avoid withdrawal symptoms	(2) A physiological withdrawal state when drinking has ceased or been reduced as evidenced by the characteristic withdrawal symptoms of alcohol (or a closely related substance) to relieve or avoid withdrawal symptoms
IMPAIRED CONTROL	(4) Persistent desire or one or more unsuccessful efforts to cut down on or control drinking (5) Drinking in larger amounts or over a longer period than intended	(3) Persistent desire or one or more unsuccessful efforts to cut down on or control drinking (4) Drinking in larger amounts or over a longer period than intended	(3) Difficulties in controlling drinking in terms of onset, termination, or levels of use

(Continued)

TABLE 3.4 (Continued)			
	DSM-III-R	*DSM-IV*	*ICD-10*
NEGLECT OF ACTIVITIES	(6) Important social, occupational, or recreational activities given up or reduced because of drinking	(5) Important social, occupational, or recreational activities given up or reduced because of drinking	(4) Progressive neglect of alternative pleasures or interests in favor of drinking, or
TIME SPENT DRINKING	(7) A great deal of time spent in activities necessary to obtain alcohol, to drink, or to recover from its effects	(6) A great deal of time spent in activities necessary to obtain alcohol, to drink, or to recover from its effects	a great deal of time spent in activities necessary to obtain alcohol, to drink, or to recover from its effects
INABILITY TO FULFILL ROLES	(8) Frequent intoxication or withdrawal symptoms when expected to fulfill major role obligations at work, school, or home	None	None
HAZARDOUS USE	When drinking is physically hazardous	None	None
DRINKING DESPITE PROBLEMS	(9) Continued drinking despite knowledge of having a persistent or recurrent social, psychological, or physical problem that is likely to be caused or exacerbated by alcohol use	(7) Continued drinking despite knowledge of having a persistent or recurring physical or psychological problem that is caused or exacerbated by alcohol use	(5) Continued drinking despite clear evidence of overly harmful physical or psychological consequences
COMPULSIVE USE	None	None	(6) A strong desire or sense of compulsion to drink
DURATION CRITERION	B. Some symptoms of the disturbance have persisted for at least one month or have occurred repeatedly over a longer period of time.	B. No duration criterion separately specified. However, three or more dependence criteria must be met within the same year and must occur repeatedly as specified by duration qualifiers associated with criteria (e.g., "often," "persistent," "continued").	B. No duration criterion separately specified. However, three or more dependence criteria must be met during the previous year.

	DSM-III-R	*DSM-IV*	*ICD-10*
CRITERION FOR SUBTYPING DEPENDENCE	None	With physiological dependence: Evidence of tolerance or withdrawal (i.e., any of items A (1) or A (2) above [is] present) Without physiological dependence: no evidence of tolerance or withdrawal (i.e., none of items A (1) or A (2) above [is] present)	None

Source: Alcohol Alert No. 30. PH 359 October. Rockville, MD.: National Institute of Alcoholism and Alcohol Abuse, 1995.

*Note: The *DSM-III-R*, *DSM-IV*, and *ICD-10* refer to substance dependence. These criteria have been adapted to focus solely on alcohol.

Major Changes From the DSM-III-R to the DSM-IV

Unlike the *DSM-III-R*, a diagnosis of dependence under the *DSM-IV* no longer requires the presence of tolerance or withdrawal. If physiological dependence, defined as either tolerance or withdrawal, is present, the *DSM-IV* indicates that it should be noted but does not consider it a defining characteristic of substance dependence. This change obviously complicates comparisons of dependence rates between studies using *DSM-III-R* and *DSM-IV* criteria. For example, even though they may have other indications of substance dependence, heavy cocaine users who stop using do not show withdrawal reactions as striking as those seen with a drug like alcohol. Consequently, under *DSM-III-R* criteria, they would not be diagnosed as dependent, but they might be classified as such by *DSM-IV* criteria.

Unlike *DSM-III-R* definitions where duration of symptoms must occur continuously over a month or repeatedly over a longer period of time, the duration requirement in the *DSM-IV* applies to individual diagnostic criteria for each disorder and not to the *categories* of abuse and dependence.

Individuals with markedly different subsets of symptoms can receive the same diagnosis in the *DSM-IV*. To be diagnosed with abuse, a drinker needs to exhibit only one of the four criteria listed in Table 3.3, *provided* there has been no previous diagnosis of dependence. The *DSM-IV* excludes a diagnosis of abuse in a person if he or she has ever been dependent.

By this definition, there are at least four different types of abusers. Diagnoses of dependence involve finding any three of seven criteria that include neuropsychological symptoms (e.g., tolerance and withdrawal), behavioral symptoms (e.g., drinking more than intended and excess time seeking alcohol), and social consequences (e.g., social and legal problems). Thus, the same diagnosis of dependence would be made for anyone with the specific three symptoms of tolerance, dependence, and much time spent seeking alcohol and for anyone with three quite different symptoms such as giving up important activities due to drinking, inability to cut down on drinking, and drinking despite persistent physical or psychological problems.

Many clinicians regard abuse as an earlier stage that eventually might develop into dependence. According to this view, a distinct abuse category is not warranted, as it is just one end of a single continuum. However, clinicians only see the relatively small percentage of people with alcohol problems who seek treatment. A review (Hasin, 2003) of several longitudinal studies with large samples from the general population, rather than clinical samples, generally found alcohol dependence was a chronic condition and one for which relatively few received treatment. In contrast, alcohol abuse cases were less likely to exhibit symptoms of abuse and unlikely to have become alcohol dependent during follow-ups. The overall evidence for the alcohol dependence category was stronger than for the alcohol abuse category. Still, the distinction between the two categories seemed warranted as illustrated by the fact that many young drinkers abuse alcohol but do not show dependence and that many older drinkers are alcohol dependent but do not show abuse.

The *DSM-IV* views of abuse and dependence beg the question of whether some drinkers develop dependency first and later become alcohol abusers because the *DSM-IV* does not permit a diagnosis of alcohol abuse for someone who has previously been diagnosed as alcohol dependent.

Analysis (Hasin & Grant, 2004) of data from respondents in the National Epidemiologic Survey on Alcohol and Related Conditions (NESARC; n = 42,392) diagnosed with current alcohol dependence found that 29.0% of men and 46.1% of women, especially those from minority groups, did not additionally meet criteria for alcohol abuse. For respondents with lifetime diagnoses of alcohol dependence, 10.1% of men and 22.1% of women did not additionally meet criteria for alcohol abuse, with highest proportions among Hispanics. One implication of these findings is that using alcohol abuse as a screener to detect alcohol dependence in large epidemiologic studies will differentially underestimate the prevalence of dependence by a subgroup, which could perpetuate a lack of services for traditionally underserved groups.

International Classification of Diseases and Related Health Problems

The 10th revision of the *International Classification of Diseases and Related Health Problems (ICD-10)* criteria for alcohol use disorders by the World Health Organization (1990) is presented in Tables 3.3 and 3.4. As the *ICD* deals with all types of physical health problems, it uses the term *harmful use* instead of the term *abuse* (used in the *DSM-IV*) to refer to problems deemed less serious than dependency. Harmful use covers both psychological and physical harm to the user.

As Table 3.3 indicates, harmful use deals only with harm to the user in contrast to the *DSM-III-R* and *DSM-IV* category of abuse that includes social harm. *ICD-10* criteria with respect to dependency are similar to those in the *DSM-III-R* and *DSM-IV* as shown in Table 3.4. However, all formulations are vague using terms such as *often, frequent,* and *progressive neglect*. Moreover, no clear time frame exists for making diagnoses. *ICD-10* specifies that the symptoms be present in the last 6 months and the *DSM-III-R* states that they be present for at least 1 month or repeatedly over a longer period, but the *DSM-IV* specifies that it occur in a 12-month period.

Relationships Among Diagnostic Taxonomies

One study (Schuckit et al.,1994) examined the relationships among *DSM-III-R*, *DSM-IV*, and *ICD-10* diagnostic criteria for substance use disorders for 1,922 adults with alcohol dependence and their relatives who participated in the Collaborative Studies on Genetics of Alcoholism (Bierut et al., 2002). Proportions of individuals diagnosed with the three diagnostic systems were similar, with the highest numbers observed for the *DSM-III-R* and the lowest for the *ICD-10*. While the same individuals generally received the same diagnosis under the three sets of criteria for dependency, diagnosis of abuse or harmful use had low agreement across the three systems.

To understand why definitions of dependence differ and also continually undergo change, it is necessary to examine the origins, functions, and goals of these major classification systems (Kendall, 1991). The *ICD-9* is a comprehensive classification covering all "diseases, injuries, and causes of death," and the *ICD-10* deals with all "diseases and related health problems" (p. 297). In contrast, the *DSM* is limited to mental and psychiatric disorders. The *ICD* deals with a broader audience of health professionals than does the *DSM*, and it is accepted in 140 countries and in at least eight languages. The *DSM* is directed more toward mental health professionals and emphasizes problems that are more prominent in Western society than in other cultures (e.g., some types of sexual dysfunction and eating disorders).

It is instructive to trace the history of both taxonomies (Widiger, Frances, Pincus, Davis, & First, 1991). In 1948, the sixth edition of the *ICD* included for the first time a classification of mental disorders, but it did not meet the needs of American psychiatrists, who developed their own nomenclature in 1952 with the first version of the *DSM*. Since then, the two organizations have revised their taxonomies several times in the light of new thinking and evidence. Although converging in their definitions, the two approaches still differ. These classification systems are advances over prior systems because they have been empirically tested, with data available on the reliability and validity of diagnostic categories. Both classification systems are periodically revised, and the hope is that eventually the definitions will converge. The increased dissatisfaction with the limitations of the categorical approach of the *DSM-IV* may lead to a shift to dimensional formulations of psychopathology that better address the complexities of psychological disorders in the *DSM-V* scheduled for 2011 (Widiger & Samuel, 2005).

ASSESSMENT OF *DSM-IV* DISORDERS

The diagnosis of alcohol use disorders based on the criteria of the *DSM-IV* utilizes either structured or semistructured interviews to obtain the necessary information to determine if an interviewee has substance use disorders (Samet, Waxman, Hatzenblehler, & Hasin, 2007). Inasmuch as comorbidity of alcohol use disorders and other *DSM-IV* psychiatric disorders often exists, these instruments also assess the presence of these problems. The time frame covered by most instruments is current as well as lifetime occurrence, although some instruments also ask about the past 12 months.

With a structured instrument, interviewers ask a standard set of questions, exactly as written, and are not allowed to probe further. This type of instrument does not require clinical judgment and takes less time to administer than semistructured instruments. Interviewers may skip some questions, based on patient characteristics or responses to earlier items. Interviewees are limited to a set of standard responses.

In contrast, with a semistructured instrument, interviewers may add follow-up queries based on their clinical skills in interpreting interviewees' initial responses to a set of verbatim questions. Thus, semistructured interviews are better suited for clinical or treatment purposes whereas structured interviews are more appropriate for research studies.

Three widely used assessment tools will be briefly described. The World Health Organization developed the Composite International Diagnostic Interview (CIDI), a structured instrument that assesses 22 *DSM-IV* and *ICD-10* diagnoses including substance use, mood, conduct, attention deficit, and anxiety disorders. A newer version, the World Mental Health Composite International Diagnostic Interview (WMH-CIDI), also includes a **screening** module, measures of 12-month as well as lifetime disorders in the same interview, a detailed assessment of clinical severity, and information on treatment, risk factors, and consequences (Kessler & Ustun, 2004). Another instrument, the **Structured Clinical Interview for *DSM-IV* (SCID;** First, 2002), assesses *DSM-IV* current and lifetime substance use and psychiatric disorders. The SCID also has a semistructured version for use by clinicians that allows them to use only those modules that they think are relevant for each interviewee. A fully structured instrument, the **Alcohol Use Disorder and Associated Disabilities Interview Schedule (AUDADIS)**, developed originally for epidemiological studies (Grant et al., 2003; Grant, Harford, Dawson, Chou, & Pickering, 1995), measures *DSM-IV* disorders involving substance use as well as major mood, anxiety, and personality disorders.

Evidence on the Validity of *DSM-IV* Use Disorders

A set of psychiatric symptoms that occur in a more or less fixed sequence supports the construct validity of the underlying category. Is there an orderly onset of the symptoms used in the *DSM-IV* criteria to define abuse and dependence? In a study of 369 clinical cases (Langenbucher & Chung, 1995), onset of alcoholism appeared to occur in three discrete stages: alcohol abuse, dependence, and accommodation to the illness. This evidence supports the construct validity of alcohol abuse as a discrete first phase from dependence, which is a distinct construct.

One analysis (Dawson, Grant, & Harford, 1995) of alcohol *consumption* examined the relationship between average daily ethanol intake and the relative frequency of drinking five or more drinks on a drinking occasion with 22,102 current drinking adults. For selected levels of consumption, drinking outcomes such as impaired control, continued drinking despite problems, and hazardous drinking were about 50% more likely than were tolerance and withdrawal. These findings support the lessened emphasis given to tolerance and withdrawal in the *DSM-IV* criteria for substance abuse and dependence.

Some evidence raises doubts about *DSM-IV* criteria that define abuse and dependence as two distinct use disorders. One analysis (Saha, Stinson, & Grant, 2007) examined the relationship between the quantity of alcohol consumed on an occasion in relation to each of the *DSM-IV* criteria for alcohol use disorders. Using a technique called *item response theory*, the frequency of hazardous drinking (five or more drinks per day for men and four or more drinks per day for women) was examined in relation to the 11 criteria used in the *DSM-IV* to define alcohol use disorders of abuse and dependence. Only one of the four *DSM-IV* criteria for abuse, *hazardous use*, was related to *lower* quantity use whereas the other three, *social/interpersonal problems*, *role neglect*, and *legal problems*, were associated with heavier drinking (five or more drinks for men and four or more drinks for women) two or more times a week. Further inconsistency with the *DSM-IV* categories was seen in the finding of less frequent heavy drinking being related to some of the criteria for dependence such as drinking larger amounts, drinking longer than planned, and inability to cut down on drinking. Abuse and dependence might be ends of a single continuum based on frequency of heavy drinking rather than two separate dimensions. The next revision of the *DSM* criteria will use this type of evidence to decide what, if any, changes will be made to the category of alcohol abuse (Hasin et al., 2003).

An analysis of alcohol-dependent individuals in the 2001–2002 NESARC study (Moss, Chen, & Yi, 2008) found that the best predictive symptom for dependence was "activities given up," which was endorsed by 95% of those classified as alcohol dependent. Only two other symptoms, "physical/psychological problems" and "time spent," were endorsed by well over 50% of the sample, suggesting that some of the other items need rewording or replacement.

Another study (Moss, Chen, & Yi, 2007) identified five subtypes among the 1,484 survey respondents from a larger sample who met the *DSM-IV* criteria for alcohol dependence, as shown in Table 3.5. The researchers applied a statistical technique called *latent class analysis* to examine the correlations among age of onset of alcohol dependency, comorbidity with

TABLE 3.5 Summary of major differences among subtypes of alcohol dependence.

SUBTYPE (percent)	Young Adult 31.5%	Young Antisocial 21%	Functional 19.5%	Intermediate Familial 19%	Chronic Severe 9%
VARIABLE					
Primary Age	Young	Mid-20s	Middle age	Middle age	Middle age
Early-Onset Drinking/Problems		Yes			Yes
Other Drug Comorbidity	Low	High	Nearly half smoke	Most smoke	High
Psychiatric Comorbidity	Low	High	One fourth have had major depression	About half	Very high
Familial/ Multigenerational Alcoholism	Low	About half	About one third	About half	About four fifths
Seek Help	Rare	About one third		About one fourth	About two thirds
Stable Job, Family, Home; High Education			Yes		

Source: Adapted from "Subtypes of Alcohol Dependence in a Nationally Representative Sample," by H. B. Moss, C. M. Chen, & H. Y. Yi, 2007, *Drug and Alcohol Dependence, 91,* 149–158.

other drugs, comorbidity with psychiatric disorders, family alcoholism history, and treatment history. Based on this information, all cases were sorted into subgroups that consisted of highly similar cases that were also highly different from the other subgroups. The results showed that the cases fell into five distinctive groups. The stereotypical skid-row alcoholic fit only about 9% of the sample. Further defying this stereotype, about 20% were functioning well and had high education, stable jobs, and stable home lives. This subtyping may be valuable in further understanding of the etiology of alcohol dependence and determining the most suitable treatment for each type. More than half of the cases were under age 30, and most of them had never sought treatment for alcohol use disorders.

Summary

Alcohol and drug use involves many different dimensions such as frequency and quantity of use (dose). First, however, before we can measure use of any substance, we must have a unit of measure for that drug. For legal substances, there are fairly uniform standards, but such is not the case for most illegal drugs. Thus, the amount of alcohol in a bottle of beer or a glass of wine can be readily estimated, but the degree of purity of illegal drugs is not standardized.

Three aspects need to be distinguished. Use simply refers to the taking of a substance, irrespective of the level of use. It assesses drug taking, without consideration of the effects of drugs. When problems arise from any type or level of use, abuse is involved. Finally, dependence involves impaired control over use, irrespective of the actual quantity or frequency of use or level of harm.

The second part of this chapter focused on the evolution of the criteria used by clinicians and researchers to assess and distinguish among use, abuse, and dependence. In the mind of the public, the disease conception is the best known due to its widespread dissemination through Alcoholics Anonymous (AA), an influential self-help recovery program that will be discussed in detail in Chapter 13. Although it originated with alcohol problems, the disease formulation has been extended to many other drugs, as well as to addictions that do not involve pharmacological substances. The disease conception involves a specific sequence of symptoms that occur over the course of the development of alcoholism or dependence on any other substance. It provides a theoretical account of the origins of the disease in terms of physical factors although it also posits that there are "spiritual" aspects. Ultimately, AA's definition requires that alcoholic individuals admit their powerlessness over alcohol before the road to recovery can begin.

In contrast, the alcohol dependence syndrome and succeeding versions of the *DSM* and *ICD* use physical and behavioral criteria but do not concur among themselves about the nature of abuse and dependence. These formulations will continue to undergo refinement as more research evidence becomes available. It is important to note that these taxonomies are only descriptions of the symptoms. As important as description is, it should not be confused with theoretical or explanatory accounts of the underlying processes, causes, and effects of drug dependence.

Stimulus/Response

1. Most measures in survey research on drugs focus on frequency, quantity, or a combined index of frequency and quantity of use. However, these measures usually do not identify situational factors such as where, when, or with whom people use drugs. Do you think this additional information would be helpful in understanding why drugs are used and what effects they have? Choose two situations and explain how the same level of drinking might have different consequences in these contexts.

2. Devise three different ways to measure how much a person drinks or smokes. Assuming your methods do not produce the same estimates, which of your methods might be likely to yield the highest estimates, and which might tend to produce lower estimates of the actual consumption? Which would be the most reliable? Which would be the most valid? Explain why estimates might depend on the method of assessment. Which method would be best for the purpose of identifying health risks from drinking?

3. How much use of a drug is "too much"? Base your answer on different criteria such as medical, legal, or social criteria by which such a judgment might be made.

4. The pattern of a given amount of total drug use over time can be stable for some while fluctuating widely for other users. What do you think might be some major reasons for these divergent use patterns?

The Extent of Alcohol and Other Drug Use

The Epidemiological Approach	Comorbidity of Alcohol and Illicit Drugs
National Surveys of Alcohol and Other Drug Use	Other Sources of Data
	The Ethnographic Approach
Stability of Alcohol Use Patterns	Summary
Abuse and Dependency Rates	Stimulus/Response

I drink when I have occasion, and sometimes when I have no occasion.

—Miguel de Cervantes Saavedra

People use alcohol and other drugs in many different contexts, and the amount they consume may vary on different occasions. Moreover, some individuals have regular use patterns while others use irregularly, depending on many factors in their lives. Alcohol and other drugs are often used together in varying combinations or sequences. Measuring the use patterns for different substances and the correlates of such activity provides important data. Identifying the relationship of patterns of use to different psychological, physical, and behavioral effects offers valuable evidence for evaluating theories about the causes and consequences of alcohol and other drug use.

A thorough description would identify the characteristics of users and specify the substances they prefer. How often and in what amounts do they use these drugs? When and where do they use, with whom do they "do drugs," and how do they get the drugs into their bodies? If they use more than one drug, what combinations do they use? What causes them to use, and what are the physiological, psychological, and behavioral effects? In addition to determining these characteristics of current use, it is important to determine the degree and direction of change over time in these aspects of use.

The first half of this chapter will parallel the first section of the preceding chapter and present some major survey findings about the epidemiology of the use of alcohol and other drugs in the general population in the United States. For the present purpose, use and abuse are not distinguished. The last part of the chapter will examine evidence regarding prevalence rates of abuse and dependency for alcohol and other drugs using standard diagnostic criteria to measure alcohol use disorders as defined in the second part of the preceding chapter.

Surveys with large representative samples of the general population do not work well in studying illicit drug use since many of these populations are "hidden" and unlikely to want to be studied. Ethnographic methods using observations and interviews with smaller samples in natural settings are necessary for obtaining detailed information about illicit drug use. Several illustrative examples of such field studies on illicit drug use will be presented.

THE EPIDEMIOLOGICAL APPROACH

Epidemiology, a specialty within the field of public health, conducts both small **case-control studies** in hospitals and large random sample surveys of the general population to describe how alcohol (and other drug) use, abuse, and dependence differ by sociodemographic variables such as age, gender, and race/ethnicity and to identify the factors that place people at elevated risk for substance use disorders. Such data are essential for developing theories, planning interventions, designing treatments, and formulating social policy. It should be pointed out, however, that surveys of alcohol or other drug use in the general population cannot determine the overall rates of *dependency*. The survey questions are not adequate to address this concern. Moreover, although some of the respondents in population surveys may indeed be dependent, national household survey procedures exclude many alcohol- and drug-dependent persons such as homeless persons, inmates of correctional facilities, and residents of other institutions including inpatient drug treatment facilities.

The majority of respondents in these large-scale national surveys use alcohol and other drugs at levels that fall within limits that are generally acceptable to society. In contrast, instances of drug use that achieve notoriety and public attention such as those associated with overdose deaths, crimes, violence, family dissolution, and other problems represent one extreme sample, typically involving heavy and frequent users or those who use drugs in hazardous environments and circumstances. While it is important to acknowledge these special subpopulations of alcohol and other drug users, at the same time we must recognize that these outcomes involve atypical users. The goal of national epidemiological surveys is to determine how many substance users exist in the general population.

Who Gets Surveyed?

One would not want to generalize about the nature of alcohol and drug use in the general population based on results from surveys conducted with convenience samples such as shoppers at a mall, occupants at a homeless shelter, or clients in a treatment facility. Nor would you want to rely on data from samples unrepresentative of the general population such as the regular patrons at the corner bar, the residents of a retirement center, the medical staff of a hospital, or the novitiates at a monastery. Instead, scientific surveys use large **random samples** that are chosen by a method that ensures that the selected respondents represent a cross section of the population about which one wishes to generalize.

National surveys of the general population of the United States usually require thousands of respondents to provide adequate representation of different major subgroups of the whole population. Such surveys entail considerable planning, time, effort, and expense. Useful survey data can also be obtained from more specialized groups, provided the sample is representative of the larger population. Thus, one need not conduct a national survey of households if one wants to draw conclusions about drug use among a special population such as college students, pregnant women, or unemployed men.

Epidemiological studies have their limitations. On one hand, the total use may be underestimated, especially for illegal drugs, because epidemiological studies tend to not include extreme cases such as inpatients of drug treatment facilities. On the other hand, they may also overestimate the total number of drug users because multiple-drug users—those who take several drugs concurrently or sequentially—get counted again for each drug they use.

Epidemiological studies measure the **incidence** (number of new cases) as well as the **prevalence** (number of existing cases) of various aspects of alcohol and drug use. Surveys usually provide estimates for the rates of incidence and prevalence of use for specific intervals such as the current month (past 30 days), the last year (past 12 months), or the duration of one's life. The relationship between the two indices can be complicated as illustrated by two scenarios. If new drinkers continue to be added at the same rate for several years, the prevalence of drinkers will accumulate even after some drinkers are removed from the total due to death from alcohol-related causes involving physical illness and accidents. On the other hand, if public health programs reduce the incidence rate of new drinkers and many current drinkers decide to quit drinking because of health concerns, the prevalence rates should decline.

Epidemiological studies indicate what use patterns exist, but they do not explain or identify the processes underlying these use patterns. However, these observations of drug use patterns are the raw data necessary to develop and test theories or explanations of drug use, assist in the planning of education and intervention programs, and influence public drug policy. These data can be examined to see how important demographic factors such as age, gender, socioeconomic class, and ethnicity are related to drug use and related consequences. The present chapter will focus on the basic methods of these surveys and the findings concerning use rates and the relationship of these rates to major demographic factors, as well as the limitations of these studies. Chapters 10–12 will explore theories that explain why alcohol and other drug use varies with age, gender, and racial/ethnic groups.

NATIONAL SURVEYS OF ALCOHOL AND OTHER DRUG USE

Numerous surveys of alcohol and other drug use exist, but we will focus on several large national surveys. Unlike many surveys that are administered only once and use small biased or nonrandom samples, these national surveys employ large random probability samples. The **National Survey on Drug Use and Health (NSDUH)** is the successor to the

National Household Survey on Drug Abuse (NHSDA) that was administered periodically since the early 1970s and annually after 1979. The name change occurred after some revisions in 2002 such as providing a $30 participation incentive to increase response rate (Substance Abuse and Mental Health Services Administration, 2002). These changes may jeopardize comparisons of the 2002–2006 estimates with those from prior surveys between 1972 and 2001.

Sponsored by a federal agency, the Substance Abuse and Mental Health Services Administration, the NSDUH uses a large (over 43,000) representative sample of the U.S. population aged 12 and older, including persons living in households and in some group quarters such as dormitories and homeless shelters. The findings may involve underestimates of use because incarcerated and inpatient treatment subpopulations, which may often include heavier users, are not included in household surveys.

The **National Epidemiologic Survey on Alcohol and Related Conditions (NESARC)**, sponsored by the National Institute on Alcohol Abuse and Alcoholism, was first administered in 2001–2002 with a follow-up in 2005. It measured rates of alcohol and other drug use but also assessed family history of alcohol use disorders, the extent and correlates of alcohol co-use and comorbidity with other drugs, psychiatric history, age of onset of alcohol dependency, and use of treatment facilities. The first wave of the NESARC in 2001–2002 used a stratified sample of 43,093 respondents across the United States that produced an excellent response rate of 81%. It also oversampled Blacks, Hispanics, and young adults aged 18–24 so that minority and special populations were well represented in the sample. To minimize reluctance of respondents to disclose information they might not want to reveal, the NESARC used computer-assisted interviews conducted in participant homes. A second wave of the survey was conducted from 2004 to 2005, but analyses of the data have not yet been published.

Prevalence rates in the NSDUH and the NESARC are not comparable because the former generally asked for use during the past 30 days whereas the latter measured use during the past 12 months. Thus, rates would be higher under the NESARC simply because it covers a longer time period.

The definition of *use* in these surveys is not as clear as it might seem. In these surveys the term applies to first-time users, continuous or long-term users, and former users who stopped for a period but resumed use during the interval in question. Use is not a measure of pathology or dysfunction although eventually some users may develop psychological and behavioral problems from drug use.

Moreover, this definition ignores the fact that "use" varies widely in quantities and frequencies. Except for the items asking about binge drinking (having five or more drinks on one occasion) and heavy drinking (defined here as having five or more drinks on one occasion five or more times in the past month), the amount or level of use is not considered in defining a user. As long as a respondent reports *some* amount of use during the period measured, he or she is counted as a user. Reports of current use for the past month may be more accurate than reports of use over longer intervals such as the past year or one's lifetime due to greater forgetting and distortion for longer periods. Frequency of use of each drug was not measured by the NHSDA until 1996 when it started including three categories of frequency of use: more than 51 times a year, more than 12 times a year, and 1 or more times a year.

Another difference preventing comparisons across surveys is that the NESARC grouped current drinkers based on the quantity of past-year consumption in some of the analyses: *light drinker* (3 or fewer drinks per week), *moderate drinker* (4–14 drinks per week for men and 4–7 drinks per week for women), and *heavy drinker* (more than 14 drinks per week for men and more than 7 drinks per week for women).

Major NSDUH 2006 Findings

Alcohol

The 2006 NSDUH rates of use for any drug were lower for the shorter time span, the past 30 days, than for past-year or lifetime use. Alcohol use occurred for 45.3% of participants in the past 30 days, 66.5% in the past 12 months, and 72.5% in their lifetime.

In the past 30 days, about half of those aged 12 or older reported being current drinkers of alcohol. More than one fifth (23.0%) of persons aged 12 or older engaged in binge drinking (five or more drinks on one occasion) at least once in the past 30 days. And 6.9% of the population aged 12 or older reported heavy drinking (five or more drinks on more than five occasions in a month). As Figure 4.1 shows, the percentage of "current drinking" (any non-binge use in the past 30 days) continues to increase with age before dropping slightly after age 65. Heavy drinking (five or more drinks on five or more occasions) and binge drinking (five or more drinks in one episode) increase with age but peak after age 30.

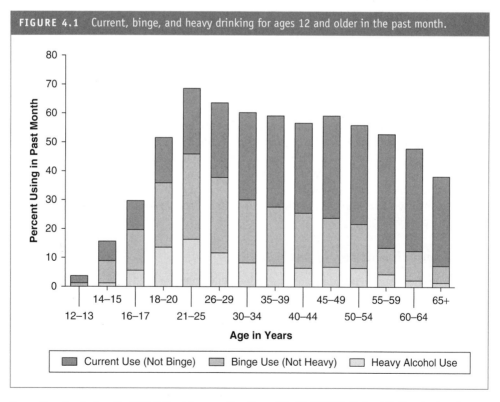

FIGURE 4.1   Current, binge, and heavy drinking for ages 12 and older in the past month.

Source: From *Results From the 2006 National Survey on Drug Use and Health (NSDUH): National Findings*, by the Substance Abuse and Mental Health Services Administration (SAMHSA), 2007, Rockville, MD: SAMHSA, Office of Applied Studies.

Tobacco

The 2006 NSDUH found that a higher percentage of males (36.4%) than females (23.3%) aged 12 or older were current (past-month) users of a tobacco product: current cigarette smokers (25.0%), cigar smokers (5.6%), users of smokeless tobacco (3.3%), and smokers of tobacco in pipes (0.9%).

Males also had higher rates of past-month use of each specific tobacco product: cigarette smoking (27.8% of males vs. 22.4% of females). However, among participants aged 12–17, the rate of current cigarette smoking did not differ significantly for females (10.7%) and males (10.0%).

Current use of any type of tobacco product among persons aged 12 or older was 16.0% for Asians, 24.4% for Hispanics, 29.1% for Blacks, 31.4% for Whites, 34.2% for persons who reported two or more races, and 42.3% for American Indians or Alaska natives. Cigarette smoking in the past month among youths aged 12–17 and young adults aged 18–25 was more prevalent among Whites than Blacks (12.4% vs. 6.0% for youths and 44.4% vs. 27.5% for young adults). Among adults aged 26 or older, however, Whites and Blacks used cigarettes at about the same rate (24.9% and 27.2%, respectively). The rates for Hispanics were 8.2% among youths, 28.8% among young adults, and 23.6% among those aged 26 or older.

Cigarette use rates were 21.6% for the past 30 days and 47.1% for lifetime, with no measure taken of use in the past 12 months. Marijuana use occurred for 18.3% of participants in the past 30 days, rose to 31.5% in the past 12 months, and increased to 42.3% for lifetime. Cocaine use occurred for 2.5% of participants in the past 30 days, 5.7% in the past 12 months, and 8.5% in their lifetime. Heroin use occurred for 0.4 % in the past 30 days, 0.8% in the past 12 months, and 1.4% in their lifetime.

While the rate of current use for any illicit drug in the past 30 days may be seen as the "bad news," the large gap between past-year and lifetime use compared with current use could be viewed as the "good news." These differences reflect the possibility that many users do not have stable patterns; some may experiment with or try a drug and then decide to stop for varying periods. Some may resume or switch to a different drug. Consequently, the higher lifetime use percentage in comparison to the lower number for past-year use reflects the fact that many of the users stopped using that drug during the past year.

Some Limitations of the NSDUH

The prevalence of polydrug use in which several drugs are used together is generally overlooked by many surveys, including the NSDUH until recently. The evidence is presented separately for each drug as if users consume one drug exclusively, but many drug users frequently use two or more drugs together. Licit drug combinations such as alcohol with tobacco, tobacco with caffeine, and alcohol followed by caffeine are not uncommon.

Users of illicit drugs report often engaging in polydrug use, typically with alcohol (Martin, Kaczynski, Maisto, & Tarter, 1996). Thus, some users combine alcohol with the use of one or more of the following drugs: marijuana, cocaine, amphetamines, benzodiazepines, and heroin. Cocaine is often combined with either heroin or amphetamine use. Often the user is deliberately choosing one type of drug to counter or reduce the effect of another drug, as in using alcohol to take the edge off of a cocaine high.

Because drugs have pharmacological **interactions**, it is not possible to identify the specific effects of each drug. For example, how a specific drug affects mood, motor coordination, sleep, and other behaviors cannot be determined when co-use occurs. Combinations of drugs from the same category—sedative-hypnotics, for example—can have additive effects whereas offsetting effects may occur with drugs from different categories such as depressants and stimulants. More smokers than nonsmokers also drink coffee, possibly due to some pharmacological effect of caffeine on nicotine (Swanson, Lee, & Hopp, 1994). Some combinations of drugs may involve potentiation where one drug amplifies the effect of another. Thus, drinking alcohol in combination with a depressant drug can be lethal because the two drugs combine to produce a larger effect than either drug would do alone.

The 2006 NSDUH compared alcohol consumption to tobacco use. Among heavy alcohol users aged 12 or older, 58.3% smoked cigarettes in the past month while only 20.4% of nonbinge current drinkers and 17.2% of nondrinkers in the past month were current smokers.

The NSDUH measured use only on one occasion, providing static portrayals that fail to reflect changes in drug use over time within given individuals. As Figure 4.2 suggests, users may move back and forth between states of use and nonuse, reflecting situational influences on their behavior. Some initiate use, find it unrewarding, and end their use. At a later time, some former users may resume their use. Still other users are "chippers," people seemingly able to control their use and engage in such activity intermittently depending on priorities and social circumstances.

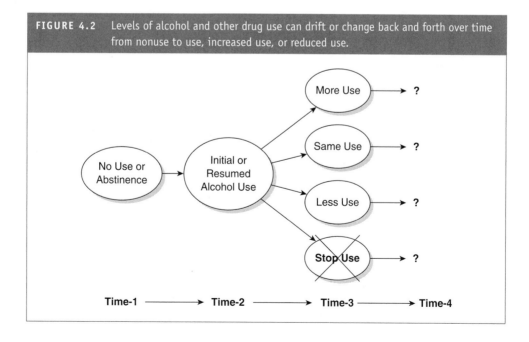

FIGURE 4.2   Levels of alcohol and other drug use can drift or change back and forth over time from nonuse to use, increased use, or reduced use.

Major Findings of the NESARC

Past-Year Prevalence

Overall, the NESARC found that about two thirds of persons aged 12 or older in the United States used alcohol and more than one quarter used tobacco during the past year. Alcohol but not tobacco use occurred for almost half of men (44.4%) and women (43.2%). Use of tobacco, but not alcohol, occurred for small percentages of men (6.4%) and women (5.6%) (Falk, Yi, & Hiller-Sturmhofel, 2006). About 1 out of every 5 adults used both substances, with a higher rate for men (27.5%) than for women (16.4%). In contrast, abstinence from both substances was higher for women (34.9%) than for men (21.8%).

Figure 4.3 provides a breakdown of the prevalence rates in the past year of any alcohol use, any tobacco use, and co-use of alcohol and tobacco for four age groupings separately for men and women.

Age by Gender

As Figure 4.3 indicates, the NESARC found higher alcohol use for men than for women in all age groups, with the highest rates for ages 18–24 and ages 25–44, lower rates for ages

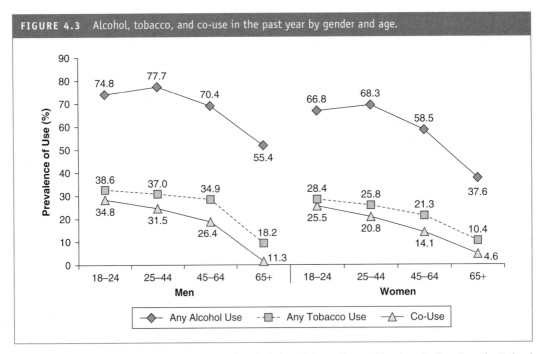

FIGURE 4.3 Alcohol, tobacco, and co-use in the past year by gender and age.

Source: From "An Epidemiologic Analysis of Co-Occurring Alcohol and Tobacco Use and Disorders: Findings From the National Epidemiologic Survey on Alcohol and Related Conditions," by D. E. Falk, H. Y. Yi, & S. Hiller-Sturmhofel, 2006, *Alcohol Research and Health, 29*(3), 162–171.

45–64, and the lowest rates for ages 65 and older. At much lower rates, however, there were parallel patterns for age and gender for use of any tobacco product as well as for co-use of alcohol and tobacco.

Race/Ethnicity by Gender

Figure 4.4 shows that alcohol use was highest for White men (74.3%) and women (65.1%) and that Asian/Native Hawaiian/Pacific Islander men (61.5%) and women (36.1%) had the lowest rates (Falk et al., 2006).

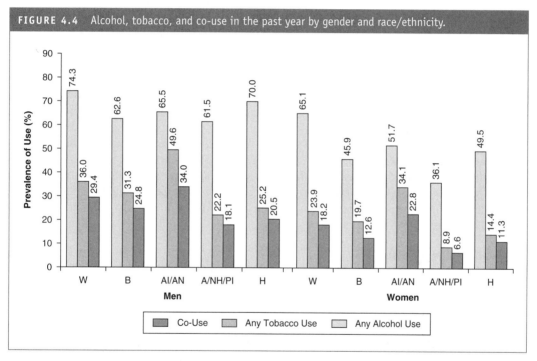

FIGURE 4.4   Alcohol, tobacco, and co-use in the past year by gender and race/ethnicity.

Source: From "An Epidemiologic Analysis of Co-Occurring Alcohol and Tobacco Use and Disorders: Findings From the National Epidemiologic Survey on Alcohol and Related Conditions," by D. E. Falk, H. Y. Yi, & S. Hiller-Sturmhofel, 2006, *Alcohol Research and Health, 29*(3), 162–171.

Co-Use of Alcohol and Tobacco

Age by Gender

The NESARC (Falk et al., 2006) found that co-use of alcohol and tobacco in the past 12 months declined with age, from the highest rate among participants aged 18–24 (34.8% and 25.5% for men and women, respectively) to the lowest rate among those aged 65 or older (11.3% and 4.6%, respectively), as can be seen in Figure 4.3.

Ethnicity by Gender

Figure 4.4 shows the NESARC prevalence of co-use of alcohol and tobacco was highest among American Indians/Alaska natives (34.0% among men and 22.8% among women) and Asian/Native Hawaiian/Pacific Islander men and women had the lowest prevalence (18.1% and 6.6%, respectively).

Simultaneous Versus Concurrent Co-Use

As in many studies of co-use, the NESARC did not distinguish between simultaneous and concurrent co-use. One study (Midanik, Tam, & Weisner, 2007) defined concurrent use as consuming alcohol and one or more drugs in the past 12 months but *never at the same time* and simultaneous use as having *alcohol and drugs sometimes or more often at the same time.* Simultaneous co-use is more problematic due to drug interactions that occur, which are less likely under concurrent co-use.

Midanik et al. (2007) studied responses from the 2000 National Alcohol Survey (n = 7,612) about use of specific drugs in the last 12 months. Rates of co-use were lower than those in the NESARC study because the researchers did not limit the analysis to co-use of alcohol and tobacco. For use of alcohol with drugs other than marijuana, about 5% of drinkers were *concurrent* users in the last 12 months, but only about 2% were *simultaneous* users. About 10% were *concurrent users* of alcohol with marijuana whereas simultaneous use was about 7%. Moreover, simultaneous use in this study of a sample from the general population was related to greater adverse social consequences, alcohol dependence, and depression in agreement with findings with clinical samples (Earleywine & Newcomb, 1997).

Illicit Drug Use

It is not surprising that there are no large-scale surveys of representative users of illegal drugs similar to those done for alcohol. First, it would be difficult, if not impossible, to identify a large and representative sample of users. Second, they would be reluctant to participate for obvious reasons, and if they did, the honesty of their answers would be suspect. Although national surveys do ask about illicit drug use and present demographic comparisons of prevalence of use, they do not provide information about patterns and conditions of use.

The 2006 NSDUH found an estimated 8.3% of respondents aged 12 or older were current (past-month) users of illicit drugs. Marijuana was the most commonly used illicit drug, used by 8.1% of males and 4.1% of females. More males than females were users of any specific drug as shown in Figure 4.5.

Cocaine use in the past month occurred for 1.4% of males and 0.6% of females aged 12 or older. Hallucinogens were used in the past month by 0.4% of those aged 12 or older, including 0.2% who had used Ecstasy. Of persons aged 12 or older, 2.8% used prescription-type psychotherapeutic drugs nonmedically in the past month while 0.3% aged 12 or older were current users of methamphetamine. However, 2006 estimates should not be compared with estimates of methamphetamine use shown in prior NSDUH reports due to changes in procedures. The rates are relatively low compared with those for licit drugs and have generally declined over this decade. However, the frequency and quantity of use were not assessed in this survey.

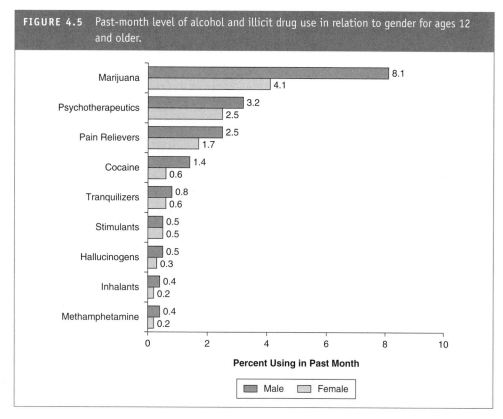

FIGURE 4.5   Past-month level of alcohol and illicit drug use in relation to gender for ages 12 and older.

Source: From *Results From the 2006 National Survey on Drug Use and Health (NSDUH): National Findings*, by the Substance Abuse and Mental Health Services Administration (SAMHSA), 2007, Rockville, MD: SAMHSA, Office of Applied Studies.

Are these rates of illicit drug use applicable to users who are in prisons, treatment facilities, and homeless shelters? And do they apply to the upper- and middle-class users whose use of illicit drugs is easier to hide? Although heavy and frequent use of illicit drugs occurs and produces harmful effects, it may be necessary to use other research methods to study these populations of illicit drug users.

Binge or Heavy Drinkers

Data from the Behavioral Risk Factor Surveillance System, a random-digit telephone survey of between 100,000 and 200,000 adults across the country each year from 1993 to 2001, indicate that binge drinking, defined as drinking episodes where five or more drinks were consumed, rose about 35% overall over the period from 1995 to 2001 (Naimi et al., 2003).

Young people between the ages of 18 and 25 as well as men of all ages were involved in the largest number of binge drinking episodes. Almost half of the reported episodes involved people classified as moderate drinkers. Binge drinkers were 14 times more likely to drive while impaired by alcohol than were nonbinge drinkers.

Abstainers

Abstainers, or nonusers, have received less study than users of drugs, perhaps because they do not create as many problems for society. It is important to recognize the heterogeneity among abstainers, with some being lifelong abstainers and others being former alcoholics. While the first group may have religious or health reasons for avoiding alcohol during their entire lives, the latter may be trying to overcome prior years of heavy drinking and may have continuing alcohol-related health problems.

Little or no change in abstention rates of about 35% occurred over the 15 years between 1964 and 1979 (Hilton, 1986; Midanik & Clark, 1994). There was no convergence in abstention rates over time for either sex or age. Regional and religious affiliation differences in abstention did not weaken either.

A comparison of the 1991–1992 National Longitudinal Alcohol Epidemiological Survey (NLAES; n = 42,862) and the 2001–2002 NESARC (n = 43,093) found no change with 34% of those surveyed being classified as lifetime abstainers (never drinking 12 or more drinks in any year during their lifetime; Grant et al., 2004). The 18–24 age group (37.0%) and those 65 or older (52.2%) were more likely to be abstainers than those in the middle age ranges. Women were twice as likely as men to be classified as lifetime abstainers (45.3% and 21.7%, respectively). Ethnic minorities were more likely than Whites to abstain from drinking. Not surprisingly, abstainers smoked cigarettes in the past year at a low level (18.5%).

Co-Use of Licit and Illicit Drugs

The NESARC found that use of alcohol was linked to use of illicit drugs. Heavy drinkers and binge drinkers were more likely to use an illicit drug than were social drinkers and nondrinkers. Among the 16.9 million heavy drinkers aged 12 or older, 32.6% were current illicit drug users in 2006. Persons who were not current alcohol users were the least likely to have used illicit drugs in the past month (3.4%). Higher rates of illicit drug use occurred for current users of alcohol who did not meet the criteria for binge or heavy use (6.4%), binge drinkers who did not meet the criteria for heavy use (16.0%), and drinkers with heavy use of alcohol (32.6%).

Similarly, as Figure 4.6 shows, current cigarette smoking was a predictor of use of other drugs. Specifically, cigarette smokers had higher binge alcohol and marijuana use.

STABILITY OF ALCOHOL USE PATTERNS

Alcohol use levels and alcohol problems have varied over time. Societal changes, economic conditions, and political factors as well as specific drug education and prevention

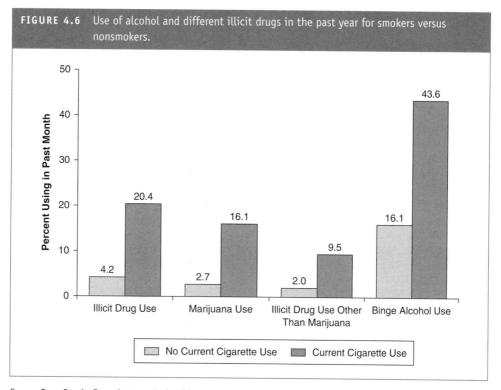

FIGURE 4.6 Use of alcohol and different illicit drugs in the past year for smokers versus nonsmokers.

Source: From *Results From the 2006 National Survey on Drug Use and Health (NSDUH): National Findings,* by the Substance Abuse and Mental Health Services Administration (SAMHSA), 2007, Rockville, MD: SAMHSA, Office of Applied Studies.

campaigns all may affect temporal changes. Historical events such as Prohibition and its repeal, women's right to vote, global wars, and economic depression are associated with change of many social attitudes and behaviors, which may directly or indirectly affect alcohol use. In addition, changes in the age, sex, and ethnic composition of the population will affect the levels of drinking.

Cross-Sectional Evidence

Comparisons (Hasin, Grant, Harford, Hilton, & Endicott, 1990) across four national surveys conducted between 1967 and 1984 showed increased drinking with a parallel rise in the prevalence of 11 alcohol-related problems among current drinkers between the ages of 22 and 59. A large increase in the percentage of men with three or more alcohol-related problems occurred over this period (from 11.4% to 17.4%). The lower rates for women increased from 2.3% to 5.2%, a doubled rate over this 20-year period in the lifetime prevalence of multiple alcohol-related problems. Current prevalence (during the past 12 months) of multiple problems increased, doubling for men and tripling for women. However, results from these cross-sectional surveys conducted over a 20-year period cannot assess whether individuals changed their drinking over this time span because each survey only assessed each individual's drinking on a single occasion.

NSDUH surveys also provide evidence of alcohol and other drug use trends over the past 25 or more years. They also show that in the 1970s there was a general increase in the percentage of respondents reporting current drug use. However, rates declined for alcohol and for *most* drugs starting about 1979.

The overall declining trend in alcohol use might be over (Greenfield, Midanik, & Rogers, 2000). A comparison of three National Alcohol Surveys from 1984 to 1995 found that rates of current drinking, weekly drinking, and frequent heavy drinking were stable from 1990 to 1995. These survey patterns corresponded with alcohol sales data. Except for a brief period during World War II, annual per capita alcohol consumption in the United States generally rose with the repeal of Prohibition in the 1930s until approximately 1980, after which it declined until about 1995 (Greenfield et al., 2000; Nephew et al., 2003) when it stabilized as Figure 4.7 shows (Greenfield et al., 2000; Nephew et al., 2003.).

However, these alcohol sales patterns hide as much as they show. Sales of alcoholic beverage types show differing patterns, with apparent consumption of distilled spirits or

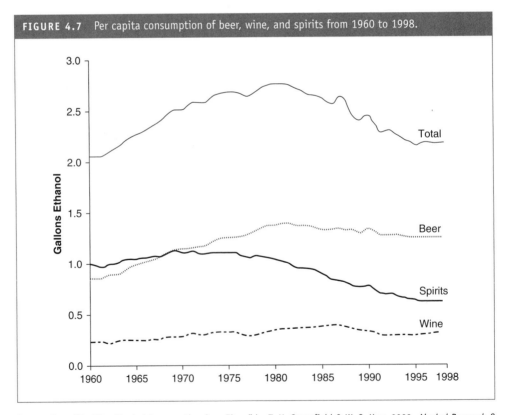

FIGURE 4.7   Per capita consumption of beer, wine, and spirits from 1960 to 1998.

Source: From "Tracking Alcohol Consumption Over Time," by T. K. Greenfield & W. C. Kerr, 2003, *Alcohol Research & Health, 27*(1), 30–38.

liquor *declining* in the past quarter-century while beer and wine consumption (sales) generally *increased* over the same period. These changes might reflect a number of different factors: changing tastes over time in societal preferences, demographic shifts in age as the older U.S. population increased, a higher percentage of women drinking than in the past, and the impact of social policy and alcohol tax changes.

Longitudinal Evidence

To what extent do patterns of alcohol use reported by *individuals* remain stable or fluctuate over time? To answer this question, the same persons must be surveyed on at least two occasions separated by a reasonable interval in a *longitudinal study*.

One such survey involved two measurements of the same persons over a 6-year period (Harford, 1993). Of the sample of 10,041 men and women between the ages of 17 and 24, a large majority of the men but only slightly more than half of the women showed stable drinking patterns over the 6 years. The demographic correlates of alcohol consumption were similar to those found in most studies, with more consumption by the young, by males, and by Whites.

Onset of current and heavier drinking declined with age over these 6 years. Shifts from drinker to nondrinker status increased with age. Abstinence was unrelated to age for both men and women. Among men, heavier drinking levels did not vary with age. Sales trends of alcohol over this period reflected the self-reported declines in drinking.

Other Drug Use Trends

In the NSDUH, the rate of cigarette use for 12- to 17-year-old males and females declined between 2002 and 2006 (12.3% to 10.0% for males; 13.6% to 10.7% for females). Among youths aged 12 to 17, rates declined significantly between 2002 and 2006 for illicit drugs in general (from 11.6% to 9.8%) and for several specific drugs, including marijuana, hallucinogens, LSD, Ecstasy, prescription-type drugs used nonmedically, pain relievers, tranquilizers, and illicit drugs other than marijuana. Current marijuana use among youths aged 12–17 declined from 8.2% in 2002 to 6.7% in 2006. Among young adults aged 18–25, the rate of current use of marijuana declined from 17.3% to 16.3% from 2002 to 2006. Past-month nonmedical use of prescription-type drugs among young adults increased from 5.4% in 2002 to 6.4% in 2006.

Comparison of drug use in different eras is of dubious validity if the potency of some drugs varies across years. Heroin, cocaine, and marijuana during the 1990s and later were more potent than they were in earlier eras. Studies of marijuana users of the 1960s involving milder cannabis have often shown no major impairment of behavior, but such users may not be generalizable to the marijuana users in more recent years if they are smoking a more potent product.

In addition, even if there are no changes in the drug over time, the effects of a drug for the initial wave of users of a specific drug may differ from those for subsequent users following in their footsteps. Thus, pioneering users of a new drug may have different personality characteristics from those who wait until it seems safe to use the drug. The effects observed may differ because of such preexisting differences among users.

ABUSE AND DEPENDENCY RATES

As noted in the previous chapter, alcohol and drug *use* per se is not equivalent to use-related problems or to dependency. What percentage of users have serious problems such as abuse and dependency, and what are the trends over time? Unfortunately, estimates derived from different sets of criteria are not in agreement. One reason that epidemiological studies offer a wide variety of estimates is because the definitions adopted by different researchers are not the same.

Specific Estimates From General Population Surveys

The (NLAES determined the prevalence rates of alcohol abuse and alcohol dependence based on 42,862 respondents in the contiguous United States and District of Columbia in 1992 (Grant et al., 1994). It was the first national survey to assess the prevalence of alcohol use disorders using the *DSM-IV*. The overall rate of alcohol use disorders was 7.41%, with 3.03% for abuse and 4.38% for dependence, which represents about 13,760,000 Americans.

Lifetime drug *use* was 15.6%, with 4.9% reporting drug use during the past 12 months. Lifetime and 12-month prevalence of *drug dependence* were estimated at 2.9% and 0.8%, respectively (Grant, 1996). Men were significantly more likely to use drugs than women, and drug use and dependence were much more common among cohorts born after World War II. Dependence among women converged with the rates among men in the younger cohorts. Women between 18 and 24 years of age (Grant et al., 2004) were more likely to use drugs, to become dependent, and to persist in dependence compared with the older cohorts.

The NLAES also provided estimates of the lifetime rates of abuse and dependency for alcohol and other major drugs (Grant, Harford, Hasin, Chou, & Pickering, 1992). Lifetime rates for alcohol dependence (13.29%) were considerably higher than those for alcohol abuse (4.88%). Cocaine dependency (1.02%) was greater than cocaine abuse (0.64%). Abuse and dependency were about equal for sedatives, tranquilizers, amphetamines, and hallucinogens. Only for cannabis was the rate of abuse (2.86%) much higher than for dependence (1.78%).

Changes in alcohol abuse over a decade and in alcohol dependence rates over the past 12 months can be inferred by comparing the 1991–1992 NLAES and the 2001–2002 NESARC. Alcohol abuse increased, especially among those aged 30 or older, whereas for males in the same age group dependency rates declined (Grant et al., 2004), as shown in Table 4.1.

It is not clear why this shift occurred. Grant et al. (2004) suggested that the trend toward lower rates of heavy drinking could explain the drop in dependence, but it is more difficult to explain the simultaneous rise in abuse. Possibly, with more negative social attitudes toward heavy drinking, heavy drinkers and their acquaintances develop more social/interpersonal conflicts. Since the *DSM-IV* criteria for abuse include such interpersonal problems, it would lead to a rise in the rate of abuse.

In addition, drinking patterns and circumstances that lead to alcohol abuse may be quite different from those associated with alcohol dependence. Such differences could be one reason that alcohol abuse is most prevalent among the youngest age groups whereas dependence is more likely among middle-aged and older groups.

TABLE 4.1 Prevalence rates for abuse and dependency by gender in 1999 versus 2001–2002.						
	Males		Females		Total	
	NLAES 1999	NESARC 2001–2002	NLAES 1999	NESARC 2001–2002	NLAES 1999	NESARC 2001–2002
Abuse	4.67	6.93	1.51	2.55	3.03	4.65
Dependency	6.33	5.42	2.58	2.32	4.38	3.81

Sources: From "Drinking in the United States: Main Findings From the 1992 National Longitudinal Alcohol Epidemiologic Survey (NLAES)," by the National Institute on Alcohol Abuse and Alcoholism (NIAAA), 1998, *U.S. Alcohol Epidemiologic Data Reference Manual* (1st ed., Vol. 6). Bethesda, MD: Author; and "An Epidemiologic Analysis of Co-occurring Alcohol and Tobacco Use and Disorders: Findings From the National Epidemiologic Survey on Alcohol and Related Conditions (NESARC)," by D. E. Falk, H. Y. Yi, & S. Hiller-Sturmhofel, 2006, *Alcohol Research & Health, 29*(3), 162–171.

There are numerous criteria for defining and diagnosing alcohol and other drug dependencies, and each set will generate different estimates. Hence, it is important to consider the particular definition used in each individual study when comparing and interpreting findings across studies. It may be useful to view drug dependency, as Jellinek (1960) did of alcoholism, as involving a number of subtypes, all of which have some common features as well as some unique characteristics. In support of Jellinek's conception, there is some evidence that five **subtypes of alcoholism** exist (Moss, Chen, & Yi, 2007), as described in Chapter 3. The causes and methods for treating each subtype may vary. If clinicians and researchers fail to recognize the existence of subvarieties, controversies and conflicting findings will continue.

Alcohol and Other Drug Use Disorders

The NESARC findings showed 8.4% of adults in the United States had an alcohol use disorder (AUD) in the form of either abuse or dependency, and 12.8% had nicotine dependence during the past year. In addition, 2.9% of all adults had both a form of AUD and nicotine dependence. Men and women had similar rates of nicotine dependence only (10.0% and 9.7%, respectively), but men were more than twice as likely as women to have an AUD only (8.2% vs. 3.1%, respectively) and more than three times as likely to have comorbid disorders (4.1% vs. 1.8%, respectively).

The NESARC collected data separately for each of four tobacco modalities (cigarettes, cigars, pipes, and snuff and chewing tobacco), but these data were aggregated across modalities. *Tobacco use* was defined as having smoked at least 100 cigarettes or 50 cigars, having smoked a pipe at least 50 times, or having used snuff or chewing tobacco at least 20 times during the course of a lifetime or having used any tobacco modality at least once during the past year.

Age by Gender

Figure 4.8 shows that the prevalence of AUDs, nicotine dependence, and comorbidity, or having both an alcohol and a tobacco use disorder, decreased with age. The prevalence of AUDs was highest among the youngest men and women (25.1% and 11.7%, respectively) and lowest among the oldest men and women (2.8% and 0.5%, respectively; Falk et al., 2006).

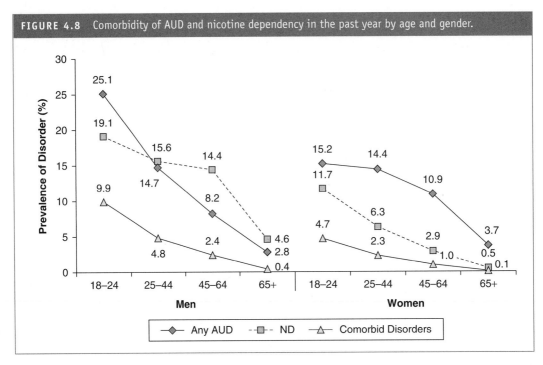

FIGURE 4.8 Comorbidity of AUD and nicotine dependency in the past year by age and gender.

Source: "An Epidemiologic Analysis of Co-occurring Alcohol and Tobacco Use and Disorders: Findings From the National Epidemiologic Survey on Alcohol and Related Conditions (NESARC)," by D. E. Falk, H. Y. Yi, & S. Hiller-Sturmhofel, 2006, *Alcohol Research & Health, 29*(3), 162–171.

Nicotine dependence was highest among the youngest men and women (19.1% and 15.2%, respectively) and lowest among the oldest men and women (4.6% and 3.7%, respectively).

Comorbid disorders decreased with age, with the highest prevalence found among the youngest men and women (9.9% and 4.7%, respectively) and the lowest prevalence found among the oldest men and women (0.4% and 0.1%, respectively).

Race/Ethnicity by Gender

American Indians/Alaska natives displayed the highest AUD prevalence (15.9% and 8.7% for men and women, respectively) while Asians/Native Hawaiians/Pacific Islanders had the lowest rates (6.8% and 2.5%, respectively).

Figure 4.9 shows high variability in the prevalence of nicotine dependence among minority racial/ethnic groups. For both men and women, the highest rates were found among American Indians/Alaska natives (26.4% and 20.2%, respectively). Among men, Hispanics had the lowest rate (7.0%), whereas among women, Asians/Native Hawaiians/Pacific Islanders had the lowest rate (4.5%). Across all racial/ethnic groups, the prevalence of nicotine dependence generally was greater than AUD prevalence with the exception of Hispanic men, in whom AUD prevalence (12.1%) exceeded that of nicotine dependence (7.0%).

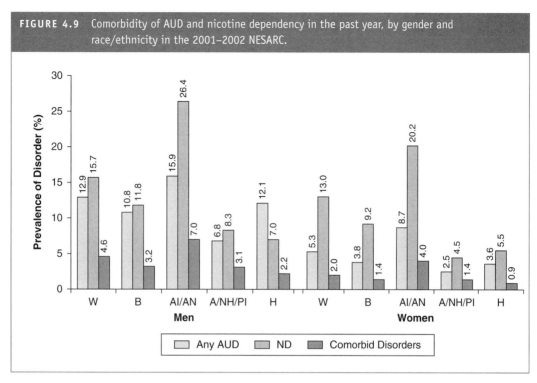

FIGURE 4.9   Comorbidity of AUD and nicotine dependency in the past year, by gender and race/ethnicity in the 2001–2002 NESARC.

Source: "An Epidemiologic Analysis of Co-occurring Alcohol and Tobacco Use and Disorders: Findings From the National Epidemiologic Survey on Alcohol and Related Conditions (NESARC)," by D. E. Falk, H. Y. Yi, & S. Hiller-Sturmhofel, 2006, *Alcohol Research & Health, 29*(3), 162–171.

The prevalence of comorbid AUDs and nicotine dependence among the racial/ethnic groups was similar for both genders: American Indians/Alaska natives displayed the highest prevalence (7.0% and 4.0% for men and women, respectively), and Hispanics had the lowest rates (2.2% and 0.9% for men and women, respectively).

Intra-Individual Alcohol and Tobacco Use

Most correlations among use of different drugs involve aggregate use over entire samples, but it is important to compare the use of different drugs by the same individuals. This type of comparison in the NESARC showed that tobacco use, daily tobacco use, and nicotine dependence all increased with higher levels of alcohol use, alcohol abuse, and alcohol dependence. Both men and women showed lowest tobacco use among lifetime alcohol abstainers (12.7% and 8.0%, respectively), but tobacco use for both genders increased with higher alcohol consumption and peaked among alcohol-dependent individuals (66.3% and 59.7%, respectively). Similar patterns occurred between individual drinking characteristics and daily tobacco use or likelihood of nicotine dependence (Falk et al., 2006).

Alcohol dependence and nicotine dependence were related. Past-year smoking was lowest among lifetime alcohol abstainers (23%) and increased to 31%, 39%, and 53% among light, moderate, and heavy drinkers, respectively (Dawson, 2000a). The NESARC (Falk et al., 2006) found lower nicotine dependence rates among male and female lifetime alcohol abstainers (3.8% and 2.9%, respectively) than among alcohol-dependent men and women (44.6% and 47.3%, respectively).

Highest dependence rates were seen in the youngest age groups, with a steady decline among older age groups. Among the racial/ethnic subpopulations, American Indians/Alaska natives had the highest rates of alcohol and tobacco co-use and comorbidity among both men and women. Overall, subgroups with higher rates of co-use showed more comorbidity.

Illicit Drug Dependence

The 2006 NSDUH survey found that the specific illicit drugs with the highest levels of dependence or abuse in the past year were marijuana, cocaine, and pain relievers as shown in Table 4.2. There was minimal change from 2005, the preceding year. Of the 7.0 million persons aged 12 or older classified with dependence on or abuse of illicit drugs in 2006, 1.7% (4.2 million) were dependent on or abused marijuana and hashish, 0.7% (1.7 million) were dependent on abused cocaine, and 0.7% (1.6 million) were dependent on or abused pain relievers. The highest rates were found among those aged 18–25 for abuse and dependency of alcohol and all illicit drugs.

COMORBIDITY OF ALCOHOL AND ILLICIT DRUGS

The prevalence of an individual with an alcohol use disorder, abuse, or dependency having the corresponding use disorder with illicit drugs (Grant & Pickering, 1996) was examined with data from the 1992 NLAES (Grant et al., 1994). Table 4.3 indicates that having an AUD greatly increases the likelihood of having the corresponding disorder with another drug. For example, the top row shows that 23.1% of those with an AUD as compared to only 2.3% of those without one also had a corresponding use disorder of any other listed drug. For each drug in Table 4.3, an **odds ratio** is presented in the right-hand column that indicates how much more likely a person was to have a use disorder (abuse or dependency) for that drug if the person also had the *corresponding* AUD. In the case of alcohol, the odds ratio is 9.6, indicating that persons with an AUD were about 10 times more likely to have a corresponding use disorder for any of the listed drugs than were those who did not have an AUD.

Odds ratios for other drugs ranged from 9.3 for cannabis to 17.1 for hallucinogens. The odds ratio for *abuse* disorders was much lower than those for *dependency* disorders, being only about 2.0 for most drugs. Thus, alcohol abusers were about twice as likely to abuse other drugs than were those who did not abuse alcohol. These findings generally agree with other studies of comorbidity of alcohol and drug problems in the general population such as the Epidemiologic Catchment Area study (Regier et al., 1984) and the National Comorbidity Survey (Kessler et al., 1994).

TABLE 4.2   Dependence or abuse rates for specific substances in the past year, by age group, in the 2005 and 2006 NSDUH.

			AGE GROUP					
	Total		12–17		18–25		26 or Order	
Past Year Dependency or Abuse	2005	2006	2005	2006	2005	2006	2005	2006
ILLICIT DRUGS[1]	2.8	2.9	4.7	4.6	8.4	7.9	1.6	1.7
Marijuana and Hashish	1.7	1.7	3.6	3.4	5.9	5.7	0.7	0.8
Cocaine	0.6	0.7	0.4	0.4	1.5	1.3	0.5	0.6
Heroin	0.1	0.1	0.0	0.0	0.3	0.2	0.1	0.1
Hallucinogens	0.2	0.2	0.5	0.5	0.6	0.6	0.0	0.0
Inhalants	0.1	0.1	0.4	0.4	0.2	0.1	0.0	0.0
Nonmedical Use of Psychotherapeutics[2]	0.8	0.8	1.3	1.4	2.2	2.0	0.5	0.5
Pain Relievers	0.6	0.7	1.1	1.0	1.7	1.5	0.4	0.5
Tranquilizers	0.2	0.2	0.3	0.2	0.5	0.5	0.1	0.1
Stimulants	0.2	0.2	0.3	0.4	0.5	0.4	0.1	0.1
Sedatives	0.0	0.0	0.1	0.1	0.1	0.1	0.0	0.0
ALCOHOL	7.7	7.6	5.5	5.4	17.5	17.6	6.2	6.2
BOTH ILLICIT DRUGS AND ALCOHOL[1]	1.3	1.3	2.2	1.9	4.2	4.2	0.7	0.7
ILLICIT DRUGS OR ALCOHOL[1]	9.1	9.2	8.0	8.0	21.8	21.3	7.1	7.2

Source: From *Results From the 2006 National Survey on Drug Use and Health (NSDUH): National Findings*, by the Substance Abuse and Mental Health Services Administration (SAMHSA), 2007, Rockville, MD: SAMHSA, Office of Applied Studies.

[1]Illicit Drugs include marijuana/hashish, cocaine (including crack), heroin, hallucinogens, inhalants, or prescription-type psychotherapeutics used nonmedically.

[2]Nonmedical use of prescription-type psychotherapeutics includes the nonmedical use of pain relievers, tranquilizers, stimulants, or sedatives and does not include over-the-counter drugs.

Psychopathology and Substance Use Disorders

Substance use disorders, especially those with illicit drugs, often accompany other forms of **psychopathology** such as antisocial personality, depression, anxiety, and affective disorders. Many who abuse or are dependent on illicit drugs may be trying to self-medicate their psychiatric problems. In turn, the psychiatric problem might be further increased by the abuse.

| TABLE 4.3 Comorbidity of lifetime prevalence of *DSM-IV* alcohol use disorders with selected drug use disorders in the National Comorbidity Survey. |

Lifetime Prevalence and Odds Ratios of Selected *DSM-IV* Drug Use Disorders Among Respondents With and Without Corresponding *DSM-IV* Alcohol Use Disorder (United States, 1992).

	Prevalence of Drug Use Disorders Among Respondents		
	With Corresponding Alcohol Use Disorders	Without Corresponding Alcohol Use Disorders	Adjusted Odds Ratio
Drug Use Disorder	Percent	Percent	
Any drug abuse and/or dependence	23.1	2.3	9.6
Any drug abuse only	10.6	2.8	2.9
Any drug dependence	14.3	1.7	10.9
Prescription drug abuse and/or dependence	8.1	0.7	10.6
Prescription drug abuse only	2.7	0.9	2.2
Prescription drug dependence	5.3	0.4	12.6
Sedative abuse and/or dependence	2.8	0.2	14.6
Sedative abuse only	0.8	0.3	2.1
Sedative dependence	2.0	0.1	22.6
Tranquilizer abuse and/or dependence	2.8	0.2	16.5
Tranquilizer abuse only	0.7	0.3	1.8
Tranquilizer dependence	1.9	0.1	22.2
Amphetamine abuse and/or dependence	6.2	0.4	11.4
Amphetamine abuse only	2.1	0.7	2.2
Amphetamine dependence	3.8	0.3	2.3
Cannabis abuse and/or dependence	18.1	1.6	9.3
Cannabis abuse only	9.7	2.5	2.9
Cannabis dependence	9.3	0.6	11.7
Cocaine abuse and/or dependence	7.0	0.5	12.0
Cocaine abuse only	2.2	0.8	2.5

| | Prevalence of Drug Use Disorders Among Respondents | | |
| | With Corresponding Alcohol Use Disorders | Without Corresponding Alcohol Use Disorders | Adjusted Odds Ratio |
Drug Use Disorder	Percent	Percent	
Cocaine dependence	5.5	0.3	13.5
Hallucinogen abuse and/or dependence	2.8	0.1	17.1
Hallucinogen abuse only	0.7	0.3	1.6
Hallucinogen dependence	1.8	0.1	23.2

Source: From "Comorbidity between DSM-IV alcohol and drug use disorders," by Grant, B. F. & Pickering, R. P. (1996), *Alcohol Health & Research World, 20* (NIAAA Epidemologic Bulletin No. 36), 67–72.

Comorbidity involves the presence of two or more psychiatric classifications in an individual. An analysis (Helzer & Pryzbeck, 1988) of data from the Epidemiologic Catchment Area study (Regier et al., 1984) showed that of the 13% of the general population diagnosed with alcohol abuse or dependence during their lifetime, about half had an additional psychiatric diagnosis. Women with AUDs were more likely than women in the general population to have diagnoses of depression (19% vs. 7%), but there was not much difference in depression between men with alcohol problems and men in the general population (5% vs. 3%). In contrast, alcohol-dependent men were much more likely to have antisocial personality disorder diagnoses than were men in the general population (15% vs. 4%). An even larger difference was found for women (10% vs. 0.8%).

The National Comorbidity Survey (Kessler et al., 1996) found that about half (51.4%) of the respondents with any lifetime *DSM-IV* substance use disorder also had at least one other lifetime *DSM-IV* psychiatric disorder. A substance use disorder and a concurrent other psychiatric disorder in a given 12-month period occurred in 42.7% of the respondents, with the rates being similar for men and women. Substance dependence disorders among men often occurred with anxiety disorders (19%) and affective disorders (15%). In contrast, substance use disorder rates for women were higher for those with anxiety disorders (31%) and affective disorders (24%) than they were for men.

A replication (Kessler, Chiu, Demler, Merikangas, & Walters, 2005) of the National Comorbidity Survey (NCS-R) with 9,282 adults in face-to-face surveys found 12-month prevalence rates for substance disorders (3.8%), anxiety (18.1%), mood (9.5%), impulse control (8.9%), and any disorder (26.2%). Comorbidity of substance use disorders with some mental disorders was projected to fall between 7 million and 10 million persons.

A comparison (Petrakis, Gonzales, Rosenheck, & Krystal, 2002) of the relationship of alcohol abuse and alcohol dependence to the prevalence of major psychiatric disorders used data from both the National Comorbidity Survey and the Epidemiologic Catchment Area study. Table 4.4 shows the extent to which alcohol abuse or alcohol dependence was linked to a greater risk of major psychiatric disorders separately for persons with and without alcohol abuse or dependence. Odds ratios in Table 4.4 with values greater than 1.0 indicate that

TABLE 4.4 Prevalence of psychiatric disorders in people with alcohol abuse and alcohol dependence.

Comorbid Disorder	Alcohol Abuse		Alcohol Dependence	
National Comorbidity Survey[1]	1–year rate (%)	Odds ratio	1–year rate (%)	Odds ratio
Mood disorders	12.3	1.1	29.2	3.6*
Major depressive disorder	11.3	1.1	27.9	3.9*
Bipolar disorder	0.3	0.7	1.9	6.3*
Anxiety disorders	29.1	1.7	36.9	2.6*
GAD	1.4	0.4	11.6	4.6*
Panic disorder	1.3	0.5	3.9	1.7
PTSD	5.6	1.5	7.7	2.2*
Epidemiologic Catchment Area[2] Study	Lifetime rate (%)	Odds ratio	Lifetime rate (%)	Odds ratio
Schizophrenia	9.7	1.9	24	3.8

Source: Petrakis, I., Gonzales, G., Rosenheck, R., & Krystal, J. H. (2002). Comorbidity of alcoholism and psychiatric disorders: An overview. *Alcohol Health & Research, 26*(2), 81–89.

Notes: *Odds ratio was significantly different from 1 at 0.05 level. The odds ratio represents the increased chance that someone with alcohol abuse or dependence will have the comorbid psychiatric disorder (e.g., a person with alcohol dependence is 3.6 times more likely to also have a disorder compared to a person without alcohol dependence).

The 1-year rate of a disorder reflects the percentage of people who met the criteria for the disorder during the year prior to the survey.

The lifetime rate reflects the percentage of people who met the criteria for the disorder at any time in their lifetime.

[1]Kessler et al. (1996).[2]Reiger et al. (1990).

comorbidity was more frequent for persons with a specific alcohol disorder than for those without it. The results show that concurrent psychiatric disorders and AUDs occurred mainly with alcohol dependence but not with alcohol abuse.

Analyses of data from the NESARC yield similar findings. *DSM-IV* substance dependence was related to current and lifetime rates of *DSM-IV* major depressive disorders, panic and generalized anxiety disorder, and several personality disorders, especially for females; middle-aged, widowed, separated, or divorced persons; Native Americans; and those with low income (Hasin, Goodwin, Stinson, & Grant, 2005). A review of research on depression (Davis, Uezato, Newell, & Frazier, 2008) found that nearly one third of patients with major depressive disorder also had substance use disorders and that this comorbidity was related to a higher risk of suicide, social and personal impairment, and other psychiatric conditions.

Causal Interpretation

When drug dependency and psychopathology occur together, different interpretations can be made. One view is that drug dependency is one of the causes of other forms of psychopathology. The substance dependency is the primary problem, and the other problem is a consequence of the drug use. Thus, excessive drug use may lead to antisocial personality or depression. A contrasting view is that those with drug dependency are premorbidly pathological or addiction prone. They have personality characteristics that led eventually to their drug dependency. According to this perspective, some form of psychopathology precedes—and perhaps contributes to—alcohol or other drug dependencies. This is a view favored by psychiatry.

For example, the association between alcohol dependency and antisocial personality might involve this process. Past studies have found antisocial personality in approximately 15%–50% of alcoholics. Antisocial personality, formerly referred to as sociopathy, is found mostly in males. It involves dysphoric moods, sensation seeking, a history of childhood misconduct, and underachievement. Such characteristics increase the risk that the individual will develop drinking problems sooner or later as a secondary outcome of his or her psychiatric problems.

Finally, it is possible that the influence is bidirectional or reciprocal, with psychopathology and alcoholism developing concurrently and each problem affecting the other. In practice, it can be difficult to identify accurately the origins of comorbidity in specific cases. These outcomes may require many years to unfold, and it is difficult to observe the process as it develops. Moreover, the criteria for the diagnosis of alcohol dependence and psychopathology categories overlap. Thus, some effects of alcohol dependency such as depression or disorientation can be mistaken for psychiatric symptoms. This overlap of criteria can lead to overestimates of the rates of comorbidity.

Follow-up of cases to observe how changes in one disorder affect the co-occurring problem can be helpful for diagnoses. Thus, if improved personality and mood problems occur following **detoxification** for alcohol dependence, it would be more likely that the alcohol problem was primary and the personality disorders were secondary. However, if a decline in drinking following psychiatric treatment for mental illness occurs, it is more likely that the psychopathology was primary and the alcohol problem was secondary.

Is psychopathology a risk factor for alcohol or other types of drug dependency? There is no simple answer to this question because the relative frequency of a characteristic or behavior influences its accuracy as a predictor. To the extent that the predictor in question is common in a given group, it should be less of a risk factor for the pathology. Thus, heavy drinking may not be viewed as a sign of psychopathology in France because drinking is commonplace there. In contrast, such behavior would be a predictor of psychopathology among Jews, for whom heavy drinking is less prevalent. But for more extreme (i.e., less common) behaviors—for example, use of illicit drugs—that behavior would be a stronger predictor of psychopathology.

OTHER SOURCES OF DATA

Methods for identifying patterns of alcohol and substance dependence and abuse in the general population do not usually involve direct observation but rely on inferences based on several different sources of information.

Official Records

One method uses official records or social indicators such as hospital admission records, arrest-for-drunkenness data, and mortality statistics such as deaths due to liver cirrhosis.

In addition, other indicators used are alcohol beverage sales figures and tax revenues from alcohol sales. Although objective, each of these indices still has its particular limitations. Thus, sales and tax revenues provide one means of determining trends in the total volume of alcohol sold each year but do not reveal patterns of actual individual consumption. The purchaser of alcohol is not always the actual consumer, so the term *apparent consumption* is used to reflect that difference. The index is computed by dividing the total amount of alcohol sold by the number of persons aged 14 or over.

Another problem in using sales statistics to infer consumption levels is that there is often a temporal lag between purchase and consumption, for example. While increased sales might imply heavier drinking if the number of drinkers stays the same—or decreases—during that interval, they call for an opposite interpretation if the number of drinkers increases over that period.

Clinical Population Data

Another index of the extent of alcoholism is more direct, using data from hospital treatment statistics to determine the number of alcoholics. However, there are economic and psychological barriers to utilization of health care facilities, so a biased and smaller sample of those with alcohol problems would be identified with this index. Also, poorer and less educated alcoholics might be less likely to utilize treatment facilities.

THE ETHNOGRAPHIC APPROACH

The study of illicit drugs relies more on qualitative techniques involving **ethnography** than on those involving epidemiology. Such studies are based on highly selective and rather small samples compared with the large representative samples often used in epidemiological surveys of legal drug use. The researcher may employ a known as technique **snowball sampling.** In this procedure, key informants, typically users, are first located. Efforts are made to establish their trust and confidence so they will identify other users to the researcher. Often, users or indigenous interviewers, rather than the researchers, are recruited and trained intensively to conduct the interviews. It may be easier to establish rapport and trust if other users conduct the confidential and intensive interviews. Users who complete the interview may introduce the researcher to other drug users. In addition, field observations of drug use are conducted to gain more detailed and precise descriptions of the conditions and consequences of such behavior than possible with surveys or questionnaires. Although this procedure has a number of problems including highly biased sampling, subjective assessment tools, legal risks, and safety concerns for the researcher, it opens a window through which the researcher can begin to observe the nature and characteristics of illicit drug use. Ethnographic methods not only are beneficial for the study of illegal drugs, but they also provide greater understanding of the meaning and function of legal drug use as illustrated by an ethnographic study of the daily lives of skid-row alcoholics (Wiseman, 1970).

Results of some ethnographic studies (Erickson, Aldaf, Murray, & Smart, 1987; Waldorf, Reinarman, & Murphy, 1991) reveal that illicit drugs such as cocaine, heroin, and marijuana may involve many "controlled users" or chippers who can use without any apparent major problems. Exactly how large this generally unseen part of the "iceberg" of illicit drug users is would be difficult to determine.

Intensive interviews with more than 200 current and long-term heavy users (both controlled and compulsive) of marijuana, opiates, and hallucinogens demonstrated that expectations, beliefs and values, and setting or social context—not the pharmacological factor alone—determined the effect of drugs. Anxiety was common among new users, but using drugs in a social setting with other users who were more experienced had a beneficial effect on the new users. Controlled users were more likely to engage in drug use for social reasons whereas compulsive users were more inclined to want to experience "highs."

Depth interviews (Waldorf et al., 1991) of 267 middle-class and mostly White heavy cocaine users recruited with a snowballing procedure revealed use levels comparable to that of the extreme 5 % in norms from national surveys. These users primarily snorted cocaine, which they used infrequently, mostly in social settings with close friends, and generally experienced no problems with their use. Most of them could be considered controlled users, consuming an average of half a gram during the past week. Most of these controlled users took cocaine for recreational rather than for stress management purposes, had structured lives and commitments to families and careers, and invoked rules and routines for controlling when and where they would use it. In addition, almost half of the sample had been able to quit, contrary to the stereotype that heavy users cannot stop. Health and financial considerations were paramount factors leading to quitting, which was facilitated by changing social circles and developing new interests. Although quitting is not easy and relapses occurred, most were able to reduce consumption significantly or reach abstinence without concomitant increases in the use of other drugs.

One ethnographic study (Singer, Romero-Daza, Weeks, & Pelia, 1995) examined heroin user participation in needle exchange programs. Users of heroin are at great risk not only because of harmful drug effects but also due to the possibility of HIV infection from use of dirty or shared needles for intravenous injections. Needle exchange programs were developed to reduce health risks for users and those they might infect by providing clean needles in exchange for used ones. An ethnographic approach revealed valuable information about potential problems in the program procedures that could not have been obtained using traditional scientific research methods.

Ethnographic studies involve small samples of highly selected participants and rely on often uncorroborated self-reports. Findings may not be generalizable to other users of these illicit drugs. Even if the sample is not random, the results show that some users can engage in controlled use. They also demonstrate that pharmacological factors are not the sole determinant of drug use outcomes because psychological and social factors also play an important role.

Summary

Epidemiological studies provide estimates of the prevalence of drug use over specific time periods such as the current month (past 30 days), an extended period such as the last year (past 12 months), or a lifetime. Findings of these studies only indicate what use patterns occurred but do not tell us what causes these use patterns. These results do, however, provide the data necessary to develop and test theories or explanations of drug use, assist in the planning of education and intervention programs, and inform public drug policy.

Started in 1971 and administered annually after 1979, the National Household Survey on Drug Abuse (renamed in 2002 as the National Survey on Drug Use and Health) measures the characteristics using large representative samples. The National Epidemiologic Survey on Alcohol and Related Conditions is a newer survey that added important questions about co-use of alcohol and other drugs.

In these surveys, the category of "users" is quite heterogeneous as it includes first-time users, continuous or long-term users, former users who stopped for a period but relapsed into use, users who vary widely in use quantity and frequency, and users who may not ever use drugs again. There are large gaps between current, past-year, and lifetime use rates of many illegal drugs. The much higher lifetime and annual use compared with current use suggests some initial use may only involve "experimenting" with a drug, which will soon cease after curiosity is satisfied.

Use of legal drugs is linked to use of illicit drugs as heavy drinkers and binge drinkers are more likely to be users of an illicit drug than are social drinkers and nondrinkers. Polydrug use and abuse is overlooked by many surveys. Researchers examine evidence separately for each drug as if users consume one drug exclusively. In fact, many drug users frequently take certain combinations of drugs. Alcohol abuse or dependency is associated with high rates of comorbidity—that is, abuse or dependency involving another drug.

Cross-sectional studies that examine only one point in time yield static portrayals that fail to capture changes in drug use over time within individuals. Drug users may move back and forth between states of use and nonuse, often in response to situational influences.

Results from annual surveys suggest that 1979 was a peak year for use of many drugs. However, the interpretation of such trends is ambiguous as there are many uncontrolled factors at the individual and societal level that are constantly changing and prevent firm conclusions.

Estimates of the prevalence of more problematic use involving alcohol and drug abuse and dependency are based on a variety of sources of information including official records and statistics, data from treatment facilities, and surveys of the general population. The findings derived from such different sets of criteria yield conflicting estimates. For example, surveys conducted in different years have used different definitions of abuse and dependency such as the *DSM-III*, *DSM-III-R*, *DSM-IV*, and *ICD-10* criteria.

Comorbidity is not limited to use of two or more drugs during the same period but also refers to the co-occurrence of a substance or drug use disorder with a psychiatric disorder such as antisocial personality or an affective disorder. Lifetime prevalence of such forms of comorbidity is high, occurring in about half of those assessed in one study. In some cases, the personality disorder precedes and increases the alcohol/drug disorder while the opposite case may apply to others where the substance disorder leads to the personality problem.

The survey method may be less useful for studying illicit drug use. Ethnographic studies, using highly selective and rather small samples, may be preferred to the large representative samples often used for epidemiological surveys of legal drug use. These studies involve small samples of highly selected participants and often depend on uncorroborated self-report, which may not be generalizable to other users of these illicit drugs.

Stimulus/Response

1. Suppose you hear a politician report that the rate of annual cocaine use has doubled in the past year. Does it matter whether this increase is from 25% to 50% or from 1% to 2%? Could you also describe the increase as a 25% gain in the first case and a 1% increase in the second case? Which depiction do you think is the fairest representation?

2. Do you think the frequency of drug use is correlated with the quantity consumed? Do people who drink more often also tend to drink larger quantities per occasion? Explain your answer.

3. What types of measures of alcohol use are more likely to be used by a distiller, brewer, or winery in reporting sales? What types of measures of alcohol use are more useful for law enforcement agencies? For moral crusaders?

4. For a given total consumption quantity in a time period, which is worse: high frequency–low quantity or low frequency–high quantity? Why?

5. Which aspect of use, frequency or quantity, do you think is the better predictor of undesirable behavioral consequences? Explain why.

6. People who smoke are more likely to drink, but the opposite is not as likely. What factors do you think contribute to these patterns?

CHAPTER 5

Neurobiology of Alcohol and Other Drug Use

What Happens After Drugs Are Taken?
How Drugs Affect the Nervous System
How Neurons Communicate
How Alcohol and Other Drugs Affect
    Neurotransmission

Changes in Neurophysiology With
    Prolonged Drug Use
Neuroadaptational Models
Physical Effects of Drugs
A Safe Level of Alcohol Use?
Summary
Stimulus/Response

Down among his nerve-cells and fibres the molecules are counting it, registering and storing it up to be used against him when the next temptation comes.

—William James, *Principles of Psychology* (1890), p. 127

People get alcohol and other drugs into their bodies through a variety of means. Whereas they swallow or sip alcoholic beverages, they typically smoke tobacco and marijuana, although some may also chew smokeless tobacco. Heroin is typically injected directly into veins while cocaine is commonly snorted, sniffed, or smoked. The specific method by which drugs are consumed is an important determinant of how rapidly specific drugs reach the brain. Eventually, drugs are detoxified by metabolic processes or eliminated from the body as waste material. **Pharmacokinetics** refers to how drugs enter, circulate, and exit our bodies whereas **pharmacodynamics** deals with the physiological and biochemical effects of drugs and the mechanisms of action.

    Irrespective of how drugs enter the body and find their way to the brain, they affect neuro-transmission processes that determine their psychological and behavioral impact. The purpose of this chapter is to provide a basic understanding of the pharmacology and neurophysiology of psychoactive drugs. As we shall see in this chapter, however, these processes are not invariant over time. They differ for the initial, intermediate, and later episodes because continued use of alcohol and other drugs creates neurophysiological changes in brain processes (Koob & Le Moal, 2005).

111

WHAT HAPPENS AFTER DRUGS ARE TAKEN?

Route of Administration

The speed with which drugs entering the body reach the brain is a major determinant of the potency of their effects. Depending on the specific drug, users prefer different methods of intake. Drugs such as alcohol and caffeine are typically consumed in beverage form. Once swallowed, they go down the esophagus before entering the stomach. Although a small loss occurs for drugs such as alcohol through perspiration or urination, the majority of drugs are absorbed directly and quickly through the linings of the stomach and small intestines into the bloodstream for distribution to the rest of the body. If food has recently been eaten before the drugs are ingested, the absorption rate will be slowed down. This mode of drug use is relatively slow, so the drug user must wait a few minutes or up to an hour before the drug reaches the brain to produce the effects typically sought by the user.

Other drug delivery methods are more direct such as by *inhalation* as in the case of cocaine snorting, tobacco snuff, or glue sniffing. These methods allow for quicker impact because the drugs reach the central nervous system rapidly. Drugs that are typically injected intravenously such as heroin also reach the brain quickly.

Smoking cigarettes containing nicotine or cannabis and inhaling crack cocaine are very fast delivery methods and produce potent effects on the brain. For example, about 90% of the nicotine in mainstream cigarette smoke is absorbed by the lungs, from which it reaches the brain in a few seconds for maximal impact because it does not have to go through the acidic content of the stomach or undergo detoxification by the liver on its first pass through the body. Smoking also produces combustion byproducts such as carbon monoxide, a poison that "captures" the hemoglobin in the blood by binding to it better than it bonds with oxygen. Thus, the ability of hemoglobin to deliver needed oxygen throughout the body is compromised.

Distribution

Most psychoactive drugs are weak acids or weak bases. They vary along a chemical dimension of acidity-alkalinity, as measured by values on a **pH scale** that ranges from 1 to 14. Scores lower than 7 reflect an acidic environment that converts drugs into an ionized or electrically charged state. As the acidic condition does not allow for easy entry of drugs into cells, they are more readily eliminated. In contrast, in an alkaline or base context with pH levels from 8 to 14, drugs are non-ionized and can easily pass through the body, increasing their retention (McKim, 2007).

Cell membranes are composed of layers of **lipid** cells, which favor the passage of fat-soluble drugs. Alcohol is a drug that is both water and fat soluble. It is rapidly absorbed from the stomach and intestines for distribution by the blood supply throughout the body. A lipid- or fat-soluble drug such as cannabis is much more slowly distributed and enters readily through cellular membranes and is retained in the body longer.

Because drugs circulate through the body until detoxified or eliminated, it should be possible to measure the concentration of drugs from blood or urine. A specific quantity of a drug consumed by individuals will be diluted for larger persons since they have more body liquids. Measures must adjust for variations in body weight across individuals. However, the feasibility of obtaining measures from blood content varies with different drugs. Thus, cocaine is not readily detectable in blood samples due to its rapid metabolism.

In contrast, levels of alcohol consumption can be inferred from **blood alcohol level (BAL) or blood alcohol concentration (BAC)**. This commonly used index measures the weight, in milligrams, of the alcohol present in a volume of 100 ml of blood. Larger units may also be used with the weight expressed in grams (1 g = 1,000 mg) and the volume measured in deciliters (1 dl = 0.10 L or 100 ml). The weight of the alcohol found in a given volume of blood is reported as a percentage such as 0.10%.

Breathalyzers are instruments such as gas chromatographs that appraise ethanol concentrations based on breath samples. They provide indirect measures but are more convenient than the use of actual blood or urine samples. However, because ethanol concentrations are not equal throughout all parts of the body, indirect measures are not without flaws. Measures from peripheral areas of the nervous system may not be accurate indices of the BAC in the brain, the organ that has the most impact on behavior. Despite this shortcoming, breath samples are reasonably reliable indices of BAL.

The relationship between BAC and the number of drinks within the past hour for persons of varying weight is depicted separately for men and women in Table 5.1. A "drink"

TABLE 5.1   Pennsylvania Liquor Control Board charts for estimated blood alcohol level for men and women differing in body weight after drinking different numbers of alcoholic beverages.

ALCOHOL IMPAIRMENT CHART

Drinks	APPROXIMATE BLOOD ALCOHOL PERCENTAGE								
	Body Weight in Pounds								
	100	120	140	160	180	200	220	240	
0	.00	.00	.00	.00	.00	.00	.00	.00	ONLY SAFE DRIVING LIMIT
1	.04	.03	.03	.02	.02	.02	.02	.02	Impairment Begins
2	.08	.06	.05	.05	.04	.04	.03	.03	
3	.11	.09	.08	.07	.06	.06	.05	.05	Driving Skills Affected —
4	.15	.12	.11	.09	.08	.08	.07	.06	Possible Criminal Penalties
5	.19	.16	.13	.12	.11	.09	.09	.08	
6	.23	.19	.16	.14	.13	.11	.10	.09	
7	.26	.22	.19	.16	.15	.13	.12	.11	Legally Intoxicated
8	.30	.25	.21	.19	.17	.15	.14	.13	—
9	.34	.28	.24	.21	.19	.17	.15	.14	Criminal Penalties
10	.38	.31	.27	.23	.21	.19	.17	.16	
Your body can get rid of one drink per hour. Each 1½ oz. of 80 proof liquor, 12 oz. of beer or 5 oz. of table wine = 1 drink.									

(left margin, vertical: NEVER DRINK AND DRIVE)

(watermark: MALE)

Source: Journal of Studies on Alcohol, Vol. 42, No.7, 1981.

TABLE 5.1   (CONTINUED)

ALCOHOL IMPAIRMENT CHART

NEVER DRINK AND DRIVE

Drinks	APPROXIMATE BLOOD ALCOHOL PERCENTAGE									
	Body Weight in Pounds									
	90	100	120	140	160	180	200	220	240	
0	.00	.00	.00	.00	.00	.00	.00	.00	.00	ONLY SAFE DRIVING LIMIT
1	.05	.05	.04	.03	.03	.03	.02	.02	.02	Impairment Begins
2	.10	.09	.08	.07	.06	.05	.05	.04	.04	Driving Skills Affected — Possible Criminal Penalties
3	.15	.14	.11	.10	.09	.08	.07	.06	.06	
4	.20	.18	.15	.13	.11	.10	.09	.08	.08	
5	.25	.23	.19	.16	.14	.13	.11	.10	.09	Legally Intoxicated — Criminal Penalties
6	.30	.27	.23	.19	.17	.15	.14	.12	.11	
7	.35	.32	.27	.23	.20	.18	.16	.14	.13	
8	.40	.36	.30	.26	.23	.20	.18	.17	.15	
9	.45	.41	.34	.29	.26	.23	.20	.19	.17	
10	.51	.45	.38	.32	.28	.25	.23	.21	.19	
Your body can get rid of one drink per hour. Each 1½ oz. of 80 proof liquor, 12 oz. of beer or 5 oz. of table wine = 1 drink.										

(watermark: FEMALE across table)

Source: University of Wisconsin Center for Health Sciences, 1998, and U.S. Dept. of Transportation, National Highway Traffic Safety Administration, 1992.

Source: Bureau of Alcohol Education, Pennsylvania Liquor Control Board (1995). Reprinted with permission.

here refers to a mixed drink containing 1.25 oz of liquor or 5 oz of wine or a 12-oz can of beer, each containing a comparable amount of alcohol. As a rough guide, each of these types of alcoholic drinks consumed within an hour increases the BAC by about 0.03%, regardless of whether it is wine, beer, or liquor.

It is commonly believed that different types of alcoholic beverages have different effects. However, whether the beverage is beer, wine, liquor, or any of the myriad variants of these three basic types, if the amount of ethanol consumed is equivalent, the same type of physiological and behavioral effects should occur if pharmacological factors are the sole determinant.

Different beverages may be associated with different effects, even when they are consumed in the same patterns. A study (Klatsky, Armstrong, & Friedman, 1990) of drinking preferences of more than 53,000 White men and women in northern California found that young males preferred beer while women, younger drinkers, and those with more education favored wine. Male drinkers, heavier drinkers, the less educated, the middle-aged or older, and those at higher risk for major diseases were more likely to prefer liquor. Consequently, it may appear that different beverages have different effects. However, this may be an erroneous conclusion because the "effects" may simply reflect differences in the types of persons who prefer different alcoholic beverages.

The effect of a given dose of alcohol depends on many factors. Consider the case of a driver who has been drinking. The impact of the dose on driving ability also depends on past drinking experience, time since last meal, use of other drugs, and so on. There will also be individual differences depending on the drinker's age, body size, gender, health, and so on.

Nonetheless, in practice the criterion that receives the critical role in judging driving legality is BAC or BAL. A BAC of 0.10 indicates that one tenth of 1% of the blood contains alcohol. Using a typical 150-lb male for illustrative purposes, this level might be obtained by drinking three to four drinks within the past hour. A female of equivalent body weight, however, will have a higher concentration due to the higher percentage of body fat in females. The unacceptable level for driving an automobile legally has changed over time. A reading of 0.10 was common after World War II, but gradually all states moved to a lower acceptable limit of 0.08.

Temporal Aspects

As alcohol or any drug is absorbed into the blood and circulated throughout the body, its concentration rises to a peak. The *ascending limb* of the BAC curve refers to the portion from the end of drinking until a peak level is obtained, as shown in Figure 5.1. As alcohol is metabolized and eliminated from the body, the BAC declines from the peak level. The *descending limb* of the BAC curve is the section following the peak until the ethanol level is reduced to zero. For any BAC less than the peak, there are two points where a specific level occurs, one on the ascending limb and one on the descending limb.

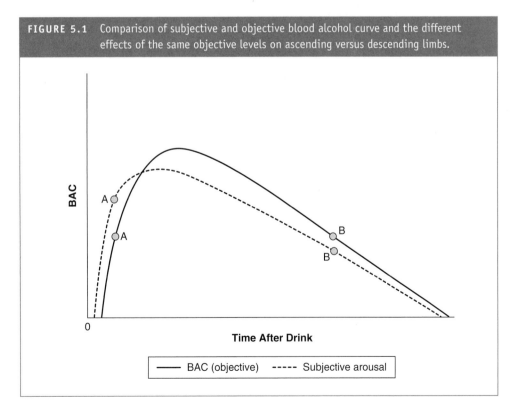

FIGURE 5.1   Comparison of subjective and objective blood alcohol curve and the different effects of the same objective levels on ascending versus descending limbs.

The *subjective effect* of a specific BAC differs, depending on whether that given value is on the ascending limb (see Point A in Figure 5.1) or on the descending limb (see Point B in Figure 5.1) of the curve. Due to the process of adaptation by which we tend to notice less and less as time goes by, we tend to feel less intoxicated at Point B during the descending limb than at Point B during the ascending limb of the curve for the same BAC. Nonetheless, the actual impairment of sensory motor functions may be the same for a given level regardless of which limb is involved. Since the subjective experience is one of less intoxication on the descending limb, the drinker may be willing to undertake risks such as driving a car even though the BAC is still dangerously high. Thus, a drinker at a party may stop drinking in anticipation of having to drive home. Shortly after that last drink, the BAC will peak and begin descending. Although the drinker may subjectively feel sober, the BAC may still be too high for safe driving.

In one lab study (Pihl, Paylan, Gentes-Hawn, & Hoaken, 2003), college participants consumed alcohol before they were tested on cognitive tasks such as abstract reasoning, organization, and planning. All participants were tested when they had a BAL of 0.08, the legal limit in most states, but half were tested at that level on the ascending and half on the descending blood alcohol curve. Compared with placebo groups, alcohol groups had impaired performance, and it was worse on the descending half of the curve.

Detoxification and Elimination

Most drugs are detoxified or broken down chemically for elimination from the body by the liver (Wing, Hofmann, & Woods, 2004). In the case of alcohol, an **enzyme** produced by the liver, **alcohol dehydrogenase (ADH)**, metabolizes alcohol (ethanol) into **acetaldehyde**. Other enzymes, **cytochrome P450** (CYP2E1) and **catalase**, convert alcohol to acetaldehyde in other tissues such as those in the brain, which lack ADH.

Acetaldehyde is toxic and may damage tissue, create **reactive oxygen species (ROS)** molecules, and alter the *reduction-oxidation* state, or **redox state**, of liver cells before another enzyme, **aldehyde dehydrogenase (ALDH2)**, can break it down into water and **acetate**, nontoxic products that are eliminated from the body (Zakhari, 2006).

The average adult can oxidize one drink in approximately one hour. If the rate of alcohol intake exceeds the capacity of the liver to detoxify ethanol, the result will be an accumulation of alcohol with an attendant "intoxicating effect" as evidenced by the drinker's slurred speech, staggering, and impaired perceptual motor coordination. Upon recovery of sobriety, the unpleasant experience of a "hangover" may be encountered as the price for the previous evening's excessive use of alcohol.

For nicotine, the primary product of metabolism by the liver is cotinine and nicotine oxide (Wing et al., 2004). During the first pass through the liver, around 80%–90% of nicotine is broken down so that orally ingested tobacco produces little effect in comparison to smoked tobacco, which takes from half an hour to 2 hours to excrete from 2% to 35%.

Cocaine users have a variety of methods—for example, smoking, intravenous injection, and snorting—that lead to easy absorption. Cocaine has a rapid metabolism, with a **half-life** of about an hour involving the liver as well as the blood. Its metabolite, benzoylecgonine, has a half-life of about 8 hours and can be detected in urine for about 48 hours. Chronic use can produce both tolerance and sensitization to the drug, with the former likely occurring under constant conditions such as infusion and the latter when use is spread out over time. Withdrawal effects are not dramatic for users, but they show other signs of addiction (Wing et al., 2004).

Marijuana is usually smoked and absorbed quickly into the lungs before it crosses the blood-brain barrier and is distributed to various organs (Wing et al., 2004). Tolerance develops rapidly to its use. The liver is the primary metabolizer of THC with about 60%–70% of the metabolites eliminated in the feces and the remaining 30%–40% through the urine. The total elimination of marijuana is relatively slow, with a half-life of around 30 hours and residual traces of its metabolite, *carboxy-THC*, found even after several days and up to a month after use because it is lipid soluble.

Dose Response Curves

A major determinant of the effect of a drug is the size of the **dose**. As the drug dose increases, assuming all else is equal, there is generally an increase in the effect of the drug on physiological and/or behavior response. The relationship between dose and response is called a **dose-response curve**. There is no universal shape of the function as it varies for different drugs, users, and conditions. In the hypothetical dose-response curve in Figure 5.2, the dose is plotted on the horizontal axis, increasing from left to right, while the magnitude of the desired response is plotted on the vertical axis, increasing from the bottom to the top of the graph. At a very low dose, there is no effect, but beyond this point or region called the threshold, the response increases as the dose increases up to a point. The increases in response are not in a linear or 1:1 relationship to the dose but typically show a leveling or

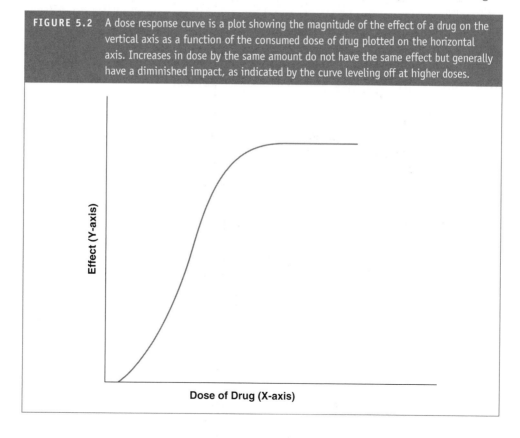

FIGURE 5.2   A dose response curve is a plot showing the magnitude of the effect of a drug on the vertical axis as a function of the consumed dose of drug plotted on the horizontal axis. Increases in dose by the same amount do not have the same effect but generally have a diminished impact, as indicated by the curve leveling off at higher doses.

Effect (Y-axis)

Dose of Drug (X-axis)

diminishing effect for the same dose increase at higher levels. Figure 5.2 also indicates "side effects" on a second curve on the right-hand side of the diagram. Such undesired effects are likely when the dose is too high.

The effect of a given dose will vary across individuals differing in metabolism, age, weight, and gender. For a given individual, the same dose may produce different effects depending on his or her physical and mental condition. Consequently, it is necessary for pharmacologists to identify *average* responses rather than rely on responses of specific individuals or use occasions.

Effective Versus Lethal Dose

Many drug abusers take drugs intended for the treatment of medical conditions for nonmedical or "recreational" use. They want to *maximize* the drug effect, so they seek strong doses despite the risk of adverse side effects. In contrast, physicians generally use lower doses that are sufficient to treat a medical condition and minimize undue risk of undesired side effects. These drugs have been tested to determine the effective dose so that the amount needed to treat a condition effectively but safely is known, especially for drugs that are expensive or have serious side effects.

At the other extreme might be dangerous levels, doses that might be *lethal,* which one would want to avoid. Using laboratory animals, the dose levels of a drug from which half of them died would be termed the *lethal dose 50*. This dose would be adjusted to estimate its equivalent for humans. Dangerous drugs are those with little room for error (i.e., the difference between the effective and the lethal dose is small). Safer drugs have a wide margin for error with a lethal dose being substantially higher than the effective dose.

HOW DRUGS AFFECT THE NERVOUS SYSTEM

What happens in the body at the neurophysiological level after alcohol and other drugs are taken is central to understanding how they affect experience and behavior. Neurochemical and neurophysiological effects occur throughout the body after consumption of drugs, which affect neuronal processes that may produce changes from prior levels, depending on the specific drug and the dose.

The Nervous System

We will first examine an overview of the nervous system followed by a description of how the neurons communicate. Then an examination of how different drugs influence neuro-transmitter substances will provide a basis for understanding how drugs affect behavior and experience. Evidence concerning the short-term or acute effects of drug use on the nervous system will be presented, followed by findings about the long-term effects of chronic drug use on major systems of the body.

Peripheral Nervous System

As Figure 5.3 indicates, the nervous system involves several components. The **peripheral nervous system (PNS)** receives stimuli from outside the body along peripheral nerve

FIGURE 5.3   Diagram of the organization of major structures of the nervous system.

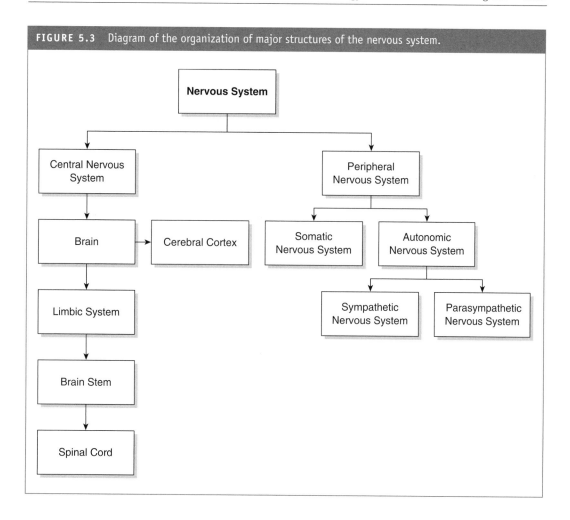

receptors to send input to the spinal cord, a set of nerve fibers, which runs along the length of the spine, and from there they are related to the brain, which sits atop it. The PNS consists of two parts, the **somatic nervous system (SNS)**, which controls the striated muscles and receptor organs that we have some voluntary control over, and the **autonomic nervous system (ANS)**, which affects smooth muscle and organs over which we have little or no control.

The ANS involves two opposing or reciprocal components, the **sympathetic** and **parasympathetic nervous systems**. In situations that threaten the well-being of the individual, the sympathetic nervous system is activated to enable behaviors to promote survival. Adrenalin or **epinephrine** is released from the adrenal gland, which activates neural receptors to increase heart rate and respiration and the release of glucose from the liver to fuel responses to cope with the situation. The parasympathetic nervous system has the opposite function, working through release of **acetylcholine (ACh)** to achieve homeostasis of bodily functions and restore resting levels when the problem is resolved.

Central Nervous System

The **central nervous system (CNS)** comprises the brain and the spinal cord. The CNS processes information from all parts of the body through the PNS to the brain. In turn, messages from the brain are sent back down the spinal cord to direct activity throughout the body.

A highly complex center, the brain is a system of interrelated structures specializing in important functions such as cognition, memory, emotion, movement, sensation, perception, eating, drinking, and sexual function. The outer covering or cerebral cortex contains a convoluted surface covering two hemispheres that serves as an association area for sensory and motor functions. Beneath the cortex in the forebrain is the limbic system consisting of several structures vital for many basic emotions involved in survival. A small but very important organ, the **hypothalamus**, plays a key role in hunger, thirst, pain, and sexual activity. The amygdala is implicated as a factor in aggressive behavior and emotional memory. A large structure, the **hippocampus**, is involved with spatial location memory. At the base of the brain or brain stem is the *medulla,* which governs respiration and vomiting, important functions that drugs may disrupt and the impairment of which may lead to fatal or serious harm. Above the medulla is the **cerebellum***,* important for motor coordination and balance.

FIGURE 5.4   Some parts of the brain involved in alcohol/nicotine dependence and psychiatric disorders.

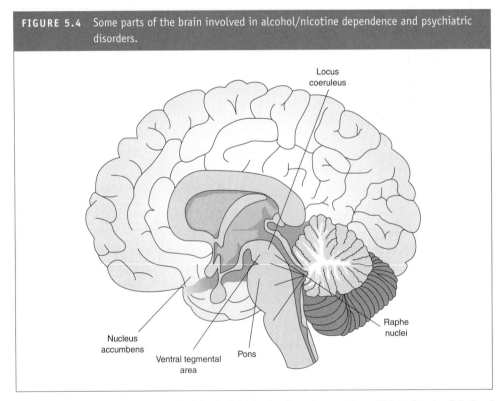

Source: From "Parts of the brain involved in alcohol/nicotine dependence and psychiatric disorders," National Institute of Alcoholism and Alcohol Abuse (2008), Rockville, MD. Available at http://www.niaaa.nih.gov/Resources/ GraphicsGallery/Neuroscience/brain_psychiatricdisorders.htm.

Figure 5.4 shows the location of several important areas of the brain affected by alcohol and other drugs and with potential damage from heavy use over long periods. A center called the *locus coeruleus* in the lower brain connects with the cortex as well as with midbrain regions such as the limbic system, which contains many of the receptors for the neurotransmitter norepinephrine (NE). These important structures regulate many basic emotional functions and fight or flight behaviors related to physical survival. The ventral tegmental area of this region connects with the **nucleus accumbens**, which contains many important sites for the neurotransmitter dopamine (DA), which is associated with pleasure. The raphe nuclei, distributed near the midline of the brainstem, include many neurons that release and selectively **reuptake** the monoamine neurotransmitter serotonin (5-HT) implicated in problems related to substance abuse such as anorexia, depression, and sleep disorders. An important midbrain center for pain receptors is the periaqueductal gray, which contains many receptors for **endogenous opiates** that are also activated by opiate drugs such as morphine and heroin. Substance abuse can damage the functioning of the pons in the brain stem region, important in affecting consciousness and sleep and linked to the cerebellum, which affects movement and posture.

HOW NEURONS COMMUNICATE

An understanding of how drugs affect the body requires an overview of how the nervous system functions, starting at the lowest level. The basic unit of the nervous system is the **neuron**, of which there are approximately 1 trillion. These cells send and receive neurochemical information to each other (Charness, 1990). Each neuron has a network of dendrites or fiber endings that extend into the spaces or gaps between cells called synapses where neural impulses are transmitted. The neuron sends this information down its axon to be received by the dendrites of as many as 1,000 adjacent neurons.

Neuronal Processes

The top section of Figure 5.5 provides a simplified view of two adjacent neurons. Within a neuron, signal transmission involves the movement of electrically charged particles or **ions** related to chemicals such as sodium (Na+), potassium (K+), chloride (Cl), and calcium (Ca+). These ions can pass through the cell membranes through channels that are specific to each type of ion. These **ion channels**, which are **proteins** in the neuron membrane, regulate the flow of ions through pores in the cell membrane. **Depolarization** occurs when the electrical charges produced by these ions involve a transient reversal of the membrane electrical potential between the outside and the inside of a neuron. This process leads to an impulse called the **action potential** that traverses the axon so that information can move through to the synapse and then on to other neurons.

Ions, in effect, create neural transmission through the cell. As shown in the bottom section of Figure 5.5, **neurotransmitters** from a presynaptic neuron pass across the synapse to adjacent postsynaptic neurons. If the entering ions have a positive electrical charge, they are termed *excitatory* as they facilitate activation of the cell processes that transmit the signal to the synapse. In contrast, other channels such as *GABA$_A$ receptors* exert *inhibitory* effects by admitting negatively charged ions such as chloride ions (Cl−) that reduce the ability of the cell to relay the signal further.

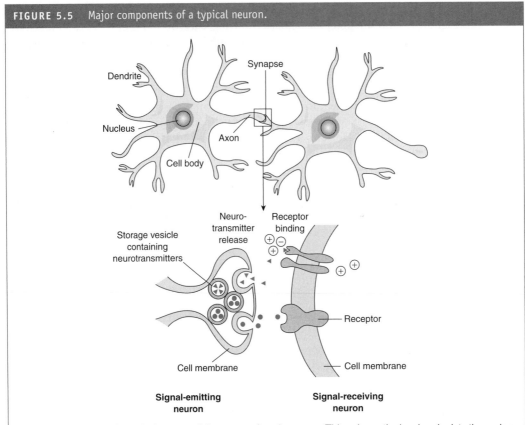

Structural features of a typical nerve cell (i.e., neuron) and synapse. This schematic drawing depicts the major components of a typical neuron, including the cell body with the nucleus; the dendrites that receive signals from other neurons; and the axon, which relays nerve signals to other neurons at a specialized structure called a synapse (see inset). When the nerve signal reaches the synapse, it causes the release of chemical messengers (i.e., neurotransmitters) from storage vesicles. The neurotransmitters travel across a minute gap between the cells and then interact with protein molecules (i.e., receptors) located in the membrane surrounding the signal-receiving neuron. This interaction causes biochemical reactions that result in the generation, or prevention, of a new nerve signal, depending on the type of neuron, neurotransmitter, and/or receptor involved.

Prepared: February 2005

Source: From "Mechanisms of Alcohol-Induced Damage to the Developing Nervous System," by C. R. Goodlett & K. H. Horn, 2001, *Alcohol Research & Health, 25*(3), 175–184.

Neurotransmitters

Neurotransmitters are chemicals created in the neurons and stored in vesicles in terminal buttons near the end of the axon as shown at the bottom of Figure 5.5. When a neuron is activated by impulses from other neurons, these neurotransmitters are released. Thus, neurotransmitters regulate the flow of information among individual neurons throughout the nervous system. Major neurotransmitters include **monoamines** such as **dopamine (DA)**, **serotonin (5-hydroxytryptamine or 5-HT)**, and **norepinephrine (NE)**. Substances like epinephrine and **glutamate** have excitatory effects, while acetylcholine (ACh) and **gamma-aminobutyric acid (GABA)** have inhibitory effects on neural activity.

Each neuron has receptor sites on its membrane that are specific for different neurotransmitters. Each type of receptor appears to recognize or accept a different type of incoming neurotransmitter across the synaptic junction, which separates each neuron from nearby neurons. For example, as Figure 5.6 shows, alcohol activates GABA, which attaches to the GABA$_A$ receptors, but it suppresses the excitatory neurotransmitter, glutamate, at the N-methyl-d-aspartate (NMDA) receptor. Additionally, alcohol blocks entry of calcium ions (CA+), essential for neurotransmitter release, at voltage-operated calcium channels (VOCC).

When a specific neurotransmitter is received at the membrane of the postsynaptic neuron, it "binds" or attaches to the receptor site in much the same way a key fits a lock. This process is like a message to the cell, which modifies its membrane permeability so that it increases or decreases the excitability of that receptor, depending on the specific neurotransmitter. The levels of these important neurotransmitters appear to be altered in various ways by the consumption of different drugs (Tabakoff, Hoffman, & Petersen, 1990).

Intraneuronal Processes

After a neuron is activated by a neurotransmitter, enzymes called second messengers, so named because they pass information from receptors on the membrane to the inner part of the neuron, further stimulate—or inhibit—synaptic transmission. This indirect process is slower and may require cascades of stimulation to be effective. One especially important messenger is cyclic guanine monophosphate (cGMP). A second messenger, cyclic adenosine monophosphate (cAMP), is valuable for its role in molecular synthesis of ribonucleic acid (RNA).

Disruption of these secondary messenger systems by the actions of ethanol (Tabakoff & Hoffman, 1987) could produce the observed acute effects of alcohol. For example, alcohol may disrupt adenyl cyclase (AC), an important enzyme affecting *cAMP*, which impedes transmission of messages from the exterior membrane of neurons to the interior.

Some drugs seem to involve phosphorylation, a process involving the addition of phosphate to the receptor sites, which, depending on the type of receptor, facilitates or impairs **G protein** activity or secondary messenger systems within the cells. These changes, which last for varying duration, improve or impede the reuptake of neurotransmitters to the originating presynaptic neurons for subsequent use.

HOW ALCOHOL AND OTHER DRUGS AFFECT NEUROTRANSMISSION

Alcohol and other drugs can alter neurotransmission in several ways at the synapse. Agonistic effects involve facilitation of neurotransmitter function in several ways: increased neurotransmitter production and blocked reuptake, increased neurotransmitter release, and activation of receptor sites that are normally stimulated by a specific neurotransmitter. In contrast, alcohol and other drugs may have antagonistic effects on neurotransmitters, either by interfering with their release, by usurping the receptor sites that a specific neurotransmitter normally occupies, or by causing neurotransmitter leakage from the synaptic vesicles.

FIGURE 5.6 Nerve cells (i.e., neurons) convert chemical messages received at the cell body (at left in this simplified neuron) into an electrical signal that is conducted along the axon to the terminal (at right). At the terminal, the electrical signal is converted back into a chemical message (i.e., a neurotransmitter) that is released from the terminal and carries the information to the next neuron in the circuit. Alcohol increases (i.e., potentiates) the effects of the major inhibitory neurotransmitter in the brain, gamma aminobutyric acid (GABA) at the $GABA_A$ receptor. GABA's effects tend to inhibit electrical signaling through the neuron. Alcohol further decreases electrical activity by inhibiting the major excitatory neurotransmitter, glutamate, particularly at a glutamate receptor protein called the N-methyl-d-aspartate (NMDA) receptor. By inhibiting glutamate at the NMDA receptor, alcohol slows the flow of calcium (Ca) into cells. Regulation of calcium balance is essential for normal cell function. In addition to its effects at the NMDA receptor, alcohol can alter the flow of calcium through voltage-operated calcium channels (VOCCs) at the cell body as well as at the terminal, where calcium is necessary for neurotransmitter release.

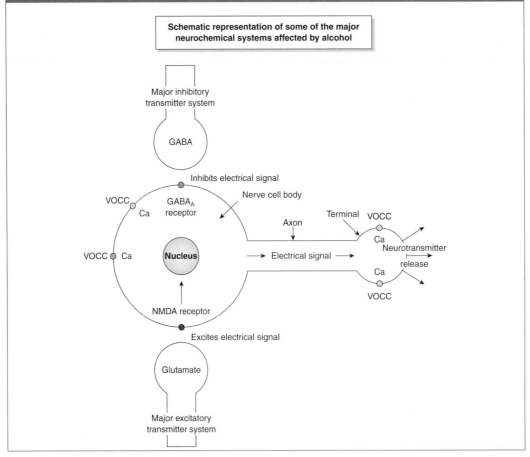

Source: From "Neurochemical Mechanisms Underlying Alcohol Withdrawal," by J. Littleton, 1998 (Updated: October 2000), *Alcohol Health & Research World, 22*(1), pp. 13–24.

Alcohol

Unlike other drugs, *alcohol* does not affect specific brain receptors but appears to influence the entire neuronal membrane (Harris & Buck, 1990). Alcohol disrupts the typical balance of the half-protein and half-lipid composition of the membrane, altering the passage of other chemicals through glutamate and GABA receptors. Alcohol increases the chloride ion entry through the actions of GABA, an inhibitory neurotransmitter, so that there is reduced neuronal excitability. Alcohol also inhibits the amino acid glutamate, the major excitatory neurotransmitter responsible for allowing higher levels of calcium ions into cells, primarily through the NMDA receptor, with the net effect of creating a sedative influence.

Dopamine (DA), which may underlie rewarding and pleasurable experiences, appears to first increase with alcohol use but to eventually show a decline with continued drinking. Norepinephrine (NE) is often higher with increasing arousal such as stressful situations. Alcohol seems to be associated with higher levels of NE. Serotonin (5-HT) is an important regulator of mood and consummatory behavior such as eating. It is diminished by heavy alcohol use, or it may be naturally lower for alcoholics. Violent and impulsive behaviors have also been associated with lowered serotonin levels (Lidberg, Tuck, Asberg, Scalia-Tomba, & Bertilsson, 1985). One conjecture is that alcoholics may drink excessively to self-medicate depression in a futile attempt to increase their serotonin levels (Tabakoff et al., 1990).

Monoamines (MA) such as dopamine, norepinephrine, and serotonin are neurotransmitters that enhance mood. Enzymes such as monoamine oxidase (MAO) break down such substances, and the mood enhancement is ended. Drugs that prevent this decomposition of MA, called **MAO inhibitors (MAOIs)**, can prolong the benefits of mood enhancers such as dopamine. A different process for prolonging the mood changes from drug-instigated release of MA involves slowing down the reuptake or removal of the synaptic junction MA back into the cell. One type of antidepressant, the tricyclics such as Elavil® and Tofranil®, works to prevent reuptake of monoamines such as dopamine and to block cholinergic receptors that receive an inhibitory neurotransmitter, acetylcholine (ACh). A newer class of antidepressant drugs such as fluoxetine (Prozac®), which selectively block the reuptake of serotonin from the synaptic area, can also prolong the improved mood states.

Barbiturates and Benzodiazepines

Sedative-hypnotic drugs such as **barbiturates** and **benzodiazepines**, designed to have sedative or anxiolytic properties, are invaluable for many medical purposes in their function as anticonvulsants and muscle relaxants (McKim, 2007). Newer drugs displaced barbiturates such as phenobarbital, which was widely used to sedate surgery patients because of its fast-acting properties. Benzodiazepines are used in treating anxiety, insomnia, agitation, seizures, and muscle spasms, as well as alcohol withdrawal.

Barbiturates and benzodiazepines created for different medical purposes vary widely in how quickly they act and how long their effects last. Abusers tend to prefer short-acting and intermediate-acting variants that can quickly pass through the blood-brain barrier and affect higher functions.

These drugs have specific receptor sites to which they bind to release chloride ion channel blockers that inhibit the CNS activity of GABA. Barbiturates bind to GABA$_A$

receptors, sites that are distinct from GABA itself and from the benzodiazepine binding sites. Both drug categories potentiate the effect of GABA, the principal inhibitory neurotransmitter at this receptor. In addition, barbiturates also block the AMP_A receptor, a subtype of glutamate receptor.

Since these drugs are often used in combination with alcohol, they are especially dangerous when abused because their effects are increased as alcohol slows down their metabolic breakdown.

Nicotine

Nicotine from tobacco is absorbed into the body and activates cholinergic receptors that are affected by the neurotransmitter acetylcholine (ACh), leading to release of dopamine, norepinephrine, and beta-endorphins.

These nicotinic receptors are found in many parts of the CNS, particularly in the brain stem. When nicotine activates nicotinic receptors at sites in the adrenal glands and reticular formation, adrenalin (epinephrine) and norepinephrine are released. These actions stimulate the CNS, as reflected by increases in heart rate, blood pressure, and brain electroencephalogram (EEG) activity (McKim, 2007).

Nicotine-stimulated dopamine (DA) release is related to increased activity in the shell of the nucleus accumbens (Pontieri, Tanda, Orzi, & Di Chiara, 1996). This region connects to the forebrain and includes the amygdala, which deals with emotional and motivational processing. After DA is released and transmits its signals, it is generally taken up by the releasing neuron. MAO B is an enzyme that breaks down DA in the brain. Pontieri et al.'s finding of lower MAO B in smokers' brains suggests that whatever is inhibiting MAO B could be working with nicotine to enhance dopamine effects by slowing its metabolism. As earlier studies have shown that nicotine does not influence MAO B, the culprit could be some of the 4,000 or so identified chemicals in cigarette smoke.

Cigarette combustion involves carbon monoxide, which forms carboxyhemoglobin when it binds with blood cells. Nicotine acts to produce electrocortical activation, skeletal muscle relaxation, and cardiovascular and endocrine effects such as the increase of catecholamines, corticosteroids, and pituitary hormones.

Cigarettes are a highly efficient "nicotine delivery system," as burned tobacco allows the nicotine to vaporize and reach the membranes inside the lungs, from which it enters the heart, bloodstream, and brain in less than a second. Nicotine has a short half-life of about 30 min and is metabolized by the liver or excreted by the kidneys.

Nicotine absorption across membranes depends on it being in its non-ionized state or alkaline form. When nicotine is in an acid environment, the psychoactive effect is weakened because nicotine is not readily absorbed from the acidic environment of the stomach. However, chewing tobacco, snuff, and nicotine gum are effective alternative delivery mechanisms to smoking because absorption of nicotine through the membranes in the mouth directly into the bloodstream maintains its alkaline state.

Caffeine

Caffeine, one of the class of alkaloids called methylxanthines, is present in coffee, tea, and cola soft drinks, as well as in chocolate. Caffeine is quickly absorbed from the stomach and small intestine and is distributed throughout the body in about 45 min. Caffeine is metabolized by the liver, and about 3 to 4 hours are required to eliminate half of the amount in the body. Caffeine is an **antagonist** that blocks adenosine receptors and slows the reuptake of neurotransmitters such as DA, 5-HT, and NE. Adenosine acts as an inhibitor of the CNS, so caffeine functions as a stimulant.

Tolerance to caffeine develops readily, which leads to increases in the number of adenosine receptors. When caffeine intake is reduced or ended, the normal physiological effects of adenosine are augmented, resulting in unpleasant withdrawal symptoms. For example, during caffeine withdrawal, adenosine dilates the blood vessels of the head, which can lead to headache and nausea. Other withdrawal symptoms such as irritability, loss of concentration, and stomachaches may appear within 12 to 24 hours after caffeine intake ends and peak at roughly 48 hours. In 4 to 5 days, these reactions end as the number of adenosine receptors in the brain return to normal levels (McKim, 2007).

Opiates

Opium is not easily absorbed from the digestive tract. Consequently, oral ingestion does not produce much effect, and opiate users experience more potent effects by injection or smoking it in pipes. Most of it is metabolized during the first pass through the liver. There are five different types of receptors to which opiates bind with different consequences: *mu, kappa, sigma, delta,* and *epsilon.* For example, analgesia is mediated mainly by opiates binding to the mu receptor (McKim, 2007). Morphine, the active pharmacological ingredient in the opium poppy, is 10 times more potent than opium. Morphine is not easily absorbed as it is not lipid soluble but is quickly absorbed and metabolized when smoked or injected.

The possibility that the body synthesizes its own opiates was raised with the discovery of receptor sites for the opiate morphine in the early 1970s (Pert & Snyder, 1973). It might seem odd that the body would have existing receptors to accept substances that come from outside the body. One hypothesis is that since opiates help the body cope with pain, the receptors for the body's natural or endogenous chemical means of reducing pain would accept exogenous substances such as morphine or other drugs because they also alleviate pain. The eventual discovery that the body has natural or endogenous opiates such as **enkephalins** and **beta-endorphins** vindicated this line of reasoning.

Heroin, developed in the late 1890s, is a semisynthetic opiate that is about three times stronger than morphine and crosses the blood-brain barrier many times faster. It is not lipid soluble. Heroin involves rapid tolerance, with a tenfold increase in dose required within a few months of use. Withdrawal reactions, which include restless agitation, twitching, sweating, drowsiness, goose bumps, vomiting, and cramping, start about 6–12 hours after use, peak in 24 to 72 hours, and last about a week. Nonetheless, the overall syndrome is relatively mild and can be confused with flu symptoms. The more intense dramatic portrayals are atypical and reflect use of either poor-quality drugs with toxic impurities or large doses.

Naloxone and **naltrexone (ReVia®)** are antagonists that block the effects of opiate drugs. They compete with opioids for their receptor sites, and by occupying these locations, they effectively neutralize the opioids by preventing them from producing their effects on the nervous system. Naloxone is used to counter overdoses whereas naltrexone, more potent and much longer lasting, is employed more as a treatment adjunct for dependence.

Methadone is a synthetic opiate that is commonly used in treating heroin addiction because its effects are longer lasting with less severe withdrawal that extends over a longer period. Methadone acts as an antagonist to heroin by competing for its receptor sites. One great health advantage is that methadone can be taken orally, avoiding the risk of infections from needle injections.

Cocaine

Cocaine produces its psychoactive effects by blocking the reuptake of dopamine as well as of serotonin. Since these neurotransmitters are retained at the synapse, their mood-enhancing and energizing effects are maintained and produce the high stimulation sought by users. When cocaine is not available to chronic users, the opposite effect of depression occurs, which is commonly referred to as a "crash."

Cocaine has a half-life of only 1 hour, with a longer half-life of 8 hours for its metabolite. A moderate dose (up to 60 mg) elevates mood, enhances performance on physical endurance, and promotes a sense of well-being. However, at higher doses, cocaine can lead to paranoid delusions as well as hallucinations. There is also a risk of overdose as well as interactions with other drugs (McKim, 2007).

Cocaine mimics the actions of the sympathetic nervous system and its neurotransmitter, epinephrine, which activates the emergency responses such as heightened arousal (increased heart rate, blood pressure, respiration rate, sweating, eye dilatation, increased body temperature). To serve the emergency needs of survival, blood flow goes to the large muscle groups and not to peripheral organs. Cocaine also has its medical functions as a local anesthetic that can be used to numb the mouth, vagina, rectum, and eyes. A potent byproduct of cocaine, crack, is the outcome when cocaine and sodium bicarbonate are combined and heated to eliminate the water content.

Amphetamines

Amphetamines are weak base substances that stimulate the release of dopamine as well as block its reuptake. Amphetamines also affect norepinephrine receptors to produce alertness and to counteract fatigue (McKim, 2007). These synthetic stimulants originally were used medically to deal with respiratory problems such as asthma, some sleep disorders, and obesity. In the workplace, they were used to increase employee productivity. During World War II, American, German, and Japanese soldiers used them to offset fatigue. Following the war, widespread abuse of amphetamines occurred, as they became a recreational drug.

A more potent form created illegally, **methamphetamine**, has high potential for wide abuse. A crystal form of meth, called "ice," has rapidly increased in use since the 1960s. It spread from the West across the nation, especially to southern rural areas. It was easily made in home labs with pseudoephedrine readily obtained from over-the-counter cough medicines until recent awareness led to controlled access.

Meth can be smoked, snorted, injected, or orally ingested, with a different impact depending on how it is ingested. Smoking leads to very fast uptake of the drug in the brain, but the pleasurable effects from the release of dopamine dissipate quickly so that abusers must binge or go on meth "runs" to maintain the highs (National Institute on Drug Abuse, 2006).

Marijuana

The active ingredient in cannabis, delta-9-THC, is lipid soluble but does not dissolve in water, so its absorption is slow. Smoking, therefore, is a much faster mode of administration since the drug moves rapidly from the lungs to the rest of the body in a few minutes. Receptors have been found throughout the CNS, especially in the nucleus accumbens.

Cannabis affects 5-HT and DA levels as well as prostaglandin synthesis. It slows turnover of ACh in animal experiments. An endogenous neurotransmitter, named anadamide (Devane et al., 1992), has been found for cannabis as well as receptor sites (Mechoulam, Hanus, & Martin, 1994) in many areas of the brain including the cortex, hippocampus, and cerebellum.

Hallucinogens

Psychedelic drugs, popular in the 1960s, include **lysergic acid diethylamide (LSD)**, peyote, and mescaline. LSD is taken orally and acts on serotonin and dopamine receptors in the cerebral cortex and locus coeruleus to block serotonin release and increase retention of serotonin at serotonin-2 receptors. Its net effect is that of a serotonin **agonist**. Psychological effects start approximately 30–60 min after ingestion, peak around 5 hours, and last for approximately 12 hours. Although tolerance occurs rapidly, it can disappear in a few days. As LSD shows no withdrawal reactions, the dangers of physical dependency are considered small (McKim, 2007).

Hallucinogenic experiences or "trips" include changes in mood and perception. Boundaries are blurred, time becomes distorted, stationary objects may seem to flow or pulsate, and color perception is intensified. These effects vary with both the individual taking the drug and the physical environment surrounding the user.

CHANGES IN NEUROPHYSIOLOGY WITH PROLONGED DRUG USE

Answers as to why drug taking is such an attractive behavior and why it is so resistant to cessation may depend strongly on the effects that drugs have on neurotransmitters, effects that vary with continued or prolonged use.

During the early use of drugs, although different drugs involve different sets of neurotransmitters, most produce either direct increases of DA or indirect effects on processes that allow DA to last longer. DA, released in the *nucleus accumbens*, is widely regarded as a major factor underlying positive reinforcement. Since drug taking is such a powerfully reinforcing behavior, it has been conjectured that drug use acts to increase and/or maintain levels of DA in the brain. Similarities exist among nicotine, heroin, and cocaine addiction as these drugs all have the ability to selectively increase dopamine transmission and energy metabolism in the shell of the nucleus accumbens (Pontieri et al., 1996). A reward deficiency hypothesis of drug taking assumes that when DA levels are low in the limbic system, due either to situations such as high stress, failure, and depression or to biological differences in the innate tendencies for DA release, drugs can serve as a substitute mechanism for restoring or elevating DA levels (Blum et al., 1995).

Stimulant drugs such as cocaine increase the presence of DA by inhibiting its reuptake so that DA's reinforcing function is prolonged. Nicotine, another stimulant, increases DA as well as ACh. Depressant drugs such as alcohol and the opiates release more DA as well as 5-HT, which may counter depressive affect, at least during early stages of drinking, although there may be a reversal as drinking continues over time.

A model of drug rewards in the early stages of drug use implicates dopamine released in the mesolimbic region. Figure 5.7 identifies the brain areas involved in this medial forebrain reward neurocircuit, described as an "extended amygdala" that incorporates the amygdala, lateral hypothalamus, and ventral pallidum loop.

FIGURE 5.7   Neuropsychological model of addiction of Koob and Le Moal.

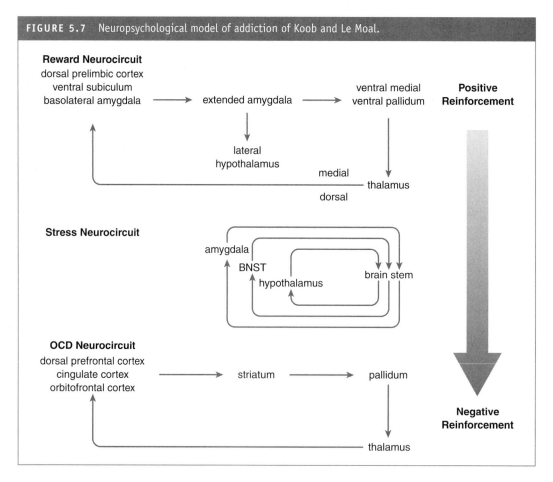

Source: From "Drug Addiction and Allostasis," by G. F. Koob & M. Le Moal, 2005, in J. Schulkin (Ed.), *Allostasis, Homeostasis, and the Costs of Physiological Adaptation* (pp. 150–163), Cambridge: Cambridge University Press. Reprinted with permission.

Psychostimulants such as cocaine and amphetamine produce their effects in the *mesolimbic dopamine system* (Koob, 1992). Cocaine blocks reuptake of dopamine by binding to a specific protein, the dopamine transporter protein, while amphetamines both enhance dopamine release and block its reuptake.

Tolerance

Continued use of most psychoactive drugs leads to neuroadaptation in which a given dose produces a diminished rewarding effect. This phenomenon is known as **tolerance**. In the case of alcohol, use of the same amount that previously produced a given effect is no longer adequate to produce the same effect on later occasions as diagrammed on the left side of Figure 5.8. One danger is that with increased tolerance the drinker underestimates the true BAC, often leading him or her to engage in riskier behaviors.

Thus, the gap between anticipated and subjective (actual) reactions to alcohol may differ with the drinker's experience with alcohol. Expected and experienced effects of alcohol in 387 male and female drinkers were compared against observer ratings (Gabrieli, Nagoshi, Rhea, & Wilson, 1991). Based on their drinking history, drinkers were classified into three levels of consumption: high, moderate, and low. They consumed alcohol in the laboratory to produce a BAC that was the equivalent of two drinks an hour over 2 hours

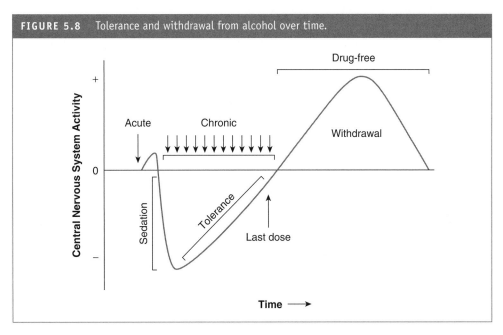

FIGURE 5.8   Tolerance and withdrawal from alcohol over time.

Source: From "Dependence and Withdrawal," by P. Metten & J. C. Crabbe, 1996, in R. A. Deitrich & V. G. Ervin (Eds.), *Pharmacological Effects of Ethanol on the Nervous System* (pp. 269–290), Boca Raton, FL: CRC Press. Copyrighted by CRC Press. Reprinted with permission.

before taking a battery of tests measuring sensory motor performance, cognitive and perceptual tasks, and autonomic responses. Assessments of their feelings of intoxication and euphoria were made by drinkers as well as by trained observers.

Anticipated sensitivity was measured by drinker ratings to determine the extent to which drinkers expected to experience intoxication, negative emotions, and euphoric emotions after four drinks. Subjective perceptions of mood after drinking were assessed with a mood inventory. In addition, observers rated the drinkers for intoxication, negative emotions, and euphoric emotions. The results showed that heavy drinkers tended to underestimate alcohol effects (objective ratings higher than subjective ratings) whereas the inexperienced light drinkers tended to overestimate alcohol effects (objective ratings lower than subjective ratings).

Based on the fact that observer ratings showed more impairment for the heavy than for the lighter drinkers, it appears that heavy drinkers may underestimate alcohol effects due to tolerance. Observer ratings of the effects of alcohol were generally greater than either the anticipated or the subjective ratings of effects made by the drinkers. Heavy drinkers may be likely to develop further problems because they deny that expected and actual effects of alcohol will be as high as they are.

Similarly, the use of other drugs involves the development of tolerance, which may be responsible for the increased size of doses of drugs consumed on subsequent occasions, although the rate at which it is achieved differs for different effects that each drug produces. In the case of drugs such as amphetamines and heroin, substantial tolerance occurs with several-fold increases in doses needed after only a few episodes of use. On the other hand, tolerance for cocaine is relatively mild.

As opposed to physiological tolerance, which occurs at the level of the neuron, behavioral tolerance involves conditioned or learned responses (McKim, 2007). Thus, expectations and learned associations acquired from using a drug in a specific setting may lead to increased future consumption in that same setting. Behavioral tolerance may occur even in the absence of physiological tolerance.

Withdrawal Syndrome

When a long-term user of most drugs abruptly discontinues its use, a **withdrawal syndrome** occurs as shown on the right side of Figure 5.8 that is usually opposite to the effect of the drug as if the nervous system attempts to compensate for departures produced by the drug on the resting balance of excitatory and inhibitory states. Acute withdrawal involves highly variable but unpleasant symptoms including sweating, tremors, agitation, seizures, and hallucinations. This pattern, **delirium tremens,** often referred to as the DTs, can be fatal. The irritability and discomfort experienced during the lack of the drug is precisely what triggers the user of some drugs to resume use. Drug taking serves as a way of self-medication to treat the unpleasant symptoms created by nonuse of some drugs. Hence, a vicious and escalating cycle is generated.

In the case of CNS depressants such as alcohol, barbiturates, and benzodiazepines, there is a tendency for a rebound effect of **hyperexcitability** when their effects wear off (McKim, 2007). With higher use levels, this withdrawal reaction is more pronounced. Stress activated by the withdrawal reactions arising from the lack of the drug triggers neurocircuits involving the hypothalamus, **bed nucleus of the stria terminalis (BNST)**, amygdala, and brain stem (refer to the middle section of Figure 5.7).

For stimulants such as amphetamines, cocaine, or crack, the withdrawal reaction seems to be relatively mild and involves the opposite effect of depression and lethargy. There is some debate as to whether the cessation of cocaine use produces a withdrawal reaction because of its mild form or whether withdrawal just takes a form that is different from the violent reactions involved in withdrawal from alcohol or heroin (McKim, 2007). Withdrawal symptoms, depending on the drug, generally start from 12 to 24 hours after the drug is no longer used and can last up to several days. The typical medical treatment for alcohol withdrawal involves use of another drug from the same class of depressants, benzodiazepines (e.g., Librium®, Valium®), and vitamins to counter the state of hyperexcitability of the nervous system. Barbiturates have also been used but are less often chosen because they involve the risk of **cross tolerance**, a condition in which the tolerance to one drug generalizes to other drugs in the same category. If alcoholic patients receive barbiturates to reduce the withdrawal to alcohol, they may adapt too quickly due to cross tolerance and fail to benefit. Clonidine and beta-adrenergic blockers have been employed with more success (Liskow & Goodwin, 1987). As the withdrawal symptoms abate, the medical treatment is gradually reduced.

Dependence

Another outcome of prolonged use of alcohol and most other drugs is dependence. Commonly called addiction, this condition often involves craving for a drug that leads to compulsive use, no longer controllable by the user. Dependence involving drugs such as alcohol or heroin is often motivated by negative reinforcement, the reduction of unpleasant withdrawal reactions rather than the increase of pleasurable states. Thus, neuroadaptation to alcohol in the form of tolerance and withdrawal leads to alcohol dependence. The drinker persists in a losing effort to consume alcohol in larger amounts and more frequently tries to escape the aversive states of physical discomfort that arise during abstinence.

Even with drugs such as cocaine that do not generally involve strong physical withdrawal reactions, dependence can develop with strong cravings for renewed or continued use. Cocaine or crack dependence may be due more to positive reinforcement such as pleasant drug experiences than to the reduction of aversive withdrawal states.

In summary, the acute and chronic use of alcohol and other drugs alter neurotransmitter levels that influence behavior and experience. Prolonged use of alcohol, for example, is assumed to lead to neuroadaptations on the major inhibitory neurotransmitter (gamma-aminobutyric acid, or GABA), the major excitatory neurotransmitter (glutamate), and the calcium channel system that regulates various processes inside neurons. Alcohol tolerance, withdrawal, and dependence are among the consequences of such neuroadaptations, which alter the neurotransmitter production and release (Littleton, 1998). Table 5.2 contains an overview of the major psychoactive drugs discussed in this chapter, listing the primary neurotransmitters affected by each drug as well as the extent to which their prolonged or repeated use leads to tolerance, dependence, and withdrawal.

TABLE 5.2 Summary of neuropsychological processes for different major psychoactive drugs: main neurotransmitters, tolerance, and dependence.

Drug	Tolerance for Main Effect	Withdrawal	Psychological Dependence	Major Neurotransmitter Actions
Alcohol	Yes	Strong, if high dose	Yes	DA, GABA, glutamate
Nicotine	Fast	Yes	Yes	ACh, DA, NE, beta-endorphin
Caffeine	Yes	Rare	Yes	Block adenosine
Barbiturates	Fast	Strong, if high dose	Yes	GABA
Benzodiazepine	Yes	Slight	Yes	GABA
Opiates, heroin	Fast	Strong, if high dose	Yes	DA, NE, glutamate
Cocaine	Yes	Weak	Yes	Block reuptake of DA, NE
Amphetamines	Slow	Weak	Yes	NE leaks, release and block reuptake of DA, 5-HT
Cannabis	Yes	Mild	Yes	DA, NE, 5-HT, GABA
Hallucinogens	Fast	No	No	Blocks 5-HT

Note: DA = dopamine; 5-HT = serotonin; NE = norepinephrine; GABA = gamma animobutyl acid; ACh = acetylcholine.

NEUROADAPTATIONAL MODELS

Opponent-Process Model

The **opponent-process theory** (Solomon, 1980) is a general model of addictive behaviors and not limited to drugs. It focuses on the affective reactions to the receipt and termination of any strong stimulus. Drug use produces an affective state, A, which dissipates after use stops. It is followed by an affective aftereffect, B, opposite in emotional tone to that produced by a drug serving as a compensatory response to restore the body to a neutral state. Together, the two states, A and B, represent opponent processes. If the drug use produced positive affect, its removal or termination would leave a feeling of negative tone, akin to disappointment. In contrast, a drug that produced negative affect would leave a positive feeling after the original affect ended, similar to relief.

With respect to alcohol, the opponent-process theory further describes changes in the relationship between these two opposing affective states over time as the drinker becomes more experienced. For beginning or light drinkers, a small amount of alcohol is capable of producing a strong positive affect (state A) while the negative aftereffect (state B) is relatively weak. However, as drug use escalates over time, tolerance, a form of habituation, develops. The small dose that originally was capable of producing a given amount of positive affect now generates a weaker positive A state, but the negative B state that follows is larger than it was previously.

Heavy users typically try to forestall both the shrinking positive affect and the escalating negative aftereffect by increasing the quantity and frequency of drug use. In essence, addiction involves the increased use of the drug to treat the unpleasant symptoms associated with withdrawal from the drug. Unfortunately, this strategy is doomed to fail, entrapping the drug user into a spiral of ever-deepening addiction.

Incentive-Sensitization Model

A model (Koob & Le Moal, 1997) that could be regarded as a neural version of the opponent-process model proposed that the rewarding A process involves activation of mesolimbic dopamine projections to the nucleus accumbens and amygdala. Tolerance to repeated drug use decreases the A state due to **downregulation** in the mesolimbic dopamine system in which the postsynaptic neuron has reduced sensitivity to the drug. Sudden cessation of drug use reduces dopamine and serotonin below normal levels temporarily, which generates an unpleasant B state, withdrawal.

An **incentive-sensitization model** of addiction (Robinson & Berridge, 1993, 2003) holds that the absence of a drug like alcohol after prolonged use heightens its *incentive salience*. Enhanced vigilance, obsessive thoughts about the drug, and compulsive behaviors aimed at obtaining the absent drug occur and activate a neurocircuit involving the dorsal striatum, pallidum, and thalamus (refer to the bottom section of Figure 5.7). Self-medication to reduce withdrawal is not the main reason users might resume use as often occurs, even in the absence of—or subsequent to the end of—withdrawal reactions.

Drugs like alcohol do damage to brain reward systems related to the nucleus accumbens such that these neural circuits involving dopamine D1 receptors may become permanently hypersensitive to specific drug effects (Everitt, Dickinson, & Robbins, 2001). Similar sensitization-related changes occur for other neurotransmitters involved in reward circuits including glutamate, serotonin, norepinephrine, acetylcholine (ACh), opioid, and GABA systems as well as for some intracellular signaling processes that they activate (Robinson & Berridge, 2000). Extended use of stimulants such as cocaine and amphetamine similarly potentiates mesolimbic dopamine levels (White & Kalivas, 1998). In addition, there is more sensitivity to contextual stimuli that were present during past drug use, but they are relatively weak factors for relapse compared with the increased motivational salience of explicit drug cues (Robinson & Berridge, 2000).

Craving, a state of "wanting" the drug, develops, even though the user may no longer "desire" the drug, which no longer provides the pleasure that it previously did. This heightened sensitivity to the drug, not any expectation of pleasurable use, is what motivates the wanting of the drug.

Allostasis

Addiction involves **allostasis** (Koob & Le Moal, 2001), a state of reduced reward with decreased dopamine, opioid peptides, and GABA at the same time there is increased stress

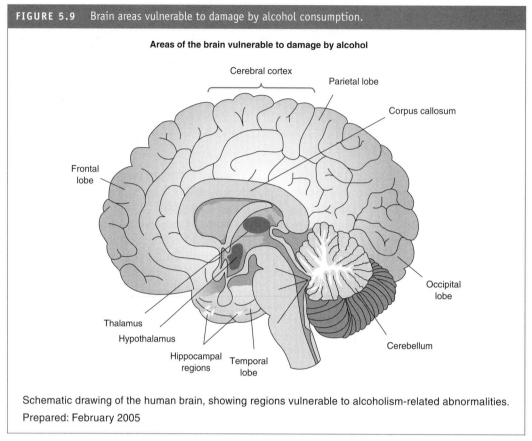

FIGURE 5.9 Brain areas vulnerable to damage by alcohol consumption.

Schematic drawing of the human brain, showing regions vulnerable to alcoholism-related abnormalities.
Prepared: February 2005

Source: From "Alcoholism and the Brain," by M. Oscar-Berman & K. Marinlovic, 2003, *Alcohol Research and Health, 27*(2), pp. 125–133.

with release of glucocorticoids, corticotropin-releasing factor (CRF), and activation of neuropeptide Y (NPY), an antistress system of hormones.

Prolonged drug use damages brain neurobiological processes, as indicated in Figure 5.9, which shows that many major brain areas harmed by drugs. Nonetheless, users experience apparent reward stability from drug use as their reward set point is permanently lowered by drug-induced neuroadaptations or adjustments in brain function. Consequently, there is high likelihood of dependence as well as relapse following abstinence.

PHYSICAL EFFECTS OF DRUGS

Methods for Getting Evidence

A variety of methods have been used to determine the long-term effects of alcohol on the nervous system, including anatomical evidence available from autopsies, neurological correlates, and behavioral evidence. The three types of evidence are not always in agreement. For example, anatomical differences observed between alcoholics and nonalcoholics or from before-after comparisons of individual alcoholics may reflect causes, effects, or simply correlates of alcoholism. These differences may or may not also be accompanied by detectable neurological and behavioral differences. Similarly, neuropsychological differences may not involve functional consequences for behavior.

The rapid development of more advanced computer techniques has offered impressive new technology for study of the relationship of brain structure, functioning, and alcohol use. A review (Pfefferbaum & Rosenbloom, 1990) described research with tools that examine anatomical structure with three-dimensional images such as scans by computerized tomography (CT) and magnetic resonance imaging (MRI) to improve our visualization of the physical structure of the brain. Research with CT has shown brain tissue shrinkage and more cerebrospinal fluid in the resulting larger ventricles in alcoholics. However, this shrinkage appears to reverse somewhat under abstinence. Findings with MRI, unlike those using CT, can distinguish between white and gray matter (two different types of brain tissue) and show that alcoholics have greater decreases in both gray and white matter than do age-matched nondrinking controls.

However, as noted earlier, structural differences do not necessarily imply functional differences. Use of techniques such as **positron emission tomography (PET)** and cerebral blood flow (CBF) enables measurement of the brain processes, as opposed to structures, by examining dynamic changes in the distribution and accumulation of blood flow, blood volume, blood oxygen, and other chemicals in the brain over time, with and without the presence of alcohol. These measures are highly indirect indices of actual physiological processes that occur during behavior or task performance under different drug conditions, obtained through the tracing of radioactive materials introduced into the body, and are still open to interpretation.

In vivo brain imaging technology (Pfefferbaum, Rosenbloom, & Sullivan, 2002) such as **functional magnetic resonance imaging (fMRI)** has enabled measurement of metabolic changes in different regions of the brain during performance of specific cognitive or motor tasks under different conditions. Using fMRI allows researchers to measure increased localized blood flow and blood oxygenation in regions of the brain involved in the tasks. In addition, fMRI allows for noninvasive study of brain changes associated with the impact of alcoholism on diseases like HIV as well as the increased vulnerability of normal aging.

In reaching conclusions about the effects of alcohol and other drug use, comparisons are often made between users and abstainers (Rehm, Gmel, Sempos, & Trevisan, 2003). However, since the category of abstainers may include former users who are not using at the time of the comparison, impairments may be underestimated if the former users have already suffered harmful effects. Restricting comparisons to lifelong abstainers has its own problems, as they may be atypical of the general population.

Another problem is the difficulty of establishing accurate evidence of the relationship between alcohol use and morbidity of health problems. For one matter, measures of alcohol use typically involve self-reports for a specific time period. Several untested assumptions are involved with these measures, which usually ask about the usual frequency and quantity of use. However, many people vary in the amount and frequency of use depending on the context even over a short time span. Changes in use patterns may be even greater over the lengthy periods that are involved when assessing the relationship between drug use and major health problems.

Chronic Effects

Brain

Comparison of alcoholics and nonalcoholics shows that wider sulci (the gaps between the convolutions of the outer layer of the cerebral cortex) and larger cerebral ventricles (cavities) exist among alcoholics. These differences parallel changes typically found with aging. Measures of the electrical activity in areas of the brain are possible with noninvasive techniques such as the **electroencephalogram (EEG) and event-related potentials (ERP)**. A widely used ERP measure is the **P300 wave**, so-called because it occurs 300 ms after a stimulus is presented. It is regarded as a measure of attention and processing of incoming sensory stimuli.

Lower amplitudes of the P300 wave have been found in response to sensory tests among adults from alcoholic families in comparison to control families, especially with males (Porjesz et al., 1998). It is possibly genetically determined rather than a consequence of drinking because nondrinking children of alcoholics (Enoch, White, Harris, Rohrbaugh, & Goldman, 2001; Patterson, Williams, McLean, Smith, & Schaffer, 1987) have also shown lower P300 responses.

Liver

The liver is the largest organ in the body and serves as the main detoxifier (Lieber, 1984, 1994) for the metabolic breakdown of alcohol. Additionally, major functions of the liver include the production of bile for digestion of fats; albumin to help regulate fluid balance in cells of the whole body; globulin, which helps fight infections; and prothrombin, which helps clot blood in order to stop wounds from bleeding. Chronic alcohol abuse can impair many vital functions of the liver. One complication, portal systemic encephalopathy (PSE), shunts the venous blood away from the liver and sends it directly into circulation. Thus, liver detoxification or elimination of waste products is prevented, which allows for the accumulation of toxins that disrupt normal neurotransmitter functions.

Chronic heavy alcohol use impairs the capacity of the liver for metabolizing alcohol. Metabolic byproducts of chronic alcohol intake can cause hepatitis or inflammation of liver tissue (Maher, 1997; Rodés, Salaspuro, & Sorenson, 1999). In some cases, the hepatitis C virus (HCV) leads to cirrhosis of the liver, which involves scarring tissue so that it can no longer effectively eliminate ethanol. Alcohol can exacerbate HCV infection, resulting in liver damage from **oxidative stress** and fibrosis, thereby accelerating progression to cirrhosis, a major cause of death.

High alcohol consumption in the presence of comorbid conditions such as hepatitis B or C, human immunodeficiency infection, type 2 diabetes, or obesity can affect response to medications. The extent to which the liver is damaged by alcohol abuse has been found to be greater for women because they have a smaller capacity for metabolizing alcohol during the first "pass" through the liver (Frezza et al., 1990).

Ironically, after heavy chronic drinking damages the liver of alcoholics, a reverse tolerance effect occurs in which less alcohol is needed to produce a given effect. Due to liver disease caused by either alcohol or other factors, there is a reduced capacity for metabolizing the alcohol consumed so that the drinker will become intoxicated at lower levels of consumption.

Gastrointestinal Tract

From the mouth, alcohol must traverse the esophagus, stomach, and duodenum to reach the small intestines where the majority of it is released into the bloodstream. Although low doses of alcohol may stimulate secretion of digestive juices, larger doses act to inhibit them as well as irritate stomach linings and produce adverse effects throughout the gastrointestinal tract. Chronic alcohol consumption is a significant risk factor for upper gastrointestinal and colorectal cancer. An enzyme, CYP2E1, in the gastrointestinal mucosa that breaks alcohol down into acetaldehyde may contribute to cancer. Heavy alcohol consumption may cause nutritional deficiencies as well as malnutrition that increase risk of gastrointestinal cancer (Seitz, Maurer, & Stickel, 2005).

Other parts of the gastrointestinal tract such as the pancreas (Apte, Wilson, & Korsten, 1997) are also adversely affected as its ducts are blocked by metabolic byproducts of chronic alcohol use. Alcohol-induced swelling of cells blocks digestive enzymes ordinarily produced by the pancreas, resulting in malnutrition. Eventually the enzymes break through the pancreatic linings, creating acute hemorrhagic **pancreatitis** leading to severe abdominal pain, nausea, and vomiting. The production of insulin, which helps convert blood sugars into stored energy, is impaired by these conditions, resulting in type 2 diabetes mellitus.

Various metabolic effects of alcohol can lead to or interact with other risk factors (genetic, dietary, environmental, and lifestyle factors) that result in acute and chronic pancreatitis and diabetes mellitus and, eventually, lead to the development of pancreatic cancer (Go, Gukovskaya, & Pandol, 2005).

Muscle Systems

Chronic alcohol abuse can harm skeletal or striated muscle that is under voluntary control producing myopathy involving muscle weakness and difficulties in gait and locomotion. Nearly half of high-dose chronic alcohol consumers develop alcoholic skeletal myopathy. Eventually alcohol decreases protein synthesis, causing loss of protein mass in the muscles (Lang, Frost, Summer, & Vary, 2005). Alcohol abuse also affects **gene expression**, as alterations have been found in over 400 genes and in the protein profile (i.e., the proteome) of muscle (Lang et al., 2005).

Cardiovascular System

The cardiovascular system includes the heart and the circulatory system of arteries and veins that extend throughout the body. The heart, which is actually a muscle, although a very vital and special type, pumps blood through this network to carry oxygen and nutrients throughout the body and removes waste materials. Cardiomyopathy is damage to the heart that impairs its ability to contract and reduces its effectiveness in pumping blood, leading to shortness of breath, fatigue, palpitations, and eventually, in many cases, congestive heart disorders (Regan, 1990). Although heart disease gradually develops from years of drinking, there is evidence it can be reversed with abstinence.

Epidemiological studies (Klatsky, Friedman, & Siegelaub, 1979) of male drinkers found that those who drank a moderate amount of beer (one to two drinks per day) were actually less likely than nondrinkers to suffer coronary arterial diseases such as myocardial infarction (heart attacks). The conclusion was made that moderate drinking might protect against coronary disease.

One study (Shaper, 1990) questioned this conclusion with findings with over 7,700 middle-aged men in the United Kingdom. Many of the "nondrinkers" had been heavy ex-drinkers who reduced their consumption for health reasons. Therefore, the long-term harm of such earlier abuse, rather than their current lack of drinking, may have contributed to the higher mortality rate found among these now nondrinkers. However, conflicting research (Klatsky et al., 1990) found mortality rates did not differ for ex-drinkers and life-long abstainers. Epidemiological evidence in many countries (Klatsky, 2002) supports a direct protective effect of moderate alcohol consumption, even after adjusting for differences between drinkers and abstainers on psychological characteristics, dietary habits, and physical exercise patterns.

Assuming that light drinking is beneficial, what might be the mechanism? One possibility is that alcohol increases high-density lipoprotein cholesterol (Criqui, 1990), which reduces the risk of heart attack. A different explanation is that alcohol may thin the blood, reducing risks of embolism (blood clots) in arteries to the heart muscle (Klatsky, 1999).

Other possible mechanisms deal with differences in lifestyle factors such as diet, exercise, or coping skills (Green & Polen, 2001). For example, a survey of 2,072 men and women in a cardiovascular disease prevention project (Barrett, Anda, Croft, Serdula, & Lane, 1995) found that men, especially nonsmokers, who were moderate drinkers had the highest participation in a community physical activity program. Women who were moderate or heavy drinkers were also more likely than nondrinkers to participate and to report attempting to lose weight.

Nondrinkers, compared with moderate drinkers, may be more susceptible to anxiety and tension. Thus, a generally lower reaction to stress rather than consumption of alcohol per se may be responsible for the presumed benefits and lower rate of heart attacks for the moderate drinkers. However, it should be noted that drinkers who had the highest consumption were at the greatest risk of heart attacks, possibly due to the acetaldehyde produced by drinking. This toxic byproduct of alcohol metabolism may cause enlargement of the **mito-chondria**, impairing their function of providing energy for heart contractions (Lange & Kinnunen, 1987).

A prospective study (Shaper & Wannamethee, 2000) tracked 7,169 men between the ages of 45 and 64 for over 12 years. Of the 655 (9.1%) having a diagnosis of coronary heart disease (CHD), there were 175 deaths from CHD. Ex-drinkers had the highest risk of CHD, cardiovascular mortality, and all-cause mortality, even after adjustment for lifestyle characteristics and preexisting disease. Compared to occasional drinking, regular light alcohol consumption (1–14 units per week) by men with CHD was not related to any significant benefit or deleterious effect on CHD, cardiovascular disease, or all-cause mortality. Moderate/heavy drinkers showed increased risk of mortality from CHD, cardiovascular disease, and all causes compared to occasional drinkers among 455 men with previous myocardial infarction.

However, drinking habits do not remain constant for many drinkers but may change drastically over time. A 20-year prospective study (Emberson, Shaper, Wannamethee, Morris, & Whincup, 2005) of 6,544 middle-aged British men free of cardiovascular disease demonstrated how changes in individuals over time might affect conclusions about the relationship between alcohol consumption and cardiovascular disease.

Over the 20 years of the study, 922 men had a major coronary event. In agreement with previous studies that showed a "protective effect" of light to moderate drinking, light drinkers had the lowest risks while nondrinkers and heavy drinkers had similar higher risks for cardiovascular disease and all-cause mortality based on their reported drinking levels at the start of the study. However, after reclassifying men based on their variations in drinking over time, risks of coronary disease declined for nondrinkers while risks for moderate and heavy drinkers increased. Light drinkers had reduced risk of CHD and risk of all-cause mortality whereas moderate and heavy drinkers had substantially higher risks of stroke, all-cause mortality, and (to a lesser degree) major CHD.

Blood

Alcohol can harm blood production and function by affecting several vital blood components produced in bone marrow that are necessary for well-being (Ballard, 1997). Deficiencies in production and function of red blood cells result in anemia, and impairment of white blood cells exposes drinkers to risk of infection. Inadequate platelet quantity or function can prevent clotting to stop loss of blood while abnormal plasma proteins can lead to harmful blood clots that increase risk of ischemic strokes. Alcoholism also affects the blood indirectly through malnutrition and loss of vitamins required for blood production.

Alcohol abuse has diverse patterns of hematological effects among alcoholics and nonalcoholics. For example, among bone marrow exam patients with low red blood cell count (cytopenia), alcoholics had more abnormal platelet and leukocyte levels (Latvala, Parkkila, & Niemela, 2004).

Endocrine System

The endocrine system releases essential hormones that control and coordinate organs throughout the body. These chemical messengers are released by nerve signals or in response to specific bodily processes. Excessive use of alcohol can disrupt these functions (Emanuele & Emanuele, 1997) by disturbing the production of hormones including cortisol, testosterone, **estrogen**, pituitary growth hormone, and prolactin that affect diverse outcomes like physical growth, bone disease, response to stress, and functioning of cardiovascular, immune, and reproductive systems.

Immune System

Alcohol abuse may disrupt the body's abilities to combat certain infectious diseases due to decreased white blood cells such as lymphocytes, **macrophages**, neutrophils, and cytokines needed to kill bacterial invasions (Szabo, 1997). Alcohol alters the *immune system* functions, increasing susceptibility to viral infections such as the hepatitis B virus, the hepatitis C virus, pneumonia, and tuberculosis (Cook, 1998; Seitz, Pöschl, & Simanowski, 1998). In addition, malnutrition, infection, and liver diseases unrelated to alcoholism may also undermine the immune system.

Thus far, there is no evidence of a direct effect of alcohol on the acquired immune deficiency syndrome (AIDS; Kaslow et al., 1989). Alcohol may indirectly affect AIDS if it serves to increase other behaviors known to contribute to AIDS such as unsafe sex practices or sharing of needles among drug users. In addition, alcohol might indirectly worsen conditions for those already infected by disrupting their already impaired immune systems.

Alcohol impairs various aspects of the immune system and increases the susceptibility to infection from the human immunodeficiency virus (HIV). Although it may not directly accelerate HIV disease, heavy alcohol use may interfere with the patient's adherence to anti-retroviral treatment regimens. Magnetic resonance imaging studies of both heavy- and light-drinking HIV-positive and HIV-negative cases found that chronic alcohol abuse exacerbates some metabolic injury in some areas of the brains of HIV-infected people (Meyerhoff, 2001).

Reproductive System

Heavy alcohol consumption reduces levels of the male hormone, testosterone, in the blood and impairs the function of the testicular Sertoli cells that affect sperm maturation (Emanuele & Emanuele, 1998). Among male alcoholics, alcohol lowers testosterone (Ruusa, Bergman, & Sundell, 1997) and is related to sexual impotence and impaired performance (Van Thiel, 1983). Even if they are able to consummate sexual activity, there may be impaired fertility because alcohol reduces the seminal fluids that enable the ejaculated sperm to travel rapidly in order to fertilize ova.

Alcohol does not spare females from sexual dysfunction either (Mello, Mendelson, & Teoh, 1993) as alcohol abuse may be related to impaired menstruation, ovarian atrophy, spontaneous abortion (miscarriage), and infertility. Levels of estradiol, a form of estrogen that contributes to increased bone density and reduced risk of coronary artery disease, increased in premenopausal women who consumed slightly more alcohol than the legal limit for driving.

It is unclear whether these outcomes are due to direct toxic effects of alcohol on the hypothalamus, pituitary gland, or ovaries or due to alcohol-induced fluctuations in hormones such as estrogen and progesterone that fluctuate over the menstrual cycle (Lex, 1991). The precise mechanisms for these disruptions are complex and may not entail direct effects of alcohol. For example, other alcohol-related diseases such as liver dysfunction or malnutrition stemming from alcohol abuse could disrupt sex hormones, menstruation, or ovulation.

Fetal Effects

For centuries, there has been suspicion that alcohol consumption holds undesirable effects for pregnant women. Children of alcoholic mothers have been observed to be impaired in physical and psychological development. In ancient Carthage, a ritual against drinking alcohol by newlyweds on the wedding night was observed as a precaution against alcohol-induced birth defects (Jones, 1986).

However, it was not until the 1970s that scientific research (Jones, Smith, Ulleland, & Streissguth, 1973; Streissguth, Herman, & Smith, 1978) produced evidence of a **fetal alcohol syndrome (FAS)**. A survey (Abel & Sokol, 1987) of 19 studies conducted in various parts of the world found rates as high as 2.9 per 1,000 in retrospective studies, compared with 1.1 per 1,000 in prospective studies. In Seattle, the estimate was 2.8 per 1,000, and the combined prevalence rate of FAS with less extreme cases with neurodevelopmental disorders for the period 1975–1981 was estimated at 9.1 per 1,000 (Sampson et al., 1997).

Another study (Larkby & Day, 1997) reported as many as 30 per 10,000 cases. Estimates depend on the methodology and definition. Prospective data based on observations at the time of birth tend to produce lower estimates because some symptoms do not appear until a few years later, whereas retrospective studies that link mental retardation to recall of the mothers' earlier drinking during pregnancy tend to yield much higher rates.

The FAS baby has a low birth weight and a retarded pattern of physical growth. Physical malformations include small head circumference, misshapen eyes, flattened midface, sunken nasal bridge, and elongated philtrum (the vertical groove between the nose and the mouth). Other malformations may occur in major internal organs as well.

The CNS shows abnormal functioning, and there is evidence of neurobehavioral impairment (Mattson & Riley, 1998; Mattson, Schoenfeld, & Riley, 2001) involving cognitive deficits and behavioral problems related to hyperactivity, impulsivity, poor socialization, and reduced communication skills. Cognitive deficits may be due to structural changes detected by brain imaging studies in various brain regions including the basal ganglia, corpus callosum, cerebellum, and hippocampus. For example, MRI measures of the corpus callosum, which separates the two brain hemispheres, reveal a wider variety of shapes among adult males with fetal alcohol exposure than among normal subjects (Bookstein, Streissguth, Sampson, Connor, & Barr, 2002). A relatively thick callosum is associated with a pattern of deficit in executive function whereas a relatively thin one is related to a deficit in motor function.

The types of impairment vary with the timing of alcohol abuse over the period of gestation. As shown in Figure 5.10, physical damage is sustained during early months of pregnancy, while the harm during later months involves cognitive and behavioral functions.

A 10-year follow-up (Streissguth, Clarren, & Jones, 1985) of 8 of the 11 young children (2 had died) in the original study of FAS revealed that their deficits were still pronounced, in both physical and psychological dimensions. They were below average in height and weight and also developed new problems such as hearing and vision problems. Four were severely mentally retarded, and the other 4 were borderline-retarded.

Whereas a drink or two might produce a BAC (e.g., 0.05 mg %) that might be considered "safe" for an adult woman, it represents a much stronger concentration for the much smaller fetus that shares the same blood content with the mother. The toxic levels may be particularly hazardous during the first trimester of pregnancy when developmental changes are greater, a period when the drinking woman is unfortunately less likely to know she is pregnant.

Only a small percentage of the children of alcoholic mothers suffer FAS, suggesting that a number of factors may combine with the alcohol abuse to exert these damaging irreversible effects. But it seems clear that there is considerable risk to those unborn children of heavy-drinking expectant mothers.

Less extreme but still worrisome problems may occur for pregnant women who drink at much lower levels than alcoholics or problem drinkers. The Seattle Pregnancy and Health Study examined about 500 children born to White middle-class married women. Subtle neurological and behavioral deficits were found in proportion to the amount of alcohol consumed during pregnancy (Streissguth, Martin, Martin, & Baer, 1981). The extent to which the mother drank during pregnancy was correlated with the degree to which newborn infants were slower to habituate to or failed to attend to a repeated stimulus and slower to begin sucking on an appropriate stimulus.

FIGURE 5.10   Alcohol affects different developmental processes in the fetus at different stages during gestation.

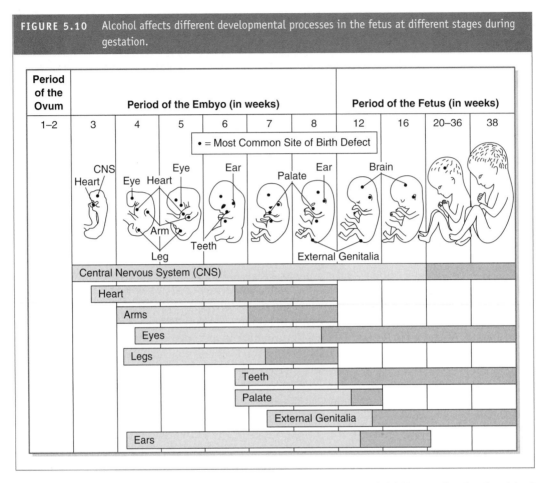

Source: From *The Developing Human* (3rd ed.), by K. L. Moore & T. V. N. Persaud, 1993, Philadelphia: W. B. Saunders. Copyrighted 1993 by W. B. Saunders. Reprinted with permission.

Follow-up studies showed that deficits on these indices of attention persist beyond childhood. At age 4, children whose mothers drank more during pregnancy scored more poorly on vigilance and reaction time tasks, suggesting that the alcohol may have impaired neonatal neurological development. From birth through age 14, cognitive impairments were observed in attention, speed of information processing, and learning problems, especially in arithmetic (Sampson, Bookstein, Barr, & Streissguth, 1994). At age 10 and 14, children born to mothers who drank an average of one drink a day during the first trimester were 4 lb lighter than those born to nondrinkers (Day et al., 2002). These less severe effects, referred to as **fetal alcohol effects (FAE)**, as opposed to the more severe FAS found with children of alcoholic mothers, occurred even for women with modest levels of drinking.

A number of behavioral problems exist among FAE and FAS children (Streissguth et al., 2004). Among 14-year-old FAS or FAE patients (n = 415), the vast majority not living with their biological mothers, more than half had major behavioral problems: disrupted school experiences (61 %); trouble with the law (60 %); confinement in detention, jail, prison, or a psychiatric or alcohol/drug inpatient setting (50%); inappropriate sexual behavior on repeated occasions (49 %); and alcohol/drug problems (35 %).

A follow-up (Baer, Sampson, Barr, Connor, & Streissguth, 2003) of 433 children at age 21 showed that their prenatal alcohol exposure adversely affected their self-reported drinking as well as scores on measures of alcohol-related problems and dependence. This relationship was independent of the effects of family history of alcohol problems, nicotine exposure, other prenatal exposures, and postnatal environmental factors including parental use of other drugs. However, prenatal nicotine exposure was not associated with alcohol problems by offspring at 21 years of age.

The study of FAS and FAE focuses on identified severe cases that are referred to clinics and hospitals. A different approach (May, 1996) to the study of **alcohol-related birth defects (ARBD)** involves the study of larger samples in the general population and measures the presence of symptoms associated with drinking and follows them over development of the child. The goal is not restricted to the diagnosis of FAS and FAE cases, which are associated with chronic heavy drinking, but to see if birth defects can occur over a wide continuum of drinking levels (Day & Richardson, 1991). One study (Day et al., 1991) compared offspring of drinking and nondrinking mothers to determine any differences in physical and behavioral symptoms that develop from birth to early childhood. Mothers who consumed one or more drinks daily on average throughout pregnancy had babies of lower birth weight, smaller head circumference and length, and slower growth.

Epidemiological studies of the rates of ARBD in the general population will give a more accurate index of the prevalence of these cases than will estimates limited to clinical cases. These data will better guide the development of prevention programs because they assess the social and cultural influences on the rates of ARBD identification (May, 1996).

In summary, the overall evidence suggests that low to moderate drinking during pregnancy does not increase the risk of fetal *physical* malformations but could produce *behavioral* impairments. There is no doubt that heavy drinking during pregnancy can produce serious behavioral and psychosocial problems, malformations, and mental retardation in the offspring.

Other Drugs and Fetal Effects

Abuse of drugs other than alcohol can also adversely affect fetal development, effects that can be misattributed to alcohol because the effects are similar. Some women use multiple drugs during pregnancy, often combining smoking and drinking with one or more illicit drugs (Chasnoff, Griffith, Freier, & Murray, 1992). Some polydrug-abusing women may not remember or admit to using certain drugs, so it is difficult to determine the effect of each separate drug used or to measure their complex interactive effects. Moreover, many pregnant women who abuse different specific drugs have poor appetite and nutrition, both of which can impair neonatal development independently of any harm specific to drugs. Low birth weight and hypoxia are common to newborns from women who used different drugs during pregnancy.

Women cigarette smokers have more pregnancies involving spontaneous abortions and stillbirths. Carbon monoxide from cigarette smoke increases fetal carbyoxyhemoglobin levels, which cross the placenta (Werler, Pober, & Holmes, 1985), possibly creating *hypoxia*, a condition involving less oxygen, which adversely affects the fetus. In this respect, crack cocaine and nicotine smoking have similar cardiovascular effects, but the harm potential may be greater for nicotine because it affects more neurotransmitters over longer duration (Slotkin, 1998).

Newborns of women who abuse opiates during pregnancy show higher irritability and withdrawal-like symptoms as well as poorer motor control, although these characteristics seem to be reduced within a month (Jeremy & Hans, 1985). Marijuana use by pregnant women also involves carbon monoxide from smoke that can produce fetal hypoxia. Evidence about the fetal harm from smoking marijuana during pregnancy is conflicting, with some suggestion of increased irritability, tremors, and sleep disturbances (Scher, Richardson, Coble, Day, & Stoffer, 1988).

There was heightened awareness and concern during the 1980s and 1990s about "cocaine-addicted babies," which is now discredited. Although some physical developmental problems such as low birth weight and small head size existed among babies born of cocaine-using women, they were not always accompanied by behavioral deficits, or the deficits were transitory and no longer apparent in later childhood (Chiriboga, 1998). Some women cocaine users had offspring with impairments of attention and arousal regulation that are not large enough to produce differences in developmental comparisons with non-cocaine-using mothers but might show problems on tasks that are more complex and demanding (Chasnoff, 1991).

The claim of fetal cocaine effects is also questioned because many cocaine users also drank alcohol, itself a fetal teratogen more harmful than cocaine (Snodgrass, 1994). When alcohol and cocaine are taken together, a metabolic toxin, cocaethylene, is produced that is stronger than cocaine.

Cancers

Cancers of the oral cavity, pharynx, and larynx appear to occur more often in heavy drinkers. Meta-analyses of combined results from numerous studies have shown that heavy drinking is associated with significantly elevated cancer risks for the following sites: oral cavity and pharynx, esophagus, stomach, colon and rectum, liver, larynx, and female breast (Bagnardi, Blangiardo, La Vecchia, & Corrao, 2001a, 2001b).

There appears to be increased **relative risk** of breast cancer with alcohol consumption (Smith-Warner et al., 1998). Compared with nondrinkers, there appears to be a 10% higher risk for women averaging one drink per day. The risk may be higher for women with a family history of breast cancer (Vachon, Cerhan, Vierkant, & Sellers, 2001) and for those on hormone replacement therapy (Zumoff, 1997).

Over 80% of squamous carcinomas of the mouth, pharynx, larynx, and esophagus are related to alcohol and tobacco use and the effect of combined use is more than additive (Thomas, 1995). Other sections of the gastrointestinal tract such as the colon and rectum have also shown higher risk for cancer (Glynn et al., 1996; Seitz, Gärtner, Egerer, & Simanowski, 1994).

However, for many cancers that show higher rates with higher average consumption of alcohol, causal inferences are weak. For example, since many heavy drinkers also tend to be heavy smokers, any link between drinking and cancer could partly be due to the effect of smoking. After controlling for smoking, the evidence on alcohol and lung cancer for men seems to vary with the type of beverage, with moderate red wine consumption actually associated with reduced risk (Chao, 2007; Chao, Slezak, Caan, & Quinn, 2008). A study of ovarian cancer risk showed similar findings, with red wine consumption inversely related for invasive tumors among current drinkers. For borderline tumors, however, risk increased with more alcohol consumption (Goodman & Tung, 2003).

Even when alcohol is related to cancers, it may not be the carcinogenic agent as other mechanisms by which ethanol might contribute to cancer have been proposed (Lieber, Garro, Leo, & Worner, 1986) including contact-related localized effects, nutritional and vitamin deficiencies, disruptions of DNA metabolism, induction of microsomal enzymes that activate carcinogens, and disruption of immune system responsiveness. Ethanol may disrupt the enzymes that control carcinogens (Driver & Swann, 1987). In addition, ethanol metabolism involves generation of acetaldehyde, which decreases DNA repair and may lead to chromosomal damage (Seitz et al., 1998).

Smoking cigarettes involves combustion, which produces over 4,000 gases and byproducts, most notably carbon monoxide and tars. Over 50 carcinogens have been identified in cigarette smoke, with the tobacco-specific N-nitrosamines (TSNA) of special significance.

The makeup of cigarettes and the composition of cigarette smoke have gradually changed (Hoffmann & Hoffmann, 1997), a development that makes comparisons over time difficult. In the United States, average tar and nicotine yields have declined. In addition, other factors such as the use of filter tips, selection of tobacco types and varieties, and use of highly porous cigarette paper have reduced exposure to some smoke constituents.

In the United States, nitrate levels in cigarette tobacco have risen from 0.3%–0.5% to 0.6%–1.35%. This change affords more complete combustion, which lowers the levels of one carcinogenic factor, polynuclear aromatic hydrocarbons. However, more combustion also increases generation of nitrogen oxides and the formation of carcinogenic **N-nitrosamines** in cigarette smoke.

Finally, it must be noted that these estimates are based on measures from cigarette smoking "machines" that are programmed to take exactly one 2-s puff with a volume of 35 ml every minute, which does not reflect the more numerous and deeper puffs (averaging two to four per minute with a mean volume of 55 ml) taken by actual smokers using low-nicotine cigarettes.

Alcohol-Related Mortality

Alcohol drinkers, especially those drinking excessive amounts, have higher death rates from injuries, violence, suicide, poisoning, cirrhosis, certain cancers, and possibly hemorrhagic stroke (Gutjah, Gmel, & Rehm, 2001). Alcohol consumption and mortality were linearly related in those under 60 years of age, even after controlling for nutritional variables and smoking in a study (Rehm & Sempos, 1995) using data from a 15-year epidemiological study of a subsample of 12,036 White men and women from two age groups (25–59 years and 60–75 years).

Studies that rely on quantity-frequency measures of drinking can overlook relationships that might exist between mortality and quantity or frequency, viewed separately. A prospective analysis (Breslow & Graubard, 2008) linked data from a cohort of 20,765 current drinkers from the 1988 National Health Interview Survey with data obtained 14 years later from the National Death Index through 2002 to examine the relationship of alcohol quantity and frequency to mortality from all causes, cardiovascular disease, cancer, and other causes in the 2,547 drinkers who had died.

For men who consumed five drinks or more (compared with one drink) on drinking days, the adjusted relative risks of mortality were higher from cardiovascular disease, cancer, and other causes. For men in the highest quartile of frequency of drinking (compared with the lowest), the relative risk for death was higher for cancer and for other causes but lower for cardiovascular disease, the opposite results to those caused by high quantity of drinking. Among women, drinking five or more drinks per drinking day increased mortality only for other causes, whereas higher frequency of drinking increased risk of death from cancer. The results show that it is important to examine quantity and frequency as separate variables in relation to mortality.

Risks also vary for different ethnic groups (Sutocky, Shultz, & Kizer, 1993). Blacks and Hispanics had higher rates of mortality from liver cirrhosis than did Whites or Asian Americans, although a higher percentage of Blacks than Whites abstain from using alcohol. The Asian/other grouping had the lowest rates of alcohol-related mortality for most causes of death.

The causes of death vary with racial/ethnic groups. For alcohol dependence and alcoholic hepatitis, Hispanics had similar or lower mortality rates than Whites. However, alcohol-related motor vehicle fatality was highest among Hispanics, followed by Whites and Blacks, and lowest for Asian/other. Among Native Americans, alcohol abuse is involved in the leading causes of death such as motor vehicle crashes, alcoholism, cirrhosis, suicide, and homicide. Among tribes with high rates of alcoholism, about 75% of all accidents are alcohol related.

Aggregate relationships between suicide and alcohol consumption were analyzed with 1,000 cases from 1969 to 1989 and 532 cases from 1975 to 1989 (Gruenewald, Ponicki, & Mitchell, 1995). Suicide rates increased significantly as a function of increased spirits sales, but beer and wine sales were not associated with suicide rates. The analyses controlled important factors such as age, gender, non-White population, per capita land area, metropolitan size, income, unemployment, religious preferences, and marital status.

The causes of alcohol-related mortality vary for different ages. For U.S. men aged 15–29, deaths from injuries and other external causes occurred for 75% of all deaths. and only 4% were from cardiovascular conditions. But for men over 60, the reverse held with only 3% of deaths from external causes and over 45% from cardiovascular conditions (Thun et al., 1997).

A SAFE LEVEL OF ALCOHOL USE?

Studies examining the harmful health effects of chronic and heavy alcohol consumption typically compare outcomes over large samples. Overall, results show that the more one drinks, the more likely there will be adverse outcomes on some medical conditions.

A separate issue is whether there is some border between safe and hazardous drinking. Evidence that heavy drinking is harmful does not address the question of whether there are safe limits or thresholds within which one can drink without harm relative to abstainers. Some suggestion that drinking not only can be safe at some level but can even be beneficial as well comes from findings that for some diseases those who engage in a small amount of drinking may receive "protective effects," with lower morbidity and mortality as compared to those who do not drink at all. This so-called J curve suggests that moderate drinking, in comparison to no drinking, might produce favorable health outcomes.

A literature review (Department of Health and Human Services, 2003) of findings about the relationship of drinking to several major health concerns concluded that consumption of two drinks a day for men and one for women is unlikely to increase health risks. The report cautioned men to not exceed four and women to not exceed three drinks per day. The report acknowledged a danger of specifying any levels of drinking as "safe" in that they may be misinterpreted as *recommended* levels needed for good health in the same way that dietary guidelines issued by government agencies are intended to be minimum daily requirements deemed necessary for good health.

Several difficulties of interpretation exist with any recommendation. One major problem is that the definition of "moderate" drinking varies widely in different studies, and there is no standard of even what one drink is. Moreover, alcohol consumption is typically measured in these studies by the volume or amount of alcohol, and the pattern of drinking and other important aspects of use are ignored. Another problem is that moderate alcohol consumption is confounded with differences on other health-related factors such as age, gender, genetic susceptibility, metabolic rate, comorbid conditions, and lifestyle factors.

Summary

Alcohol and other drugs enter the body in different ways, depending on the drug, but once absorbed into the bloodstream they affect the functioning of the nervous system. By altering the membranes of neurons, alcohol affects the normal balance of neurotransmitters. These changes produce effects on the central nervous system, either depressing or stimulating activity, depending on the drug. Low or moderate amounts of drugs can be detoxified or eliminated from the body by the liver efficiently so that the toxic byproducts of drug metabolism are prevented from accumulating and causing physical damage.

Unlike many other drugs, alcohol does not affect specific brain receptors but appears to influence the entire neuronal membrane. Sedative-hypnotic drugs such as barbiturates and benzodiazepines, designed to have sedative or anxiolytic properties, are invaluable for many medical purposes in their function as anticonvulsants and muscle relaxants. Benzodiazepines are used in treating anxiety, insomnia, agitation, seizures, and muscle spasms, as well as alcohol withdrawal. Barbiturates and benzodiazepines created for different medical purposes vary widely in how quickly they act and how long their effects last. Nicotine from tobacco is absorbed into the body and activates cholinergic receptors that are affected by the neurotransmitter, acetylcholine (ACh), leading to release of dopamine, norepinephrine, and beta-endorphins. Caffeine, a class of methylxanthines, is present in coffee, tea, cola and soft drinks, as well as in chocolate. Caffeine is quickly absorbed from the stomach and small intestine and gets distributed throughout the body in about 45 min. Caffeine is metabolized by the liver and requires about 3 to 4 hours for half of the amount in the body to be eliminated. Caffeine is an antagonist that blocks adenosine receptors and slows the reuptake of neurotransmitters such as DA, 5-HT, and NE.

Opium is not easily absorbed from the digestive tract. There are five different types of receptors to which opiates bind with different consequences: mu, kappa, sigma, delta, and epsilon. For example, analgesia is mediated mainly by opiates binding to the mu receptor. Morphine, the active pharmacological ingredient in the opium poppy, is 10 times more potent. Morphine is not easily absorbed as it is not lipid soluble, but it is quickly absorbed and metabolized when smoked or injected. Heroin is a synthetic opiate developed in the late 1890s, which is about three times stronger than morphine, and crosses the blood-brain barrier many times faster. It is not lipid soluble. Heroin involves rapid tolerance, with a tenfold increase in dose required within a few months of use. Cocaine produces its psychoactive effects by blocking the reuptake of dopamine as well as of serotonin. Since these neurotransmitters are retained at the synapse, their mood-enhancing and energizing effects are maintained and produce the high stimulation that users seek.

Amphetamines are a weak base substance that stimulate release of dopamine as well as block its reuptake. Amphetamines also affect norepinephrine receptors to produce alertness and to counter fatigue. The active ingredient in cannabis, delta-9-THC, is lipid soluble but does not dissolve in water, so its absorption is slow. Smoking, therefore, is a much faster mode of administration since the drug moves rapidly from the lungs to the rest of the body in a few minutes. Psychedelic drugs, popular in the 1960s, include *LSD* (lysergic acid diethylamide), peyote, and mescaline. LSD is taken orally and acts on serotonin and dopamine receptors in the brain cortex and locus coeruleus to block serotonin release and increase retention of serotonin at serotonin-2 receptors.

Tolerance for drugs develops with continued use so that the same dose produces a diminished effect, which often leads to increased usage at higher doses. However, when the drug is not available, highly unpleasant withdrawal reactions involving physical discomfort, agitation, and irritability occur. Chronic heavy use can damage brain centers, leading to changes in the neurophysiological processes involved with drug use. Neuroadaptational processes occur to lower the reward set point as the user increases amount and/or frequency of use in a losing attempt to restore rewarding and offset negative withdrawal effects during absence of the drug.

Prolonged and excessive alcohol and other drug use can produce a number of serious physical and medical problems over most major systems of the body. While some of the effects may be direct, as in the case of fatty liver production from chronic alcohol use, other effects may be indirect, such as malnutrition or bodily injury due to accidents and falls. Chronic effects may occur even for those for whom the acute effects may have been minimal. Long-term excessive alcohol consumption impairs the functioning of all major organs so that eventually most alcoholics will be confronted with a physical toll of damage stemming from the cumulative effects of alcohol. In particular, damage to the liver disrupts the ability to detoxify alcohol as efficiently as in the past so that reversal in tolerance occurs, with less alcohol producing the same effect that formerly required more alcohol. Due to the long delay usually involved between drinking and these types of adverse effects, it is not surprising that chronic excessive drinking and these types of physical consequences are difficult to detect and prevent.

Alcohol consumption, as well as abuse of many other drugs by pregnant women, may have profoundly damaging irreversible birth effects involving the physical and mental condition of the developing fetus. Higher alcohol use also shows a positive relationship with indices of many causes of mortality as well as increased likelihood of suicides.

Stimulus/Response

1. Have you had the subjective effect of alcohol or another drug vary with the physical and social setting in which it was consumed? Describe the experience and explain how it affected your subsequent use.

2. Has the effect of alcohol or another drug on your behavior varied with factors such as time of day or with your physical condition or health? What conditions make drugs more potent in their effects on you?

3. Suppose that psychopharmacologists developed an "antibody" or a substance that could offset a drug's normal neurophysiological effect. Do you think most individuals with problems with that drug would voluntarily take it? Would it be ethical for a judge to order that someone with drug problems be treated with such an "antibody"?

4. "Crack babies" have been reportedly born to some women who abused cocaine and crack during pregnancy. Is a control comparison necessary to allow for the conclusion that the use of this drug during pregnancy caused these problems for the babies? If so, what do you think would be the appropriate control comparison?

CHAPTER 6

Heredity and Environment

Alcohol and Other Drug Use

Heredity deals the cards; environment plays the hand.

—Charles L. Brewer

Questions about the role of heredity and environment provoke strong and heated debate for many psychological phenomena. The understanding of the determinants of alcohol and drug use, abuse, and dependency is certainly no exception. In this chapter, we will first examine the role of hereditary factors with regard to differences in the use of alcohol and other drugs. Then, we will see how environmental factors, especially early experiences within the family, might affect the likelihood of alcohol and other drug use.

In thinking about heredity as a factor, we do not mean that genes determine the use of, abuse of, or dependency on a specific drug in the same way that they determine physical features such as eye color. The relationship between genetics and behavior is much more complex. Genes may indirectly affect behavior by determining how drugs are metabolized or by creating temperamental characteristics such as impulsivity or anxiety. In turn, these characteristics can influence the likelihood that exposure to drugs may eventually lead to abuse or dependency.

MOLECULAR GENETICS

As illustrated in Figure 6.1, individuals receive genetic material from both parents that influences their physical and psychological characteristics. This information is encoded in a molecule, **deoxyribonucleic acid (DNA)**, present in the nucleus of all cells and transmitted by 46 **chromosome** pairs, one member from the father and one from the mother. An individual's sex is determined by one pair of these chromosomes. Males have an X and a Y chromosome while females have two X chromosomes.

When Gregor Mendel, the founder of modern genetics, did his pioneering studies around 1860, the existence of chromosomes was unknown; in fact, it was not proposed until half a century later. These stringlike chains of DNA contain thousands of rather than single genes, but Mendelian genetics assumed that single genes determine a specific outcome like eye color. However, modern views realize that complex behaviors are not determined by a single

FIGURE 6.1 Genotype and environment jointly determine phenotype.

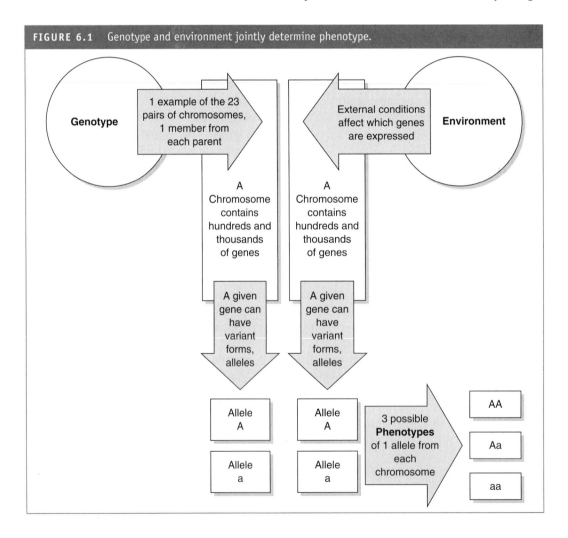

gene but by multiple genes **(polymorphism),** with each gene adding a relatively small influ-ence. Such genes, termed **quantitative trait loci (QTL)**, determine outcomes on a proba-bilistic basis rather than as certainties. These genes are expressed or activated only if their level exceeds some threshold. Most behaviors that affect alcohol consumption—and how it affects drinkers—involve QTL rather than single genes. Polymorphic genes also interact with environmental influences to determine the likelihood of alcohol dependency.

A **genotype** refers to the underlying combination of genes from each parent as shown in Figure 6.1. The gene or genes underlying alcohol dependency, referred to as markers, do not directly "cause" the disorder in the way that hair color is determined genetically. Instead, the process is indirect, as genes affect enzymes and neurotransmitters affect metabolic processes, which in turn affect behavior.

Behaviors such as drug use for individuals with a given genotype can still vary consid-erably due to environmental differences. A gene may assume different forms known as alleles. These variants of a given gene are called phenotypes and represent the observable expression of the influence of genes, which are not directly seen. **Endophenotypes** are similar to phenotypes but are often physiological in nature such as event-related potentials, which reflect electrical brain activity.

Alcoholism is the consequence of genetically determined factors such as differences in physical reactions to alcohol, metabolism of alcohol, or personal traits that lead individuals to seek higher risks or react more strongly to stressors. It is such inherited differences as these that increase the likelihood that alcoholism will develop. Genes do not act automatically but only have the potential for being activated or "expressed" when certain environmental conditions exist as well.

Differences in biological predispositions that may be genetically determined can lead to wide variations in the reactions of users to the pharmacological ingredients in drugs. While many users experience unpleasant sensations and reactions to their first use of a drug, some users report positive initial experiences. These initial reactions may also be influenced by expectations learned from others but still suggest that some unlearned or biological differences are involved.

Environment is a complex factor that includes cultural setting, societal context, interpersonal relations, and physical surroundings. In a broad sense, any factor that is not hereditary could be viewed as environmental. Together, both types of factors affect the likelihood that indi-viduals will use drugs as well as the consequences of such actions.

INDIRECT EVIDENCE OF HEREDITARY INFLUENCES ON ALCOHOLISM

It is further remarkable that drunkenness resembles certain hereditary . . . diseases.

—Benjamin Rush, *An Inquiry Into the Effects
of Ardent Spirits Upon the Human Body
and Mind,* 1785/1943

Family Studies

Observations that family members often tend to have similar alcohol and other drug use patterns could be—and have been—used to argue that heredity is a major factor underlying drug dependency. But because family members often share a similar environment, particularly during formative years, as well as a common heredity, such evidence can also support environmental explanations. Thus, by observation and **modeling** of one or both drug-dependent parents, children may acquire attitudes and norms that may increase their susceptibility to similar drinking and drug use lifestyles. In addition, growing up with parents who are alcohol or drug dependent, children may develop poor self-esteem, experience abuse or neglect, and later as adults turn to drinking and use of other drugs to cope with life stressors.

In research on possible familial links to alcohol and drug problems, *proband* or *index case* is used to refer to those individuals assumed to be at risk for alcohol and other drug dependency due to having at least one biological parent with a similar problem. Numerous studies show consistent gender differences in alcoholism. First-degree male—but not female—relatives of alcoholic probands exhibit a higher probability of being alcoholic than do first-degree male relatives of members of the general population (Reich, Cloninger, Van Eerdewegh, Rice, & Mullaney, 1988; Winokur, Reich, Rimmer, & Pitts, 1970). Thus, Figure 6.2 shows that fathers, brothers, and sons of both male and female alcoholics are at greater risk of being alcoholic than are first-degree female relatives such as mothers, sisters, and daughters (Reich, Earls, & Powell, 1988). In addition, the wives of alcoholic men are less likely than the husbands of alcoholic women to also have alcoholism. While female relatives are at lower risk for alcoholism (Winokur et al., 1970), they are at greater risk than male relatives for affective or mood disorders such as depression.

FIGURE 6.2   Transmissibility of risk of alcoholism for spouses and first-degree relatives for males and females.

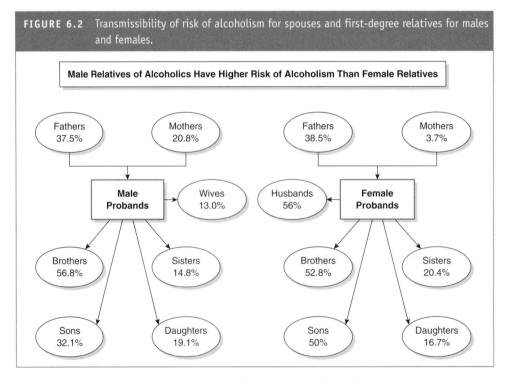

Source: Based on data from "Secular Trends in the Familial Transmission of Alcoholism," by T. Reich, C. R. Cloninger, P. Van Eerdewegh, J. P. Rice, and J. Mullaney, 1988, *Alcoholism: Clinical and Experimental Research, 12,* pp. 458–464.

Although relatives of alcoholics may share some common genetically transmitted tendencies for different emotional or affective reactions to stressors, there are societal and cultural conditions that may allow for different forms of expression for males and females. Since most societies tolerate and even encourage more drinking by males, these tendencies may lead to heavier use of alcohol for them whereas females who traditionally have been culturally restricted from drinking may turn to other drugs such as tranquilizers to deal with stress.

Transmissibility, or the influence of family history of alcoholism, is greater for males (Reich, T., et al., 1988). Furthermore, this effect is greater for more recently born cohorts in terms of a higher lifetime prevalence as well as an earlier age of onset of alcoholism. These cohort effects may reflect changes in society that now increase drinking or encourage drinking at an earlier age.

The risk for relatives of drug- and alcohol-dependent persons having similar problems can be examined in studies comparing dependence among relatives of dependent and non-dependent individuals. One study (Merikangas et al., 1998) on this issue found that the higher risk for relatives of dependent persons varies for different substances. Risk of alcoholism was greater in relatives of alcohol- and cannabis-dependent subjects but not in those of opioid- or cocaine-dependent probands. The *same* drug disorder, compared with cross-drug associations, occurred at a higher rate in relatives of the probands, with relative risks of 10.2% for opioids, 4.4% for cocaine, and 5.8% for marijuana.

Another study (Bierut et al., 1998) examined alcohol, marijuana, cocaine, and tobacco dependence rates among 1,212 probands (persons classified as dependent) and their 2,755 siblings. A non-alcohol-dependent comparison sample contained 217 probands and their 254 siblings. Siblings of alcohol-dependent probands, compared with siblings of non-alcohol-dependent controls, had higher rates of marijuana dependence, cocaine dependence, and habitual smoking, with higher rates among males for all substances.

Analysis of age-adjusted interview data, family history, and medical records from the Collaborative Study on the Genetics of Alcoholism of 8,296 first-degree relatives of alcohol-dependent probands and 1,654 controls showed that the former were at greater risk for dependence on a variety of drugs as well as for some forms of psychopathology such as antisocial personality disorder, anxiety disorders, and major depression (Nurnberger et al., 2004).

Table 6.1 compares the risk of a disorder for relatives of alcohol-dependent probands with the risk for those of controls. If the risk was the same, the relative risk (RR) = 1, but values greater than 1 indicate higher risk for alcohol probands. As Table 6.1 indicates, the RR was higher for alcohol dependence when assessed with four different criteria. For example, for *DSM-IV* alcohol dependence, the RR was 2, reflective of the finding (not shown in the table) that 28% of the relatives of alcohol-dependent probands but only 14% of the relatives of controls had the same diagnosis.

Rates of specific substance dependence were markedly higher in relatives of alcohol-dependent probands for dependence on cocaine, drugs, marijuana, opiates, sedatives, and stimulants. In contrast, rates of *DSM-III-R* abuse for different drugs did *not* show significant differences between alcohol-dependent probands and control relatives. Rates for abuse were overall low, which may contribute to the failure to find differences, or it may be that abuse and dependence involve different processes. Research about the relationship between alcohol abuse and alcohol dependence is still unresolved, and their definitions differ under different versions of the *DSM* (Hasin & Grant, 2004; Saha, Stinson, & Grant, 2007).

TABLE 6.1 Relative risk (RR) of substance use and psychiatric disorders for relatives of alcohol-dependent probands in comparison to the RR for relatives of controls.

Substance Use Disorders	(RR)	Psychiatric Disorders	(RR)
Alcohol Dependence	1.81	Antisocial Personality Disorder	1.41
Alcohol Dependence *DSM-IV*	2.08	Major Depression	1.14
Alcohol Dependence *ICD-10*	2.16	Obsessive Compulsive Disorder	2.23
Alcohol Dependence (Feighner)	1.77	Panic Disorder	1.57
Cocaine Dependence	3.10		
Drug Dependence	2.28		
Marijuana Dependence	1.75		
Opiate Dependence	2.53		
Sedative Dependence	1.96		
Stimulant Dependence	2.73		

Source: Based on data from "A Family Study of Alcohol Dependence: Coaggregation of Multiple Disorders in Relatives of Alcohol-Dependent Probands," by J. I. Nurnberger Jr., R. Wiegand, K. Bucholz, S. O'Connor, E. T. Meyer, T. Reich, et al., 2004, *Archives of General Psychiatry, 61*(12), pp. 1246–1256.

Note: Disorders are based on *DSM-III-R* criteria unless otherwise indicated. For equal risk, RR = 1; values greater than 1 indicate higher risk for relatives of alcohol probands.

Psychiatric disorders such as antisocial personality disorder, panic disorder, and major depression also showed aggregation (higher occurrence) among family members of alcohol-dependent probands than among those of controls. These findings suggest that some common genetic mechanisms may exist for substance use and psychiatric disorders among these families.

Twin Studies

The study of twins, a longstanding strategy used by researchers trying to marshal evidence for hereditarian views for a variety of characteristics and behaviors, originated with Sir Francis Galton in the late 1800s. Concordance rates, or the extent to which both members of a set of twins show the same outcomes, are compared among identical or **monozygotic (MZ) twins**, fraternal or **dizygotic (DZ) twins**, and siblings.

Whereas MZ twins share the same genes, family environment, and age, DZ twins share the same family environment and age but only half of their genes. Nontwin siblings share family environment and half of their genes but not age. If genetic factors play a greater role than environmental factors in alcoholism, the concordance rates should be highest for MZ twins, followed by those for DZ twins and then siblings. If environmental factors are more important than genetic ones, the difference in concordance rates of MZ twins compared with that of DZ twins will be small.

Scandinavian countries, with their extensive and thorough registries of birth and medical treatments and temperance board records of alcohol problems, have provided an excellent source of data for testing theories about the role of heredity in alcoholism as well as other forms of psychopathology. Concordance rates of alcoholism among identical (MZ) twins have typically been higher than those for fraternal (DZ) twins or siblings (Partanen, Bruun, & Markkaners, 1966).

A Finnish study (Kaprio et al., 1987) of more than 2,800 pairs of male twins between 24 and 49 years of age found higher concordance of alcoholism among identical than among fraternal twins. However, the frequency of social contact between identical twins was greater than it was between fraternal twins, so the higher concordance of their drinking patterns may not be entirely due to genetic factors but also may be partly attributable to the greater common environment created by their higher social contact. However, a different study (Heath, Jardine, & Martin, 1989) of almost 2,000 female twins in Australia also found higher concordance of alcoholism among identical than among fraternal twins but did not find frequency of social contact was related to the alcoholism concordance rates. The Finnish study used only males while the Australian study used only females, so gender may have made a difference in their findings.

Studies (Pickens et al., 1991) of both male and female same-sexed twins at alcoholism treatment centers revealed a stronger genetic basis for alcoholism for men than for women. Alcoholism rates were higher for MZ than for DZ twins (0.59% vs. 0.36% for male twins but only 0.25% vs. 0.05% for female twins). A study (Kendler, Heath, Neale, Kessler, & Eaves, 1992) of a nonclinical population of female twins identified through the Virginia Twin Registry also found higher concordance among MZ than among DZ twins. However, a study (Heath et al., 1997) with Australian twins (n = 5,889) found no sex differences in the higher concordance rates of alcohol dependence based on *DSM-III-R* criteria for MZ over DZ twins.

Twin studies have also shown a genetic basis for dependency on drugs other than alcohol. The Vietnam Era Twin Study (Tsuang et al., 1998) of American men in military service during the Vietnam War era conducted telephone interviews of 1,874 MZ and 1,498 DZ twins with a completion rate of about 80%. The results supported a general genetic factor (common to five different drugs) as dependency on one substance generally involved dependence on other substances, especially for marijuana but less so for opiates.

Several causal models were proposed and tested in this study. A **causal model** is similar to a theory in that both hypothesize which factors will lead to certain outcomes. Two of the models supported in this study were a common pathway model and an independent pathway model. A common pathway model holds that the same factors are involved in leading to all forms of substance use whereas an independent pathway model suggests that the factors affecting use of each type of substance differ. Evaluation of these models involves complex statistical methods such as **structural equation modeling (SEM)** to account for the obtained pattern of correlations among variables. The researcher makes a statistical evaluation of the goodness of fit between patterns of relationships in the observed data with predictions derived from alternative models that make different assumptions about the causes. Models with predictions that do not "fit" the observed data are rejected, but any models whose predictions are close matches to the observed data are retained as viable explanations. If more than one model fits, as was the case in this study, the one that is more parsimonious, or makes fewer assumptions, is adopted. Even though the observed relationships provided some support for both models, this study accepted the common pathway model because it requires fewer assumptions.

The extent to which genetic and environmental factors were related to dependency varied widely for specific drugs. Heroin had a unique genetic basis whereas marijuana, stimulants, and sedatives had a shared genetic basis. Familial environment was unique for marijuana, but stimulants, sedatives, and heroin shared common family environment influences. These drugs shared nonfamilial environment in addition to having some smaller drug-specific nonfamilial environmental influences. Overall, these findings point to both general and drug-specific genetic and environmental determinants of substance abuse.

The Virginia Adult Twin Study of Psychiatric and Substance Use Disorders (VATSPSUD) is a large-scale project using population samples of MZ and DZ twins to develop and test structural equation models of the roles of genetic, environmental risk factors and their interaction in the etiology of a range of common behavioral disorders (Kendler & Prescott, 2006). The VATSPSUD studied over 4,500 pairs of same-sex and opposite-sex MZ and DZ twins, including a longitudinal component, to obtain prevalence rates for alcohol dependency as well as for other drug and psychiatric disorders and for comorbidity among them. More important, it provided an index called **heritability** that reflects the proportion of genetic variability relative to environment variability for comparing MZ and DZ twins in demographic subgroups *within* a specific study. This index is not comparable *across* studies as the index is based on the genetic and environmental variance *within* each study. Thus, a larger hereditability score in one study does not necessarily mean it reflects greater genetic influence than a lower score in a different study does.

The VATSPSUD researchers distinguished between two types of environments, shared common environment (C) and a specific environment (E) unique to each twin (Prescott & Kendler, 1995). These two environments, combined with the *genetic* factor (A), which is summed over all inherited determinants, determine the difference between MZ and DZ twins. Figure 6.3 shows that the higher *total* influence from all three sources, the genetic factor and the two environments, leads to higher liability of alcohol dependency for MZ over DZ twins. The logic is that if MZ rates exceed DZ rates of alcohol use disorders, genetic factors play the major role. However, if MZ and DZ twins have similar rates, environmental factors must be more important. Finally, if dissimilar rates occur for members within MZ twins, the individual environments of each twin are more important.

Overall, regardless of the drug, the VATSPSUD found higher heritability estimates for dependence among MZ than among DZ twins. For both alcohol abuse and dependence, heritability ranged from 0.50% to 0.61% for both men and women, unlike early studies that found lower genetic influence for women. For alcohol dependence, the heritability estimate for men and women combined was 56%; for shared environment, it was 0%; and for individual environment, it was 34%.

Similarly, MZ twins had greater similarity than DZ twins for nicotine dependence. No sex differences were found, and the overall variance for genetics was 55%; for shared environment,

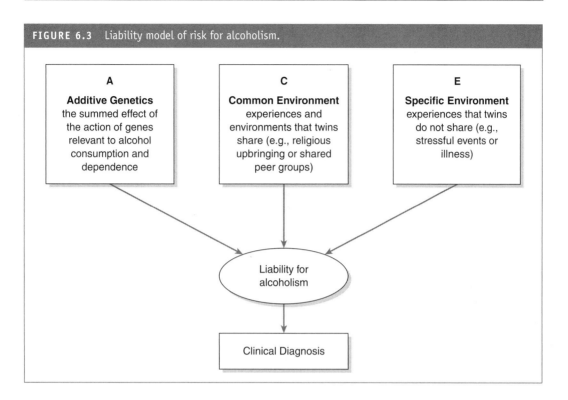

FIGURE 6.3   Liability model of risk for alcoholism.

Source: From "Twin Study Design," by C. A. Prescott and K. S. Kendler, 1995, *Alcohol Health and Research World, 19,* pp. 200–205.

it was 11%; and for individual environment, it was 34%. Caffeine dependence, based only on female twins, was higher for MZ twins. Heritability of the genetic factor was estimated using four indices: monthly use (43%), heavy use (77%), tolerance (40%), and toxicity (45%). Shared environment was not a factor. Hereditability for a wide range of illicit drugs with the genetic factor ranging from 60% to 80% for MZ twins was always greater than that for DZ twins, except for opiate use by males. Otherwise, genetics had similar influence on men and women. Shared environment was not a factor except for cocaine use disorders for men.

The rich VATSPSUD data set allowed for examination of many other types of hypotheses about the origins of alcoholism. One example is the question of how drinking motives might be related to genetics. Because alcohol and antianxiety drugs affect the brain receptors in similar ways, there may be genetic factors that are similar. One analysis (Prescott, Cross, Kuhn, Horn, & Kendler, 2004) using 2,529 female and 3,709 male adult twins examined how social anxiety might contribute to alcoholism.

Models of genetic risk factors for common drug dependencies were also developed (Kendler, Myers, & Prescott, 2007) based on data from 4,685 men and women twins. Specifically, two separate genetic factors were proposed, one for a predisposition largely to illicit drug dependence and one primarily to licit drug dependence. A large proportion of the genetic influences on nicotine and particularly caffeine dependence appear to be specific to those substances. The models proposed for men and women were similar.

Adoption Studies

When children grow up in the homes of their birth parents, it is not possible to isolate the impact of genetic and environmental factors on their chances of becoming alcohol or drug dependent. In contrast, when children are adopted out at an early age, a "natural experiment" exists that offers a somewhat controlled test of the relative role of heredity and environment.

In the case of alcohol dependency, adoption records maintained in Scandinavia allowed for precisely such an opportunity. The reasoning is that if alcoholism has a strong genetic basis, children from alcoholic parents who are adopted out to nonalcoholic homes should still be more likely to become alcoholics as adults than should control adoptees who have no alcoholic parent. On the other hand, if environment plays a strong role in alcoholism, they should have a lower probability of becoming alcoholics due to their adoption into non-alcoholic homes. This analytical advantage afforded by studies of adoptees has led to several influential investigations.

Danish Adoption Studies

A pioneering study using adoption records from Denmark, (Goodwin, Schulsinger, Hermansen, Guze, & Winokur, 1973) studied male offspring of 55 alcoholic parents, primarily fathers, who were adopted during the first few weeks of life by nonalcoholic families. In Phase 1, comparisons of the adult alcoholism rates of these 55 alcoholic probands with 78 control adoptees from nonalcoholic parents revealed four times greater alcoholism among those adoptees who had at least one alcoholic parent.

Thus, the male alcoholic probands became alcoholics later as adults at a higher rate—and at an earlier age—than did sons of nonalcoholics even though both were adopted into apparently nonalcoholic environments. They also had a much higher rate of divorce than did sons of nonalcoholics, a factor that could have contributed to their alcohol problems as well as any genetic influence. Comparisons of other factors such as psychiatric disorder did not show differences.

Phase 2 (Goodwin et al., 1974) compared the same 55 sons of alcoholics who were adopted out with 35 other sons who grew up in the homes of their alcoholic biological parent. The nonadopted and adopted siblings did not differ in alcoholism rates, suggesting that being raised in an alcoholic home of a biological parent does not add to the risk of alcoholism among persons known to be at risk biologically. Thus, the biological factor appeared to be the major factor responsible for determining alcoholism rates.

A third phase examined biological factors involved in alcoholism among women (Goodwin, Schulsinger, Moller, Mednick, & Guze, 1977). In contrast to the study of males, no differences were found in alcoholism among 49 female adoptees from alcoholic biological parents in comparison to those observed among 48 control adoptees from nonalcoholic parents.

These early adoption studies were highly influential, but they are not without problems. The foster parents who adopted the children showed high rates of psychiatric problems as well as a high divorce rate; these problems may have added to the influence that any genetic factor of alcoholism would have had. Although alcoholism rates were higher among adopted sons of alcoholics, it should be noted that only about 20% of the probands had become alcoholic at the time they were studied. When the two heaviest drinking categories, alcoholics and problem drinkers, were analyzed as one group, there was little difference between the adoptees from alcoholic and nonalcoholic parentage.

The majority of the alcoholic parents were the fathers, but no information was obtained about the mothers' status regarding alcoholism (Searles, 1988). It is not unreasonable to expect that some of them were alcoholic as well or at least drinking during pregnancy. If so, this factor of prenatal alcohol abuse complicates the interpretation since any deficits may not reflect only genetic influences.

Swedish Adoption Studies

Subsequent studies in Sweden with larger samples corroborated the conclusions from the Danish studies. Alcoholism rates in adoptees and their biological parents among persons born out of wedlock and adopted before the age of 3 by nonrelatives were examined (Bohman, 1978). Alcohol abuse was defined objectively based on the number of times an individual had been registered for insobriety with the Swedish Temperance Board and whether or not treatment had been recommended. Three levels of severity of abuse were defined based on this type of information rather than using any clinical or psychiatric criteria. It is likely that use of more conventional diagnostic criteria would have yielded different classification of cases.

Adopted sons with alcoholic biological fathers were three times as likely to be alcoholic as were adopted sons of nonalcoholic fathers. The ratio was still 2:1 if the alcoholic parent in question was the mother. The proportions of alcoholism for adopted-out daughters were not related to parental alcoholism.

However, a genetic influence for alcoholism in women was suggested in a study of female adoptees (Bohman, Sigvardsson, & Cloninger, 1981) that showed an overall prevalence of alcoholism of around 4%. The risk of alcoholism was four times greater if the biological mother was alcoholic. The level of alcohol abuse of the foster parents in the adoptive environment did not play as great a role as the alcohol abuse of the birth parent.

A study (Cloninger, Bohman, & Sigvardsson, 1981) with 862 male adoptees with alcohol problems had an overall prevalence rate of alcoholism of about 18%. Alcohol abuse of sons and daughters in some families where both biological parents had mild but untreated alcohol abuse varied in proportion to the amount of environmental demands the children faced. A replication study (Sigvardsson, Bohman, & Cloninger, 1996) of 577 Swedish men adopted at an early age by nonrelatives confirmed the distinction between Type 1 and Type 2 alcoholism based on Swedish adoption studies (Cloninger et al., 1981) that was described earlier in Chapter 2. These two types of alcoholism were independently heritable forms of alcoholism in male adoptees. Adopted men from a Type 1 alcoholism background had a lifetime risk of severe alcoholism among 11.4% of the sample, about four times greater than those with a nonalcoholic background. In contrast, the risk of Type 2 alcoholism was 10.7%, about six times higher in adopted sons with a Type 2 genetic background compared with those from a nonalcoholic background irrespective of their postnatal environment.

U.S. Adoption Studies

Although the documentation about the biological parents of adoptees is less complete in the United States and the criteria for adoption involve nonrandom assignment of adoptees to homes, adoption studies conducted in Iowa show agreement with the Scandinavian research about the relationship of alcoholism between parents and adopted children. Male and female adoptees separated at birth from parents with psychiatric disturbance were compared to adoptees with biological parents without mental disturbances (Cadoret & Gath, 1978). The psychiatric background of the parent was not associated with adoptee alcoholism status. Although alcoholism rates were low among the adoptees, there was nonetheless a pattern suggesting that adoptees with alcoholism were more likely to have an alcoholic biological parent than were those without alcoholism. However, a weakness of the study is that the criteria for diagnosing parental alcoholism were subjective and based on ratings by social workers rather than by psychiatrists.

Studies of adoptive families examine if there is a stronger link between parental alcohol use and family functioning with alcohol involvement by birth children than by adopted children. One such study (McGue, Sharma, & Benson, 1996) found stronger associations for birth children with their parents but only weak or low relationships between adopted children and their parents. Other comparisons that assessed the effect of shared environment involved sets of siblings where there was no biological commonality. Among the families, there were 255 sibling pairs that were not biologically related, some involving two adopted children and others with a birth child and an adopted child. The impact of environment on the similarity of alcohol use patterns between siblings was modest but stronger for siblings closer in age and of the same sex.

Adoption and twin studies involve atypical cases that have limited generalizability to the general population. At best, they provide indirect or suggestive answers to the question of the relative importance of heredity and environment on alcoholism. Heredity and environment operate jointly, and it is difficult to separate the influence of one factor from that of the other. These types of studies can only make inferences about heredity but do not have access to actual genetic information.

DIRECT EVIDENCE OF HEREDITARY INFLUENCES ON ALCOHOLISM

Substantial advances in genetics culminated with the completion in 2003 of the mapping of the human genome, or total human genetic makeup (Schuler et al., 1996). This major achievement made it possible to more precisely specify the genetic bases of alcoholism as well as of other psychological outcomes and conditions, opening important new research possibilities to actually study genetic mechanisms.

Linkage Studies

Linkage studies search for genetic differences between family members and relatives of alcoholics (called **probands**) and those of nonalcoholics. The entire genome is tested to find associations between genes and some characteristic or disorder such as substance abuse. Linkage analyses first identify chromosome regions rather than specific genes that may be related to alcohol dependence. Guided by past research that identified which genes might be related to the disorder, or because they are located in chromosome regions that previous linkage studies have found to be correlated with the disorder, **candidate genes** are identified.

Association Studies

Association studies are then conducted to measure the correlation between the hypothesized candidate gene(s) and a specific outcome or disorder. These studies often use samples of individuals with a known frequency of a certain gene. Association studies look for polymorphisms, which are genetic differences between individuals at specific locations of the genome. They may be found within a gene (different gene variants, or **alleles**) but also outside of genes. Association studies can identify **single-nucleotide polymorphisms**, referred to as **SNPs**, which are individual differences in the building blocks of DNA. They provide more precise determination of genes related to the disorder under study by comparing cases with the disorder to control cases without it.

Association studies can identify QTL (multiple genes) that are correlated with a specific trait such as alcohol sensitivity or alcohol preference (Crabbe, Phillips, Buck, Cunningham, & Belknap, 1999). Experimental procedures needed to identity effects of genetic manipulations that would not be possible with humans are often dependent on the use of animal models involving laboratory rats (Crabbe, 2002; Tabakoff & Hoffman, 2000).

The Collaborative Studies on Genetics of Alcoholism

The Collaborative Studies on Genetics of Alcoholism (COGA) comprise a large-scale study (Bierut et al., 2002) to determine the genetic bases of alcoholism using data from 105 multigeneration families and 1,200 families with at least three first-degree relatives of each alcoholic obtained from six sites across the United States. One study from this large data set (Reich et al., 1998) with 987 siblings from these 105 families examined siblings who met the criteria for alcoholism to see if they shared more genes than expected based on chance.

Chromosomes 1, 7, and to some extent 2 held genes with higher risk for alcoholism. A replication study (Foroud et al., 2000) with 1,295 people from 157 families did not yield total agreement. There was stronger support for chromosome 2 than in the initial sample, and the greatest support occurred for chromosome 3, which was not identified in the initial sample. Given the complexity of alcoholism, such findings are not necessarily in conflict but may reflect the genetic bases of different aspects of the disorder.

Using SNPs, the COGA found several candidate genes that may contribute to the development of alcohol and/or nicotine dependence. It identified linkages to alcohol dependency on chromosomes 1, 4, and 7. These genes encode parts of the receptors through which gamma-aminobutyric acid (GABA) blocks other nerve signals from crossing to those neurons by interacting with $GABA_A$ and $GABA_B$ receptors embedded in neuron membranes. In contrast, no SNPs related to alcohol dependence were identified in the neighboring genes, which encoded other $GABA_A$ receptor components (Edenberg et al., 2004). The overall evidence supports the view that the $GABR_{A2}$ gene contributes to the development of alcohol dependence.

The COGA also identified endophenotypes, markers of alcohol dependency that are more physical than behavioral in nature. In these studies, the P300 component of an event-related potential (ERP) was the endophenotype. A reduced amplitude or delayed appearance of the P300 brain wave when a sudden stimulus is presented has been found both in alcohol-dependent people and in people at increased genetic risk of becoming alcohol dependent (Porjesz & Begleiter, 2003). Hence, both linkage results and molecular biological studies have suggested that variation in the $GABA_A$ receptor might be involved in alcohol dependence.

COGA research (Edenberg, 2002) has also demonstrated how genetic factors may serve a protective role against alcoholism. In alcohol metabolism, if acetaldehyde dehydrogenase is low, the buildup of toxic acetaldehyde will cause nausea and **facial flushing**. Such outcomes might lead a person to stop drinking and, in effect, reduce his or her likelihood of becoming an alcoholic. Whereas about a third to a half of East Asians have a recessive allele (ALDH2*2) that seems to have this protective function, this allele is rare for European populations.

Nicotine dependence also has been linked to candidate genes (Grucza & Bierut, 2006). Several linkage studies have implicated a region on chromosome 9, which includes genes for the $GABA_B$ dependence receptor involved with nicotine dependence (Gelernter et al., 2004; Li et al., 2003). Based on these linkage analyses, a candidate gene association study (Li, 2006) of the $GABA_{B2}$ gene, which lies within the area of chromosome 9 and encodes a component of the $GABA_B$ receptor, identified several SNPs associated with nicotine dependence.

Thus, GABA receptors play a role in the development of both alcohol and nicotine dependence. Nicotine enhances the rewarding effects of other drugs by interfering with inhibition that GABA produces. However, whereas alcohol acts directly on the $GABA_A$ receptor, the effect of nicotine on $GABA_B$ function appears to be indirect. In summary, variations in the $GABA_{A2}$ gene are associated with differences in electrophysiological measures (e.g., the P300 wave) that are indicative of vulnerability to a variety of addictions. In addition, several association studies have implicated $GABA_{A2}$ in alcohol dependence.

Marker Studies

If, as assumed by a genetic model, children from families with an alcoholic parent are more likely to develop drinking problems, perhaps there are some genetic, physical, biochemical, or neurophysiological differences even prior to the development of drinking problems. Persons with positive family histories (FH+) and those with negative family histories (FH−) for alcoholism may have different levels on these marker variables. However, marker variables are not necessarily causes. Some markers such as indicators of ethanol metabolism may indeed play a causal role since they affect differences in reactions to alcohol. In this type of research, children from FH+ and FH− families are compared to see if they differ on factors that might point toward future differences in drinking behavior.

Genetic Markers

One study using **genetic markers** (Schuckit, 1987) tested the view that sons of alcoholics with a positive family history for alcoholism (FHP) may differ in their sensitivity or reaction to alcohol from sons of nonalcoholics with a negative family history for alcoholism (FHN). Sons of alcoholics were less sensitive than were sons of nonalcoholics in response to an alcohol challenge (drinking a moderate dose of alcohol in the laboratory). This difference in reaction to alcohol could allow sons of alcoholics to drink larger amounts of alcohol before they feel its effect and might partly explain why they are at higher risk of becoming alcoholics.

However, studies of alcoholic family history and sensitivity to alcohol vary in their findings about the risk for alcohol use problems. Alcohol use disorders are absent for some men despite their having both of these attributes; furthermore, other men who lack both characteristics can also become alcoholics. These cases that are inconsistent with the model may in part be due to inaccurate assessment of family history. For example, one follow-up study of sons of alcoholics (Schuckit, Klein, & Twitchell, 1995) discovered that as many as 7% of FHN and another 5% of FHP males were misclassified at the time of original assessment.

A prospective study (Schuckit & Smith, 2001) of 411 men, sons of alcoholics and controls, in a 15-year follow-up assessed differences in alcohol use disorders. As expected, men who had both a positive family history (FHP) and a low level of response (LR) to alcohol had the highest rates of alcohol use disorders, followed by men who had only one of these two characteristics, men with either an FHP background or a low LR to alcohol, and men with an FHN background and a high LR to alcohol.

This difference in LR to alcohol challenges has also been found with a sample of 40 men between 18 and 29 years of age from the following generation (Schuckit, Smith, Kalmijn, & Danko, 2005). FHP, compared with FHN, men had significant positive correlations between subjective feelings of intoxication and body sway after receiving alcohol.

Biochemical Markers

Monoamine oxidase (MAO) is a genetically controlled enzyme that influences mood states through its regulation of the levels of neurotransmitters such as dopamine, serotonin, and norepinephrine. MAO level in blood platelets has been found to be lower in alcoholics even after they abstain for long periods. Members of alcoholic families also show lower platelet MAO levels than those from nonalcoholic families.

Lower MAO levels among alcoholics might contribute to drinking by interfering with production of serotonin (5-HT), a neurotransmitter found to be low in alcoholics (Anthenelli & Tabakoff, 1995). MAO level differences between normals and alcoholics may be limited to certain subtypes of alcoholics (Pandey, Fawcett, Gibbons, Clark, & Davis, 1988; Von Knorring, Bohman, Von Knorring, & Oreland, 1985). Furthermore, the difference in platelet MAO may not be specific to alcoholism but due to general psychopathology or other correlates of drinking. For example, since alcoholics also tend to smoke heavily, it is inconclusive as to whether alcohol is the main factor (Snell, Glanz, & Tabakoff, 2002). In fact, several factors such as cigarette smoking, lifetime history of alcohol dependence, gender, and recruitment site were found to be associated with lower platelet MAO activity levels. In a study of more than 1,500 Australian twins that controlled for smoking (Whitfield et al., 2000), alcohol dependency was not related to MAO activity.

Adenyl cyclase (AC), an enzyme that synthesizes cAMP, is another potential marker (Anthenelli & Tabakoff, 1995). This important enzyme affects neurotransmission of messages from the exterior of neurons to the interior portions. AC has been found to be lower in alcoholics, which suggests that they have less cAMP, the secondary messenger inside cells that can affect neural transmission. One possible effect is that the reinforcement process involving production of dopamine is impaired.

Electrophysiological Markers

Differences in brain wave patterns have been observed between FH+ and FH– groups. When visual or auditory stimuli are presented, they trigger an electrical charge in the cortex known as the P300 wave, so named because it peaks about 300 ms following stimulus detection. Also called P3, this response is assumed to reflect attention to the presentation of stimuli, and it is typically found to be of smaller amplitude for FH+ groups given a dose of alcohol (Porjesz & Begleiter, 2003). P300 studies at six different COGA sites (Porjesz et al., 1998) comparing alcoholics and their relatives against control families without alcoholism confirm prior findings of reduced P300 in alcoholics, especially males.

The Biological Risk Factors Family Study (Hill, 1995) provided substantial evidence for the role of genetic factors in familial alcoholism among females. An electrical charge, N2, which involves a negative peak about 200 ms after a stimulus is presented, is assumed to occur when individuals have a task where they have to discriminate between stimuli. N2 can be a marker for genetic differences since it is lower among women with FH+ backgrounds.

Inconsistencies in some studies suggest additional factors such as psychopathology could be important. Female alcoholics had reduced P300s but only for those having a comorbid lifetime diagnosis of depression. Male alcoholics did not show a reduction in amplitude in either the auditory or the visual modality (Hill, Locke, & Steinhauer, 1999).

Neuropsychological Markers

Evidence on the relationship between alcohol family history and cognition is conflicting. Some studies (Nagoshi & Wilson, 1987) suggest that offspring of alcoholics have impaired cognitive abilities in comparison to controls prior to—but not after—consuming a moderate dose of alcohol.

Cognitive differences between FH+ and FH– groups were not found after controlling for age, intelligence, and level of drinking (Hesselbrock, Hesselbrock, & Stabenau, 1985). Similarly, no major differences occurred between FH+ and FH– groups on a number of cognitive tests assumed to require different levels of neuropsychological functioning (Workman-Daniels & Hesselbrock, 1987).

Problems With Marker Studies

Overall, the evidence on markers for alcoholism has been inconsistent. One ignored factor throughout this research that may contribute to the conflicting array of findings is the temporal point of measurement following alcohol administration. FH+ and FH– sons may differ in their sensitivity to alcohol in different ways, depending on whether the blood alcohol level is on the ascending or the descending phase at the time of observation (Newlin & Thomson, 1990). Specifically, sons of alcoholics (SOAs) experienced more arousal than sons of nonalcoholics (SONAs) on the ascending limb, which would give them more incentive to drink. In addition, they also differed on the descending limb where SOAs had greater acute tolerance within the test session and returned to baseline levels more quickly than SONAs did, a difference that could lead to less anxiety and also promote more drinking by SOAs. During about the first 30 min after a drink, the SOAs showed more intoxication and physiological changes than the SONAs, but as time since drinking passed, they had fewer negative effects of intoxication compared with the SONAs.

The primary interest of most lab studies of autonomic responses to alcohol is in changes over the course of drinking, but these experiments do not take into account the baseline resting autonomic levels prior to receipt of alcohol (Newlin & Thomson, 1991). However, these baseline or tonic levels are important as they might change with repeated exposure to alcohol due to anticipation of the drug, conditioned responses, and long-term effects of the drug. In turn, these baseline levels might affect the phasic responses that occur over the course of alcohol metabolism. Such effects may also vary for low- and high-risk individuals.

Young men with alcoholic fathers showed *sensitization* or increased autonomic responses to a moderate dose of alcohol with successive test sessions as compared to men from similar backgrounds with only one lab exposure to alcohol. In contrast, men from nonalcoholic homes showed *tolerance* or lowered autonomic response to alcohol over successive sessions. Reanalysis of the data from the initial study a decade later (Newlin & Thomson, 1999) still found *opposite* physiological reactions to alcohol for men from alcoholic and nonalcoholic homes. Specifically, over repeated sessions involving alcohol, high-risk men showed increasing tonic levels (sensitization) whereas low-risk men showed decreasing tonic levels (tolerance). However, these opposing relationships for low- and high-risk individuals are not invariant but depend on their baseline levels just prior to drinking. These findings may help identify physiological factors by which paternal alcoholism increases risk for substance abuse disorders in male offspring.

How do markers act as contributors to or as "causes" of alcohol consumption? For example, morphological characteristics such as body size could be viewed as a marker of drinking for adolescents since boys who are physically larger for their age might start drinking sooner because they can more easily be perceived as older (Tarter, Moss, & Laird, 1990). But we would not conclude that large body size is a direct cause of drinking differences. Instead, body size, for sociological and psychological reasons, is an indirect facilitator of underage drinking.

FAMILY ENVIRONMENT INFLUENCES

> *But the father lies drunk on the floor,/ The table is empty, the wolf's at the door,/ And mother sobs loud in her broken-back'd chair,/ Her garments in taters, her soul in despair.*
>
> —From *Ruined by Drink* by Nobil Adkisson, c. 1860

Genetic factors are not the only basis for children of alcoholics being at risk for alcohol and other drug problems. Growing up, their alcoholic parent(s) may create a home environment that entails high risk for developing psychological problems during childhood and subsequent alcohol and other drug problems. Observation of parental attitudes and behaviors related to alcohol and drugs may influence alcohol and drug use by children as they enter adolescence. In addition, alcoholic parents have been found to abuse or mistreat their children in many ways including neglect, emotional abuse, physical aggression, and sexual abuse. Research on this issue compares children from families where there is a positive history of alcoholism (FH+) with children from families with a negative history of alcoholism (FH−).

General Population Studies

Alcohol-Specific Influences

Parents may influence their children's drinking through both direct modeling of alcohol use and the transmission of their values about drinking (Kandel & Andrews, 1987). It is not surprising that similarities in the drinking patterns of parents and their adult children have generally been found in studies with large samples of the general population (Barnes & Welte, 1990; Dawson, Harford, & Grant, 1992) as well as with smaller clinical samples (Orford & Velleman, 1991).

Non-Alcohol–Specific Influences

In addition to alcohol-specific family influences, children in alcoholic homes also face influences that are not alcohol related, as shown in Figure 6.4. Children from alcoholic homes have more parental psychiatric problems, lower socioeconomic status, and higher instances of family psychopathology, family violence, and parental cognitive impairment than do children from nonalcoholic homes (Ellis, Zucker, & Fitzgerald, 1997). Both alcohol-specific and alcohol-nonspecific factors must be considered as having adverse effects on the development of children in alcoholic homes.

The adverse impact of family conditions on children in alcoholic homes may extend over several generations. Using measures of grandparental and parental alcohol use disorder from a three-generation database, one study (Fuller et al., 2003) examined the relationship between marital aggression and aggression in offspring to early- and later-childhood aggression in third-generation offspring. Family data collected at baseline and at 6 years later from 186 young SOAs and both biological parents were compared to age-matched sons from 120 control families without substance abuse from the same neighborhoods.

The results showed a cycle of aggression occurred across three generations. The marital aggression of grandparents predicted parental antisocial behavior, which predicted their alcoholism and marital aggression and partially mediated aggression levels of their sons when they were preschoolers. Marital aggression was the best predictor of sons' preschool aggression, but direct parental aggression toward sons was more important at ages 9–11. Thus, risk for alcohol problems among children of alcoholics is not only mediated by parental alcoholism but also increased by other aspects of family functioning such as aggression.

Children of alcoholics also suffer poorer academic achievement (McGrath, Watson, & Chassin, 1999). Greater drinking frequency and quantity during a laboratory competitive task was related to lower academic achievement for young males from an FH+ background than for those from an FH− home (Conrod, Petersen, & Pihl, 1997) irrespective of being tested under sober or alcohol drinking conditions.

FIGURE 6.4 High- and low-risk environments for sons of alcoholic fathers.

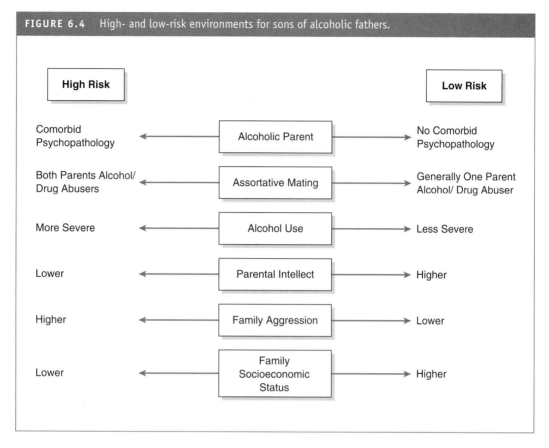

Source: From "The Role of Family Influences in Development and Risk," by D. A. Ellis, R. A. Zucker, and H. E. Fitzgerald, 1997, *Alcohol Health & Research World, 21,* pp. 218–226.

Although cross-sectional studies that compare adult children of alcoholic and non-alcoholic parents on their *current* behavior or status generally show that the offspring of alcoholics are impaired on a variety of cognitive, emotional, and physical health measures, it is not possible to make any interpretation that the parents' alcohol problems "caused" the condition of their adult children. Other variables may be involved that produced both the parental drinking problems and the characteristics of the adult children.

High-Risk Populations

Children from alcoholic homes are assumed to be at high risk for developing psychological problems during childhood and subsequent alcohol and other drug problems. Research on this issue compares children from families with a positive history (FHP or FH+) with those from families with a negative history (FHN or FH–) of alcoholism.

Retrospective Studies

Studies based on retrospective recall of alcoholics determine the extent to which parents had alcohol problems while their children were growing up (see Figure 6.5). Self-reports of alcoholics who had an alcoholic parent suggest that alcohol had a stronger effect for them when they first started drinking, as compared to accounts of alcoholics from nonalcoholic homes. For example, alcoholics with an alcoholic parent or grandparent recalled starting drinking at a younger age and having more problems due to alcohol than did either alcoholics without a drinking parent or alcoholics whose drinking relative was someone other than a parent or a grandparent (Penick et al.,

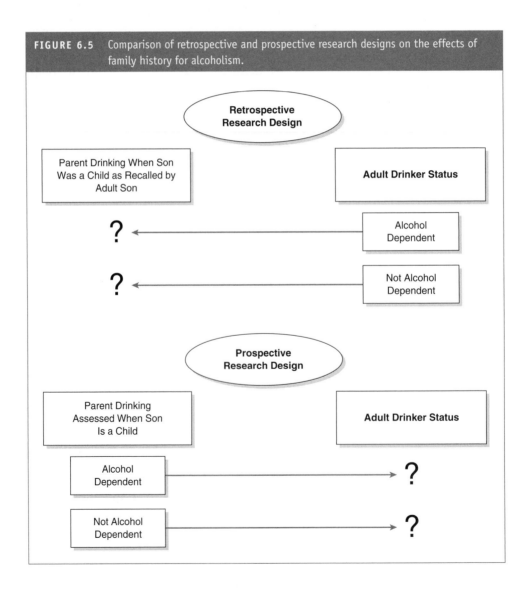

FIGURE 6.5   Comparison of retrospective and prospective research designs on the effects of family history for alcoholism.

1987). Thus, the individual's own level of alcohol abuse and a family history of alcoholism appear to produce independent and additive effects. Either factor places one at higher risk, and having both factors increases the likelihood of alcoholism even more.

Inclusion of FH+ subjects who were not alcoholic as a control group in this study allowed for an evaluation of the effects of family history of alcoholism on persons not yet afflicted by alcoholism. Since FH+ subjects were found to be more susceptible to problems on most measures than were the FH– controls, the study supports the view that a family history of alcoholism places one at higher risk for a variety of psychological and physical health impairments.

A study (MacPherson, Stewart, & McWilliams, 2001) of 213 college students examined current anxiety in relation to the extent to which their parents had alcohol problems when the students were children. It was assumed that distress in children over parental problem drinking behavior may elevate anxiety and psychological concern, which in turn may generate anxiety disorder symptoms as was found among students who recalled that their parents had drinking problems.

Similar effects of alcohol family background occur for other drugs. For example, daily smoking over longer periods was greater among adolescents from an FH+ home (Chassin, Presson, Sherman, & Mulvenon, 1994). They saw themselves as more addicted to cigarettes, had more positive beliefs about the effects of smoking, and reported stronger relaxation and stimulation motives for smoking compared with peers from FH– backgrounds. A study (Rodriguez, 1994) of young heroin users found cognitive test scores were within the normal range, but those with a family history of alcoholism started using illicit drugs at earlier ages and performed worse on tasks involving attention, memory, verbal-conceptual abstraction, and nonverbal reasoning. These deficits were attributed to these family antecedents rather than to drug consumption per se.

Using data from a national sample of adults (n = 42,862; 58.4% female), one study (Dawson, 2000b) examined the relationship between alcohol family history and the risk of initiating drinking and of moving later into dependence. Whereas many family history studies use a dichotomous measure (positive or negative) that requires only one parent be alcoholic, this study used a *saturation* measure, defined as the percentage of alcoholic first- and second-degree relatives. Among those who had been alcohol drinkers at some time in their lifetime (n = 27,616; 50.7% male), higher family history saturation was related to a greater risk of initiating drinking prior to age 15, but the relationship weakened with age. When early initiation of drinking was controlled, family history saturation increased the risk of progressing to dependence as age increased.

An index of family history density (FHD) for alcoholism (Stoltenberg, Mudd, Blow, & Hill, 1998) also provides a continuous variable that can make more graduated measures of family environments than the FH+ versus FH– dichotomy. FHD was a better predictor of alcohol problem severity than was the dichotomous FH measure, especially for women. Similarly, children from homes with a higher family density of alcoholism (Conway, Swendsen, & Merikangas, 2003) had a stronger relationship between their alcohol expectancies and problem drinking symptoms and their level of alcohol use.

Prospective Studies

Prospective studies assess children of alcoholics prior to the onset of alcoholism among them, as well as follow them afterward (see Figure 6.5). Such before-after comparisons of individuals from FH+ and FH– backgrounds offer a stronger basis for inferences about the effects of FH background on the offspring than do retrospective studies.

A comparison of college students examined how parental drinking and parental comorbidity affected them over their 4 years of college (Sher, Walitzer, Wood, & Brent, 1991), controlling for other psychological disorders often found among alcoholics so that the specific effect of parental alcoholism could be made independent of these other contributors to alcohol use by their offspring. One limitation was that measurement on these variables was based only on student descriptions. The results revealed that a family history of alcoholism is associated with more alcohol and drug problems, stronger expectancies for alcohol use, more behavioral undercontrol, and more psychiatric distress. In addition, FH+ students showed poorer academic performance and lower verbal ability. These differences were present for both men and women for most variables.

A 10-year longitudinal study (Beseler, Aharonovich, Keyes, & Hasin, 2008) assessed the relationship of family background of alcohol use disorders and of drinking motives at baseline among 423 participants who met *DSM-IV* alcohol dependence criteria by the end of the study but not at baseline. A similar analysis was made among 301 participants who met the criteria for *DSM-IV* alcohol abuse at follow-up but had not met these criteria at baseline nor met *DSM-IV* criteria for dependence at the follow-up.

Those participants with a positive family history and who had baseline drinking motives for negative affect reduction and for social facilitation were more likely to meet *DSM-IV* alcohol dependence criteria at the 10-year follow-up. In contrast, new onsets of alcohol abuse were not predicted by either alcohol family history or drinking motives.

Problems of Interpretation

Retrospective studies are often based on samples of individuals seeking help for problems not necessarily related to alcohol. They may be likely to search earlier memories for signs of family problems such as parental alcoholism that might account for their own problems. This bias in recall is hard to rule out since most studies rely on self-report of family history rather than objective or independent assessment. This tendency might produce overestimates of the extent of alcoholism in family backgrounds. Furthermore, these study participants may be more extreme cases seeking counseling or clinical treatment and hence not be representative of all children from alcoholic families.

Prospective studies have their own limitations. Repeated and anticipated testing may alter the behavior under study. Participants discontinue involvement in studies that require several sessions for varied reasons. Some forget, others lose interest, and still others move away, become incarcerated, or die. The remaining participants may not be representative of the original sample, so interpretation of differences over time is difficult. Are those who continue in the study the "cream of the crop," the "bottom of the barrel," or from some place between the extremes?

Overall, evidence from retrospective and prospective studies shows higher risk of alcohol use disorders among those from families with one or more alcoholics. However, many studies, both retrospective and prospective, use a before-after approach that involves only two points in time that do not permit an examination of temporal patterns of change.

Studies of the trajectory of alcohol drinking patterns, which address this issue, will be deferred until Chapter 10, which deals with age changes in alcohol use but will include discussion of the relationship of family history to drinking changes over age.

Variations in Response to Parental Alcohol Use Disorders

Responses to heavy parental drinking can have varying effects. Aversion may occur in which the child adopts a negative attitude toward alcohol use, or polarization may occur where the child goes to one extreme, abstinence, or the other, heavy use (Webster, Harburg, Gleiberman, Schork, & DiFranceisco, 1989). As some heavily drinking parents may often be abusive toward their children, for example, the tendency to model after the drinking of such parents may be reduced. Thus, 56 % of the low-volume male drinkers had a heavily drinking mother whose drinking violated cultural norms. Daughters of heavily drinking parents were found to be more likely to show the polarization effect.

Aversion effects were more likely when the opposite-sex parent was a heavy drinker with alcohol-related problems (Harburg, DiFranceisco, Webster, Gleiberman, & Schork, 1990). However, daughters often imitated the drinking levels of heavily drinking fathers without problems related to their drinking. Daughters showed a polarization effect if their mothers were heavy drinkers, with most of them being abstainers and a sizeable minority becoming heavy drinkers themselves. Overall, the highest correspondence of drinking levels between parents and children occurred for abstaining parents, especially if the father was abstinent.

Despite having one or two alcoholic parents, some children of alcoholics (COAs) seem to avoid alcohol and drug problems. A study (Hussong & Chassin, 1997) using a subsample of 267 COAs from a 3-year prospective study of 454 COAs and matched control families found that COAs with greater perceived control or extreme (very low or high) levels of cognitive coping were less likely to initiate substance use than their peers. Highly organized families and behavioral coping efforts may deter substance use initiation.

Perhaps one or both parents might cope with the alcoholism in a way that buffers or is "protective" for the children. If a father is alcoholic, perhaps a nonalcoholic mother is more vigilant and monitors the children's behavior, provides more social support, and uses consistent discipline. However, one study (Curran & Chassin, 1996) failed to find support for parental behavior that protected the child against alcohol and drug use or externalizing symptoms such as antisocial behaviors.

Other research (Orford & Velleman, 1991) found that the relationship of heavy parental drinking to the drinking of offspring varied with the interpersonal relationship between drinking parent and child. Daughters were more likely to have drinking problems if they had a close relationship to their heavily drinking fathers. Sons were more likely to have drinking problems if they had heavily drinking mothers and poor relations with their fathers. These findings, similar in many respects to previous research (Harburg et al., 1990), suggest that the impact of heavy drinking by parents on the drinking of their children is greater for offspring of the opposite sex. However, it also appears that some children from alcoholic homes prove to be resilient in not being adversely impacted by developing protective strategies (Velleman & Orford, 1999; Velleman & Templeton, 2007).

A prospective study (Zhou, King, & Chassin, 2006) also found that the relationship between family history of alcoholism and drinking problems among young adult children was lower if there were harmonious family relations. Similarly, a study with 665 children between the ages of 13 and 17 years (Ohannessian et al., 2004) found that the adverse impact of family history of alcoholism was present mainly if the parent had a comorbid psychopathology.

Finally, it should be noted that some effects attributed to early alcoholic home environment may actually involve processes that precede birth. A 14-year prospective study (Baer, Barr, Bookstein, Sampson, & Streissguth, 1998) of pregnant women showed that the level of prenatal alcohol use measured during pregnancy was a better predictor of adolescent alcohol use than was the family alcohol environment during childhood.

Problems With Studies of Children of Alcoholics

Overall, the evidence suggests children from FH+ backgrounds are more likely to use more alcohol or to develop alcohol problems. One problem with family history studies is the wide variation in the criteria used to define FH levels. Some studies use stringent criteria such as a parent diagnosed and treated for alcoholism while other studies rely on vague and uncorroborated criteria such as the offspring's judgment that a parent had drinking problems sometime in the past. Thus, in some studies, the magnitude of the difference between the FH+ and the FH− levels is rather small and unreliable.

The likelihood of finding differences between FH+ and FH− groups should vary with the criteria used for defining the two groups along the continuum that ranges from nondrinking to moderate drinking to heavy drinking. If groups selected to represent FH− and FH+ groups are too close together or at the lower end of the dimension, it should be harder to find drinking differences between them.

Another problem is that researchers have not generally reported the levels of alcohol use in any absolute or standard values that can be compared across studies. The reported lack of differences could reflect either equally low *or* equally high drinking by FH+ and FH− groups. It is conceivable that any effect of FH level among young samples is masked by the tendency for FH− individuals to drink because of adolescent curiosity about alcohol and as a result of peer pressure. If other factors such as these influences combine with family drinking history to determine drinking levels, the effect of FH level will be ambiguous. Finally, the studies, thus far, that show no relationships between parental and offspring drinking cannot rule out the possibility that future alcoholism will be greater for children from the FH+ homes because it may take more time to occur.

These studies cannot separate hereditary and environmental contributions. Instead they assess the joint influences of heredity and environment on the children from alcoholic and nonalcoholic families. The assumption is that both genetic and home environment factors represent a higher risk for alcoholism for persons from families with a parental drinking problem. However, the genetic and environmental factors could even offset each other in some families. As depicted in Figure 6.6, there may be families where a genetic factor favoring alcoholism is countered by a home environment that lowers the risk for alcoholism and other families where a low genetic potential for alcoholism is offset by a home environment that raises the risk for alcoholism.

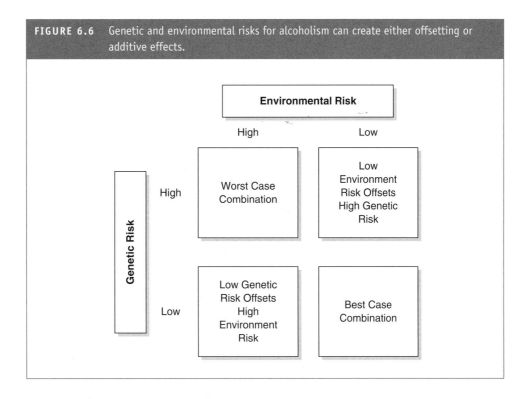

FIGURE 6.6 Genetic and environmental risks for alcoholism can create either offsetting or additive effects.

In other words, the vulnerability or susceptibility of an individual toward alcoholism is based on a combination of both genetic and environmental factors. If either factor is sufficiently strong, alcoholism may occur even if the other factor is weak. For children from FH+ families, both factors are assumed to generally be high. However, it is conceivable that although COAs may have a high genetic potential for alcoholism, some may have an environment that does not foster alcoholism. Similarly, although children of nonalcoholics may have a low genetic potential for alcoholism, some of them may live in an environment that fosters alcoholism.

INTEGRATIVE MODELS OF HEREDITY AND ENVIRONMENT

Instead of pitting heredity and environment against each other, it may be more fruitful to develop models that show the joint influence of both sets of factors and examine how they affect each other. As Figure 6.7 illustrates, genes that affect sensitivity to alcohol, metabolic processes, and neurotransmitter regulation play a role in determining whether people drink and how their bodies react to alcohol. These processes may also be affected by factors in the physical environment such as pollutants, crowding, and noise that generate stress. In addition, numerous environmental factors ranging from cultural and social norms to

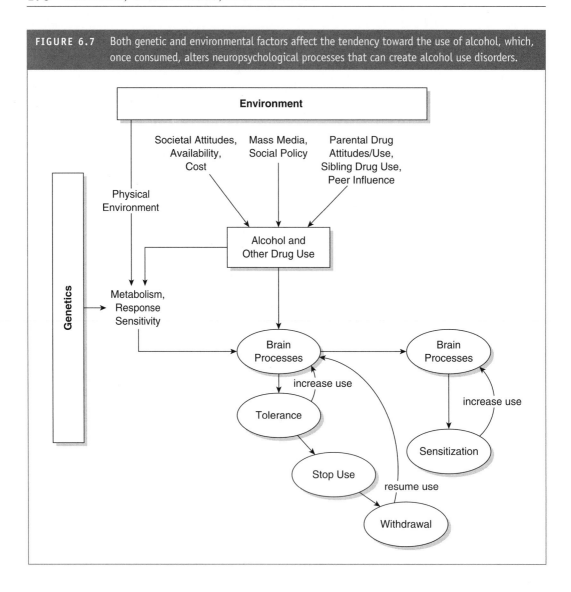

FIGURE 6.7 Both genetic and environmental factors affect the tendency toward the use of alcohol, which, once consumed, alters neuropsychological processes that can create alcohol use disorders.

interpersonal interactions to coping with personal stressors may influence the likelihood that alcohol and other drugs will be consumed. Together, the genetic and environmental factors determine whether people drink alcohol, how often, in what quantity, and with what consequences.

Gene–Environment Interactions

Genetic influences are complicated by their interactions with environmental factors. For example, individuals with different inherited tendencies for alcohol or drug use may not be equally likely to grow up in the same types of environments. While many COAs may grow up in circumstances that add to their chances of developing alcohol problems (e.g., child neglect, abuse, poverty, low self-esteem), other COAs do not encounter these stressful environments and hence may be less likely to develop alcohol dependency.

Genetic factors seem to be more influential in the development of alcohol use disorders for adolescents and young adults than for middle-aged and older adults. Adolescents who have their first drink before age 15 are more likely to develop alcohol problems (McGue, Iacono, Legrand, Malone, & Elkins, 2001). They may have genetic characteristics that promote externalizing behaviors such as more use of alcohol and other drugs, more impulsive and sensation-seeking behaviors, and conduct disorders. In contrast, other adolescents with the same genetic background might escape these tendencies because of better parental monitoring that delays their initiation into drinking until they are older. Since their lives will not center on drinking, these adolescents may achieve better academically. Thus, the social environments created by these two groups of adolescents are markedly different. Alcohol problems can still occur later in life for those who do not start drinking early, but they may be more in response to environmental stresses and social demands for drinking than to genetic factors.

Comparisons of alcohol problems among adolescents in rural and urban environments also illustrate the importance of **gene–environment interactions** at least for males in a study of over 1,200 17-year-old twins in Minnesota (Legrand, Keyes, McGue, Iacono, & Krueger, 2008). In urban environments, externalizing behavior, including alcohol and drug use, conduct disorder, and antisocial personality behavior, was strongly related to genetic factors, whereas shared environmental factors were more important in rural environments with populations of fewer than 10,000. Possibly, rural communities offer fewer opportunities for alcohol and drug use as well as greater parental awareness and monitoring of the behavior and social contacts of their adolescent children.

Because gene-environment interactions determine eventual behaviors, a clear separation between effects attributable to genes and effects attributable to environment is not possible. Prospective studies of MZ and DZ twins, by examining biological and environmental factors more precisely, have potential for the achievement of a more comprehensive understanding of the determinants of alcohol and drug use in real-life conditions.

The question of the relative influence of genetic and environmental factors on the development of alcoholism has generated considerable interest and controversy. An explanation emphasizing heredity is more fatalistic since it implies that the "die has already been cast" and offspring cannot alter or control their destiny. Environmental explanations allow for more optimism in the sense that interventions can be attempted to counteract or reduce the damage. COAs might receive earlier counseling or be placed under foster care, for example. Another possibility would be more education and counseling of parents as to the dangers of parental alcoholism.

At the level of the individual, the answer to this issue would have implications for assignment of blame or responsibility between parents and children. If alcoholism were regarded as primarily of genetic origin, the alcoholic would be seemingly absolved of personal responsibility for the problem. At the societal level, the answer to the question carries implications for social attitudes and social policy. If genetic factors were assumed to be the primary determinants of alcoholism, society would be more tolerant than if the alcoholic was seen to be personally responsible.

Summary

Genetic information is encoded in a molecule, DNA, in the nucleus of all cells and transmitted by 46 chromosome pairs, one member from the father and one from the mother. Alcohol consumption—and how it affects drinkers—is affected by multiple rather than single genes that combine with environmental influences to determine the likelihood of alcohol dependency.

Genetic factors do not act in a vacuum but are activated or "expressed" under certain environmental conditions. For example, personality differences in reactions to stressors can affect individual use of alcohol. In turn, genetic factors can affect alcohol metabolism and the physical and psychological reactions to alcohol.

Alcohol and other drug use for individuals with a given genotype can still vary considerably due to environmental differences such as cultural setting, societal context, interpersonal relations, and physical surroundings. Together, both genetic and environmental factors affect the likelihood of alcohol and other drug use as well as their consequences.

Naturalistic evidence about the relative role of heredity and environment is difficult to evaluate since it is impossible to disentangle the effects of each factor from the other. Studies in the late 1800s comparing rates of alcoholism among identical and fraternal twins with those among siblings and the adoption studies of the 1950s in Denmark and soon after in Sweden provided "natural experiments" for evaluating the role of heredity as a risk factor for alcoholism. However, the generalizability of twins and of adoptees to the larger population may be questioned. The circumstances and the types of individuals who place children for adoption and accept adopted children are likely to be significantly different from the more general population. For example, infants placed for adoption are not a random sample of infants but often come from unwed mothers, probably adolescent girls. They may have lower income, poor nutrition, and so on. The types of individuals who apply for adoption are not a random sample of the general population either, being screened by social agencies to ensure that they can afford to care for the child and appear to be psychologically stable. Certainly the answer to these questions may vary in different countries and eras, depending on the social-legal conditions and cultural attitudes related to adoptions.

Studies of samples from the far larger number of children who grow up in the homes of their biological parents are also inconclusive about the relative role of heredity and environment. Differences between children from FH+ and FH– families have to be viewed as due to the joint or combined effects of heredity and environment. Overall, the findings of family studies question the widely held view that children who grow up in alcoholic families are at greater risk than those from nonalcoholic families for alcoholism and other types of psychological and behavioral problems. There is some support for the conclusion that children from alcoholic environments are different from other children. However, they do not always differ with respect to their drinking practices or the effects of drinking on them. Some of the contradictory findings across different studies about the relationship of parental alcoholism and characteristics of their children may be due to the variety of criteria used to define an alcoholic parent in different studies. It is also possible that under some conditions—or for some types of individuals—the potentially adverse effects of parental alcohol dependency can be offset, but the nature of these protective factors is not yet fully understood. However, because alcohol dependency may require years to emerge, continued follow-up over another 10 or 20 years may yield other conclusions.

When the human genome map was completed, research based on **molecular genetics** allowed for more direct measures of genetic factors that might differentiate alcoholics and their relatives from nonalcoholics and their relatives. Recent research using linkage analyses and association studies is beginning to identify QTL (multiple genes) on specific chromosomes that may underlie processes that increase an individual's risk for alcohol abuse and dependency.

Stimulus/Response

1. Similar patterns of alcohol or drug use may seemingly occur among family members; for example, children of alcoholics become alcoholics themselves when they grow up. Psychologists call it a confirmation bias when we notice cases that fit our expectations: You know Joe is an alcoholic, and you then learn his father was also one. "Aha," you say, "just as I suspected. So that's why Joe drinks so much!" But are we as likely to also notice disconfirming instances? For example, do you notice that Bill, also an alcoholic, has a nonalcoholic father? Is Bill just an exception to the rule?

2. Do you know anyone who is a total abstainer from alcohol? Do most members of his or her immediate family also not drink? Would such observations support a genetic or an environmental basis for abstinence?

3. You are seriously considering marriage and having a family with someone special. You visit your potential mother- and father-in-law for dinner several times at their home and at restaurants and notice that one of them tends to drink heavily. Would this behavior bother you enough to make you reconsider marrying into this family? Assuming that only one of the parents engages in heavy drinking, would it be more worrisome if it were the mother or the father who was the alcohol abuser? Do you think the males and the females in the class will have different answers, as a group, to any aspect of this thought exercise?

4. Imagine one of your parents has a serious drinking problem that worries you because you know there are some genetic factors involved in drinking tendencies. What effect, if any, would this have on your drinking? Would it worry you more if the parent in question was of the same or the opposite sex as you?

Basic Psychological Processes

Methodological Issues	Structural Neuropsychological Explanations
Mood and Emotion	Process Neuropsychological Explanations
Emotional Regulation and Drinking	Summary
Sensory Motor Activity	Stimulus/Response
Cognition	

When I read about the evils of drinking, I gave up reading.

—Henny Youngman

People drink alcohol and use other drugs for many different reasons. They may expect to achieve pleasurable outcomes or reduce painful experiences, impress others or yield to social pressure, escape boredom, and forget about problems. Many users seek these goals by consuming these substances, but unfortunately there are often unforeseen detrimental effects when large quantities are consumed, especially if repeated often over an extended period.

In this chapter we will examine research findings about the relationship between alcohol and other drug use and several important psychological processes and outcomes. Pharmacological explanations attribute these effects to chemical factors. However, psychological factors may also be partly or entirely responsible for many "effects" of alcohol and other drugs that are attributed to the pharmacological factors. Due to the social context in which these substances are used—and to the expectations of the user—effects attributed to alcohol and other drugs may actually represent the influence of psychological factors. For example, people expect to have a good time when they go to a party. Alcohol and other drugs may be consumed there, and people may later believe these substances were a major factor responsible for the pleasant experiences they had at the party. However, these substances may not have been the primary cause of the happy experiences because most of the people present would have had some degree of positive experience anyway because they came expecting to have fun.

Nonetheless, beliefs that alcohol promotes good times, that tobacco relieves social anxiety, that cigarettes aid both concentration and relaxation, and that marijuana makes people mellow may produce **attributions** that it was the alcohol, tobacco, or marijuana that produced—or at least enhanced—the positive experiences associated with its use. Because these substances may relieve anxiety or tension, they may facilitate the occurrence of pleasurable experiences by "allowing" the user to forget conscious controls and inhibitions, but they may not be sufficient alone to produce these effects. In other contexts, drugs can lead to quite different effects. For instance, when people in an angry and frustrated crowd drink heavily, aggressive, hostile feelings and violent behavior may be unleashed instead.

Expectancies about the effects of alcohol and other drugs, which were discussed in Chapter 2, are determined by the individual's background, knowledge, and past experiences with the substances. Whatever the source, these factors are psychological rather than pharmacological in nature. To understand how alcohol and other drugs affect experience and behavior, it is necessary to analyze the contributions of both types of factors.

In this and the next two chapters, we will focus on research on the effects that alcohol and other drugs have on important psychological processes. Before examining any research findings, however, it is necessary to consider some methodological concerns and problems faced in research measuring alcohol and drug effects on behavior. Understanding the strengths and weaknesses of these methods is essential for analyzing controversies about causal inferences of the effects of alcohol and other drugs.

METHODOLOGICAL ISSUES

Uncontrolled Observation

Two major research methods have been used to examine how alcohol and other drugs affect behavior and experience. *Naturalistic* or **uncontrolled observation** examines correlations between drug use and behavioral outcomes. Often, several alternative interpretations of an observed relationship are possible, and caution is needed to rule out rival explanations.

As an example, suppose we observed that those who drank more alcohol during lunch worked less efficiently after lunch. One interpretation for this evidence is that alcohol impaired work performance. In jumping to this conclusion, we assumed that these workers were more productive prior to drinking, but we had no direct evidence to support this view. As the top line in Figure 7.1 shows, demonstration of a causal influence of alcohol or any other drug requires that the work quality *before* the drug use is better than it was *after* the drug use. In addition, even if the work quality was lower after drinking for this group of workers, we also would like to know what the level of work quality was like for comparable peers who did not drink during lunch. This group would serve as a baseline for comparison. If these nondrinking peers also showed reduced work quality after lunch, the drinking workers' deficits could not be due entirely to drinking. Perhaps everyone has a postlunch letdown at work.

On the other hand, if the sober workers did better work than the drinking workers after lunch, as shown by the lower line in the hypothetical example in Figure 7.1, we would be safer in attributing the reduced work quality of the drinkers to the effects of the alcohol they drank with their lunch.

FIGURE 7.1 Evidence needed to infer causal effects of alcohol.

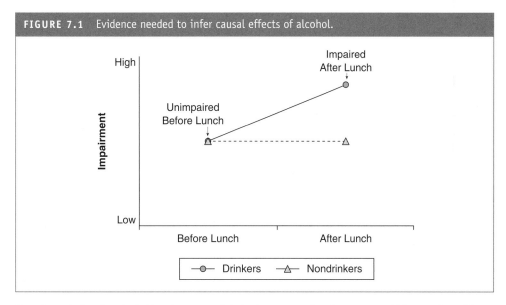

Note: A conclusion that alcohol impairs someone's behavior *assumes* that the person would have performed better prior to drinking, as shown in the top line. Also, comparable persons who did *not* drink are assumed to perform at better levels than the drinker, as shown in the bottom line. However, causal inferences are often made without evaluating these two assumptions.

Self-Selection

An alternative explanation for the findings in our example does not attribute the work impairment to any causal effect of alcohol at all. Instead, it proposes that a selective process may be operating, with those workers who drank more alcohol during lunch being different from those who drank less—or not at all—in some important ways that affect work productivity. For instance, workers who are less motivated, less capable, or under more stress might be more likely to drink more at lunch. Thus, even without the influence of alcohol, their work would likely be inferior to the typical performance of those who drank less. Consequently, we cannot safely attribute the differences in work performance of the two groups to the effects of differences in alcohol consumption.

Whenever some selective process occurs, we may mistakenly conclude that some difference such as poor work quality by drinkers is an outcome or effect caused by drug use. Instead, some preexisting difference distinguishing drug users and nonusers is responsible for the observed outcome differences when **self-selection** occurs. Or both factors may be operative, with some initial differences between drug users and nonusers being enlarged or increased by the influence of the drug.

When we compare individuals who differ in how much they choose to drink on differences in their work, we do not have a before- and after-drinking comparison. Instead, we are measuring whether individuals who choose to drink more also do poorer work than those who prefer to drink less or not at all. Individuals who tend to drink more may also, on average, be more likely to suffer impaired behavior *even when they are not drinking* than those who drink less or not at all. One basis for this prediction is that drinkers are more impulsive and undercontrolled than nondrinkers (Sher & Trull, 1994; Tarter, 1988). For similar reasons, when drinking does occur, the same amount of alcohol may produce a bigger effect on those who typically drink and/or drink in large quantities than on those who ordinarily do not.

Controlled Observation

The second major method for obtaining evidence about alcohol and other drug effects is the *experiment* or **controlled observation**. An experimental study of the question described above could create two groups of workers using **random assignment** to determine group membership. One group would arbitrarily be assigned the task of drinking a specified amount of alcohol during lunch. The other group would be instructed to drink an equal volume of a nonalcoholic drink. Under this method, self-selection on the basis of drinking history would be prevented. Any differences in work performance observed after lunch between the two groups could not be attributed to preexisting differences and would be interpreted as stemming from the effect of alcohol consumption.

Because the only systematic difference between the two groups would be the amount of alcohol consumed during lunch, it would be more likely that differences in work performance after lunch could be explained as the effects of alcohol. Although the logic of the experimental method is sound, a practical problem with experimental evidence is that it may not be highly generalizable to behavior under natural conditions. In other words, in the real world the level of drinking, for example, is not an "assigned" activity but is one that involves choice or voluntary behavior.

It is important, when evaluating and interpreting the research findings, to note the strengths and weaknesses of the methodology used. Uncontrolled observations are often useful in generating ideas or hypotheses that can then be evaluated more carefully through controlled observations to rule out alternative explanations. Thus, if smokers are more productive than nonsmokers, is the difference due to smoking per se or to some other factor that also differs between smokers and nonsmokers such as some personality characteristic? To disentangle the two alternative explanations, one would compare the performance of two groups of workers, one of which contained smokers and the other of which contained nonsmokers, who were similar in personality traits. This type of controlled observation allows any observed differences to be more safely attributed to smoking rather than to personality. Combining evidence obtained from both methods is often useful to arrive at stronger conclusions.

Expectancy Controls

The mere *expectancy* of receiving drugs can be an influential factor affecting behavior, separate from any pharmacological influence. Laboratory or controlled experiments of the effects of drugs typically try to measure any influence of expectancy by including **expectancy controls**, control groups or conditions in which participants are told that they are receiving a drug but in fact they are actually given a **placebo** (nondrug). In this traditional design, any differences in behavior between these participants and those in the experimental group, who expected to receive *and* received the drug, are attributed to the effect of the drug. A variant of this method uses only one group but tests participants on more than one occasion by applying the experimental (drug) and control (nondrug) conditions in different sequences to different subgroups.

But this research paradigm fails to assess any influence that **expectancy** of receiving the drug per se contributes since both groups expect the drug. Because this type of expectancy is the same for both groups, investigators cannot detect any impact that the mere expectancy of consuming the drug might exert on psychological experiences and behavior. Indeed, if the actual drug has no pharmacological effect, all of the behavior will be due to the expectancy effect.

Participants in laboratory studies may be suspicious when they receive alcohol or other drugs and respond differently from the way they normally would. For this reason, in some alcohol studies participants are told that the experiment involves a taste-rating task to hide the true purpose for having them drink alcohol. Participants are led to believe that they will be sampling different wines to assess their taste preferences; in actuality, the goal is to see if more alcohol is consumed when the experimental task involves higher stress.

Some researchers (Testa et al., 2006) have concerns that an alcohol placebo condition might prompt some recipients to compensate for the expected effects of the anticipated alcohol consumption by altering their behavior. However, it is difficult for researchers to know precisely how such responses affect the results of a study because individuals might compensate in different ways. In addition, individuals may react differently across situations. This predicament calls for caution in the use of placebos. For example, where prior findings show that a placebo generally has no effect, it might be better not to use one because it could activate compensatory reactions that would obscure any effect of any variable being evaluated.

Balanced Placebo Design

A research design known as the **balanced placebo design** was developed (Marlatt, Demming, & Reid, 1973) to assess the role of expectancy in the effects of consuming alcohol. As shown in Figure 7.2, this design isolates pharmacological and psychological effects by using four different test conditions. Half the participants receive an alcoholic beverage such as vodka mixed with tonic in a 1:5 proportion, and half receive a nonalcoholic beverage such as tonic water disguised to resemble a cocktail lounge drink. To increase credibility, a small amount of alcohol may be rubbed around the top of the glass to provide the odor of alcohol. In addition, half of participants in each of these two groups are told that they have an alcoholic drink while the other half are told that they have a nonalcoholic beverage.

This complex design allows for the evaluation of a consumption effect by a comparison of the combined two groups that receive alcohol (Groups 1 and 3) with the combined two groups that do not (Groups 2 and 4), regardless of whether they expect alcoholic beverages. In addition, it allows for an assessment of an expectancy effect by comparison of the combined two groups that expect alcohol (Groups 1 and 2) with the combined two groups that do not expect alcohol (Groups 3 and 4), regardless of what they actually receive. Interaction effects also can be examined with this design to see if the effect of alcohol varies, depending on the type of expectancy. Thus, alcohol consumption might produce a difference in some behavior if the drinkers believe they are drinking (expect to receive) an alcoholic beverage but might not have an effect if they believe they are consuming a nonalcoholic drink.

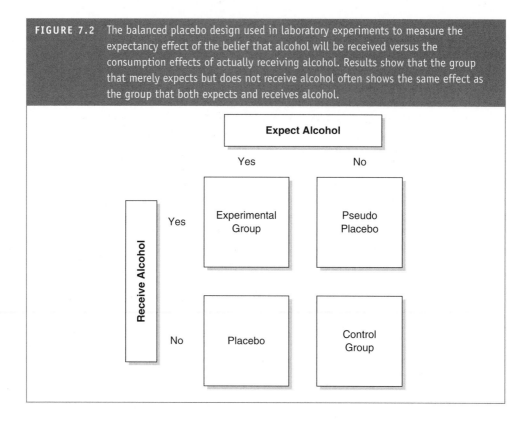

FIGURE 7.2 The balanced placebo design used in laboratory experiments to measure the expectancy effect of the belief that alcohol will be received versus the consumption effects of actually receiving alcohol. Results show that the group that merely expects but does not receive alcohol often shows the same effect as the group that both expects and receives alcohol.

To minimize confusion, it is important to keep in mind that two different types of expectancy will be discussed in this chapter, expectancies about the *effect of alcohol* and expectancies about the *type of beverage* that will be received, alcoholic or nonalcoholic. In natural settings, we receive the type of beverage that we expect to have; hence, we cannot isolate the pharmacological effect of alcohol from the effect of expecting to receive an alcoholic beverage. In contrast, the balanced placebo design used in the laboratory is able to separate these effects. Some drinkers receive the type of beverage that is *expected,* while others do not receive the type of beverage expected. When the term *expectancy* is used in connection with experiments, it usually refers to the expectation about the type of beverage that will be consumed and not to the expected effects of alcohol.

Among light to moderate drinkers, the expectancy of having received even a small dose of alcohol such as one drink has a stronger effect on cognitive processes than whether alcohol was in fact consumed (Marlatt & Rohsenow, 1980). Two experiments (Fillmore & Vogel Sprott, 1995) examined the degree of performance change after one session on a motor skills task with alcohol during a second session on another motor skills task where alcohol was expected but a placebo was received. A control group completed the second task without expecting alcohol. Those with expectancies of greater impairment from drinking alcohol performed worse than the control group on the second task even though they received a placebo. Thus, expectancy plays a major role in affecting outcomes, effects that would have been attributed entirely to pharmacological factors in studies that did not use a placebo condition as a control.

One limitation of the balanced placebo design is that not everyone may have identical beliefs or expectancies about alcohol's effects. And, in the few experiments where different expectations about alcohol's effects are provided to different groups, they may not be equally credible. All the balanced placebo design can do is control expectancies about receiving or not receiving alcohol; it does not determine different expectancies about the effects of alcohol. Another limitation is that it can only be used with low doses of alcohol below a BAC of around 0.04% to be effective (Martin, Earleywine, & Finn, 1990). Thus, problems of credibility (as well as ethics) arise if large doses of alcohol are given to participants who are misinformed and told that they are receiving nonalcoholic beverages when in fact they are given alcohol.

However, some evidence suggests the balanced placebo method may not be accurate even at moderate blood alcohol concentrations (Sayette, Breslin, Wilson, & Rosenblum, 1994). Although misinformed that they were *not* drinking alcohol, 44% of participants who did receive alcohol correctly reported consuming alcohol. Only 6% of those in the placebo control group who were misinformed that they had consumed alcohol but actually were given tonic water saw through the deception.

Absolute or Relative Effects

Researchers using laboratory experiments want to compare performance of a group that receives a specific amount of a drug with that of a control group that does not receive any drug to draw conclusions about the *effect* of the drug, free from self-selection that may occur with uncontrolled experiments or observations outside the lab. Consequently, participants in experiments on use of licit drugs must abstain from their normal use of alcohol, nicotine, and caffeine overnight. Since participants begin the session in a virtually drug-free condition, researchers know the drug levels in participants during the session with reasonable accuracy.

While this procedure makes sense from the researcher's perspective, it creates some problems in interpretation of findings. When moderate to heavy users of drugs go for an extended time without their customary dose, they generally experience discomfort or withdrawal, states that ordinarily may disrupt many behaviors. However, once the experiment commences and they receive the drug that they have been without overnight, their task performance seems to improve and is better than that of control subjects who do not receive the drug.

But is this superior performance under the drug an *absolute* improvement or merely a *relative* one whereby users improve relative to the impaired level induced when experiencing withdrawal from the absence of the drug? This issue is important because it affects the conclusion made about the effects of specific drugs. If improved outcomes occur under the influence of drugs, does this mean that the performance is superior to the nondrug condition, or does it merely mean that the drug is bringing the drug user from an impaired withdrawal level back to performance that is probably not different from—and sometimes still worse than—the performance of the nondrug group?

The Example of Caffeine Effects. The issue of whether effects are absolute or relative is often a concern in drug research as can be illustrated using caffeine as an example. In one controlled study of the effects of caffeine on attention (Yeomans, Ripley, Davies, Rusted, & Rogers, 2002), moderate caffeine consumers received a drink containing 0, 1, or 2 mg/kg caffeine at breakfast followed 60 min later by a second drink containing either 0 or 1 mg/kg caffeine.

The first moderate dose of caffeine improved performance on a sustained attention task and increased rated mental alertness when participants were still caffeine deprived, but the second moderate dose when consumers were no longer caffeine deprived had no such benefits, suggesting that the observed benefits of the first dose of caffeine may have been merely the reversal of caffeine withdrawal to some extent.

But other studies did not show withdrawal alleviation effects. One study (Haskell, Kennedy, Wesnes, & Scholey, 2005/2006) investigated the acute cognitive and mood effects of caffeine in 24 habitual users consuming an average of 217 mg/day and 24 habitual nonusers with an average of 20 mg/day of caffeine. Mood or performance did not differ at the baseline measure taken in the morning after they had refrained from using caffeine since the previous night. Each group then received a 150-ml drink containing either 75 or 150 mg of caffeine or a matching placebo. Tests given 30 min later showed significant improvements in simple reaction time, digit vigilance reaction time, numeric working memory reaction time, and sentence verification accuracy in both groups. Self-rated mental fatigue was reduced, and ratings of alertness were significantly improved by caffeine independent of group. Habitual consumers outperformed nonconsumers on rapid visual information processing and spatial memory accuracy. Caffeine improved mood more in consumers than in nonconsumers while performance improved more in nonconsumers than in consumers.

A study (Hewlett & Smith, 2007) that led to a similar conclusion gave repeated caffeine doses to 120 volunteers, 36 of whom were nonconsumers. A baseline session measured mood and a range of cognitive functions at 8:00 a.m. following overnight caffeine abstinence. Volunteers were then given 0 or 1 mg/kg caffeine in a milkshake, a glucose solution, or water (at 9:00 a.m.), followed by a second 0- or 1-mg/kg caffeine dose (at 9:40 a.m.), and tested again at 10:00 a.m. There was no effect of overnight caffeine withdrawal on mood or performance at baseline. Caffeine improved vigilance performance and prevented decreases in alertness, and these effects increased with the higher doses of caffeine.

MOOD AND EMOTION

Use of alcohol and other drugs is often motivated by the desire to reduce some prevailing undesired moods such as depression and boredom or to enhance some positive moods such as pleasure and joy. Many drugs such as alcohol, nicotine, and marijuana can serve both functions, depending on the dose, the situation, the user, and the intended effect on the user. Other drugs such as benzodiazepines are generally used in the belief that they can lower negative affective or mood states such as anxiety and tension. For other drugs such as cocaine or amphetamines, the primary goal is to increase arousal or produce positive or pleasurable moods. Even though the goals for using different drugs are markedly different, it is clear that a primary goal in use of all drugs is to influence affective feelings or mood states, changing negative states to less negative or to positive ones, at least for the moment.

Although the present section will focus on how drug use affects mood or affective states, it is important to keep in mind that different psychological processes often occur concurrently and affect each other. Mood, for example, can alter cognitive processes such as memory, reasoning, and decision making. Mood can also affect motivation and attention. Mood may also have an indirect impact on behavior through its influence on cognition, sensory processes, and motivation. In turn, these processes can also influence mood in a reciprocal manner. It is not possible to single out one process as more important, but since alcohol and other drugs are typically sought specifically to influence mood, we will first discuss mood states in relation to alcohol and other drug use.

EMOTIONAL REGULATION AND DRINKING

A motivational model of alcohol use (Cooper, Frone, Russell, & Mudar, 1995) assumed that drinkers try to regulate positive and negative emotions with alcohol. This model held that two factors, coping (with negative emotions) and enhancement (of positive emotions), are major factors for alcohol use and eventually, for some, abuse. Expectancies that alcohol consumption can both reduce stress and increase positive experiences and sensations may be associated with greater use of alcohol.

Some support was found for the hypothesized model with both adolescent and adult samples, showing the important role of these two opposing motives for alcohol use. However, whereas about 25%–30% drank primarily for one primary motive, either to cope with negative emotions or to enhance positive emotions, the majority engaged in drinking for both motives, depending on the situation or context.

One study examined how drinking motives to cope with negative emotions were related to moods in college students. For individuals with low motives to cope by drinking (Hussong, Galloway, & Feagans, 2005), as might be expected there was no relationship between drinking and mood. However, mood and drinking were related for individuals with high motives to cope by drinking, but the relationship was counterintuitive as there was *less* drinking on days of greater sadness, except for shy and fearful individuals.

However, this was a correlational study, which cannot rule out other interpretations. The men with higher motives to cope with alcohol may have differed from the men who were less likely to drink to deal under negative mood in other ways such as fewer social skills or resources for dealing with stress. Some of these differences, rather than their drinking motives, may have produced the inverse relationship between drinking and negative mood. In short, there are many uncontrolled variables in naturalistic studies to consider as rival causes.

A problem with studies of mood is the reliance on retrospective recall of moods and reasons for past drinking occasions. These self-reports may be distorted by forgetting and self-serving motives, and there is usually no way to corroborate them. A second problem of most survey and questionnaire research on drinking is that analyses are based on group average levels of alcohol use, stressors, and negative affective states. However, correlations between *average* drinking and *average* stress levels across groups can occur even if individuals do *not* drink more on the occasions when they experience stressors than when they do not. A direct examination within each individual's behavior over time is needed to see how many and what types of individuals drink more shortly after they encounter stressors.

To avoid these problems, some studies (Armeli, Todd, & Mohr, 2005) had participants maintain daily drinking diaries over 1–2 months, yielding multiple reports of stress levels measured closer in time to the drinking episodes. Analyses were based on ratings of stress and reports of drinking within individuals rather than on correlations of group averages. In one study, individuals who reported using avoidance coping strategies regularly to deal with stress did not demonstrate stronger positive within-individual associations between daily event stress and level of drinking. In fact, some analyses indicated that an avoidance coping style was actually related to a *lower* tendency to drink on high-stress days.

Experiments on Mood

In seeking more definitive evidence about causal roles of drugs, we turn from naturalistic observations to controlled experiments. This approach can be illustrated with a hypothetical example of how one would use experimental control to investigate the relationship between drug use and mood among autoworkers. We could form equivalent groups of men and then subject them to different levels of life stressors to see if smoking or drinking occurs more for those faced with higher stress. If so, mood should improve after the drug use. Another hypothetical approach would be to "require" different equivalent groups to smoke or drink in different amounts and then observe to see if the levels of stress that develop in their lives are higher for those who use drugs more. In this case, mood should worsen with increased drug use.

For ethical and practical reasons, these examples of experiments would probably be unlikely to be conducted. Hopefully, these fictitious cases help clarify the differences between naturalistic and experimental evidence. Now, we turn to some examples of actual experiments that examine how alcohol and other drugs affect behavior.

The effect of alcohol—or any other drug—can vary widely depending on many variables surrounding its use. Some moderators of the nature and extent of a drug's influence on behavior include time since initiation of use, the circumstances surrounding its use, and individual factors such as personality, age, or gender.

Dose Level

An important and obvious aspect of alcohol consumption that affects mood is dose level. Unfortunately, many studies that examine the effect of alcohol on mood with college participants have used only one dose, usually a small amount consisting of 1–2 drinks, but the results may differ with larger amounts.

Setting

Drinking in the laboratory experiment setting can be an anxiety-producing experience because the subject is aware of being evaluated. There is typically no assessment of the subject's existing mood at the start of the experiment, a factor that can influence mood levels during the experiment.

In contrast, in real-life circumstances drinkers ordinarily consume alcohol under a wide variety of moods, both positive and negative. Alcohol may magnify these existing moods when drinking is initiated. The angry or depressed individual may decide to drink to forget problems while the happy individual may engage in drinking to celebrate a positive event with loved ones. These different types of motives must be considered in determining how alcohol will affect subsequent moods. In addition, an individual may drink for different reasons in different contexts, and these factors must be examined in predicting the effects of alcohol.

Ascending Versus Descending Blood Alcohol Curve

One factor that may lead to conflicting findings across different studies on any behavior is the level on the blood alcohol curve when the experimenter assesses the effects of alcohol. Alcohol effects differ over the course of the curve because alcohol is being metabolized and eliminated over time. In addition, the drinker habituates to the test situation and the subjective influence of the alcohol over time. Because blood alcohol level is a joint function of dose and time since drinking, mood should be assessed at several time points, at baseline before drinking starts and during the ascending as well as the descending limbs of the blood alcohol curve.

As blood alcohol concentration (BAC) increases after drinking, drinkers feel elation and stimulation, but when BAC peaks and then declines, they typically feel fatigue or depressed. This biphasic effect of alcohol may reflect both physical and psychological factors. At the physical level, the central nervous system is depressed by alcohol, which allows for disinhibition of restraints and the experience of pleasurable feelings. After drinking stops and BAC starts to decline, an opposite rebound of negative feeling states occurs. At the psychological level, anticipation of tension relief may occur during the early part of a drinking episode, followed by fatigue after drinking ends and BAC declines.

Individual differences may exist. Light versus moderate/heavy drinkers may experience alcohol differently, with more stimulation occurring for the moderate/heavy group. A test of this assumption measured acute subjective and objective responses to ethanol (0.6 or 0.8 g/kg) or placebo at baseline and during rising and falling blood alcohol levels (Holdstock, King, & de Wit, 2000). Moderate/heavy drinkers reported greater stimulant-like and fewer sedative-like and aversive subjective effects after ethanol than did lighter drinkers. These differences occurred in the absence of any group differences in breath alcohol levels, performance effects, neuroendocrine changes, or overall reports of feeling any drug effects.

Another study (Erblich & Earleywine, 2003) found personality differences among 100 college drinkers in the effects of consuming 0.85 ml/kg of alcohol (approximately four drinks) in a lab setting. They gave self-reports of the extent that drinking had stimulating and sedating effects before drinking, 15 min after drinking during the ascending limb of the blood alcohol curve, and 45 min after drinking during the descending limb of the curve. As expected, behavioral undercontrol (i.e., sensation seeking) was strongly related to more stimulation during the ascending limb as well as to heavier drinking habits. Such patterns were more evident in drinkers who generally experience stimulation from drinking than in those who do not.

Mood ratings of students were compared at baseline, after alcohol consumption, and during anticipation of a self-disclosing speech (a stressor; Wilkie & Stewart, 2005). Relative to baseline levels, alcohol consumption increased elation and energy. During the waiting period prior to the stressor, the alcohol group reported sedation relative to the placebo group, which reported increased energy. The simulation during the ascending limb and the sedation during the descending limb were similar for those who primarily drink to cope with stress and those who drink to enhance positive affect.

Attentional Demands

An important additional factor that must be considered is the extent to which the drinker has other tasks to perform. One theory holds that alcohol reduces our capacity to deal with demands on our attention processing. Consequently, when someone is busy with a demanding task that might ordinarily generate tension, consumption of alcohol would serve to reduce tension by interfering with the capacity for attention to it (Steele & Josephs, 1988). In contrast, if the drinker has few distractions when drinking, alcohol may increase tension since the drinker may focus on worrisome problems.

In one experiment (Josephs & Steele, 1990), intoxicated and sober participants were instructed they would have to make a speech in 15 min about aspects of their body and appearance that worried them. Half were kept busy with another task while waiting to make their speech, and half were not. As predicted, anxiety was reduced in the group that was both busy and intoxicated while it increased for the groups that were not busy, not intoxicated, and neither busy nor intoxicated.

The extent to which alcohol might alter stress may also depend on the temporal sequence in which the alcohol and the stressor are experienced (Sayette & Wilson, 1991). Most laboratory studies of the effects of alcohol on stress expose the participants to stress after they have consumed the alcohol. Many real-life drinking situations involve this temporal order, but in other real situations stress is encountered after drinking has taken place.

The relationship of alcohol to stress may vary depending on which of these two types of situation is involved. Since alcohol reduces attention, it was predicted (Sayette & Wilson, 1991) that receiving alcohol first would involve less stress because the subject would not attend to the stressor as closely. In contrast, exposure to a stressor prior to receiving alcohol would produce a stronger stress because more attention would be focused on the stressor.

Male moderate-to-heavy social drinkers, given either an alcoholic or a placebo beverage, were required to give a speech for 3 min about what they "disliked about their body and appearance." During the waiting period, measures of heart rate were recorded before and after the drink. As predicted, a stress-dampening effect of alcohol on heart rate occurred only when the drink preceded the stressful speech. A replication (Sayette, Martin, Perrott, Wertz, & Hufford, 2001) with both males and females also showed that receiving alcohol prior to a stressor disrupts the appraisal process of a social stressor and leads to reduced stress.

Cigarette smoking is also linked to mood alteration. Since nicotine is a stimulant on the central nervous system, it may seem odd that smokers report that sometimes they smoke to relax. A psychological explanation is that the situation or context of smoking (e.g., study or work break, social interactions) may promote the positive mood. In addition, the relief experienced can be pharmacologically based because the smoking occurs following some period of nicotine deprivation, a condition that will produce negative states.

The ability of smoking to relieve anxiety created by a stressful task was measured either with or without a concurrent distraction (Kassel, 1997). A control group of nonsmokers was also given the task to see how distraction would affect their performance. A distractor reduced anxiety for smokers but did not help the nonsmokers. Thus, cognitive factors such as distraction, rather than pharmacological factors, may account for the anxiety relief of smoking. By narrowing the focus of attention, smoking relieves anxiety by distracting the smoker from stressful cognitions.

Smoking cigarettes may often enhance attention (Kassel, 1997). According to the stimulus-filter model, nicotine facilitates cognitive performance by screening irrelevant and annoying stimuli from the smoker's awareness. In contrast, consistent with the attention-allocation model (Steele & Josephs, 1988), nicotine enhances information processing by narrowing attention as well as by increasing perceptual processing capacity.

Smoking improved speed and accuracy of college students on verbal and spatial learning tasks relative to nonsmoking controls (Algan, Furedy, Demirgoeren, Vincent, & Poeguen, 1997), especially for men. Smoking improved verbal task performance for females and increased their confidence on the spatial task.

One interpretation of these studies is that by improving mood, cigarette smoking can enhance performance. But is the improvement a net gain in performance or just the restoration of normal function in smokers who perform poorly when deprived of smoking? The issue is identical to the one raised earlier in this chapter about whether the improvements with caffeine reflect absolute gains or relative changes back to baseline following withdrawal. Smoking may boost performance but only to a level comparable to what would have occurred if smoking had not previously occurred. Nicotine may only be relieving the unpleasant tension suffered by smokers when they have been abstinent from smoking.

One study compared cigarette smokers who either smoked as they usually would or were deprived of smoking overnight with 20 nonsmokers on a battery of mood questionnaires. Before and after a cigarette/rest period, they performed on cognitive tasks (Parrott & Garnham, 1998). At the initial session, deprived smokers reported significantly greater feelings of stress, irritability, depression, poor concentration, and low pleasure, compared with both nondeprived smokers and nonsmokers. After the rest/cigarette break, the mood states of all three groups became generally similar, although the previously deprived smokers still reported elevated depression.

A study in which some smokers were allowed to continue smoking while others had to quit for a month showed less negative mood such as depression, anger, and tension among those allowed to continue smoking (Gilbert et al., 1998). These findings also support the view that mood gains after smoking merely reflect reversal of abstinence distress.

One experiment (Perkins et al., 2008) examined the role of expectancy versus actual nicotine on mood alleviation. Male college smokers were randomly assigned to one of four conditions in a balanced placebo design that varied actual nicotine received (a mild dose of 0.6 mg vs. a denicotinized placebo with 0.05 mg) and expected dose (nicotine vs. denicotinized). A fifth group was a no-smoking control.

When negative mood was induced, the smoking groups, irrespective of nicotine content, reported negative affect as well as withdrawal and craving. Whether they expected a nicotine cigarette or a placebo had little effect. Psychological rather than pharmacological factors seemed more potent in reducing negative mood as even smokers who expected—and received—a denicotinized cigarette reported less negative affect.

Concurrent Use of Different Drugs and Mood. Smoking and drinking often occur together rather than separately in the general population (Anthony & Echeagaray-Wagner, 2000). In a clinical sample with anxiety and alcohol use disorders (Morissette et al., 2008), daily smokers reported higher levels of alcohol dependence and drank more per occasion than nonsmokers. Similarly, in a college sample (Reed, Wang, Shillington, Clapp, & Lange, 2007), smokers drank more often and in larger amounts than nonsmokers.

The causal relationships among smoking, drinking, and negative mood states are complex. One possibility is that concurrent use of alcohol and cigarettes may help some cope with negative moods, but it is also likely that the moods lead to the drug use. For example, one study (Saules et al., 2004) found that college women experiencing increased depression during the first year of college, dieting concerns, and alcohol-related problems were more likely to initiate smoking.

Alcohol and marijuana are also used together, but the effects of this drug combination on mood and behavior has not received much study. In one experiment (Chait & Perry, 1994), four conditions were compared: alcohol alone, marijuana alone, alcohol and marijuana in combination, and no drug treatment. Each drug alone produced moderate levels of subjective intoxication and some degree of behavioral impairment. The combination of drugs produced the greatest impairment on most tasks and the highest overall subjective ratings. These effects of moderate doses of alcohol and marijuana, consumed either alone or in combination, showed no residual behavioral or subjective impairment on the following day.

In another study (Heishman, Arasteh, & Stitzer, 1997), moderate alcohol and marijuana users were administered different doses of alcohol, different doses of marijuana, and different doses of a placebo in random order. Double-blind tests in which neither the experimenter nor the participant knew what conditions were being administered were given over seven separate sessions. Alcohol and marijuana had dose-related changes in subjective measures of drug effect. Ratings of perceived impairment were identical for the high doses of alcohol and marijuana. Both drugs produced comparable impairment in digit-symbol substitution and word recall tests but had no effect on time perception and reaction time.

Overview

Abundant naturalistic evidence shows that alcohol and other drugs are related to mood states. However, interpretation of the causal role of these substances is difficult especially due to self-selection affecting drug use. More precision is potentially possible with controlled experiments. However, as Table 7.1 shows, there are many important differences between alcohol and other drug use in the laboratory and under natural conditions that make it difficult to compare results obtained under the two methods.

Under either method, mood and emotional states are not easy to study. Under natural conditions, it is difficult to be on the scene to observe the drug use, so one must often rely on retrospective accounts. In experiments, this problem is avoided, but studying moods is

TABLE 7.1 Some major differences between studies of drug effects on mood in laboratory and naturalistic conditions.						
	Mood Prior to Drug Use	**Motivation to Use Drug**	**Dose Level**	**Setting for Observation**	**Duration of Observation**	**Mood After Drug Use**
Natural Conditions	Varies widely from positive to negative	User decides; varies widely with individual	Varies widely with individual, setting	Varies widely from public to private, alone or group	Varies, can be several hours	Varies widely with drug, dose, setting, individual; can reverse over time
Laboratory Experiment	Mildly negative or neutral, but not usually measured	Use is a requirement of participation in study	Usually low for ethical concerns	Neutral lab setting, usually alone or with researcher	Short duration, usually an hour or less	Mildly negative or neutral

difficult because they can be subtle, subjective, and hard to measure verbally. Moods can change rapidly and can be easily altered by the very attempt of a researcher trying to observe or measure them.

In the laboratory, the researcher administers drugs to participants to see their effects. There is no need to ask why the participant is using the drug; use is a requirement of participation. Dose levels are often much higher in the real world than in the laboratory for some users. Anxiety or suspicion may be activated when drugs are given in the laboratory setting because the participant is aware of being evaluated. Often there is no assessment of the mood prior to or at the start of the experimental session, a factor that could affect how drugs influence subsequent mood states during the session.

In contrast, in the real world, many different moods may exist for different individuals or on different occasions and settings at the point when the choice is made to use drugs. Also, individuals may consume drugs under many moods, positive as well as negative, and these drugs may alter these moods. Thus, an angry or a depressed person may decide to drink to forget problems whereas a happy individual may drink to celebrate a positive occasion with loved ones. These different motives can help determine how the alcohol will affect subsequent moods.

SENSORY MOTOR ACTIVITY

Unlike mood research, studies of sensory motor skills, especially reaction time, typically are conducted in laboratory settings since equipment to present stimuli and record responses is generally essential for this research. Laboratory situations are highly controlled but also greatly simplified from the real-life situations to which we would hope to apply experimental findings. However, laboratory experiments allow for firmer conclusions about causal influences on alcohol and other drugs on these processes.

Visual Search

In many situations, a signal or an object must be detected from among a larger set on many tasks. An athlete searches the visual field to locate teammates, and a quality control inspector examines products to identify those with flaws. In one study (Hoyer, Semenec, & Buchler, 2007) of the effects of alcohol and expectancies on visual search, participants searched for a target in large arrays of homogeneous distractor stimuli that were either high or low in similarity to the target after receiving a low dose (0.5 g/kg) or a high dose (0.7 g/kg) of alcohol or a placebo. Targets were systematically placed at a fixation point and at angles of 2.5, 5.0, 7.5, and 10.0 degrees in the visual field.

The effects of alcohol on visual search did not differ at the lower dose or the placebo. The higher dose of alcohol impaired the accuracy of target detection as the visual angle increased when targets appeared among highly similar distractors but not when they were dissimilar. Alcohol expectancies also impaired search as the placebo condition led to poorer performance than in a no-beverage control group.

Attention and Reaction Time

Alcohol has not been found to affect simple reaction time where a person has to detect or react to a single stimulus, but these results may not be highly relevant to tasks outside the laboratory. *Divided attention* tasks where several competing stimuli are present simultaneously, however, are more commonly encountered in naturalistic situations such as driving an automobile or operating equipment in the workplace.

When the situational demands for task performance require divided attention, alcohol use, even at low to moderate levels below the legal level for driving, may contribute to a high percentage of automobile accidents (Moskowitz, Burns, & Williams, 1985). Divided attention tasks are similar to the demands placed on automobile drivers when they have to attend to other vehicles in the periphery of their visual field, read street signs while steering through heavy traffic, or talk on a cell phone while merging onto a crowded freeway. Laboratory experiments create divided attention tasks where participants attend to a primary auditory or visual target and press a key when other distractor stimuli are presented at random peripheral background locations after drinking either alcohol or a placebo. The detrimental effect of alcohol on this task may be indirect, working through its influence on information processing of the central nervous system and brain rather than directly from toxic effects on motor coordination or gross muscle movement.

Motor Coordination

Studies to determine how alcohol and other drugs affect sensory motor coordination have obvious implications for understanding factors contributing to important real-life problems such as driving accidents. One study (Finnigan, Hammersley, & Millar, 1995) assessed the acute effects of alcohol and expectancy on male social drinkers on a dual tracking and reaction time task analogous to some driving skills, as well as on choice reaction time. A high dose of alcohol had large effects on both tasks, but a low dose had no significant effects. Expecting and receiving a high alcohol dose led to better performance on the primary tracking task than expecting a placebo but receiving the high alcohol dose.

Risk Perception

A controlled laboratory experiment used young drivers, ranging from nondrinking drivers to DWI (driving while intoxicated) offenders, to study alcohol's effects on their driving skill (hazard perception latency) and driving style (perceived level of risk in hazards; Deery & Love, 1996). Young adults underwent two experimental conditions, no alcohol and moderate alcohol (0.05% BAL), in a counterbalanced design. Under alcohol, subjects took longer to detect hazards and responded to them in a more abrupt manner, and these effects were particularly pronounced for DWI offenders. In general, subjects perceived active hazards (as being under their control) as less dangerous than passive hazards (environmental factors).

Driving Simulator Performance

Attention, reaction time, and motor coordination are all involved in situations like driving an automobile, and it is important to determine how alcohol affects each of them. In one experiment (Liu & Fu, 2007), eight licensed drivers, aged between 20 and 30 years, performed simulated driving tests under high- and low-load conditions at BAC levels of 0.00, 0.25, 0.4, and 0.5 mg/L. The effect of BAC varied with the task. Performance of driving tasks that involved divided attention, information processing, and short-term memory showed significant deterioration as BAC increased, while dangerously impaired driving behavior did not occur until the BAC reached 0.4 mg/L.

The effect of a small dose of alcohol (0.05%) on simulated driving performance of young healthy individuals while they performed divided attention tasks over a hands-free mobile phone was assessed at different levels of wakefulness (Iudice et al., 2005). Participants received four counterbalanced conditions: alcohol, alcohol after 19 hours of sustained wakefulness, alcohol after 24 hours of sustained wakefulness, and sober. The combination of alcohol and 24 hours of sustained wakefulness produced the highest driving impairment. Alcohol and 19 hours of wakefulness significantly affected only driving time to collision. No significant changes occurred following alcohol intake under unrestricted sleep conditions. Thus, blood alcohol levels that are regarded as "safe" after normal sleep produced significant driving impairments under prolonged wakefulness.

Driving and Other Drugs

Insofar as many alcoholics are regular smokers, the stimulating effects of nicotine may be masking some of the detrimental effects of alcohol on cognitive tasks relative to smokers who are not alcoholic (Nixon, Lawton-Craddock, Tivis, & Ceballos, 2007), Smokers performed better on a driving simulator task involving tracking and braking skills when they received nicotine than when they had a placebo treatment (Sherwood, 1995). Smoking cigarettes enhanced motor performance, but the results seemed to involve a relative rather than an absolute improvement. In other words, performance of experienced smokers was impaired when smoking was prevented but restored when smoking was possible (Sherwood, 1993). Nonsmokers and light smokers showed only small benefits of nicotine.

Alcohol receives the major concern about impaired driving, but it is not the only drug that may harm driving ability. The effects of marijuana (0%, 1.77%, or 3.95% THC) on equilibrium and simulated driving were compared (Liguori, Gatto, & Robinson, 1998). Marijuana users smoked one marijuana cigarette at the beginning of each session. After 2 min, they began a 60-min test battery that included a computerized test of body sway and brake latency in a driving simulator.

The high—but not the low—marijuana dose increased body sway. The high dose also marginally increased brake latency by a mean of 55 ms, which is comparable to an increase in stopping distance of nearly 5 ft (about 1.5 m) at 60 mph. The equilibrium and brake latency data with 3.95% THC were similar to results from past studies using a moderate dose of alcohol (0.05%).

Drinking and Driving: The Role of Self-Selection

Although alcohol and other drugs do contribute to accidents, to what extent is self-selection involved in who drives under the influence (DUI) of substances? Clearly, not everyone who drinks and drives gets arrested or in an accident. Aside from the differences in their involvement in drinking and driving behavior, do DUI offenders and non-DUI offenders differ in important other ways such as their driving skills, attitudes, speed, and circumstances? For example, if DUI offenders tend to drive more recklessly than non-DUI offenders even when sober, they might get more tickets and have more accidents than non-DUI offenders anyway.

Perhaps a subset of drinking drivers may be reckless, impulsive, and irresponsible and hence more likely to be involved in collisions and traffic violations. One approach to this question is to compare drivers with the following: collisions and having been drinking, no collisions but having been drinking, clear driving records, or a previous DUI arrest.

Some research (Perrine, 1990) on this issue involved roadside stops of drivers to measure their drinking frequency and quantity. Although 14% of the drivers in the group with no collision or arrest had measurable blood alcohol levels, only 2% had blood alcohol concentrations above 0.10, the legal limit at that time. DUI offenders had the highest percentage of heavier drinkers whereas the other categories of drivers primarily consisted of lighter drinkers (for those who died in car accidents, drinking data were obtained from next of kin). DUI offenders may not just be "unlucky" in getting arrested or into accidents. For example, they might drive faster or more aggressively than other drinking drivers, attracting the attention of law enforcement officers as well as increasing risks of accidents.

COGNITION

Alcohol and many other drugs affect cognitive functions such as memory, verbal skills, and visual-spatial-motor coordination. These skills, like sensory motor skills, are more easily studied in controlled laboratory experiments than are mood states. We will examine some examples of controlled studies of the effects of alcohol and other drugs on these functions and the explanations proposed for the effects of both short-term or acute and long-term or chronic use.

Acute Effects on Memory

How does alcohol affect memory of information or events that occur in close proximity to the drinking event? Several different aspects of memory receive the attention of researchers such as the distinction (Tulving, 1983) between memory for general information (**semantic memory**) and memory for specific information (**episodic memory**) that is available to persons who experienced an event. For example, knowledge like the major holidays or the words or melodies of popular songs would be part of semantic memory whereas what you ate for dinner last night or whom you went to the ball game with last week would be part of your episodic memory.

Memory experiments use tasks that tap different aspects of memory such as encoding, storage, and retrieval of information. Encoding refers to the active involvement of the learner in processing the information presented in the lab. It is held in memory (**storage**). A test is given either after a very short interval (immediate or short-term memory) or after up to a week or two later (long-term memory). The test of memory involves **retrieval** of the information by different methods including **recognition** where the person must select the correct material from a set of stimuli, **free recall** without any hints or prompts, and **cued recall** where some stimuli related to the material to be recalled are provided as aids.

Working memory refers to the present memory capacity and processes rather than stored memories from the past. One study (Saults, Cowan, Sher, & Moreno, 2007) compared the effects of alcohol on working memory for spatial arrays of colors or spoken digits that involved simultaneous item display versus temporal sequences of colors or spoken digits that presented items in succession. Moderate doses of alcohol impaired memory for material presented in temporal sequences but did not affect memory of simultaneous or spatial arrays. Alcohol appears to disrupt more difficult mnemonic strategies rather than shrink the overall capacity of working memory. Thus, greater impairment of recall of sequentially presented material occurs because it involves rehearsal and other executive functions whereas memory for simultaneously presented materials such as spatial arrays is less disrupted as it relies on attention span or capacity.

As compared to placebo, rising BAC levels impaired working memory with increased errors, slowed mental scanning, and slowed reaction time (Grattan-Miscio & Vogel-Sprott, 2005). However, offering a reward for good performance during the ascending limb of the blood alcohol curve counteracted impairment in scanning rate and reaction time but did not reduce errors.

Explicit memory is retention about events that occurred with the full awareness of the participant whereas **implicit memory** involves events that occurred when participants had no awareness that they would be tested later for memory. However, the distinction between the two systems in normal subjects is not accepted universally as some researchers believe there is only a single memory system.

One study (Duka, Weissenborn, & Dienes, 2001) compared the effects of a moderate dose of alcohol (0.8 g/kg) on explicit and implicit memory. Forty-eight participants were tested in one of four drug conditions varying in whether or not alcohol was given at encoding and at retrieval: alcohol-alcohol, placebo-placebo, placebo-alcohol, or alcohol-placebo. Participants had to encode and remember 80 word pairs, half with strong associates (e.g., *table-chair*) and half with weak associates (e.g., *table-horse*). They then received an implicit memory test consisting of a stem completion task in which they had to give the first word they thought of when a stimulus word was presented. Next, they received an explicit memory test with a cued recall task (stem completion). Participants also had to judge whether the items from the studied list were consciously recollected ("remembered") or were known as having been present in the studied list ("known"). Implicit memory was defined by the number of completed items that participants gave from the studied list but that they did not recognize as having been on the list.

In the cued recall task of explicit memory, alcohol did *not* affect overall performance. However, participants who had the *same* drug-state conditions at both the encoding and the retrieval stage (either alcohol or no alcohol) reported greater recollection than familiarity with study material. In contrast, participants who had *different* drug-state conditions for encoding and retrieval had equivalent recollection and familiarity judgments. For implicit memory, alcohol did not affect overall correct completion rates. However, participants who received alcohol prior to encoding reported lower *awareness* of correctly completed study items. Implicit memory was better if the drug states during encoding and retrieval were not the same.

In contrast, explicit memory was better if the drug state at encoding and retrieval was the *same,* sober both times or intoxicated both times. This phenomenon, called **state-dependent learning,** implies that memory involves both the information *and* the context in which it is learned. Thus, crime witnesses and victims often remember more details about an incident when they revisit the crime scene than if they are questioned at the police station. For similar reasons, memory for events experienced while under the influence of a drug may suffer when the individual tries to recall later when sober, or vice versa. **Blackouts**, where heavy drinkers are unable to recall events that occurred during intoxication when they are sober, are a case of **state-dependent learning**.

Expectancy Effects and Memory

Studies with the balanced placebo design have generally shown expectancy but not consumption effects of alcohol on memory (Marlatt & Rohsenow, 1980). Poorer memory occurred if participants believed they had consumed alcohol. In other words, what they believed they drank, whether an alcoholic or a nonalcoholic beverage, was more important than what they actually received.

Expectancy regarding the specific effects of alcohol can also affect behavior (Friedman, McCarthy, Bartholow, & Hicks, 2007). Individuals who expected that alcohol lowers tension were asked to meet with an opposite-gender stranger under anxiety-producing conditions. Prior to this encounter, half attended to alcohol-related words and half to non-alcohol-related words on an unrelated task. Participants holding the same expectancy about alcohol were more willing to meet the stranger if they had been primed with the alcohol- than with the non-alcohol-related words. A second study showed a similar priming effect of expectancy among individuals who expected that alcohol would increase aggression. After participants were "provoked" by a stranger, the likelihood of hostile responses toward the stranger was higher if they had first attended to alcohol-related rather than non-alcohol-related words on an unrelated task.

Alcohol effects can depend on the joint influence of dose level and task difficulty (Lloyd & Rogers, 1997). Cognitive tasks and mood ratings were completed before lunch and during the 4 hours following lunch by participants consuming drinks with no alcohol, a low alcohol dose, or a high alcohol dose with a small lunch in counterbalanced order on 3 different days. Low alcohol (approximately 0.12 g/kg) significantly increased performance on a difficult vigilance task in comparison to the no-alcohol condition. In contrast, the high-alcohol dose (approximately 0.35 g/kg) tended to impair performance of this task. No effects of alcohol on performance occurred on less demanding tasks. The low dose of alcohol also improved mood by reducing tension. Thus, the calming effects of alcohol mediated higher performance on the difficult task.

Chronic Effects on Memory

A comparison (Williams & Skinner, 1990) of heavy drinkers with moderate to infrequent drinkers matched for age, sex, socioeconomic level, and education showed much poorer performance by the heavy drinkers on a battery of cognitive, verbal, and logical reasoning tasks. Deficits were even greater among those with lower education.

A study (Weissenborn & Duka, 2003) of pattern and spatial memory examined acute effects of alcohol but also made comparisons of drinkers who differed in their chronic use levels. They used a pattern recognition task that involved a series of geometric patterns presented sequentially. Then 5 s later participants had to identify which of two geometric patterns was from the previous set. For a spatial recognition task, subjects were presented with five empty boxes at different locations on the screen. After 5 s they had to identify which of two boxes was the one positioned in a location previously shown.

Alcohol (0.8 g/kg) or a placebo was administered to social drinkers. Overall, there were no effects of alcohol on either task. However, among the participants with moderate to heavy use of alcohol, "bingers" had poorer spatial working memory and pattern recognition than "nonbingers." Thus, the acute effects of alcohol, for the dose of alcohol used, did not impair memory. However, the comparison of the bingers and nonbingers agrees with a review of other studies (Parsons & Nixon, 1998) showing impairment of cognitive processes will occur with long-term drinking of five to six or more drinks daily.

One possible physical basis for cognitive deficits stemming from chronic heavy alcohol use is the **Wernicke-Korsakoff syndrome**, a set of disorders attributed to organic brain damage (Berman, 1990). Wernicke's disease, a disorder involving confusion, ataxia (body sway), and ocular disturbances such as diplopia (double vision), is assumed to be due to thiamine deficiency and other vitamin deficits associated with prolonged alcohol use. Korsakoff's psychosis involves a short-term memory impairment (alcohol amnestic disorder) that occurs despite the ability to engage in other intellectual activities. In this disorder, also known as **anterograde amnesia**, alcoholics have difficulty remembering recent events and learning new information. In addition, alcoholism may result in a **dementia**, or global deficit of intellectual function, so that abstraction and judgment are impaired.

A different interpretation (Berman, 1990) of these impairments views the memory deficits as part of a syndrome of interrelated disruptions due to alcohol that also involves emotion and motivation. Thus, poorer attention, lower motivation, and diminished affect due to alcohol consumption might all contribute to poorer performance on memory tasks. Memory is not a function that operates independently of other processes.

Other Drugs and Cognition

Performance on cognitive tasks showed no significant differences in letter cancellation performance among smokers, deprived smokers, and nonsmoker groups, either before or after smoking. Deprived and nondeprived smokers attempted more mental arithmetic problems than nonsmokers, both before and after the rest/cigarette break. This pattern suggests that smokers have faster cognitive processing, irrespective of their nicotine status (Parrott & Garnham, 1998).

A balanced placebo design study (Kelemen & Kaighobadi, 2007) using low-nicotine-dose (0.60-mg) cigarettes examined nicotine and expectancy effects on memory and subjective feelings about the effects of smoking among 120 male and female college student smokers. Neither memory nor predicted memory performance differed from that of controls for either expectancy or nicotine conditions. The pharmacological effect exceeded the expectancy effect for most ratings of the effects of cigarettes, but expectancy enhanced ratings of cigarettes on increased wakefulness, concentration, calming, cigarette satisfaction, and hunger reduction. The presence of nicotine significantly reduced smoking urges, but expectancy alone reduced tension after smoking.

STRUCTURAL NEUROPSYCHOLOGICAL EXPLANATIONS

Two main approaches (Nixon, Tivis, & Parsons, 1995), structural and process, have been used to develop evidence for neuropsychological explanations of cognitive deficits from alcohol as summarized in Table 7.2. The structural approach attempts to find a correspondence between behavioral deficits and structural damage created by alcohol to areas of the brain assumed to underlie such behavior. It is assumed that the greater the extent of brain damage, the more impaired the functions governed by the damaged area of the brain should be. One limitation of structural approaches, until relatively recently, was that one could not determine the types of structural problems until after the person died and autopsies were performed. Now, with more advanced neuroimaging tools such as evoked response potentials, magnetic resonance imaging (MRI), functional magnetic resonance imaging (fMRI), and positron emission tomography (PET), it is possible to observe physical differences in structure in vivo.

TABLE 7.2	Predicted cognitive impairment from alcohol according to different neuropsychological models.	
	Models of Alcohol and Cognition	**Main Impairment**
Structural Theories	Generalized/diffuse hypothesis	Functions governed by both hemispheres of the brain
	Frontal lobe hypothesis	Perseverative errors
	Right hemisphere hypothesis	Visual-spatial abilities
Process Theories	Premature aging hypothesis	Similar to that found with older persons who are not alcoholic
	Increased vulnerability hypothesis	Occurs in older but not in younger alcoholics

Frontal Lobe Hypothesis

Alcoholics, compared to nonalcoholics, have poor attention, require longer to process visual-spatial information, have difficulty with abstract problem solving and learning new information, and show loss of emotional control. These deficits suggest that alcohol may have disrupted vital executive functions controlled by the frontal system. Lesions and injury to this area are associated with poor impulse control, planning, and abstraction (Kolb & Wishaw, 1990). There is evidence that alcoholism damages the **frontal lobe**, especially among older alcoholics (Oscar-Berman & Marinlovic, 2003).

One study (Pfefferbaum et al., 2001) that supports the **frontal lobe hypothesis** examined whether or not alcoholics invoked the same brain systems as controls did when performing working memory tasks that both groups were able to perform equally well. The task required participants to press a button when a target position was in the center of the field (match to center), to press a button when a target position matched the spatial position presented two items earlier (match 2-back), or to rest. Whole-brain fMRI showed diminished activation of frontal cortical systems in alcoholics relative to controls when responding 2-back as compared to resting.

The frontal lobe hypothesis may account for deficits often found among alcoholics in social cognition such as inability to detect or decipher meaning from facial expressions or speech intonations (prosody). Such impairments would reduce their ability to accurately judge the feelings or intentions of others and create misunderstandings. In one study (Uekermann, Daum, Schlebusch, & Trenckmann, 2005) comparing alcoholics and healthy controls on a comprehensive neuropsychological test battery, alcoholics had more impairment on a naming task with incongruent semantic content and on a task where they had to match affective feeling to facial expression. Alcoholics showed deficits of affective prosody processing in ambiguous situations where no additional cues were available simultaneously to help them interpret emotional prosody. A literature search (Uekermann & Daum, 2008) over a 30-year period (1977–2007) supported the view that alcoholism is associated with impaired understanding of facial emotional expression, speech intonations, and humor comprehension, all of which could stem from neurotoxic effects of alcohol on the prefrontal areas of the brain.

Overall, higher consumption of alcohol is related to more impaired cognitive performance, consistent with the frontal lobe hypothesis. However, different measures of alcohol consumption (e.g., duration, frequency, and quantity consumed) have not shown consistent relationships with the degree of neuropsychological dysfunction (Parsons, 1993). Furthermore, the presumed neurotoxic effects of alcohol on the frontal lobe may also be due to other factors such as thiamine deficiency and liver disease, two disorders associated with alcoholism. It is also important to note that the frontal lobe is not an isolated part of the brain but has important connections to other areas of the brain that may also be compromised by alcohol.

Right Hemisphere Hypothesis

The lateralization of brain function has been well documented with evidence showing that the left hemisphere governs verbal functions while the right hemisphere controls visual-spatial-motor skills. Verbal skills have been usually found to be less impaired than the visual-spatial-motor functions (Ellis & Oscar-Berman, 1989). Therefore, this lateralized pattern of impairment found with alcoholism led to the hypothesis that the right hemisphere is an area where damage is likely. Alcoholics, relative to controls, have little impairment on tasks controlled by the left side of the brain (verbal) whereas performance on tasks involving the right side of the brain (nonverbal or spatial) is disrupted. Some researchers concluded that chronic alcohol use may have impaired the functioning of the right hemisphere, but others question the validity of the right hemisphere hypothesis as an explanation for these findings of performance deficits (Ellis & Oscar-Berman, 1989). For one matter, visual and verbal tasks are heterogeneous categories. The brain may not control all tasks of either category in the same manner.

Possibly, when less impairment occurs on verbal than on visual tasks, factors other than differential damage to brain hemispheres may be operating (Ellis & Oscar-Berman, 1989). Thus, the two tasks (verbal and nonverbal) are confounded with task difficulty, with the nonverbal being more difficult. Consequently, the complexity of strategies used by participants will differ for the two types of tasks. Thus, alcoholics may do less well whenever the tasks involve elaboration of strategies, as do many verbal tasks. But if a verbal task does not require such elaboration, they should not be as impaired.

Generalized/Diffuse Hypothesis

An alternative view to the right hemisphere hypothesis is the **generalized/diffuse hypothesis**, which regards alcohol as impairing both hemispheres of the brain more or less equally with all functions disrupted by alcohol to the same extent.

Beatty, Tivis, Stott, Nixon, and Parsons (2000) found performance deficits on several widely different tasks including digit symbol, abstraction, and vocabulary tests that suggested alcohol creates widespread (i.e., diffuse) cognitive impairment by damaging multiple brain areas, each of which regulates distinct but related abilities, rather than harming localized areas. While it might be assumed that the duration of alcoholism might make a difference, comparisons of alcoholics who differed in the chronicity (duration) of their alcoholism (4 to 9 vs. 10 to 33 years) showed negligible differences.

The diffuse effects hypothesis can account for more findings than other models, but at the same time it is difficult to disprove because it covers all types of deficits (Tarter, Ammerman, & Ott, 1998).

PROCESS NEUROPSYCHOLOGICAL EXPLANATIONS

A process approach (see Table 7.2) emphasizes the underlying cognitive functions rather than the anatomical areas of the brain assumed to be affected by alcohol. Even if alcohol does not produce measurable structural changes, it might still disrupt behavioral and cognitive processing. For example, memory involves several cognitive operations such as storing of information, as indexed by errors on tasks, and retrieval of information, as reflected by speed or latency of response. In addition, a process approach examines efficiency of performance, as reflected by the ability to ignore irrelevant stimuli when performing a task. Alcohol may impair these processes so that memory is poorer even though no structural damages can be detected.

Premature Aging Versus Increased Vulnerability Hypotheses

Alcoholics have impaired performance on tasks involving the right hemisphere. An earlier explanation is that alcoholism produces accelerated or premature aging. However, the overall evidence seems to favor the **increased vulnerability hypothesis** that older brains are more vulnerable than younger brains to alcohol impairment—hence, the poorer performance of older alcoholics (Oscar-Berman, 2000).

Recovery of Functions

Some deficits in cognitive functioning found in alcoholics may be recovered following a period of abstinence. Since recovery of cognitive deficits from aging does not generally occur, such evidence would challenge the **premature aging hypothesis**. One study (Reed, Grant, & Rourke, 1992) tested memory defects in non-Korsakoff alcoholics matched for years of drinking but who had different lengths of abstinence varying from 29 days to about 2 years to 7 years. Recently detoxified alcoholics showed memory impairment relative to that of controls, but demographically matched long-term abstinent alcoholics with similar drinking histories had performance comparable to that of controls.

A review of studies of frontal lobe deficits among alcoholics (Moselhy, Georgiou, & Kahn, 2001) suggests that impairments are potentially reversible to some degree with abstinence for several months or years, but even after several years the brain may still not fully recover.

One study (Bartels et al., 2007) examined whether impaired functioning of the hippocampus in alcoholics can show recovery with abstinence. At the start of the study, 30 of the 50 severe chronic alcoholic patients showed impaired performance on verbal and spatial memory tasks, suggestive of hippocampal dysfunction. A subgroup of 32 alcoholics was observed for 2 years under conditions of strictly monitored alcohol abstinence. The

17 alcoholics who originally had distinct hippocampal dysfunction returned to normal function. The 6 alcoholics with additional causes of brain damage failed to show functional recovery while there was no change in the remaining 9 alcoholics with initially normal hippocampal function.

Elderly alcoholics also seem to recover some cognitive functions following abstinence. A study (Fein & McGillivray, 2007) compared 91 elderly alcoholics (an average age of 67.3) who had been abstinent for an average of 14.8 years with age- and gender-matched controls on an array of cognitive tasks including attention, verbal fluency, abstraction/cognitive flexibility, psychomotor, immediate memory, delayed memory, reaction time, spatial processing, and auditory working memory. Overall, the groups performed comparably to controls on the assessments of cognitive function. The researchers recognized that the results may partly be due to selective survivorship. Cognitively healthier alcoholics may be more likely to maintain intact cognition for more years.

Overview

Cognitive impairment from alcohol falls along a continuum. Impaired neurological functioning can slow processing of information, impede new learning, interfere with abstraction, and reduce visual spatial performance (Evert & Oscar-Berman, 1995). At the extreme end of impairment is the Wernicke-Korsakoff syndrome, which is distinguished by anterograde amnesia. Support for a continuum hypothesis would be strengthened if evidence showed a positive correlation between the amount of alcohol consumed and the degree of cognitive impairment. However, such evidence is not available. A clear test is difficult to devise, however, as cognitive impairment is also due to other factors such as age. Gender differences could also be a factor but have not been studied much. It is difficult to devise a comparable test due to greater body fat for women (Nixon, 1995). Motivational and emotional factors as well as diet and the presence of other diseases also play a role.

A component-process model of alcohol effects on memory (Garland, Parsons, & Nixon, 1993) involved a distinction between an episodic store of specific events and facts and a knowledge information store of general concepts and ideas. Alcoholics may be impaired in either store in three different aspects of memory: the *availability* or persistence of information, the access or speed of *retrievability* of memory, or the *efficiency* of memory (ability to distinguish between relevant and irrelevant information). Efficiency may be particularly sensitive to impairment among alcoholics.

In one test of this model (Nixon & Parsons, 1991), alcoholics and controls received descriptions of four plants, two that were healthy and two that were unhealthy. Information was provided about the type of care each plant had been receiving such as type of plant food and amount of watering. Based on this information, participants were told how another plant had been treated. Their task was to predict and explain what the health of the other plant would be. Although alcoholics and controls were equal in predicting the physical condition of the plant, the alcoholics were less efficient, as they had more difficulty in determining the relevant treatment variable, type of food or amount of watering that was responsible for the condition of the plant.

In addition, there may be complex interactions between different cognitive functions such as compensatory adjustments. Alcoholics with deficits in one area of cognitive functioning may adapt through use of other intact capacities (Ham & Parsons, 1997). Verbal skills are generally intact among alcoholics whereas visual-spatial abilities are impaired. On visual-spatial tasks, alcoholics may try to use verbal skills to compensate for their inability to perform well. On the other hand, deficits in cognitive abstraction are closely related to verbal skills so that deficits in problem solving, which involve abstraction, cannot be as readily compensated for by verbal abilities. Tests of male and female alcoholics (detoxified 3–6 weeks before testing) and nonalcoholic controls gave some support for a compensatory model of cognitive functioning.

Summary

A variety of methods, naturalistic and experimental, have been used to test hypotheses about the effects of alcohol and other drugs. With experiments, it is possible to "separate" effects of drug use from the influence of beliefs about drug use's effects to determine how much each factor contributes to the observed behavior. An experiment can also help rule out self-selection biases such as when observed differences are not caused by drug use but merely reflect the possibility that those who tend to use drugs more may also differ in other important respects from those who use them less or not at all.

But on the negative side, experiments are usually limited to legal drugs. Experimental situations are artificial, and the behavior may not be reflective of behavior outside the laboratory. Sampling is limited to a small number of participants as well as to unrepresentative samples of the general population; observations are of short duration, and participants know their behavior is being observed. In laboratory settings, participants may be administered drugs, quite unlike the situation in real life when the person decides when or whether to take a drug.

The balanced placebo design is one method aimed at examining the combined as well as the separate influences of the expectancy of consuming alcohol and the pharmacological factor. Studies using this paradigm have shown that for light to moderate drinkers, many behaviors are altered by the belief or expectancy that they have consumed alcohol. However, the method is limited to the study of acute effects of small doses of alcohol due to ethical problems as well as to issues of credibility. Outside the laboratory and its controlled experiments, expectancy and pharmacological effects are inseparable and may even reinforce each other.

In laboratory experiments, opportunity for alcohol consumption is determined on a random basis by the researcher. But under naturalistic circumstances, individual psychological and physiological factors determine who may be more disposed to use as well as abuse alcohol. Consequently, the reactions to alcohol consumption may differ for light and heavy drinkers, even before drinking problems develop. Thus, the psychological effects of alcohol cannot be fully understood without including consideration of other differences among individuals who differ in their voluntary levels of alcohol consumption.

The psychological effects of a given amount of alcohol for chronic abusers and alcoholics differ from those for light to moderate drinkers. Depending on the extent of alcohol abuse, chronic use may have produced tolerance, organic damage, and nutritional deficits. Also, the psychosocial deterioration associated with alcoholism may alter the expectancies and motives for drinking. Such differences should lead to different behavioral and experiential consequences of alcohol consumption for those who are alcohol dependent versus those who are not.

Use of alcohol and other drugs is often motivated by the desire to reduce some prevailing undesired moods such as depression and boredom or to enhance some positive moods such as pleasure and joy. Many drugs such as alcohol, nicotine, and marijuana can serve both functions, depending on the dose, the situation, the user, and the intended effect on the user. Other drugs such as benzodiazepines are generally used in the belief that they can lower negative affective or mood states such as anxiety and tension. For other drugs such as cocaine and amphetamines, the primary goal is to increase arousal or produce positive or pleasurable moods. Even though the goals for using different drugs are markedly different, it is clear that a primary goal in use of all drugs is to influence affective feelings or mood states, changing negative states to less negative or to positive ones, at least for the moment.

Alcohol and many other drugs affect cognitive functions such as memory, verbal skills, and visual-spatial-motor coordination. These skills, like sensory motor skills, are more easily studied in controlled laboratory experiments than are mood states. Some examples of controlled studies were examined regarding the effects of alcohol and other drugs on these functions, and explanations were proposed for the effects of both short-term or acute and long-term or chronic use.

We hope to ultimately understand real-life drug use, but too many uncontrollable variables impede our comprehension. Laboratory studies afford a more precise form of observation but at the cost of reduced generalizability. Using evidence from both methods may enable us to gradually refine our models and derive more valid conclusions from our observations.

Stimulus/Response

1. Use your own experience to describe how mood states have been both antecedents to and consequences of alcohol and other drug use.

2. Students who drink excessively have been found to get lower grades. Does this prove that alcohol impairs learning? Suggest alternative explanations for this correlation. Design a study to provide more conclusive evidence.

3. Stimulants such as cocaine, crack, and methamphetamines are thought to cause hyperactivity. Marijuana is thought to cause an "amotivational syndrome" and mood changes. Could self-selection be involved in these examples? How can you test this possible alternative explanation for these correlations?

4. Mothers Against Drunk Driving (MADD) conducted a survey in 1998 and found that Americans support tougher anti-drunk-driving laws. Most Americans (70.1%) support lowering the legal drunk driving limit to a blood alcohol level of 0.08. More than 80% support impounding repeat offenders' vehicles, and 65% support permanent vehicle confiscation. Alcohol treatment was backed by 91% and jail sentences by 85%. How effective do you think each of the proposed changes would be in deterring drinking and driving? Can you think of other measures that might be as effective? Are there some measures that you think would be especially relevant for younger drivers?

Interpersonal Processes

Aggression
Moderators of the Alcohol-Aggression
   Link
A Moderator Variable Model

Sexual Activity
Summary
Stimulus/Response

Beer glasses are by far the most common weapon of assault . . .

—Jonathan Shepherd

Alcohol and other drugs are often consumed, publicly or privately, in a social context. In some situations, such as at a party, almost everyone may be using alcohol or other drugs, but in other circumstances, there may be few or no other users. In both situations, use of these substances can produce immediate and delayed consequences, both positive and negative, on the nature of social interactions between the users and those around them.

In this chapter, we will examine the relationship between the use of alcohol and other drugs and two important forms of interpersonal behavior, aggression and sexual behaviors. Although they are highly dissimilar, they share one common feature: Societal restrictions and prohibitions against their expression often exist for both behaviors. Aggressive behaviors, which will be discussed first, refer mainly to conduct that involves harm to others or, at least, intent to harm. In extreme cases, these actions involve violence against others. Then, we will examine the relationship of alcohol and other drugs to sexual behavior, both consensual sexual relationships and unwanted sexual advances.

AGGRESSION

What is the relationship between the use of alcohol and other drugs and the occurrence of aggression? Because alcohol is commonly believed to be a disinhibitor, expectations or learned beliefs may increase aggressive tendencies that often occur with drinking in addition to any pharmacological effects operating at the neurophysiological level.

Correlational Evidence

Ample naturalistic evidence suggests that alcohol use often precedes or accompanies violent behavior. Almost daily, one hears about homicides, assaults, attempted murders, burglaries, and robberies in which the perpetrators, the victims, or both had been drinking. Victims of violent drinkers typically are acquaintances of the aggressors. They tend to be similar to the aggressors, being young, never married, and frequenters of bars (Fillmore, 1985). Despite the many accounts of incidents of violence reported in the news and portrayed in dramatic presentations, violence occurs relatively infrequently (Roizen, 1997). Most people, fortunately, either do not commit violent actions or commit them rarely.

In more than half to two thirds of homicides and assaults, the offender, the victim, or both had been drinking (Welte & Abel, 1989). In cases where victims appeared to have been instigators of the fatal incidents, they were more likely to have been intoxicated than when defendants were the provokers. In a large-scale study (Pernanen, 1991) in Thunder Bay, Ontario, about half of the sample (n = 900) reported being victims of violence, although in about 40% of cases, the incident had occurred as long as 8 years ago. In about half of these violence incidents, alcohol was involved for at least one party, with the offender being the drinker in 51% of these cases, whereas the victim was the solitary drinker in 30% of the cases.

A national clinical survey (Shaw et al., 2006) based on the 1,594 people convicted of homicide in England and Wales between 1996 and 1999 found that more than one third (42%) had a history of alcohol misuse or dependence and 40% had a history of drug misuse or dependence. Alcohol was judged to have had a major role in 52 (6%) and a minor role in 364 (39%) homicides. Drugs played a major role in 6 (1%) and a minor role in 138 (14%) homicides. Persons who were comorbid for severe mental illness and substance misuse committed 42 homicides (17%).

A high incidence of alcohol use has been reported in date or acquaintance rape (Abbey, 1991). Estimates vary widely, depending on how it is measured. Overall, studies suggest about 25% of American women have experienced sexual assault, including rape with alcohol consumption by the perpetrator, the victim, or both involved in about half of the incidents (Abbey, Zawacki, Buck, Clinton, & McAuslan, 2001).

Prison Populations

A different large source of available data is from prison inmates among whom there are high rates of alcohol use and problems. The Arrestee Drug Abuse Monitoring program (Martin, Bryant, & Fitzgerald, 2001) at 39 prisons for men and 25 for women assesses alcohol and drug use of arrestees in city and county detention facilities. The 2003 findings for men showed these rates: positive alcohol urinalysis, 9.5%; binge drinking in the last 30 days, 47.9%; heavy drinking in the last 30 days, 26.1%; and alcohol dependency risk, 28.6%. The rate of positive urinalysis was much higher for women than for men (86.4%), but women had lower rates of binge drinking in the last 30 days (34.9%), heavy drinking in the last 30 days (15.8%), and alcohol dependency risk (23.8%).

The high rates of drinking are not necessarily evidence that alcohol is causally linked to violent crimes. Although many inmates were arrested for violent crimes, the actual *percentage* of inmates involved in violent crimes is relatively small. A survey with a stratified sample of state and federal correctional facility inmates in the United States (Mumola, 1999) found only 22% of state inmates—and even fewer federal inmates (16%)—had a prior violent offense. Almost half of these inmates claim to have been using alcohol, other drugs, or both alcohol and other drugs at the time they committed their offenses. The 2004 report (Mumola & Karberg, 2006) provided drug but not alcohol use rates. Drug use rates were stable in 2004 for state inmates while they rose for federal inmates. About 25% of violent offenders reported using drugs at the time of their crime. These reported rates of violence must be viewed cautiously as they were not verified by evidence obtained at the time of arrest. Thus, the low rates of violent crimes associated with drug use do not mean that these cases are infrequent but that on a *percentage* basis of total drug-related arrests they are low, possibly because a high percentage of drug-related arrests are for possession rather than use.

A survey of a stratified sample of 465 jails selected from 3,365 facilities examined the role of alcohol and other drugs during criminal offenses (Karberg & James, 2005). Among 440,570 inmates, violent as compared to property crimes were more likely committed while using alcohol (37.6% vs. 28.5%) whereas the reverse held for using drugs, which was lower for violent than for property crimes (21.8% vs. 32.5%). Violent and property crime rates did not differ for those reporting use of "alcohol or drugs" at the time of the crime (47.2% vs. 46.8%).

The U.S. Department of Justice Bureau of Justice Statistics compared the relationship of using alcohol versus illicit drugs to crime. The 1997 report (Mumola, 1999) concluded that there was a relationship between past use of illicit drugs, but not of alcohol, with crime.

However, the report used *different* criteria in defining alcohol use and illicit drug use, leaving the conclusion in question. Whereas juvenile *illicit drug use* was defined in terms of rates of monthly and lifetime use, *alcohol use* was more stringently defined in terms of problematic use levels, such as binge drinking and alcohol dependence. These different criteria bias the results in favor of alcohol because a heavier level of alcohol than illicit drug use was required before it was linked to crimes.

When comparable criteria were used, such as the extent of use occurring *at the time of the offense* for which an individual was incarcerated, there were no differences between the relationship of crime to alcohol versus illicit drugs. They have roughly equal roles in crime: 37% of state inmates reported using alcohol, and 33% of state inmates said they were using drugs at the time of their crimes. About 34% of federal inmates reported being under the influence of alcohol at the time of their offenses, and 22% of federal offenders said they were under the influence of illicit drugs when they committed their crimes.

In the 1997 survey of the inmates of federal prisons (Mumola, 1999), 51% reported the use of alcohol or drugs while committing their offenses. Although only one fifth of inmates in state prisons were drug offenders, 83% reported past drug use, and 57% were using drugs in the month before their offense, compared with 79% and 50%, respectively, in 1991. Also, 37% of state prisoners in 1997 reported drinking at the time of their offense, up from 32% in 1991.

Alcohol may be more dangerous than illicit drugs in some situations such as those involving violent crime such as assault, murder, and sexual assault. In fact, 42% of state prisoners and 25% of federal prisoners convicted of violent offenses reported using alcohol at the time they committed their crimes, compared with 29% of violent state offenders and 25% of violent federal offenders who said they were high on drugs when they committed their crimes. Many drug offenders were in prison primarily or only because of drug law violations. One in six drug offenders reported that they committed their crimes to get money to buy illicit drugs.

Illicit Drugs and Aggression

Due to the illegal status of many drugs, there is less objective evidence and research about their relationship to aggression or, for that matter, many other behaviors. Much of the evidence is anecdotal, involving case examples, and is not based on large samples representative of the general population.

The most widely used illicit drug, marijuana, is stereotypically viewed as a drug that may lead to reduced aggression and "mellow" feelings. One study with young users (Lee, Neighbors, & Woods, 2007) found different use patterns and consequences for individuals motivated to use by different goals. "Experimenters" used marijuana less and with fewer problems compared with those seeking enjoyment, activity enhancement, or altered perceptions or those who used it habitually. Heroin is commonly seen as producing lethargy and, except for some violent crimes to obtain drug money, is thought unlikely to provoke aggression as a direct pharmacological effect. However, due to the street conditions of use of injected drugs like heroin, users may be vulnerable to being victims of physical violence. More than two thirds of injection drug users, both men and women, were targets of physical violence (Marshall, Fairbairn, Li, Wood, & Kerr, 2008).

In contrast, stimulants such as methamphetamines, cocaine, and crack generally are believed to produce heightened arousal as well as feelings of paranoia that can lead to higher levels of violent aggression. In particular, the agitation and confusion accompanying withdrawal from the lack of access to stimulant drugs may activate aggression in chronic users and not reflect a pharmacological effect of the drugs. A study (Cohen et al., 2003) with 1,016 methamphetamine users seeking treatment at several sites found extensive abuse and violence, with 80% of women reporting abuse or violence from a partner. Men were more likely to report experiencing violence from friends and others. The occurrence of violence among drug users in treatment was related to cocaine and alcohol problems as well as to other factors such as disrespect for the law and aggressive personality (Macdonald, Erickson, Wells, Hathaway, & Pakula, 2008). The combined use of alcohol and cocaine has been found to be particularly associated with greater violence (Pennings, Leccese, & Wolff, 2002).

Benzodiazepines (minor tranquilizers) were related to less violence than alcohol because these drugs are sedatives and reduce anxiety (Haggard-Grann, Hallqvist, Langstrom, & Moller, 2006). Paradoxically, there is also clinical evidence that some users of this class of drugs may display anger and hostility and become violent (Daderman, Fredriksson, Kristiansson, Nilsson, & Lidberg, 2002).

The circumstances surrounding drug dealing also contribute to violence. Battles over turf or territory, fraudulent selling of inferior grades of an illicit drug, or disputes over money from drug transactions lead to "systemic violence." Although these violent behaviors are nonetheless serious problems associated with illicit drug use, they must be recognized as socially and psychologically, rather than pharmacologically, determined.

Critical Evaluation

The overall evidence would appear to establish alcohol and drugs as dangerous substances that contribute to many undesirable social consequences. One limitation to this evidence, however, is that it is largely based on self-reports, which may be inaccurate due to faulty memory or deliberately distorted to reduce punishment.

In addition to forgetting, overestimates of drinking may occur if drunkenness is invoked as an *excuse* (MacAndrew & Edgerton, 1969). Thus, if offenders think they may receive lighter punishment when their misdeeds are perceived as due to the influence of alcohol, they may claim they were drinking more than they actually were.

Measurement Issues

Assessing the level of alcohol use is difficult. With retrospective recall, there is often no accurate information about how close in time the drinking occurred in relation to the offense. The accuracy of measuring drinking may not be equivalent for all offenses, being higher for offenses in which the offender is apprehended on the scene or shortly thereafter than for those in which weeks or months have passed since the incident. Often, only dichotomous yes-no assessments, rather than measures of degree of drinking, are used to determine if drinking occurred in association with a violent incident. Thus, the evidence usually cannot accurately answer the question of whether alcohol and other drugs directly *caused* criminal activities.

Sampling Issues

A problem with evidence from prison inmates is that it involves atypical samples that may not be easily generalizable to the general population. The relationship of alcohol to violent crimes may be inflated among inmates because intoxicated offenders may be more likely to be apprehended than lighter drinkers or nondrinkers (Murdoch, Pihl, & Ross, 1990). In addition, some cases could involve mistaken or false charges.

Control Comparisons

Regardless of whether a general or a prison population is studied, a sample of sober individuals is needed as a baseline comparison to determine how much aggression occurs in the absence of drinking (Lipsey, Wilson, Cohen, & Derzon, 1997). Often, this control group is absent when statistics are cited about the extent of alcohol use among offenders (Roizen, 1997). To argue that a link exists between violence and drinking, one must realize that it is not sufficient to demonstrate that a certain percentage of violent offenders had been drinking at the time of arrest. In Figure 8.1, the percentage of violent offenders among drinking arrestees (Cell 1) should be compared with the percentage of violent offenders who were

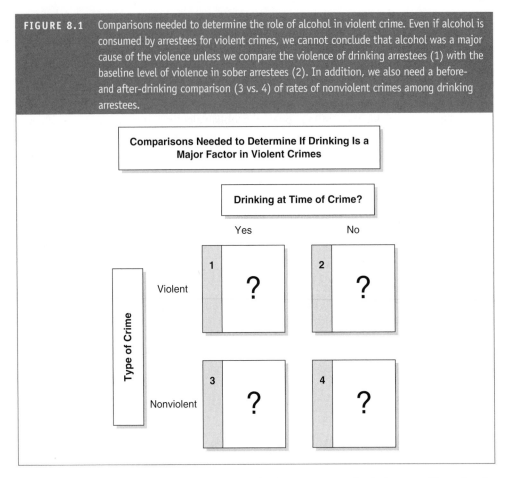

FIGURE 8.1 Comparisons needed to determine the role of alcohol in violent crime. Even if alcohol is consumed by arrestees for violent crimes, we cannot conclude that alcohol was a major cause of the violence unless we compare the violence of drinking arrestees (1) with the baseline level of violence in sober arrestees (2). In addition, we also need a before- and after-drinking comparison (3 vs. 4) of rates of nonviolent crimes among drinking arrestees.

sober when arrested (Cell 2) and found to be higher. Even so, alcohol may still not be the primary cause of the violence and drinking combination; third-variable explanations also might account for why some people both drink more and are more violent. For example, some psychiatric conditions might lead some individuals to engage in more drinking and more violent behavior. Assuming that alcohol use is related to violent crimes, is the relationship any stronger than that between drinking and nonviolent crimes (Cells 3 vs. 4 in Figure 8.1)? Hypotheses about the type of processes that enable alcohol to increase crime would depend on whether drinking increases violent and nonviolent crimes to the same extent.

Since it is not possible to have the control conditions of a lab experiment when studying naturally occurring events, one study (Phillips, Matusko, & Tomasovic, 2007) employed a case control design with 100 men arrested for an aggravated assault or homicide during a conflict with another man. In this method, each arrestee served as his own control comparison by describing both the violent outcome incident for which he was arrested as well as a conflict that had a nonviolent outcome. A key difference between the two situations was whether the assailant had a gun with him. Thus, drinking per se was not as likely to provoke lethal male-male violence in conflicts as when it was combined with carrying a gun.

Solitary Versus Dyadic Drinking

An analysis of the alcohol-aggression correlation also must distinguish between situations in which only the offender or only the victim was drinking (**solitary drinking**) and situations in which both were drinking (**dyadic drinking**). The first situation implicates alcohol as a possible cause of violence by the drinker, the second situation is somewhat at odds with a causal interpretation, and the third situation is ambiguous about causality (Murdoch et al., 1990). Thus, if both parties involved in an assault had been drinking, it is difficult to determine whether alcohol instigated violence on the part of the offender, the victim, or both. Also, in some cases, it may not be certain which party was the offender and which party was the victim. Finally, in addition to alcohol possibly leading to aggression, an opposite consequence also may occur for heavy drinkers. They themselves become targets for violent victimization because their intoxication may render them more vulnerable.

A similar problem arises in explaining cases of acquaintance rape in which both parties have been drinking. Alcohol does not automatically activate sexual aggression but may facilitate it through many processes that could be affected by drinking (Abbey, 1991), as suggested by Figure 8.2. In this model, culturally learned aspects of gender roles serve as background factors. The male's expectation that alcohol increases sexual feelings may encourage his advances. The female's drinking may act as a stereotypical signal of sexual readiness that the male misinterprets. Once the male consumes alcohol, he may be less likely to interpret resistance as refusal and regard it as playing hard to get. As for the female, her drinking also might lower her ability to continue her resistance.

Pharmacological Versus Psychological Factors

Alcohol and other drugs may influence behavior through either pharmacological or psychological processes or both. Drugs such as alcohol, barbiturates, and benzodiazepines act as central nervous system depressants whereas other drugs such as amphetamines and cocaine increase arousal and stimulation. All psychoactive drugs alter mood and conscious experience in some manner, and these effects may influence social behaviors such as aggression and sexually intimate behaviors.

In addition—or alternatively—alcohol and other drugs may influence social behavior through their influence on cognitive and affective factors that determine the appraisal and meaning of social situations. These *psychological* factors, such as beliefs and expectations about drug effects, may affect social interactions.

For example, a comment made in jest that would ordinarily be taken in stride by a sober person may be misinterpreted as hostile by someone who has been drinking. In contrast, someone who is lighthearted from drinking might ignore criticism or not regard the comments as threatening.

Experimental Evidence

Studies using an experimental group that receives alcohol and a control group that receives a nonalcoholic placebo beverage generally find that the alcohol condition leads

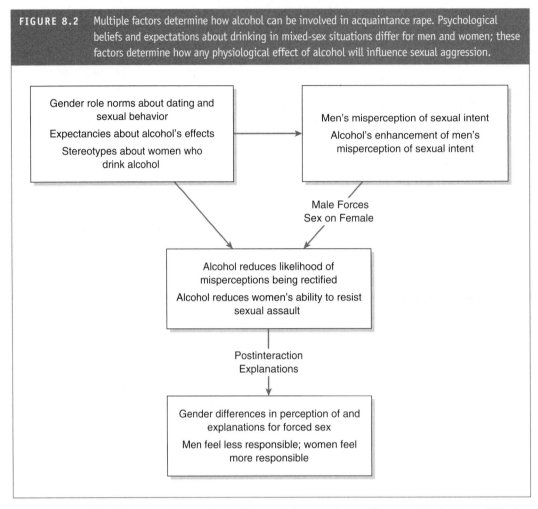

FIGURE 8.2   Multiple factors determine how alcohol can be involved in acquaintance rape. Psychological beliefs and expectations about drinking in mixed-sex situations differ for men and women; these factors determine how any physiological effect of alcohol will influence sexual aggression.

Source: From "Alcohol's Role in Sexual Assault," by A. Abbey, L. T. Ross, and D. McDuffie, 1994, in R. R. Watson (Ed.), *Drug and Alcohol Abuse Reviews, Vol. 5: Addictive Behaviors in Women,* Totowa, NJ: Humana Press. Copyrighted 1994 by Humana Press. Reprinted with permission.

to more aggression than the control condition (Bushman & Cooper, 1990). However, a review (Hull & Bond, 1986) of balanced placebo design studies, which control for expectancy as well as for alcohol per se, found that the effects of both consumption and expectancy of alcohol on aggression were inconsistent across different studies. The heterogeneous results about expectancy effects on aggression could be due to individual differences in the need for expressing aggression. For example, among individuals expecting alcohol, only those who have experienced recent frustration might display aggression.

Laboratory Paradigms

The experimental method allows for objective and standard measurement of the intensity and duration of the stimuli. In experiments, for ethical as well as legal reasons, actual harmful aggression is not inflicted. The situation in these studies is staged to provoke participants by having an accomplice insult or criticize their task performance. Next, these "victims" receive an opportunity to retaliate against their provokers.

For example, with a so-called *aggression machine* (Buss, 1961), real participants are supposed to teach a concept to a bogus participant over a series of trials. Whenever a mistake is made, the participants' task is to use the machine to select an intensity of electric shock to the learner as a form of corrective feedback. Unknown to the participants, the learner in an adjoining room does not actually receive shocks. This paradigm allows the researcher to measure how different factors, including alcohol, affect participants' level of aggressive responses, as defined by the shock intensity used.

Another widely used procedure (Taylor & Chermack, 1993) has an accomplice in an adjoining cubicle pretend to compete with a real participant on several trials on a reaction time task. The real participant is led to believe that the winner of each trial can select some level of electric shock to punish the loser. In actuality, the shock levels are selected in a predetermined sequence of increasing intensity that is independent of actual performance. The real participant receives shock on trials when *he loses*. When the real participant *wins* a trial, he gets to see what shock level his opponent had intended for him. It is assumed that the participant will be more likely to retaliate with high-shock intensities on subsequent trials when the fake participant loses if he learns his opponent had intended to give him high rather than low shocks, had the opponent won the trial.

Although these tasks are intended to measure analogues of aggressive behavior, their generalizability to real-life situations may be questioned for many reasons. For example, the two opponents do not have face-to-face interactions. These studies of aggression are mostly limited to the use of electric shock as the form of aggression, and most of them only use same-gender pairs of opponents. Finally, although the deceptions may seem realistic, some participants may not fully believe they are harming the other participant because they may assume that the researchers would not have them perform a task that inflicts real harm on others.

Expectancy Controls

A comparison (Chermack & Taylor, 1995) of the influences of pharmacological and expectancy effects on the alcohol-aggression relationship involved interviews of males about their alcohol expectancies. They were randomly divided into two groups: placebo and high-alcohol dose. They had the opportunity to behave in an aggressive manner (administer shocks) toward an unseen *opponent* on a competitive reaction time task.

High doses of alcohol resulted in higher levels of aggression compared to the placebo condition, regardless of participants' expectancies about the type of beverage they received. Thus, pharmacological factors are needed to fully account for the relationship between alcohol ingestion and aggression. Similarly, a study (Giancola, 2006) with both men and women found that for men the BAC level was a more important factor than expectancy or aggressive traits in predicting aggression on the competitive reaction time task, in line with the view that alcohol's pharmacological effect, combined with aggressive predisposition, determines aggressive behavior.

MODERATORS OF THE ALCOHOL–AGGRESSION RELATIONSHIP

Alcohol does not automatically release aggression, as often implied in typical accounts of associations between drinking and aggression. If alcohol only acts by releasing inhibitions for aggression, we should find more aggression across all situations for all individuals when aggressive feelings are activated. However, many situational and personal factors exist that appear to moderate the effect of alcohol.

Provocation

Many studies using a competitive reaction time task, with the winner in each trial getting to shock the loser, have found an alcohol-aggression link under certain conditions such as provocation, threat, and dose. Provocation was necessary for alcohol to increase aggression on the Taylor (1967) competitive reaction time task as defined by the intensity of the shock level delivered to a fictitious unseen opponent. When there was no provocation, both the alcohol and the sober conditions were low on aggression (Chermack & Giancola, 1997).

In one study (Giancola & Zeichner, 1995), 60 young, White, intoxicated social drinkers were tested using the Taylor (1967) aggression task. In a high-provocation condition, aggressive personality traits, subjective intoxication, and blood alcohol level were effective predictors of physical aggression for males. In a low-provocation condition, only aggressive personality traits and blood alcohol level predicted male aggression. None of the variables was related to aggression for intoxicated females.

The relationships among provocation, acute alcohol intoxication, and aggressive behavior were studied in men who had impaired cognitive performance on tasks associated with frontal lobe function to see if reduced cognitive functioning may reduce inhibition of aggression (Lau, Pihl, & Peterson, 1995). Half completed an aggression task while intoxicated, and the other half performed the task while sober. Aggression increased with provocation, alcohol consumption, and poorer cognitive performance. Furthermore, men with the lower cognitive performance—and presumably more frontal lobe damage—showed the greatest aggression when provoked.

Situational Conflict

The context or situation can also influence the likelihood that alcohol consumption increases aggression. If the situation is one where an individual has ambivalence about expressing aggression, alcohol may contribute to its expression. When social cues suggest that retaliation or social disapproval will occur for aggression, anxiety may be aroused that may inhibit aggression. Alcohol consumed before receiving these cues may weaken the anxiety and hence increase the level of aggression. When an individual is sober, increased anxiety cues act to inhibit aggression, whereas when an individual is intoxicated, these cues may be less noticed and hence fail to inhibit aggression. For example, if external cues in a situation that might ordinarily inhibit aggression (e.g., presence of police) are not noticed, aggression is not blocked. Alcohol consumption in sufficient amounts can increase aggression by blocking awareness of inhibitors so there is less conflict about expressing aggressive feelings. Thus, alcohol consumption increases aggression when the situation involves high but not low conflict (Steele & Southwick, 1985).

This tendency of alcohol to release our inhibitions of aggression leads to **alcohol myopia** (Josephs & Steele, 1990), a term that describes situations where our short-sighted impulses dominate our long-range interests. This effect is due to the disruptive effects of even a few drinks on our attention. When we are sober, we can weigh the pros and cons of engaging in a specific behavior, but when we are intoxicated, attention allocation is diminished and prevents such considerations.

In the attention-allocation model, alcohol has a "myopic" effect on attention that may facilitate aggression in hostile situations because the individual focuses on the more salient aggression-provoking, rather than the less salient inhibitory, cues. Aggression might be reduced if the individual can be distracted or occupied by other tasks that prevent this myopia. In one experiment (Giancola & Corman, 2007), mild electric shocks were exchanged with a fictitious opponent. One experiment showed that a moderate-load cognitive distractor task (i.e., holding four elements in sequential order in working memory) suppressed retaliatory aggression in intoxicated subjects to levels below those of a placebo control group. A second experiment compared aggression in the alcohol and placebo conditions under varying amounts of distracting cognitive load. A moderate-load distraction suppressed aggression, but cognitive loads of larger and smaller magnitudes did not.

Temporal Factors

Any effect of alcohol on aggression that might occur due to stress may depend on the temporal relationship between drinking and the stressor. For example, how alcohol affects aggression may depend on whether the drinking precedes or follows a stressor. In one study (Sayette & Wilson, 1991), more anxiety reduction occurred when alcohol was consumed *before* rather than *after* facing the stressor. Although aggression was not examined in this study, one might infer that the greater anxiety reduction due to drinking prior to the stressor would be associated with less aggression.

Ascending Versus Descending Blood Alcohol Level

In a controlled experiment (Giancola & Zeichner, 1997), male college students, under no alcohol versus 0.08% alcohol competed on a modified aggression machine against a fictitious opponent. Half of participants in each group were tested on the ascending and half on the descending limb of blood alcohol level. More aggression occurred when participants were tested on the ascending limb (when alcohol has an activating effect), but alcohol had a sedating influence on the descending limb, reducing energy.

A MODERATOR VARIABLE MODEL

Figure 8.3 (Chermack & Giancola, 1997) is a model of many factors that affect whether alcohol use leads to aggression. Childhood experiences with aggression, family history of substance abuse (SA), executive cognitive function (ECF) skills, and temperament are among the distal factors affecting the likelihood in a given situation that an individual's

FIGURE 8.3 Model of moderators of aggression. Note that the immediate setting and psychological factors are proximal determinants of the effects of alcohol on aggression. In addition, distal background factors from childhood and family experiences also play a role.

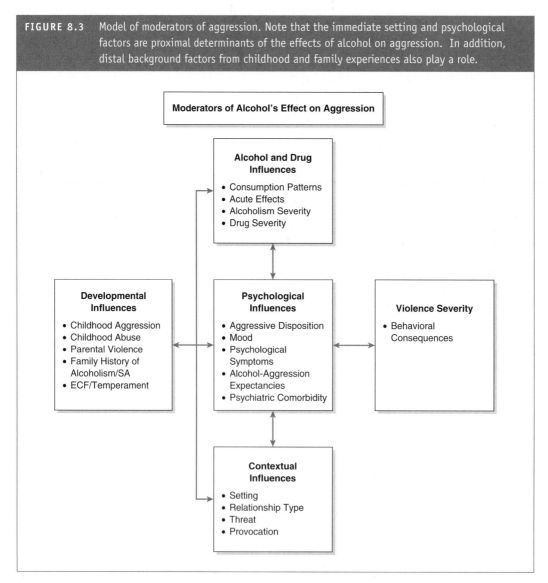

Source: From "The Relation Between Alcohol and Aggression: An Integrated Biopsychosocial Conceptualization," by S. T. Chermack and P. R. Giancola, 1997, *Clinical Psychology Review, 17*(6), pp. 621–649. Copyright 1997 by Elsevier Science. Reprinted with permission.

alcohol use will lead to aggression. Contextual determinants include the physical setting, the relationship to the other person or persons, and the amount of threat involved. The individual's own personality and present mood combine with these situational factors to determine the use of alcohol and drugs as well as how such use may lead to the expression of violence. There are many reciprocal, rather than unidirectional, effects among the components. Thus, alcohol consumption can affect mood, which in turn can affect violent behavior, but the reverse may also occur. Violent behavior can alter mood, which in turn can determine alcohol and other drug consumption.

As Figure 8.4 further suggests, proximal factors affect the extent to which provocation while under the influence of alcohol will evoke aggressive or nonaggressive behaviors. First, the individual's cognitive appraisal such as the perceived intent of the offending person can affect whether aggression or nonaggression is the appropriate reaction. The likelihood of aggression when provoked while drinking might also be reduced by consideration of the possible adverse effects on the victim as well as those that might befall the aggressor. In addition, reactions of others who witness the aggressive incident can either intensify or reduce the likelihood of continued aggression.

Causal Explanations

Correlational evidence linking alcohol and aggression is ambiguous as to causality. Drinking may reduce inhibitions, releasing aggressive behaviors. Conversely, aggressive behaviors

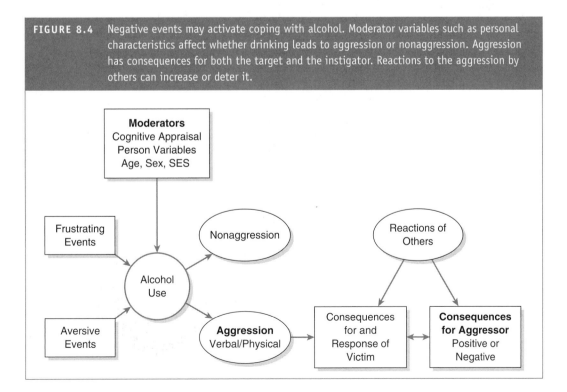

FIGURE 8.4 Negative events may activate coping with alcohol. Moderator variables such as personal characteristics affect whether drinking leads to aggression or nonaggression. Aggression has consequences for both the target and the instigator. Reactions to the aggression by others can increase or deter it.

could activate guilt or fear that may increase drinking. Finally, a process involving a third factor, such as personality, could increase both drinking and aggression independently.

A prospective longitudinal study can provide some answers. Behaviors that precede other behaviors are eligible to be considered causes of the later behaviors. In contrast, later behaviors cannot logically be viewed as causes of earlier behaviors. One such study using a random telephone survey (White, Brick, & Hansell, 1993) was conducted over 3 years to examine the transition in alcohol use, aggression, and their relation to each other during early adolescence. Three different cohorts consisting mainly of White working-class and middle-class samples, ages 12, 15, and 18, were tested. They were selected to assess the temporal sequence of aggression and alcohol consumption, the stability of the relationship, and how changes in one affect the other.

The results do not support a reciprocal model whereby alcohol and aggression affect each other. Instead, at least for males, early aggression tendencies at age 12 appeared to lead to early alcohol use by age 15, but this early use of alcohol did not increase later aggression. Furthermore, early aggression was a better predictor of later alcohol problems than was early alcohol use.

The results favor the model in which early aggressive tendencies lead to increased later drinking. This naturalistic study shows that over an extended period of several years, more aggressive individuals tend to drink heavily and behave aggressively when intoxicated. These findings might seem in conflict with laboratory experiments in which the opposite sequence occurs, with higher alcohol use preceding the aggression. However, it must be kept in mind that laboratory experiments deal with behavior within a specific short-term period, whereas naturalistic studies typically span months or years.

SEXUAL ACTIVITY

Candy is dandy but liquor is quicker.

—Ogden Nash

Intimate sexual encounters, especially with new partners, often involve the use of alcohol and other drugs because they are widely believed to enhance sexual arousal and lower inhibitions. Alcohol and other drugs are widely believed to act as aphrodisiacs, so suitors ply their potential partners with these substances to weaken any resistance. Drinking thus may increase the advances and passion of the individual initiating the sexual encounter and also increase the recipient's acceptance of overtures. Drinking may precede, accompany, and follow sexual intimacy. The questions of research interest are whether drinking or using other drugs directly or indirectly increases sexual activity and, if so, what the underlying psychological or physiological processes are.

The urgency created by the severity of the HIV/AIDS crisis shifted the focus of alcohol in sexuality research from the study of its effect on sexual behaviors to the concern with identifying sexual behaviors directly related to disease transmission. A priority is to determine whether alcohol use increases the likelihood of engaging in risky sex (i.e., sexual behaviors that increase the risk of contracting HIV) such as intercourse without condom protection, with multiple partners, and with partners of unknown HIV status. The likelihood of unsafe sex practices might be greater because alcohol may impair judgments and sexual decision making.

Studies on these concerns have been conducted almost exclusively with survey methods designed to assess sexual knowledge, sexual attitudes, and sexual behaviors. Sexual arousal, on the other hand, which obviously is a key factor leading to sexual engagement, has been relatively abandoned after early laboratory experiments conducted around the late 1970s.

Survey Evidence

As adolescents mature, they become involved in activities that were previously forbidden to them and are generally restricted to adults, such as alcohol consumption and sexual intimacy. An analysis (Finer, 2007) of data in the National Survey of Family Growth found that from 1982 to 2002, the incidence of premarital sex was over 75% for youth under 20 years of age. Because alcohol is popularly viewed as a disinhibitor, it is hardly surprising that alcohol is associated with increased sexual activities. One study (Baskin-Sommers & Sommers, 2006) found adolescent use of alcohol and methamphetamines was linked to unprotected sexual intercourse and multiple sexual partners. A study (De Genna, Larkby, & Cornelius, 2007) of pregnant adolescents found that an early age of first alcoholic drink predicted problem alcohol use before pregnancy and drinking during pregnancy.

The annual Youth Risk Behavior Surveillance System (YRBSS) report provides information about a broad set of six health risk behavior categories from a representative sample of public school students in the United States. An analysis (Lowry et al., 1994) of the 1990 report, based on more than 11,000 students, found that students who reported no substance use were least likely to report having had sexual intercourse, having had four or more sex partners, and not having used a condom during the last incidence of sexual intercourse.

The 2007 YRBSS report (Centers for Disease Control and Prevention, 2008) showed that in the past 3 months 35% of high school students nationwide had been sexually active (with one or more partners). These rates increased for males from 22% for 9th grade to 48% for 12th grade and for females from 18% for 9th grade to 56.7% for 12th grade. About 68.5% of males and 54.9% of females reported use of a condom during the most recent sexual intercourse. Among these currently sexually active students, 27.7% of males and 17.7% of females reported use of alcohol or drugs during the most recent sexual intercourse. These rates varied by race, showing 21.8% for White, 21.3% for Hispanic, and 16.4% for Black students.

A survey (Meilman, 1993) of 439 randomly selected college students found that 35% reported some form of sexual activity after starting college that was influenced by drinking. While under the influence of alcohol, 18% had engaged in sexual intercourse, and 15% had not used safe-sex techniques. Three measures—any form of sexual activity, sexual intercourse, and abandonment of safe-sex techniques—had a positive association with heavier alcohol use and binge drinking.

Alcohol use was related to inconsistent condom use among college students with multiple sexual partners according to a survey (Desiderato & Crawford, 1995) of 398 undergraduates.

In a 3-month period, two thirds of the students had engaged in sexual intercourse, and one third of these reported having more than one sexual partner. Almost half of the sexually active students did not use a condom during their last sexual encounter, and only one fourth reported using condoms consistently.

Alcohol use and sexual risk taking in specific events involving first and repeat oral and vaginal sex encounters were reported by 80% of 221 at-risk male and female college student drinkers (Goldstein, Barnett, Pedlow, & Murphy, 2007). Alcohol use was associated with riskier sex with new as compared to repeat sexual partners. For new sexual partnerships, regardless of the type of sex experience, knowing the partner for less time was associated with an increased likelihood of drinking as well as a tendency for new vaginal sex experiences to be associated with a lower likelihood of contraceptive use. For recent vaginal sex experiences with a repeat partner, alcohol use was more likely among those who were less committed to the relationship.

Role-Playing Risky Sex Decisions

Alcohol's effect on risky sex decisions has also been studied in hypothetical situations where participants role-played condom negotiation skills (Maisto, Carey, Carey, Gordon, & Schum, 2004). Sixty heterosexual women were randomly assigned to one of four beverage conditions: control, alcohol-low (0.35 g alcohol/kg), alcohol-moderate (0.70 g alcohol/kg), or placebo. Then all participants completed measures of motivation to engage in risky sex and condom use negotiation skills. A higher dose of alcohol and stronger alcohol expectancies were associated with greater motivation to engage in risky sexual behavior. However, perceived intoxication, rather than actual alcohol consumption or expectancies, was the best predictor of condom use negotiation skills.

A study (Maisto et al., 2004) randomly assigned 48 young heterosexual males to one of three beverage conditions: control, alcohol (0.65 g alcohol/kg), or placebo. Then participants completed measures regarding attitudes toward condom use, intention to engage in risky sex, and condom use negotiation skills. Alcohol impaired negotiation skills and increased intention to engage in risky sex, as compared to controls, but did not affect attitudes regarding condom use.

Young heterosexual men and women rated their *perceptions* of unprotected sex consequences in one study (Davis, Hendershot, George, Norris, & Heiman, 2007). They received alcoholic (BAL, 0.10%) or nonalcoholic drinks before completing a risky sexual decision-making task that included a quantitative measure of sexual decision-making cue attention. Intoxicated participants reported greater sexual risk intentions than sober participants.

Specific Incidents

Most surveys of sexual activity are based on correlations of overall rates of sexual activity and drinking. However, the study of specific sexual incidents can provide stronger evidence about the role of alcohol use in sexual behavior because it can establish whether drinking and sexual activities occurred together during specific incidents.

In one survey of specific incidents of sexual activity, 968 adults were asked about the circumstances of two sexual encounters: their most recent sexual experience and their most recent encounter involving a new sexual partner (Temple & Leigh, 1992). Encounters with new partners were more likely to involve alcohol, but the use of alcohol was not significantly associated with risky sexual activity. Sexual attitudes proved to be a stronger predictor of unsafe sex.

A clearer picture of any causal relationship between drinking and sexual practices may be obtained if data are obtained on a daily basis rather than retrospectively. A study (Leigh & Stall, 1993) based on daily diaries of drinking and sexual events of 99 men and women over a 10-week period showed that alcohol consumption was associated with a general reduction of sexual activity and had no effect on risky sexual behaviors related to AIDS transmission. Apparently, lapses in judgment about sexual practices due to alcohol consumption may not be as strong as retrospective recall studies suggest.

A review (Weinhardt & Carey, 2000) of studies of specific events involving alcohol and sexual behavior together found no clear evidence that alcohol is a cause of or major contributor to risky sexual behavior. The tendency to use or not use condoms during sexual relations seems to be consistent within individuals whether they have or have not been drinking. Personality traits, attitudes, and beliefs may be "third variables" that lead to both behaviors. Thus, people likely to drink heavily may also be more likely to engage in more sexual risk behavior because of a specific personality trait or a constellation of attitudes and beliefs rather than because of a causal unique relationship between alcohol use and sexual risk behavior.

Overview

Overall, the evidence shows that alcohol and other drug use is related to early sexual activity, more frequent sexual involvement, and riskier sexual practices such as unprotected intercourse among sexually active adolescents. However, these correlational studies are cross-sectional and do not prove that alcohol per se causes adolescents to take greater risks such as engaging in unprotected sexual intimacy. A third factor such as personality characteristics might contribute to higher alcohol and other drug consumption as well as to earlier sexual intimacy and risky sexual behaviors. For example, among young adolescents, both activities can be viewed as normatively deviant behaviors. Hence, both behaviors might occur in rebellion to parental and societal norms and expectations, leading to the early development of both drinking and risky sexual activity as separate forms of delinquency.

Clinical Evidence

Clinical studies deal with a more restricted population of individuals who are seeking treatment for alcohol abuse. They may also have other problems, such as **sexual dysfunction**, that may stem from their alcohol abuse. In research that directly measures sexual dysfunction with couples in a laboratory setting, the reverse situation exists. The pioneering team of Masters and Johnson (1966) studied a sample of individuals who were seeking treatment for sexual dysfunction, not for alcoholism. However, alcohol was found to be a possible contributing factor in many instances. Impaired sexual performance among this population may have been due to the acute effects of alcohol in some cases but may have been due to the chronic effects of alcohol abuse in other instances. As the gatekeeper observed in Shakespeare's *Macbeth*, Act II, Scene 3, "Much drink may be said to be an equivocator of lechery."

Alcohol abuse eventually may lead to risky sexual behaviors and to sexual dysfunction. In turn, sexual impairment could activate a cycle of further alcohol abuse as a form of self-medication to cope that actually further impairs sexual performance. Thus, among chronic alcoholics, impaired sexual performance and fertility occur as a consequence of alcoholism (Emanuele & Emanuele, 1998) as alcohol abuse can interfere with testosterone production, disrupt sperm maturation, and reduce male secondary sexual reproductive hormones.

A survey of women in the general population (Wilsnack, Klassen, & Wilsnack, 1984) found that those who drank at high levels had greater sexual dysfunction (lack of sexual interest, low frequency or lack of orgasm) than light drinkers. Moderate levels of drinking were associated with the lowest frequency of sexual dysfunction.

In identifying the causes of sexual dysfunction, most views have placed the blame on some aspect of the impaired individual. However, because dysfunction also may be a function of the partner, this may be an oversimplification. Thus, alcoholic wives are often married to alcoholic husbands. If the wives are sexually unsatisfied, to what extent are these conditions created or influenced by the alcoholism of their husbands? If the husbands themselves are physiologically impaired by alcohol or are less attractive psychologically due to their intoxicated condition, they may contribute to the wives' lack of sexual responsiveness.

Conversely, sexually inhibited wives may turn to alcohol or be encouraged by their husbands to drink to overcome inhibitions. Reliance on alcohol to engage in sex for many years may eventually lead the wife to become alcoholic and, in turn, become less attractive to her husband. This creates a vicious cycle, with further impairment of sexual interest and performance.

Marital Conflict

Although marital conflict probably exists in most marriages involving alcohol dependency, most studies have not explicitly examined the role of marital conflict in male alcoholics' sexual satisfaction. One study (O'Farrell, Choquette, Cutter, & Birchler, 1997) on this issue included married couples with an alcoholic husband, maritally conflicted couples, and nonconflicted couples without alcohol-related problems on both sexual dysfunction and sexual satisfaction.

In comparison to the nonconflicted couples, male alcoholics and their wives experienced less sexual satisfaction across a range of variables and more sexual dysfunction, including diminished sexual interest, impotence, and premature ejaculation for husbands and painful intercourse for wives. However, when contrasted with maritally conflicted couples, impotence was the only area in which alcoholics reported more difficulties. Also, there was a greater decline in the frequency of intercourse with older age among the alcoholic than among the conflicted couples. Thus, marital conflict is a major contributing factor to most of these problems. For alcoholic couples, both marital conflict and the physical effects of chronic alcohol abuse combine to create sexual dysfunction.

Sex Offenders

Some studies of alcohol's influence on sexual activity involve retrospective analysis of special populations. One example is a study of sex offenders such as rapists and pedophiles (Gebhard,

Gagnon, Pomeroy, & Christianson, 1965). The researchers attempted to determine whether drinking had been involved in these offenses. Interviews showed that about two thirds of offenders reported being intoxicated at the time of the offense, but this type of evidence is suspect due to its self-serving nature. It does not explain how the alcohol contributed to the offense. Many drinkers do not commit such crimes even when they have the opportunity. A more complete picture of the role of alcohol in these crimes also requires data about the effects of alcohol use on sex offenses by a control group of sex offenders who did not get caught.

Sexual Victims

Although males also can be sexual victims, it is a much greater problem for females. Hence, the discussion will focus on alcohol in relation to sexual victimization of females. These risks begin at an early age. A Web-based, self-administered survey (Young, Grey, Abbey, Boyd, & McCabe, 2008) collected data from 7th- through 12th-grade students (n = 1,037) in a large Midwestern metropolitan area. Students reported their sexual victimization experiences and involvement of alcohol within specific assault events. The sample was equally distributed by gender and ethnicity (White vs. Black), and the average age was 14.

Alcohol was involved in approximately 12%–20% of the sexual assault cases, depending on age and gender. For females, the presence of alcohol during assault differed significantly based on the location at which the assault occurred, ranging from 6% (at the survivor's home) to 29% (at parties or someone else's home). Furthermore, alcohol-related assault among females was more likely to involve physical force than non-alcohol-related assault.

A national probability sample of 4,008 women in the National Women's Study (Kilpatrick, Resnick, Saunders, & Best, 1998) indicated that victims of violence were more than twice as likely as nonvictims to have had one major alcohol problem and more than four times as likely to have had two or more major alcohol problems. For 54%, the first intoxication occurred after the first violence experience. About two thirds of sexual abuse victims had their first intoxication after their first sexual abuse.

Different interpretations can apply to these findings. One possibility is that alcohol-abusing women increase the likelihood of being sexually victimized if their lifestyles place them in situations of higher risk for assault. In addition, sexual and physical abuse of women also may lead them to alcohol abuse. It is, of course, possible for a third factor, such as parental alcohol abuse, to increase the likelihood that daughters will face more alcohol abuse and sexual victimization.

Women who drink heavily are perceived to have loose sexual standards, making them at greater risk for sexual advances and possible victimization (Klassen & Wilsnack, 1986). Women report feeling more sexually uninhibited when drinking especially if large quantities are consumed (Wilsnack, Klassen, Schur, & Wilsnack, 1991). Under the influence of alcohol, they may be less likely to avoid or resist victimization due to blackouts or loss of motor control. A review of past research (Rickert & Wiemann, 1998) indicated that alcohol use was a factor contributing to acquaintance or date rape, rape, and other forms of victimization.

Alcohol may alter cognitive processing of pornographic material and make men more susceptible to engaging in sexual violence and lower the resistance of women to such actions (Norris & Kerr, 1993). After drinking alcohol or no alcohol, men and women viewed pornographic films involving coerced or forced sexual intercourse. Women receiving alcohol, compared with sober women, rated the male's behavior as more acceptable and as involving less force while men receiving alcohol had higher self-reported likelihood of engaging in similar sexually violent behavior.

Undoubtedly, both processes may be involved in the relationship between problem drinking and sexual victimization. Thus, a study using a 5-year follow-up (Wilsnack et al., 1991) compared mostly White, middle-aged women who were either problem or non-problem drinkers. Data collection involved face-to-face interviews with female interviewers. Problem drinkers, reporting sexual dysfunction at the initial interview, were more likely than those without sexual dysfunction to have more drinking problems at the 5-year follow-up.

The opposite causal sequence also was supported in the same study. Women who were nonproblem drinkers at the start of the study but who experienced sexual abuse during the 5-year period were more than twice as likely to develop drinking problems over this interval as those who did not encounter sexual abuse.

A different explanation for this relationship between victimization and alcohol problems is that excessive drinking develops as an escape from guilt, shame, and loss of self-esteem stemming from victimization (Wilsnack, 1984). Posttraumatic stress disorder (PTSD), a set of adverse reactions to severe trauma, may occur in some victims of violence (Miller, Downs, & Testa, 1993). Some women may respond to PTSD by excessive use of alcohol and other drugs.

Evidence From Lab Experiments

Experiments, unlike surveys, can be used to directly study the effect of alcohol on physiological aspects of human sexual response. In lab experiments conducted during the late 1970s, college students received alcohol drinks that produced low to moderate blood alcohol levels or placebos before viewing an erotic film. For males, a device called a plethysmograph attached around the penis measured the degree of penile tumescence or erection continuously during the film viewing. For females, a vaginal plethysmograph consisting of a photocell inside a Plexiglas tube recorded changes in vaginal blood pressure as an index of sexual arousal while film viewing.

A review (George & Stoner, 2000) of this type of research spanning more than a decade concluded that, overall, alcohol decreases both men's and women's genital reactions to sexual stimuli in the laboratory. Except at very low dosages, alcohol suppressed penile tumescence (Wilson & Lawson, 1976b; Wilson, Lawson, & Abrams, 1978). For women, alcohol suppressed vaginal blood volume (Wilson & Lawson, 1976a; Wilson & Lawson, 1978). Higher alcohol doses produced larger effects.

Researchers used the balanced placebo design to try to separate the pharmacological and psychological influences on sexual arousal. This design has four conditions, and this particular study varied the expectancies about the type of beverage that college subjects were told they would receive, alcoholic or nonalcoholic, as well as the type of beverage they actually received, alcoholic or nonalcoholic.

Males expecting alcohol showed greater penile tumescence (Wilson & Lawson, 1976a) and subjective arousal (George & Marlatt, 1986) than those receiving or expecting no alcohol. For males, the belief that alcohol enhances sexual arousal was self-fulfilling. A different explanation for the expectancy effect is that men expecting to receive alcohol use intoxication as an excuse for otherwise disapproved behavior. However, no such expectancy effects occurred for females. Expectancy did not affect vaginal arousal, whereas alcohol reduced it; yet subjective arousal correlated positively with estimates of intoxication level (Wilson & Lawson, 1978). Under alcohol, women's objective and subjective sexual arousal indices were not related (Wilson & Lawson, 1976a; Wilson & Lawson, 1978); their self-reported sexual arousal after drinking alcohol in the laboratory bore no relationship to their concurrent vaginal response.

However, studies in laboratory settings are highly artificial and involve, for ethical reasons, relatively low doses. Low doses are also necessary to achieve credibility when the balanced placebo is used. These studies rely on samples of college students who are hardly representative of the general population. Even among college students, they can be viewed as a biased sample because those who volunteer for sex research have more sexual experience, more liberal sexual attitudes, and more sexual problems (Wolchik, Braver, & Jensen, 1985).

The implication of these findings is that contrary to popular belief, alcohol's effect on sexual arousal is not mediated through a physiological basis but through a psychological process in which one's expectancies are more critical, at least at low dose levels. The correspondence between physiological and psychological sexual arousal is much weaker for women than it is for men. Social and anatomical factors could account for this difference (Wilson et al., 1978). Men may form stronger associations between genital sensations and cognitive information, such as the type of beverage consumed, because it may be easier for males to label or identify penile arousal than it is for females to detect vaginal arousal.

The pattern of results from laboratory studies of alcohol effects on sexual arousal is compatible with the excuse function of alcohol use (Crowe & George, 1989). Sexual arousal may be increased by alcohol expectancy when excuses are needed (i.e., when inhibition may exist). Thus, in one study (George & Marlatt, 1986), participants viewed slides showing erotic, violent, and violent-erotic content, materials that presumably create inhibition in the participants during a research study. Both the amount of viewing time and self-reported sexual arousal for a set of slides depicting highly deviant behaviors were higher for the group that expected alcohol than the group that did not. Viewing of such stimuli, especially in an experiment conducted at a university, is a type of *deviant* activity that is likely to generate inhibition. Therefore, the expectancy of alcohol should disinhibit or enhance sexual arousal.

The societal context should be considered when interpreting the pattern of findings (Crowe & George, 1989). Society imposes a double standard, with greater tolerance of sexual arousal and deviance among men than among women; it should not be surprising that alcohol expectancy generally produces less sexual arousal among women than among men.

The fact that alcohol at higher doses can often increase sexual responsiveness, even when it is socially unacceptable, may be due to the impairment of cognitive processing. A model of alcohol-related disinhibitory effects proposes that higher doses disrupt awareness of inhibitory cues that ordinarily restrain antisocial behaviors such as sexually inappropriate behaviors (Steele & Southwick, 1985). Evidence for the model came from previous studies of the effects of alcohol that were classified in terms of whether the observed behavior or situation involved high or low conflict. A method, known as meta-analysis, was used to combine results from different studies to evaluate the effects of alcohol consumption and expectancy for low- and high-conflict contexts. Consistent with the model, expectancy effects exceeded consumption effects in low-conflict situations, but the opposite was found for high-conflict situations.

Overall, experiments on alcohol and sexual response seem to yield paradoxical effects, with both enhanced and suppressed sexual responses (George & Norris, 1991). Although *psychological* arousal may increase with more alcohol, there is an inverse relationship between the amount of alcohol consumed and the level of *physical* sexual arousal. With higher blood alcohol levels, sexual arousal diminishes.

There are also questions of generalizability of the findings due to the artificial nature of the laboratory setting and the types of students who would participate in this type of study that invades their privacy.

Other Drugs and Sex

Associations between the development of adolescent alcohol, cigarette, and marijuana use and risky sexual behavior were examined over an 18-month period (Duncan, Strycker, & Duncan, 1999). Participants were 257 adolescent boys and girls assessed at three time points. Use of all three substances was significantly related to risky sexual behavior. Similar patterns in these relationships occurred for boys and girls.

Substance use and risky sexual behavior were examined for 125 substance-abusing female adolescents and 78 controls between ages 14 and 18 (Castillo Mezzich et al., 1997) in relation to psychological variables. Uncontrolled behavior, negative affectivity, and childhood victimization were related to both substance use and risky sexual behavior. Antisocial behavior mediated the associations among uncontrolled behavior, negative affectivity, and childhood victimization with substance use and risky sexual behavior. Affiliation with an adult boyfriend was directly associated with substance use involvement and accounted for the relationship between chronological age and risky sexual behavior.

The Massachusetts Youth Risk Behavior Survey was administered to a sample of 3,054 students from randomly selected high schools and classrooms (Shrier, Emans, Woods, & DuRant, 1997). More than one third of the sample had experienced sexual intercourse. Increased frequency and severity of use of drugs such as marijuana, cocaine, crack, and alcohol, as well as more years of sexual intercourse, were associated with an increased number of sexual partners and recent condom nonuse.

Substance use and sexual activity were studied with a nationally representative, probability-based sample of young adults aged 18–30 in 1990 (Graves & Leigh, 1995). Respondents who drank more frequently, were heavy drinkers, smoked cigarettes, and used marijuana in the past year were more likely to be sexually active. Those who had five or more drinks at a sitting and who used marijuana were more likely to have had more than one sexual partner. Heavy drinkers were also less likely to use condoms; however, no association occurred between alcohol use and engaging in unsafe sexual practices.

Overview

Although behaviors involving aggressive violence and risky sexual practices are markedly different, there are some similarities in how alcohol and other drugs may affect these behaviors. Figure 8.5 illustrates a model involving how either aggression or risky sexual behaviors might be increased by heavy alcohol use.

FIGURE 8.5 Hypothetical model of the relationship between impulsivity and either aggression or sexual activity. Each behavior can have aversive consequences and lead to subsequent continued/increased alcohol consumption.

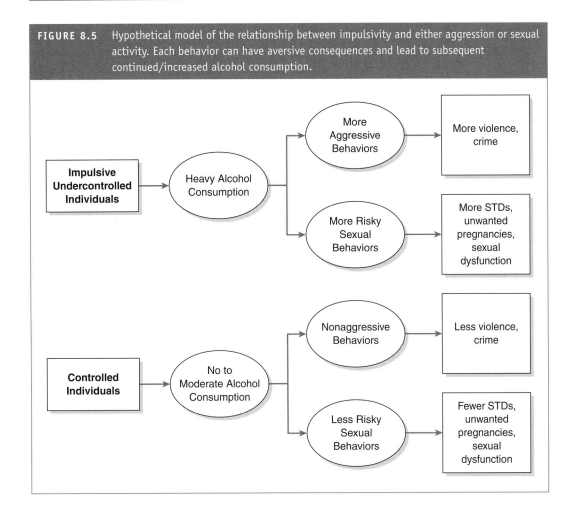

Initially, impulsive or undercontrolled individuals drink heavily, and this behavior eventually increases the instigation of violence or the initiation of sexual risk taking. Heavy involvement with alcohol at an early age may increase other delinquent activities. Risks of violence increase, with attendant risk of criminal offenses. Early entry into drinking increases having sexual intimacy, which can lead to complications such as sexually transmitted diseases, unwanted early pregnancies, and, in some cases, sexual dysfunction. Young females also may become sexual victims, exploited by older men. For females who become pregnant, there are the additional physical and psychological risks of abortion.

To deal with guilt and anxiety, harmful consequences, and stresses associated with aggression and sexual intimacy that are facilitated by early and heavy alcohol use, individuals may increase subsequent alcohol use (not diagrammed in Figure 8.5) as a form of self-medication to help escape or forget their miserable lives. Such drinking responses may be more likely for aggression among males, but for females, it may occur in relation to sexual activities.

Summary

Alcohol is popularly viewed as a disinhibitor, so it is not surprising that its use is associated with behaviors that are ordinarily inhibited or restrained in most circumstances, such as violence or sexual intimacy. Incidents of natural aggression are difficult to interpret due to many uncontrolled variables. Much of the evidence is retrospective recall and not easily validated. The number of incidents that are available for researchers to study is relatively infrequent and may not involve random samples. Evidence from studies of prison inmates convicted of violent crimes, which suggest that use of alcohol and other drugs may have played a role in these crimes, may not be generalizable to the general population.

Laboratory studies allow for controlled observation to help rule out alternative explanations for the correlation between alcohol use and aggression. Alcohol generally releases aggression in laboratory studies, although the situation is also an important factor. The more conflict involved in the situation, the more likely alcohol will produce higher aggression.

Depending on the dose, different effects may occur. At levels that produce intoxication, some drinkers may perceive certain situations as more threatening and therefore may react in ways that either evoke or provoke aggression. Cues such as anxiety, which ordinarily would inhibit an individual from aggressive behavior, might not be noticed when intoxication occurs, so these inhibitors no longer function to keep violence under control. Or if a person is more likely to become angered when drinking, the likelihood that he or she may initiate aggression may increase in certain circumstances.

Control of aggressive tendencies may be less effective after drinking occurs because alcohol may restrict attention and reduce the salience of inhibiting cues. Higher cognitive controls in the forms of self- and social criticism that ordinarily restrain behaviors also may be weakened under the influence of alcohol.

Sexual intimacy can be affected by alcohol and other drugs. Cues and behaviors during interactions that might lead to sexual relations may be interpreted differently when one or both parties are under the influence of alcohol than when they are not. These differences have implications for how an individual reacts to sexual overtures or signals from potential sexual partners. Anxiety, fear, and guilt, which might inhibit sexual behavior, might be reduced by alcohol consumption. Alcohol use also can serve as an *excuse* later if sexual activities are condemned. Risky sexual practices associated with potential HIV infection are higher for those with more alcohol involvement. Among alcoholics, alcohol use has been found to be associated with sexual dysfunction.

Due to the correlational nature of the evidence on alcohol and sex, however, it is unclear if—and how—alcohol use affects sexual conduct or vice versa. It is difficult, if not impossible, to separate the pharmacological and psychological effects in natural circumstances, so researchers turn to controlled experiments to determine their relative contributions. Laboratory studies of the effects of alcohol on sexual arousal are limited to relatively small doses given on single occasions to a select group of college students who are willing to volunteer for studies that most students might not. Although the generalizability to real-life sexual behavior is questionable, these studies demonstrate the influence of alcohol expectancies on sexual arousal, apart from any pharmacological effect.

Aggression and sexual intimacy are similar in that they are both often highly restricted behaviors. When alcohol is consumed at levels and in circumstances that narrow the attention of the drinker, these inhibitors are less effective in restraining either of these behaviors. Both pharmacological and psychological factors may affect how people behave when they consume alcohol and other drugs.

Alcohol or other drugs per se may not be the primary factor responsible when their use is associated with incidents having negative outcomes. Instead, some combination of the personality of the transgressor and the use of alcohol may be responsible. To blame alcohol or other drugs, without considering the characteristics of the user who commits the crime, is to scapegoat the substance.

Stimulus/Response

1. Think of different methods that you could use to determine the effect of alcohol or some other drug on a specific crime.

2. How accurately do you think you could determine the effect of alcohol for the following hypothetical cases?

   a. A man murders his wife but is not apprehended for 3 weeks.
   b. A bank robber is arrested as he flees the bank.
   c. A clerk, known to be an alcoholic, confesses to embezzlement.

3. On the basis of your *practice* on these criminal cases above, how accurate do you find the following statement? "In 2002, jail inmates convicted of robbery (56%), weapons violations (56%), burglary (55%), or motor vehicle theft (55%) were most likely to have reported to be using drugs at the time of the offense" (Bureau of Justice Statistics, 2005).

4. Research shows a correlation between heavy use of some drugs and violent crime. Do the drugs cause these forms of aggression, or do aggressive persons both use more drugs and commit more aggressive acts?

5. The popular media often present sensationalistic depictions of drug use. Headlines such as "Drug-Crazed Man Commits a Crime" are often used to describe events. How can we know that a drug caused a specific man to commit a crime? Maybe he would have done it even if he were drug free. And could it be that a person could actually be less likely to commit the crime under the influence of a drug?

6. Do you think that alcohol releases sexual inhibitions due to a pharmacological effect on sexual arousal or because of expectations and beliefs? How could you determine the relative influence of each factor?

7. Sexual assault and rape are often associated with drinking by the offender. Discuss possible alternative processes that might be responsible for this relationship.

CHAPTER 9

Family Processes

Alcohol and Marital Status	Adult Children of Alcoholics
Effects of Parental Alcohol Use Disorders on Children	Codependency
	Summary
Alcoholic Family Interactions	Stimulus/Response

'Mid pleasures and palaces, though we may roam, be it ever so humble, there's no place like home.

The well-known last phrase of this expression about the security and comfort of home actually comes from a lament composed around 1860 about the domestic ravages of alcoholism, titled "Ruined by Drink," by Nobil Adkisson. It goes on to describe the domestic tragedy: "But the father lies drunk on the floor, The table is empty, the wolf's at the door, and mother sobs loud in her broken-back'd chair, Her garments in tatters, her soul in despair." This depiction dramatically shows the devastation that parental alcoholism may wreak on the well-being of the family. It is not surprising, then, that considerable efforts are devoted to understanding the impact of the father's alcoholism on the mother as well as on the children.

Due to the rapid and major changes in the structure of the family that have occurred over the past quarter-century, previous perspectives may need revision. The model of the nuclear family—two parents and two children, possibly one of each sex—has become a rarity. Research in this area needs to recognize the wide variety of family constellations and arrangements (McCubbin, McCubbin, Thompson, & Han, 1999). According to the 1994 U.S. census, married-couple families in 1994 represented only 55% of households, down from 71% in 1970. Single-parent households, of which single-mother households were 86%, represented about 31% of families in 1994, and they are increasing. At the same time, the average size of families declined from 3.14 persons per household in 1970 to 2.62 in 1994. These statistics are averaged over the entire population and are not accurate for different racial/ethnic groups.

The definition of the term *family* has changed as first-marriage rates have declined and cohabitation has increased. In addition, remarriages are commonplace; 67% of Blacks and 55% of Whites live in stepparent families. Marriage occurs at high rates for cohabiting stepfamilies, with 25% marrying within 1 year. More than a third of children are born to unwed mothers, and more than half of all children will live in a single-parent household at some time (Bumpass, 2004). These and many other changes in the definition of *family* may yield different rates of alcohol and other drug use from those found in traditionally defined families.

ALCOHOL AND MARITAL STATUS

How alcohol might influence decisions to marry is a complex issue (Leonard & Eiden, 2007). On one hand, excessive use of alcohol may promote earlier sexual intimacy and often produces unplanned pregnancies that could lead to earlier-than-planned marriages. In addition, chronic heavy use of alcohol could impair education, leading to school dropouts and early entry into low-paying jobs that make it difficult to support families adequately. In contrast, marriage may be delayed or not occur for some excessive drinkers. They may lack the skills to develop a long-term intimate relationship or be unwilling to commit to a marriage. Furthermore, their alcohol problems may lead prospective mates to reject them as undesirable prospective marriage partners.

Selection Into Marriage

Mate selection in our society is obviously not a random process but often involves a process called **assortative mating**. People do not select mates on a random basis; rather, they prefer to choose their marriage partners, and usually they select mates who are similar to themselves in important ways such as values, interests, and demographic background.

Drinking might be one of the many dimensions of similarity that is related, even if indirectly, to sexual attraction. Thus, impulsive and aggressive males who also drink heavily may be more sexually attractive to females, especially if they also are actively engaged in a drinking lifestyle. Although drinking problems may not exist or be apparent during courtship or early years of marriage, eventually drinking problems may arise for some of these couples. Past clinical research suggests that if one member of a marriage has a drinking problem, there is a greater chance that the partner also has a drinking problem. However, studies of treatment samples may overestimate the extent to which couples in the general population are similar in drinking.

There is mixed support for assortative mating with respect to drinking. An analysis (Mudar, Leonard, & Soltysinski, 2001) of newlyweds found that for couples where the husband was not a heavy drinker, only 7% of wives were heavy drinkers, but among couples with a heavily drinking husband, 25% of the wives were also heavy drinkers. However, the finding that 58% of heavily drinking wives were married to men who were not heavy drinkers does not support the assortative mating view.

In a study of 5,310 young adult women in a national longitudinal survey (Windle, 1997), problem-drinking women were twice as likely to be married to problem-drinking husbands than were nondrinking women. The overall problem-drinking prevalence rate was only about 10%, much lower than reported in other studies. However, this sample used women younger than age 30. Rates should be higher for older samples because more time may be needed for alcohol problems to develop. In addition, women who had heavier lifetime use of marijuana and cocaine were twice as likely to have husbands who were problem drinkers. There were some racial/ethnic differences, with assortative mating being lowest among African Americans. Similar ethnic group patterns existed for other drugs such as marijuana and cocaine.

Marriage Effect

The "**marriage effect**" (Leonard & Das Eiden, 1999) refers to the lower drinking rates found among married than among single individuals. Many cross-sectional studies have demonstrated this relationship. However, because single and married groups differ in their average age and young persons tend to drink more heavily, one might suspect that the drinking differences attributed to marital status could be due more to age differences. However, the marriage effect remains even after controlling for age, gender, and socioeconomic status.

A study (Leonard & Das Eiden, 1999) of 500 newlyweds in their first year of marriage found that drinking within couples was at similar levels. This similarity could reflect their common interests, values, and lifestyles. It might also stem from their similar reactions to shared experiences, both positive and negative.

Husbands seem to influence wives more, as the typically heavier drinking of men may lead their wives to increase their drinking level. On the other hand, the typically lower level of drinking of women does not seem to have any protective effect in reducing the alcohol consumption of heavier-drinking husbands. This asymmetrical influence could be due to many factors. Husbands may drink with men at work and be more influenced by them than by the drinking of their wives. Wives, on the other hand, may not have other drinking partners; their drinking may be primarily influenced by their husbands' drinking.

Recovery of alcoholics may be enhanced by marriage. An analysis (Dawson, Grant, Stinson, & Chou, 2006) using a sample of 4,422 adults with *DSM-IV* alcohol dependence in the past year found that entering a first marriage increased the likelihood of nonabstinent recovery (low-risk drinking) during the following 3 years.

Reduced use of other drugs also may occur for married as opposed to single individuals (Burton, Johnson, Ritter, & Clayton, 1996). However, studies (Horwitz, White, & Howell-White, 1996) that have measured drinking over 5 years after marriage have not shown a consistent marriage effect.

Cross-sectional studies showing lower drinking among married than among single persons may not reflect actual reductions in drinking due to marriage. An alternative explanation is self-selection. The "marriage effect" might be due to lighter drinkers marrying sooner than heavier drinkers, thus leading to a difference in drinking levels of marrieds and singles. The evidence on this issue is mixed (Leonard & Das Eiden, 1999). Longitudinal studies that examine the drinking levels of the same individuals before and after marriage are needed to determine if the differences between single and married individuals actually reflect temporal changes within individuals.

Longitudinal studies demonstrate that within a year or two after marriage, many individuals have indeed decreased their drinking. Studies conducted within a year or two after marriage (Leonard & Das Eiden, 1999; Miller-Tutzauer, Leonard, & Windle, 1991) find reductions for men and women during the first year after marriage but not for single individuals in the same period.

Why might marriage reduce drinking? An analysis (Bachman et al., 2002) of results of a national longitudinal survey on alcohol and drug use suggests that many changes that occur during marriage could be responsible. Shifts in religiosity, social-recreational activities, friends' alcohol use, and normative views of alcohol use are all important. Married couples spend fewer "evenings out," and they disapprove of occasional heavy drinking for both men and women.

Drinking and Marital Satisfaction

How is drinking by husbands and wives related to their satisfaction with their marriage? Newlywed couples were assessed for marital satisfaction and drinking behaviors shortly before marriage and then reassessed at their first and second anniversaries (Homish & Leonard, 2005, 2007). Both times, husbands and wives who usually drank with their partners reported greater levels of marital satisfaction. However, over time, marital satisfaction declined for both husbands and wives. Nondrinking wives as well as those who more often drank *apart* from their spouses experienced a greater decline in marital satisfaction than the wives who drank *with* their husbands. Possibly, the couples that drink together stay together because their drinking leads to more positive social interactions.

In marriages where heavy drinking continues over long periods, marital quality eventually deteriorates. Husbands' drinking quantity and problem drinking by either spouse were inversely related to marital quality for newlyweds (Leonard & Roberts, 1998). Among those who marry at a young age, heavy drinking creates a high risk; most of these marriages dissolved by age 23 in a British study (Burton et al., 1996).

Continued heavy drinking by one spouse may increasingly lead to conflict. Heavy drinkers may be abusive or depressed, which may lead to divorce at a higher rate among couples with a heavy drinker. However, the influence could be in the opposite direction as well with some dissolved marriages leading to excessive drinking.

Drinking and Domestic Violence

Domestic violence (also called intimate partner violence, or IPV) is a major concern. A national household survey (Schafer, Caetano, & Clark, 1998) of 635 representative couples living in the 48 contiguous states used face-to-face reports of both partners to estimate IPV rates. Although male-to-female IPV receives more publicity, instances of female-to-male IPV occurred at a higher rate, 18.21 %, than male-to-female IPV, 13.61 %.

Alcohol abuse has been found to be related to the occurrence of IPV in many studies. For example, the level of the husbands' drinking was directly related to greater spousal abuse in a comparison (Van Hesselt, Morrison, & Bellack, 1985) of wife-abusive, maritally discordant but nonabusive, and happily married couples. The level of drinking by wives was not a predictor of the spousal abuse received. In contrast, another study found that alcoholic wives were more likely than nonalcoholic wives to be victims of spousal violence (Miller, Downs, & Gondoli, 1989), possibly because they were perceived as not deserving better treatment due to their alcoholism. In one study (O'Farrell & Murphy, 1995), married men in alcoholism treatment were four times more likely to have physically abused their wives than were demographically matched nonalcoholic males.

A cross-sectional study (Lipsky, Caetano, Field, & Larkin, 2005) examined 182 IPV cases among women treated at an urban emergency room. A woman was more likely to have experienced violence from her partner if he had a higher number of drinks per week, had five or more drinks per occasion, showed evidence of alcohol abuse and dependence, and used illicit drugs. During incidents where the abused women perpetrated violence, the drinking of both members of the couple was similarly high. The likelihood of an abused woman drinking while she perpetrated violence was higher for women who drank more each week.

For a household probability sample of the 48 contiguous states, most married or cohabiting couples reporting IPV had experienced bidirectional rather than unidirectional incidents (Caetano, Ramisetty-Mikler, & Field, 2005). Whereas in cases of unidirectional IPV it is fairly clear who the perpetrator is—and that the intent is offensive—in bidirectional IPV incidents it is difficult to determine who initiated the violence and whether it was primarily offensive or defensive.

As in other studies, females were more likely than males to engage in unidirectional IPV. Unidirectional male-to-female IPV was related to a single risk factor, male childhood physical abuse. In contrast, bidirectional IPV and unidirectional female-to-male IPV were related to the female partner having heavier drinking, alcohol-related problems, and a family-of-origin history of violence. In addition, there were ethnic differences as Blacks were more likely than Whites to report bidirectional IPV. Severe unidirectional and bidirectional IPV were more prevalent among Blacks and Hispanics.

Evaluation

Domestic or intimate partner violence is usually attributed to the amount of alcohol consumed by the abuser (Leonard & Senchak, 1996). However, distal factors such as social class, personality, and upbringing also must be considered as determinants. These "third variables" should be controlled for because any of them might lead to both the violent tendencies and the drinking levels. When these distal factors have been controlled for, the amount of alcohol consumed still is found to contribute to the probability of violence.

The direct pharmacological effects of alcohol might account for the alcohol-violence relationship. In a specific episode, alcohol abuse may alter cognitive and emotional processes that ordinarily inhibit aggression and facilitate attention to cues that instigate aggression. However, pharmacological effects of alcohol and psychological factors such as the drinker's expectancies about the influence of drinking cannot completely explain marital aggression because wide individual differences in IPV exist among alcoholic husbands. As suggested by the multiple threshold model (Fals-Stewart, Leonard, & Birchler, 2005), personality may be a moderator of the alcohol-IPV relationship in that men diagnosed with antisocial disorder were more likely to engage in severe IPV after drinking than were men without this trait.

Violent and nonviolent alcoholic men may have different drinking patterns. Thus, binge drinkers are more likely to be violent than steady drinkers (Murphy & O'Farrell, 1994). Binge drinking could create a higher level of intoxication than steady drinking. Finally, the effect of intoxication on spousal communication differs for violent and nonviolent alcoholics, with greater defensiveness and hostility among those who resort to violence (Murphy & O'Farrell, 1996, 1997).

Another explanation for the correlation between drinking and IPV is self-selection. Alcoholics who are prone to domestic violence might differ from nonviolent alcoholics in their beliefs and expectancies about the relationship between drinking and violence or in their temperamental dispositions toward aggression or hostility. Thus, men with antisocial personalities not only may be more prone to aggression but also may show increases in aggression with alcohol, whereas other men may not.

However, explanations based on self-selection in which some types of persons prone to violence also tend to drink excessively cannot explain easily why violence often declines after alcoholics stop using alcohol following **behavioral marital therapy** to levels comparable to those found with nonalcoholics (O'Farrell, Van Hutton, & Murphy, 1999). Additional mechanisms must be involved. Reduced information processing under the influence of alcohol can only account for short-term effects of drinking because the intoxicating effects of drinking eventually wear off. An explanation of the effect of long-term drinking on marital quality is also needed.

A third model examines the mediating processes that might lead to violence following heavy drinking. For example, marital difficulties might mediate the relationship between alcoholism and marital violence. One or both partners may turn to drinking to cope with the stress over financial, work, or legal problems, which may weaken the quality of the marriage and increase the likelihood of violence after drinking.

A meta-analysis of the research on IPV (Foran & O'Leary, 2008) found only a modest relationship between alcohol and IPV, but a closer analysis showed that some studies showed very strong relationships but the overall pattern was reduced because other studies found weak associations. A major factor for the divergent findings was that the criterion of drinking used differed widely across studies, ranging from a quantity-frequency measure to heavy drinking to alcohol dependence. Stronger alcohol-IPV relationships occurred mainly in studies that used measures reflecting more problematic drinking such as dependence.

Conflicting findings were also due to methodological problems. Whereas some studies of the alcohol-IPV relationships used extreme groups such as only impaired individuals or only well-functioning individuals, other studies included individuals from both clinical and nonclinical settings. All else being equal, one would expect to find a smaller relationship in the first type of comparison simply because there is a "restricted range" in the sample. For example, overall, adult height and weight are correlated (i.e., taller people generally weigh more than shorter ones). But if this comparison is made only for a sample of short people or tall people, the correlation will be weaker than if the sample covers the entire range of height.

Drinking and Divorce

If, as suggested earlier, marriage tends to reduce drinking, does divorce tend to increase drinking? Cross-sectional studies of the relationship between drinking and divorce provide equivocal evidence. While some individuals may increase their drinking after divorce, increased drinking may also be a cause of some divorces. Longitudinal studies are necessary to observe the temporal order of divorce and drinking.

One national longitudinal study of young women (Hanna, Faden, & Harford, 1993) found that those who were separated or divorced increased their alcohol use subsequently although short-term reductions in drinking occurred for both men and women with family histories of alcoholism (Harford, Hanna, & Faden, 1994).

Why might divorce lead to more alcohol-related problems? One hypothesis holds that alcohol abuse is a means of coping with depression and low self-esteem following divorce. If there are children involved, custody disputes and single parenting are added stressors. A different explanation focuses on changes in roles and lifestyles (e.g., being single again often places one in situations such as clubs and bars that promote drinking).

It is likely that there is a bidirectional influence between divorce and alcohol dependency. Thus, as alcohol abuse increases, divorce is more likely; after a divorce, alcohol abuse may be a response for dealing with the emotional problems related to the failed marriage. The findings, based on samples of couples, are supported by analyses of aggregated measures over the entire nation between total alcohol sales and consumption, divorce rates, and expenditures on alcohol (Caces, Harford, Williams, & Hanna, 1999). As consumption increases by an average of 1 liter, divorce rates increase by 20%. Increased divorce rates of 1 in 1,000 were associated with a 10% rise in alcohol expenditures.

Divorce may also have the opposite effect for some individuals, leading to reduced drinking. Leaving a "bad" marriage may reduce the need to drink. Thus, problem-drinking women, following divorce or separation, had a reduced risk for alcohol problems (Wilsnack, Klassen, Schur, & Wilsnack, 1991). Similarly, the earlier-cited analysis (Dawson et al., 2006) showing that *DSM-IV* alcohol-dependent adults reduced drinking when they married also found that exiting a first marriage increased the likelihood of recovery (low-risk drinking) during the ensuing 3 years.

Sampling Problems

It must be kept in mind that the families available for studies of family processes in alcoholic homes are not a random sample (Leonard, 1990). Families in which one or both parents have reduced previous problem drinking to acceptable levels would not be included. Also excluded would be families with extreme or prolonged alcohol problems because they would probably have divorced. The remaining families most likely would be those managing to put up with or tolerate the alcoholic's drinking thus far.

It is also more likely that the families that agree to be studied will seek treatment or counseling, but those that do not seek help would not be studied. In some of these families, the problems may not be sufficiently serious for the family to seek counseling or treatment, but in other families, other factors such as attitudes may be preventing treatment, even though the problems warrant help

EFFECTS OF PARENTAL ALCOHOL USE DISORDERS ON CHILDREN

Children of alcoholics (COAs) might be expected to be at higher risk than children of nonalcoholics (NCOAs) for developing personality disorders, behavior problems, and eventually alcohol and other drug use disorders for several reasons. As discussed in Chapter 6, genetic factors increase risk factors for these problems in the COAs. In addition, the family environment of alcoholic homes can increase the likelihood of these problems for COAs.

A review of early studies (West & Prinz, 1987) suggested that COAs have more alcohol problems than NCOAs. Children in alcoholic homes faced more parent-child conflict and had more psychiatric problems, possibly due to their alcoholic parents having more marital conflict and poor adaptive functioning. Many studies were inconclusive about causality as they used cross-sectional evidence or clinical observations based on small samples that were unrepresentative of both the alcoholic and the general population. The use of poor measurement instruments and retrospective self-reports yielded observations of unknown unreliability and validity. Later studies with improved research methods generally upheld the hypothesis that COAs are at risk for impaired psychological development during childhood, which can lead to alcohol and other drug problems in adolescence and adulthood.

Children's self-esteem may be one casualty of living with alcoholic parents. One mechanism by which alcoholic parents generate adverse effects on their children's development might be poor parenting. For example, alcoholic parents, especially when drinking, may fail to monitor or supervise children's behavior or their choice of friends, so they may develop delinquent behaviors and fall under the influence of persons who may lead them astray (Chassin, Curran, Hussong, & Colder, 1996).

Alcohol-abusing parents show less warmth and sensitivity toward their children, which in turn could impede the development of self-regulation during preschool years. Using a sample of kindergarten children with alcoholic (n = 130) and nonalcoholic (n = 97) parents, one study (Eiden, Edwards, & Leonard, 2007) found that COAs engaged in more externalizing behavior than NCOAs. Moreover, the father's alcoholism when the child was 12–18 months old predicted lower maternal warmth and sensitivity at 2 years of age. Warmth and sensitivity of the mother, but not of the father, predicted poorer children's self-regulation as indexed by more externalizing behavior or conduct and discipline problems in kindergarten.

A study of adult COAs (Rangarajan, 2008) examined the relationship of their self-esteem to parental alcoholism, family stress and communication patterns, and parental attachment. Based on a total of 515 participants, almost 60% college students and 40% respondents on a Web site, the findings showed that paternal but not maternal alcoholism impaired attachment with the offspring and mediated lowered self-esteem, possibly because alcoholic fathers may have been less available or less responsive to their children. However, open family communication reduced the effects of family stressors on attachment insecurity.

Children's Later Drinking

Impaired personality development may increase the likelihood that COAs will develop alcohol problems as adolescents and adults. Alcoholic parents may influence their children's drinking by direct modeling of alcohol use and by the transmission of their values about drinking. Hence, it is not surprising that similarities exist between the drinking patterns of parents and those of their adult children in studies with large general population samples (Barnes & Welte, 1990; Dawson, Harford, & Grant, 1992) as well as with smaller clinical samples (Orford & Velleman, 1991).

Typically, these studies agree that children of heavier-drinking parents also develop more frequent and heavier patterns of alcohol use as adults. However, some studies with nonclinical samples of college students (Engs, 1990; Wright & Heppner, 1991, 1993) have found no relationship between the drinking of parents and that of their college-age children.

A study with a community sample of 1,744 adolescents from schools in South Wales (Chalder, Elgar, & Bennett, 2006) found almost one fifth of the sample had a parent with alcohol problems. These COAs drank more frequently, more heavily, and more often alone than children of parents without alcohol problems. Internal motives to drink such as drinking to feel intoxicated or to forget about problems were good predictors of alcohol consumption and frequency for COAs.

Not only might COAs drink more than NCOAs, but their drinking initiation-to-disorder trajectories are shorter or "telescoped." A longitudinal study (Hussong, Bauer, & Chassin, 2008) with a community-based sample found that COAs progressed more quickly from initial adolescent alcohol use to the onset of disorder as compared to matched controls. Stronger telescoping effects were observed for COAs if parents were comorbid for either depression or antisocial personality disorder. This risk for telescoping was also evident for drug disorders.

However, conflict and stress are by no means specific or limited to alcoholic homes but also may occur in families with nonalcoholic psychiatric problems. Thus, impairments observed in COAs may reflect the effects of growing up in a dysfunctional family rather than one with alcoholism per se. Conclusions about the extent to which COAs have more personality impairments, conduct behavior problems, and alcohol abuse would be more persuasive if studies included not only a control group of children of normal-functioning parents but also one consisting of children from families with problems other than parental alcoholism (West & Prinz, 1987).

Child Abuse

Under the influence of alcohol, some parents may act abusively toward their children (Langeland & Hartgers, 1998; Widom, Ireland, & Glynn, 1995). One category of abuse is nonsexual and involves behaviors such as hitting or slapping, verbal abuse such as insults or threats, and physical harm with a weapon. Such treatment could have serious harmful consequences that continue into adulthood.

A second form of violence involves sexual abuse, when unwanted sexual behaviors, from exposure to touching to penetration, are inflicted on the child. Unlike cases of physical abuse, most sexual abuse incidents involve perpetrators other than the parents. Within the family, the most likely instances involve sexual abuse of fathers or stepfathers toward their daughters.

One reason why children of alcoholic parents have a higher risk for sexual abuse is that the parents are less able to protect them from sexual predators. For example, if the father is the perpetrator, mothers may be unable or unwilling to call authorities, leave the home with the children, move the children to a safe place, or make the husband leave. In some cases, the mother herself may have been sexually abused as a child, have substance abuse problems herself, and have an abusive partner and therefore be unable to protect her children.

In addition to the immediate but long-lasting harmful consequences such as physical and psychological trauma for the children who are abused, there may be delayed consequences. In effect, a perpetuating cycle may develop across generations, as shown in Figure 9.1, in which parental alcohol abuse may increase the likelihood of physical and/or sexual abuse of their children. When these children later grow up, they will have a higher likelihood of abusing alcohol, which in turn may lead them to abuse their own children.

Child Abuse and Children's Later Alcohol Abuse

Victims of child abuse may subsequently develop alcohol and other drug dependency to cope with the shame, fear, and pain of these experiences (Miller, Maguin, & Downs, 1997), particularly in women who have been victims of childhood abuse (Widom & Hiller-Sturmhofel, 2001). Most research on this topic uses clinical samples of individuals with alcohol abuse problems. These cases may represent the extreme cases, assuming recall is valid, which may not be generalizable to the general population.

Clinical Samples

Self-reported childhood abuse by women who were in alcohol treatment, drinking and driving programs, and mental health facilities was compared to that of a control group of

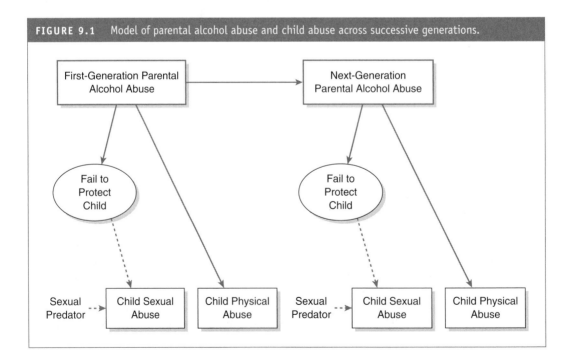

FIGURE 9.1 Model of parental alcohol abuse and child abuse across successive generations.

women from a household sample (Miller & Downs, 1993; Miller, Downs, & Testa, 1993). Substantially higher percentages of the women in the alcohol programs reported experiences of some form of nonsexual violence as well as sexual abuse toward them as children.

Women in alcohol treatment programs were also more likely to have been sexually abused than were women in mental health clinics for problems that were not alcohol related or women in the general population. However, women in mental health treatment programs who also had alcohol problems were more likely to have been victimized as children than those without alcohol problems (Miller et al., 1993).

The effects of childhood victimization for women seem to differ depending on race, whether the abuse was physical or psychological, and whether it came from the mother or the father. A study (Downs, Capshew, & Rindels, 2004) of women in alcohol treatment or receiving services for domestic violence found that mother psychological aggression was related to alcohol dependence. Father psychological aggression was related to alcohol dependence only for non-White women. Both mother and father physical abuse were related to alcohol dependence but only for women who did not report childhood sexual abuse.

A prospective examination into young adulthood and middle age (Widom, White, Czaja, & Marmorstein, 2007) of 500 women with documented histories of child physical and sexual abuse or neglect showed more past-year drinking and past-month heavy drinking (more than eight drinks) among these women than among a matched control group of nonabused/nonneglected women. For both men and women, parental alcohol/drug problems had an indirect effect on their children's drinking in middle adulthood through young adult alcohol diagnosis. When parental drinking levels were controlled, there was no relationship between child abuse and neglect and excessive drinking in middle adulthood for women, although excessive drinking by women in middle adulthood was related to having a diagnosis of alcohol use disorder in young adulthood. For men, child abuse and neglect was not related to either alcohol use disorder in young adulthood or excessive drinking in middle adulthood.

Childhood abuse can lead to alcohol use disorders in adulthood, and in turn, such outcomes may increase their potential for violence. A prospective **cohort study** (Widom, Schuck, & White, 2006) involving documented cases of child abuse and neglect and a matched control group found that child maltreatment increased the likelihood of violence for men through aggressive behavior and problematic alcohol use. For women, a stronger relationship between childhood victimization and violence occurred with greater problematic alcohol use.

Community Samples

Clinical and community samples may yield different findings. Studies on samples of problem drinkers in treatment suggest an association between severe alcohol problems and previous sexual abuse, at least in women, especially for earlier and more severe forms of sexual abuse (Moncrieff & Farmer, 1998). But those who have not yet sought or received treatment may have less serious problems, although it is also possible that some could have serious problems that they will not report.

The relationship of childhood sexual abuse to alcohol problems of women in the general population was explored through interviews of 917 adult women as part of the National Study of Health and Life Experiences of Women (Wilsnack, Wilsnack, & Klassen, 1984).

Retrospective reports of childhood sex abuse by women with problem drinker parents were more than twice those for women without problem drinker parents.

An analysis of several studies found a higher prevalence of alcohol problems in the general population among females if they had been sexually or physically abused as children (Langeland & Hartgers, 1998). For men, the evidence about relationships between child sexual or physical abuse and alcoholism was inconclusive.

A study of childhood sexual abuse and alcohol and drug abuse conducted with 4,790 students in Washington state public schools in Grades 8, 10, and 12 (Bensley, Spieker, Van Eenwyk, & Schoder, 1999) found the strongest association was between combined sexual abuse/molestation and heavy drinking for the eighth graders. For drug use, the associations with reported abuse history were slightly stronger, at higher levels of severity, and for combined abuse and molestation compared to nonsexual abuse.

Several possible explanations might account for the complex findings from different studies on this issue, including that sexual abuse leads to alcohol misuse, alcohol leads to sexual assault, sexual assault and alcohol misuse both stem from a third factor, and sexual abuse leads to other conditions associated with alcohol misuse.

Gender Differences Among Sexual Abuse Victims

Most child sexual abuse studies have focused on female victims because they constitute the large majority of cases, but it must be recognized that males also can be targets of sexual abuse. A study of a psychiatric sample (Windle, Windle, Scheidt, & Miller, 1995) found that 49% of the women and 12% of the men reported sexual abuse, 33% of the women and 24% of the men reported physical abuse, and 23% of the women and 5% of the men reported dual abuse.

Although both women and men had higher rates of antisocial personality disorder and suicide attempts, other reactions to such abuse may not be the same for male and female victims. Females may develop generalized anxiety and cope with alcohol and other drugs, but males may be more likely to display violent and aggressive responses as well as depression. One reason for the gender differential is that the norm for male drinking is already so high that it may not increase much for victims of child abuse. In contrast, females generally drink at a lower rate, so higher drinking by child sexual abuse victims may be more detectable.

Gender Differences Among Child Abusers

Although most child sexual abusers are probably males, such may not be the case for physical abuse. Most research on the relationship of alcohol abuse and child abuse does not identify which parent is the primary perpetrator of the physical abuse. Fathers with alcohol problems are often assumed to be the perpetrators, perhaps because more males than females seem to be treated for alcohol-related problems (Blume, 1994).

However, women with alcohol and other drug problems are also more likely to physically abuse their children (Miller, Smyth, & Mudar, 1999). Many of these mothers themselves reported being victims of abuse when they were children or being abused by their spouses (Hotaling & Sugarman, 1986), suggesting intergenerational cycles of family violence

(Velleman, 1992a, 1992b). Mothers who had been victims of childhood *physical* abuse or spousal abuse were harsher in their punitiveness toward their children than those who had been victims of childhood *sexual* abuse.

Methodological Problems

There are variations in the definition of *sexual abuse* as well as in the degree and timing of abuse that make comparisons across studies difficult. Similar problems exist in lack of agreement on the definition of alcohol misuse or dependence. Other problems involve the methods of data collection, sample selection, the presence or absence of control groups, possible recall bias, and difficulties with conducting prospective studies.

Retrospective studies are more common because they are easier to conduct, but they generally involve clinical samples. However, the relationship between child abuse and adult alcohol abuse can be obscured if the treatment interventions are highly effective. Prospective studies with samples from the general population avoid this problem but are expensive and require more time to complete.

One prospective study (Widom et al., 1995) compared documented court cases (611) of child abuse, neglect, or both with a control group of 457 nonabused and nonneglected children. Most cases were from lower socioeconomic status levels. The sexual abuse rate was about three times that found in a national survey. Examination of these cases showed a relationship between childhood victimization and subsequent alcohol abuse about 20 years later for women but not for men, even when controlling for parental alcohol or drug problems, childhood poverty, race, and age. Consistent with findings of other research (Dunn et al., 2002), child neglect, not abuse, was a better predictor of later alcohol problems for women.

Another study used data from a national survey of women's drinking in which 1,099 women were asked about their sexual experiences prior to age 18. Those who reported abusive sexual experiences were compared to women who did not (Wilsnack, Vogeltanz-Holm, Klassen, & Harris, 1997). Controlling for age, ethnicity, and parental education, women with histories of childhood sexual abuse were more likely than women without such histories to report recent alcohol use, intoxication, drinking-related problems, alcohol dependence symptoms, and lifetime use of prescribed psychoactive drugs and illicit drugs. These national sample findings were consistent with those from clinical samples.

In addition to alcohol abuse, women who suffered childhood sexual abuse also had more problems in other areas. They had higher depression and anxiety, pain that prevented intercourse, sexual intercourse before age 15, less sexual satisfaction, and more sexual dysfunction. One might conjecture that some of these problems either stemmed from or contributed to the alcohol abuse.

Problems of Causal Interpretation

Although the evidence generally agrees that childhood sexual abuse and, to some extent, physical abuse are related to later alcohol abuse, the underlying process for this relationship is not clear. Causal interpretation of research on the relationship between childhood sexual and physical abuse and subsequent alcohol abuse has numerous problems. Some studies do not include a control group of nonabused children. Such control groups need to be matched with the abused group on important demographic variables that are related to child abuse. Thus, it is useful to match for age, socioeconomic level, and parental education because more sexual abuse has been found for younger individuals and for those from families with lower socioeconomic status and lower parental education. Those studies that do include a control group may not be able to rule out other factors that are associated with child abuse, such as family problems unrelated to alcohol abuse, child neglect, or other forms of victimization.

Most analyses of childhood abuse have focused on the factors that increase the likelihood of dysfunctional consequences such as alcohol abuse while not examining other "protective factors" related to lower alcohol abuse. For example, one study (Fleming, Mullen, Sibthorpe, Attewell, & Bammer, 1998) of 710 Australian women who reported childhood sexual abuse illustrates the importance of an additional factor, family background. Specifically, adult alcohol problems among women with childhood sexual abuse were more likely only for women who also had a mother perceived to be cold, had an alcoholic partner, or believed that alcohol was a sexual disinhibitor.

In sum, the alcoholic parent may adversely affect the child in several different ways. Nonetheless, some children do not seem to be harmed by living with an alcoholic parent. They deal with the stress of living with an alcoholic parent well, just as some children who must deal with problems of a parent unrelated to substance abuse can cope well. Identifying the sources of this resiliency of some children is an important task for researchers.

ALCOHOLIC FAMILY INTERACTIONS

Observing the interactions of members of alcoholic families may provide important insights about the process of family disruption from the alcoholic's drinking. Correlations of retrospective self-reports of parent and child behaviors, even if they do not withhold embarrassing admissions, do not examine the actual dynamics of family interactions. Accordingly, some researchers (Steinglass, Bennett, Wolin, & Reiss, 1987) bring families into the clinic or the laboratory and observe their interactions directly. This type of research is expensive and time-consuming but offers the advantage that the observations are made directly by the researchers. One shortcoming is that the clinic may involve biased samples of families.

Moreover, family interactions in the laboratory or the clinic may yield artificial or atypical behavior because participants know they are being observed. However, direct observation of families in their own homes is difficult to achieve due to the amount of time required and the intrusiveness of the observers, which may distort the typical behaviors.

Wet Versus Dry Interactions

A series of studies (Steinglass, 1981) involved direct observations of family interactions. In one study, an alcoholic who was being treated in a residential facility volunteered to be a research participant. However, he was reluctant to give up alcohol and had stated his intention to resume drinking following discharge. He agreed to be observed in an interview session while sober, along with his wife and two teenage children and a psychiatrist. The session, representing a **dry interaction**, was marked by confrontations between him and the other family members who attacked his behavior.

A week later, another interview occurred with one important difference. Prior to the interview, the alcoholic was allowed to drink 6 oz of alcohol and was told he could drink during the interview. Family members were informed about this procedure and agreed to participate as part of a research project. The alcoholic was less depressed than in the first interview and was assertive with his family. Similarly, the family members were more animated, whereas in the first interview, they had sat rigidly in their seats, avoiding eye contact with each other. Verbal interactions increased dramatically. Surprisingly, during this **wet interaction** there was also considerable laughter among all members, even when references were made to some of the alcoholic's past alcoholic behaviors.

The difference in behavior in the two interviews may reflect a cyclical pattern of behaviors associated with sobriety and those related to intoxication (Steinglass, 1981). The family acts as if it believes that certain behaviors are caused by the alcohol, but such behaviors do not occur when the alcoholic is sober. These intoxicated-state behaviors are highly predictable over drinking occasions for any given family, although the specific behaviors may vary across alcoholic families.

More important than their regularity is the use of these behaviors as short-term problem-solving strategies for dealing with family problems (e.g., feelings, role conflicts, sexual difficulties, or problems external to the family such as neighbors or work issues). Thus, alcohol might act to make one person assertive in dealing with a problem when assertion is desirable, or it might lead another person to withdraw from conflict when such retreat helps promote interpersonal harmony. Such habits or strategies inspired by alcohol become stronger over time. The family is not typically aware of this function served by the alcohol. In fact, the family usually views the alcoholism as the problem rather than as the strategy for coping with everyday problems. Although alcohol may work for short-term solutions, it does not work in the long run and also creates the additional problems of alcohol dependency and its disintegrative effects on the family.

In one study (Jacob & Leonard, 1992), researchers videotaped interactions between the members of alcoholic couples to study the sequences of responses between them. Alcoholic husbands reacted with negative behavior to problem-solving attempts of their wives; when the husbands' behavior was positive, it had no effect on their wives. In comparison, with depressed couples, alcoholic husbands were less positive in their responses to the problem-solving efforts of their wives. Even during sober interactions, there were differences between alcoholic and other couples, with more complaints and hostility in marriage for the alcoholics. Alcoholic husbands were less unhappy than their wives were, and they were also less aware of wives' complaints.

Audio recordings of dinnertime conversations of 96 alcoholic and 47 control families were assessed (Jacob, Haber, Leonard, & Rushe, 2000). Two subgroups of alcoholics were formed based on the male alcoholic's level of antisociality. Across all groups, mothers' rate of communication to children was greater than that of fathers for all communication variables; similarly, children's rate of communication to mothers exceeded their rate to fathers across all communication variables. Contrary to expectation, families of alcoholics with higher levels of antisociality expressed lower levels of positivity, disagreement, and instrumentality than did families of alcoholics with lower antisociality.

Episodic Versus Steady Drinker Interactions

A distinction between *episodic* (binge) and *steady* (regular pattern) drinkers may improve our understanding of the effects of alcoholism on family interactions (Jacob & Leonard, 1988). Drinking comes to serve as a strategy for facilitating problem solving among steady drinkers. In contrast, for episodic drinkers, it functions as a means of avoidance and expressing hostility in conflicting situations. Observations of sober interactions showed no differences between these two types of alcoholics. However, after drinking occurred, more problem solving was found for couples with a steady drinker, possibly because pattern drinking is more predictable than **episodic drinking**.

Overall, these studies suggest that alcoholic family interactions when the alcoholic is drinking differ from those observed under sobriety, but the exact pattern may differ for alcoholics with different drinking styles. The assumption that all alcoholic couples are similar should be questioned (McCrady & Epstein, 1995) because the **drinking style** is an important factor in the couples' interactions.

ADULT CHILDREN OF ALCOHOLICS

Clinical observations have suggested that children from an alcoholic home can have insecurity, low self-esteem, and extreme needs to please others (Beattie, 1987; Cermak, 1986). They judge themselves without mercy, feel different from other people, and have difficulty having fun. These consequences could lead these children to alcohol and other drug abuse as they grow up. Understanding how COAs are affected by growing up in alcoholic families may be useful in seeing how alcohol-related problems continue from one generation to the next.

Alcoholism of parents leads to a dysfunctional family (Black, 1981). However, children react in various ways to their parental drinking (Wegsheider, 1981). Many experience anger and resentment or even suppression of feelings. Some children cope by withdrawal, and others may try to placate and mediate. Many children may come to blame themselves for the problem. These different reactions are adaptations to a dysfunctional family situation that will eventually entail serious psychological cost to the well-being of the child.

COAs show wide variations in how they are affected by growing up in alcoholic homes. They face many stressful experiences including family arguments, conflicts, shame, and in some cases violence. In early childhood, coping varies from distancing and avoidance to conflict to assuming parental functions.

The overall evidence regarding adverse outcomes for children from alcoholic families is mixed. Some early studies found COAs have more mental health problems (Moos & Billings, 1982) and engage in substance abuse more often (Beardslee, Son, & Vaillant, 1986). Some studies (Roosa, Sandler, Beals, & Short, 1988) found that adolescent COAs have lower self-esteem, more depression, and heavier drinking in comparison to NCOAs, but the evidence involved mostly self-report about the parental drinking. Other factors such as physical abuse and other family psychopathologies were not considered as causes.

A middle-aged, middle-class community sample of female COAs had higher levels of depression and lower levels of self-esteem than NCOAs (Domenico & Windle, 1993). COAs also reported lower levels of perceived social support, family cohesion, control over their children, and marital satisfaction and higher levels of marital conflict. No significant differences in alcohol use were found.

Sons of alcoholics drank significantly more heavily, experienced problems earlier, and developed alcohol dependence more extensively than daughters of alcoholics or NCOAs, according to an analysis over 5 years with 12,686 young adults from the National Longitudinal Survey of Youth (Jennison & Johnson, 1998).

Mothers with alcohol abuse or alcohol dependence may have adverse effects on the mental health of their children (Jones, 2007). A study was conducted with 2,193 children, half boys and half girls, in the 1994 National Longitudinal Survey of Youth whose mothers showed alcohol abuse or dependence. The sons had higher behavior problem scores while the daughters received less emotional support and cognitive stimulation at home.

Documented cases of childhood physical and sexual abuse and/or neglect (n = 500) and matched controls (n = 396) in the Midwest were contacted and interviewed in middle adulthood (Widom et al., 2007). Women who experienced child abuse or neglect reported higher past-year typical quantity and past-month number of days of drinking eight or more drinks than nonabused/nonneglected women. For men and women, parental alcohol/drug problems had a significant indirect effect on the offspring's drinking in middle adulthood through young adult alcohol diagnosis.

Other research, however, found that many COAs function as well as or better than NCOAs from control families (Velleman & Orford, 1999). Sampling differences may account for some inconsistencies because only those COAs seeking counseling were included, and they may have had other problems not directly derived from the parents' alcoholism.

When COAs were compared with children from families that experienced a different major problem (divorce), no differences were found on current outcomes of functioning; nor did they differ from a control group (Senchak, Leonard, Greene, & Carroll, 1995). This similarity occurred despite the fact that COAs were more likely to remember that their fathers were cold than were children from divorced or control families. Children from families with divorce or alcoholism both recalled more parental conflict than did the controls.

The degree of risk for children may differ, depending on the type of alcohol-dependent parent. One study (Zucker & Ellis, 1996) compared family life of fathers who were antisocial alcoholics (AAL), nonantisocial alcoholics (NAAL), and nonalcoholics. The AAL fathers came from families with a greater density of alcoholism, lower intellectual functioning, and higher levels of nonalcoholic psychopathology in comparison to NAAL fathers. Moreover, the wives of AAL fathers had higher levels of antisocial behaviors than those of NAAL fathers. AAL families showed more aggressive behavior and conflict and had lower socioeconomic status than NAAL families.

Paternal depression and alcohol problems were higher in AAL than in NAAL families, and the nonalcoholic control families were lowest. The differences were not as wide among mothers but were apparent for antisocial behavior and current depression levels. Finally, spousal aggression was highest for AAL families, followed by NAAL families and then by controls.

These differences could provide a basis for greater risk of problems for the children of AAL families. The different backgrounds and experiences of AAL and NAAL families affect how parents treat their children and possibly affect the degree of risk their children face for subsequent alcohol problems. Table 9.1 shows that for preschool children, as well as for early elementary schoolchildren, aggression (externalizing behavior), depression (internalizing behavior), hyperactivity, and risky temperament (a composite index of activity and emotional reactivity level) were highest for COAs from AAL families, lower for children from NAAL families, and lowest for children from control nonalcoholic families.

One hypothesis is that hyperactivity in children, rather than parental alcoholism, is the basis for the relationship between parental alcoholism and problems in children. Because hyperactive children suffer from attention deficit, they may exhibit behavioral undercontrol and have inadequate coping skills to deal with the stress of living in the home with an alcoholic parent (Sher, Walitzer, Wood, & Brent, 1991).

TABLE 9.1   Differences in risk factor levels for children of alcoholics and children of nonalcoholics.

Differences in Childhood Risk Among Boys From Families With Different Alcoholic Subtypes and From Nonalcoholic Control Families

Childhood Risk Indicators	**Degree to Which Indicator Is Present in Children**
Preschool Years (ages 3–5)	
Child Externalizing Behavior Problems[1]	AAL > NAAL > Control
Child Internalizing Behavior Problems[2]	AAL > NAAL > Control
Child Hyperactivity[3]	AAL > NAAL > Control
Child Risky Temperament	AAL > NAAL > Control
Early School Years (ages 6–8)	
Child Externalizing Behavior Problems	AAL > NAAL > Control
Child Internalizing Behavior Problems	AAL > NAAL = Control

[1]Aggressivity and delinquency
[2]Depressed or uncommunicative behavior
[3]Restlessness and short attention span

AAL = Antisocial alcoholics
NAAL = Nonantisocial alcoholics
Control = Matched nonalcoholics from the same communities

Source: Adapted from "The role of family influences in development and risk" by Ellis, D. A., Zucker, R. A., & Fitzgerald, H. E., 1997, *Alcohol Health & Research World, 21*(3), 218–226.

Weak support was found in a review (West & Prinz, 1987) of seven earlier studies for the idea that COAs are more hyperactive. Some later evidence (Molina, Pelham, Gnagy, Thompson, & Marshal, 2007) from a comparison of 142 adolescents with childhood attention deficit hyperactivity disorder (ADHD) with 100 matched controls without this diagnosis found that ADHD moderated the alcoholic parental influence as only the children with ADHD showed impairment.

Adverse effects of ADHD may not be apparent until adolescents are older. A study (Molina et al., 2007) did a follow-up of 364 ADHD probands after an average of 8 years, either when they were adolescents (11–17 years old) or young adults (18–28 years of age). Heavy drinking and *DSM-IV* dependence symptoms were elevated among 15- to 17-year-old but not among 11- to 14-year-old probands in comparison to age-matched adolescents (n = 120) without ADHD or to adults (n = 120).

Developmental Trajectories

Increased research now examines developmental trajectories because differences between children of COAs and NCOAs may not be invariant but change with age (Chassin, Fora, & King, 2004). A heavy drinking/heavy drug use group was at risk for alcohol and drug dependence, persistent dependence, more familial alcoholism, negative emotionality, and low constraint. In contrast, a moderate drinking/experimental drug use group was at risk for alcohol dependence but not comorbid or persistent dependence. This group exhibited less negative emotionality and higher constraint.

COAs depart from more normative trajectories for externalizing behaviors such as aggression. Typically, childhood aggressive behavior of NCOAs increases from 18 months to 3 years, but then declines sharply from age 3 to 4. In contrast, COAs with two parents with alcohol problems did not show the normative decline from 3 to 4 years of age (Edwards, Eiden, & Leonard, 2006). A longitudinal study (Wong et al., 2006) of a community sample of 514 preschool COAs and matched controls found that children slower in developing behavioral control or with lower initial levels of resiliency were more likely to use alcohol and other drugs during adolescence.

There are gender differences in trajectories. For boys, disruptive behavior declines from preschool to age 12, but those with alcoholic fathers are consistently higher in disruptive behavior than those with nonalcoholic fathers, even after controlling for maternal alcohol problems, family conflict, and child temperament (Loukas, Zucker, Fitzgerald, & Krull, 2003). In contrast, daughters of alcoholic fathers as compared to those of nonalcoholic fathers show lower social competence at age 6, but the difference is gone by age 15 (Hussong, Zucker, Wong, Fitzgerald, & Puttler, 2005). This change was primarily due to decreases in social competence among girls of nonalcoholic fathers rather than to increases in social competence by girls of alcoholic fathers.

Which COAs Become Alcoholics?

Fortunately, not all COAs become alcoholics. What are the underlying mechanisms for those who do become alcoholics? Many COAs develop low self-esteem from the greater amount of life stresses experienced in the home, which in turn leads to depression and other symptoms (Roosa et al., 1988). Eventually, this process might increase the risk of alcohol abuse as a means of coping with the low self-esteem. However, for those children in alcoholic homes who do not experience as many threats to their self-esteem, there may be a weaker adverse impact of parental alcoholism.

The family environment may affect the likelihood of COAs becoming alcoholics as adults in complex ways. A follow-up of a classic longitudinal study of adolescent boys started in the 1940s examined factors that affected the drinking of sons of alcoholics (McCord, 1988). If the mother had held the alcoholic father in high esteem, the sons were more likely to show alcoholic tendencies. In nonalcoholic families in which sons became alcoholics, a better predictor than the mother's attitude toward the father was the extent to which the sons were undercontrolled during adolescence. Thus, different pathways to alcoholism may exist in different families.

Consistent with this view, an analysis (Bijttebier, Goethals, & Ansoms, 2006) of the relationship between parental alcoholism and self-esteem of COAs found that family cohesion was a mediator of the relationship. Low global self-worth among COAs was more likely if the family lacked cohesion.

Invulnerables

More variability exists among COAs than the formulations of self-help organizations such as **Adult Children of Alcoholics (ACOA)** would suggest (Werner, 1986). A large percentage of these children seem to function ably and have been termed **invulnerables**. It would be worthwhile to examine the factors that enable them to do so well while others do not.

All alcoholic parents do not have the same severity of alcoholism, and the alcoholism does not lead to divorce or a splitting of the family in all cases. The age of the child when a parent develops alcoholism, the child's relationship in general with parents, the size of the family, and other forms of parental psychopathology are additional factors that might prove important in determining how detrimental the alcoholism of a parent is on the mental health of the child.

Protective Factors

In addition to the risk factors presented by alcoholism in the family, shown in Figure 9.2, there may also be counterforces that protect against the development of alcohol and other drug use. For example, children might be protected by nonalcoholic mothers who might offset the negative influences of alcoholic fathers (Curran & Chassin, 1996).

COAs could be protected in several ways by their parents. For example, parental monitoring of adolescents' involvement with peers who abuse drugs seems to help prevent their adoption of such practices (Chassin et al., 1996). However, alcohol-abusing parents are probably less likely to practice this vigilance.

The nonalcoholic parent, other relatives, older siblings, and friends could nurture COAs to help offset the negative impact of the alcoholic parent on the children's self-esteem. COAs also may develop a sense of self-worth through associations with nonalcoholic friends. In addition, the children may be fortunate enough to encounter some

FIGURE 9.2   A model showing how positive factors outside the alcoholic family may counter the adverse effect of family alcohol abuse on the child's self-esteem. The total set of factors determines the likelihood of use of drugs to cope.

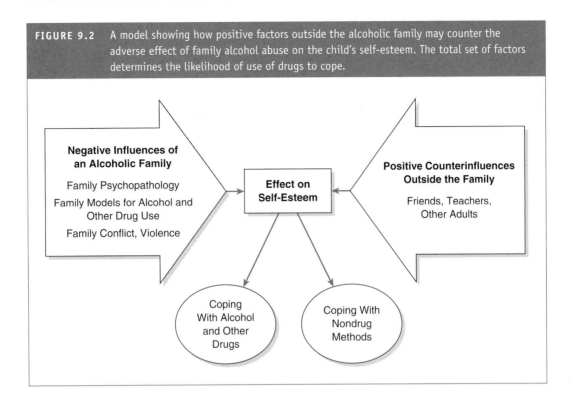

sources of rewarding experiences from adults at school or in the community that may offset any adverse effects of an alcoholic home.

Parenting by COAs

How do COAs relate to their own children when they become parents? After the experience of having been reared by one or more alcoholic parents, do they differ from NCOAs in how they bring up their children?

One study of COA and NCOA mothers and their children (Bensley, Spieker, & McMahon, 1994) showed COA mothers had less problematic mother-child interactions during teaching a task to their children at 1 year of age, during structured play at preschool age, and in child attachment behavior at preschool age. Although COAs reported more historical life stress, more family disruption, and more drug use, these problems did not appear to be related to their own performance as parents. They recalled feeling relatively more rejection than love from their alcoholic parent, but this was not related to their own parenting behaviors. Perhaps some COAs, as parents, make more efforts to avoid the shortcomings of the parenting they received themselves.

A Critique of COA Studies

There is a risk of overgeneralizations from studies of COAs based on those receiving counseling (Velleman & Orford, 1999). Those COAs who do not have adjustment problems are overlooked, as suggested by Figure 9.3. There is a lack of controlled research to evaluate the validity of COA typologies, and few comparisons are made between children of alcoholic parents and children of nonalcoholic parents (Blane, 1988). The definition of the alcoholic parent is often vague and varies widely across different studies (Searles & Windle, 1990).

In studies where controls are included, only small differences in psychological functioning and well-being have been found between COAs and NCOAs. For example, a comparison (Tweed & Ryff, 1991) of 114 adults who were COAs with 125 adult NCOAs found that although the COAs showed higher anxiety and depression scores than the NCOAs, possibly due to their awareness of the risks of growing up in an alcoholic home, no differences were found in the overall functioning of the two groups.

Moreover, research evaluating various types of interventions is sorely needed. It is important to determine whether different types of programs are needed, depending on the age of the child. Psychological interventions might even have harmful effects for some COAs, especially if the labeling of such individuals promotes self-fulfilling prophecies. Studies (Burk & Sher, 1990) have demonstrated that adolescents hold more negative

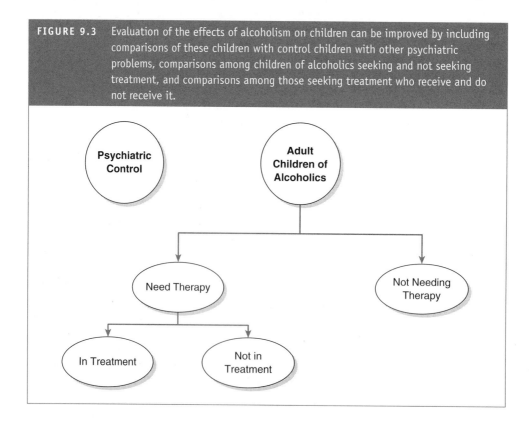

FIGURE 9.3 Evaluation of the effects of alcoholism on children can be improved by including comparisons of these children with control children with other psychiatric problems, comparisons among children of alcoholics seeking and not seeking treatment, and comparisons among those seeking treatment who receive and do not receive it.

stereotypes of COAs than they hold of "typical" teenagers. Adolescents gave lower evalua-tions of an adolescent they viewed on video who was labeled on the soundtrack as a child from an alcoholic rather than a nonalcoholic home, regardless of whether the depiction of the adolescent was positive or negative. A similar bias affected ratings of mental health pro-fessionals on the same task.

Most naturalistic and clinical studies of adolescent and adult COAs are retrospective, rely-ing on inferences and self-reports about earlier events (Sher et al., 1991). The implication is that the present differences in characteristics that distinguish between children of alco-holic parental environments and children of nonalcoholic parental environments can be attributed to this factor alone. However, objective and thorough comparisons of early-life events experienced by children of alcoholics and those of nonalcoholics are rarely available. Nevertheless, strong beliefs are widely held that COAs are uniquely dysfunctional. This sit-uation could be an example of a "Barnum effect" in which vague descriptions of character-istics caused by growing up in an alcoholic home are accepted readily as true by anyone with low self-esteem (Sher, 1997).

Many research studies of COAs first identify alcoholic parents, usually in treatment, and then compare their children with those of nonalcoholic parents. One problem with the use of a sample of alcoholic parents in treatment is that they may not be comparable with nontreated alcoholics who could be either more or less impaired as a group in their alcoholism. Similarly, the children of treated alcoholics may not be equivalent to those of nontreated alcoholics.

Another major problem with these methods, each of which involves cross-sectional comparisons of different groups at one point in time, is the difficulty of establishing causal inferences. If there is a correlation between the drinking levels of the parents and those of the children, it could be that the parents' alcoholism is producing the problems in their children or vice versa or that both processes are involved. The use of longitudinal designs in which measures are taken of the same individuals at different points in time would permit such infer-ences, but these methods are expensive and obviously require a longer time frame.

It also might be important to differentiate among alcoholic families in which one versus both parents are alcoholic. If both parents are alcoholic, this might appear to be worse than if only one parent is alcoholic. On the other hand, if one parent is alcoholic and the other is not, there might be more conflicts between the two parents. More research is needed that examines the effect of discordant drinking patterns of the couple and how it influences mar-ital satisfaction, conflict, and child neglect (Leonard & Eiden, 2007).

When only one parent is alcoholic, comparisons of the effect of the sex of the alcoholic might prove important. Furthermore, the effect of the alcoholic parent could very well differ for sons and daughters. Whether the alcoholic parent is the same or the opposite sex of the child may have different implications for that child. Unfortunately, little research has examined these aspects of the alcoholic parent-child relationship.

CODEPENDENCY

The discussion thus far has focused on the family environment of an alcoholic home as it might affect the children and nonalcoholic members of the family. It is assumed that the family wants the drinking to stop or be reduced and that the family will try to influence the alcoholic in this direction. However, it is also important to examine the possibility that the reactions of the nonalcoholics may paradoxically contribute to or enable the continued or increased drinking of the alcoholic.

A systems theory view of the family (Bowen, 1974) focuses on the influence of each member's behavior on other members. This model holds that, in general, families achieve a balance or homeostasis from which they resist change. In alcoholic families, alcoholism becomes the focal point to which adjustments are made, and family interactions can become highly dysfunctional in maintaining this equilibrium. The concept of **codependency** (Wegsheider, 1981) refers to this reciprocal relationship between the alcoholic and one or more nonalcoholics who may unwittingly aid and abet the alcoholic's excessive drinking and irresponsible nondrinking behaviors created by the drinking.

Change occurs within the family as it adjusts to the drinking problem (Jackson, 1954). There is an understandable tendency for nonalcoholic family members to deny that there is a problem for a long time. The alcoholic becomes the focus of the family, and adjustments are made to accommodate the alcoholic. Thus, the codependents sacrifice their own independence and autonomy by reacting to the alcoholic's behavior in a futile attempt to regain control. By covering up and excusing the alcoholic's shortcomings, the codependent becomes an accomplice.

Due to the stigma of alcoholism, it is not surprising that many nonalcoholic family members are inclined to hide the fact of alcoholism from the outside world by making up excuses for the alcoholic when necessary. In addition, they may blame themselves or be blamed by others for their role in facilitating and maintaining the drinking of the alcoholic member. Codependent behavior, however, generally has not been seen in a negative light until recently. Indeed, in the past, a heroic vision of the martyred family members of the alcoholic was a more prevalent portrayal. However, the view that the nonalcoholic members of a family could contribute to maintaining the alcoholic's drinking has gained acceptance.

Codependency is regarded as a problem in its own right (Cermak, 1986). By continually adjusting and reacting to the alcoholic's drinking but without success, the codependent suffers a loss of self-esteem and experiences a mixture of depression, helplessness, and self-blame. As the alcoholic becomes less able to perform his or her family roles, the codependent may try to rescue the family and assume responsibility by trying to perform those tasks in addition to his or her own. Using concepts from Twelve-Step programs such as Alcoholics Anonymous, Adult Children of Alcoholics has actively called attention to the dysfunctional aspects of codependency among codependents and encouraged them to toss aside the need to control the lives of others.

This line of thinking is not limited to alcoholism but has been applied to an array of addictions, including dependency on other people as well as on substances. Pop psychology and self-help books call for codependents to recognize and overcome their codependent relationships. Critics (Gordon & Barrett, 1993) of the construct condemn it as a popular social movement that tends to stigmatize and blame the victim for being dysfunctional.

Codependency quickly achieved wide acceptance in the psychiatric, psychological, and addiction literature (Stafford, 2001). It was initially developed to describe the reactions of wives of men who abuse alcohol, but codependency has been transformed into a generic term to refer to any dysfunctional style of relating to others. There have been clinical observations and anecdotal evidence about the nature of codependency, but few rigorous scientific investigations validate these impressions, identify correlates, and determine consequences. One study compared couples in which one member was a recovering alcoholic with a group of matched couples without an alcoholic member. Higher codependency levels occurred for the clinical sample (Prest, Benson, & Protinsky, 1998). Moreover, within the clinical group, alcoholics and their spouses had similar dysfunction in their families of origin, current families, and codependency levels.

Wives of Alcoholics

Alcoholism often has been referred to as a family disease in the sense that all members are adversely afflicted. It was not until the 1950s that the family dynamics of alcoholism began to receive attention. The early focus came from clinical studies of alcoholic men and their nonalcoholic wives (Ablon, 1984). At that time, it was suspected that the wife often might have been a factor causing the alcoholic to drink because she was frequently observed to have psychological problems. Thus, the alcoholism of the husband was blamed on the wife as if her psychological disturbances somehow drove him to drink or as if she had some characteristics that facilitated her husband's drinking.

Comparisons (deBlois & Stewart, 1983) of wives of alcoholics and wives of nonalcoholics found that those whose first husbands had been alcoholics had married at an earlier age after knowing their husbands for briefer periods. They had more marital problems, lower education, and lower socioeconomic status. However, the study was unrepresentative in that the sample had women who were mothers of boys attending a child psychiatry clinic, and assortative mating could also account for the link between husbands' drinking and the psychological problems of their wives. Certain types of people are attracted to each other and marry. Thus, antisocial and rebellious men who drink excessively may tend to be matched with women who have psychological problems (Stewart & deBlois, 1981).

Yet another explanation is that some of the psychological problems of the wife of an alcoholic might be viewed as the consequences of living with an alcoholic husband (Jackson, 1962). Support for this view can be found in a study (Dawson, Grant, Chou, & Stinson, 2007) of over 11,000 women in the first wave of the 2001–2002 National Epidemiologic Survey on Alcohol and Related Conditions (NESARC) that found that those with partners having alcohol problems were more likely to experience victimization, injury, mood disorders, and anxiety disorders and to be in poorer health than women whose partners did not have alcohol problems. They also experienced more life stressors and had lower mental/psychological quality-of-life scores even after the fact that many of the women also had their own drinking problems was controlled for.

The emphasis on wives of alcoholic husbands was appropriate for previous generations, but with the changed sex roles and increased drinking among women, more research needs to be directed at how alcoholic wives affect the well-being of non-alcoholic husbands.

Summary

Marriage partners tend to use alcohol at similar levels, as people may tend to select mates who share similar characteristics and behavior patterns. Initially, alcohol consumption declines during marriage. Over time, alcohol use will increase for some individuals. Those marriages in which one or both partners develop alcohol abuse or dependency may generate conflict and even end in divorce. Following divorce, alcohol abuse may begin or continue to increase.

Children living in alcoholic family environments may be affected in several ways by the alcoholism of one or both parents. Direct effects on early childhood development may occur because the parents' drinking behavior serves as a model for the children to imitate later. However, it appears that for some children, there is a drop-off in the tendency to imitate the opposite-sex parent's drinking if it is heavy. Parental alcoholism may produce adverse effects in the form of neglect or abuse of children, consequences that may eventually lead to excessive drinking in the children when they become older.

Indirect paths of influence are also possible when alcoholism leads to domestic strife or divorce, which could create a home environment that might impair the children's psychological development of self-esteem, regardless of whether they eventually develop drinking problems.

In addition to affecting the levels of alcohol abuse in their children, some alcoholic parents may harm their children with physical and sexual abuse. Some evidence shows that childhood sexual abuse and, to some extent, childhood physical abuse are related to adult alcohol abuse, especially for women.

Direct observations of interactions of alcoholic families reveal that the family members behave differently when the alcoholic is dry versus sober, but the nature of the differences may vary with the family or whether the alcoholic is a binge or steady drinker. Alcohol may function as a short-term coping response for problems that eventually fails. These studies are based on small samples that volunteer to be observed; thus, the findings may not be generalizable to other alcoholic families, but they offer important opportunities to develop hypotheses about the impact of alcoholism on family interactions.

Nonalcoholic family members may inadvertently maintain the alcoholic's drinking. Thus, in adjusting their behavior to accommodate the alcoholic's needs, they may hope to avoid conflict but ironically may facilitate its continuance.

COAs are hypothesized to have higher risks of becoming alcoholics themselves than are NCOAs. Although some research supports this view, many COAs do not appear to be harmed by having alcoholic parents. It is important to also study which factors are protective in preventing these at-risk children from following in the footsteps of their alcoholic parents.

Codependency may develop when nonalcoholic family members try to please or not annoy the alcoholic. Thus, the blame is shifted, partially at least, from the alcoholic to the nonalcoholic family members.

Stimulus/Response

1. Marriage partners generally seem to be similar in their levels of drinking. Do you think this outcome involves conscious awareness of similarity of their alcohol use by the couples during courtship, or do you think a more subtle process is involved?

2. Have you been seriously involved in a romantic relationship where your partner's alcohol or drug use was a major deterrent for you to continue with this person?

3. Some research indicates that, following divorce, alcohol consumption may increase due to the feeling of loss following the breakup. Can you make any arguments for predicting *reduced* drinking by some individuals following divorce?

4. How does drinking alter the pattern and nature of interactions between drinkers and nondrinkers in a family? Can you identify both positive and negative interactions after drinking?

5. Do you think that parents who drink heavily treat their children differently when they are sober versus when they have been drinking? If so, describe the nature of the different treatment and speculate on why such differences exist.

6. If one or both of your parents was a heavy drinker when you were growing up, did you act differently toward them when they were sober versus intoxicated? If so, can you explain why?

Age and Alcohol
and Other Drug Use

Adolescents

College Students

Young Adults

Older Populations

Age, Cohort, and Period Effects

Summary

Stimulus/Response

The nature of alcohol and other drug use, abuse, and dependency changes over the course of life. When children become adolescents, they want to—and usually are expected to—become more independent. Eventually adolescents move out of the home for many reasons, and they are no longer directly under the observation or control of their parents. They get a job and live on their own, drop out of high school, leave to attend college, join the military, or get married, for example. Many engage in new activities, some of which their parents may disapprove of, including use of many drugs. Not all adolescents will take this route, but for many others the temptation may be irresistible and the peer pressure overwhelming.

Later, as individuals assume adult roles, they take on the responsibilities of jobs and careers. Most also enter marriage and possibly eventual parenthood. Changes occur in their views of normative drinking, friends' alcohol use, social and recreational activities, and religious involvement. Consequently, many of them reduce the extent of their drug use as it might interfere with the fulfillment of the obligations and commitments associated with these roles (Bachman et al., 2002; Johnston, Wadsworth, O'Malley, Bachman, & Schulenberg, 1997). In midlife, other role transitions occur. Some will divorce, others will experience widowhood, and some will enter new marriages. Their children will grow up and leave the home. During later years, they may change jobs, reduce their workload, or retire. In addition, with age, physical decline and major health problems occur that may alter the effect of alcohol and other drugs. Smaller doses of alcohol and other drugs may produce greater physical and behavioral impairment. Accordingly, some older drinkers may reduce their drinking to compensate.

Alcohol and other drug use must be studied across the life span because use patterns can change over these life transitions. Such evidence could help identify and modify the antecedents and consequences of alcohol and other drug use patterns and problems. The present chapter focuses on factors involved in alcohol and other drug use for different age groups. First, findings about alcohol and other drug use and problems among adolescents will be presented, followed by a similar analysis for college students. Finally, evidence on the nature of alcohol and other drug use and problems among middle-aged and older populations will be discussed.

Age differences in alcohol use and consequences will not be the same for men and women or across all racial/ethnic groups. However, it would be difficult to examine all three of these key factors—and their combinations—in relationship to alcohol and other drug use in a single chapter. To simplify the presentation, evidence about gender and racial/ethnic group differences in alcohol and other drug use will be presented separately in the next two chapters. However, whenever generalizations are made about one factor such as age, it should be kept in mind that there may be variations for subgroups along the two other factors, gender and race/ethnicity.

ADOLESCENTS

Adolescence is a stage of development with rapid biological, physical, and psychological changes when young people learn the expectations and norms of the adult society into which they will soon be entering. This period involves discovery about oneself and the formation of values and goals. The process of identity development involves trying out different roles and encountering different experiences before deciding what behaviors best fit. This process occurs with respect to a variety of important concerns such as careers, marriage, and parenthood. Thus, adolescents typically date a variety of persons before entering marriage. They work at a variety of jobs to gain knowledge and experience before making commitments about careers.

A similar attitude of experimentation lies behind the initial use of alcohol and other drugs for many youth. Although drinking and smoking is a legal activity for individuals over the age of 21 and 18, respectively, in most states, the same behavior is prohibited for minors who are considered "too young" to use these drugs. The added incentives of challenging authority might increase the appeal of drinking and smoking for some younger adolescents. Doing what you are not supposed to do might be a way of asserting independence and gaining peer approval.

For underage adolescents, unlike for most adults, alcohol and other drugs are lower in availability or accessibility due to legal, economic, and social factors. Thus, not using drugs may be due not to choice but to lack of opportunity. If adolescents cannot buy licit drugs because they are too young or because they do not have enough money, their drug use may be sporadic rather than continuous. Because their alcohol use is of relatively recent onset, dependency involving physical damage may be less likely for adolescents than for older drinkers. Even when alcohol use involves harmful consequences, they may often be immediate and short in duration. In contrast, the toll on physical health from prolonged drug use over many years may occur mainly in older people.

Most adolescents, prior to having their first drink, already have acquired firm expectations about how alcohol alters behavior and feelings (Miller, Smith, & Goldman, 1990). They know that when adults are depressed or angry they often consume more alcohol. Adolescents also recognize that adults also drink at social gatherings and parties to become less inhibited and to have more fun. Adolescents also have learned that drinking too much or too often has ruined many lives and created problems for others, but until they have actually used these drugs adolescents do not know what the actual effects of drinking will be for them physically and psychologically.

Faced with this background, most young adolescents approach alcohol with curiosity and fascination as well as some fear and anxiety. Alcohol advertising and media images promise that drinking will make life more exciting, alleviate negative moods, and impress peers. On the other hand, they realize that there are costs and benefits to drinking. Drinking could be detrimental to academic, social, or athletic success. In addition, many parents and other adults might strongly disapprove of drinking by adolescents.

Although a minority of adolescents abstain completely, sooner or later most adolescents will at least "experiment" with alcohol and other drugs. Some will satisfy their curiosity quickly and discontinue use or use infrequently and in small amounts. However, others will increase their frequency of use as well as use higher amounts. A variety of personal and social problems may result from drug use ranging from accidents to impaired work and school performance to physical health problems to interpersonal conflicts and aggression. Adolescents may believe that because they are young and relatively healthy, they can use drugs without losing control over their use.

Similar processes may be involved for the experimental use of illicit drugs but for a much smaller percentage of adolescents (Johnston, O'Malley, & Bachman, 1997). The same blend of curiosity, conformity to peer pressure, and fear may be present, perhaps coupled with rebellion and defiance among some.

Prevalence of Adolescent Alcohol and Other Drug Use

Since 1975, an annual national survey called **Monitoring the Future (MTF)** has documented the extent to which high school students, college students, and adults up to age 45 use different drugs (Johnston, O'Malley, Bachman, & Schulenberg, 2007b). We will focus on the data collected in classrooms from a total of 48,500 students in the 8th, 10th, and 12th grades from 400 schools across the United States. Participation was voluntary, and responses were anonymous.

Table 10.1 shows that past-30-days, past-12-months, and lifetime rates for alcohol, cigarette, marijuana, and any illicit drug use increase for the 8th, 10th, and 12th grades in the 2006 MTF survey. Data on the same variables for a decade earlier from 1995 are included as a comparison to show that all indices have shown a decline over that decade.

Alcohol was by far the most frequently used drug reported in the 2006 MTF survey. Table 10.1 shows that about 3 of every 4 students in the 12th grade had used alcohol at one time in their life, but only about half had used alcohol in the past month. Over half had been drunk,

TABLE 10.1 Comparison of 2006 and 1995 past-30-days, past-12-months, and lifetime percentages of use among 8th-, 10th-, and 12th-grade students for any illicit drug, marijuana, alcohol, "ever drunk," and cigarettes.

	8th Grade			10th Grade			12th Grade		
	30 days	12 months	Lifetime	30 days	12 months	Lifetime	30 days	12 months	Lifetime
Any Illicit Drug									
2006	8.1	14.8	20.9	16.8	28.7	36.1	21.5	36.5	48.2
1995	12.4	21.4	28.5	20.2	33.3	40.9	23.8	39.0	48.4
Marijuana									
2006	6.5	11.7	19.5	14.2	25.2	31.8	18.2	31.5	42.3
1995	9.1	15.8	25.3	17.2	28.7	24.1	21.2	34.7	41.7
Alcohol									
2006	17.2	33.6	43.5	33.8	55.8	61.5	45.3	66.5	72.7
1995	24.6	45.3	54.5	38.8	63.5	70.5	51.3	73.7	80.7
Ever Drunk									
2006	6.2	13.9	19.5	18.8	34.5	41.4	30.0	47.9	56.4
1995	8.3	18.4	25.3	20.8	34.1	46.9	33.2	52.5	63.2
Cigarettes									
2006	8.7	NA	24.6	14.5	NA	36.1	21.6	NA	47.1
1995	19.1	NA	46.4	27.9	NA	57.6	33.5	NA	64.2

Source: From *Monitoring the Future National Survey Results on Drug Use, 1975–2006: Volume I: Secondary School Students*, by L. D. Johnston, P. M. O'Malley, J. G. Bachman, and J. E. Schulenberg, 2007, Bethesda, MD: National Institute on Drug Abuse.

and just under half had smoked cigarettes during their lifetime. Close to half had used an illicit drug during their lifetime, but this rate was due mainly to marijuana (42%) use.

Unless they were involved with other forms of problem behavior, adolescents were likely to later lower their drinking levels (Donovan, Jessor, & Jessor, 1983), suggesting that their earlier use was a reflection of curiosity or experimental use rather than a precursor to heavier use. Over half of the adolescent problem drinkers who became nonproblem drinkers by young adulthood had married during the period in contrast to only 20% of the adolescent problem drinkers who remained so during young adulthood. Similar changes have been found with adolescents during the transition period from late adolescence to adulthood. Alcohol, cocaine, and marijuana use peaked in the mid-20s for both males and females compared to their use rates as high school seniors. Only cigarette use levels tended to persist (Johnston et al., 1997).

The National Survey on Drug Use and Health (NSDUH), described in detail in Chapter 4, examined a wider age range than the MTF survey. Only the alcohol section of the 2006 survey (Substance Abuse and Mental Health Services Administration [SAMHSA], 2007) will be presented here (refer to Figure 4.1). Among persons over age 12, rates of current alcohol use increased from 3.9% for ages 12–13 to a peak of 68.6% for ages 21–25. Drinking may peak around that age because many young adults begin to assume the adult responsibilities of careers, marriage, and childrearing.

The 2006 NSDUH found drinking by persons under the minimum legal age for drinking (persons aged 12–20) occurred in the past month for 10.8 million members (28.3%) of this age group. An estimated 7.2 million (19.0%) were binge drinkers, and 2.4 million (6.2%) were heavy drinkers. There was a gender difference in underage drinking, with higher current use for males than for females (29.2% vs. 27.4%, respectively); binge drinking (21.3% vs. 16.5%); and heavy drinking (7.9% vs. 4.3%). These patterns are similar to those found since 2002.

Long-Term Trends

Figure 10.1 presents the 30-year trend of annual prevalence rates in the MTF survey between 1976 and 2006 (Johnston et al., 2007b) separately for alcohol use and "been drunk" for grades 8, 10, and 12. After a peak around 90% in 1979 for 12th graders, the alcohol use

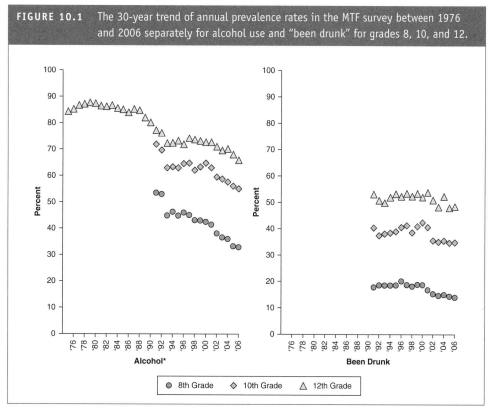

FIGURE 10.1   The 30-year trend of annual prevalence rates in the MTF survey between 1976 and 2006 separately for alcohol use and "been drunk" for grades 8, 10, and 12.

Source: From *Monitoring the Future National Survey Results on Drug Use, 1975–2006: Volume I: Secondary School Students*, by L. D. Johnston, P. M. O'Malley, J. G. Bachman, and J. E. Schulenberg, 2007, Bethesda, MD: National Institute on Drug Abuse.

*Beginning in 1993, a revised set of questions on alcohol use was introduced. From 1993 on, data points are based on the revised questions.

rate dropped steadily over the 1980s to around 70%. It increased slightly during the 1990s before declining after 2000 to around 70% and lower for younger students.

Age of First Drink

The age of first use of alcohol is a good predictor of future problems with alcohol (Dawson, Goldstein, Patricia Chou, June Ruan, & Grant, 2008; Zucker, Donovan, Masten, Mattson, & Moss, 2008). Early onset of drinking seems to be associated with future likelihood of heavy drinking, binge drinking, alcohol abuse, and alcohol dependence. Figure 10.2 shows the percentage of adults over age 21 with alcohol abuse or dependence in the 2006 NSDUH. Those who started alcohol use by age 14 had substantially greater risk of subsequent alcohol abuse and alcohol dependence than those who started at an older age.

Exactly what the relationship means is not clear. Does early drinking simply reflect a symptom, or marker, of high risk-taking tendencies in some children? Or might early use of alcohol cause later dependence on alcohol possibly by altering neurophysiological reactions and sensitivity to alcohol to increase its use? A prospective study (McGue, Iacono, Legrand, Malone, & Elkins, 2001) of 1,343 11-year-olds found that oppositionality, hyperactivity/impulsivity, and inattentiveness predicted drinking onset by age 14. These adolescents had high levels of disinhibitory behavior and psychopathology prior to their first use of alcohol, which suggests that they may have contributed to their subsequent drinking problems.

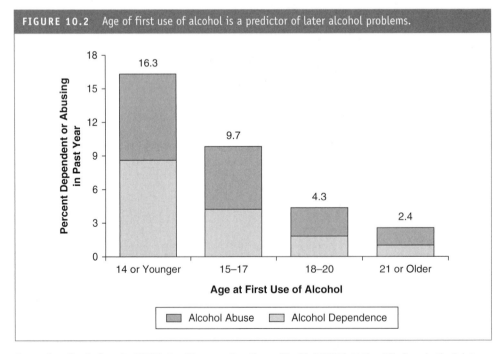

FIGURE 10.2 Age of first use of alcohol is a predictor of later alcohol problems.

Source: From *Results From the 2006 National Survey on Drug Use and Health (NSDUH): National Findings*, by the Substance Abuse and Mental Health Services Administration [SAMHSA], 2007, Rockville, MD: SAMHSA Office of Applied Studies.

Early age of drinking may only be a marker of subsequent alcohol dependence among children from alcoholic families, according to findings from a prospective study (King & Chassin, 2007) of adolescent children of alcoholics and matched control children of non-alcoholics (n = 395) at age 20 or 25. When other risk factors were controlled for, first use of alcohol at or before age 13 was not related to the odds of alcohol and drug dependence provided hard drugs were not used. However, early users of hard drugs were more likely to develop drug dependence by young adulthood, even while shared risk factors were controlled for.

Underage drinking is of great concern for many reasons. Early drinking may lead to poor school achievement, dropping out of school, and other forms of delinquency that may jeopardize users' futures. Underage alcohol use may increase the chances of subsequent alcohol and drug consumption and possible development of abuse and dependence.

Findings based on animal models suggest that heavy alcohol use may disrupt and alter important neurophysiological functions and processes in developing organisms related to alcohol metabolism, absorption, elimination, and sensitivity ("The Effects of Alcohol on Physiological Processes and Biological Development," 2004/2005). Early and extensive alcohol consumption can also produce serious physical harm to the adolescent's liver, bones, growth, and endocrine functions ("Genetics, Pharmacokinetics, and Neurobiology of Adolescent Alcohol Use," 2004/2005).

Gateway Drugs

Alcohol and tobacco have been dubbed "gateway drugs" since use of these drugs precedes the use of illicit drugs in many adolescents. The term implies that use of drugs such as alcohol and tobacco opens the way to use of illicit drugs and involvement in other forms of socially deviant behavior. Hence, these drugs are deemed additionally dangerous because of what they portend by way of future illicit drug use.

Numerous studies have shown that adolescents who drink or smoke are more likely to experiment with illicit drugs. For example, adolescents of high school age who either smoked or drank during the past month were much more likely to use other drugs (Department of Health and Human Services, 1997). Use of any illicit drug, for example, was reported by 35.3% of cigarette smokers but only by 4.7% of nonsmokers. Heavy users of alcohol (54.9%) were more likely to use any illicit drug than nondrinkers (4.3%).

A test of the gateway drug model (Tarter, Vanyukov, Kirisci, Reynolds, & Clark, 2006) compared boys who consumed licit drugs only (n = 99), boys who consumed licit drugs before marijuana use (gateway sequence; n = 97), and boys who used marijuana before using licit substances (n = 28) from ages 10–12 years through 22 years to determine what psychological, family, peer, school, and neighborhood characteristics were associated with each drug use pattern. Contrary to the gateway model, 22.4% of the participants who used marijuana did not exhibit the gateway sequence. Delinquency was more strongly related than licit drug use to marijuana use among those following the gateway pattern. Deviance proneness and drug availability in the neighborhood promoted marijuana use more than prior alcohol use.

Although use of alcohol and/or tobacco does not guarantee use of marijuana and other drugs, it seems to increase the chances substantially as the use of illegal drugs is much lower for those who have not first used alcohol or tobacco. In a temporal sense, it is undoubtedly true that most users of illicit drugs started with alcohol, tobacco, and/or marijuana. However, there is no evidence for a *pharmacological* gateway in the sense that use of these drugs alters the nervous system in ways that facilitate the use of illicit drugs. Use of licit drugs such as tobacco and alcohol is apt to precede most use of illicit drugs simply because of their easier availability and lower cost. Labeling them as "gateway" drugs only *describes* the sequence in which users move from one drug such as alcohol or tobacco to other drugs such as cocaine. However, to call them gateway drugs does not *explain* the underlying mechanisms for how they contribute to or influence the use of other drugs. It may mislead us to think that if social policies restricted access to the gateway drugs, there would be less eventual use of the illicit drugs.

The relationship of the use of gateway drugs to the use of other drugs is not necessarily a causal one. Some "third variable" such as a predisposing factor related to different personal backgrounds may determine which minority of gateway drug users move on to illicit drugs while the majority do not. Most adults engage in alcohol use to some extent, but only a relatively small percentage ever go on to use illicit drugs. Use of alcohol does not open a gate to use of illicit drugs in the sense of facilitating movement. Most illicit drug users started using alcohol before using other drugs, but the implication of the gateway metaphor that most alcohol users later take illicit drugs is obviously false.

Cross-Sectional Versus Longitudinal Studies

Most major surveys of adolescent drinking have been cross-sectional in design, comparing individuals from different age groups. However, this method does not allow for firm inferences about underlying processes responsible for the age differences. Several explanations can be considered for observed patterns. One explanation is that the level of alcohol and drug involvement leads to different consequences as age increases. Thus, high use may contribute to poor school achievement and work performance at a later age. Alternatively, it may be just the reverse, with low school and work accomplishments leading these individuals to cope by using alcohol and other drugs. Age differences might just reflect individual differences on factors that exist prior to initiation of alcohol and other drug use, such as personality traits, and that continue to operate at older ages.

To identify the processes involved in the initiation and development of alcohol and other drug use over age, we need *longitudinal* studies that assess the same individuals before substance use begins and observe how it changes over time. One example of the value of longitudinal studies is a study (Shedler & Block, 1990) covering individuals from preschool to age 18. Adolescents who engaged in some experimentation and temporary use of alcohol and other drugs were better adjusted with lower anxiety and higher social skills than those who did not. At the other extreme, frequent users were maladjusted and alienated, with more emotional distress. These differences in drug use were related to differences in parenting; adolescents who experimented with drugs but did not become heavy users had closer ties with parents than did either heavy users or nonusers.

Developmental Trajectories

Longitudinal studies examining change in use of alcohol and other drugs have increased efforts to identify variations in the developmental course of alcohol and other drug use patterns over the life span. Figure 10.3 diagrams a small sample of hypothetical **developmental trajectories**, or patterns of change over age. Whereas some drinkers start at low frequencies and/or amounts and remain at that level for many years, other drinkers may start at high frequencies and/or amounts, and still others may continue to drink at even higher levels. Others may start low and then increase later while still others may start high but later sharply reduce their use. The number of years that different individuals spend drinking also varies from a few to many years. Some start in their youth, others at midlife, and some during old age. Of course, many more complex patterns are possible as well. The value of identifying these trajectories is that the antecedents and consequences of different trajectories probably differ in important ways. Knowledge of these factors may prove valuable in designing more effective prevention and intervention strategies by tailoring them for drinkers with different use trajectories (Maggs & Schulenberg, 2004/2005).

Studies that identify trajectories apply complex statistical modeling techniques known as **latent growth curve models** and multilevel models. These tools search for trends in the temporal pattern of changes of alcohol and other drug use over three or more time points spanning several years. Some trajectory studies are primarily descriptive and designed to identify a normative or general trajectory across an age span. These studies seek to identify subgroups or define a taxonomy of distinct trajectories that describe the use patterns for the entire sample under investigation. An example is a model (Auerbach & Collins, 2006), based on data from the Reducing Risk in Young Adult Transitions Study (n = 1,143), that identified five dimensions of alcohol use among young adults: no use, occasional low use, occasional high use, frequent high use, and frequent high use with heavy episodic drinking. All categories of participants showed increased alcohol use over the 4 years. While low-alcohol users were more likely to remain at that level, moderate- and higher-level users were more likely to eventually be in the frequent high use with heavy episodic drinking group.

The most common trajectory subgroup observed across different studies of adolescents and young adults contains abstainers, light drinkers, or very rare heavy drinkers across all time periods measured (Maggs & Schulenberg, 2004/2005). Depending on the ages and other characteristics of the sample, the size of the low-risk group varies widely from as low as one fifth to over two thirds of the sample. Stable-moderate drinkers are heavy drinkers across adolescence and young adulthood but do not escalate—or even decrease—their use dramatically into middle age. About one third of adolescents and young adults fall into this group. Chronic heavy drinkers typically are early-onset heavy drinkers and generally do not decrease their drinking in their 20s. Late-onset heavy drinkers start to drink later (i.e., middle to late high school) than stable-moderate and chronic heavy drinkers, but their use escalates steeply. Decreasers begin heavy drinking at an early age, such as in middle school, but reduce their consumption significantly during high school. About 10% of adolescents and young adults fall into this subgroup.

These different trajectories or categories of users may have different causes and consequences of their alcohol and drug use. For example, do adolescents who are heavy

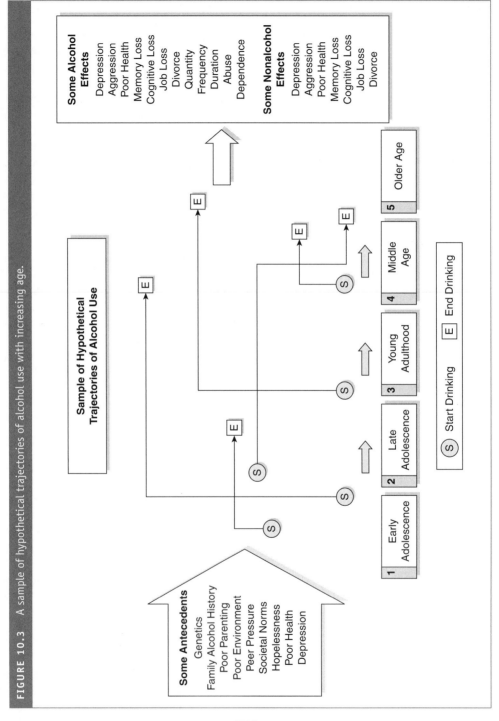

FIGURE 10.3 A sample of hypothetical trajectories of alcohol use with increasing age.

drinkers differ from low-level drinkers in home background, parental drinking, and delinquency? If so, do these factors cause or are they merely correlates of alcohol use patterns? With respect to drinking consequences, do heavy versus light adolescent drinkers have greater alcohol problems as adults, differ in future school achievement, and have more psychiatric problems later?

Trajectories help show how aspects of early alcohol experience are related to subsequent problem drinking (Warner, White, & Johnson, 2007). Three trajectory groups of drinkers were identified through analyses of five waves of data from 438 12-year-old respondents who were followed until age 30 or 31. About two thirds of the respondents were classified as no- or low-problem drinkers, one fifth as adolescence-limited problem drinkers, and one eighth as escalating problem drinkers. Several aspects of early drinking—age at drinking onset, feeling drunk during the first alcohol experience, and family history of alcoholism—were associated with significantly greater odds of being in a problem trajectory group relative to the no- or low-problem trajectory. The two problem-drinker groups did not differ on their early alcohol experiences.

Another trajectory study (Chassin, Fora, & King, 2004) examined how adolescent personality traits and family alcoholism were related to alcohol dependence later in life. Using 454 adolescents ranging in age from 10.5 to 15.5 years from an earlier ongoing study of parental alcoholism, 246 adolescents who had an alcoholic biological parent as their custodial parent and 208 demographically matched adolescents with no alcoholic biological or custodial parents were compared on three annual assessments of their alcohol and drug use. Two follow-ups were made when the adolescents were older (median age of 20 and 25).

A model was developed that identified three trajectories: heavy drinking/heavy drug use, moderate drinking/experimental drug use, and light drinking/rare drug use. The heavy drinking/heavy drug use group was at risk for both alcohol and drug dependence, which were persistent. It also showed more familial alcoholism, negative emotionality, and low constraint. Although the moderate drinking/experimental drug use group was also at risk for alcohol dependence, it was not at risk for drug dependence. It showed less negative emotionality and higher constraint than the heavy drinking/heavy drug use group. Having an alcohol-dependent custodial parent elevated the risk for both alcohol and drug dependence in part because of impulsivity, neuroticism, and lowered agreeableness.

Trajectory studies do not provide definitive conclusions at this relatively early point in their use. Different studies of trajectories may often produce contradictory or inconsistent conclusions because they do not cover the same age span or the same type of population, study the same potential causes, or examine the same outcomes (Schulenberg, Maggs, & O'Malley, 2003). These variables will limit the generalizability of these models. As a whole, however, these longitudinal studies of developmental trajectories increase the understanding of factors related to patterns of alcohol and other drug use over long periods.

Defining Adolescent Problem Drinking

One limitation of past research is the assumption that adolescent problem drinking can be accurately described with the traditional measures and conceptions of alcohol use and abuse developed for adult samples. For example, items on questionnaires designed for adults focus on typical drinking quantities and frequencies. While these types of questions may be appropriate for many adults, they may be of limited validity for understanding adolescent drinking behavior. A similar problem applies to comparisons of drug use in general among adolescents and adults.

The context and meaning of drinking for adolescents is different from that of their parents and other adults. Drinking patterns of adolescents, in that drinking alcohol is a relatively new behavior for them, fluctuate more over time than those of adults for many reasons. Adolescents may be more likely than adults to encounter problems from a single drinking episode, perhaps due to inexperience or lack of knowledge. In contrast, numerous drinking episodes over many years of chronic alcohol use are more likely associated with the likelihood of problems for alcoholic adults. Physical and medical impairments stemming from such adult drinking histories are less applicable to young people, who, as a group, have a briefer history of drinking. In addition, some problems associated with drinking are unique to young people such as troubles with parents or with the law due to underage drinking.

Due to the legal inaccessibility of alcohol for underage adolescents, their problems with alcohol may be more often related to having consumed too much on specific drinking *occasions or episodes* as compared to adults for whom the problem often involves chronic consumption, sometimes at less extreme quantities consumed per occasion. In short, the nature of alcohol problems for nonclinical populations of adults and adolescents may be quite dissimilar.

Relation to Family Structures

Adolescent alcohol and drug abuse may vary in different family structures. Family structure in America has changed rapidly over the past generation, with a shift from the nuclear family with two parents and their two children toward more single-parent, stepparent, and extended-family homes.

The relationship of family structure to adolescent alcohol use was studied with data from the 1995 National Household Survey on Drug Abuse survey (n = 17,747; Department of Health and Human Services, 1997). Compared to the two-biological-parent home as the baseline, adolescents from one-parent or stepparent families were at higher risk for a number of problems including poorer school performance, lower college attendance, early sexual initiation and parenthood, later marital problems, delinquency, and use of alcohol and most other drugs. A general explanation for this pattern is that if families are dissolved due to parental conflict and spousal abuse, the children may experience stress, anxiety, depression, and low self-esteem, which in turn may lead to use of alcohol and other drugs.

Complications arise in the causal interpretation of the relationship of family structure to outcomes in studies unless there is control for variables that covary with family structure. Thus, the lower income of single-parent families due to a large percentage of single-mother families may contribute to the adolescent problems more than the nature of the family structure per se.

Still, even with controls for important demographic variables such as age, race/ethnicity, and family income, the finding of lower alcohol use for adolescents from two-parent families persists. Females from mother-only and mother/stepfather families are more likely to abuse drugs, even after demographic factors are controlled for.

However, the study was limited to examining only family structure but not the *quality* of family interaction, which can vary within each subgroup. Quality of family life may be a more important or at least an additional determinant of adolescent alcohol use. Moreover, it is not possible to rule out reverse causation in a cross-sectional study. Thus, instead of family structure affecting adolescent drug abuse, it is possible that adolescent alcohol abuse may contribute to family dissolution by placing stress on the parents. Longitudinal data are needed to see the temporal relationship between important changes in the family structure and adolescent initiation, continuation, escalation, or reduction of substance use.

COLLEGE STUDENTS

After high school, students head off into different directions that have a profound impact on their futures. Those with academic talent—or at least leanings—seek entrance to colleges and universities, others enter careers or trades, and yet others enter military service. These alternative life paths may in part reflect existing drug use patterns, and they may also determine future drug use styles. For example, high school students who are heavily into drugs, especially illicit drugs, may be less likely to become college students. College students, if they live away from home, come under the influences of dormitory, fraternity, and sorority norms of alcohol and other drug use that may differ markedly from the practices acceptable in their parents' home. Thus, college students increase rates of heavy drinking and use of marijuana during their college years, although use of cocaine does not increase. Cigarette use is relatively low among college students and does not change much during college (SAMHSA, 2007).

Prevalence of College Alcohol and Other Drug Use

Although most college students are over 18 years of age, those who are not living at home, which is a large percentage, would not be included in national probability surveys. Therefore, surveys of college students may yield different results from surveys of high school students. In comparing use patterns of high school and college samples, differences in drinking between high school and college students should not be attributed entirely to age differences since the two populations vary in many respects other than age that might affect drinking.

High alcohol use rates were found in a synthesis (O'Malley & Johnston, 2002) of the findings from several large surveys of college student drinking conducted since the 1980s including the College Alcohol Study, the Core Institute Survey, Monitoring the Future, the National College Health Risk Behavior Survey, and the National Household Survey on Drug Abuse. About 40% of American college students were heavy drinkers, based on the definition of five or more drinks in a row in the past 2 weeks. Males drank more often and in larger amounts with more alcohol-related problems than female students. The percentage of heavy drinking was highest for White, lower for Hispanic, and lowest for Black students.

Survey Findings

A mail survey of about 7,000 college students at 34 New England colleges and universities (Wechsler & McFadden, 1979) with a return rate ranging from 51% to 87% across different campuses showed that men drank more frequently and in larger quantities than women, with a third of men being classified as frequent-heavy drinkers in comparison to a tenth of the women. The extent to which they drank in high school and the level of parental drinking were related to more college drinking. There was an inverse relationship between academic performance and amount of drinking. Over a third of the men and a sixth of the women were drunk at least once a month. Physical fights and difficulties with authorities due to drinking occurred for a fifth of the men.

A replication study (Meilman, Stone, Gaylor, & Turco, 1990) was conducted at a private rural New England university with a random sample of 350 mostly White respondents between the ages of 17 and 21 (about 60% males and 40% females). The results suggested a lower rate of daily consumption, especially among males, than found 10 years earlier (Wechsler & McFadden, 1979). In fact, a quarter of the respondents drank less than a drink per week. Nonetheless, alcohol-related problems were still frequent with over a quarter of the respondents reporting having a "hangover" and 30% indicating some disruption of normal functioning due to drinking within the past week. The 30-day prevalence rates showed that alcohol, tobacco, and marijuana were the most frequently used drugs, followed by amphetamines, hallucinogens, and cocaine. Use of alcohol, tobacco, and marijuana was higher for males.

A longitudinal study (n = 7,083) with measures at three time points over a 6-year period (Timberlake et al., 2007) found a higher percentage of college students were binge drinking and consuming higher quantities than their peers who did not attend college, just the reverse of the pattern in high school. A comparison of another sample of 855 sibling pairs compared the magnitude of genetic influences on alcohol consumption for college and noncollege youth. Concordance rates for drinking among identical twins, fraternal twins, siblings, and half-siblings varied more among college students than among noncollege peers, possibly because college environments allow for a wider range of drinking opportunities for youth.

Long-Term College Student Drinking Trends

Figure 10.4 shows the trend over 26 years from 1980 to 2006 in the MTF survey for rates of the occurrence of at least one heavy drinking occasion (five or more drinks) within the past 2 weeks (Johnston et al., 2007b). College students consistently had higher drinking rates than age-matched noncollege students and 12th-grade students. Since college students are a select group with higher intelligence, aspirations, and expectations for achievement than their high school classmates who are not attending college, one might expect their alcohol and other drug use to be lower because it may interfere with college success. One explanation (Johnston, O'Malley, Bachman, & Schulenberg, 2007a) for increased binge drinking after leaving high school and entering college is that many of these students no longer are under parental surveillance. Moreover, college students are less likely to get married in the 4 years after high school than their noncollege age mates, which may lead them to spend more time in drinking situations such as parties.

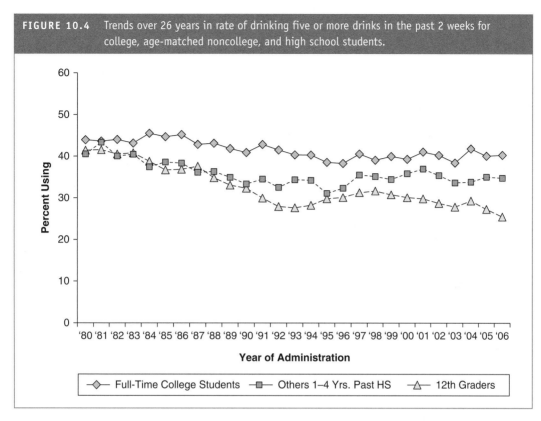

FIGURE 10.4   Trends over 26 years in rate of drinking five or more drinks in the past 2 weeks for college, age-matched noncollege, and high school students.

Source: From *Monitoring the Future National Survey Results on Drug Use, 1975–2006: Volume I: Secondary School Students*, by L. D. Johnston, P. M. O'Malley, J. G. Bachman, and J. E. Schulenberg, 2007, Bethesda, MD: National Institute on Drug Abuse.

Over this 26-year period, as Figure 10.4 shows, the rates of consuming five or more drinks per occasion tended to be slightly lower whereas the rates of alcohol use in the past year (not shown) showed a downward trend for college as well as noncollege students.

Trajectories of College Student Drinking

Using data from the National Longitudinal Survey of Youth (n = 1,265), patterns of heavy drinking of college and noncollege samples were compared at four ages: high school, college, young adult, and adult (Lanza & Collins, 2006). Heavy drinking occurred in eight patterns: young adulthood only (3.7%); young adulthood and adulthood (3.7%); college age only (2.6%); college age, young adulthood, and adulthood (8.7%); high school and college age (4.4%); high school, college age, and young adulthood (6.3%); persistent heavy drinking (16.9%); and no heavy drinking (53.7%).

College and noncollege students showed no differences in heavy drinking at any of the four examined developmental ages. Those college-enrolled individuals who showed heavy drinking during college ages were less likely to do so prior to and after college. In contrast, those not enrolled in college who did not drink heavily during high school or college ages had a greater risk for heavy drinking later as adults.

A similar comparison (Harford, Yi, & Hilton, 2006) of the relationship between educational attainment and drinking suggested a protective effect of education. In a 10-year prospective follow-up of a sample of 8,661 respondents drawn from the National Longitudinal Survey of Labor Market Experience in Youth, education beyond high school was related to a lower risk for alcohol dependence whereas high school dropouts had a higher long-term risk for alcohol dependence.

Binge Drinking

A survey (Wechsler, Dowdall, Davenport, & Castillo, 1995) conducted at 140 colleges and universities involving 17,592 students measured the extent of binge drinking (defined as five or more drinks in a row for men and four or more drinks in a row for women in the 2 weeks prior to the survey). A different criterion of binge drinking was used for men and women to reflect the gender differences in metabolism and body mass, as women who typically drink four drinks in a row had about the same likelihood of experiencing drinking-related problems as men who typically drink five drinks in a row (Wechsler, Dowdall, Davenport, & Rimm, 1995). Also referred to as frequent heavy drinking in some studies, binge drinking may be more serious in its adverse consequences for both these drinkers and those around them because it produces more impaired functioning.

About 50% of men and 39% of women binged, although the percentage varied widely across different campuses. About half of these drinkers were considered frequent binge drinkers, defined in this study as engaging in three or more such binges in the past 2 weeks. Prior bingeing in high school was related to college binge drinking, suggesting that, for many students, binge drinking begins before college. Those who binged in high school were three times as likely to do so in college. Being White, membership in fraternities and sororities, and involvement in athletics were risk factors.

Despite the high percentage of binge drinkers, less than 1% felt they had a drinking problem. Still, binge drinkers had more alcohol-related problems than nonbinge drinkers during the school year. In a follow-up survey (Wechsler et al., 2002), about a third (34.9%) of the men and a fourth (24.3%) of the women reported having been intoxicated three or more times in the past month, with similar percentages indicating that getting intoxicated was a primary reason for their drinking. The follow-up found that drinkers in the past 30 days reported more adverse consequences such as injury (12.8%) and property damage (10.7%), arguments with friends (22.9%), driving after drinking (29%), and unprotected sex (10.4%).

Binge drinkers not only suffer harmful psychological consequences from their own behavior but also produce detrimental psychological consequences for others (Wechsler, Moeykens, Davenport, Castillo, & Hanson, 1995). A survey of 28,709 students at 140 campuses across the nation assessed the adverse impact of heavy drinkers on other college students. A response rate of 69% was obtained from the predominantly White (81%) sample. Nonheavily drinking students living on campuses that were among those with the highest drinking levels (campuses with over 50% classified as heavy drinkers) were 3.6 times as likely to report having experienced a serious problem such as violence, vandalism, or unwanted sexual advances caused by another student's drinking than were students at campuses with lower drinking levels (campuses with less than 50% classified as heavy drinkers).

Nondrinking students in a follow-up survey in 2001 (Wechsler et al., 2002) reported that their interactions with a drinking student had caused them to be insulted or humiliated (29.2%); to be pushed, hit, or assaulted (8.7%); to have to take care of a drunken student (47.6%); to have studying or sleeping interrupted (60.0%); or to experience an unwanted sexual advance (19.5%).

Drinking Setting

Do aspects of college residential environments contribute to drinking among college students? Alcohol use and related problems in heavily drinking students between their senior year in high school and their first autumn in college were studied (Baer, Kivlahan, & Marlatt, 1995). Increases in the frequency of drinking over the college years were strongly associated with residence in a fraternity or sorority, possibly reflecting the drink-friendly environments of these social organizations. However, this difference could also reflect a selection process where fraternal organizations and students with interests in drinking parties choose each other. In contrast, the students' family history of alcohol problems was not consistently related to changes in use rates or problems.

Drinking After College

Many heavy drinkers in college show a reduction or stability in drinking levels only a few years after leaving college. The change in drinking may result from the departure from the college environment where the norm is for many students to drink frequently and heavily. The assumption of adult roles requires greater responsibility as well as independence. Many abandon their youthful alcohol and drug patterns because they are incompatible with their career and life objectives. Dropping out of school because of involvement in drugs, for example, limits opportunities for successful careers and jobs.

Follow-up surveys of high school seniors from the MTF studies assessed their changes in drinking after they became young adults (Schulenberg, O'Malley, Bachman, Wadsworth, & Johnston, 1996). Many heavy drinkers (five or more drinks on one or more occasions in the past 2 weeks) "matured out" during their 20s, with the frequency of heavy drinking dropping from 55% for 21- to 22-year-old males to about 36% by the time they were 31 or 32. Young women showed even greater declines, going from 33% at age 19 or 20 to about 15% at age 31 or 32. However, others (12% of males and 3% of females) maintained their heavy drinking between ages 18 and 24 while some (14% of males and 7% of females) showed increased heavy drinking over this period.

Thus, most young adults seem to reduce their alcohol and other drug use as they assume the responsibilities of work, marriage, and parenthood. These adult roles serve as protective rather than risk factors for substance abuse. These roles may be stressors for most people, but some cope without abuse of alcohol and other drugs. Exactly why these life transitions lead to different consequences for different people is an important issue for further research.

Other Drug Use

Cigarette Smoking

Cigarette smoking in the past month started during the early teen years and was most prevalent for ages 21–24 before gradually declining with increasing age in the 2006 NSDUH, as Figure 10.5 shows. Figure 10.6 presents the 30-year trends in the MTF survey of student smoking rates from 1976 to 2006 (Johnston et al., 2007b) separately for use in the past 30 days and for daily use for that period. Since 1976 when rates were highest for all grade levels, rates have generally declined sharply. Twelfth graders were highest, with around 40%

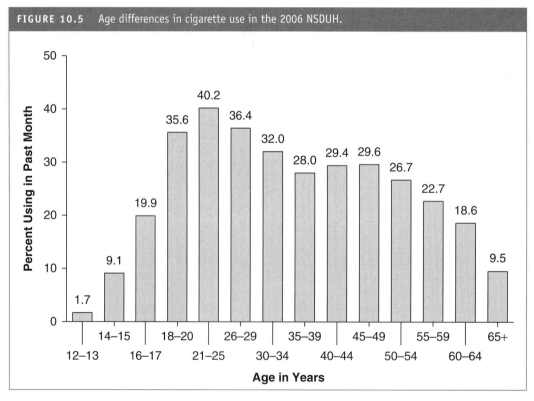

FIGURE 10.5 Age differences in cigarette use in the 2006 NSDUH.

Source: From *Results From the 2006 National Survey on Drug Use and Health (NSDUH): National Findings*, by the Substance Abuse and Mental Health Services Administration [SAMHSA], 2007, Rockville, MD: SAMHSA Office of Applied Studies.

FIGURE 10.6   MTF 30-year trend cigarette use among 8th, 10th, and 12th graders for the past 30 days and daily in the past 30 days.

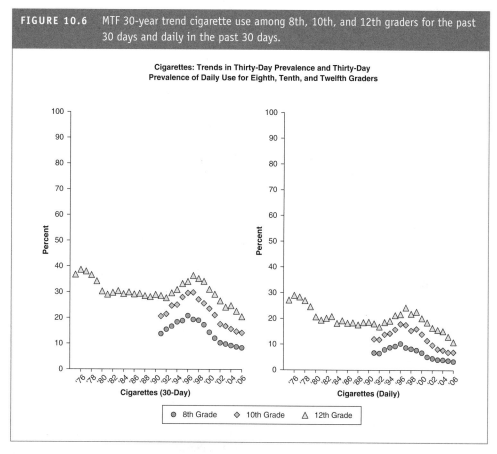

Cigarettes: Trends in Thirty-Day Prevalence and Thirty-Day Prevalence of Daily Use for Eighth, Tenth, and Twelfth Graders

Source: From *Monitoring the Future National Survey Results on Drug Use, 1975–2006: Volume I: Secondary School Students,* by L. D. Johnston, P. M. O'Malley, J. G. Bachman, and J. E. Schulenberg, 2007, Bethesda, MD: National Institute on Drug Abuse.

reporting use in the past month and about 30% having used daily in the past month. Cigarette smoking then declined before rising again in the late 1990s, after which it declined again to a 30-year low of around 10% for 12th graders and lower for 10th and 8th graders.

Illicit Drugs

Due to the illegal nature of many drugs, there have not been as many surveys of their use as there have been of alcohol use. Figure 10.7 presents rates of illicit drug use in the past 30 days as a function of age from the 2006 NSDUH. The group of 18- to 20-year-olds had the highest percentage, 22%, who used illicit drugs, but the NSDUH did not measure the quantity or frequency of use. Rates declined in half to 10% for the group of 30- to 34-year-olds, continued to drop slightly until ages 50–54, and then significantly declined to less than 1% for those over age 65.

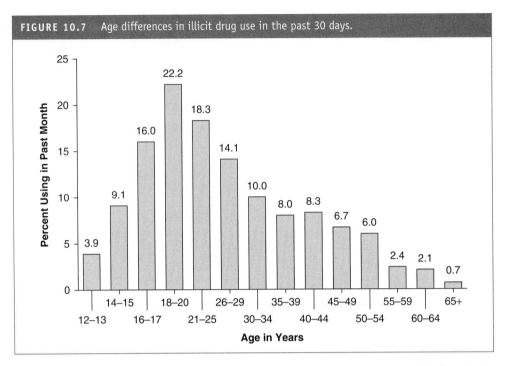

FIGURE 10.7 Age differences in illicit drug use in the past 30 days.

Source: From *Results From the 2006 National Survey on Drug Use and Health (NSDUH): National Findings*, by the Substance Abuse and Mental Health Services Administration [SAMHSA], 2007, Rockville, MD: SAMHSA Office of Applied Studies.

Figure 10.8 displays the 30-year trend in the MTF survey data (Johnston et al., 2007b) from 1976 to 2006 for the past-month use by 12th graders of *any illicit drug* (any use of marijuana, LSD or other hallucinogens, crack, cocaine, heroin, or any other drug that is not under a doctor's orders). However, due to changes in the survey items in 1982, the data for "any illicit drug other than marijuana" before and after 1982 are not comparable. Use rates were highest in the early 1980s and generally declined to a low in the early 1990s. They rose gradually over the rest of the decade and have been fairly stable since.

A study of the relationship among self-reported level of use of alcohol, that of tobacco, and that of several illicit drugs was based on 28,709 predominantly White college students from 140 different colleges and universities with predominantly White enrollments (Wechsler, Dowdall, et al., 1995). About equal numbers of men and women were included. Heavier drinkers were more likely to use illicit drugs as well as cigarettes. Only a small percentage of nondrinking students reported use of illegal substances. Marijuana was the most widely used illicit drug, although the percentage of students who used marijuana varied widely across colleges, ranging from 0% to 52% of the respondents (Bell, Wechsler, & Johnston, 1997). These findings are limited in that the survey did not assess frequency or quantity of marijuana use.

A study involving four waves of measurement examined the trajectory of marijuana use among 1,205 adolescents (Windle & Wiesner, 2004) and identified five different patterns of

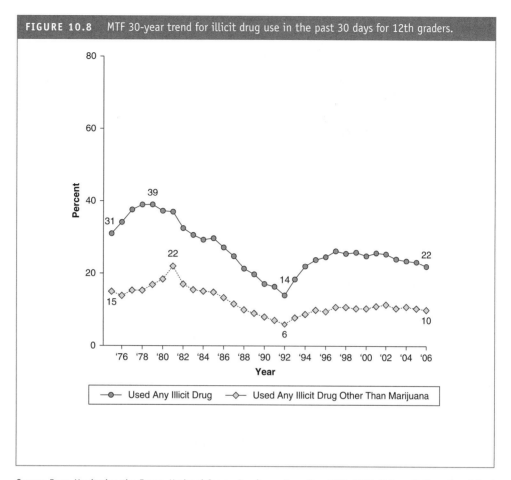

FIGURE 10.8   MTF 30-year trend for illicit drug use in the past 30 days for 12th graders.

Source: From *Monitoring the Future National Survey Results on Drug Use, 1975–2006: Volume I: Secondary School Students*, by L. D. Johnston, P. M. O'Malley, J. G. Bachman, and J. E. Schulenberg, 2007, Bethesda, MD: National Institute on Drug Abuse.

change in the frequency of marijuana use: abstainers, experimental users, decreasers, increasers, and high chronics. The high chronic group had higher levels of delinquency, lower academic performance, more drug-using friends, and more stressful life events than the other four groups. Comparisons of the five groups on 10 risk behaviors as young adults (mean age, 23.5 years) showed that adolescent risk factors predicted marijuana use and substance abuse but not depressive or anxiety disorders in young adulthood.

Problems of Interpretation

Most studies of college drinking are cross-sectional in design, so trends and changes cannot be determined. However, cross-sectional findings are often interpreted as if they involve longitudinal evidence (Liljestrand, 1993). Moreover, most studies give only mean scores for the entire sample presented. This failure to disaggregate the data might hide some differences among subgroups that are buried in the overall means. Alternatively, if changes in some subgroups are large enough, aggregated data will make it appear that the same trends exist for all groups. Therefore, it is difficult to determine from these studies if rates of drinking are increasing, unchanging, or decreasing. Another problem is that surveys vary as to whether they report the percentage of participants who drink during a specific time period, the percentage who drink different quantities, or both (Liljestrand, 1993). These variations in measures make it difficult to compare across studies.

YOUNG ADULTS

Cross-Sectional Evidence

Table 10.2 shows age differences on several aspects of alcohol and other drug use in the 2006 NSDUH (SAMHSA, 2007). In addition to measuring the past-month, past-year, and lifetime rates of alcohol use, the study determined rates in the past-month binge use of alcohol, heavy use of alcohol, cigarette use, and any illicit drug use. Table 10.2 shows that the younger groups, ages 12–17 and 18–25, had the highest rates on all variables, while there were lower rates except for lifetime alcohol use for those aged 26 and older.

Longitudinal Evidence

A follow-up study (Bachman, Wadswirth, O'Malley, Johnston, & Schulenberg, 1997) over 14 years after high school with a sample of more than 33,000 respondents from the MTF survey found evidence of decreases in alcohol and other drug use. The declines are not surprising because with each year following college, increased numbers of individuals marry

TABLE 10.2	Age differences in lifetime, past-year, and past-month alcohol use and in past-month binge and heavy use of alcohol, cigarettes, and any illicit drug.						
Age Group	Alcohol Use Lifetime	Alcohol Use Past Year	Alcohol Use Past Mo	Alcohol Binge Past Mo	Heavy Alcohol Past Mo	Cig. Past Mo	Any Illicit Drug Past Mo
12–17	40	33.3	16.5	9.9	2.4	10.4	9.8
18–25	85.7	77.9	60.9	41.9	15.3	38.4	19.8
26 up	88.2	69.0	55.1	21.0	5.6		6.1
35 up						22.5	

Source: From *Results From the 2006 National Survey on Drug Use and Health (NSDUH): National Findings*, by the Substance Abuse and Mental Health Services Administration [SAMHSA], 2007, Rockville, MD: SAMHSA Office of Applied Studies.

and start families. In line with new responsibilities of this new role, alcohol and drug use should decline, particularly for women when they become pregnant.

Changes in smoking were examined in a 10-year study of 5,115 young adults, aged 18–30, who were taking part in a coronary artery risk study (Wagenknecht et al., 1998). Results with this sample, of course, may not be representative of the general population of this age, but they show how different subgroups may change in different patterns. Smoking rates declined in White men and women and remained stable in Black women but increased in Black men, possibly due to more new smokers among the youngest birth cohort in this group.

A model (White, Pandina, & Chen, 2002) of trajectories for cigarette smoking from early adolescence into young adulthood that used five interviews from 374 participants from age 12 until age 30 or 31 identified three groups: heavy/regular, occasional/maturing out, and non-/experimental smokers. In comparison to nonsmokers, the probability of belonging to a smoking group was higher for females and those who had higher disinhibition, received lower grades, and had more frequent use of alcohol or other drugs.

Sex differences in developmental trajectories and in smoking behavior among regular smokers were notable. Socioeconomic status, parent smoking, and friend smoking were related to smoking for females but not for males. Between adolescence and adulthood, cessation and escalation of smoking may be affected by different factors for males and females.

According to a model using data from 5,115 participants (55% women) in the CARDIA (Coronary Artery Risk Development in Young Adults) Study, a longitudinal study of young adults conducted from 1985 to 1995 (Costanzo et al., 2007), heavy-drinking trajectories from early to middle adulthood generally declined between 18 and 40 years of age for White men and women. Trajectories over these ages were flat for Blacks and did not change; Black women had the lowest rates of heavy drinking while Black men had high rates of heavy drinking. High rates of heavy drinking persisted longer for individuals high in hostility, anxiety, or depressive symptoms.

Among those who did not go to college, similar changes occurred in the decade following high school graduation as the new responsibilities of employment, marriage, and parenthood were assumed after high school. In comparison to use during high school, those who entered military service were likely to increase smoking and heavy drinking. However, dramatic declines in rates of use of marijuana and cocaine occurred, perhaps in part due to the strong antidrug policies of the military. Women who became full-time homemakers rather than attending college showed lower rates of smoking increase but greater reduction of alcohol consumption, heavy drinking, and illicit drug use. These changes were probably not due to the status of homemaker per se but to the fact that typically homemakers were married, sometimes with children, or pregnant, all conditions that could account for their changes in alcohol and drug use.

OLDER POPULATIONS

As the "graying of America" increases with the baby boomer post–World War II generation reaching old age, it becomes even more important to understand the nature of alcohol and drug problems among the elderly. In 1990, persons over age 65 represented 12% of the total U.S. population, but it is estimated to increase to 65 million persons, or 22% of the total population, by the year 2030 (Spencer, 1989).

Physiological changes due to normal aging can alter the effects of drugs. Older persons have a higher percentage of body fat and less dilution of a given dose of alcohol relative to younger persons. Consequently, a specific dose of alcohol produces a higher blood alcohol level for older persons (Kalant, 1998). However, whether or not a given dose produces greater impairment for older persons depends on other factors. It is commonly assumed that older persons are more sensitive to alcohol, so a given dose should have more impact on older persons. For example, a dose that would not be problematic for a younger person may be disruptive for an older person. Alcohol-impaired motor coordination among older drinkers occurs possibly because a given dose produces a higher blood alcohol level in older than in younger drinkers (Vogel-Sprott & Barrett, 1984). However, the impairment is not due entirely to the alcohol. Age and correlated factors, such as diseases related to aging and use of more medications, act like alcohol in that they generally impair performance. However, whether alcohol has a *greater* impairment for older persons is not yet firmly established. Comparisons of younger and older persons receiving the same dose under equivalent conditions are needed to test this assumption.

As older persons face these psychosocial adjustments of normal aging coupled with physical aches and pains, they may increase their use of drugs and medication in the form of legal prescription and proprietary over-the-counter drugs. The combination of alcohol with many drugs and medicines taken for old-age-related health problems may produce some dangerous outcomes and cross-tolerances between the substances. There are also reasons to assume that many older individuals drink less due to lower tolerance for alcohol, medical problems that may be seriously affected by alcohol use, and lower income.

An overview (Brennan & Moos, 1996a) of the major factors influencing late-life drinking and its effects showed the role of personal factors, life context, and treatment factors. Personal factors include demographic variables and past drinking history as well as modes of coping with stress. The life context or environment of the person includes negative life events and chronic stressors, the availability of social resources (perceived social support), and the attitudes about and use of alcohol by significant others. Finally, treatment refers to past experiences with alcohol treatment, including treatment seeking and the characteristics of treatment programs. Together these factors determine drinking behavior and outcomes.

Difficulties in Studying Aging and Alcohol Problems

Conceptual and methodological problems exist in research on alcohol problems of the aged. There is a lack of consensus about when an adult becomes "elderly." Usually an arbitrary chronological age is imposed—such as 65, the age for receiving Social Security payments in the United States—rather than one based on physical or biological factors. Many measures and criteria of alcohol problems that may be appropriate for younger ages may not be valid for older ages.

Causal interpretation of the relationship of alcohol use to stresses such as accidents, health problems, poor work performance, weak relationships with family and friends, and criminal behavior are always difficult to make for any age group. The view that major life stressors may increase drinking among the elderly has an intuitive appeal, but one must recognize that a large percentage of the older population copes with these stressors without becoming problem drinkers. It is important to include an analysis of sociodemographic and personal factors when analyzing problem drinking among the elderly (Finney & Moos, 1984). The social status and background, as well as the level of self-esteem, coping skills, cognitive appraisal, and availability of social resources, may alter the impact of stressful events and moderate the need for alcohol abuse as a means of coping.

Prevalence of Older-Population Alcohol Use

Surveys of older persons yield a wide range of estimates about the prevalence of alcohol problems as they vary in their definitions of old age and drinking problems and whether the source of respondents is from the community or clinical settings. In this section, we will examine age differences with few comparisons between men and women, a topic deferred until the next chapter on gender differences because much of the early research did not examine this variable among the older population.

The 2006 NSDUH (SAMHSA, 2007) found that use in the past month declined to 48.0% for ages 60–64 and dropped to 38.4% for those over 65. Problematic types of alcohol use, binge and heavy drinking, showed similar age declines. For those over age 65, "binge" use (five or more drinks on the same occasion on at least 1 day in the past 30 days) occurred for 7.6%, and heavy alcohol use (five or more drinks on the same occasion on each of 5 or more days in the past 30 days) occurred for 1.6%.

An analysis (Breslow & Smothers, 2004) based on 40,556 adults aged 60 years and older pooled from five cross-sectional National Health Interview Surveys in 1997–2001 found that 52.8% of men and 37.2% of women were current drinkers. For older age groups, the proportions of men and women drinking higher quantities of alcohol (two drinks or more) decreased whereas the proportions consuming lower quantities (one drink) increased. The proportions of men and women drinking on both fewer than 12 days per year and between 260 and 365 days per year were higher for older age groups. In sum, quantity and frequency measures of alcohol consumption showed strikingly different patterns of age-related change.

Overall, alcohol use and heavy alcohol use were lower among older than among younger age groups. However, the implications of such reductions are unclear because of the lack of equivalent criteria to define problematic consequences for different age groups. Thus, older drinkers have fewer job-related difficulties due to alcohol use than younger drinkers simply because many of them are retired.

An alternative to cross-sectional research where different ages are compared during a given year for assessing age effects is a longitudinal design in which the same individuals are assessed at two or more different time points. As diagrammed in Figure 10.9, an example of a longitudinal study with a retrospective comparison of ages 30–50 might compare present data collected in 2010 from 50-year-olds with information collected about them at an earlier date, 1990, when they were 30 years old. However, sometimes this is not possible as this earlier information was not collected or no longer exists. Figure 10.9 also shows a longitudinal design from age 30 to age 50 from 2010 to 2030 with a prospective comparison

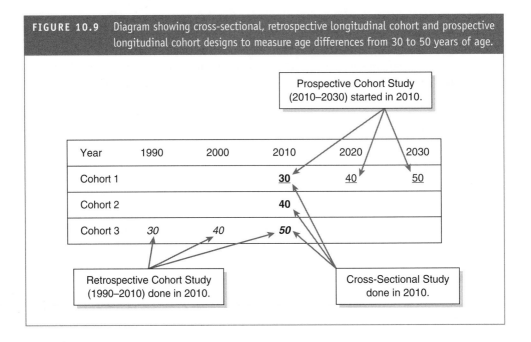

FIGURE 10.9 Diagram showing cross-sectional, retrospective longitudinal cohort and prospective longitudinal cohort designs to measure age differences from 30 to 50 years of age.

of present data with information to be collected in the future. A limitation to this method is that we would have to wait for many years before the comparison could be completed.

Another problem for longitudinal studies that extend over many years is the likelihood of **differential attrition**. Over the course of a longitudinal study, heavier drinkers may be less likely to continue in the study for many reasons. Problem drinkers may be more transient, be less likely to be married, or have unstable employment, so they would be difficult to follow up on (Temple & Leino, 1989). Heavy drinking may lead to more accidents, diseases, and other sources of fatality among younger groups. Although drinking declines with increased age for most people, this elimination of the heavier drinkers artificially inflates the extent of the decline.

Early- Versus Late-Onset Problem Drinking

It is important to distinguish between those older alcoholics who developed their problems with alcohol very early in life and those who had a later onset. In addition, there may exist a third group of intermittent or episodic problem drinkers whose levels of drinking have fluctuated widely over their lifetimes. The cumulative effects of alcohol should be greater for those who have been drinking longer, all else being equal. Unfortunately, many age comparison studies do not include the distinction based on **age of onset** of drinking problems.

Early-onset alcoholics will have had many more years of abusive levels of drinking than other older drinkers. According to a model of accelerated aging (Ryan & Butters, 1984), early-onset alcoholics might have cognitive deficits at later ages. But an alternative model of increased vulnerability holds that the impairment of alcoholics is relatively small at younger ages and widens with increased age. Thus, we would expect early-onset alcoholics who maintain a lifetime of alcohol abuse to show large deficits compared to nonalcoholic elderly cohorts.

Late-onset problem drinkers, or reactive drinkers, are defined as not having problems with alcohol until after about age 40. They may be using alcohol to cope with the medical and physical impairments associated with aging as well as social status changes such as retirement or widowhood. These specific stressors encountered at older ages may precipitate the development of drinking problems. With a definition of late onset set at age 40, however, by age 65 many so-called late-onset alcoholics would have had drinking problems for as long as 25 years (Gomberg, 1990)! Perhaps a more useful comparison would be between distant and recent onset.

Since late-onset problem drinkers have shown no evidence of a lifelong drinking lifestyle, there is a tendency to assume the drinking is reactive or a coping response to stress. We may tend to search for a specific overwhelming negative life event to blame for the drinking. However, stress was not related to heavy drinking in general or to late-onset heavy drinking in one study of heavy drinkers aged 60 and older (Welte & Mirand, 1995) in a random telephone survey (n = 2,325). Chronic stress was, however, positively related to alcohol dependence and consequences.

In contrast, we may fail to detect specific stressors that instigate drinking for early-onset problem drinkers simply because it is more difficult to recall specific stressors from the distant past associated with problem drinking. Thus, it may only seem that specific stressors are more often involved in late- as opposed to early-onset problem drinking.

A 4-year prospective study (Brennan & Moos, 1996b) of late-life problem drinkers (n = 581) found that heavier baseline alcohol use and being male predicted more alcohol consumption later. More drinking problems were found at follow-up for those with early-onset and a higher number of drinking problems at baseline. Those who used avoidance coping strategies had *more* drinking problems if their friends' approved of their drinking. However, individuals with more drinking problems at baseline had *fewer* subsequent drinking problems if they experienced negative health events and friend stressors.

Stress and Coping

A community study of older persons living in New York state did not find higher drinking for persons with more health-related stressors (Welte, 1998). Instead, those who were sick or ill actually drank less while those who were active and healthy tended to drink more. Although these findings might be interpreted as showing that higher stress, fewer social resources, and avoidance coping "causes" problem drinking, it is also possible that the opposite process is involved whereby problem drinking increases stress, reduces social resources, and leads to avoidance coping.

The type of stressor was also important in a community sample of older persons (Brennan, Moos, & Mertens, 1994). Those with higher levels of health-specific stressors at the start of the study had fewer drinking problems 1 to 4 years later. However, non-health-related stressors were associated with increased drinking problems over the period of 1 to 4 years.

How stress affects drinking also appears to be affected by the individual's coping method and level of alcohol use. Increased stress led to more alcohol-related problems for those who relied more on avoidance coping (Brennan & Moos, 1996a) or drank at higher levels (Brennan et al., 1994). Heavy drinking can be viewed as a form of avoidance coping that is used when stressed if few alternative solutions for dealing with life stressors exist. In contrast, persons with personal and social resources for dealing with their stress were less likely to drink. Lighter drinkers showed reduced drinking a year later if their stress level was higher (Moos, Brennan, & Schutte, 1998). In contrast, those who were heavier drinkers reacted with increased drinking a year later if they had higher stress.

Many older problem drinkers eventually stop drinking. In a study with 330 untreated remitters, 120 treated remitters, and 130 untreated nonremitters, about 3 in 4 of the older problem drinkers showing **remission** did so without any formal treatment. Compared with remitters who received treatment and to untreated nonremitters, they had completed more schooling, reached their peak alcohol consumption, and stopped having new drinking problems earlier. Moreover, untreated remitters were more likely to be women, more likely to have less severe drinking and depression histories, and less likely to have been advised to reduce consumption. Finally, untreated remitters were more likely than untreated nonremitters to have reduced their drinking because of late-life health problems.

Effects of Retirement on Drinking

The effect of retirement on drinking may vary. On one hand, boredom and increased leisure time may allow for more drinking, but retirement may reduce the stresses of work as well as contact with the drinking companions from the workplace. One study (Ekerdt, Labry, Glynn, & Davis, 1989) compared drinking in men over a brief period of 2 years after retirement with a group of men from the same age cohort who remained employed. Retirees showed more variability in drinking levels during this period but overall were not different from the working group. However, retirees were more likely to report problems caused by their drinking toward the end of the 2 years. These results suggest that problems associated with drinking may become more evident with increased time since retirement began.

A study (Bacharach, Bamberger, Sonnenstuhl, & Vashdi, 2008) of retirement-eligible employees (n = 1,122) in construction, manufacturing, and transportation work examined the relationship between positive alcohol expectancies and drinking problems. Employees still working despite retirement eligibility had increased drinking problems 4 years later if they held high positive alcohol expectancies. In contrast, those with low positive alcohol expectancies had decreased drinking problems. The work environment in many occupations contributed to this effect, as workers used alcohol to cope with work stress as well as to promote camaraderie among coworkers (Sonnenstuhl, 1996). Fully retired workers, no longer exposed to these stressors, had a weaker relationship between positive alcohol expectancies and drinking problems.

Retirees may not be regarded by society—or by their families—as requiring treatment for alcohol and drug problems because no jobs are jeopardized. Family members, embarrassed by excessive drinking of their elders, may find it more convenient to deny or cover up the problem. A retired person may drink to the point of intoxication, but unless he or she becomes aggressive or annoying, this behavior may be tolerated whereas the same impairment in a younger person would be considered a problem because it could impair job performance. Thus, the criterion of what constitutes a substance problem may vary with age.

Older persons are underrepresented in alcohol and drug abuse treatment, suggesting that they may not perceive themselves as having abuse problems. Such perceptions are not entirely independent of societal standards and values. In addition, the elderly may face social and economic barriers to treatment access.

Older Populations and Other Drugs

National Health Interview Survey results from almost 30 years, 1965–1994, provide prevalence rates of smoking for older persons (Husten, McCarty, Giovino, Chrismon, & Zhu, 1998). Current smoking among 65-year-olds and older individuals declined over this period from 17.9% to 12.0%. Among older adults, the prevalence of smoking cessation rose with higher educational attainment and was consistently higher for men than for women and for Whites compared with Blacks. There were no racial differences among women, but older White and Hispanic men were more likely to be former smokers than older Black men.

Less is known about the use of illicit drugs such as cocaine and heroin among older populations (Rosenberg, 1995). Available evidence suggests that very low rates of illicit drug use exist for those over 60 years of age, except among special groups such as psychiatric and criminal populations (Caracci & Miller, 1991).

The 2000 National Household Survey on Drug Abuse (SAMHSA, 2001) found that 1% of adults over age 55 had used illicit drugs in the past month, with psychotherapeutics used nonmedically by 0.5% of users and marijuana by 0.4%. Among older adults, the rate of past-month illicit drug use was highest for those aged 55–59, irrespective of gender. The successor to this survey, renamed the National Survey on Drug Use and Health, found higher rates ranging from 1.9% to 3.4% from 2002 to 2006 among those aged 55–59 (SAMHSA, 2007).

Since excessive use of any harmful substance lowers life expectancy, a selective process in which heavy drug users are literally eliminated may occur so that on average, those with a lower average level of use are more likely to survive. It is also possible for health concerns related to aging to motivate many users to reduce their use of illicit drugs as they age. They may switch to alcohol or prescription drugs, which are less expensive, and they may have fewer contacts and sources in relation to illicit drugs. In some cases, they may have received effective therapy and counseling so that they are no longer dependent on drugs.

AGE, COHORT, AND PERIOD EFFECTS

A major problem of interpretation of age differences in alcohol and other drug use is whether they reflect a true **age effect** (i.e., differences due to aging processes) or whether they instead represent a generational difference or *cohort effect*. A cohort refers to a generational grouping such as baby boomers or Generation X. Since different age cohorts grow up under different historical circumstances, their substance use may be a reflection of differing attitudes and values toward alcohol and other drugs held in those different eras.

A hypothetical comparison of 20- and 40-year-old groups of individuals born in different years is diagrammed in Figure 10.10. For example, in any given year, we could assess age differences by a cross-sectional comparison of persons who are 20 with a different set of

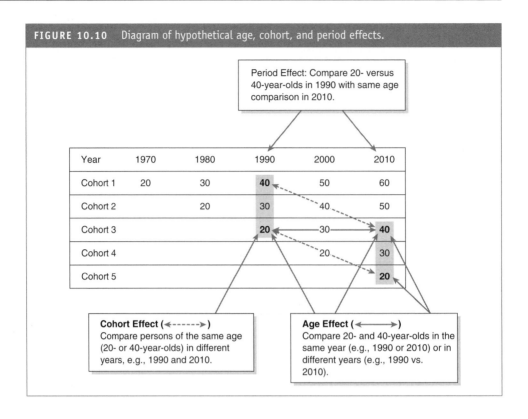

FIGURE 10.10 Diagram of hypothetical age, cohort, and period effects.

persons who are 40. Alternatively, we could use a single cohort consisting of the same persons and compare them longitudinally when they were 20 versus when they were 40.

Assume that the first comparison shows a difference. Are the differences due entirely to age, or could they reflect differences between cohorts, those who were age 20 in 1990 versus those who will be age 20 in 2010? Different age groups in the year 2010 will have grown up in different social climates with different attitudes and patterns of drinking. A 40-year-old group in 2010 will have been born in 1970 and grown up during an era when drug use was peaking relative to the prior decade. Thus, members of the 40-year-old group in 2010 not only would be older than those of the 20-year-old group in 2010 but also would hold the drug attitudes and values of the 1990s when they were 20, which will not be the same as those of people who will be 20 in 2010. These generational differences or **cohort effects**, rather than age differences, could be responsible for some of the drinking differences between 20- and 40-year-old groups in a cross-sectional study. Age and cohort are inherently confounded, and it is important to examine age differences across different cohorts to obtain a more conclusive view of age effects.

Additionally, **period effects** due to social climate differences may occur. A comparison of 20- versus 40-year-olds in 1990 may yield different results for the same age comparison conducted in 2010 due to conditions in different historical periods rather than to age (see Figure 10.10). Drinking attitudes and practices during Prohibition of the 1930s were markedly different from those during the drug heyday of the 1960s. As an example, two different longitudinal studies, one done between 1920 and 1940 and one conducted between 1990 and 2010, could each assess age effects. Any observed age differences would not be due to cohort effects since each study would use the same individuals at all of its time points. However, since the historical periods of the two studies would differ, some or all of the differences attributed to age might actually reflect a period effect.

The Normative Aging Study measured drinking as a function of age, cohort, and period (Levenson, Aldwin, & Spiro, 1998). This longitudinal study involved 2,280 men first studied in the 1960s. They received follow-up mail surveys in 1973, 1982, and 1991. A total of 1,267 men, who were primarily White, from middle and lower socioeconomic levels, from the Boston area, and between the ages of 46 and 72 years, responded to all three follow-ups. The findings about age effects varied. Only one cohort, those men born between 1919 and 1927, had a consistent decline in drinking as they aged.

In contrast, period effects were strong with all eligible cohorts showing increased drinking between the 1973 and 1982 surveys and a decline between the 1982 and 1991 surveys. Cohort effects were weak, as only the cohort born between 1928 and 1936 showed consistently higher drinking across age and period. In general, problem drinking showed the same patterns as alcohol consumption, with the exception of the 1928–1936 cohort, which had the highest problem drinking at all ages and periods, even though their consumption levels showed a decline in the 1991 survey. Both the cohort and the period are important as drinking is affected by changes in society as well as in individuals.

The relationship of age and alcohol consumption was evaluated for several cohorts over a 20-year span with data from 14,105 adults from the first National Health and Nutrition Examination Survey I (NHANES I) and its three follow-up surveys conducted between 1982 and 1992 (Moore et al., 2005). A majority, 74%, were consistent in being drinkers or abstainers over the entire period. The amount of alcohol consumption declined as age increased even after cohort and period were controlled for. A cohort effect was found, with the reduced consumption being greater for earlier cohorts.

The interpretation of any changes in alcoholism rates observed over long periods can be complicated by other factors unrelated to aging, psychological attitudes, or values. For example, if alcoholism treatment quality or availability becomes lower over these years, we might expect a rise in the number of alcoholics due to that factor alone. In contrast, if alcoholism treatment improves or becomes more available over these years so that more alcoholics receive care, we might find a lower percentage of the older population with drinking problems. Thus, age differences in prevalence of alcohol problems may reflect society's response in addition to the biological and psychological differences associated with different ages.

Summary

One's first drink is a rite of passage from adolescence into adulthood. By the time we have our first opportunity to drink, we have already learned many expectations from adults and the media about the effects of alcohol as well as of other drugs.

Early-onset drinkers differ from late-onset drinkers or abstainers even before the first drink. They are often more rebellious, undercontrolled, impulsive, and poorer in academic achievement. Because underage drinking itself is a mild form of social deviance, it is not surprising that many early-onset drinkers also engage in a number of other behaviors that violate social norms such as use of other drugs, sexual activity, delinquency, and even criminal activities.

Attempts by adults to restrict or prohibit underage drinking may backfire by providing the added challenge to some adolescents of defying parental controls. Adolescents who have important activities and goals that would be jeopardized by excessive use of alcohol seem better able to avoid alcohol-related problems. However, those adolescents with low self-esteem and little hope of being able to achieve success may be more likely to find excessive use of alcohol and other drugs a convenient means for coping with their frustrations and failures.

The trajectory of alcohol and drug use is not the same for all adolescents, and these patterns have been useful in predicting future problems. Age of the first experience is highly related to future drinking problems, for example. This relationship has led to alcohol being dubbed as a gateway drug, as if its use "causes" the user to move on to use of illicit drugs.

Many college students, living away from home for the first time, are exposed to more peer pressure and opportunities for drinking than they might be if they lived at home. The academic pressures are more demanding and may be related to alcohol abuse as either a cause or an effect of poor academic performance. After students leave college, many return to settings where heavy alcohol use is not expected or tolerated, and drinking levels may decline. Many students who engage in heavy drinking due to participation in fraternity and sorority life, for example, may revert to lighter drinking after graduation because they are in new environments that are not conducive to excessive drinking.

At the other end of the age distribution, one might expect the transition from full-time work schedules to retirement to affect drinking opportunities. But while the demands of employment might keep drinking in control for most people, the freedom of retirement may be boring and unstructured and allow more drinking to occur without adverse work consequences.

Older persons are underrepresented in alcohol and drug abuse treatment. The reasons for this situation are diverse. Elderly persons may not perceive themselves as having abuse problems. In addition, they may face social and economic barriers to treatment access. Furthermore, societal beliefs and attitudes do not consider them to be problems for society.

Comparisons of age effects are complicated by the fact that most studies involve cross-sectional comparisons of groups of different-aged participants who also grew up with their own set of historical and cultural experiences. Since our attitudes and behaviors related to alcohol are formed by the norms that prevailed during our formative years, comparisons of the drinking of persons who differ in age are difficult to interpret because differences could be due to either physiological or sociological differences.

The majority of the findings, however, suggest that alcohol-related problems decline with age. Some of the decrease may reflect the medical complications created by drinking. Thus, if alcohol is recognized as a threat to health, older samples may voluntarily—or be advised by physicians to—cut down consumption. In addition, if alcoholism is a self-limiting disease so that the worse cases die at an earlier age, part of the decline could be due to this attrition process.

Stimulus/Response

1. Based on your own experience and observations of your friends, do you agree with the view that friends tend to have similar drug attitudes and use patterns because "birds of a feather flock together"? Or do you favor the position that one's peer group shapes and molds the behavior of its members? Can you see how both positions could be valid as well?

2. Using your own experiences, how did your drinking attitudes and practices change after the transition from high school to college? What factors do you see as leading to these changes? Do you think your drinking will increase, decrease, or stay the same after you complete college and start a job?

3. Many previous studies suggest that children who begin drinking before age 21 are more than twice as likely to develop alcohol-related problems than those who do not start drinking until after age 21. Do you agree that this evidence warrants the conclusion that teen drinking is a major source of adult alcoholism? Can you suggest other—and possibly better—evidence to support or refute this conclusion?

4. In 2008, the presidents of 130 U.S. colleges and universities introduced the Amethyst Initiative, a proposal that it was time to consider lowering the minimum drinking age from 21 to 18 because the law was ineffective as many underage youth used alcohol. What pros and cons do you see for such a change? Suggest the design of a study that would provide evidence to answer the question of what impact such a change would have on several different outcomes such as alcohol-related accidents, interpersonal violence, drinking and driving infractions, or academic performance.

5. Some estimates indicate that underage youth purchase cigarettes successfully 70% of the time over the counter, and 90%–100% of the time through vending machines. Think of several possible methods that might have been used to obtain these estimates. For each method, how reliable and valid do you believe these estimates are?

6. What factors do you think account for the greater amount of alcohol use by members of fraternities and sororities? Do you think that these social organizations tend to attract individuals who have tendencies toward alcohol excess in the first place or that new members change their behavior in ways expected by these organizations to gain acceptance?

7. Many people curtail their alcohol and other drug use as they get older. What evidence would you need to determine the extent to which this reduction is determined by biological, psychological, and sociological factors? Some older people seem to increase their alcohol and other drug use with increased age. How do you think biological, psychological, and sociological factors produce this effect?

8. Have you noticed any change in your parents' drinking patterns as they have gotten older? Have they increased or decreased in amount of drinks or the conditions leading to drinking? What factors do you think played important roles in creating these changes?

Gender Differences in Alcohol and Other Drug Use

Alcohol and other drug research has typically focused on men with less attention to women. To some extent, this imbalance reflects the social reality that alcohol and other psychoactive drug use generally has been more prevalent among men (Lex, 1991). The influential disease concept of alcoholism (Jellinek, 1952, 1960), which will be described in detail in Chapter 13, was developed with male alcoholics starting in the late 1930s and did not include female alcoholics, a largely invisible group. Moreover, alcoholic men, more so than women, appeared to more frequently create more serious social problems, especially involving aggressive acts and criminal activities. Estimates from the National Longitudinal Alcohol Epidemiologic Survey of a nationally representative sample of 42,862 adults aged 18 years and older in 1992 found that twice as many men (18.6%) as women (8.4%) met the *DSM-IV* criteria for alcohol dependence during their lifetime (Grant, 1997b).

However, many women do suffer alcohol use disorders, a trend that has steadily increased since the end of Prohibition (Fillmore, 1986). This chapter describes gender variations in the use of alcohol and other drugs and examines theories that have been proposed for these differences. Factors that may lead to alcohol and drug use, use-related problems, and dependency are examined. The conclusions about gender differences and alcohol are generally applicable as well to many other drugs such as marijuana, cocaine, and opioids (Lex, 1994).

METHODOLOGICAL AND CONCEPTUAL ISSUES

Comparisons of alcohol and other drug use levels between males and females, however, can be misleading. Due to the greater stigma associated with female alcohol and other drug abuse, many alcohol- and other drug-dependent women may go undetected. Self-reports of men and women may differ in the extent to which they rationalize their actions. Self-reports of consumption may underestimate drug use and related problems by women. Because alcohol and other drug use and abuse are more acceptable for the male sex role, women may be more motivated to try to excuse their deviant drug use by calling attention to extenuating stressful events.

Studies of consumption levels often fail to consider sex differences in body weight and composition, leading to underestimates of alcoholism among women. Because women weigh less and have a higher proportion of body fat to water, the same dose of alcohol should result in greater impairment for women than for men (Lex, 1991). Consequently, the definition of the number of drinks that constitutes heavy drinking on one occasion is typically higher for men (five) than for women (four). The reasoning is that since women reach higher blood alcohol levels than men when consuming the same amounts of alcohol, women's hazardous alcohol consumption would be underestimated and lead women to underestimate the behavioral and health effects of their seemingly moderate levels of consumption. However, there are arguments against using a gender correction or adjustment (Graham, Wilsnack, Dawson, & Vogeltanz, 1998). Some feel that gender adjustments for volume of alcohol are not that accurate or useful. Higher blood alcohol levels from a given amount of alcohol in women due to their lower proportion of body water may or may not produce a greater effect on behavior. Gender differences exist in many other aspects of drinking such as drinking style, drinking pace, amount of food consumed while drinking, drink size, and type of alcoholic beverage and may have greater physical and psychological effects than the gender difference in blood alcohol level created by the same number of drinks.

For example, a higher percentage of men than women drank beer (93.6% vs. 71.4%), but for wine (57.0% vs. 77.6%), the opposite was true (Dawson, Grant, & Chou, 1995). A slightly lower percentage of men than women drank liquor (70.0% vs. 73.4%). Men drank beer on more days in the past year than women did (94.0 vs. 56.0 days) and in larger amounts (3.2 vs. 2.3 drinks per occasion). Men drank liquor on more days in the past year (48.7 vs. 40.3 days) and in larger amounts (2.5 vs. 2.0 drinks per occasion). The opposite was the case for wine, which men drank on fewer days than women in the past year (37.5 vs. 44.9 days) but in equal amounts per occasion (1.7 drinks).

Drinking styles may differ for men and women. One study (Olenick & Chalmers, 1991) examined the role of mood and marital problems in drinking by alcoholic and nonalcoholic women. Among alcoholics, women were more likely than men to drink to alter mood or deal with marital problems. In contrast, nonalcoholic women drank to alter mood more than nonalcoholic men did, but marital problems did not differ in their effect on the drinking of nonalcoholic men and women.

Women, relative to men, generally drink on less frequent occasions and consume a lower maximum number of drinks per day (Johnson, Gruenewald, & Treno, 1998). Women tend to develop alcohol-related problems a few years later than men but have fewer years between the onset of problems and seeking help, a phenomenon known as "telescoping" as illustrated in one **retrospective study** (Johnson, Richter, Kleber, McLellan, & Carise, 2005) of 1,252 males and 785 females from many substance user treatment facilities. Women generally moved from initiation of regular alcohol use to problem use in less time than men. The age of initiation of regular alcohol use may also be important as telescoping occurred in the older but not the younger cohort.

Fewer female alcoholics have legal, job, or personal problems related to alcohol. However, the temporal sequence in which these problems occurred did not differ much between men and women in a sample of alcohol-dependent respondents in treatment (Schuckit, Anthenelli, Bucholz, Hesselbrock, & Tipp, 1995; Schuckit, Daeppen, Tipp, Hesselbrock, & Bucholz, 1998).

The context or setting in which men and women typically drink also has been found to differ, and the types of risk that they experience may differ even for the same level of drinking. Thus, males often drink in public places such as bars and, compared with women, may be more prone to drive after drinking, exposing themselves (and others) to higher risks of accidents. Past research indicates that women list social reasons more frequently than men do for drug use, and the use patterns of their male partners are a major influence on their own level of drinking (Lex, 1994). The same considerations may apply to gender differences in the conditions for using illicit drugs. Furthermore, women who drink or use illicit drugs while pregnant risk damage to the fetus, a biologically based hazard that men are obviously spared.

Measurement biases also may affect studies comparing the drinking of men and women. A review (Schmidt, Klee, & Ames, 1990) of research on women's drinking found that most indicators of alcohol problems such as public intoxication, fights, and arrests while intoxicated may be more applicable to males than to females. The reliance on such male-oriented measures may have underestimated the extent of women's alcohol problems.

Even if there were no methodological problems in obtaining comparable indices, there would be the question of gender differences in the meaning or impact of drinking. Does a given level of heavy drinking have the same degree of adverse social and psychological consequences for male and female drinkers? Women suffer greater biological harm from alcohol and face more social sanctions than men (Nolen-Hoeksema, 2004).

GENDER AND PREVALENCE OF ALCOHOL USE

Cross-Sectional Evidence

Annual national surveys such as the National Survey on Drug Use and Health (NSDUH) (Substance Abuse and Mental Health Services Administration [SAMHSA], 2007) find that a higher percentage of men than women report alcohol use. In 2006, for persons over age 12, more than half of males (57%) but less than half of females (45.2%) reported using alcohol.

Table 11.1 shows the gender comparison for the youngest group, ages 12–20, over the years between 2002 and 2006. During this period of 5 years, overall gender differences were negligible for lifetime, past-year, and past-month alcohol use. However, gender differences exist for younger ages with adolescent males engaged in heavy and binge drinking at higher rates than females. Among young adults aged 18–25, 65.9% of males and 57.9% of females reported current drinking in 2006.

TABLE 11.1 Gender differences in lifetime, past-year, and past-month use of alcohol, heavy drinking, and use of any illicit drug.

Gender/Alcohol Use	2002	2003	2004	2005	2006
TOTAL					
Lifetime	56.2[b]	55.8[b]	54.9	53.9	53.9
Past Year	47.0	46.8	46.6	46.3	46.1
Past Month	28.8	29.0	28.7	28.2	28.3
Binge Alcohol Use[1]	19.3	19.2	19.6	18.8	19.0
Heavy Alcohol Use[1]	6.2	6.1	6.3	6.0	6.2
MALE					
Lifetime	56.5[b]	55.0	54.9	53.7	54.0
Past Year	46.6	45.6	46.3	45.6	46.0
Past Month	29.6	29.9	29.6	28.9	29.2
Binge Alcohol Use[1]	21.8	21.7	22.1	21.3	21.3
Heavy Alcohol Use[1]	8.1	7.9	8.2	7.6	7.9
FEMALE					
Lifetime	56.0[b]	56.6[b]	54.8	54.2	53.7
Past Year	47.5	48.0[a]	46.9	46.9	46.2
Past Month	28.0	28.1	27.8	27.5	27.4
Binge Alcohol Use[1]	16.7	16.5	17.0	16.1	16.5
Heavy Alcohol Use[1]	4.2	4.3	4.3	4.3	4.3

Source: From *Results From the 2006 National Survey on Drug Use and Health (NSDUH): National Findings,* by the Substance Abuse and Mental Health Services Administration [SAMHSA], 2007, Rockville, MD: SAMHSA Office of Applied Studies.

[a] Difference between estimate and 2006 estimate is statistically significant at the 0.05 level.

[b] Difference between estimate and 2006 estimate is statistically significant at the 0.01 level.

[1] Binge Alcohol Use is defined as drinking five or more drinks on the same occasion (i.e., at the same time or within a couple of hours of each other) on at least 1 day in the past 30 days. Heavy Alcohol Use is defined as drinking five or more drinks on the same occasion on each of 5 or more days in the past 30 days; all heavy alcohol users are also binge alcohol users.

Similar gender differences occur in the National Epidemiologic Survey on Alcohol and Related Conditions (NESARC) in rates of use (refer to Figure 4.5) and dependence (see also Figure 4.8) for alcohol and tobacco (Falk, Yi, & Hiller-Sturmhofel, 2006).

For young adults (ages 18–25), past-month use of any *illicit* drug in the NSDUH was higher for men in 2005 and 2006 (24.6% and 23.7%, respectively) than for women (15.6% and 15.8%, respectively). Past-year use was higher for men (38.2% and 38.4%, respectively) than for women (30.1% and 30.3%, respectively). Lifetime use was higher for men (62.5% and 61.4%, respectively) than for women (55.8% and 56.5%, respectively). Although use levels have declined for both genders for most drugs since 1979 when these national surveys began, the higher use for men compared to women is a reliable finding.

An analysis (Wilsnack et al., 2000) of population surveys from 10 major countries found consistent gender effects across these nations regarding alcohol consumption and alcohol-related problems. Although men and women were generally equally likely to drink, men had greater alcohol consumption and increased risk of alcohol-related problems than women in all 10 countries. Men consistently exceeded women in their average drinking frequency and average quantity of drinks per drinking occasion in agreement with the general finding of increased consumption and adverse consequences in men.

Although these cross-sectional studies identify differences in drinking among men and women who differ in age at a given point in time, longitudinal designs in which the same individuals are retested more than once are needed to reveal how prevalence, duration, and remission of drinking and problems are related to drinking changes in given individuals.

Women's drinking was compared across three different decades with data from national surveys administered in 1981, 1991, and 2001 (Wilsnack, Kristjanson, Wilsnack, & Crosby, 2006). Cross-sectional comparisons were used, so it was not possible to measure changes over time in specific individuals. The study gives a view of how drinking differed for different age groups across three consecutive decades. The analysis examined whether differences existed in women's drinking from 1981 to 2001 for six 10-year age groupings (21–30, 31–40, etc.) with respect to the extent of heavy episodic drinking (six or more drinks per day) in the past 12 months and in the past 30 days, as well as to subjective intoxication experiences.

For 21- to 30-year-old women, there was not much change between 1981 and 1991, but in the following decade to 2001, both the prevalence of drinking and heavy drinking *declined,* especially for ages 21–30, while 30-day abstinence rates *increased*. Paradoxically, even though it appears young women were drinking less, their rates of intoxication *increased* especially among ages 21–30.

One interpretation is that increased awareness and publicity campaigns led women to "report" experiencing more frequent intoxication episodes despite evidence that heavy drinking declined. In other words, they may have been sensitized to intoxication by the media messages and consequently may have reported having these experiences at a higher level than seems warranted by their levels of reported drinking. Findings in many different cultures agree that gender differences in drinking have been generally consistent over time, according to a review of recent research (Holmila & Raitasalo, 2005).

Longitudinal Evidence

A survey of 696 women administered first in 1981 and again in 1991 (Wilsnack, 1996) used the same questions to assess quantity and frequency of drinking to allow for a longitudinal comparison. No men were surveyed, so a gender comparison is not possible. Some women had considerable changes in problem drinking over the interval. Thus, 11 % of the women who were problem free in 1981 had developed problems associated with drinking by 1986. In the other direction, one third of those who had two or more drinking problems in 1981 were free of those problems by 1986. Such shifts were greatest among younger women, which might reflect the strong effect of situational and contextual factors on their drinking such as social roles and drinking characteristics of their partners.

The percentage of abstainers increased over the 10 years, but there was no clear relationship with age, whereas the percentage of heavy drinkers declined with age. Frequency and quantity of drinking at low (one or more drinks a day) and high (six or more drinks a day) levels declined over this interval especially for women older than age 40. Problems associated with drinking and symptoms of alcohol dependence declined for all groups, especially for women of younger ages, for whom these conditions were higher than for women older than age 40. Younger women tended to drink larger quantities per occasion, often with negative consequences, whereas older women consumed lower quantities, even though they drank as frequently as younger women.

Convergence Hypothesis

The view that rapidly changing sex roles since the 1960s may have led more women to drink in styles similar to those of men suggests that the gender gap should have decreased since then (**convergence hypothesis**). However, a lack of convergence of rates for several indices of alcohol consumption or alcohol-related problems for men and women was reported in earlier national surveys conducted between 1964 and 1984 (Hilton, 1988).

In support of the convergence of rates, age differences were found (Reich, Earls, & Powell, 1988) in the estimated lifetime prevalence of alcohol abuse for men and women that varied with their date of birth. Prevalence rates were 12.3% for males and 4% for females, respectively, for cohorts born before 1940. In contrast, for individuals born after 1955, the estimated rates were higher but more similar, at 22% and 10% for males and females, respectively. Thus, men were only twice as likely to be alcoholic in the younger cohort, whereas they were three times as likely in the older cohort. A similar comparison (Holdcraft & Iacono, 2002) similarly found that individuals with *DSM-III-R* alcohol dependence who were born after 1951 had an earlier onset and a longer duration of alcohol-related problems and that these effects were stronger for women than for men.

Further evidence for convergence in alcohol outcomes between men and women comes from a large-scale study (Keyes, Grant, & Hasin, 2008) based on face-to-face survey data from the 2001–2002 NESARC that compared four cohorts born in different periods: 1913–1932, 1933–1949, 1950–1967, and 1968–1984. The gender gap was smaller for more recently born cohorts on several drinking measures: lifetime largest drinks, frequent binge drinking, alcohol abuse, and alcohol dependence. This pattern suggests that the age differences are not due entirely to age and is evidence of a period effect, such that the age differences vary with the era when the study was conducted.

GENDER CORRELATES OF ALCOHOL AND OTHER DRUG USE

A number of factors may be related to gender differences in drinking and alcohol-related problems. Biological factors, exposure to and reactions to stress, developmental transitions, gender roles, and family background experiences all may have a bearing on gender differences in alcohol use (Holmila & Raitasalo, 2005). We will examine each type of factor in this section.

Biological Factors

Due to lower total body water in women, gender differences in alcohol metabolism, and effects of alcohol on postmenopausal estrogen levels, the effect of a given dose of alcohol will be greater in women (Lex, 1994). Consequently, women are at risk for some medical problems from lower consumption levels than men are (Bradley, Badrinath, Bush, Boyd-Wickizer, & Anawalt, 1998). In general, chronic higher alcohol consumption by women is associated with hypertension, stroke, breast cancer, and mortality.

Some biological processes related to the reproductive system can be affected by alcohol for both men and women because regulation by the hypothalamic-pituitary-gonadal axis is disrupted by alcohol (Mello, Mendelson, & Teoh, 1993) either by direct toxic effects or indirectly by influencing sex hormones such as testosterone, estrogen, and progesterone. Men suffer impotence and lowered sexual interest, and women have menstrual problems as well as childbearing difficulties. Knowledge that heavy drinking can increase infertility and spontaneous abortion may affect drinking by some women. The awareness that adverse fetal effects can occur after alcohol consumption during pregnancy may reduce drinking levels (Bradley et al., 1998).

Alcohol's effect on menstruation, limited to women, may contribute to the later onset of drinking and smaller consumption by women than by men, but it may also contribute to the greater impairment for women than for men when drinking the same amount (Lex, 1994). A common belief is that the discomfort during the premenstrual stage might motivate more drinking for women. Poor methodological design and inadequate means of cycle phase identification in this research have produced contradictory results. Drinking was unrelated to menstrual cycle among college women in some studies (Charette, Tate, & Wilson, 1990; Tate & Charette, 1991), and considerable variations in the drinking–menstrual cycle pattern occurred with a small sample of social drinkers (Mello, Mendelson, & Lex, 1990). Those who drank more had more hostility and anger during the premenstrual stage, whereas those who drank less experienced more physical discomfort.

Alcohol impairs some functions such as memory and cognition, but the amount of disruption was unrelated to three different points in the menstrual cycle (Brick, Nathan, Westrick, & Frankenstein, 1986). However, impairment of functions such as reaction time and sensory acuity did vary. Because women eliminate alcohol more rapidly during the mid-luteal phase of the cycle (Gill, 1997), studies conducted at different points in the menstrual cycle might have conflicting results. A review of studies (Mumenthaler, Taylor, O'Hara, & Yesavage, 1999) comparing gender differences in alcohol absorption, distribution, elimination, and impairment does not support the view that gender differences in alcohol pharmacokinetics or alcohol-induced performance impairment is due to variations in female sex hormones over the menstrual cycle.

Stress and Drinking

Analysis (Dawson, Grant, & Ruan, 2005) of the number of past-year stressors with several measures of heavy drinking showed a positive relationship among respondents in the 2001–2002 NESARC. Overall, stress did not lead to drinking more often but to consuming higher quantities of alcohol when respondents drank, and the relationship was stronger for men than for women. With each additional stress, frequency of heavy drinking increased 24% for men and 13% for women. Drinking for men showed a stronger relationship than for women to legal and job-related stress.

Gender Roles

Gender roles have changed dramatically since the middle of the past century as more women entered the workplace instead of remaining in the home. Increasingly, both husbands and wives held jobs or pursued careers outside the home. These changes also affected marriage, childbearing, and parenting patterns. However, because women traditionally have the responsibility of rearing children, working mothers had to choose between giving up their jobs or trying to both work and bring up their children, adding a stress that might lead some to cope with alcohol or other drugs. Thus, parenting may affect the use of alcohol and other drugs to a greater degree for women than for men. However, it is difficult to separate the extent to which the role changes for women in work, marriage, and parenting affected alcohol and other drug use because the multiple roles are so closely intertwined.

Both men and women may drink in response to work pressure, but women often carry the double burden of holding a full-time job and being a homemaker, which might contribute to more drinking. Career women face situations where opportunities to drink alcohol are readily available—and expected—as in business lunches. In one study (Wilsnack, 1996), employed women were not found to have more drinking problems than women who did not work outside the home, but they did drink more frequently, which over time could become more problematic.

Married women who work outside the home have higher rates of alcohol problems than homemakers or unmarried working women (Johnson, 1982). One explanation is that the stress of competing with men in the workplace may increase drinking for working women as found in one study (Svare, Miller, & Ames, 2004) of 1,105 workers (11% women) in a heavy machinery assembly plant. Women reporting a negative social climate in this study had a greater propensity to drink at work.

A large scale study (Cho, 2004) with 11,783 currently working women, aged 21–65, from the 1990 National Health Interview Survey (NHIS) assessed the relationship between gender composition in different occupations and the level of alcohol consumption. The results suggested that women working in occupations with male coworkers rather than in jobs with predominantly female coworkers were more likely to drink. It was suggested that male dominance in an occupation with both male and female coworkers may create job stress for women, which may increase their alcohol consumption.

Marital Status and Alcohol Use

The relationship between marital status and drinking might depend on women's drinking history. For some, drinking could produce marital problems, but for others, domestic problems could be a cause of drinking. Thus, for some married women with drinking problems, divorce might be an eventual effect of their drinking. For married women without drinking problems, divorce may sometimes lead to drinking problems. Yet, for other women who leave an unhappy marriage, the drinking may be reduced.

A study (Hanna, Faden, & Harford, 1993) of drinking patterns of 24- to 32-year-old women for the years 1982–1988 in relation to changes in their marital status used data from respondents in the National Longitudinal Survey of Youth (NLSY). Marriage seemed to have a "protective effect" as women who got married or remarried showed less drinking, whereas those who became separated or divorced increased drinking over the 6 years of the study. Another study (Harford, Hanna, & Faden, 1994) based on the National Longitudinal Survey of Labor Market Experience of Youth found that married women had lower drinking over an extended period of 11 years, except among women with a history of heavy drinking. Separation and divorce were not associated with long-term effects on current drinking, but divorce was associated with decreased drinking, at least in the short term, for men and women with a family history of alcoholism.

Similar findings occurred in a longitudinal study of a birth cohort born in 1958 (Power, Rodgers, & Hope, 1999) in England that examined the relationship between alcohol consumption and marital status changes between ages 23 and 33 for both men and women. At both ages, the divorced showed increased drinking and had the highest levels whereas the married showed declines and had the lowest levels. Separation was accompanied by short-term increases in heavy drinking. High rates of heavy drinking persisted for never-married men and women.

Women living alone and cohabitating women (living with and having sexual relations with someone to whom they were not married) had the highest levels of heavy drinking and dependence (Joutsenniemi et al., 2007). Until relatively recently, cohabitation was an unacceptable lifestyle to society, which added stress for women with more rebellious or independent attitudes. Social norms and values have changed significantly over the past 50 or so years. Cohabitation, previously regarded as flouting social convention, has become more acceptable and widespread, and it may no longer predict drinking problems as well.

When additional factors are examined together with marital status, its relationship to drinking levels is much lower. A longitudinal study (Matzger, Delucchi, Weisner, & Ammon, 2004) of 600 dependent and 992 problem drinkers in treatment programs examined the relationship of several individual and social factors in addition to marital status and amount of drinking over a period of 5 years. For problem drinkers, factors such as age, income, education, age of initiation into drinking, problem severity, and size of alcohol- and drug-using social network were better predictors of alcohol use than marital status. For those with alcohol dependence, income, number of alcohol dependence symptoms, higher drug severity, and a heavy alcohol- and drug-using social network were more important than marital status in predicting consumption.

Family Background Experiences

Growing up in an alcoholic home can be a stressful and traumatic experience, not only because of the adverse effect of alcohol on the parent but also because of child neglect and abuse, divorced or absent parents, and financial hardships that may contribute to future vulnerability. Some risk factors associated with the development of alcohol dependency, such as a positive family history of alcoholism, may be similar for men and women. Other factors may be more likely to differ (Gomberg, 1994). Thus, women alcoholics recall experiencing more family disruptions during their early years than men alcoholics do, although alcoholics have more such memories than nonalcoholics. Possibly, family problems may be more closely related to drug problems for women because interpersonal ties and relationships are more important to women than to men.

A study (Chermack, Stoltenberg, Fuller, & Blow, 2000) examined gender differences in the effect of family history of alcoholism and violence on the development of childhood and adult behavioral problems in a sample of men and women entering treatment for substance abuse or dependence. Women for whom family violence occurred with family alcoholism were more prone to childhood conduct problems and adult problems with alcohol. For men, family alcoholism was not directly associated with child conduct problems or adult problems with alcohol and violence but was associated with adult drug problems.

Adverse Effects of Alcohol

A household survey identified gender differences in the nature of problems associated with the use of alcohol and other drugs (Robbins, 1989). The assumption was that men tend to cope with problems by external responses, including antisocial behaviors, whereas women are more likely to internalize problems and suffer emotional distress. Thus, women might hide their use of alcohol and drugs to cope with problems but feel more guilt and anxiety from their use. In contrast, men who abuse alcohol and other drugs were expected to engage in more aggressive and belligerent behavior. The results supported the view that men and women engage in different styles of deviant behavior, with alcohol-abusing women showing more depression and irritability and men having more difficulties with work, school, financial issues, and the law.

Gender and Drinking Among Older Populations

The prevalence of alcohol use among individuals over age 65 was compared with data from three nationally representative cross-sectional surveys: the 2000 National Health Interview Survey, the 2001 Behavioral Risk Factor Surveillance System, and the 2000 National Household Survey on Drug Abuse (NHSDA; Breslow, Faden, & Smothers, 2003).

For men over age 65, the prevalence of "moderate drinking" (defined as one drink or less per day) in the three surveys ranged between 27.2% and 38.7%. "Heavier drinking" (defined as more than one drink per day) among men ranged from 9.2% to 10.1%. Women over age 65 had lower rates than men, with the prevalence of "moderate drinking" ranging from 21.5% to 32.3% and that of "heavier drinking" ranging between 2.2% and 2.6% among women across the three surveys.

Older groups of men showed stable moderate drinking rates while heavier drinking rates decreased in two of the three surveys. In contrast, all three surveys showed that older groups of women had lower levels of moderate drinking while heavier drinking remained stable. Another study (Karlamangla, Zhou, Reuben, Greendale, & Moore, 2006) focused on age trajectories of heavy drinking, defined as five or more drinks per occasion for men and four or more drinks per occasion for women. In general, with increased age, heavy drinking declined, especially for married women and those who quit smoking but less so for men.

Older women may drink less than men of similar age because they adhere to the traditional sex roles for women (Wilsnack & Wilsnack, 1992). The study found that motivations for drinking among women generally were to be sociable, to feel good, and to forget worries. However, younger women were much more likely to drink for relaxing effects and forgetting of worries. They were also more likely to report negative consequences of drinking such as physical health consequences, adverse effects on family and social life, and financial consequences.

In contrast to the evidence for alcohol, evidence exists that older women are more likely to use psychoactive drugs (e.g., benzodiazepines such as Librium® and Valium®) and prescription medication than men (Finlayson, 1995). Use of psychoactive drugs among older women was related to widowhood, lower education, higher religiosity, poorer health, higher stress, lower income, and less social support. Since alcohol may have dangerous side effects as well as interactions and cross tolerances with many of these prescription drugs, use of alcohol may be particularly disruptive for women.

One study (Gomberg, 1993) compared men and women over age 55 who were classified as alcohol abusers or as alcohol dependent. In a sample of 124 men and women in treatment (mean age in middle 60s), three times as many women as men were widowed. Education level was comparable, but twice as many men were employed or temporarily laid off; about one third of the women were "homemakers."

An examination of family history revealed that the women were more likely than the men to have had fathers, mothers, and siblings who also had drinking problems. As for their own drinking history, the women had later onsets of both initial drinking and their first drinking problem. There were different psychological consequences for older problem-drinking men and women, with men reporting generally positive effects, aside from family conflicts, and women experiencing negative effects such as depression. Older women in alcohol treatment, especially those who were divorced, separated, or widowed, were also found to be more likely than older men to have had a significant other (spouse/lover) who was a heavy problem drinker.

In comparison to men, women were more likely to have heavily drinking current or previous spouses, less frequent public drinking, and greater use of psychoactive drugs such as prescribed medications. Problem drinking occurred for 38% of the women during the last 10 years (late onset) but for only 4% of the men. Finally, women alcoholics were more likely to be also diagnosed with affective disorder whereas men alcoholics were more frequently diagnosed as also having antisocial personality.

A longitudinal study examined the relationship between depressive symptoms and drinking behavior for 621 late-middle-aged women and 951 late-middle-aged men (Schutte, Moos, & Brennan, 1995). Follow-ups occurred after 1 and 3 years showing gender differences in the relationship between depression and drinking. Among women, heavier alcohol consumption predicted less depressive symptomatology 1 and 3 years later, as if drinking was a form of self-medication. In contrast, among men, more depressive symptoms were related to less alcohol consumption on the follow-ups, as if the depressive mood interfered with drinking.

Studies (Brennan & Moos, 1990; Brennan, Moos, & Kim, 1993) of 55- to 65-year-old problem drinkers in the community found they had more stress or negative life events and tended to use avoidance coping responses in dealing with such stressors in comparison to nonproblem drinkers who had more social resources and social support and tended to use approach or problem-solving responses in dealing with stressors.

Problem drinkers were more likely to be unmarried and male. Women problem drinkers used psychoactive medicines more—and alcohol less—relative to men. Compared with men, they had more recent onset of drinking problems as well as greater depression. The women had more family-related stressors, but they had fewer financial stressors and more social support.

Stress studies often use indices of global or total stress. However, specific types of negative life events may not produce the same effects on drinking, as illustrated by a study (Glass, Prigerson, Kasl, & Mendes-de-Leon, 1995) of 798 men and 1,242 women (aged 65 years or more). Measures of drinking and negative life event stressors were taken, and a follow-up was conducted 3 years later. In general, alcohol consumption declined over the 3-year period, but how it related to life stressors depended on the type of stressor as well as on gender. Among men, only 4 of the 11 stress events were associated with higher alcohol consumption, while 2 others were associated with decreased alcohol consumption. Among women, 2 events were found related to higher drinking while 2 other negative events were associated with decreased drinking at follow-up. Another 4 events had more complex relationships, with higher drinking depending on the level of some other variable.

Gender differences exist in the types of social influences and stressors experienced and the extent to which increased drinking occurs in response. Drinking histories were obtained from a community sample of 831 older adults (347 women and 484 men; average age = 69) that included both problem and nonproblem drinkers (Lemke, Schutte, Brennan, & Moos, 2008). Overall, women tended to report drinking in relation to exposure to a partner's drinking, family interpersonal problems, death of someone close, and emotional distress. Men drank in response to peers' drinking and workplace problems more than women did in these situations. Similar relationships between stressors and drinking occurred for problem drinkers and nonproblem drinkers, but gender differences in reactivity for problem drinkers were minimal.

Among couples, when a problem drinker stops drinking, it creates a new stressor that may differ for men and women. Not only did remission of drinking problems fail to improve relationships with others for men; it also seemed to increase family stressors for women (Brennan et al., 1993). This gender difference may be due to men problem drinkers receiving more spousal support than women problem drinkers get from their husbands. A year after remission, however, women reported fewer spousal problems and men reported fewer conflicts with friends. One possible reason is that the crisis created by problem drinking produced short-term increases in family communication as they struggled with the problem.

As noted in the previous chapter, retirement presents major role changes and challenges that may affect the use of alcohol and other drugs by both men and women. Furthermore, the physiological processes involved with alcohol use differ for men and women, especially if they are taking drugs for medical purposes (Epstein, Fischer-Elber, & Al-Otaiba, 2007). While older women may benefit from the buffering effect of low levels of alcohol on menopausal hormonal declines—and perhaps from its protection against coronary heart disease and osteoporosis—heavier drinking may negate these benefits as well as increase the risk for breast cancer.

GENDER AND ALCOHOLISM TREATMENT

Interviews with 7,359 adult men and women from the 1992 National Longitudinal Alcohol Epidemiologic Survey (NLAES) with *DSM-IV* alcohol abuse or dependence in their lifetime revealed a gender disparity in receiving treatment, with only 23.0% of men and 15.1% of women ever having been treated (Dawson, 1996). Even 30 years after onset of the alcohol problem, men (42.4%) were more likely than women (35.6%) to have had treatment.

Possibly, women are more likely to be hidden or closet alcoholics, which delays treatment until the problems become more severe. However, the existence of a gender disparity may not be due mainly to barriers or biases to treatment access. For example, if the percentage of men in need of treatment exceeds that of women, it should not be surprising that more men receive treatment. Hence, it is necessary to control for this factor. In the analysis of NLAES results, the proportions of males to females in treatment closely matched their proportions with diagnoses of *DSM-IV* alcohol use disorders, 2.7 to 1.0, respectively.

After treatment, unfortunately some alcoholics eventually return to drinking. Relapse, a problem that Chapter 15 will discuss in detail, is mentioned briefly here in terms of gender differences. Overall, it appears that men and women suffer the same rates of relapse (Walitzer & Dearing, 2006). Still, the causes and consequences of relapse may not be the same for men and women. Alcoholic women seem to be more at risk for relapse from marital stress and interpersonal conflict than men. In some cases, the husbands' drinking generates marital stress that leads their wives to drinking. In contrast, alcoholic men are less likely to relapse and may be "protected" by marriage because of their wives' support, although only if they are non- or light drinkers.

THEORIES OF GENDER DIFFERENCES IN ALCOHOL AND OTHER DRUG USE

Most psychological theories about the function of alcohol have developed from observations of males, often those who were alcoholic. These explanations were assumed to be valid for women as well, an assumption that has been largely untested. Theories that have focused specifically on women have attempted to explain their drinking in terms of their conformance or nonconformance to sex roles. We will look at both clinically based psychodynamic theories and behaviorally based sex role theories to see how well they can account for gender differences in the use of alcohol.

Psychodynamic Theories

Early theories about the origins of drinking problems focused on males. Alcohol was seen as a way to deal with dependency conflicts, according to traditional psychoanalytic theories (McCord & McCord, 1960). In addition, drinking was viewed as a means of fulfilling the need for a feeling of power (McClelland, Davis, Kalin, & Wanner, 1972).

Based heavily on observations of clients in therapy, these views focused on unconscious determinants of behavior, ignoring intentional and conscious processes. The emphasis on biologically determined and early-childhood experiences did not recognize the role of current situational and personal factors affecting the individual's use of alcohol and other drugs. Many of the formulations are vague and difficult to test scientifically.

In addition, psychodynamic views seem limited because many factors for drinking are gender specific. Biological differences in the metabolism of alcohol and hormones related to reproductive function may be one source of gender differences in alcohol use. Learning experiences play a vital role in determining sex roles that affect gender differences in attitudes and beliefs about the use of alcohol. In addition, societal values offer different opportunities, encouragement, and approval of drinking for males than for females. It is important to formulate and test other theories that can explain alcohol use by women as well as by men.

Sex Role Theory

Sex role theory offers explanations for gender differences in drinking that emphasize sex roles, a set of learned beliefs and attitudes about the societal roles for men and women. In the past, male drinking, even to excess on occasion, generally was acceptable, whereas it was frowned on for females. A man was expected to be able to hold his liquor, but it was deemed unladylike for a woman to get high from drinking. In contrast, women used alcohol to achieve feelings of womanliness or fulfill a feminine sex role (Wilsnack, 1976). A comparison of fantasies of women before and after they consumed a small amount of alcohol found that after drinking, women decreased imagery related to achievement but increased thoughts about traditionally feminine activities. Women who drink heavily may feel particularly insecure about their femininity, resorting to alcohol to achieve more fantasies about being more womanly. The traditional sex role for women, centered on hearth and home, might create frustration and depression, leading some women who feel restrained to turn to alcohol as an escape.

Sex Role Conflict

The changes in sex roles achieved by feminist activism since the 1970s may have altered the picture. Social changes toward more equality of sex roles would place the traditionally feminine woman under **sex role conflict**, either between her traditional domestic role and her actual nontraditional behavior or between her nontraditional behavior and the traditional expectations of society. Either conflict might lead to more alcohol use. Consistent with this view, alcoholic women had traditional feminine scores on sex-typed attitudes but masculine tendencies on measures of interpersonal and expressive style. Thus, drinking may be a means to relieve conflict related to sex roles. Married women working outside the home had higher drinking-problem rates than unmarried working women or married women not working outside the home (Johnson, 1982). Women who reject values of traditional femininity might experience social ostracism from those expecting them to adhere to feminine values. These women also might experience stress, as a result, and turn to alcohol to cope with this problem (Wilsnack, 1976).

Multiple Sex Role Stress

A different aspect of sex roles that might be involved in increasing women's drinking is the stress of the dual roles of pursuing a career and being a traditional homemaker. In other words, **multiple sex roles** can create more stress and lead to drinking problems. Some support for this view, as well as for the sex role conflict view, is that among 1,367 employed men and women, greater alcohol use occurred for working women with traditional sex roles and for working men with nontraditional sex roles (Parker & Harford, 1992). These women and men, who had substantial obligations at home and also intense competition at the workplace, consumed more alcohol.

Sex Role Deprivation Stress

Sex role deprivation rather than multiplicity of roles was more likely to be associated with problem drinking among women at all ages in one study (Wilsnack & Cheloha, 1987). The youngest women were more likely to drink if they lacked stable marital and work roles; middle-aged women drank more if their marriages dissolved or they had children growing up and moving out. An additional risk factor for women older than age 50 was working outside the home. Role deprivation may create alienation and feelings of loneliness that allow for more time to drink as a coping response for their feelings of despair. An alternative explanation, however, is that women who drink excessively may cause the loss of domestic and job relationships.

Overview

Thus, a variety of processes related to sex roles have been proposed that create stress and might produce alcohol problems among women. The risk of alcoholism exists not only for women who accept traditional sex roles and for those who do not feel sufficiently feminine (Wilsnack, 1974) but also for women who reject traditional values of femininity (Wilsnack & Wilsnack, 1978).

Findings from retrospective studies with women who are already encountering drinking problems are difficult to interpret because the drinking could be a cause or a consequence of sex role problems or both. Information on this question that would be less ambiguous might come from a prospective study of adolescent girls who have not yet developed strong drinking patterns.

As sex roles for women continue to evolve, their relationship to drinking should be expected to change also. In the days when most married women with children were home-makers, it may have been more stressful to also be employed. However, now that many married women with children also have employment outside the home, it could be that the women who are homemakers or have no work outside the home experience more stress. In the future, if the need for males to drink to prove their masculinity decreases and if social acceptance for female drinking in more contexts increases, the relationship between gender roles and drinking should disappear. Currently, however, drinking is still more compatible with sex roles for males than for females.

Generational Differences

Due to the large changes in sex roles in America over the past generation, it is difficult to interpret age-related differences because they are often intertwined with changing cultural values. These generational differences may be greater for women because the relation of drinking to sex roles has changed to a greater extent for women than for men.

An illustration of this issue comes from a study of age-related differences in alcohol problems (Gomberg, 1984) that examined alcoholic women and age-matched controls in their 20s, 30s, and 40s. Some of the differences among these groups might not be due to age, per se, but to generational differences. In other words, the era in which each group was a given age was not the same, and some of these social conditions may have led to different drinking behavior among these groups. Thus, the younger women grew up in an era of greater freedoms for women, with more women working outside the home, more single-parent families, and more couples cohabitating rather than being married.

Alcoholic women in their 40s did not develop their alcoholism until late in their 30s whereas those in their 20s began their alcoholism in their teen years. Differences in drinking behavior between alcoholic women and the controls were smallest for the women in their 40s. On average, these women were born in 1936, an era of traditional femininity. Alcohol may have been a means of reducing frustration and resentment from lack of fulfillment for some women confined by traditional feminism.

Women in their 20s in this study, born on average in 1956, showed many problems of impulse control and strained relationships with parents. They were more likely to drive after drinking, use other drugs, have potential fetal harm, face workplace problems, and encounter assaults and other violence. The women in their 30s were born, on average, in 1946 and represented the baby boom generation. This group showed more conflict than the other two age groups, perhaps due to the rapid social transition in sex roles during their adolescence. Middle-aged problem drinkers had fewer problems of impulsivity in their childhood, greater acceptance of traditional sex roles, more use of psychoactive drugs, and more private drinking.

The differences among the women from different eras illustrate how the social context may alter the role of alcohol for different generations. Although all of the alcoholic women drank excessively, it may have stemmed from different types of psychological reasons because of the varying nature of society's demands and expectations for women over this period.

Another example of generational or cohort differences measured the alcohol consumption of 468 men and 132 women with lifetime alcohol dependence who were born between 1941 and 1960 (Holdcraft & Iacono, 2002). Alcohol dependence rates were higher for those born after 1951. This younger cohort, especially the women, also had earlier onset and longer duration of alcohol-related problems.

SMOKING AND GENDER

"You've come a long way, baby."

—Virginia Slims cigarette slogan

Smoking by women increased to a peak of about one third of the population in the early 1970s. However, the 1964 Surgeon General's report (U.S. Department of Health Education and Welfare, 1964) on the health risks of cigarette smoking eventually led to a decline over much of the 1970s and 1980s for both men and women. During the period from 1985 to 1995, the NHSDA found that smoking in the past month dropped from 34.5% to 26.8% for women and even more for men, from 43.4% to 31.1% (Department of Health and Human Services, 1997).

The decline continued to the present, and the prevalence of smoking is only slightly higher for men than it is for women. Between 2002 and 2007, the NSDUH rate of current cigarette smoking among youths decreased for both males (from 12.3% to 10.0%) and females (from 13.6% to 9.7%; SAMHSA, 2007). For young adults aged 18–25 during the same 5-year period, the NSDUH rate of cigarette use declined for both males (44.4% to 40.5%) and females (37.1% to 31.8%). In 2007, males aged 12 or older still had higher rates of cigarette smoking (27.1% vs. 21.5%) in the past month than females, and the disparity of less than 6% was comparable to the difference of a decade earlier.

This convergence in gender smoking differences partly reflects higher rates of women than men becoming smokers (Pierce, Fiore, Novotny, Hatziandreu, & Davis, 1989) especially among those with less education (U.S. Department of Health and Human Services, 2001). Initiation of smoking among teen girls remains high, with 3 out of 10 high school senior girls reporting having smoked within the past 30 days in 2001. In addition, the gender gap narrowed because women were less likely than men to quit.

However, gender comparisons of smoking that rely only on the percentage of smokers or number of cigarettes smoked are misleading. Men tend to inhale more deeply, so for the same number of cigarettes, they receive more nicotine and other harmful substances from combustion. Men and women prefer different types of cigarettes. Women tend to smoke lower-tar, filtered cigarettes and in smaller amounts than men do. Men are more likely to use smokeless tobacco, pipes, and cigars. Cultural factors also affect gender differences in using specific tobacco products within some cultures but not others. In addition, this gender gap varies over time, depending on culture and type of tobacco product (Grunberg, Winders, & Wewers, 1991).

Gender differences in the neurophysiology of nicotine must be considered (Pomerleau, Pomerleau, & Garcia, 1991). Women may differ from men with regard to nicotine intake, nicotine effects, or both, especially depending on the menstrual cycle phase, oral contraceptive use, and estrogen replacement therapy. Chronic nicotine use may affect female reproductive endocrinology in ways that affect the extent to which smoking is reinforcing. Finally, pharmacological agents used to treat smoking may have different effects in women than in men.

Daily diaries of smoking maintained by 22 females showed that smoking did not differ as a function of menstrual phase. There was no systematic correlation between symptomatology and smoking within individuals (Pomerleau, Cole, Lumley, Marks, & Pomerleau, 1994). Alcohol and caffeine intake was highly stable across the menstrual cycle in these female smokers.

Women smokers face the risk of reduced fertility, gynecological problems, and earlier menopause, which is a risk factor for other problems including osteoporosis, cancer in the reproductive system, and heart disease (U.S. Department of Health and Human Services, 1990). Smoking women who are pregnant have fetuses of lower birth weight, retarded fetal growth, and premature birth, presumably from nicotine and carbon monoxide toxicity, which crosses the placenta and creates carboxyhemoglobin, reducing blood transport of oxygen.

Some health consequences of smoking such as lung cancer and coronary heart disease are similar for men and women but may occur at different rates. Among women, lung cancer is more likely than breast cancer. Women who smoke have greater risk for cardio-vascular disease (U.S. Department of Health and Human Services, 1990). A longitudinal study of more than 199,000 nurses found that the more cigarettes they smoked, the greater the likelihood of coronary heart disease (Willett et al., 1987).

Cigarette smoking has been related to depression in past research although it is unclear how they might be causally related (Korhonen et al., 2007). The relationship between smoking and depression may differ for men and women. A prospective study with over 9,000 male and female twins in Finland found that men who smoked or had previously smoked had higher risk for depression, but among women only quitters had increased risk for depression. Persistent smoking was a stronger risk for men.

Information about smoking during the past 12 months, drinking, and recent depression was obtained from 14,063 Canadians by random-digit dialing and computer-assisted telephone interviewing (Massak & Graham, 2008). Using *DSM-IV* criteria for depression, smoking and depression were more closely related for women for all categories of smoking. However, for men, only midlevel and heavier smoking was related to depression.

Similar differences occurred in the NESARC, Wave 1 (Husky, Mazure, Paliwal, & McKee, 2008). Current or prior smoking was more closely associated with current or prior diagnoses of *DSM-IV* depression among women than among men.

GENDER AND OTHER DRUG USE

Drug abuse among women has been recognized only recently for the serious problem it represents historically (Kandall, 1998a, 1998b). Drugs were widely used for medical purposes in the 19th century, especially in treating pain. Virtually all diseases were treated with opiates. Because women were regarded as the "weaker sex" during this period and were subject to diagnoses of neurasthenia involving a weak nervous system, leading to chronic mental and physical weakness, cocaine, opiates, and cannabis were routinely dispensed to women for medical purposes. With advances in medical knowledge and recognition of the addictive properties of many drugs, opiate use in the treatment of women declined over the 20th century.

Prevalence Rates

Comparisons of gender differences in the use of different drugs among the general population can be obtained from national probability surveys such as the NHSDA and NSDUH. However, these surveys underestimate the extent of heaviest drug users because many of them are among incarcerated and hospitalized populations, which are not included in population surveys.

Rates of any illicit drug use for young adults (aged 18–25) in the 2005 and 2006 NSDUH (SAMHSA, 2007) for lifetime, the past year, and the past month were higher for males, as Table 11.2 shows. One exception was males' use of stimulants, which was at about the same or a slightly lower rate than for females.

Studies of young women methadone patients found that a male partner initiated a small percentage of their drug use. In contrast, males were more likely to be introduced to drugs in a larger group context (Anglin, Hser, & Booth, 1987; Hser, Anglin, & Booth, 1987). This process probably holds for many other drugs.

Gender differences exist in the time course of substance use problem development as women require less time from starting use before dependence occurs. A study of 271 men and women (mean age of 32.6) receiving treatment for substance abuse found women had

TABLE 11.2 Gender differences in past-month, past-year, and lifetime illicit drug use for ages 18–25 in 2005 and 2006.

	TIME PERIOD					
	Lifetime		Past Year		Past Month	
Demographic Characteristic	2005	2006	2005	2006	2005	2006
TOTAL	59.2	59.0	34.2	34.4	20.1	19.8
GENDER						
Male	62.5	61.4	38.2	38.4	24.6	23.7
Female	55.8	56.5	30.1	30.3	15.6	15.8

Source: From *Results From the 2006 National Survey on Drug Use and Health (NSDUH): National Findings,* by the Substance Abuse and Mental Health Services Administration [SAMHSA], 2007, Rockville, MD: SAMHSA Office of Applied Studies.

fewer years of regular use of opioids, cannabis, and alcohol before entering treatment than men even though there were no gender differences in the age at which they started use (Randall et al.,1999). A study using retrospective recall with a larger sample of 2,037 men and women in alcohol treatment (Johnson, Richter, Kleber, McLellan, & Carise, 2005) found similar "telescoping" or a shorter time between regular use and entering treatment for women, but age was also a factor as this difference was found only among older women.

Men and women also differ in the progression of drugs that they will use (Kandel, Warner, & Kessler, 1998). For men, alcohol use generally precedes marijuana use, which in turn may lead to illicit drug use. In contrast, for women, cigarette smoking or alcohol use is more often the precursor of marijuana use and subsequent use of other illicit drugs.

The justification and conditions for drug use also may differ for men and women (Lex, 1991). For example, women attribute their use of cocaine to depression, feeling unsociable, family and job pressure, and health problems, whereas men attribute their use to the desire for intoxication. Women may not spend as much money on drugs because they are living with a drug-using male partner who provides the drugs. For example, due to the high price of crack, some women may exchange sex for the drug.

Psychotropic drugs are widely prescribed for psychological distress, especially for women. They are viewed as safe methods of treating the affective or mood disorders of women but soon become drugs of abuse and dependency. Of all groups, older women receive the most psychoactive prescription drugs (Graham, Carver, & Brett, 1995). The evidence is mixed, but physicians may diagnose men and women differently even when the same symptoms exist (Gomberg, 1995a), which would lead them to prescribe different drugs for men and women. At older ages, both men and women may use more psychoactive drugs as well as medications such as cardiovascular drugs, analgesics, sedatives, and tranquilizers (Gomberg, 1995b). The danger is increased because these drugs can have adverse interactive effects with each other.

Gender Dependence on Different Drugs

The National Comorbidity Survey (Kessler et al., 1994), based on interviews with a national representative sample of more than 8,000 individuals ages 15–54, measured the extent of comorbidity of alcohol and drug dependence in the United States. Dependence was measured using the criteria of the *DSM-III-R* (1987), which requires a respondent to meet at least three of nine possible criteria, some of which must exist for at least a month or repeatedly over a longer period.

Gender differences exist in dependence for different drugs (Anthony, Warner, & Kessler, 1994). Men and women do not differ much in dependence for tobacco, heroin, and cocaine. However, men are twice as likely as women to experience dependence for alcohol and marijuana during their lifetimes. The reverse holds for psychotropic drugs such as sedatives and tranquilizers, for which women are twice as likely to develop dependence as men. For both men and women, dependence was most frequent for tobacco, followed by alcohol and then illicit drugs for men. However, for women the opposite held, with dependence for alcohol at a lower rate than for illicit drugs (Anthony et al., 1994). These data refer only to dependence rates. If one combines dependence with abuse, the rates are about 18% for women but much higher, at 35%, for men.

Gender and Psychiatric Comorbidity

About half (51.4%) of the respondents with a substance use disorder in their lifetimes also had at least one other psychiatric disorder in their lifetimes. Concurrent occurrence of a substance disorder and another psychiatric disorder in a given 12-month period was found in 42.7% of respondents, with the rates being similar for men and women.

Table 11.3 shows the comorbidity of drug dependence with other psychiatric disorders in the National Comorbidity Survey for men and women, ages 15–54 (Kandel et al., 1998). For women, anxiety, alcohol, and affective disorders had the highest rates of comorbidity with drug dependence. In contrast, the order for men was alcohol, antisocial personality, and conduct disorder, followed by anxiety disorders and then affective disorders.

Gender and Comorbidity of Alcohol With Other Drugs

Studies of alcohol use typically ignore an important contextual aspect of drinking, the extent to which polydrug use occurs. **Polydrug abuse** occurred in 61% of the 212 problem drinkers in a treatment program (Martin, Kaczynski, Maisto, & Tarter, 1996). They were primarily young, male, and unmarried in comparison to those who did not use multiple drugs. The most common combinations were alcohol and cocaine (60%), alcohol and marijuana (51%), and alcohol and a sedative (31%).

TABLE 11.3   Gender differences in comorbidity of drug dependence and other psychiatric disorders from the National Comorbidity Survey.

	Women		Men		
	Percent	**Standard Error**	**Percent**	**Standard Error**	**z**
Anxiety	70.6	(3.5)	43.8	(3.8)	5.2
Affective	55.3	(4.1)	32.7	(3.4)	4.2
Alcohol	68.1	(4.3)	82.2	(2.7)	2.8
Other	34.4	(5.1)	59.2	(4.0)	3.8
Total Number	(241)		(369)		

Source: From "The Epidemiology of Substance Use and Dependence Among Women," by D. B. Kandel, L. A. Warner, and R. C. Kessler, 1998, in C. L. Wetherington and A. B. Roman (Eds.), *Drug Addiction Research and the Health of Women* (pp. 105–130), Washington, DC: National Institute of Drug Abuse.

Summary

Although sex roles have undergone substantial changes in U.S. society over the past generation, men are still allowed or encouraged to drink more often, in greater amounts, and in a greater variety of contexts than women are. In addition, the motives and meaning of drinking may vary for men and women.

Epidemiological studies still show more frequent consumption and larger quantities of alcohol consumed by men in the general population. Men are still more likely than women to be seen in alcoholism treatment facilities, although to some degree, the differences may reflect biases of access rather than sex differences in prevalence of alcohol problems.

The role of alcohol and its effects on women may vary markedly at different ages. During adolescence, drinking may be associated with increased sexual activity, and the patterns of drinking developed at this stage may well serve as "scripts" that influence drinking throughout life. Early drinking also may create conflicts with parents. Adolescents face increasingly greater influence from peers and social norms. Boys traditionally have been encouraged to be more independent and are allowed more deviance from social norms, leading to earlier onset of use, more frequent use, and greater quantity of alcohol consumption than for girls. Although adolescent males still drink more often and more heavily than females do, the gap has been closing.

Changes in sex roles over the past generation may affect the risks of alcohol abuse for women. On one hand, greater career opportunities outside the home offer more freedom for women and reduce the frustration of being limited to domestic roles. For some women, such opportunities might lessen the potential for alcohol and drug use by offering new avenues for personal fulfillment. For other women, the new roles may not be appealing and could create added or at least different types of stress that also might lead to drug abuse for them just as the traditional roles did for women in the past.

As women marry and begin to have children, most women reduce their drinking and drug use. However, for other women, these role demands may be pressures that increase drinking, which in turn may impair a woman's relationship with her children and spouse, especially if she neglects, rejects, or abuses them.

At middle age, the empty-nest syndrome, along with the decline of physical health and youthfulness, may be a stressor that leads to increased alcohol and other drug use. Finally, elderly women who become widowed may experience stigma and loneliness. In addition, the physical aches and pains of aging increase. All of these factors could lead to more alcohol and other drug use as a coping response.

Historically, drugs now considered illicit were legal means of treating women medically. Opiates were acceptable for pain medication until early in the 20th century. Although these substances are now illegal, other psychoactive medications such as tranquilizers and benzodiazepines have been widely prescribed for women since the 1960s to deal with psychological distress. Consequently, a growing concern exists about the higher prevalence of comorbidity, in which dependence on two or more drugs exists at the same time, such as between alcohol and psychotropic drugs such as sedatives. In addition, comorbidity can occur when drug dependence exists with other psychiatric disorders such as depression or anxiety. There are gender differences in the nature of comorbidity, with women more likely to combine alcohol dependency with affective disorders and men more likely to suffer from alcohol dependency with antisocial personality and conduct disorders.

Stimulus/Response

1. In the past, men consumed more alcohol and many other drugs than women. What factors do you think would lead to convergence of alcohol and other drug use levels by men and women?

2. Convergence could involve the use level of men moving lower toward that of women, or it might involve the use level of women moving higher toward that of men. Is one direction more preferable, and why? Which direction seems to be the actual one?

3. The recognition that drinking increases the risk of fetal alcohol harm leads doctors to advise women to stop or at least curtail drinking during pregnancy. What methods do you feel are appropriate in dealing with women who disregard such advice during pregnancy?

4. Smoking has tended to increase for adolescent females, but it has declined for most other groups as more information about the health risks has become available. What might account for this pattern? What do you think might change this trend for adolescent females?

5. Among couples, the level of alcohol and other drug use by females is more likely to be influenced by their male partners' level of use, but females' use level is less likely to influence males' level of use. What reasons do you think account for this differential influence?

Minority Groups

Alcohol and Other Drug Use

Racial/Ethnic Minority Groups and
 Alcohol
Racial/Ethnic Minority Groups and Smoking
Racial/Ethnic Minority Groups and Illicit
 Drugs

Influence of Acculturation on Alcohol
 and Other Drug Use
Sexual Minority Groups and Alcohol
Summary
Stimulus/Response

Alcohol and other drug use patterns, the consequences of such behavior, and the effective treatment for use-related problems vary for racial/ethnic subpopulations. Much research ignores or overlooks such differences; it either primarily studies White, middle-class, European Americans or uses aggregated data, which obscures many subgroup differences among racial/ethnic minorities (Caetano, Clark, & Tam, 1998). However, findings based on overall averages may not be valid for groups of lower social status that encounter prejudice, suffer stigma, and sometimes experience violence such as racial/ethnic minority groups (Galvan & Caetano, 2003).

Although it is not a racial/ethnic category, homosexual populations, popularly referred to as the "gay community" or "gay and lesbian community," face similar marginalization in society that may increase their risk for alcohol and other drug problems. It is important to study the use of alcohol and other drugs among these populations, now often grouped with bisexual and transgender persons and referred to as the "LGBT community," because their substance use patterns and related problems may be quite different from those of the overall population.

The racial and ethnic face of the United States has changed and will continue to change rapidly over the 21st century. Projections for the U.S. population from 1992 to 2050 forecast a continued decline in the non-Hispanic White population. In contrast, there will be a doubling of African Americans, a quadrupling of Hispanic Americans, and a fourfold increase for Asian Americans and Pacific Islanders (U.S. Bureau of the Census, 1992b). Determining the size of LGBT subgroups is a far more difficult undertaking. Estimates suggest that these groups are growing in size, partly due to greater willingness for self-disclosure and increased social tolerance.

The major part of this chapter will describe research on racial/ethnic group variations, as there is still little reliable evidence available on alcohol and other drug use and problems from large unbiased samples from LGBT populations. Many conclusions about alcohol and other drug use among these groups come from anecdotal and clinical evidence with small samples, evidence that may not be representative of LGBT individuals.

Historically, minority racial/ethnic groups in the United States have suffered psychological harm from social injustices inflicted by racism, lack of economic opportunities, and poor living conditions. In the United States, except for Native Americans, these groups descended from immigrants or, in the case of African Americans, slaves. Because of their different cultures, languages, and usually darker skin color, these groups were easy to identify, which helped make them targets for prejudice. Ethnic minority groups, in comparison to each other as well as to Whites, have racial or biological as well as ethnic or cultural differences. We will use the term *racial/ethnic group* to acknowledge this complexity.

In the following discussion of drug use and abuse among racial/ethnic minority groups in America, it must be emphasized at the outset that each of the minority groups to be examined—African Americans, Hispanic or Latino Americans, Native Americans, and Asian Americans—is far from homogeneous, as often implied. Considerable heterogeneity exists within ethnic minority groups, which is often overlooked (Cheung, 1993).

Until 2000, the basic racial categories used in the U.S. Census since 1977 had been defined by Directive No. 15 of the Office of Management and Budget (U.S. Department of Commerce, 1978) as follows: Blacks or African Americans include persons with origins from any of the racial groups of Africa. Latino Americans originate from such diverse regions as Central and South America, Cuba, Puerto Rico, and Mexico or any Spanish culture. Asian and Pacific Islander Americans include persons with origins from the Far East, Southeast Asia, the Indian subcontinent, and the Pacific Islands. American Indians and Alaska natives have origins in any of the original peoples of North America. Whites or European Americans comprise persons with origins from peoples of Europe, North Africa, and the Middle East. These arbitrary ethnic glosses (Trimble, 1991) are often very misleading. It should be readily apparent that each racial/ethnic group is diverse and that any depiction of drug use practices and consequences will not accurately represent all of the ethnic groups that have been assigned to each major category.

The 2000 U.S. Census made some major changes from the race/ethnicity categories used in 1990 and 1980. It created seven mutually exclusive and exhaustive racial categories: *American Indian/Alaska native alone, Asian alone, Black or African American alone, Native Hawaiian and Other Pacific Islander alone, Some Other Race alone, White alone, and Two or More Races.* The latter category is highly varied as it includes all 57 possible combinations of two or more races. The largest change was that respondents were allowed to identify one or more races to indicate their racial identity. The category, *Some Other Race,* was used for groups like Mulatto, Creole, and Mestizo that did not fit the main categories. The *American Indian/Alaska native* category combined what previously had been three groups, American Indian, Eskimo, and Aleut, while the former Asian and Pacific Islander category was split into two categories: *Asian* and *Native Hawaiian and Other Pacific Islander*.

Alcohol and other drug use will be examined among the major racial/ethnic minority groups within the United States. Causal interpretations of ethnic group differences must be taken with caution, however, because some of the observed differences can be attributed to other factors that vary across ethnic groups, such as social class and religious differences, rather than to ethnicity per se. Thus, comparisons of race and ethnicity often fail to control for socioeconomic status and religious affiliation, two factors that can independently affect drug use. Ethnic differences in drug problems vary with social class (Jones Webb, Hsiao, & Hannan, 1995). For example, among the less affluent, African American men report more adverse drinking consequences and total drinking problems than White men. However, among affluent men, just the reverse is true.

Generalizations about ethnic minority groups are often based on observations of a limited subset of those populations, primarily those who are male, unemployed, or with low income (Lex, 1987). However, it is essential to also examine alcohol and other drug use among other subgroups within each of these ethnic minority groups on factors such as gender, age, employment status, income level, education, and acculturation.

Another important factor not to overlook is the impact of minority status in the host culture. Thus, Asians would be majority group members in China, Korea, and Japan but would be minority group members in the United States, as well as targets of racial prejudice and discrimination. Lack of education and unfamiliarity with the English language, especially for recent immigrants, would be additional burdens relegating these groups to lower incomes. Thus, minority group members would differ from majority group members not only in culture and heredity but also in social status. These multiple differences make the task of explaining the factors producing differences in drug use among ethnic groups difficult.

RACIAL/ETHNIC MINORITY GROUPS AND ALCOHOL

Surveys such as the annual National Survey on Drug Use and Health (NSDUH) using large representative samples from the general population show that the patterns and consequences of drinking differ widely across racial/ethnic minority groups. Table 12.1 presents the 2006 NSDUH past-month alcohol use results separately for adolescents (ages 12–17) and young adults (ages 18–25). The racial/ethnic group differences in alcohol use in the past month started from an early age during adolescence. For ages 12–17, the highest rates were for Whites followed by Native Americans/Alaskans, multiracial individuals, Hispanics, Blacks, and Asians. The rates increased substantially for all groups among the 18- to 25-year-olds, but the rank order among the racial/ethnic groups was similar with the exception that the multiracial group became second highest.

TABLE 12.1 Racial/ethnic differences in past-month alcohol use.	Ages 12–17	Ages 18–25
Past-Month Alcohol Use		
Total	**16.6%**	**61.4%**
Whites/non-Hispanics	18.9	68.6
Blacks/African Americans	11.1	47.4
Native Americans/Alaskans	16	49.4
Native Hawaiians/Pacific Islanders	8.3	57.1
Asian Americans	7.3	48.7
Multiracial individuals	14.6	63.6
Hispanics	16	51

Source: From *Results From the 2006 National Survey on Drug Use and Health (NSDUH): National Findings,* by the Substance Abuse and Mental Health Services Administration [SAMHSA], 2007, Rockville, MD: SAMHSA Office of Applied Studies.

Table 12.2 compares the rates for ages 12–20 from the 2005 and 2006 NSDUH for three different levels of drinking in the past month: current use (at least one drink), binge use (five or more drinks on the same occasion at least once), and heavy use (five or more drinks on the same occasion on at least 5 different days). In 2006, the highest rates occurred among Whites: heavy use (8.2%), binge use (22.7%), and current use (32.3%). Nondrinkers, by inference, were 67.7% for 12- to 20-year-olds. For other age groups, the order for all three drinking levels was similar, with Whites highest, followed by Native Americans/Alaskans, multiracial individuals, Hispanics, Blacks, and Asians.

Within each racial/ethnic group, however, there were wide variations reported in earlier surveys. For example, in the 2001 National Household Survey on Drug Abuse (Substance Abuse and Mental Health Services Administration [SAMHSA], 2002), alcohol use for 12- to 20-year-olds of Hispanic background varied for those with different countries of origin: Cubans (26.9%), Mexicans (25.6%), Central/South Americans (23.1%), and Puerto Ricans (22.8%). Among Asians, there was even wider variation: Koreans (18.6%), Filipinos (15.5%), Chinese (15.1%), Asian Indians (13.9%), and Vietnamese (10.5%).

Focusing on binge and heavy drinking, the more problematic forms, the highest rates were among European Americans, Native Hawaiians/Other Pacific Islanders, and American Indians/Alaska natives; lower rates were found among Hispanics/Latinos and African Americans; and rates were lowest for Asian Americans.

It is important, however, to examine *patterns* rather than only the quantities and frequencies of use. For example, although Hispanics and Blacks still drank a smaller total quantity and with lower frequency than Whites did, the quantities consumed *per occasion* were higher for these two minority groups, especially among older persons (Johnson,

TABLE 12.2 Racial/ethnic differences in current alcohol use, binge use, and heavy use for ages 12–20 in the 2005 and 2006 NSDUH.						
	TYPE OF ALCOHOL USE					
	Alcohol use		**Binge Alcohol Use**		**Heavy Alcohol Use**	
Demorgrahic Characteristic	**2005**	**2006**	**2005**	**2006**	**2005**	**2006**
TOTAL	28.2	28.3	18.8	19.0	6.0	6.2
HISPANIC ORIGIN AND RACE						
Not Hispanic or Latino	28.7	29.0	19.0	19.5	6.4	6.5
White	32.3	32.3	22.3	22.7	7.8	8.2
Black of African American	19.0	18.6	9.1	8.6	1.8	1.3
Native American or Alaska Native	21.7*	31.3	18.1	23.6	6.0	4.7
Native Hawaiian or Other Pacific Islander	12.0	*	8.4	*	1.4	*
Asian	15.5	19.7	7.4*	11.8	1.2	1.3
Two or More Races	24.0	27.5	16.6	20.7	7.1	6.3
Hispanic or Latino	25.9	25.3	17.9	16.5	4.2	4.8

Source: From *Results From the 2006 National Survey on Drug Use and Health (NSDUH): National Findings*, by the Substance Abuse and Mental Health Services Administration [SAMHSA], 2007, Rockville, MD: SAMHSA Office of Applied Studies.

*Low precision; no estimate reported.

Note: Binge Alcohol Use is defined as drinking five or more drinks on the same occasion (i.e., at the same time or within a couple of hours of each other) on at least 1 day in the past 30 days. Heavy Alcohol Use is defined as drinking five or more drinks on the same occasion on each of 5 or more days in the past 30 days; all heavy alcohol users are also binge alcohol users.

Gruenewald, & Treno, 1998). Since higher quantity consumed per occasion produces more impaired functioning from intoxication, it may be of more concern than the frequency or quantity consumed over extended periods.

Heavy frequent drinking, a pattern often found among young males, decreased with increased age but only for Whites. Abstention increased over this period for all subgroups except Hispanic women, who showed a stable level of drinking. These racial/ethnic group differences occurred even though education level and socioeconomic status were controlled for (Johnson et al., 1998).

The 2006 NSDUH (SAMHSA, 2007) reported a combined estimate of rates for abuse of and dependence on alcohol and other drugs by persons over age 12. The prevalence rate for

American Indians/Alaska natives (19.0%) was higher than for all other racial/ethnic groups, followed by Native Hawaiians/Other Pacific Islanders (12%), multiracial individuals (12%), Hispanics (10%), Whites (9.2%), Blacks (9%), and Asians (4.3%).

Alcohol and other drug use prevalence and trends between 1976 and 2000 were measured for high school seniors from different racial/ethnic groups (Wallace et al., 2002). Alcohol, tobacco, and illicit drug use rates were highest for Native American. Cuban American and White students also had high use levels, followed by Mexican American and Puerto Rican students. The lowest levels of drug use were reported by other Latin American, African American, and Asian American students. Most of these differences have been consistent over the past 25 years, but some have widened and others have narrowed.

Parental Influence

Racial/ethnic groups differ in how parents try to influence their children's drinking. Thus, parental disapproval of drinking is associated with higher risk of initiating alcohol use by fifth graders for European Americans (Catalano et al., 1992). Parental influence shows an opposite effect for Asian Americans, serving as a protective factor against their alcohol use. Among African American students, a different factor is more important. For this group, parental influence in the choice of friends, rather than parental drinking, acts as a protective factor against alcohol abuse.

Among racial/ethnic minority groups such as Hispanic/Latino and Asian Americans, drinking is much more prevalent for fathers than for mothers in comparison to European Americans who regard drinking by mothers as more acceptable. This gender difference leads to the hypothesis that parental influence may be limited to fathers among minorities, especially for sons. However, for majority-group students, both parents are likely to affect their children's drinking, with fathers' drinking affecting that of sons and mothers' drinking affecting that of daughters. However, the relationship between parental and adolescent alcohol use is rather similar for both African Americans and European Americans (Peterson, Hawkins, Abbott, & Catalano, 1994). Even though African American parents drank less frequently, had stronger norms against alcohol use, and involved their children less frequently in family alcohol use than European American parents, there were no differences in the relationship between parent and adolescent drinking.

In surveys of community samples, no differences were found between European Americans and African Americans in the parental influence on drinking attitudes and norms of children (Herd, 1994). Similarly, a comparison (Li & Rosenblood, 1994) of Chinese Canadians and European Canadians found that even though Chinese Canadians drank at a lower level, parental alcohol attitudes and drinking patterns predicted the drinking of students for both groups.

Methodological Issues

Two approaches, which differ widely in methodology, are widely used to provide evidence about the drinking behavior of ethnic minorities (Lex, 1987). The community or population survey uses standard and objective methods to obtain self-reports from a representative sample of the total population, including members from all minority groups.

In contrast to community and population studies, ethnography uses the methods of field researchers such as anthropologists. They make field observations and inferences about the meaning or role of drinking in the context of an ethnic group's values and traditions rather than focus narrowly on quantitative descriptions of the quantity and frequency of consuming various types of alcoholic beverages. Moreover, ethnographers typically have used non-random samples and relied on indigenous reports about drinking. Despite these important differences, each approach is useful, and the data can be meaningfully combined to further understanding of drinking behaviors.

African Americans

African Americans, numbering about 29.28 million and representing 11.8% of the U.S. population in 1990 (U.S. Bureau of the Census, 1992a), increased to 37.1 million (12.4%) in 2006 (U.S. Census Bureau, 2007). This ethnic minority group has suffered heavily from the adverse effects of alcohol. Economic factors may be related to heavy drinking among Blacks both as antecedents and consequences. Living in poverty in crowded and crime-ridden neighborhoods without much hope for improvement might contribute to or exacerbate drinking. Black drinking has been viewed as a reaction to stress or a form of escape to deal with poverty and racism. Yet alcohol abuse and dependence also can further reduce one's economic condition by jeopardizing the ability to gain or hold employment, creating family conflict, and increasing risk of involvement with the criminal justice system.

Alcohol Consumption

The 2006 NSDUH (SAMHSA, 2007) found lower drinking in the past 30 days for young (ages 12–20) Blacks than for young Whites, among both males (18.7% vs. 33.2%) and females (18.4% vs. 31.4%). Similarly, binge drinking for this age group was higher for White than for Black males (9.7% vs. 25.2%) and females (7.5% vs. 20.0%). Abstention rates were higher for Black than for White men and women.

Analysis of a survey (Herd, 1994) of 1,947 Black and 1,777 White Americans with a 1984 national sample of 5,221 men and women showed that parental influences had a moderate influence on drinking norms and attitudes. They were the best predictors of drinking for both Blacks and Whites. However, the exact relationships among social characteristics and norms, parental demographics, parental drinking attitudes and behavior, and drinking patterns depended on race.

The ratio of men to women drinkers was slightly higher among Blacks (1.3 to 1) than among Whites where there was virtual gender equality (Herd, 1997). A higher percentage of women than men (49% vs. 26%) abstained among Blacks than among Whites, who had lower rates of abstinence for women (34%) and men (24%). Blacks were higher than Whites on a measure based on the quantity and frequency of drinking, reflecting a tendency for males to drink more frequently and in larger quantities relative to women.

Variations in alcohol use may be related to the degree of ethnic or racial identity (Herd & Grube, 1996). Thus, those who were more involved with Black social networks and had greater Black social and political involvement drank at lower levels. These characteristics may be related to greater religiosity and more conservative drinking norms for this segment of African Americans. However, those with greater exposure to Black mass media, which emphasize drinking, tended to drink at higher levels.

The importance of racial identity to reduced drinking was confirmed with a sample of 488 African American adolescents (Caldwell, Sellers, Bernat, & Zimmerman, 2004). The extent to which race was a central part of one's identity, the extent to which there were positive feelings about Blacks, and fathers' support was related to less drinking.

Research (Cooper et al., 2008) on the changes in alcohol use from adolescence into young adulthood suggests that these trajectories differ for Black and White youth. Among Black adolescents, drinking motives to cope with negative emotions were predictive of alcohol involvement into their early 30s. In contrast, motives to drink for the enhancement of positive emotions were better predictors of drinking among Whites 15 years later.

Alcohol Problems

The relationship between drinking patterns and problems related to drinking, however, differed for Blacks and Whites. For the same level of drinking, White women were more vulnerable to problems than White men, but among Blacks, women were less susceptible to problems than men were. Drinking problem rates were comparable for Black and White women, but the rates for Black men were much higher than for White men. The ratio of males to females was higher for Blacks than for Whites for binge and symptomatic drinking, job problems, belligerence, financial problems, and problems with relatives.

The lower rates of drinking for Black women are not compatible with the mechanisms posited for White women's drinking. There might be higher levels of body weight for Black women (Herd, 1997) so that the same amount of alcohol when consumed by White women produces a lower effect. In addition, excessive drinking among Black women may be more acceptable or less stigmatized.

Blacks developed higher rates of physical health problems than Whites from alcohol use (Herd, 1987). This disparity could be due to factors such as racial prejudice, unemployment, poor health, and poor living conditions. Physical health hazards, which are increased by heavy drinking among Blacks, include higher liver cirrhosis mortality for Blacks than for Whites that may result from higher hepatotoxicity of alcohol for them (Stranges et al., 2004).

Cultural Factors

It is difficult to define a single Black drinking style in that both heavy drinking and abstinence orientations exist (Herd, 1985). The strong influence of fundamentalist Protestant beliefs among many Blacks may contribute to the high level of abstainers, but racial prejudice and poverty might contribute to the high level of problem drinking.

An ethnohistorical understanding is needed to explain Black alcohol use. In the early days of slavery, alcohol was valued and was a part of an Afro American tradition that was not accompanied by high rates of disorderly drunkenness. Then came a shift toward temperance in the United States, partly in concert with the move toward abolition of slavery. Blacks assumed a strong attitude of abstinence because alcohol was viewed as a symbol of oppression under White supremacist and segregationist views. The Black church emerged as a powerful factor for temperance. During Prohibition, Black attitudes toward alcohol shifted back to viewing it as a form of oppression. Later, mass migration from the rural South to the industrial cities of the North served to loosen Blacks from social forces such as the church, which had discouraged excess drinking. Surrounded by the urban environments of nightlife and tavern drinking, alcohol again shifted in its significance and came to be a symbol of urbanity and freedom. Even today, alcohol represents sophistication, prestige, and affluence for many urban Blacks.

Studies that fail to recognize the historical context tend to focus on deviant drinking by Blacks, particularly by youth who are assumed to engage in alcohol abuse due to alienation with society. In part, this misrepresentation stems from the use of small and usually unrepresentative samples. Thus, the impact of religion has a strong relationship with drinking for African Americans (Collins & McNair, 2002). A study of about 1,200 Black and White women (Darrow, Russell, Cooper, Midar, & Frone, 1992) found that drinking was unrelated to church attendance among White women but was inversely related among Black women. In agreement with this finding, abstention was more likely among Black women if they attended church more often, were older, or came from a lower socioeconomic background.

A relationship between religious involvement and alcohol use problems was found in a longitudinal study of a Black community population comprising ages 6–32 (n = 1,242; Bowie, Ensminger, & Robertson, 2006). Alcohol-use-related problems among Blacks were related to not attending church monthly as well as to being male, having a major depressive disorder, completing fewer years of education, being unemployed, and moving more frequently. Depressed individuals who attended church monthly had no more alcohol problems than nondepressed individuals. However, for those who did not attend church frequently, depression was strongly associated with alcohol problems.

Overall, heavier drinkers were more likely to be White and younger and have a family history of alcoholism. The social setting for drinking also varied for Black and White women. Black women do more of their drinking at home in comparison to White women, who drink more often in restaurants, in bars, and at parties (Herd & Grube, 1993). However, the relationship between drinking setting and alcohol-related problems may not be an effect of race per se but may be attributable to race differences in attitudes about drinking and socioeconomic status.

The primary measures of alcohol consumption in most studies focus on the quantity and the frequency of use, but for Blacks it is especially important to consider the quality of the beverage and the place of consumption (Gaines, 1985). A concern with quality can be seen in the focus on brand-name liquors as the only suitable beverages. Drinking in public places is disfavored because drinking is regarded as more appropriate for private social gatherings to enhance conviviality. Whether drinking is viewed as a problem is not a simple matter of the amount; rather, it is defined more in terms of type and context of drinking and the impact of drinking on family relationships and job performance.

Another important aspect of Black drinking is a high rate of binge drinking, consuming five or more drinks per occasion, which creates greater risk for health impairments and higher mortality. Even though average alcohol consumption per *week* was comparable for African Americans and Whites, both African American men and women drank a higher average amount over a *24-hour period* than White men and women in the National Health and Nutrition Examination Survey I and the 19-year follow-up that included 2,054 African American men and women (Sempos, Rehm, Wu, Crespo, & Trevisan, 2003).

Analysis of data from a 1984 national probability survey by Herd (1989) found evidence suggesting some major changes in Black drinking behavior. During the 1980s, Black men reared in dry areas such as the rural South were drinking more than those growing up in the urban North. No such pattern reversal was found for Whites who drank more heavily if they came from traditionally "wet" areas. Arrests for public drunkenness and driving while intoxicated were more comparable for Blacks and Whites than in the past, when Blacks showed a higher incidence.

The rapid changes in Black drinking behavior suggest that it may be highly responsive to social conditions and changes (Herd, 1987) rather than a reflection of some enduring psychopathology. Analysis of the social meaning of drinking may be needed to understand these patterns and to plan effective interventions. The past emphasis on the familial environment as the main determinant of Black drinking may be wrong as legal, political, and economic factors may be stronger factors. The high availability of alcohol outlets in Black communities must also be recognized as a contributing factor (Jones-Webb, 1998).

Treatment for Black alcoholism has not considered the definition of alcoholism as it is viewed in Black communities, and more culturally sensitive approaches are advocated (Brisbane & Wells, 1989). For example, the conception of alcoholism as a disease, held by Alcoholics Anonymous, is not consistent with a common view in Black communities of alcoholism as immoral or sinful behavior. The Black church and family strongly support a view that the alcoholic person, not the alcohol, is responsible for the problems and that alcoholics could, if they wished, control their behavior.

Hispanic/Latino Americans

Hispanic/Latino Americans comprise a heterogeneous population of almost 22 million persons primarily with Mexican, Cuban, Puerto Rican, or Central and South American heritage. Using the new 2000 Census definitions, the Hispanic/Latino population increased to over 40 million (14.8%) in 2006, making it the largest racial/ethnic minority group in the United States (U.S. Census Bureau, 2007), from 9% of the U.S. population in 1990 (U.S. Bureau of the Census, 1992a). The largest subgroup at 23.1 million were White Hispanics, 18.2 million were "Some other race," 1.7 million were of two or more races, and slightly over 1 million were from "Other races." It is a young population with over 40% under age 21, low income with 23% below the federal poverty line, and low educational attainment with over half of those over age 25 without a high school diploma (Ramirez & de la Cruz, 2002).

Earlier national surveys on drinking in the general population generally did not give much attention to ethnic subgroups such as Hispanics (Caetano, 1990). Early anthropological and sociological studies that focused on Hispanics in the Southwest dealt mostly with deviant drinking. Most epidemiological research on drinking with larger samples of Hispanics are limited in that they dealt mainly with Mexican Americans as they represent about 60% of Hispanics.

Analysis of survey data collected in the 1984 National Alcohol Survey (Caetano, 1988) showed that Mexican Americans have a more serious problem with alcohol than the other Hispanic groups and have a higher incidence of alcohol-related problems such as accidents, homicides, and arrests than the general population. The 1984 National Alcohol Survey showed that Hispanic male drinking was higher among those with higher education and higher income, contrary to expectations based on views that Hispanic drinking might be due to social deprivation.

Alcohol Consumption

Findings with middle and high school students in the annual nationwide Monitoring the Future (MTF) survey (Johnston, O'Malley, Bachman, & Schulenberg, 2008) have generally shown that Hispanic students have much higher rates of alcohol, cigarette, and illicit drug use than White and Black students, although the extent varies with different Hispanic subgroups (Turner, Lloyd, & Taylor, 2006).

In national samples of the adult Hispanic population (Caetano, 1988), drinking levels appeared to peak before middle age and then decline. However, the peak was at a later age, 30–39, for Mexican American males. Unfortunately, these age differences are based only on cross-sectional studies for Hispanics and do not permit firm conclusions that the patterns of younger drinkers will persist as they grow older. This tendency for alcohol use to increase or stay high with older men resembles the pattern in Mexico (Roizen, 1983).

Gender is another important factor. Differences were found between Mexican American and Anglo women in consumption level, with higher percentages of Mexican American women being abstainers or low consumers and a higher percentage of the Anglo women falling into the two heavy-drinker categories. As with the men, regional differences also played a role, with fewer abstainers and infrequent drinkers among urban Mexican American women than among those from the barrio and rural areas. Many studies of Hispanic alcohol and other drug use combine data from such diverse groups as Mexicans, Puerto Ricans, Cubans, and Central and South Americans. This tendency ignores the wide variations that exist among these groups. The overall evidence from several studies shows that prevalence rates vary across subgroups and with the specific substance (Caetano et al., 1998; Randolph, Stroup-Benham, Black, & Markides, 1998; Warner et al., 2006).

Alcohol Problems

According to the National Drug and Alcoholism Treatment Unit Survey (NDATUS) report (NIDA/NIAAA, 1990) on alcoholism treatment in the United States in 1989, 10% of alcoholism clients were of Hispanic heritage. These statistics indicate that Hispanic clients are slightly overrepresented in the proportion of their percentage of the national population, 9%.

Although the percentage of the Hispanic population younger than age 20 is greater than in the total population, the treatment data do not include many clients younger than that age. Hence, adult Hispanics receiving treatment represent a much larger percentage of the much smaller adult segments among Hispanic populations. A comparison (Cervantes, Gilbert, de Snyder, & Padilla, 1990–1991) was made of drinking among U.S.-born Mexican Americans and a mixture of immigrants from Mexico and Central America enrolled in community adult schools in Los Angeles. High levels of depression were found, and depression was predictive of drinking levels among the men but not among the women. Higher positive expectations about the effects of alcohol occurred among men, a factor that may have contributed to greater use of alcohol by men to cope with depression.

General population household surveys with a random sample of respondents 12 years of age and older indicated that 4.6% of currently drinking male adolescents (aged 12–17 years) met criteria for past-year dependence, as did 8.5% in the group of 18- to 23-year-olds, before dropping with higher ages (Caetano & Babor, 2006).

Surprisingly, younger age groups reported higher rates of tolerance and withdrawal symptoms than older age groups. This finding might be an artifact if young adults report tolerance and withdrawal symptoms partly because the wording of structured interview items leads them to confuse binge drinking and its effects with the physical symptoms of alcohol dependence.

A large scale study (Caetano, Ramisetty-Mikler, & Rodriguez, 2008) based on the 2006 Hispanic Americans Baseline Alcohol Survey (HABLAS) determined the prevalence of alcohol abuse and dependence for the past 12 months among a total of 5,224 individuals, 18 years of age and older, from households in five metropolitan areas of the United States: Miami, New York, Philadelphia, Houston, and Los Angeles.

The results showed that Mexican American and Puerto Rican men had much higher rates than Cuban American and South/Central American men. Rates of alcohol dependence for Mexican American and Puerto Rican men were higher than those for men in the U.S. general population, especially for ages 40–49 and 50–59.

Cultural Factors

Machismo makes alcohol consumption an integral component of Mexican American males' behavior patterns but stigmatizes it for females. Machismo is a cultural value that emphasizes strength, personal autonomy, and honor but also connotes masculine virility. Machismo is popularly thought to promote heavy drinking, but the relationship between them is not well supported (Neff, Prihoda, & Hoppe, 1991). Most studies have not clearly defined machismo or measured how it changes over time in conjunction with alcohol usage. Cultural explanations for male Hispanic drinking using vaguely defined constructs such as exaggerated machismo are simplistic and endorsed in a national survey by only 16% of Hispanic males, 15% of Hispanic females, and even fewer acculturated Hispanics (Caetano, 1990).

Native Americans

The minority group most afflicted with alcohol abuse is Native Americans, estimated to represent 2.02 million people, constituting less than 1% of the 1990 U.S. population (U.S. Bureau of the Census, 1992b).

By 2006, Native Americans had increased to 2.4 million members (0.8%) of the U.S. population (U.S. Census Bureau, 2007). Despite the widely held stereotype of the "drunken Indian," a wide diversity of drinking attitudes and patterns exists among various Native American tribes, as documented by ethnographic or field observations (Weibel-Orlando,

1985). Although there are high rates of heavy drinking among Native Americans, there are also high rates of abstinence.

Not only do Native American tribes vary in their alcohol use, but those living on reservations may differ from those in the general population as well (O'Connell, Novins, Beals, & Spicer, 2005). Data from a study of two culturally distinct tribes of Native Americans, the Southwest Indians and the Northern Plains Indians, living on or near reservations were compared with findings from the National Longitudinal Alcohol Epidemiologic Survey (NLAES), which included data from a geographically dispersed sample of Native Americans as well as the U.S. reference population.

After controlling for demographic characteristics, the prevalence of drinking during the past year was similar among males from the Northern Plains tribe, Native Americans in the NLAES, and the U.S. population. Northern Plains females were twice as likely as U.S. females to be current drinkers. Southwest Indian tribe males and females were less likely to have drank during the past year. Among past-year drinkers, Native Americans consumed a larger quantity of alcohol per drinking day than the U.S. reference population. However, the reservation-based Native Americans consumed alcohol less frequently than those in the NLAES and in the U.S. population.

Alcohol Consumption

Native American adolescents consume alcohol at levels that create problems for 42% of the males and 31% of the females in comparison to 34% of White males and 25% of White females. However, prevalence rates of drinking among Native American adults vary considerably for different tribes, ranging from 30% to 84% (May, 1996). Males between ages 25 and 44 consume the most alcohol, and after age 40, consumption level declines (Lex, 1985).

Alcohol Problems

One index of the severity of alcoholism problems for Native Americans is their disproportionate representation in treatment programs. Although representing less than 1% of the total population, they constitute about 6% of the outpatients treated in federal treatment facilities (National Institute on Alcohol Abuse and Alcoholism, 1981). Another index of the extent of alcoholism among Native Americans is the high liver cirrhosis mortality rate, which is three times the national rate (Indian Health Service, 1982). Other health problems related to alcohol abuse such as pancreatitis, malnutrition, fetal alcohol syndrome, and heart disease are also prevalent (Westermeyer, 1972). Suicide rates (Heath, 1988) as well as homicide rates (Lex, 1985) were twice as likely for Native Americans as for members of the general population.

Cultural Factors

One sociological theory for this situation is that alcohol was new to the American Indians of colonial times, and their culture had no traditions for regulating its use. Another explanation is that the loss of their land and hunting prey as the White settlers expanded the development of the West produced a frustration that was assuaged by excessive use of alcohol. In addition, the U.S. government destroyed Native American communities with forced relocations such as the removal of Cherokees from North Carolina to Oklahoma in 1838 in what came to be known as the Trail of Tears. Federal authorities imposed mandatory boarding schools on Native American youth from the late 1800s to the middle 1900s where as part of a plan to indoctrinate them with Euro American values and customs they were not permitted to speak their native languages, practice their religions, or wear customary clothing (Churchill, 1996).

Unable to assume traditional social roles and practices such as talking circles, sweat lodges, and sacred dances that serve therapeutic functions by connecting tribe members with nature, some Native American tribes have experienced cultural losses that place them at more risk for alcohol problems (Szlemko, Wood, & Thurman, 2006). Although Native Americans are viewed by outsiders as a homogeneous ethnic group and assumed to have common features to their drinking, there are important variations in their attitudes related to alcohol.

Anthropologists such as Levi-Strauss (1966) have distinguished between the sacred or spiritual elements and the profane or undesired. Thus, some tribal Native Americans adhere to the myth of the noble savage, of the unspoiled Native Americans as they suppos-edly were before the corruptive influence of the European settlers when they arrived on this continent. Alcohol would be the prime example of such a profane influence of the White man that should be scrupulously avoided, especially at any sacred ceremony such as Fifth Sunday Sings, when Native American Christian churches convene. Profane separation or deviant solidarity is a second stance that might be adopted, one in which there is a collec-tive and public display of flagrant abuse of alcohol. This attitude apparently derives from a rebellion against what may have been once paternalistic Prohibitionist policies restrict-ing Native American access to alcohol, long after it was allowed to every other group. Violating laws and wreaking social havoc, these Native Americans presented a unified reac-tion to discriminatory policies of the government.

Finally, maintaining or controlling one's liquor consumption is a third possible response to alcohol. In the past, powwows, Native American ceremonial events of tribal music and dance, often involved heavy drinking and antisocial behaviors. However, a change toward better monitoring and control of drinking has been observed at powwows through greater physical separation of space allocated for the sacred and the profane activities (Weibel & Weisner, 1980). There is not, as popularly thought, a single drinking style among Native Americans. For example, among the Navajo, there are both recreational and anxiety drinkers (Ferguson, 1968). In the former style, males drink in groups on weekends and spe-cial occasions in large quantities for long periods, with the intent to become intoxicated. The latter style is typified by the solitary and regular use of alcohol by socially marginal indi-viduals, akin to skid-row alcoholics, who are rejected by their tribes.

Among the Chippewa (Westermeyer, 1972), both unrestrained Native American and restrained "White styles" of drinking exist, even in the same individuals, depending on the time and place. Native American drinking styles vary by time and location. One recreational style is accompanied by loud talking, warm interpersonal relationships, and hilarity, which may continue until all financial resources are depleted. This style is generally reserved for drinking among other Native Americans. These different perspectives hold implications for the types of treatments that might be successful for Native Americans with drinking problems. First, "alcoholic" is not a label used by most Native Americans, although they recognize that some people drink "too much." Typically, Native Americans in an alcoholism treatment facility do not think they are there because they see themselves as alcoholics but because they feel that the alternative, usually jail, is worse.

Due to the lack of correspondence between Native Americans' view of their drinking and that of the treatment facility, the high failure rate is not surprising. Differences of philosophy exist in various facilities, many of which are culturally sensitive but still short of meeting the needs of typical Native American clients (Weibel-Orlando, 1985). It must be kept in mind that some forms of intoxication have traditionally been an integral part of Native American sacred ceremonies. In contrast, today alcohol is associated with secular or nonreligious activities to a greater extent. Successful treatment programs for Native Americans seem to combine spiritual elements and activities with their treatment procedures (Spicer, Bezdek, Manson, & Beals, 2007).

In support of this view is part of a study (Stone, Whitbeck, Chen, Johnson, & Olson, 2006) of four American Indian reservations in the upper Midwest and five Canadian First Nation reserves based on 732 adult respondents. One goal examined the impact of three component dimensions of Native American traditional culture (traditional practices, traditional spirituality, and cultural identity) on cessation of alcohol use. The findings suggested that older adults, women, and married adults were more likely to have quit using alcohol if they participated in two of the three components (traditional activities and traditional spirituality).

Asian Americans and Pacific Islanders

Americans coming from or having a family background from Asian countries represent a wide variety of cultural traditions, but the total population is quite small compared to other ethnic minority groups, despite rapid growth in the past decade. In the 2000 Census, Asian Americans are referred to as Asians. Combined, all Asians constituted less than 3% of the 1990 U.S. population (U.S. Bureau of the Census, 1992a) but increased to 13.1 million people (4.4%) in 2006 (U.S. Census Bureau, 2007).

As a whole, Asians in America come from cultures that have traditionally emphasized Confucian ideals of moderation. Consistent with these views, moderate use of alcohol for males and little or no alcohol consumption for females have been the norm. Public drunkenness is highly frowned on as disgraceful and unacceptable conduct. In view of these cultural roots, one would expect that these groups would have low to moderate use of alcohol and be relatively free from alcohol problems.

Alcohol Consumption

Considerable diversity of drinking exists among Asian groups (Makimoto, 1998). A survey (Kitano & Chi, 1986–1987) of four different Asian cultures in Los Angeles found that Chinese American males drank alcohol in smaller quantities than the general U.S. population, with a higher percentage of abstainers as well. Indirect evidence of low alcoholism rates was found in the low rates of admission for alcoholism treatment for Chinese, although this might reflect a cultural bias against seeking treatment rather than an absence of problems. Another study (Sue, Kitano, Hatanaka, & Yeung, 1985) showed that of four Asian groups, Chinese American males had the highest number of abstainers and the lowest number of heavy drinkers.

In contrast, higher levels of drinking closer to those of the general population were found in the other Asian American groups. Japanese American drinking practices were surveyed using random households in Los Angeles (Kitano, Hatanaka, Yeung, & Sue, 1985). Rates for both the abstainer and the heavy drinker categories were higher for Japanese American males than for other Asian American groups. However, drinking level was not closely related to problem behavior.

A comparison of drinking of Korean American and Chinese American men and women showed that Korean Americans had higher rates of alcohol use for both sexes (Weatherspoon, Danko, & Johnson, 1994). Men of both groups drank more often and in larger amounts than women. A study (Lubben, Chi, & Kitano, 1988a) of drinking of Filipino Americans, one of the largest Asian American groups, found that a high percentage of Filipino males, more than 29%, were found to be heavy drinkers. Among Korean American males, both extreme use levels occurred frequently, with more than 25% heavy drinkers but almost 45% abstainers (Lubben, Chi, & Kitano, 1988b).

Ninth-grade students in California and 10th-grade students in Hawaii showed considerable variation in alcohol, tobacco, and other drug use rates for Chinese, Filipino, Japanese, and Pacific Islander/Native Hawaiian adolescents. Chinese reported the lowest rates while Whites, Pacific Islanders, and Native Hawaiians reported the highest (Wong, Klingle, & Price, 2004).

Among Asian American females, alcohol use is low overall (Chi, Lubben, & Kitano, 1989). The highest percentage of heavily drinking females occurred among Japanese Americans (11.7%), but this category was virtually nonexistent for the Chinese, Koreans, and Filipinos.

Biological Factors

The lower use of alcohol by Asian Americans has been attributed to a greater physiological reactivity to alcohol among Asians, especially among women (Collins & McNair, 2002), as reflected by *facial flushing* that occurs in substantially more Asian than Caucasian adults (Wolff, 1972) and infants (Zeiner & Paredes, 1978). The facial flushing created by vasodilation due to alcohol is one indication that alcohol has a stronger or quicker effect on peoples of Asian descent.

Genetic differences may be involved. Asians seem to metabolize alcohol differently from other ethnic groups because they have a variant of the aldehyde dehydrogenase (ALDH2) gene that helps metabolize alcohol.

Asians, overall, have a slower rate of elimination of toxic byproducts of alcohol metabolism leading them to experience an adverse physiological reaction to relatively small amounts of alcohol, which acts in a protective manner by inhibiting their drinking.

In one study (Wall, Thomasson, & Ehlers, 1996), Asian American men (ages 21–25) received a placebo beverage or a 0.75-ml/kg alcohol beverage. The extent of observed flushing was a sensitive and specific predictor of the presence of the allele for the ALDH2 genotype, which is related to alcohol metabolism.

A study (Luczak, Wall, Shea, Byun, & Carr, 2001) compared the association of ALDH2 status with binge drinking in 328 Chinese, Korean, and White college students. Whites had the highest rate of binge drinking, followed by Koreans and then Chinese. Chinese have higher prevalence rates of the ALDH2*2 allele than Koreans. The presence of an ALDH2*2 allele and being Chinese were protective factors whereas being White or being Korean without an ALDH2*2 allele was a risk factor for binge drinking. These results suggest that ALDH2 status, as well as other factors that differ in Koreans and Chinese, contribute to higher binge drinking among Koreans than Chinese.

A retrospective study (Doran, Myers, Luczak, Carr, & Wall, 2007) further examined the role of ALDH2 on the stability of heavy episodic drinking among Chinese and Korean American college student drinkers (n = 336; 51% female) during their first 2 years in college. In addition, it looked at how a temperamental variable associated with conduct disorder, behavioral undercontrol, was related to continued heavy drinking.

Drinkers were classified into four groups: stable nonheavy drinkers, regressors who drank less over time, progressors who drank more over time, and stable heavy drinkers. Stable nonheavy drinkers were more likely than progressors to have ALDH2*2 alleles. Stable heavy drinkers had the most alcohol-related problems, whereas progressors had more problems than either regressors or stable nonheavy drinkers. Students with behavioral undercontrol had a higher frequency of heavy drinking, whereas those with ALDH2*2 tended to drink less.

Cultural Factors

Asian cultures strongly discourage public intoxication, and the alcohol abuser is highly ostracized. The family traditionally plays a strong role in Asian cultures influenced by Confucian ideals, and it discourages public drunkenness in favor of moderation. Asians place a premium on maintaining *face*, so the threat of losing control due to alcoholic excess may lower the risk for drinking problems (Ja & Aoki, 1993).

Although most Asian cultures have low alcoholism rates, there is still some variability among them. For example, men in Japan seem to drink at higher levels than in the United States, but the opposite is true for women (Kitano, Chi, Rhee, Law, & Lubben, 1992). Differences in cultural values, norms, and institutions regulating alcohol use exist among Asian cultures. A comparison (Akutsu, Sue, Zane, & Nakamura, 1989) was made of relative effects on drinking of both physiological differences and cultural differences between Asian Americans and European Americans. Physiological reactivity and attitudes toward drinking were the best predictors of ethnic differences in drinking levels.

Commonalties Across Racial/Ethnic Groups

The focus has been on differences among major racial/ethnic groups, but there are also some factors affecting alcohol use that transcend all minority groups such as social disadvantage in terms of poverty, racism, and unfair treatment. Data for White, Black, and Hispanic Americans (n = 6,631) from the 2005 U.S. National Alcohol Survey, a nationally representative telephone-based survey of adults aged 18 and older showed that Blacks and Hispanics reported greater exposure to social disadvantage than Whites. Greater exposure to disadvantage was associated with from two to six times more problem drinking in all three groups. Although Blacks and Hispanics had greater exposure to such experiences of disadvantage, social disadvantage had similar adverse effects on problem drinking among racial/ethnic minorities as well as Whites (Mulia, Ye, Zemore, & Greenfield, 2008).

RACIAL/ETHNIC MINORITY GROUPS AND SMOKING

Tobacco use differs for U.S. racial/ethnic minority groups and non-Hispanic Whites. (U.S. Surgeon General, 1998). Among four major racial/ethnic minority groups, Table 12.3 shows that, in 2005 and 2006, the highest prevalence of past-month cigarette smoking for youth ages 18–25 occurred for Native Americans and Alaska natives, followed by multiracial individuals, Whites, Native Hawaiians/Pacific Islanders, Hispanics, African Americans, and, lastly, Asians. Other than for Native Americans/Alaska natives, men had higher prevalence rates of smoking than women.

Table 12.4 compares cigarette use for the past month for racial/ethnic groups, for two age groups, 12–17 and18–25, from the 2005 and 2006 NSDUH. Sizeable increases occurred between adolescence and young adulthood. In general, American Indians/Alaska natives had the highest rates for both age groups, followed by Whites, multiracial individuals (two or more races), Hispanics/Latinos, Blacks, and Asians.

TABLE 12.3 Racial/ethnic differences in percent use of cigarettes in lifetime, past year, and past month for ages 18–25 (2005 and 2006).

| | TIME PERIOD | | | | | |
| | Lifetime | | Past Year | | Past Month | |
Demographic Characteristic	2005	2006	2005	2006	2005	2006
TOTAL	67.3	66.6	47.2	47.0	39.0	38.4
HISPANIC ORIGIN AND RACE						
Not Hispanic or Latino	68.7	68.1	48.7	48.9	40.5	40.5
White	73.3	73.2	53.2	53.4	44.2	44.4
Black or African American	54.4	51.4	33.5	33.0	28.7	27.5
Native American or Alaska Native	78.5	*	56.9	*	51.0	*
Native Hawaiian or Other Pacific Islander	*	*	*	*	*	*
Asian	47.5	47.2	31.1	33.1	24.0	25.0
Two or More Races	72.8	72.6	54.0	52.5	44.0	46.6
Hispanic or Latino	61.0	59.4	40.6	38.3	31.9	28.8

Source: From *Results From the 2006 National Survey on Drug Use and Health (NSDUH): National Findings,* by the Substance Abuse and Mental Health Services Administration [SAMHSA], 2007, Rockville, MD: SAMHSA Office of Applied Studies.

*Low precision; no estimate reported.

TABLE 12.4	Cigarette use for past month by race/ethnicity for ages 12–17 and 18–25 (2005 and 2006 NSDUH).	
	Ages 12–17	**Ages 18–25**
Past-Month Cigarette Use		
Total	**10.6%**	**38.7%**
Whites/non-Hispanics	12.6	44.3
Blacks/African Americans	6.3	28.1
Native Americans/Alaskans	19.5	49.5
Native Hawaiians/Pacific Islanders	6.1	41.7
Asian Americans	4.1	24.5
Multiracial individuals	11.9	45.3
Hispanics	8.6	30.4

Source: From *Results From the 2006 National Survey on Drug Use and Health (NSDUH): National Findings*, by the Substance Abuse and Mental Health Services Administration [SAMHSA], 2007, Rockville, MD: SAMHSA Office of Applied Studies.

RACIAL/ETHNIC MINORITY GROUPS AND ILLICIT DRUGS

The reasons for illicit drug use among minority groups are complex. Cultural and historical explanations suggest that past traditions and beliefs account for why some groups use illicit drugs. Mexican migrant workers in the early 1900s in the American Southwest used marijuana, and later it became popular among Black jazz musicians. Chinese immigrants who came to California in the mid-1800s favored opium, which the British had introduced to them in China. For many Native American tribes, hallucinogens such as peyote and mescaline have been used for centuries as part of their ceremonies and rituals.

A different explanation, based on social status, attributes the use of illicit drugs among some members of minority groups to the lack of opportunity, racial prejudice, unemployment, and poverty. In the MTF study (Johnston, O'Malley, & Bachman, 1996), racial/ethnic differences in drug use varied somewhat with drug type. As a whole, among 12th graders, Whites had the highest illicit drug use rates, whereas Blacks generally had the lowest rates for illicit drugs. Among 12th graders, Hispanics had the highest rates for many illicit drugs such as cocaine, crack, marijuana, and heroin. Asian Americans generally had the lowest rates.

The MTF surveys show increased drug use among girls, with highest use among Native American girls and lowest among Black and Asian American girls (Wallace et al., 2003).

344   ALCOHOL, OTHER DRUGS, AND BEHAVIOR

Comparisons of surveys since the late 1970s show important changes in girls' drug use to levels that are converging with those of boys.

The NSDUH, which included multiracial and Native Hawaiian groups that were not in the MTF, showed a slightly different order among groups. The 2005 and 2006 findings for these groups were similar and combined (see Table 12.5). Table 12.5 shows the prevalence rates of illicit drug use in the past month among adolescents (ages 12–17) and young adults (ages 18–25) for major racial/ethnic groups. Use rates increased over the two age groups by at least twofold. For both age groups, three groups were comparably highest in use: Native Hawaiians/Pacific Islanders, multiracial individuals, and Native Americans/Alaska natives; Whites and African Americans were lower in use, and Hispanics and Asians were lowest.

Table 12.6 shows how racial/ethnic groups differed in past-month, past-year, and lifetime illicit drug use in the 2005 and 2006 NSDUH. The use of any illicit drug reported in these surveys was generally highest for Native Americans/Alaska natives and multiracial individuals, followed by Whites, Hispanics, Blacks. and Asians.

INFLUENCE OF ACCULTURATION ON ALCOHOL AND OTHER DRUG USE

Although some stability in drinking patterns occurs over successive generations for several ethnic groups (Greeley, McCready, & Theisen, 1980), the influence of **acculturation** is

TABLE 12.5   Illicit drug use by race/ethnicity among 12- to 17-year-olds and 18- to 25-year-olds in the past month.

	Ages 12–17	Ages 18–25
Past-Month Drug Use		
Total	**9.8%**	**20%**
Whites/non-Hispanics	10.1	22.6
Blacks/African Americans	10.6	17.7
Native Americans/Alaskans	19	24.3
Native Hawaiians/Pacific Islanders	10.8	25.8
Asian Americans	5	8.5
Multiracial individuals	10.8	27
Hispanics	9.1	14.8

Source: From *Results From the 2006 National Survey on Drug Use and Health (NSDUH): National Findings*, by the Substance Abuse and Mental Health Services Administration [SAMHSA], 2007, Rockville, MD: SAMHSA Office of Applied Studies.

TABLE 12.6 Past-month, past-year, and lifetime illicit drug use by race/ethnicity in 2005 and 2006.

| | TIME PERIOD | | | | | |
| | Lifetime | | Past year | | Past month | |
Demographic Characteristic	2005	2006	2005	2006	2005	2006
TOTAL	59.2	59.0	34.2	34.4	20.1	19.8
HISPANIC ORIGIN AND RACE						
Not Hispanic or Latino	61.0	61.2	35.6	36.4	21.1	21.1
White	64.1	64.7	38.2	38.9	22.6	22.7
Black or African American	54.0	51.9	29.7	29.2	18.1	17.3
Native American or Alaska Native	66.9	75.7	35.2	45.7	20.8	28.5
Native Hawaiian or Other Pacific Islander	*	*	*	*	*	*
Asian	36.9	37.3	17.4	20.5	8.1	9.0
Two or More Races	72.7	70.0	42.6	40.2	31.8[a]	22.4
Hispanic or Latino	50.8	48.7	27.9	25.0	15.7	13.9

Source: From *Results From the 2006 National Survey on Drug Use and Health (NSDUH): National Findings*, by the Substance Abuse and Mental Health Services Administration [SAMHSA], 2007, Rockville, MD: SAMHSA Office of Applied Studies.

*Low precision; no estimate reported.

[a]Difference between estimate and 2006 estimate is statistically significant at the 0.05 level.

highly evident for most immigrant groups. Drinking patterns move away from those in the country of origin toward those found for the U.S. general population (Blane, 1977). Thus, Irish Americans drink less than the Irish in Ireland, whereas the Jews in America drink more than those in Israel. Similarly, a comparison (Kitano et al., 1992) of alcohol use among Japanese in Japan, Hawaii, and California found that the acculturated Japanese Americans in California drank more in line with American than with Japanese norms.

Hispanic/Latino Acculturation

One study (Caetano & Mora, 1988) investigated the changes in drinking among Mexican immigrants due to acculturation after they moved to the United States. Responses to a drinking questionnaire by Mexican Americans in a national probability sample were compared to those of men living in the surroundings of Morelia, Mexico. Although Mexican American men drank more frequently than the Mexicans, they typically drank smaller amounts, suggesting a shift toward U.S. drinking norms. Despite lower amounts of drinking by Mexicans, they reported experiencing more problems related to alcohol than did Mexican Americans. Thus, the impact of drinking is not entirely due to the consumption levels but also depends on cultural values and reactions of the drinker's ethnic group. Mexican American women tended to drink more often as well as in larger quantities than Mexican women, suggesting that acculturation involves greater change for Mexican women. Hence, a greater increase in drinking occurs among women than among men (Caetano, 1990).

The relationship between acculturation and Hispanic drinking is inconsistent across studies, being associated with more abstention as well as more frequent drinking (Caetano, 1990). The nature of the effect may depend on national origin (Puerto Rico, Mexico, Cuba) and the relocation site (Warner et al., 2006). For example, Hispanics residing in California report heavier drinking than those in Texas. These different drinking norms are reflected in greater instances of drunkenness and alcohol-related problems in California than in Texas. Analyses (Caetano, Ramisetty-Mikler, & Rodriguez, 2009) of the HABLAS data cited earlier in this chapter found that men among heavier drinking Hispanic groups such as Mexicans and Puerto Ricans with greater acculturation had a higher risk of alcohol abuse.

Gender may moderate the association between acculturation and alcohol use. A study (Raffaelli et al., 2007) of 148 Mexican American students (67% female; mean age 23 years) from three state universities in California and Texas used self-report surveys to examine if social context, family conflict, and psychological functioning mediate the relationship of acculturation and drinking. After controlling for age, maternal education, living situation, and geographical site, linguistic acculturation was found to be related to increased alcohol use and misuse among women but not men. However, these results conflict with findings from 126 Mexican American college students in a Midwestern university (Zamboanga, Raffaelli, & Horton, 2006) showing that less acculturated men (those with higher levels of ethnic identity) had a higher frequency of heavy alcohol use but that for women acculturation was not related to heavy alcohol use.

A survey (Caetano, Ramisetty-Mikler, Wallisch, McGrath, & Spence, 2008) of 472 male and 484 female Hispanic adults living along the Texas-Mexico border found that higher acculturation was related to lower rates of alcohol use disorders among men but a higher frequency of heavy episodic drinking among women. Men engaged in heavy episodic drinking and those who were less acculturated were at higher risk for alcohol abuse and/or dependence. Acculturation level did not predict alcohol disorders for women.

According to a review of 24 studies (Zemore, 2007a) of Hispanics, overall, the relationship between acculturation and alcohol use was stronger for women than for men. Higher acculturation was consistently related to greater total volume, drinking frequency, typical quantity, heavy/problem drinking, drinking problems, and abuse/dependence, even when demographic factors were controlled. Among men, acculturation and drinking were weakly related; however, this result was possibly due to small samples and other measurement problems.

Acculturation is related to higher use of illicit drugs among Hispanics, especially women (Vega, Alderete, Kolody, & Aguilar-Gaxiola, 1998). A survey of a stratified sample of 3,012 subjects between 18 and 59 years of age assessed use of marijuana, cocaine, hallucinogens, heroin, and inhalants. Men had higher rates of use than women for every drug (men = 46.3 %, women = 23.2 %). Urban rates were higher than rural rates for both men and women. Men were more likely than women to have ever used illicit drugs or inhalants, cocaine, or marijuana. However, acculturation and U.S. birthplace were more strongly related to more illicit drug use among women than among men, especially among urban rather than rural residents.

Acculturation may increase use of illicit drugs by both men and women because it weakens the influence of *familism,* a Hispanic emphasis on family that traditionally protected against behaviors such as drug abuse that weaken family influences. Less is known about the impact of the larger community context, but it is possible that residence in predominately Hispanic communities may help prevent the erosion of familism by acculturation (Warner et al., 2006).

Asian Americans and Acculturation

Drinking among Asian American youth was examined in relation to acculturation with data from boys (n = 332) and girls (n = 382) in grades 7–12 obtained from a prospective study, the National Longitudinal Study of Adolescent Health (Hahm, Lahiff, & Guterman, 2003a). Overall, higher acculturation was associated with greater alcohol use. However, the strength of parental attachment was a moderator of the impact of acculturation. Acculturation increased drinking for those with low parental attachment while it had no relationship to drinking among adolescents with moderate or high parental attachment. Analyses of the same data set (Hahm, Lahiff, & Guterman, 2003b) showed that increased binge drinking occurred for both boys and girls with higher levels of acculturation. This higher binge drinking was mediated by higher friends' use of alcohol and tobacco.

Alcohol use in relation to Asian American acculturation was examined for 112 Chinese American and 108 Korean American male and female undergraduates (Hendershot, Dillworth, Neighbors, & George, 2008). Whereas acculturation had a protective influence in reducing drinking for Korean Americans, it did not reduce alcohol use for Chinese Americans, possibly because their level of drinking was not initially as high as the level of the Korean Americans.

The process underlying acculturation to the ways of a new culture is a complex change involving two concurrent processes (Landrine & Klonoff, 1998). First, extinction of the norms, attitudes, and use patterns of alcohol and tobacco of the country of origin occurs. Concurrently, acquisition of the norms and attitudes of the host culture takes place. Whether an individual group shows increased or decreased use depends on the relative degree of drug use in the host and origin countries. Thus, someone coming from a country where drug use is higher than in the United States will gradually tend to decrease his or her level of use, and vice versa for someone from a country where drug use is lower than in the United States. In accord with this model, smoking and drinking rates of ethnic minority groups coming from countries with lower use than that of the United States *increased* as these groups acculturated to American norms. In contrast, smoking and drinking rates of those coming from countries with higher use *decreased* the longer they lived in the United States.

This model also can account for the situation where acculturation has opposite effects for men and women. Increased acculturation generally leads to more drinking and smoking for women, but it is associated with declines for men. In most cultures from which U.S. racial/ethnic minorities originate, men drink and smoke at a much higher rate than women do. Hence, when they move to the United States, men show a drop in use, whereas women show a rise in use.

Moreover, immigrants come in different waves or cohorts during different time periods. Acculturation effects can vary with the specific cohort from the same country. Thus, immigrants from Japan to the United States at the turn of the 20th century came from a different background than those coming at the turn of the 21st century. In addition, the drinking norms they encountered in the United States when they came in the early 1900s have changed drastically and differ for the 21st-century immigrants.

SEXUAL MINORITY GROUPS AND ALCOHOL

Lesbian, gay, bisexual, and transgender populations (LGBT) are, of course, not ethnic/racial groups, but both groups suffer the disadvantages of having minority group status in society. The prejudicial treatment they encounter might contribute to greater use of alcohol and other drugs among some members of these groups as they attempt to cope with the social disadvantages they face.

Early studies with clinical samples found rates of alcohol problems to be around 30% for homosexual men (Lohrenz, Connelly, Coyne, & Spare, 1978), which is much higher than the 10%–15% estimates usually found for men in **general population surveys**. However, estimates based on clinical samples may be elevated relative to the entire population of homosexuals.

Gay bars have been another major source of evidence because they have served as a major social gathering place for homosexuals. However, drinking might still be expected to be higher among gay bar patrons than among the homosexual population as a whole. Previous estimates may be artificially high, although alcohol problem rates have been found to be higher for homosexuals than for the general population (Paul, Stall, & Bloomfield, 1991).

Among gay and lesbian populations, one review of problem-drinking research (Bux, 1996) found that gay men did not have a significantly higher risk for drinking heavily or for developing drinking problems than heterosexual men. Lesbians had higher problem drinking than heterosexual women but at lower rates than reported in earlier studies. However, both gay males and lesbians appear to be less likely to abstain from alcohol than their heterosexual counterparts.

Population Studies

One study (Cochran, Keenan, Schober, & Mays, 2000) compared the alcohol use patterns and alcohol treatment utilization of sexually active adults, 194 with a same-gender sexual partner and 9,174 with an opposite-gender sexual partner in the 1996 National Household

Survey on Drug Abuse. Alcohol use patterns or related problems did not differ significantly between the two groups. However, lesbians reported using alcohol more frequently, in greater quantities, and with more alcohol-related problems than did exclusively heterosexually active women.

One analysis (Drabble, Midanik, & Trocki, 2005) compared homosexual men, lesbians, and bisexuals to heterosexuals in a sample of 7,612 adults in the 2000 National Alcohol Survey selected through random digit dialing. Four categories of sexual orientation were used: homosexual identified, bisexual identified, heterosexual identified with same-sex partners, and exclusively heterosexual. These four groups were compared on past-year mean number of drinks, days with five or more drinks on a single occasion, drunkenness, negative social consequences (two or more), and *DSM-IV* alcohol dependence. Few significant differences were found among men by sexual orientation. Both lesbians and bisexual women were more likely to report alcohol-related social consequences, alcohol dependence, past help-seeking for an alcohol problem, and lower abstention rates.

A prospective study (Hatzenbuehler, Corbin, & Fromme, 2008) assessed the trajectories and determinants of alcohol use of 111 lesbian, gay, and bisexual individuals and 2,109 heterosexual men and women for a few months after they graduated from high school. Lesbians consumed more alcohol than their heterosexual peers during high school, whereas gay men increased their alcohol use at greater rates than heterosexual men during the initial transition to college.

Lesbian-Only Samples

A literature review (Abbott, 1998) comparing lesbians with women from the general population shows that lesbians tend to drink more than other women. The rates of drinking for lesbians did not decline with age as they did for women in the general population. Moreover, lesbians reported greater difficulties related to alcohol consumption even when the drinking levels were equivalent to that of general population women.

Lesbian rates of heavy alcohol use and alcohol-use-related problems were much lower than in early studies in a comparison (Hughes, 2003) of a race- and age-diverse sample of lesbians with a matched group of heterosexual women. These findings are surprising, given the high rates of childhood sexual abuse, depression, and suicidal ideation reported by lesbians, which should increase their risk for heavy drinking and drinking-related problems. However, these observed lower rates for lesbians are difficult to interpret because the lesbian sample was more likely than the heterosexuals to be in recovery or prior treatment for alcohol-use-related problems.

Lesbians and bisexual women may be at especially elevated risk for the harmful health effects of alcohol and tobacco use (Burgard, Cochran, & Mays, 2005). The California Women's Health Survey (1998–2000), an annual statewide health survey, found that lesbians were more likely than exclusively heterosexual women to currently smoke and to drink alcohol more frequently and in larger quantities, especially in the 26- to 35-year-old group.

Analyses of drinking patterns and problems in a large and diverse sample of lesbians (Hughes et al., 2006) compared the prevalence of lifetime and 12-month problem-drinking indicators across four age and three racial/ethnic groups in the Chicago Health and Life

Experiences of Women Study. The study used structured interviews with 447 community adult women (ages 18–83) who self-identified as lesbians. About half were non-Hispanic White, 28% were non-Hispanic Black, 20% were Hispanic/Latina, and 4% belonged to another racial/ethnic group. Almost half (42%) of the lifetime drinkers had at some point thought they might be developing a drinking problem, 17.7% had received help for a drinking problem, and 7.9% described themselves as being in recovery. Women aged 40 and younger were more likely to report potential alcohol dependence (65.4%).

Unlike general population surveys, in which women's rates of drinking tend to decrease with age, few differences existed across the four age groups of respondents. There were no significant differences between Hispanic and White lesbians on any of the lifetime or 12-month problem-drinking indicators and only a few significant differences between White and Black lesbians. As with heterosexual women, patterns of drinking and drinking-related problems among lesbians vary by age and race/ethnicity.

A comparison (Wilsnack et al., 2008) of women representing five different types of sexual orientation—exclusively heterosexual, mostly heterosexual, bisexual, mostly lesbian, and exclusively lesbian—used face-to-face interviews with 405 self-identified lesbians from the Chicago area and 548 urban women from a U.S. national sample. Exclusively heterosexual women had the lowest rates of hazardous drinking (heavy episodic drinking, intoxication, drinking-related problems, alcohol dependence symptoms). Differences were found between subgroups of sexual minority women, with bisexual women reporting more hazardous drinking indicators and depression than exclusively or mostly lesbian women. Sexual minority women as a group reported higher rates of childhood sexual abuse, early drinking, and depression although it is not clear how these events affected their subsequent drinking or sexual orientation. Such information may guide assessment of drinking-related problems, their treatment, and development of prevention and early-intervention strategies.

Alcohol and Sexual Risks

It is widely believed that heavy alcohol use may increase risks of unsafe or unprotected sexual practices for both homosexuals and heterosexuals. Thus, risky sexual practices such as engaging in anal intercourse without a condom in a 90-day period were reported by 55% of 383 sexually active gay and bisexual men (ages 18–60) entering substance abuse treatment (Paul, Stall, Crosby, Barrett, & Midanik, 1994).

A study (Ryan, Huggins, & Beatty, 1999) of 187 gay men who knew their HIV serostatus (31 were HIV+) found that lifetime rates of *DSM-III-R* alcohol dependence and drug dependence disorders among this sample were two to three times higher than those among the general population. HIV serostatus was predicted by presence of both alcohol and drug dependence. For seronegative men, no relationship was found between recent alcohol use and unprotected anal sex.

Men who have sex with men (MSM), injecting drug users (IDUs), and heterosexual men and women were compared on the association between substance use and sexual behaviors in a national sample of patients in treatment for HIV (Beckett, Burnam, Collins, Kanouse, & Beckman, 2003). Substance use was most prevalent among MSM. Substance use and current dependence were associated with being sexually active among MSM but not among IDUs.

Marijuana use, alcohol use, and hard drug use were most strongly associated with being sexually active among MSM.

Several caveats are in order about the difficulty of drawing sound conclusions about the role of alcohol in sexual risk taking. Based on a review (Donovan & McEwan, 1995) of the research about the relationship between alcohol use and sexual risk taking among young people, it was noted that most studies that concluded that higher alcohol use is related to risky sexual behavior cite correlations based on aggregated or group data. Event-specific studies, which measure how often alcohol use and risky sex co-occur for specific sexual interactions, were rare and generally found no relationship. Secondly, risky sex is defined typically in terms of behavior such as having anal or vaginal sex without a condom. This definition ignores the context of the sexual act. For example, monogamous couples may engage in unprotected sex but not regard it as entailing risk for HIV.

Finally, studies that compare the role of alcohol in sexual behavior between heterosexuals and homosexuals are making invalid comparisons. Many heterosexuals having sexual intercourse without a condom may not think that HIV is a risk for them because they may believe the disease occurs only for unprotected homosexual sex. For heterosexuals, an unwanted pregnancy would be a perceived greater risk of unprotected sex than HIV.

Summary

Although alcohol is consumed almost universally, consumption patterns and problems related to its use vary widely across different cultures. Within U.S. society, racial/ethnic minority subgroups differ among themselves and from the Anglo norms of drinking. In addition to the biological and psychosocial factors that might influence the drinking patterns of any ethnic group, minority groups face the stress of marginality, poverty, and racial prejudice as factors affecting drinking and drinking consequences.

Comparisons of drinking levels and alcohol-related problems between minority groups and Whites can be highly misleading if socioeconomic disparity is not considered. As is true for Whites, social class differences among minority groups also influence drinking styles and consequences.

As among Whites, women drink much less than men among the ethnic minorities examined. Whereas males in some ethnic minorities match or exceed the drinking levels of Whites, female minorities typically drink less than White females.

Among most racial/ethnic minorities, the distribution of drinking appears to be more bimodal than for Whites, with more abstainers as well as more heavy drinkers. Also, the age at which drinking seems to reach its peak is generally later for racial/ethnic minorities than for Whites. Overall, Latino American and Asian American college students generally consume alcohol less frequently and in lower amounts than European Americans. The highest percentage of heavy drinkers was found among Native Americans, followed by European Americans, Hispanic Americans, and then Asian Americans. Use of other drugs also varies with racial/ethnic minorities. Cigarette smoking is highest for Native Americans and Alaska natives and lowest among Asian Americans and Pacific Islanders, with men generally smoking at higher rates than women. Illicit drug use is often thought to be prevalent in racial/ethnic minority groups, but there are wide variations. Among high school students, Whites had the highest rates, but among racial/ethnic minorities, Hispanics and Native Americans had the highest rates, and Blacks, Asian Americans, and Pacific Islanders had the lowest rates. These patterns shift slightly with adult populations.

To understand the nature of substance use among minorities, one should consider the historical background of drugs within specific ethnic groups. The factors that lead to alcohol and other drug use and the role it plays are not the same for each minority group. As immigrant groups become acculturated to the United States, their drinking and smoking patterns begin to increase or decrease to resemble more closely those of the host culture than those in the country of origin.

Although not a racial/ethnic group, lesbians, gays, bisexuals, and transgender persons experience some similar minority group stigma and discrimination, which may lead to increased use of alcohol and other drugs to cope. Lesbians and, to some extent, gays have been found in clinical and general population studies to use alcohol more frequently and in greater quantities, experience more alcohol-related problems, and show more dependence than heterosexuals. Such substance use in turn increases the likelihood of risky sexual practices among some LGBT members that expose them to greater risk of sexually transmitted diseases.

Stimulus/Response

1. To what extent are racial/ethnic group differences in alcohol and other drug use due to socioeconomic factors versus cultural attitudes and values? Can you design a study to evaluate the effect of these different factors?

2. Using Asian Americans as an example, consider cultural and historical factors that might contribute to different alcohol and other drug use/problems among subgroups such as Chinese, Korean, Japanese, Indian, and Vietnamese Americans.

3. What factors do you think will contribute to different alcohol and other drug use levels and consequences among Hispanic American subgroups such as Mexican, Puerto Rican, and Cuban Americans? For example, will differences in their acculturation rates exist, and if so, how might that affect alcohol and other drug use?

4. Do you think acculturation to U.S. alcohol and other drug use norms will be faster for men or for women? Will this gender difference vary for different racial/ethnic groups? Explain why or why not.

5. Which immigrant racial/ethnic groups will acculturate faster to American alcohol and other drug use norms, and why?

6. Do you think the factors that create alcohol problems among heterosexuals and LGBT individuals are basically similar or different? Explain.

7. As societal attitudes toward LGBT individuals become more accepting, do you think their alcohol and other drug use/problems will change? In what ways, and why?

CHAPTER 13

Recovering From Alcohol and Other Drug Dependencies

Motivating Change	Self-Help Treatment for the Family of
Methods of Recovery	Alcoholics
Alcoholics Anonymous and Related	Natural Recovery
Mutual Help Groups	Summary
Behavioral Model	Stimulus/Response

One drink is too many for me and a thousand is not enough.

—Brendan Behan

The problem facing the treatment of alcohol and other drug abuse and dependence is just the opposite from the one involved with getting the proverbial horse to drink water. How do you lead the alcoholic *away* from alcohol, and how can you *prevent* the drinking? Addictions are well ingrained and extremely difficult to overcome.

Many users of alcohol and other drugs will experience serious impairment sooner or later. There is no single pattern of development for the transition from recreational and casual use of alcohol and other drugs to abuse and dependency. Unfortunately, the user is often the last to recognize the problem, which deteriorates from bad to worse. Alcohol-dependent and other-drug-dependent persons often inflict harmful consequences on themselves as well as on others. Even friends and family may ignore or fail to recognize the problem, or when they do recognize it, they may be reluctant or unable to confront their loved ones about their alcohol or other drug problem.

Irrational thought processes allow alcoholics to defend their drinking (Denzin, 1987). Alcoholics could be said to hold a "lay theory" of drinking that centers on denial. Alcoholics believe that alcohol conveys power and control; any challenge to their drinking evokes powerful rationalizations and defenses of their drinking. They often shift blame from themselves to others such as their nondrinking spouses, whom they sometimes accuse of being the cause of their drinking. Instead of viewing alcohol use as the problem, alcoholics reverse things and regard alcohol as the solution. Even alcoholics in treatment may nostalgically recall earlier days when their drinking was associated with positive outcomes, a tendency that may sustain the denial. Alcoholics may think that they can still regain the power to indulge in successful drinking, despite the present setbacks associated with drinking.

Eventually, many individuals who drink alcohol excessively will develop problems that necessitate intervention and treatment. They may experience physical symptoms such as craving and withdrawal or suffer alcohol-related health problems. In addition, some may manifest antisocial or violent behavior, poor work performance, depression, and/or hostility. Eventually, they will be referred or mandated by legal authorities to attend some form of alcoholism treatment and counseling.

MOTIVATING CHANGE

Until an alcoholic is diagnosed, the process of treatment and rehabilitation cannot be effective. Even then, there is often much resistance. How do alcohol-dependent and other-drug-dependent individuals break their addictions? The answer to this problem involves a series of questions. First, what motivates or prevents alcohol-dependent and other-drug-dependent individuals from even considering quitting? Next, what moves them to actually try to quit? What procedures do they use in trying to quit? Why is quitting so difficult to maintain, with many attempts ending in relapse? Finally, how do alcohol-dependent and other-drug-dependent individuals achieve success in quitting over the long term?

In extreme cases in which alcohol and other drug abuse leads to legal difficulties, the motivation may involve coercion in the form of court-mandated treatment. In other cases, individuals may come to recognize that the dependency is costing them too much in the form of work and school performance, mental and physical well-being, and interpersonal relationships. Irrespective of the original impetus for change, individuals will seek a variety of treatment methods ranging from self-help groups such as Alcoholics Anonymous to more formal treatment from professional treatment providers in clinics and hospitals.

On the other hand, there are obstacles to wanting to stop. Fear of not being able to quit also may deter some from trying. Embarrassment in admitting addiction and the inability to control one's drug use are other factors. For example, one impediment to successful long-term smoking cessation is weight gain, especially among women (Murray & Lawrence, 1984).

Stages of Change

Quitting is often discussed as if it is an all-or-none process, leading to a user or nonuser outcome. An alternative conceptualization (DiClemente et al., 1991) views quitting as a process involving different stages of change, as diagrammed in Figure 13.1. Originally proposed to deal with self-change in smoking, the **stages of change model** also can be applied to other

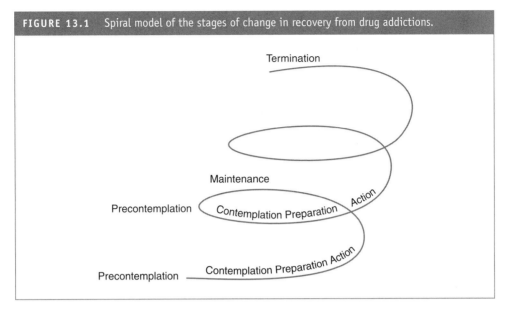

FIGURE 13.1   Spiral model of the stages of change in recovery from drug addictions.

Source: From "In Search of How People Change: Applications to Addictive Behaviors," by J. O. Prochaska, C. C. DiClemente, and J. C. Norcross, 1992, *American Psychologist, 47,* pp. 1102–1114. Copyright 1992 by the American Psychological Association. Reprinted with permission.

drug dependencies. The progress through stages is not without occasional reversals, when setbacks to an earlier stage occur. Hence, the model involves a spiral, rather than a linear, pattern over time. First, there is a *precontemplation stage* when drug abusers do not see any problem and feel that everything is under control. In this period, they may seriously consider quitting but do not actually try to quit. They are ambivalent, but the seeds of change may be beginning to grow.

However, if problems associated with alcohol and other drug use start to develop, a process of self-change may begin. Hints and negative feedback from others, interpersonal conflict, poor school and work performance, and so on may serve to raise consciousness to the possibility that they may have a substance abuse problem. During this contemplation stage, they may consider cutting back on their drug use to see if the situation improves. It is a period of identifying and weighing the costs and benefits of change.

Some move on to the preparation or *determination stage* in which they not only think seriously about change but also start making efforts to cut down. Over the next 6 months, an action stage occurs in which serious efforts to stop using are made. Efforts may or may not involve or require professional treatment, depending on individual circumstances, and sometimes self-change or support groups may be effective. Next, the *maintenance stage* begins about 6 months after action is initiated and continues until successful quitting is achieved. However, because drug habits are difficult to eliminate, considerable vigilance must be employed during this stage to prevent a breakdown or relapse. Social support is important in helping those who want to quit using alcohol and other drugs adhere to their goals.

Motivational Interviewing

There are some similarities among the approaches used by friends, counselors, clergy, and other laypersons who are not professionally trained to treat alcohol and other drug abusers. By helping friends with alcohol and drug problems appraise the consequences of their current alcohol or drug lifestyle, they can sometimes get individuals with drug problems to take that first step.

Motivational interviewing (Miller, 1996) is one technique developed for use by professional therapists to help alcohol and other drug abusers that is very similar to methods also used by laypersons. Whether used by a counselor or a friend, the strategy involves guiding the individual into completing a decision balance sheet by identifying the perceived pros and cons of continuing to use or stopping the use of drugs. This process can help the individual move from the precontemplation to the contemplation stage for taking action against alcohol abuse and dependency.

Motivational interviewing uses structured interviews that avoid confrontation or argument; instead, the approach is to plant seeds or ideas in the minds of individuals that their drug dependency is creating problems. When individuals analyze the costs and benefits of their alcohol and other drug use, it increases their awareness of the extent to which this behavior affects their current lives. The hope is to create sufficient discomfort to motivate them to want to change. In contrast to widely used informal methods of help for alcohol abuse and dependency such as Alcoholics Anonymous, the approach does not require admission of powerlessness or acceptance of the label of alcoholic. It encourages personal choices and responsibility about the role of future drug use in their lives.

METHODS OF RECOVERY

Various approaches exist for the treatment of alcoholism and alcohol abuse, but they can be grouped under two major categories: informal self-help groups such as Alcoholics Anonymous and related Twelve-Step programs and formal or professional treatment that includes individual or group psychotherapy, cognitive-behavioral methods, and pharmacologically based treatments. Typically, some combination of approaches will be used.

This chapter focuses on informal treatment through mutual help groups such as Alcoholics Anonymous. Many of the issues discussed below apply more or less to the development and treatment of problems associated with the use of other drugs. It is hardly surprising, then, that similar mutual help groups (McCrady & Delaney, 1995) based on Twelve-Step concepts such as Nicotine Anonymous, Cocaine Anonymous, and Narcotics Anonymous have been developed for people with problems with other drugs such as tobacco, cocaine, and narcotics, respectively. In addition, we will describe newer recovery programs that have challenged and provided alternatives to the approach of Alcoholics Anonymous, such as Rational Recovery®, SMART Recovery, and Women for Sobriety. Then, in the following chapter, we will examine more formal treatment approaches involving professionally trained therapists using psychotherapy, behavioral methods, and pharmacotherapy.

ALCOHOLICS ANONYMOUS AND RELATED MUTUAL HELP GROUPS

Alcoholics Anonymous

During the temperance and Prohibition eras, the prevalent view of alcoholism involved the moral judgment that excessive drinking was sinful behavior and reflected a lack of willpower. Blame was placed primarily on the alcoholic, who was held to be responsible for his or her own predicament. Little sympathy was given to the drunkard, who was ridiculed as a "skid-row bum," ignoring the reality that many otherwise respectable citizens who were gainfully employed might also be drinking excessively.

It was in this social climate in the mid- to late 1930s that two strange bedfellows fostered the movement that led to a major shift in the societal stance toward alcoholism away from the moral model. One party consisted of perhaps the most influential grass-roots mental health development in U.S. history, Alcoholics Anonymous (AA). In addition to its impact on alcoholism, it also has served as a model for innumerable other self-help groups formed to deal with a variety of other psychological and societal problems throughout the world.

The inauspicious founding in 1935 of this organization in Akron, Ohio, involved informal meetings that developed from a chance encounter of two alcoholics, a stockbroker named Bill Wilson and a physician, Dr. Bob Smith. They discovered they were able to help each other achieve something that had eluded each of them individually, sobriety. By first acknowledging their powerlessness over alcohol, they were able to start on the road to recovery. Many of the ideas and the philosophy underlying AA had been developed by earlier temperance groups, including the Washingtonians in the 1840s, and by an evangelical religious movement known as the Oxford Group in the early part of the 20th century. However, it was not until AA emerged that the underlying philosophy of these approaches achieved its highest success. Bill W. and Dr. Bob, as they called themselves to protect their anonymity because of the stigma of alcoholism, discovered that meeting with other alcoholics to share personal accounts of their drinking problems and to read and discuss inspirational materials were keys to recovery. Through this program for recovery, alcoholics achieved a spiritual reawakening and regained control of their lives with the support of one another.

From this humble beginning was born the self-help program of AA. Bill Wilson began to disseminate this ideology and these techniques to any alcoholic who sincerely wanted to stop drinking. The original publication of Alcoholics Anonymous in 1935 (Alcoholics Anonymous World Services, 1935), now in its third revision, was a major factor in spreading the AA program. This book, affectionately termed the "Big Book" by AA members, contains the story of Bill Wilson's battle with alcoholism as well as personal stories of the recovery of other alcoholic men and women that provide inspiration for many alcoholics toward recovery.

AA meetings are now held throughout the world, not only for alcoholism but for other forms of addiction as well. At the same time, challenges have come from alternative approaches such as Rational Recovery® and SMART Recovery, which regard AA as a cult that emphasizes fatalistic views.

Scientific Models

Another party opposing the moral model of alcoholism, scientific researchers, had fewer personal motives for their interest in alcoholism. As objective observers, they wanted to apply the empirical methods of rigorous science to study alcoholism and alcohol abuse just as scientists do when studying any type of phenomenon. The approach espoused by scientific investigators emphasized reliance on objective data, quantifiable variables, controlled experiments, and theories that generated testable hypotheses. This approach encompassed several different models.

Medical Model

In the influential formulation of a noted scientist, E. M. Jellinek (1960), alcoholism is regarded as a disease, one that can be and should be amenable to treatment and cure in much the same manner as many physical diseases. The idea that alcoholism is a disease was not original with Jellinek but dates back as early as 1785, with the views of Benjamin Rush, an eminent American physician. However, during the 1800s, the moral view prevailed, and drunkenness was regarded as sinfulness. If alcoholism had been recognized as disease rather than a character defect, a number of significant implications would have followed. The medical profession, due to its commitment to the treatment of diseases, could no longer justify ignoring the plight of alcoholics. Society would not be able to continue to blame alcoholics for their problem because diseases are medical problems and uncontrollable by those afflicted. This view of alcoholism as a disease fit AA's views on the physical nature of the origins of alcoholism and wholeheartedly promoted the AA philosophy.

The original formulation (Jellinek, 1952) distinguished between addictive and nonaddictive forms of alcoholism, maintaining that the disease model applied only to the addictive variety in which there is the susceptibility to eventual loss of control over drinking after years of excessive drinking. As to the causes of the differences between addictive and nonaddictive forms, Jellinek speculated that a so-called "Factor X" existed, possibly a predisposing metabolic or physiological difference, although he did not rule out differences in lifestyle as a determinant either. But Jellinek (1960), hoping to direct more awareness to alcohol problems, later modified his definition of alcoholism by broadening its scope to cover any use of an alcoholic beverage that causes any damage to the individual or to society.

Stages of Alcoholism

From a small sample of 98 AA members who completed a questionnaire about the course of development of their drinking problems, Jellinek (1952) proposed a model of alcoholism by identifying a syndrome of symptoms to describe its temporal course through the four **stages of alcoholism**, as shown in Figure 13.2. Later, a larger sample of about 2,000 AA members was used to refine the model (Jellinek, 1960).

In the early stage, referred to as the *prealcoholic phase*, social factors often lead to drinking for relief from tension. Eventually, tolerance to alcohol develops so that a larger dose is

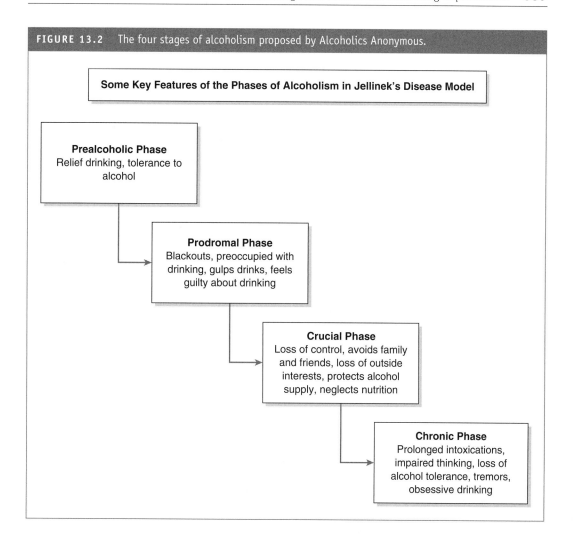

FIGURE 13.2   The four stages of alcoholism proposed by Alcoholics Anonymous.

Some Key Features of the Phases of Alcoholism in Jellinek's Disease Model

Prealcoholic Phase
Relief drinking, tolerance to alcohol

Prodromal Phase
Blackouts, preoccupied with drinking, gulps drinks, feels guilty about drinking

Crucial Phase
Loss of control, avoids family and friends, loss of outside interests, protects alcohol supply, neglects nutrition

Chronic Phase
Prolonged intoxications, impaired thinking, loss of alcohol tolerance, tremors, obsessive drinking

needed to produce the same level of relief previously generated by a smaller amount. The disease enters the *prodromal phase* with the occurrence of blackouts, a type of amnesia for events experienced during drinking episodes, especially when the drinker is physically fatigued. Later, when sober, the drinker may not recall experiences encountered during previous drinking bouts. Surreptitious drinking begins in which the alcoholic sneaks drinks to prevent others from knowing. Preoccupation with drinking develops so that the alcohol takes on a greater importance than previously.

In the third phase, the *crucial phase*, loss of control occurs in which drinking is difficult to stop once it begins. There may still be control over whether to start drinking on a specific occasion. As drinking takes over, the alcoholic begins to rationalize his or her drinking more frequently, often with defensiveness and hostility. Other major changes occur in the life of the alcoholic, including family frictions, loss of friends, work impairment, poor nutrition, and medical problems, which might also increase drinking.

Finally, in the fourth phase, the *chronic phase*, prolonged intoxication or "benders" occur, along with a reversal in tolerance for alcohol so that less alcohol is needed to produce impairment than previously. When alcohol is not available, withdrawal reactions occur involving pronounced physical discomfort, anxiety, shakes, tremors, and irritability. Although the length of the phases may vary with the individual and other factors, the sequence of the phases is regarded as universal (Jellinek, 1952).

This model, proposed by one of the leading alcohol researchers of the time, was important because it provided a disease model as an alternative to the then-prevailing moral model, which held that alcoholics drank because they lacked willpower. Instead of condemning the alcoholic and denying compassion and treatment, the disease model called for a nonjudgmental response and treatment just as for other physical diseases.

The views of AA and Jellinek were not developed independently of each other because, as noted earlier, Jellinek relied heavily on the personal experiences of alcoholism from AA members. It should hardly be surprising, then, if the self-reports of self-labeled alcoholics fit the primary model proposed by Jellinek and AA very closely. Interestingly, it also may be noted that none of the interview responses of females was included because they often differed from those provided by males (Fingarette, 1988).

Subtypes of Alcoholics

If other types of alcoholics than those studied by Jellinek exist who, for whatever reason, do not participate in AA, the disease model may have less validity for them. In his 1960 formulation (derived from interviews with AA members), Jellinek described several types of alcoholics, using Greek letter designations to identify them. The *gamma alcoholic*, characterized by psychological and physical dependence as well as loss of control, is the type most commonly seen by AA and is assumed to be the prototypical American male alcoholic. Chronic and progressive in nature, this type of alcoholism involves psychological and physical dependence on alcohol. The alcoholic loses control over drinking and is unable to voluntarily stop.

Jellinek (1960) also proposed the existence of several other types: The *alpha alcoholic* is a purely psychologically dependent case and presumably does not exhibit loss of control or show evidence of physical addiction to alcohol. In contrast, the *beta alcoholic*, an infrequent variety, shows only organic damage and nutritional deficiencies, probably due to heavy drinking, but no psychological or physical dependence. The *delta alcoholic* is similar to the gamma alcoholic but without loss of control. This drinker seems to drink continuously throughout the day but not in quantities that typically produce intoxication. This type is more commonly observed in wine-consuming nations such as France. Finally, there is the *epsilon* (or periodic) *alcoholic*, described as an infrequent binge drinker but one who shows no chronic physical dependence. This type of alcoholic can go for long periods without drinking, but when drinking occurs, it is excessive. Although the types seem to be mutually exclusive, Jellinek allowed that individuals drink in different patterns at different times and hence might be classified as a different type on various occasions.

Instead of acknowledging some type of variation among alcoholics, many conceptions about alcoholism assume that all alcoholics are alike and that an individual can readily be identified as either an alcoholic or a nonalcoholic. Jellinek's typology was generally ignored, and alcoholism was viewed as a homogeneous disease. Recognizing the value of examining subtypes of alcoholics is warranted because it may provide a better understanding of both the origins of and the treatments for the different types of alcoholism than possible under a unitary model of the disease.

The **medical model** or disease conception of alcoholism has proved influential in altering negative societal attitudes toward alcoholics, leading to a more humane concern with their plight. Treatment and rehabilitation, not condemnation and ostracism, have been accepted as the more appropriate response to alcoholism.

In addition, during this era when the medical model was being developed, other important strides toward greater scientific investigation of the biomedical and psychological aspects of alcoholism were made. Jellinek and other researchers developed a Center of Alcohol Studies at Yale University, later relocated to Rutgers University, which has been at the forefront in encouraging and promoting scientific research on alcohol problems as a legitimate goal. The establishment of a major scientific periodical (now named the *Journal of Studies on Alcohol and Drugs*) provided a prestigious and influential outlet for researchers to disseminate their findings.

The Alcoholics Anonymous Program

Alcoholics Anonymous, undoubtedly the most publicized and familiar recovery program, is unique because of its self-help orientation and philosophy that alcoholics are the ones who can best help other alcoholics recover. Since its beginnings in the mid-1930s, it has offered hope to countless alcoholics all over the world. The concepts underlying Alcoholics Anonymous are not entirely original, having been used by earlier social reformers (Trice & Staudemeier, 1989). The 19th-century temperance movement in the United States produced one of the forerunners of AA in the mid-1800s: the Washingtonians, a group of alcoholics who took a pledge of abstinence and relied on mutual support and hope as a means for recovery. A later movement of a quasi-religious nature, called the Oxford Group, emphasized the importance for alcoholics of recognizing or admitting their powerlessness over alcohol. As with the Washingtonians who preceded it and with AA, which followed it, the Oxford Group strongly believed in the value of mutual support and help.

AA is a program based on **Twelve Steps** (Alcoholics Anonymous, 1952), a set of practices (see Table 13.1) designed to help the alcoholic achieve a lasting recovery. Although not based on any formal religion, concepts and processes resemble features of many religious ceremonies and rituals. First is the recognition that the alcoholic is powerless over alcohol because the belief of control over drinking ensures defeat by it. The alcoholic must move from arrogance and pride to humility. Unless this first step is achieved, the prognosis for improvement is poor because individuals will feel that others are imposing the treatment on them for a nonexistent problem. In contrast, once they can change their self-perception and admit frailty, progress can begin. Critics of the view that alcoholics are powerless sometimes have interpreted this as implying that alcoholics are not responsible.

TABLE 13.1 The Twelve Steps of Alcoholics Anonymous.
1. We admitted we were powerless over alcohol in that our lives had become unmanageable.
2. Came to believe that a Power greater than ourselves could restore us to sanity.
3. Made a decision to turn our will and our lives over to the care of God as we understood Him.
4. Made a searching and fearless moral inventory of ourselves.
5. Admitted to God, to ourselves and to another human being the exact nature of our wrongs.
6. Were entirely ready to have God remove all these defects of character.
7. Humbly asked Him to remove our shortcomings.
8. Made a list of all persons we had harmed and became willing to make amends to them all.
9. Made direct amends to such people wherever possible except when to do so would injure them or others.
10. Continued to take moral inventory and when we were wrong promptly admitted it.
11. Sought through prayer and meditation to improve our conscious contact with God as we understood Him, praying only for knowledge of His will for us and the power to carry that out.
12. Having had a spiritual awakening as the result of these steps, we tried to carry this message to alcoholics, and to practice these principles in all our affairs.

Source: The Twelve Steps are reprinted with permission of Alcoholics Anonymous World Services, ("AAWS"). Inc. ("AAWS"). Permission to reprint the Twelve Steps does not mean that AAWS has reviewed or approved the contents of this publication, nor that AAWS agrees with the views expressed herein. AA is a program of recovery from alcoholism only; use of the Twelve Steps in connection with programs and activities that are patterned after AA but address other problems—or in any other non-AA context—does not imply otherwise.

Alcoholics are then encouraged to believe that a **higher power** (Step 2) can restore them to sanity and next, in Step 3, to decide to turn their lives over to the care of the higher power or God "as we understood Him." These two steps often represent major hurdles for those who do not believe in the concept of God, even though AA expands the definition of God to allow for even nonreligious conceptions. A spiritual awakening and an attitude of surrender to a higher power infuse this step in which the drinker seeks and accepts help.

Some of the Twelve Steps involve highly specific behavioral objectives, starting with the making of a fearless moral inventory (Step 4) to increase awareness of one's strengths and weaknesses. This is a difficult hurdle because it entails admission of failures. Although alcoholics may admit to excessive drinking, they often think that sobriety alone will restore their lives. The drinking, in their eyes, is the cause of any character defects they might have; therefore, they try to avoid a moral inventory.

Step 5 involves confession not only to oneself and a higher power but also to another person of the wrongs committed against others. As with religious confessions, humility is achieved by such admissions. In confessing to another person, one may be embarrassed but still benefit from the relief. Knowledge of one's faults is not enough. Step 6 calls for the readiness for change with the help of the higher power. This requires submission because the alcoholic must admit the need for the assistance of the higher power.

Step 7 directs the alcoholic to humbly ask for the removal of shortcomings. AA feels that without the attitude of humility the alcoholic cannot maintain sobriety. Humility comes about only through repeated humiliations that stem from overreliance on self-sufficiency.

Step 8 calls for a commitment to make amends whenever possible to the persons alcoholics have harmed. Some find this difficult and become defensive, or they focus instead on the harm that these persons may have done to them.

Step 9 requires actual fulfillment of these good intentions. At first, the experience might prove exhilarating because of the sense of relief, but AA warns against resting on one's laurels and procrastinating in making amends for more serious offenses. Hence, Step 10 reminds the alcoholic to continue taking personal inventory and admitting errors.

Step 11 invokes a religious tone, reminding the alcoholic of the importance of prayer and meditation to maintain contact with the higher power. This step is spiritual and urges the alcoholic to pray not for what he or she wants but for insight into what the higher power wants. By working the Twelve Steps of the program, the alcoholic achieves humility and atonement and eventually carries forth the message to help other alcoholics, as specified in the 12th step.

Aspects of the AA program could easily be related to other approaches. A behaviorist would notice that AA uses procedures that are the same as self-monitoring, social learning, and covert sensitization. Although the theoretical foundations, view of the change process, and treatment practices of AA are often seen as at odds with those of behavior therapy, many similarities may allow for integration of the two models (McCrady, 1994). Similarly, the focus of psychotherapy on the development of insight or the reliance on realistic goal setting is compatible with the AA attitude of taking "one day at a time."

As shown in Figure 13.3, the stages of the change model (DiClemente, 1993) parallel the processes advocated by AA. Whereas AA speaks of the need for "hitting rock bottom" before change can begin, the change model refers to precontemplation. Some of the first few steps of AA, such as recognizing that one's life has "become unmanageable," correspond to the contemplation stage of change. When AA calls for reliance on a higher power, the change model calls for preparation for change. Participation in AA meetings and "making amends" to those harmed by one's drinking are comparable to the action stage of change. Continuing to work the AA program is essentially the maintenance stage in the change model.

Members attend free AA group meetings as often as they wish. These meetings are held in most communities throughout the week in public facilities such as churches, community centers, and hospitals. Some meetings are open to any interested person with or without a personal drinking problem, but other meetings are closed to nonmembers. During the typical speaker's meeting, one or more recovering alcoholics will make a personal statement about their own lives and how they were adversely affected by drinking before they came to AA. They will then relate how their lives were changed through "working the program" of AA to achieve sobriety. There is a formal structure, beginning with an inspirational reading from an AA publication and ending with a prayer, "God grant me the serenity to accept the things I cannot change, the courage to change the things I can, and the wisdom to know the difference."

FIGURE 13.3 Parallels between AA and stages of the change model.

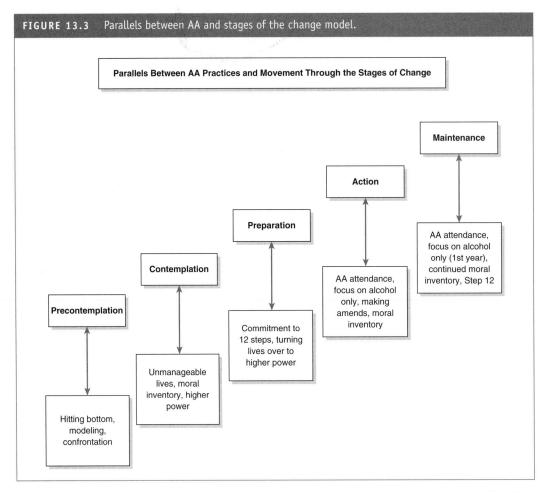

Source: From "Alcoholics Anonymous and the Structure of Change," by C. C. DiClemente, 1993, in B. S. McCrady and W. R. Miller (Eds.), *Research on Alcoholics Anonymous: Opportunities and Alternatives* (pp. 79–98), Piscataway, NJ: Rutgers Center of Alcohol Studies. Copyright 1993 by Alcohol Research Documentation, Inc., Rutgers Center of Alcohol Studies, Piscataway, NJ 08854. Reprinted with permission.

This prayer makes the important distinction between those things that are not changeable and those that are. It then urges appropriate responding by asking one to learn to accept the things that cannot be changed. Failure to accept things that cannot be changed leads to anger, frustration, and resentment, conditions often associated with excessive drinking. However, it is also important to act to modify those things that can be changed. Passive acceptance of a bad marriage, a boring or an unfulfilling job, and modifiable health status can all lead to escape through excessive drinking. Finally, the prayer recognizes the difficulty in sometimes accurately knowing which situations are unchangeable and which are changeable by asking for wisdom in being able to distinguish the two.

Some of the benefits of AA participation can be interpreted in terms of attributions (Beckman, 1980). AA involvement helps alcoholics modify their attributions of responsibility for their drinking. Alcoholics' realization that many drinkers do not suffer the harmful effects of alcohol that are experienced by alcoholics leads them to blame themselves for their plight. The feeling that "I'm a no-good drunk" adds to their burden and sustains the drinking. By affiliating with AA, alcoholics reinforce each other's belief that the disease of alcoholism, not their own doing, is responsible for their condition. Acceptance of AA ideology allows for a shift of attributions about their drinking from internal to external factors, a change that may be helpful in reducing their self-blame and facilitating recovery.

Critics and skeptics often have rejected the religious connotation of many tenets of AA, especially the requirement of surrendering to God, even though AA allows for considerable latitude in defining God or a power greater than ourselves. The AA group itself could represent the power that is greater than the self. The concept of a higher power should not be an obstacle for alcoholics because, in a sense, alcohol is their higher power: The trick is for the addict to switch from a destructive higher power to a constructive and beneficial one (Wallace, 1996). Nevertheless, the view that AA is a type of religious cult with rigid rules and ideas dies hard and is often an obstacle to newcomers. This image acts as a barrier for many nonreligious alcoholics from participation in AA. Skeptics also ridicule AA participants for their excessive smoking and coffee drinking, arguing that even if they give up alcohol, they are still addicts to other substances or to AA meetings themselves.

Who Goes to AA?

It should not be assumed that everyone referred to AA attends regularly or at all. Only around 20% of those referred to AA actually attend (Brandsma, Maultry, & Welsh, 1980). Some studies described the typical AA member as male, older than age 40, White, middle upper class, and with an authoritarian personality, strong affiliative needs, susceptibility to guilt, external locus of control, field dependence, cognitive simplicity, formalistic thinking, low conceptual level, religious orientation, existential anxiety, and a tendency to conform (Ogborne & Glaser, 1981). However, other studies (Emrick, 1987) refuted this negative profile by showing there was no relationship between AA involvement and socioeconomic status, social competence, social stability, or religion. Treated alcoholics who were AA members were psychologically healthier than those whose treatment did not include AA (Hurlburt, Gade, & Fuqua, 1984).

These conflicting views could all be tenable if the nature of AA membership changes over time. AA conducts its own anonymous survey of participants. These surveys, conducted every 3 years, are not based on random samples, and some bias may exist in who chooses to complete them. The two most recent AA surveys involving around 8,000 members in over 700 locations (Alcoholics Anonymous, 2005, 2008) found that the mean age was between 47 and 48 years. The age range was wide: 8% were under age 30 in 2004, increasing to 13.6% in 2007, while those over age 70 were stable at 4.8% in 2004 and 5.3% in 2007. There were about twice as many males as females, and although the latter had increased greatly from around 20% in 1968 to over 30% by the mid-1980s, that rate seems to have stabilized in the 2004 and 2007 surveys in the mid-30% range. These changes are difficult to interpret as they could reflect both changing drinking norms and changes in the demographic composition of the population.

The 2007 survey also obtained data on ethnicity and marital status. The results revealed that the overwhelming majority of AA members were White (85%), with only 5.7% Black,

4.8% Hispanic, 2.8% Asian, and 1.6% Native American. Slightly over one third were single, another third were married, 28% were divorced, and 8% identified as "Other." In terms of length of sobriety, about one third had been sober over 10 years, but slightly under one third were also newcomers with less than 1 year of sobriety. On average, members in the survey reported attending 2.4 meetings per week.

A secondary data analysis (Tonigan, Connors, & Miller, 1998) found no differences in AA attendance for White versus Hispanic and African American participants if they had no previous inpatient treatment. Although Hispanic clients attended AA less frequently than White clients, their involvement with and commitment to AA was paradoxically higher than among White clients. However, for both Hispanics and Whites, higher AA involvement was related to greater abstinence.

The reputation of AA as a therapeutic as well as cost-effective program (Humphreys, 2003) has led many treatment facilities and social agencies to refer alcohol-dependent individuals to AA more often than in the past. The 2004 AA survey findings showed 39% of members reporting that professional treatment had helped lead them to AA. The majority, 64%, had had some other form of treatment before going to AA. This level was almost identical in the 2007 survey when 63% reported receiving some type of counseling after they participated in AA.

Attendance at AA was attributed to various influences including advice from treatment facility, 31%; AA member, 31%; family members, 23%; court order, 11%; counseling agency, 8%; and health care provider, 8%. These levels were virtually identical in the 2004 and 2007 surveys. This cooperation between professionals and AA is not surprising, given that many therapists are also members of AA.

Evaluation of AA

Due to the anonymous nature of AA participation—a feature intended to facilitate the seeking of help by protecting individuals with this highly stigmatized problem—it is not possible to obtain scientifically rigorous evidence about the benefits of AA (McCrady & Miller, 1993). Little is known about who drops out or who continues to attend but does not benefit. Of course, an abundance of testimonials and anecdotal evidence attests to the many positive changes achieved through AA, so it is likely that benefits are real and substantial for large numbers of participants. Nonetheless, without more thorough information, it is difficult to understand the underlying basis for improvement.

One strategy for evaluating the effectiveness of AA involves comparing alcoholics in a treatment program who have and have not participated in AA. A serious problem, however, is that these two groups may differ in many other aspects, such as severity of their alcoholism or motivation for improvement, so interpretations must be cautious.

The fact that many AA participants benefit and achieve abstinence might reflect a selective process in which those who are more motivated or ready to accept the goal of abstinence are more likely to attend AA meetings than those who are not. However, no demographic variables were identified that distinguished between those who did and those who did not benefit from AA participation (Emrick, 1989). This analysis of AA survey responses showed that the degree of AA involvement before, during, or after a treatment program was unrelated to drinking levels.

A review (Brandsma et al., 1980) of early controlled studies of the effectiveness of AA that randomly assigned alcoholics to AA and several other types of formal treatment found no differential improvement. However, these studies may have underestimated the effects of treatment because they used poorly motivated clients who were court-referred to AA, as suggested by high dropout rates. Moreover, the extent to which AA attendees actually practiced the steps advocated by AA was not measured in these evaluations (Ogborne, 1993).

A longitudinal study extending over 16 years (Moos & Moos, 2005) compared three groups of untreated alcoholics (n = 362) that either attended AA only, entered professional treatment only, or entered professional treatment and AA together. They were surveyed at baseline, 1 year, 3 years, 8 years, and 16 years later about their AA participation, treatment, and current alcohol-related functioning. They also described their reasons for entering AA and/or treatment and the perceived benefits of these experiences.

The overall analysis showed benefits for earlier and longer participation in AA. Alcoholics who entered treatment and AA together participated in AA longer and more frequently. They had more remission relative to those who initially participated only in treatment but later entered AA. Individuals who entered treatment but delayed participation in AA did not appear to obtain any additional benefit from AA. Longer duration of participation in AA was associated with a higher likelihood of remission at all four follow-ups while individuals who dropped out of AA were more likely to relapse or fail to improve. However, since the alcoholics were not randomly assigned to these different activities, it is not clear how AA participation affected drinking outcomes. Alcoholics who had less serious problems and were more hopeful may have attended AA for longer periods, so AA attendance may have been an "effect" rather than a "cause" of improvement in sobriety.

Other evidence that the heterogeneity of AA participants is an important correlate of outcomes is a study (Kaskutas et al., 2005) that used an advanced statistical procedure, latent class growth curve modeling. Analysis of data from 349 alcohol-dependent drinkers who attended AA at least once between entering treatment and one or more follow-up interviews at 1, 3, and 5 years later identified four subgroups with different patterns of AA attendance: a low AA group that mainly attended AA during the first 12 months following treatment entry, a medium AA group with stable attendance at around 60 meetings a year, a high AA group with attendance of over 200 meetings per year at the 3- and 5-year follow-ups, and a declining AA group that initially doubled its meeting attendance after a baseline period to almost 200 meetings during the first year but was only attending about 6 meetings on average by the fifth year.

Frequency of AA attendance was related to greater abstinence as in the fifth year. Abstinence rates (for the past 30 days) were 43% for the low AA group, 61% for the declining attendance group, 73% for the medium attendance group, and 79% for the high attendance group. Unfortunately, however, rates of dependence symptoms and social consequences of drinking did not differ between the groups in the fifth year. Furthermore, many who attended at a low level still had improvement.

The difficulty in evaluating AA is due not just to anonymity of participants or to methodological problems but also to vague definitions and concepts (Bradley, 1988). These problems add to the lack of scientific progress in understanding how AA works. The scientific approach to evaluating AA attempts to measure processes of disease and recovery with behavioral indices rather than subjective reports.

However, in response, AA holds that its program is holistic and phenomenological and not best evaluated by scientific methods. The "outcome" is not something that is achieved at a specific, measurable point in time. Dropouts should not be viewed as "failures" because the definition of "dropout" can be relative, as someone not ready at that point for AA, rather than an absolute failure incapable of ever recovering.

AA believes that recovery from alcoholism involves more than the reduction of drinking. Thus, AA believes a spiritual awakening is an essential aspect of recovery, an outcome that behavioral researchers have ignored or discounted.

One investigation that focused on spirituality (Tonigan, Miller, & Schermer, 2002) examined the relationship between "God belief" at intake with subsequent AA attendance and drinking reduction (n = 1,526). Not surprisingly, atheist and agnostic clients attended AA significantly less often relative to clients self-labeled as spiritual and religious. AA attendance, however, was related to increased abstinence and reductions in drinking intensity regardless of God belief. No differences in the percentage of abstinent days and drinking intensity were found between atheist/agnostic and spiritual/religious clients, but the latter had lower drinking frequency.

Although it did not directly examine AA, some evidence on the relationship of spirituality to improvement was obtained from 405 clients at alcohol treatment facilities that differed in their emphasis on spirituality (Sterling et al., 2006). It was predicted that better outcomes would occur for clients with spirituality views congruent with their treatment program than for clients with views on spirituality that conflicted with those held by their treatment program. Overall, client-program matching of spiritual values was not related to outcomes, although clients with lower levels of spirituality in programs that deemphasized spirituality had poorer treatment outcomes.

Correlations between participation in Twelve-Step programs and spirituality cannot answer questions of causality or whether the two factors may jointly facilitate recovery. A prospective treatment study (Zemore, 2007b) addressed this concern using a baseline interview and 1-year follow-up of 733 alcoholics in five outpatient hospital and seven residential substance abuse treatment programs. The results showed that clients with increased Twelve-Step involvement were more likely to achieve total abstinence a year later. Spiritual change or awakening was correlated with this improvement, but the study does not rule out the possibility that other factors associated with Twelve-Step programs also contributed to recovery.

An example showing that spiritual processes may occur and benefit alcoholics even without participation in Alcoholics Anonymous is a longitudinal study (Robinson, Cranford, Webb, & Brower, 2007) of 123 White middle-aged outpatients (66% male) with alcohol use disorders. Regardless of their level of involvement with AA, gains in spirituality and/or religiousness occurred, and these changes were related to an absence of heavy drinking after 6 months of treatment for both men and women.

Racial/Ethnic Minorities and AA

It is somewhat surprising, given the history of AA and the middle-class Protestant and Anglo-Saxon roots of the movement, that racial/ethnic minority group members would find AA participation effective (Caetano, 1993). Although no official statistics are available about the ethnic background of participants, there is sufficient observational evidence that racial/ethnic minorities attend AA in sizable numbers. For example, AA meetings that consist of predominantly Hispanic members (Gilbert & Cervantes, 1987) may be more acceptable to this minority group. However, without further study, it is unclear which aspects of AA minority participants embrace (Glaser & Ogborne, 1982). These groups may participate in AA in different ways than do White middle-class attendees, adapting the program to meet their values. For example, not all participants may accept the higher power concept of AA, even though they might recognize the usefulness of humility or the value of social support (Morgenstern & McCrady, 1993).

Challenges for AA

It is important that more longitudinal and comparative outcome studies on AA and on professional Twelve-Step treatment programs be conducted to determine the extent to which participation in Alcoholics Anonymous and in Twelve-Step treatment reduces substance abuse. Use of larger samples, with greater inclusion of African Americans and women, and use of better measurement tools are needed. A priority is research that identifies the processes involved in self-help groups and Twelve-Step treatment programs that bring about recovery (Humphreys, 2003).

Contrary to the voluntary nature of AA attendance, courts, prisons, and substance abuse treatment programs have increasingly mandated alcoholics under their jurisdiction to attend meetings or face severe sanctions. When such coerced participation occurs, it can be disruptive and detrimental to the recovery process for alcoholics who are voluntary participants at AA meetings. Because AA offers "free" and ubiquitous meetings, the control of its membership and the conduct of meetings are often compromised.

Alternatives to AA

Alcoholics Anonymous has acquired a dominant place among substance use disorder recovery programs despite the sparse scientific evaluation. However, as a group-oriented approach involving self-disclosure, some may find it to be a threat to personal privacy. Others object to its formal structure and authoritarian tone. Consequently, alternative approaches have developed that make different assumptions about the nature of addiction and the appropriate methods for recovery. However, like Alcoholics Anonymous, they too have not received much evaluative research.

Rational Recovery. An organization, **Rational Recovery® (RR)**, created in the late 1980s, vehemently opposes AA and the Twelve-Step program philosophy (Trimpey, 1992). RR is a for-profit organization that believes individuals can quit without help and are not powerless over alcohol as AA dogmatically proclaims. Based on concepts from rational emotive therapy (Ellis, McInerney, DiGuiseppe, & Yeager, 1988), RR teaches individuals how to recognize and ignore what they call the addictive voice of AA ideology. Alcoholism is not a disease, according to RR. Learning skills to cope with problems can lead to plans for achieving abstinence.

RR attacks the vast addiction treatment industry that has developed as an indication that society is hooked on the concept of addiction, as much as it is on drugs. Unlike AA, no group meetings are involved. RR refers to its primary reading resource, the "Small Book," to emphasize its differences from AA and its "Big Book."

SMART (Self-Management and Recovery Training). In the early 1990s, a split developed among the leaders of RR, and one group separated to form SMART, which is maintained as a nonprofit organization. Like RR, **SMART Recovery** opposes AA's emphasis on powerlessness and relies on the rational emotive therapy (Ellis et al., 1988) and urges independence and self-reliance in recovery using techniques related to cognitive-behavioral modification.

Women for Sobriety. AA started as and still is a male-oriented organization. Middle-class, middle-aged, White, educated women may find the requirements of AA that alcohol-dependent women must make atonements and strive for humility objectionable because women generally have lower power in many aspects of their lives (Beckman, 1993). In 1975, Jean Kirkpatrick started **Women for Sobriety**, a self-help organization for women with alcohol problems that emphasizes taking responsibility for one's actions and adopting positive thinking (Kaskutas, 1996). The philosophy also emphasizes self-reliance; feelings of competent, emotional, and spiritual growth; and abstinence. The meeting format is less hierarchical than that of AA. All women at a meeting take turns sharing their recent experiences, especially positive events, rather than dwelling on presenting historical accounts of their personal drinking. Although not highly publicized, this small and relatively new mutual aid organization provides an alternative to AA for women with alcohol dependency problems.

BEHAVIORAL MODEL

In the 1960s, the study of alcohol use was based on a different emphasis in the work of behaviorally oriented researchers who focused more on the drinking behavior of alcoholics than on an underlying internal disease leading to drinking. They conceptualized alcoholism as a learned response that, like any other form of acquired behavior, could be reinforced or controlled by its consequences. They avoided speculation about intrapsychic states such as denial, craving, and loss of control that were major aspects of lay beliefs about alcoholism as well as of influential organizations such as Alcoholics Anonymous.

Behaviorists questioned the validity of the disease conception of alcoholism. Although they did not deny that alcoholics might develop physical diseases from drinking, they rejected the view that alcoholism itself is a physical disease. They held that medical diseases have an identifiable set of symptoms that develop in a certain sequence, whereas alcoholism does not. Defenders of the disease conception countered that the behaviorists held too narrow a definition of disease and that many physical diseases involve substantial variations in symptomatology.

These researchers studied alcoholics in clinical and experimental settings and used laboratory animals under better-controlled but artificial conditions. They emphasized objective observation of quantifiable aspects of behavior under the influence of alcohol, in comparison to behavior under a sober state. The goal was to find methods of modifying drinking behavior to bring it to acceptable levels.

The controversy between AA and behaviorists over the question of whether alcoholism is a disease, a continuing issue of debate, is complicated by the common use of disease as a metaphor. Disease is often used to symbolize any pathological condition. Thus, *dishonesty* is a term used to refer to someone who engages in behaviors such as lying and cheating. Metaphorically speaking, we condemn dishonesty as a cancer or disease because as it spreads, it destroys the quality of our social relationships.

The metaphorical use of the term *disease* should be distinguished from the view that alcoholism is a medical disease. Thus, one would not call on a surgeon to treat dishonest persons for this disease with a scalpel. Instead, one might try to modify these behaviors through a variety of psychological techniques, including counseling, punishment, guilt, and social modeling. The dishonest person would be expected to assume responsibility for changing these behaviors. In the same respect, staunch critics (Peele, 1989) of the disease concept of alcoholism viewed excessive drinking behavior, or dependence on alcohol, as an unacceptable and harmful form of behavior, not as a disease in the medical sense.

SELF-HELP TREATMENT FOR THE FAMILY OF ALCOHOLICS

As noted in the preceding chapter, family members are seriously damaged by the drinking of the alcoholic member of the family and are often in need of counseling and psychological treatment. Al-Anon, a program that borrows heavily from AA concepts, was developed for the treatment of the family members separately from the treatment of the alcoholic.

The Al-Anon Program

Al-Anon is a recovery program related to AA in approach that was developed for the significant others of alcoholics. Started in 1935 by Lois Wilson, the wife of the cofounder of AA, its philosophy closely mirrors that of AA and its Twelve Steps. Al-Anon (1984, 1986) encourages its members to admit their powerlessness over their alcoholic family members and the unmanageability of their lives as the first step toward recovery. Without this first step of detachment, members might continue to find ways to stop the alcoholics from drinking or feel guilty that they have failed.

Al-Anon holds that nonalcoholic family members need to be concerned about their own recovery from strong tendencies toward overcontrolling and assuming too much responsibility for the lives of others. Before the term *codependency* was coined, Al-Anon was dealing with the underlying phenomenon in which the nonalcoholic unintentionally enables or contributes to the maintenance of the alcoholic's drinking. Many nonalcoholics try to prevent their alcoholic spouses from drinking, using a variety of means such as hiding the bottles or emptying the alcohol down the sink. These attempts to control the drinking of the alcoholics are rarely effective in changing the drinking; eventually, the codependents feel despair, resentment, and a sense of hopelessness. At the same time, they deny that alcoholism exists. They are embarrassed by the stigma associated with alcoholism. They also cover for and clean up after the alcoholics, despite the physical and psychological damage created by the drinking. Because the alcoholics are spared some of the adverse effects of the drinking, they are unlikely to assume responsibility for it.

Al-Anon recognizes that nonalcoholic spouses have problems separate from those of alcoholics, and to meet those problems, it is first necessary for them to recognize that they are not personally responsible for their alcoholic spouses' drinking or for getting them to stop. As in AA, alcoholic drinking is viewed as a disease, not a willful act. According to Al-Anon, family members cannot stop an alcoholic's drinking regardless of how much they try. The task of the nonalcoholics or codependents is to learn to "release with love" their alcoholic family members and to stop overcontrolling them. After the first step of detachment, the codependent is urged to turn the matter over to a higher power. As with AA, members of Al-Anon gain support from each other to facilitate recovery through a Twelve-Step program of self-improvement and personal growth based on similar concepts developed by AA.

Evaluation of Al-Anon

A 1984 survey conducted across the United States by Al-Anon showed that most participants were White (96%) and predominantly female (88%; Cermak, 1989). They were mostly middle-aged, with about half of them having had some college education. There may be some bias in the types of persons who completed the survey, so this demographic portrait of membership may only be a rough approximation.

As is true of AA, little objective evaluation of the effectiveness of Al-Anon participation has been done. Self-reports of wives who participated in Al-Anon claimed a reduction of enabling behaviors—making excuses, covering up, checking up on spouses' drinking—as well as fewer emotional outbursts and nagging about the spouses' drinking (Gorman & Rooney, 1979). However, even assuming these self-reports are valid, it is unknown if such changes by wives reduced the husbands' drinking behavior.

NATURAL RECOVERY

Natural recovery or remission may occur for some alcoholic and drug-dependent persons who did not receive formal treatment but still managed to end their substance abuse (Tuchfield, 1981). Interviews (Ludwig, 1986) of alcoholics who experienced spontaneous recovery suggested that certain life events motivated change, but there is a wide variety of such events, ranging from social pressure and major life changes on one hand to "strangely trivial" events that work in mysterious ways (Knupfer, 1972, p. 272) on the other.

The pioneering 18th-century American physician, Benjamin Rush, described several cases of natural recovery in his discourse on the effects of alcohol (Jellinek, 1943). In one instance, a farmer who was habitually drunk happened to rush home from the local tavern one day due to an impending storm before he had a chance to become intoxicated. Surprised by his unusual sobriety, his 6-year-old son announced his father's arrival to his mother, emphasizing that he was not drunk. Shamed by his realization of how he was regarded by his son, the farmer suddenly reformed his drinking habits.

Another tale of a natural recovery involved a drunkard who was followed one day to the tavern by his goat, whom he proceeded to drench with liquor so that they both had to stagger home. The next day, the loyal goat again followed the master to the tavern but balked at the entrance despite the master's entreaties to enter. The apparently greater intelligence of the goat so shamed the master that from that point he ceased to drink liquor.

These anecdotes suggest that sudden changes in drinking attitudes and behaviors can occur. Overall, however, not much attention has been given to such natural recoveries. Some problem drinkers may not need formal treatment to recover. Natural recoveries may be much more frequent than suspected. One study (Sobell, Sobell, & Toneatto, 1991) recruited 120 ex-drinkers through newspaper ads that asked, "Have you successfully overcome a drinking problem without formal treatment?" After screening, there were 71 who were abstinent and 49 who were nonabstinent. In addition, a group of 28 alcoholics was identified that had had some formal treatment but did not consider it a factor in their recovery.

Unlike in previous studies of natural recoveries, this one used a control group of 62 problem drinkers recruited with newspaper ads that asked, "Do you have a drinking problem now?" The ad indicated that this was a research study to obtain information to help those with problems and seeking treatment, but participants in this study would not be given a treatment program. Only those who never had sought formal treatment were studied.

More than 96% of the 182 participants in the study met the *DSM-III-R* (American Psychiatric Association, 1987) criteria for alcohol dependence, although only 21% were considered highly dependent. The demographic profile of the participants was similar to that found for alcoholics in seven major outcome studies (Foy, Nunn, & Rychtarik, 1984).

The first phase of the study identified the variables related to stopping and maintaining the cessation of drinking, distinguishing between those who achieved abstinent and nonabstinent—or **controlled drinking**—recovery. The reasons for choosing abstinent or controlled drinking were related to the respondents' self-confidence that they could control their drinking, with those choosing abstinence being less optimistic.

Not seeking formal treatment was related to embarrassment, no perception of a problem, unwillingness to share the problem with others, and stigma. Almost all claimed that they felt they could handle the problem themselves. Paradoxically, they also admitted having a drinking problem. Failure to identify with the stereotype of an "alcoholic" was often a barrier to seeking treatment. Perhaps there should be more attempts to offer programs for those who recognize that they have drinking problems but do not want formal treatment.

An intervention study compared two different methods for helping alcohol dependents reduce drinking without formal treatment (Sobell et al., 2002). Media solicitations recruited 825 problem drinkers who had never sought formal treatment. They were randomly assigned to one of two interventions delivered by mail. The bibliotherapy group (n = 411) received two pamphlets with information about the effects of alcohol and guidelines for low-risk drinking and self-monitoring. The motivational enhancement group (n = 414) received personalized advice/feedback about their drinking on the basis of the participants' assessment of their drinking and related behaviors.

Significant reductions in drinking from 1 year before to 1 year after intervention occurred for both groups, but there were no significant differences between the two interventions for any variable. These results, coupled with the low cost to deliver the intervention, suggest that public health campaigns could have a substantial effect.

The effectiveness of natural recovery may differ for men and women (Bischof, Rumpf, Hapke, Meyer, & John, 2000). Reasons for not seeking help, triggering mechanisms, and maintenance factors of remission were compared for women (n = 38) and men (n = 106) who remitted from *DSM-IV* alcohol dependence without utilization of formal help (treatment or self-help groups).

Prior to remission, women, as compared to men, experienced lower extents of social pressure to change drinking behavior, drove less often under the influence of alcohol, revealed less satisfaction with different life domains, and reported a higher impact of health problems on the remission process. They also confided in fewer individuals about their former drinking problems.

Alcohol dependents recovering without formal treatment are a heterogeneous population. Interviews with 178 media-recruited natural remitters revealed three types based on severity of dependence, level of social support, and adverse problems due to drinking (Bischof, Rumpf, Hapke, Meyer, & John, 2003). One cluster had high severity of dependence, low alcohol-related problems, and low social support ("low problems–low support"; n = 65); another group had high severity of dependence, high alcohol-related problems, and medium social support ("high problems–medium support"; n = 37); and a third group had high social support, late age of onset, low severity of dependence, and low alcohol-related problems ("low problems–high support"; n = 76).

Follow-up interviews after 2 years (Bischof, Rumpf, Meyer, Hapke, & John, 2007) found that the differences in social support among the three clusters of remitters diminished. However, the "low problems–low support" group was still lowest in social support, and it had higher rates of relapse and utilization of formal help than any other group. Social support appears to be an important correlate of the maintenance of natural recovery.

Natural Recovery Among Smokers

Is it possible to quit smoking without formal treatment? Self-reported and observer-rated nicotine withdrawal in self-quitters after 30 days showed that anxiety, difficulty concentrating, hunger, irritability, restlessness, and weight increased and heart rate decreased after cessation for up to 180 days (Hughes, 1992). Except for hunger and weight gain, these symptoms returned to original levels by 30 days after quitting. Craving, depression, and alcohol or caffeine intake did not reliably increase. Relapse was predicted by postquitting depression rather than by withdrawal symptoms, craving, or weight gain.

A comparison of 10 large-scale studies at different research sites studying self-quitting found widely varying success rates at typically low levels (Cohen & Shiffman, 1989). Part of the variation in success rates may depend on the severity of the smoking. Heavier smokers are less likely to succeed in quitting on their own. Failing to quit on their own may lead them to eventually turn to clinical treatment, but their success rates may be low compared to those of self-quitters simply because self-quitters may be relatively light or infrequent smokers.

In addition, success rates depend on the definition of quitting. For example, the duration of quitting must be considered. The longer the follow-up interval, the more likely there will be more relapse to resumption of smoking. Thus, it is impossible to evaluate a study of psychology faculty members who reported high rates of successful self-quitting (Schachter, 1982) because the duration of quitting was not examined.

Even when the same time interval is used, rates of quitting can depend on how continuous each success is. Someone who quit and did not smoke continuously over a 6-month period would be counted as only one success, whereas someone who quit on four different occasions over the same period, having relapsed on three of the attempts, would get counted as four successes. When longer duration of cessation is used as the criterion, the rates of successful self-quitting are lower.

Natural recovery also has been reported with heroin addicts (Biernacki, 1986). These middle-class users, who led otherwise normal lives, were able to stop using heroin without formal treatment. After facing many crises from their drug use, they managed to modify their social settings by dissociating themselves from other users and developing new social networks that supported their recovery, often participating in self-help groups with other recovering users.

A study of natural recovery (Granfield & Cloud, 1996) of middle-class male and female alcoholics and drug addicts found that despite little or no exposure to either formal treatment or self-help groups, they reported being abstinent for more than 5 years, on average. They reported an average period of more than 9 years of prior drug dependency. It must be recognized, however, that this nonrandom sample was small and that self-report was the only evidence of prior dependency and present abstinence.

Summary

Alcoholics Anonymous is the best-known and most widely publicized approach to the treatment of alcoholism and alcohol abuse. Although it describes itself as a program of spiritual recovery more than as a "treatment" for alcoholism, AA's philosophy and methods have exerted a strong influence on formal treatment programs. Through self-evaluation and mutual support, AA members engage in a spiritual program to abstain from alcohol as they rebuild their lives. Countless numbers of individuals have attended AA group meetings all over the world. The Twelve Steps, beginning with an admission of powerlessness over alcohol, provide a structured series of tasks of self-examination and improvement that will help overcome alcoholism.

Due to its informal and subjective nature, the program of AA is difficult to evaluate objectively. Nonetheless, professional or formal treatments often involve AA participation as an adjunct to a treatment package consisting of education and counseling as well as more specialized components that differ across programs. The failure to include control groups makes it impossible to determine the relative effectiveness of different parts of a treatment package. AA's reputation as an effective means for recovery from alcoholism, although difficult to rigorously evaluate, has led to the development of similar organizations for other types of psychological problems.

Rational Recovery®, a for-profit organization created in the late 1980s, vehemently opposes AA and the Twelve-Step program philosophy. RR believes individuals can quit without help and are not powerless over alcohol as AA dogmatically proclaims. Based on concepts from rational emotive therapy, RR teaches individuals how to recognize and ignore what they call the addictive voice of AA ideology. Alcoholism is not a disease, according to RR. Learning skills to cope with problems can lead to plans for achieving abstinence.

Since AA has historically been a male-oriented organization, Women for Sobriety, a self-help organization for women with alcohol problems that emphasizes taking responsibility for one's actions and adopting positive thinking, was formed in 1975. Its philosophy emphasizes self-reliance; feelings of competent, emotional, and spiritual growth; and abstinence.

Al-Anon is a self-help organization for family and friends of alcoholics. It is modeled after AA in concept and offers a similar Twelve-Step program for codependents to help them realize that they are powerless over the drinking of their alcoholic family members. It is believed that this first step of detachment is needed before codependents can begin to recover from their own addiction to trying to control their alcoholic family members' drinking. Alcoholism is viewed as a family disease, not limited to the alcoholic family member, because the nonalcoholic family members are also dysfunctional. The codependents must be led to focus primarily on their own recovery, not that of the alcoholic.

Natural recovery from drug dependency apparently happens, but most of the evidence is anecdotal. The existence of such successes does not mean that everyone is capable of natural recovery, but it does suggest that formal treatment is not always necessary. It is possible that some types of personality or environmental circumstances are more likely to be associated with such successes. Such cases warrant more investigation to identify the techniques and factors that are involved.

Stimulus/Response

1. Motivating change: Have you ever tried to get someone to reduce his or her frequency or quantity of drinking? Which tactics have you found to work best, and which tactics have you found to be ineffective? Has anyone tried to get you to reduce the use of any drug? If so, which tactics worked, and which did not?

2. AA maintains that alcoholics must admit that they are helpless over their drinking and must seek a higher power. Do you think this approach is compatible with or in opposition to a view that everyone has to take responsibility for and control over their own lives?

3. Because there are many parallels between the ideology and rituals of AA and those of organized religion, do you think AA would be more effective with individuals who also hold firm religious commitments?

4. Do you know someone who has or have you ever overcome a strong bad habit without any formal intervention or treatment? Describe which processes were helpful in this natural recovery. Do you see any similarities in the processes that lead to natural recovery for alcohol or tobacco addiction and nondrug addictions?

Treatment of Alcohol and Other Drug Dependencies

I went on a diet, swore off drinking, and in 14 days, I lost 2 weeks.

—Joe E. Lewis

Professional treatment of alcohol and other drug abuse and dependency is markedly different from the approach used by grassroots or lay organizations such as Alcoholics Anonymous, Cocaine Anonymous, and Narcotics Anonymous. Formal treatment requires specialized professional knowledge of fields such as psychology, pharmacology, and neurophysiology.

Most approaches involve one or more of three emphases—pharmacological, psychotherapeutic, and behavioral. This chapter will focus on psychotherapeutic and behavioral approaches, although the distinction between them is often blurred because they overlap or are often used together. Most formal treatment programs employ a wide range of techniques including psychotherapy, cognitive-behavioral skill training, aversive conditioning, pharmacotherapy, hypnosis, physical exercise, and social skill training rather than a single technique (Institute of Medicine [IOM], 1990).

TYPICAL 28-DAY INPATIENT TREATMENT

Although variations exist among programs, some common features exist among most 28- to 30-day inpatient alcoholism and drug treatment programs that follow the **Minnesota model** of treatment (Miller, 1998). First, if the patient enters the hospital in a crisis due to excessive drug use, detoxification for several days is necessary before counseling and psychotherapy can begin. Severe withdrawal reactions may occur when treatment begins because of the sudden unavailability of drugs such as alcohol and heroin. Medical supervision, drug treatment with benzodiazepines, and nutritional treatment are required for safe management of the detoxification phase. Then, a mixture of individual and group therapy follows that includes didactic educational films and lectures about the physical effects of the patient's specific drug problem. Cognitive processes are impaired after prolonged use of alcohol or other drugs, leaving some question as to how well the cognitive information is comprehended following detoxification (McCrady, 1987). Recreational and occupational therapy often supplement the primary components of inpatient treatment programs. Self-help in the form of Alcoholics Anonymous, Cocaine Anonymous, or Narcotics Anonymous meetings serves as an adjunct and as aftercare to formal treatment.

During the 1970s, health insurance covered most inpatient treatment costs, but use of inpatient or residential programs declined sharply by the 1980s as the cost for the typical 28-day hospital stay for alcoholism was often about 10 times as great as the cost for outpatient treatment. With the increased efforts toward containment of health care costs, increased reliance fell on outpatient care, especially since there was evidence that inpatient care was generally no better than outpatient treatment according to a review (Miller & Hester, 1986) of 26 controlled studies of alcohol treatment. Managed care and health maintenance organization policies aimed at cost containment reduced insurance coverage and limited access to treatment for many vulnerable subpopulations (Stockdale, Tang, Zhang, Belin, & Wells, 2007). In 2000, 54% of treatment facilities involved managed care contracts.

In contrast, therapy for abuse of illegal drugs such as cocaine or heroin has been primarily based on outpatient programs and residential treatment facilities known as therapeutic communities (TCs) such as Synanon and Phoenix House that not only dealt with drug problems but provided counseling, education, and discipline as well. These publicly funded programs offer a supportive and highly structured living environment. However, there is considerable variability among drug treatment facilities in their underlying philosophy on issues such as the use of counselors, self-reliance, vocational training, and family participation (Melnick, De Leon, Hiller, & Knight, 2000). Many TCs are not residential, and some residential drug abuse treatment programs are not TCs (De Leon, 1995).

SIZE OF THE TREATMENT POPULATION

Although the number that receives treatment is only the tip of the iceberg of those in need, it is still useful to identify characteristics of those who seek and receive treatment. While an estimated 27% of the general population has suffered some type of drug abuse or dependence during their lifetimes, only 8% have received formal treatment (Kessler et al., 1994).

The National Drug and Alcoholism Treatment Unit Survey (NDATUS) estimates the number of alcohol and other drug abusers under treatment in the United States each year. Started in 1974 by the National Institute on Drug Abuse, it was jointly conducted periodically since 1979 with the National Institute on Alcohol Abuse and Alcoholism to determine the number and type of treatment facilities in the United States and the extent to which they are used. Tracking this information can be useful in forecasting future needs and costs for substance abuse treatment. The NDATUS was redesigned in 1995 to improve reporting and analysis, was renamed the Uniform Facility Data Set (UFDS), and included a telephone follow-up survey of all nonresponders for critical survey items.

The NDATUS data are no longer up to date, but the 1992 findings provide a baseline measure of the scope of the demand and supply of treatment facilities. Those results showed that alcohol abuse together with abuse of one or more illicit drugs was the most common pattern of substance abuse across the United States, with 38% of clients abusing both alcohol and drugs. A slightly smaller fraction (37%) abused only alcohol, and a smaller fraction (25%) abused only drugs. Whites accounted for the largest share of clients (60%) in 1992, followed by Blacks (22%) and Hispanics (15%). The racial and ethnic composition of NDATUS clients changed little between 1980 and 1992 as women increased from 25% to 29% whereas men declined from 75% to 71%. From 1987 to 1992, the fastest growing segment was between the ages of 35 and 44, increasing from 23% to 28% of all clients over these 5 years.

Outpatient services accounted for 87% of all clients. The other broad category of services was 24-hour or round-the-clock care. Outpatient clients were mostly in drug-free programs (75%), but some also received methadone (12%). Outpatient services may include the same services that are delivered in 24-hour care, although outpatient treatment episodes are typically less intensive and are stretched out over a longer period of time. From 1980 to 1992, there was a gradual shift toward outpatient services increasing from 84% in 1980 to 87% in 1992, while 24-hour care declined from 16% to 13%.

The NDATUS statistics show the prevalence of treatment but give no information about the relative supply and demand for such services. What percentage of the population needs treatment, and how many seek and receive it? Table 14.1 addresses some of these questions with findings of the 2006 and 2007 National Survey on Drug Use and Health (NSDUH). The definition of need included persons who had actually received treatment. In 2007, for example, 9.4% of persons aged 12 or older (23.2 million persons) needed treatment for an illicit drug or alcohol use problem. Of these, only 1.0% (2.4 million persons) actually sought and received treatment from a specialty facility. Table 14.1 does not show this information, but in 2007, 952,000 persons received treatment for alcohol use only, 728,000 received treatment for illicit drug use only, and 615,000 received treatment for both alcohol and illicit drugs, and these estimates were comparable to those for 2006 and 2007. Estimates of the number of individuals needing treatment were inflated by those who had both problems.

Those receiving treatment were the tip of the iceberg as Table 14.1 shows that 8.4% of the general population aged 12 or older (20.8 million persons) needed treatment in 2007 for an illicit drug or alcohol use problem but did not receive it at a specialty substance abuse facility as compared to the 1.0% of that population receiving treatment. Only around 10% of most subgroups received treatment from a specialty treatment facility during the year. To what extent was this gap due to a shortage of affordable treatment, to a reticence of those in need seeking it, or to some combination of these factors?

TABLE 14.1 Percentage of persons aged 12 or older needing treatment for an illicit drug or alcohol problem* in the past year by demographic characteristics (2007).

	NEEDED TREATMENT FOR AN ILLICIT DRUG OR ALCOHOL PROBLEM IN THE PAST YEAR									Percentage Who Received Treatment at a Specialty Facility Among Persons Who Needed Treatment	
	Total		Received Treatment at a Specialty Facility		Did Not Receive Treatment at a Specialty Facility						
Demographic Characteristic	2006	2007	2006	2007	2006	2007				2006	2007
TOTAL	9.6	9.4	1.0	1.0	8.6	8.4				10.8	10.4
AGE											
12–17	8.2	7.9	0.7	0.6	7.5	7.3				8.7	7.6
18–25	21.8	21.1	1.5	1.5	20.3	19.7				7.0	7.0
26 or Older	7.6	7.5	1.0	0.9	6.7	6.6				12.9	12.4
GENDER											
Male	12.7	13.0	1.4	1.4	11.4	11.5				10.7	10.9
Female	6.6*	6.0	0.7	0.6	5.9	5.4				10.9	9.3
HISPANIC ORIGIN AND RACE											
Not Hispanic or Latino	9.4	9.5	1.0	1.0	8.5	8.4				10.1	11.0
White	9.5	9.7	0.9	1.0	8.6	8.8				9.6	9.9
Black or African American	9.6	9.3	1.4	1.7	8.2	7.6				14.2	18.2
Native American or Alaska Native	20.2	14.5	2.3	3.4	18.0	11.1				*	*
Native Hawaiian or Other Pacific Islander	12.3	9.9	0.8	0.1	11.5	9.9				*	*

NEEDED TREATMENT FOR AN ILLICIT DRUG OR ALCOHOL PROBLEM IN THE PAST YEAR

Demographic Characteristic	Total		Received Treatment at a Specialty Facility		Did Not Receive Treatment at a Specialty Facility		Percentage Who Received Treatment at a Specialty Facility Among Persons Who Needed Treatment	
	2006	2007	2006	2007	2006	2007	2006	2007
Asian	4.4	4.9	0.3	0.2	4.2	4.7	6.2	*
Two or More Races	12.4	11.7	1.1	1.8	11.3	9.8	8.6	*
Hispanic or Latino	10.7[a]	8.6	1.5[a]	0.5	9.1	8.0	14.3[a]	6.0

Source: From *Results from the 2007 National Survey on Drug Use and Health (NSDUH): National Findings,* by the Substance Abuse and Mental Health Services Administration (SAMHSA), 2007, Rockville, MD: SAMHSA Office of Applied Studies.

*Low precision; no estimate reported.

Note: Respondents were classified as needing treatment for an illicit drug or alcohol problem if they met at least one of three criteria during the past year: (1) dependent on illicit drugs or alcohol; (2) abuse of illicit drugs or alcohol; or (3) received treatment for an illicit drug or alcohol problem at a specialty facility (i.e., drug and alcohol rehabilitation facilities [inpatient or outpatient], hospitals [inpatient only], and mental health centers). Illicit Drugs include marijuana hashish, cocaine (including crack), heroin, hallucinogens, inhalants, or prescription-type psychotherapeutics used nonmedically, based on data from original questions not including methamphetamine use items added in 2005 and 2006.

[a]Difference between estimate and 2007 estimate is statistically significant at the 0.01 level.

Table 14.1 also shows the breakdown by major demographic variables. Males had greater treatment need than females, and 18- to 25-year-olds had the highest need of any age group. American Indians/Alaska natives had the highest while Asians had the lowest need for both alcohol and illicit drug abuse treatment. Blacks had the second highest need for illicit drug treatment, and Hispanics had the second highest need for alcohol treatment.

REASONS FOR NOT SEEKING TREATMENT

The NSDUH asked respondents who needed but did not seek treatment for reasons for this failure. Data were reported separately for treatment of alcohol and illicit drug abuse. According to combined 2004–2007 NSDUH findings, the most common barrier to seeking treatment was "not being ready," reported by 38.7%. About a third of respondents cited cost and lack of health coverage as impediments. In addition, a small percentage cited reasons such as a "negative effect on their job" or "negative opinion of neighbors" and "not knowing where to go."

PSYCHOTHERAPY

Psychotherapy comes in many forms, but the emphasis is on verbal communication between patient and therapist, in either individual or group settings. The communication focuses on the patient's background, current life situation, and motives for drinking or other drug use in an attempt to give the patient an understanding of the causes of their behavior. After achieving insight about the psychological origins of the drinking or other drug use, presumably the alcoholic or other drug user can gain control over the problem.

Psychodynamic Approaches

Psychodynamic schools of thought interpret alcohol and other drug abuse as a reflection of conflicts (often unconscious) or character defects during earlier stages of development. For example, psychoanalytic views hold drug use to be a sign of a negative fixation at the oral stage of development due to negative experiences associated with feeding during infancy. They regard the drug abuser as adept at the use of defense mechanisms and unconscious processes such as denial, rationalization, and projection to cope with the threat represented by the excessive drug use.

Interpretation of the past by the therapist is assumed to break down client defenses, provide insight, and facilitate recovery. However, it may be unwise to strip away the "preferred defense mechanism" (Wallace, 1985, p. 26) of alcoholics too early during the therapeutic process. These defenses, although maladaptive in the long run, are the only immediate means of coping that the alcoholic has. Other methods must be developed before they will give them up.

Psychodynamic approaches view alcoholism and other drug abuse as a symptom of underlying conflict (Leeds & Morgenstern, 1996). Personality precursors are assumed to cause the excessive drinking and drug use. Research to evaluate the validity of therapy for alcoholism and other drug abuse often has involved poor methodology, with reliance on single cases and no controls. The degree of severity and heterogeneity of alcoholics and other drug abusers has been ignored in drawing conclusions.

One proposal for improvement in identifying the underlying factors of alcohol and other drug abuse calls for an integration of psychoanalytic concepts with aspects of cognitive behavior modification therapy (Keller, 1996). This approach is a mixture of a psychodynamic model with a behavioral model (Marlatt & Gordon, 1985) for **relapse** prevention.

Therapy involves a working alliance (Greenson, 1967) in which the clients come to identify with the therapist as they work together on agreed goals. Patient resistance, which refers to patient defenses that impede the operation of the working alliance, is a psychoanalytically based concept. The task of the psychodynamic therapist is then to explore defenses and unconscious conflicts to help establish a working alliance so that the behaviorally based relapse prevention skills can be developed (Keller, 1996).

Critics of psychodynamic approaches question the usefulness of concepts such as denial, which is assumed to be characteristic of alcoholics and other drug abusers. This assumption may be unwarranted as a survey (Grant, 1997a) of a sample of respondents with a lifetime *DSM-IV* alcohol use disorder (American Psychiatric Association [APA], 1994) revealed that only 12.7% had at some time recognized a need for alcohol treatment but had not undertaken it.

It was also enlightening to learn what the respondents reported as the reasons for failure to seek treatment. Instead of denial or a failure to realize they had a drinking problem, many indicated ambivalence, fear, or embarrassment about public disclosure of a stigmatized problem such as alcoholism. Other reasons reflected feelings that they should be strong enough to handle the problem or that the problem would get better by itself. Because the study relied on self-reports, some of the reasons may have been excuses or rationalizations, but overall they do not support widespread denial among those who did not seek treatment. The use of denial as an explanation for failure to seek treatment is somewhat circular. "Denial" is suspected when others think a person should be in treatment but the person disagrees.

Rational Emotive Therapy

Rational emotive therapy (RET) places more focus on increasing the client's awareness of present and future motivators of drug use rather than on past or unconscious factors. Based on the views of Albert Ellis (Ellis, McInerney, DiGuiseppe, & Yeager, 1988) that many psychological problems stem from irrational beliefs, the therapist attempts to dispel and correct misconceptions about alcoholism or other drug abuse held by the client. By continually questioning and confronting the alcoholic or other drug abuser with evidence, the goal is to help the clients realize their illogical and erroneous views. Alcoholics, for example, often react to such confrontation with thoughts like "I can't be alcoholic because I don't drink in the morning" or "I only drink wine and beer."

Later, if the alcoholic or other drug abuser admits that he or she has a problem, the goal is to help the client realize why he or she is drinking or using other drugs and to find alternative ways to reach their goals. RET also helps the client understand the need for abstinence and learn how to overcome irrational beliefs such as "I need alcohol to relax" or "I am too weak to handle the situation without a drink." Abstinence is difficult to maintain because of other irrational beliefs such as "No one will like me if I don't drink" or "I never have any fun without alcohol." The therapist tries to modify these cognitions by helping the client obtain disconfirming evidence.

Motivational Enhancement

Motivational enhancement training (MET; Miller, Zweben, DiClemente, & Rychtarik, 1995) emphasizes the use of nonconfrontational techniques to help alcohol and other drug abusers develop their own motivation for reducing their reliance on these substances. Behavior change is regarded as an active process involving cognitive appraisal by the client rather than as a passive process where therapists control outcomes. The goal is to have the client assume responsibility for wanting to make changes rather than to require change or to directly teach techniques for change.

An initial assessment battery determines the client's drinking or other drug use patterns, the client's performance on some neuropsychological tasks, results of the client's blood tests, and negative consequences of the client's drinking or other drug use. Feedback and explanations are provided to the client—and often a significant other—during the first of four sessions. In these few counseling sessions, the therapist tries to help the client recognize discrepancies between his or her current life situations and how he or she would like his or her life to be. The therapist is empathic and supportive. When the client shows resistance by arguing or sidetracking from the issue, the therapist does not challenge the client but instead rolls with the situation. By suggesting ways to change and encouraging the client to actively decide which route to take, MET helps the client develop self-efficacy or the belief that he or she can influence outcomes.

BEHAVIORAL APPROACHES

Behavioral orientations toward treatment of alcohol and other drug abuse view these behaviors as similar to any other learned behavior. Behavior followed by reinforcement will increase. Use of alcohol and other drugs can lead to desirable outcomes as diverse as peer acceptance, arousal and stimulation, release of tension, and lower anxiety. Continued use, especially if excessive, may develop into abuse and dependency so that the user no longer can control the drug taking. Absence of the drug produces negative consequences including physical discomfort and social ostracism. These adverse consequences then lead many to intensify their drug use to cope with their discomforts. Use of alcohol and other drugs that initially was motivated by expectations of pleasurable states now becomes compelled by hopes of relief from negative states.

The behavioral approach to treating alcohol and other drug dependency is based on principles of learning and conditioning theory, many of which were discovered with laboratory studies of humans and other animals. This approach assumes that behaviors such as use of drugs are sustained or reinforced by outcomes such as the physiological and psychological states they produce. Stimuli such as the physical and social context associated with these outcomes from drug use acquire the power to activate future drug use. The same processes should allow us to unlearn prior associations and habits or to develop new ones. Hence, one general strategy for treatment might be to attempt to remove these sources of reinforcement, drugs, and the associated stimuli that trigger the motivation to use them. This strategy could be supplemented by the reinforcement of alternative behaviors that interfere with drug taking.

Treatment Goals: Abstinence Versus Moderation

An emotionally charged issue is the question of whether the treatment goal for alcoholics and other drug abusers should be abstinence. The ideology of Alcoholics Anonymous (AA) and other self-help groups clearly insists on abstinence as the goal. Behavioral psychologists, on the other hand, have argued that more alcoholics and other drug abusers will be willing to undergo treatment if they are allowed to use their drug moderately rather than required to stop completely.

Some early clinical studies (Davies, 1962; Lovibond & Caddy, 1970) found evidence suggesting some alcoholics can achieve "controlled drinking," contrary to the views held by AA. These alcoholics seemed to function normally at work without relapse, even though they had consumed, on average, up to 5 oz of absolute alcohol daily, thus refuting the assertion that abstinence is a necessary goal for recovery.

Advocates of abstinence goals maintain that it is dangerous for recovering alcoholics to drink at all because they might lose control. Whether recovering alcoholics should drink, even at a moderate level, and whether they can drink moderately are separate questions. Behaviorists have insisted that the latter issue be resolved empirically by comparison of alcoholics treated under the two different criteria of abstinence and controlled drinking.

Controlled Drinking Controversy

The disease conception of alcoholism that held that alcoholics have to achieve abstinence before treatment can be successful was challenged by evidence of controlled drinking. In one major study using a randomized control group design (Sobell & Sobell, 1973), male alcoholics received treatment for 4 weeks in an inpatient hospital. Two experimental groups received a package of treatments that included blood alcohol content discrimination training, aversive conditioning, assertion training, and counseling; one group had a criterion of abstinence and the other a goal of controlled drinking. Two control groups received the conventional programs used at the hospital, again with one having a controlled drinking goal and one given an abstinence criterion.

At both the 6-month and the 1-year follow-up, the treated groups showed better improvement than the control groups. Importantly, the abstinent groups were no better than the groups that had been allowed to drink moderately, leading to the conclusion that alcoholics could achieve controlled drinking.

This study created a heated controversy and much research that did not resolve the issue. Some of the evidence conflicted because the severity of alcoholism may determine which goal works, with controlled drinking succeeding only for those with lower dependence and abstinence being more effective for those with severe dependence (Miller, Leckman, Delaney, & Tinkcom, 1992). The interest in controlled drinking as a treatment option declined after the 1970s. Abstinence now appears to be the preferred treatment goal.

Treatment Based on Classical Conditioning

Aversive conditioning is one method of treating alcoholism and other drug abuse. Based on classical conditioning, a major tradition of learning theory pioneered by Pavlov (1927), it involves a relatively passive role for the individual. In classical conditioning, a participant receives stimuli that have naturally positive (e.g., food) or negative (e.g., electrical shock) consequences in the presence of stimuli (e.g., a tone or light) that do not produce those effects. Through repeated pairing of these two types of stimuli, neutral stimuli such as lights or tones acquire the ability to elicit positive or negative effects similar to those created by food or shock, respectively.

Aversive conditioning pairs unpleasant stimuli with alcohol or other abused drugs on the assumption that eventually alcohol and other drugs will elicit aversive consequences that will reduce the desire to use them (Rachman & Teasdale, 1969). It is assumed that repeated pairing of drugs or stimuli associated with their use, such as taste and visual cues, with a negative or painful stimulus will make drug users want to avoid the drug in the future. External cues associated with drug use such as hypodermic needles, in the case of injected drugs, could similarly be paired with aversive consequences to create negative associations to drug use. The technique is not exactly a modern development. For example, Benjamin Rush (1745–1813) long ago observed that mixing a tartar emetic with rum produced a strong aversion to alcohol in a man who loved to drink (Jellinek, 1943).

One review (Wilson, 1987) of research on aversive conditioning concluded that the benefits of chemical aversion conditioning are low in comparison to the physical risks. Another study (Elkins, 1991) found that emetic conditioning has a success rate of around 60% in private hospitals. Since its introduction, research and practice with this method have declined substantially, especially as patients are not eager to accept this type of treatment where they risk physical harm if the noxious stimuli are too strong.

Treatment Based on Operant Conditioning

Another major tradition in learning theory, **operant conditioning**, holds a view of the learner as an active participant in behavior change. Trial-and-error behavior may be involved in which the learner comes to identify which responses lead to which outcomes (Thorndike, 1911). The outcomes serve as reinforcers (Skinner, 1938) that are contingent on the responses made by the individual. Alcohol and other drug use is similar to any other behavior in that it is reinforced by consequences of that behavior. The user experiences positive or pleasurable outcomes and begins to use more often or more heavily. According to learning theory, alcohol and other drug use should be reduced if it leads to negative consequences. Some treatment programs employ contingency management to reinforce substance abusers of many different drugs for abstinence, adherence to treatment goals, attendance, and compliance with medication. Vouchers exchangeable for retail goods and services function as reinforcers for patients meeting the goals of treatment and maintenance programs (Stitzer & Petry, 2006).

One treatment study (Petry, Martin, Cooney, & Kranzler, 2000) randomly assigned 42 alcohol-dependent veterans to standard treatment or standard treatment plus contingency management (CM), in which they earned the chance to win monetary prizes for having negative blood alcohol readings. Many more CM participants (84%) stayed in the 8-week treatment than those receiving only standard treatment (22%). At the end of treatment, 69% of those receiving CM—but only 39% of those receiving standard treatment—were still abstinent.

Social reinforcements from the patient's social network can reinforce either drinking and other drug use or sobriety. In one controlled study (Litt, Kadden, Kabela-Cormier, & Petry, 2007), 210 alcohol-dependent men and women from the community were randomly assigned to one of three outpatient treatments: network support, network support combined with contingency management, or control. Network support conditions increased behavioral and attitudinal support for abstinence as well as AA involvement. These changes helped improve drinking outcomes. After 15 months, both conditions involving network support had better outcomes than the control condition.

Treatment Based on Social Learning

Social learning theory (Bandura, 1977, 1999) emphasizes processes that allow alcoholics and other drug abusers to learn through observation of consequences to others. Seeing that reductions in drinking or drug use lead to desirable consequences such as social approval or better work performance can motivate a desire to curb these behaviors. By imitating other people who have successfully reduced their drinking or drug abuse, alcoholics and drug abusers acquire self-efficacy, the feeling that they can control these behaviors.

Cognitive–Behavioral Learning Treatment

This related approach views excessive drinking or drug use as a maladaptive and avoidance form of coping with problems. The goal is to teach active forms of coping that do not involve alcohol or other drugs when the individual is in situations that entail high risk for using these substances. Accordingly, this approach applies learning principles to teach alcohol and other drug users to modify their behavior by changing the outcomes or contingencies of alcohol or other drug consumption. In addition, they are taught alternative coping behaviors for reducing stress by techniques such as relaxation training and stress management. By mastering these skills, self-control develops. Instead of a unidirectional influence in which the environment controls the individual, they discover there can be a bidirectional relationship involving reciprocal determinism by which the individual's behavior can also alter the environment.

An investigation (Monti et al., 2001) of the effects of coping skills training combined with communication skills training compared outcomes with an education and relaxation control treatment in a 2-week program with 165 alcoholics. The skill training groups were less likely to report relapse days and reported fewer heavy drinking days at the 6- and 12-month follow-ups than patients in the control treatment. These improvements were correlated with more use of the prescribed coping skills, fewer cue-elicited urges, and more self-efficacy during a posttest role-play test.

FAMILY THERAPY

Family therapy, an approach that shifts the focus of treatment from the individual to the family, has grown rapidly since the 1950s. Originally developed for a variety of psychological problems, it also has been increasingly used for the treatment of the alcoholic family. There is no single type of family therapy because diverse orientations such as psychodynamic and behavioral approaches exist. They differ from the view of Al-Anon, the self-help group described in the preceding chapter, which regards alcoholism as a family disease. Al-Anon urges the nondrinking family members to detach from the alcoholic rather than remain as enabling codependents who might contribute toward continued drinking by the alcoholic.

In contrast, theories of family systems emphasize the dynamic interactions among family members and require a treatment program involving the entire family. Family therapists believe it is insufficient to treat only the substance abuser. If other family members know about the drug abuse, which in most cases involves alcohol, they are part of a system of interrelated members who interact with the alcoholic. Just as the alcoholic's drinking and behavior affects them, family members can in turn have a strong effect on the alcoholic.

Comparisons of interactions when alcoholics have been drinking with those that occur when alcoholics have not been drinking are a central goal. Families come to see how their alcoholic family members' drinking disrupts their interactions in harmful ways. Therapy focuses on changing family communication and interaction patterns that occur when alcoholics have been drinking to more constructive and positive behavior.

Psychodynamic Approaches

Ackerman (1958) was a pioneer in family therapy. Coming from a Freudian psychoanalytic orientation, which emphasizes unconscious intrapsychic conflicts and defense mechanisms as underlying alcoholism, he recognized the need to work with the entire family as an interrelated system in treating any type of psychological problem. Each member of a family system has a role, and boundaries or rules more or less define each member's function. When conflicts arise among family members, communication may break down. Family members may become defensive, anxious, and unable to deal with each other. The therapist must help the family overcome resistance and achieve a new balance of roles among members after its homeostasis has been disrupted by disturbances such as alcoholism.

Structural Family Therapy

Bowen (1974) also viewed many psychological problems as rooted in family relationships. Tensions between any two family members may spread to include a third member, a process called **triangulation**. When two persons have a breakdown of communication, one party may draw a third party into the conflict, someone who may take sides. This process may be repeated so that more interlocking triangles are created, until eventually all family members become enmeshed in the problem.

In the case of alcoholism, family members who have the greatest dependence on the alcoholic member are assumed to be the most overly anxious about the problem. This anxiety may lead to criticism of the drinker and emotional isolation from the drinker, factors that might increase the drinking, creating an escalating cycle of events. The family therapist's task is to interrupt and reverse this process by helping family members lower their anxiety and restore emotional contact with the alcoholic member (Bowen, 1978).

Despite clinical evidence of the usefulness of family therapy, the comparative effectiveness of different approaches to family therapy has not been determined (Kaufman, 1985), and controlled evaluations are rare (Thomas, 1989). One problem in comparing studies of family therapy is that there are so many variables in family composition such as marital status, number of children, living arrangements, and number of drinkers or other drug users in the family. Also, there is the generalizability issue of whether families willing to enter family therapy differ on other important factors from those who do not enter family therapy (IOM, 1990).

Behavioral Family Therapy

Marital family treatment programs involve highly structured sessions with both spouses present to work together on improving their relationship (O'Farrell, 1995). The first goal is to reduce abusive use of alcohol or other drugs. Couples discuss their feelings about the drug use of one member and may form written contracts about goals for their behavior. In later sessions, the focus is on repairing the marital relationship and increasing positive behavioral exchanges between the spouses. The long-term goal is to help prevent relapse and deal with other marital issues.

Behavioral treatment methods for family therapy (McCrady, 1989) emphasize the reciprocal reinforcement system between spouses. The development of improved positive communications involves the non-drug-using spouse providing reinforcement to the alcoholic or drug-using spouse for achieving sobriety. Spouses are taught how to reinforce abstention from alcohol and other drug use and to cope with spouses when they fail to abstain.

Studies comparing recovering alcoholics with nonalcoholic controls from the community suggest that marital therapy could be effective in improving the psychological functioning of the spouses and children. One study (Moos, Finney, & Chan, 1981) compared the family environments of alcoholics 2 years after marital therapy with those of nonalcoholic community controls. Two subgroups of alcoholics were identified: the remitted group that had maintained sobriety and the relapsed group that had not. Cohesive, expressive environments relatively free of conflict were found in the homes of both the remitted alcoholics and controls. In contrast, the home environments of the relapsed alcoholics were not cohesive, expressive, organized, or free of conflict. Remitted patients were similar to controls in some respects such as depression and physical symptoms, but they still were poorer in other respects such as more use of medical treatment and greater anxiety. The relapsed patients were poorest on all dimensions.

Follow-up studies (Finney & Moos, 1991, 1992) of the 83 members of the original sample of 113 alcoholics who were alive 10 years later upheld the findings observed after the first 2 years at the 10-year follow-up. For more than two thirds of the patients, drinking status and remission at the 10-year follow-up were at the same level as they were 2 years after treatment.

Alcoholics with more cohesive families, with lower life stress, and using active cognitive coping at the 2-year follow-up were more likely to have better 10-year outcomes. At 10 years, those who showed remission functioned at a level comparable to the matched community control group, and both were superior to the relapsed group.

Unfortunately, evaluative studies, especially those involving random assignment, have high attrition rates and inadequate follow-ups. As more research is conducted that is free from these methodological problems, a better understanding of the factors affecting the usefulness of family therapy will be achieved.

BRIEF INTERVENTION THERAPY

In addition to the major approaches to therapy already discussed, some forms of "brief intervention" may be effective, at least for some individuals. For example, a provocative study of 99 married male alcoholics (Orford & Edwards, 1977) suggested that conventional treatment involving abstinence for a randomly selected subgroup was no more effective than a single session of advice and counseling regarding the need to reduce drinking. Each couple in the advice group met with a psychiatrist who told them that the husband had alcoholism and should abstain from drinking. In the treatment group, couples were offered a yearlong program, including AA and access to prescription drugs to reduce withdrawal symptoms. By the end of the treatment, only 11 of the total sample were abstainers, and there was no difference between the advice and treatment groups.

Two brief interventions, face-to-face self-efficacy enhancement and a self-help booklet, were compared with usual care to see if they could reduce heavy alcohol consumption (Holloway et al., 2007). Participants were 215 of 789 inpatients, aged 18–75 years, in a large general hospital who screened positive for alcohol consumption for the past 7 days in excess of national recommended limits.

Changes were observed at the 6-month follow-up on measures that included self-reported alcohol consumption on a 7-day retrospective drinking diary, number of alcohol drinking days in the last week, and maximum units of alcohol consumed on any one day in the last week. The self-efficacy enhancement group and the self-help booklet group brief interventions both had greater reductions in self-reported weekly alcohol consumption than the usual care group.

Emergency rooms have employed the use of a standardized screening, brief intervention, and referral to treatment (SBIRT) intervention for patients coming for treatment of injuries. A quasi-experimental comparison group design (Academic ED SBIRT Research Collaborative, 2007) was used in which control and intervention patients who drank above the National Institute on Alcohol Abuse and Alcoholism guidelines for low-risk drinking were recruited at 14 different sites. Control patients received a written handout. The intervention group received the handout and a brief intervention, the Brief Negotiated Interview, aimed at reducing unhealthy alcohol use. Follow-up surveys were conducted at 3 months by telephone using an interactive voice response system.

Of 7,751 patients screened, about 26% exceeded the low-risk limits. Slightly over half of these patients consented to be in the study (581 control, 551 intervention), and 62% completed a 3-month follow-up survey. Those receiving a brief interview reported consuming 3.25 fewer drinks per week than controls and a maximum number of drinks consumed per occasion that was almost three quarters of a drink less than that of controls. Although the findings suggest that brief interventions can be effective in reducing drinking, self-reported drinking may not reflect actual changes. Furthermore, evidence on how durable such effects are is needed.

EARLY DETECTION AND SCREENING

For any type of psychological disorder, earlier detection allows for earlier participation in treatment. A major goal of alcohol and other drug treatment, therefore, has been to find ways of early detection in hopes that more severe problems can be prevented from occurring.

For instance, if individuals simply complete a short written questionnaire and self-diagnose the extent to which they may be having problems, it might help identify alcohol and other drug problems at an earlier stage. Such an instrument would be inexpensive and readily available so that large numbers of people could, if they wished, be tested. Early screening, if accurate, could facilitate early intervention.

The Michigan Alcoholism Screening Test (MAST; Selzer, 1971) was one of the first such surveys. It consists of 25 items dealing with questions about individuals' drinking, opinions of friends and relatives about their drinking, alcohol-related problems, and symptoms of alcohol dependence. This screening test has been effective with alcoholics in accurately identifying a high percentage. However, the test requires that honest answers be given, and it is easy to fake. Treated alcoholics already have come to admit or accept their diagnosis of alcoholism; however, whether the scale would be as successful in identifying alcoholics who are not yet in treatment is a different issue. A test with high sensitivity is one that can identify a high percentage of people who have alcohol problems. At the same time, the test needs to be specific in identifying alcoholics and minimize false positives where individuals are misclassified as alcoholics.

A review (Storgaard, Nielsen, & Gluud, 1994) of studies of the MAST found wide variations in validity for studies conducted over 20 years. This result may partly be attributed to the considerable variation in the prevalence of alcohol problems, diagnostic criteria, and examined patient categories. Factors with the largest effect on predictive values were the prevalence of alcohol problems, the diagnostic method against which the MAST was validated, and the populations to which the MAST was applied.

The Alcohol Use Disorders Identification Test (AUDIT) developed by the World Health Organization in 1992 to screen for alcohol dependence is a 10-item screening test that takes 2 min to complete. It is a paper and pencil test with three questions on the amount and frequency of drinking, three questions on alcohol dependence, and four questions on problems caused by alcohol. The typical procedure of a single cut-off score of 4, however, is called into question (Karno, Granholm, & Lin, 2000) by findings of one validation study. Another validation study (Doyle, Donovan, & Kivlahan, 2007) using two large national samples of *DSM-IV* alcohol-dependent individuals in the Project MATCH and COMBINE studies showed that the AUDIT actually assesses two separate factors, alcohol consumption and alcohol-related consequences.

PHARMACOLOGICAL APPROACHES

The use of drugs for the treatment of alcoholism has typically served to ensure the physical safety of intoxicated patients undergoing the adverse effects of withdrawal reactions during detoxification. Benzodiazepines such as Librium® or Valium® are used as an adjunct to relieve anxiety and depression in patients to facilitate their psychological treatment.

A different application of drugs such as disulfiram (**Antabuse**®) is to block the elimination of acetaldehyde, a toxic byproduct of alcohol metabolism by the liver. Antabuse® deters drinking by patients in treatment because alcohol consumption while taking this medication produces strong unpleasant physical reactions (Brewer, 1993).

Newer drugs such as naltrexone, an opioid antagonist that is believed to block the effects of alcohol (Kranzler, Tennen, Penta, & Bohn, 1997; Volpicelli, Clay, Watson, & Volpicelli, 1995), have shown promise in reducing craving and relapse among alcoholics. A review (Pettinati et al., 2006) of 29 double-blind studies based on 5,997 alcohol-dependent patients examined the effect of naltrexone on two outcomes, reduction of "heavy or excessive drinking" and abstinence. In 19 of 27 clinical trials that measured reductions in "heavy or excessive drinking," naltrexone showed an advantage over placebo, whereas only 9 of 25 clinical trials that demanded abstinence found an advantage for medication over placebo.

COMBINING BEHAVIORAL AND PHARMACOLOGICAL TREATMENT

The advancements in the development of effective methods of pharmacological treatment of alcoholism generated interest in combining behavioral and pharmacological methods to see if even greater benefits are achievable. The National Institute on Alcohol Abuse and Alcoholism funded a major investigation to compare different combinations of pharmacological and behavioral treatments for alcohol dependence in a multisite study (Anton et al., 2006) named *Combining Medications and Behavioral Interventions (COMBINE)* that involved randomized assignment of patients to treatments and placebo control conditions. Double-blind conditions were used so that neither the therapists nor the patients knew the treatment condition involved.

The COMBINE study treated 955 men and 428 women classified as alcohol dependent by *DSM-IV* criteria. The multisite study involved patients at 11 outpatient alcoholism treatment clinics across the United States. Most patients were White, middle-aged, educated, married, and employed, and about half of them had received prior treatment. On average, they drank on 75% of the past 90 days, with a mean of 12 drinks per day. To qualify for the study, men had to have 21 or more drinks and women had to have 14 or more drinks per day.

This ambitious study used two major forms of pharmacological treatment, naltrexone (ReVia®), which acts as an opioid antagonist that blocks the pleasurable effects of alcohol and reduces craving, and acamprosate (Campral®), which acts as a glutamate receptor modulator to restore neurotransmitter balance to alleviate the physiological and psychological distress experienced during withdrawal in the absence of alcohol.

Each drug treatment group was compared with a placebo group. In addition, each of those four groups also received one of two behavioral treatments, medical management (MM) or Combined Behavioral Intervention (CBI). The latter is a manual-guided therapy that is more intensive than MM. Manuals are akin to cookbook recipes in that they provide highly specific procedures, requiring less training to implement. CBI includes Cognitive Behavioral Training (CBT), and is modeled after community reinforcement and the couples therapy approach.

Overall, four groups received MM while another four received CBI. Of the four groups receiving each type of behavioral treatment, one also received both naltrexone and acamprosate, one received only naltrexone, one received only acamprosate, and one received neither drug. The ninth group received CBI without any pills or MM to represent the type of treatment that is widely used in clinics.

The program involved 16 weeks of treatment. Drinking behavior and clinical status were assessed at the end of treatment (Week 16) with follow-ups at Weeks 26, 52, and 68. The efficacy of pharmacological and behavioral interventions was assessed 1 year later in the COMBINE study (Donovan et al., 2008). Several outcomes were examined: percentage of days abstinent, number of days before first heavy drinking day, and overall improvement. Compared to controls treated with double placebos and no CBI, higher percentage of days abstinent occurred for groups treated with active naltrexone, without active acamprosate or CBI, with active acamprosate combined with CBI, and with CBI combined with double placebo.

All groups showed substantial reduction in drinking with a higher percentage of days abstinent than for those receiving placebos and MM-only conditions. Naltrexone also reduced risk of a heavy drinking day over time whereas acamprosate showed no significant effect on drinking in any treatment combination. Overall, patients had better drinking outcomes if they received MM with naltrexone, CBI, or both.

The hypothesis that combining pharmacotherapy with behavioral interventions will produce greater improvement in treatment outcome was not confirmed by the COMBINE study. It is possible that the improvements in the treatment groups stemmed from common mechanisms underlying the treatments rather than from the pharmacological interventions and the specific behavioral intervention (Bergmark, 2008).

EVALUATION OF TREATMENT PROGRAMS

The primary goals of clinical practitioners who conduct psychotherapy with alcohol and other drug abusers are not the same as those of research-oriented evaluators of treatment outcomes. Therapists, depending on their years of training and actual practice in dealing with drug abusers, may be convinced that an effective program does not need scientific evaluation. Practitioners who treat alcoholics and other drug abusers do not use controlled studies of the effectiveness of procedures or seek to verify the underlying processes responsible for any improvement in patients. Instead, psychotherapists rely on clinical experience and expertise and attribute any improvement to treatment. Although effective treatment indeed may occur in the absence of objective and rigorous evaluation, such evaluation is a primary goal for researchers. These investigators want objective evidence about treatment effectiveness, which can also help eliminate ineffective or even harmful treatments.

Many alcohol treatment programs follow counseling models of untested validity—or worse—that have been shown to be harmful or lacking in cost-effectiveness. The increased concern for evidence-based therapies calls for proof that treatments have been empirically validated and demonstrated as effective (Carroll & Rounsaville, 2007). Procedures used to meet this objective involve random clinical trials in which alcoholics are randomly assigned to a treatment or a no-treatment placebo condition. The procedures of a specific treatment are clearly defined and described in manuals for practitioners to follow. Therapists are monitored to determine how faithfully they follow these procedures. Outcomes are measured with valid and reliable instruments.

Controls

In practice, sound evaluation of therapy is difficult for a number of reasons. In its simplest form, it requires the use of a research design that compares the outcomes for a group of treated drug abusers (experimental group) with those for an otherwise comparable untreated group of drug abusers (control group). However, most treatment facilities do not permit clients to be assigned to untreated control groups, partly because they are convinced that their program is valid and partly because they feel they cannot ethically justify withholding treatment from persons in need.

Sometimes outcomes for treated alcoholics are compared with similar indices for alcoholics who did not receive treatment. For example, as Figure 14.1 indicates, some alcohol or other drug users may not seek or accept treatment. Still others may want treatment but be unable to afford or obtain it. However, if outcomes for treated groups are better than for these untreated groups, it is not proof that the treatment was the primary underlying factor for the differences. Because patients (as well as therapists) are not randomly assigned to the treated and untreated conditions, they are quite likely to be unequal in respects other than the treatment. Thus, some selective bias may be involved in determining who gets which treatment or who even gets treated at all. Another possibility is that the treated patients may be more motivated than the untreated ones. Or they may differ in social class, education level, or some other factor that affects drug use. This selective process is not wrong or undesirable, from a practical perspective. If, for whatever reason, those alcoholics who receive treatment show improvement, it is a desirable outcome. On the other hand, this bias in the

FIGURE 14.1   Who gets which treatment, if any, and what happens to them. Nonrandom samples make causal interpretation of outcomes difficult, especially if the attrition from different treatments is not comparable.

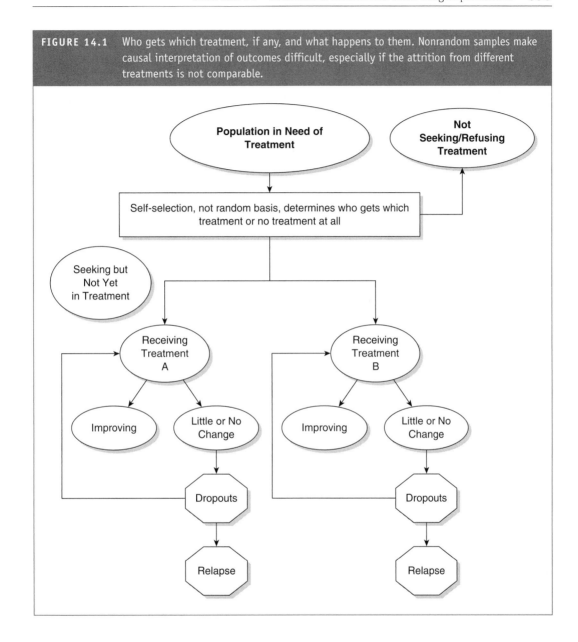

methodology jeopardizes the identification of the factors responsible for the treatment outcomes and limits the generalizability of outcomes.

Figure 14.2 presents a model illustrating how treatment outcomes are affected jointly by various aspects of the treatment such as its length, setting, or method and by client characteristics such as alcohol or drug use patterns, physical and psychological attributes, and social background. Additionally, the rapport or therapeutic alliance established between the

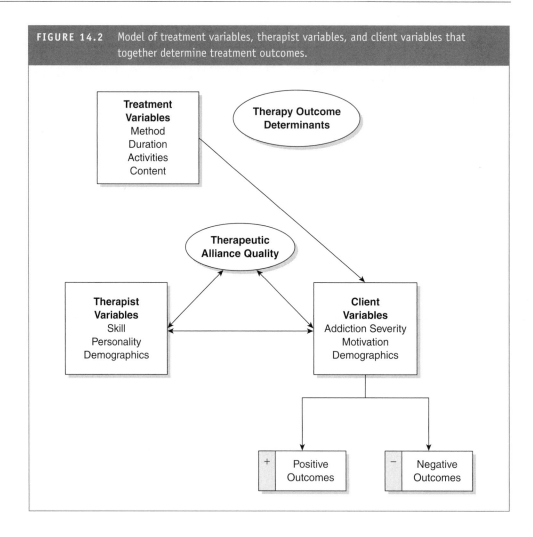

FIGURE 14.2 Model of treatment variables, therapist variables, and client variables that together determine treatment outcomes.

therapist and the patient affects the impact of treatment. A focus on one set of these variables to the neglect of the others yields an incomplete picture that can restrict the understanding of the factors determining success or failure from treatment.

Another problem in evaluating treatment is identifying the most effective aspects of a program. Treatments usually involve a package or set of components, as illustrated by Figure 14.3. A typical program may include individual and group psychotherapy, family therapy, exercise, nutrition, and educational films and lectures. If changes occur following treatment, can we determine how much each component contributed to the changes? It is conceivable that some of the components even could have had adverse effects that were masked by the beneficial effects of other components. It is rare to include any types of control groups that do not receive treatment to establish baselines for change over time. Without appropriate control groups, it is not possible to determine the type of effect each treatment component has on client status outcomes so that only the total effect can be established.

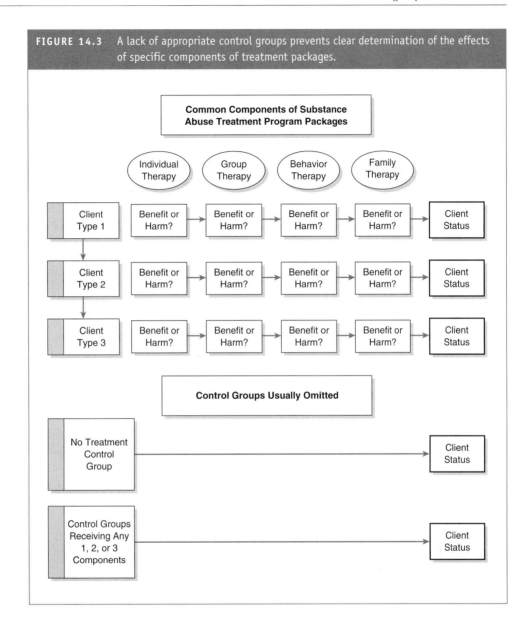

FIGURE 14.3   A lack of appropriate control groups prevents clear determination of the effects of specific components of treatment packages.

Attrition

A program will invariably have attrition where some clients drop out before completion, as shown earlier in Figure 14.1, which creates serious difficulties for program evaluation. Thus, if the more severe cases drop out, leaving cases that are more amenable to improvement, one may conclude erroneously that the treatment was the sole factor responsible for the success. If, for the two programs in Figure 14.1, Treatment A has a greater reduction in drinking than Treatment B, the conclusion that it was more effective would be incorrect if the heavier drinkers dropped out of Treatment A.

Long-term follow-ups, essential for evaluation, are difficult to conduct for alcohol and other drug treatment populations. Once released from treatment, those patients who have no families to return to or steady employment opportunities may become transients with little chance of being relocated later. If contacted, they may have little interest in participating in research, especially if they have suffered relapse from their treatment gains.

Assessment Reactivity

Starting from the intake evaluation and continuing through the course of a treatment program, participants receive assessments by numerous surveys to evaluate their status, help determine next steps, and inform therapists on the success of the treatment. Similarly, research studies require numerous assessments. There is increased concern that these assessments may have unintended effects on the motivation of participants (Clifford, Maisto, & Davis, 2007). On one hand, assessments might serve to motivate participants because they realize the staff is involved in their progress, but on the other hand, the assessments can be tedious and repetitive, which can lower motivation.

One experiment (Clifford et al., 2007) measured how two salient components of research assessments, specifically the frequency and comprehensiveness of interviews, might be related to alcohol use and treatment involvement. The study randomly assigned 235 participants from hospital-based alcohol outpatient and other substance abuse clinics to one of four assessment exposure conditions: (a) frequent-comprehensive, (b) frequent-brief, (c) infrequent-comprehensive, and (d) infrequent-brief. The poorest outcomes (i.e., more alcohol use and less treatment participation) occurred when assessment was infrequent and brief.

A second study with the same procedures (Maisto, Clifford, & Davis, 2007) examined reactive effects of assessment on drug treatment engagement across a 1-year follow-up. The results varied for different outcomes and for the first and second half of the year. More assessment increased participant presentation for outpatient treatment but had no effect on the number of days in outpatient treatment. Frequent assessment increased participation and number of days of attendance in intensive treatment during the first 6 months of follow-up, but the reverse was true in the last 6 months.

Evaluation Findings

A review (Maisto & Carey, 1987) of 26 published evaluation studies of alcoholism treatment avoided the problem of selective bias affecting the assignment of subjects to treatment conditions. The review looked only at either studies involving random assignment of clients to two or more treatment groups or studies in which clients in different treatment groups were matched on variables related to the outcome measures. A wide variety of treatment approaches were represented in this set of studies. The treatments usually were added as supplements to other prior forms of treatment. Furthermore, pretreatment measures were obtained before the treatments were administered. The evaluation was made from 1 to 19 or more months later, depending on the study, with the modal period being 12 months.

The review revealed that the type of treatment was not a factor in effectiveness. Observed improvements across the 26 studies were stable over the observed period of 1 to 2 years. One conclusion might be that improvement was due to a few common aspects embedded throughout the variety of methods used and that some of the differences in treatment were not having any effect. However, the lack of differences in improvement may reflect a "ceiling effect" in that the level of improvement was already approaching the maximum when these supplemental treatments were imposed. Another explanation involves mismatches of patients to the type of therapy. Treating all alcoholics with the same treatment method may have masked some genuine effects. Thus, if some alcoholics benefit more from one technique but others improve more with a different procedure, the overall results obtained with a single method applied to both populations would show a less impressive average effect.

A comparison (Miller et al., 1995) of therapy evaluation studies published since the late 1970s attempted to determine the effectiveness of different treatment programs by combining the results across studies. Each of the 211 studies that were acceptable for the analysis had to have at least two groups, an experimental (treated) group and a control (untreated) group or two experimental groups, each receiving a different treatment. In addition, a study must have used random assignment of patients to the different treatments to be included in the analysis. This requirement helps rule out other explanations for any differences between the treatment groups.

Results from all studies evaluating a specific type of treatment were combined to provide a measure of overall effectiveness that was based mainly on two factors. One factor, based on several indices, reflected the quality of the evaluation methodology as measured by low attrition and the use of objective methods, follow-up, collateral corroboration, appropriate statistical analyses, and replication. The second factor was based on whether the research design included a no-treatment control or not.

If a no-treatment control was used, the study scored +2 if the treatment was better than the control. If a no-treatment control was not used, the study scored +1 if one treatment was better than the other treatment. The basis for a greater weight when a no-treatment control group was included was that this design can inform if the treatment being evaluated was better (or worse) than no treatment. In contrast, the design without a no-treatment control group can only inform regarding relative benefits (or harm) of the two treatments. It cannot indicate if either of the two treatments differed from no treatment. Conversely, if the treatment being evaluated provided poorer outcomes, the study received a score of −2 when there was a no-treatment control and −1 when there was no control group. If no differences were obtained, the study received a 0 score. The scores on the two factors, method quality and research design, for each study were multiplied and totaled across all studies using a specific treatment.

The results showed that the most widely used procedures were among the lowest in demonstrated effectiveness. Thus, educational films, general alcoholism counseling, and psychotherapy—the major components found in the widely used general alcoholism treatment programs following the Minnesota model—were among those with the lowest scores. It must be kept in mind that this index does not prove they were ineffective; it means the studies did not convincingly show that they were effective. In contrast, studies evaluating brief intervention, social skills training, and motivational enhancement and community reinforcement were able to demonstrate high effectiveness. Because no controlled evaluation studies of AA exist, it was not possible to evaluate AA with this procedure.

The criteria and definitions used in this or any other specific evaluation of the effectiveness and methodological rigor of studies may not be acceptable to everyone. Also, conclusions based on cumulative results rather than on specific studies may be misleading. Another caveat about treatment evaluation is that lack of effectiveness after brief treatments may not mean that they will never work. Over half of the patients entering publicly funded treatment programs require multiple episodes of treatment over many years to achieve and sustain recovery (Dennis, Foss, & Scott, 2007; Dennis, Scott, Funk, & Foss, 2005). The process for many patients involves cycles of recovery, relapse, and repeated treatments, often spanning many years before stable recovery, permanent disability, or death is achieved.

DETERMINING HOW EFFECTIVE THERAPIES WORK

Over the course of therapy for alcoholism, improvements in alcoholic drinking may occur for many reasons, some related to specific procedures of the therapy and some due to nonspecific factors such as rapport with the therapist in creating a working alliance. If a therapy leads to better outcomes than those obtained for a no-treatment comparison group, it is still essential to determine the underlying process or mechanism.

Several strategies are suggested that may help achieve this goal (Longabaugh, 2007). One form of evidence used to support the view that specific aspects of a therapy contribute to reduced drinking involves mediational analyses. It is useful to look into the black box to observe if the putative agent of change (e.g., coping skills, spirituality, improved self-esteem) underlying the treatment is in fact present. For example, a treatment program teaching coping skills is assumed to help reduce drinking for those alcoholics who drink excessively when they are confronted with stress. However, without direct evidence that the therapy actually increased the level of coping skills, it is possible that the improvements were really due to some other factor. Factors unrelated to coping skills such as strong rapport with the therapist might have been responsible for the gains.

Many treatments may involve the same mediating processes but have different strategies to activate them. CBT might increase self-efficacy by teaching coping skills, where Twelve-Step treatment might reach the same goal by teaching reliance through self-help groups.

Moderational analyses provide another form of evidence that can test the validity of a treatment. One therapy should not be equally effective for all patients. In other words, "one size should not fit all." Some categories of patients benefit more than other patients from most therapies. For example, a therapy focusing on enhancing coping skills should work better for those lacking these skills than for those who already have them.

Choosing Among Therapies

An approach that relies heavily on the use of standardized treatment manuals has not yielded clear evidence that they are highly effective or that any one method is superior to alternative methods (Morgenstern & McKay, 2007). This model assumes that alcohol-dependent patients will respond in a uniform and linear fashion over the course of treatment, but the evidence shows there are large individual differences in patient responsiveness even when therapists adhere strictly to standardized treatment manual protocols. There is a need for a dynamic rather than static conceptualization of change in behavioral treatments for addiction that must consider the relationship and interactions between the patient and the therapist in addition to the specific procedures in a therapy. Since many different therapies yield comparable results, features that are common to them, rather than specific mechanisms of each technique, may be responsible for much of the individual changes.

Client Views of "What Works"

Among clients who do improve, it not always clear what processes occur during treatment to produce benefits. It may be instructive to study the perceptions of clients about their experiences during treatment, recognizing, though, that these subjective views may not always be accurate and could reflect biases of retrospective memory. One study using this approach (Orford, Hodgson, Copello, Smith, & Black, 2005) interviewed clients with positive changes in their drinking during the previous 3 (n = 211) or 12 (n = 198) months to identify their attributions for improvement. Unfortunately, the study did not analyze explanations from clients who relapsed or showed lack of improvement.

Interestingly, even after treatment, many clients emphasized the role of the life experiences that propelled them to seek or enter treatment initially. It might have been a dissolving marriage, a run-in with the law, problems at work, social pressure, or other factors. Because these circumstances preceded treatment, treatment evaluations do not consider their role on treatment processes, but these events may affect the extent to which treatment is effective (Willenbring, 2007).

Once into treatment, eventually several factors came into play. Counseling and education sessions during treatment led them to *think differently* about alcohol. While some clients emphasized the impact of learning new information (e.g., physical harm of drinking), others described their realization that their drinking was having harmful effects on others.

In addition, during treatment, they recalled that they began to *act differently*. Some reflected on their reduced drinking and described tactics they used to achieve these outcomes. Others did not specifically refer to reduced drinking but described behavioral changes that indirectly reduced drinking, such as spending more time doing non-drink-related activities and with nondrinking friends than with former drinking companions.

Over the course of treatment as these cognitive and behavioral changes occurred, clients realized that their lives had improved, which many attributed to changed attitudes about alcohol and reduced alcohol use. However, some clients credited changes to self-direction, feeling that treatment had not been a factor.

Irrespective of the type of explanations clients made, almost all who succeeded in reducing drinking were aware of improvements in their lives such as better family relationships, improved finances, better health, and more energy. Many felt greater confidence, were less arrogant, assumed more responsibility, and felt they had a sense of purpose and clearer objectives for their lives.

They acknowledged the influence of friends and family was an additional factor that enhanced their changes during treatment. They felt that treatment helped produce more open communication with their loved ones. Friends and family provided support for reduced drinking and in some cases took over control of the client's drinking.

Thus, treatment does not operate in isolation. A fuller understanding of how change is produced must recognize that formal treatment is only part of a myriad of interacting events and processes that occur outside of the clinic. In addition to treatment per se, change is affected by the client's increased awareness of accumulating harms and triggering occurrences for drinking, supports and pressures from other people to reduce drinking, and factors that affect their degree of engagement in treatment programs.

MATCHING PATIENTS AND TREATMENTS

All alcohol- and other-drug-dependent individuals do not have the same patterns, causes, or consequences of use. Moreover, individual differences exist in the types of treatments acceptable to different drug-dependent persons. Consequently, a given treatment method might be effective for some patients but prove useless for others. Accordingly, the strategy of treatment "**matching**" was developed in the hope of providing different types of alcoholics with treatment methods best suited for them (Miller & Hester, 1986). There is nothing to be gained from trying to treat patients with a specific program if they probably will not benefit from it. If treatment resources are scarce, as is usually the case, matching might allow someone who could benefit from a specific treatment to have a better chance of receiving it.

One study (Longabaugh, Wirtz, Beattie, Noel, & Stout, 1995) compared three different treatments over 18 months—brief broad spectrum (BBS), extended relationship enhancement (ERE), and extended cognitive-behavioral (ECB)—with 188 patients randomly assigned to one of the three treatments. The ERE treatment was significantly more effective in increasing abstinence of patients entering treatment with a network unsupportive of abstinence or with a low level of investment in their network whereas the BBS treatment was more effective for patients with either (a) both a social network unsupportive of abstinence and a low level of network investment or (b) high investment in a network supportive of abstinence. Outcomes for the ECB condition were neither as good as for those who were matched nor as bad as for those who were mismatched to the different exposures of relationship enhancement. This suggests that dose of relationship enhancement should be determined after assessing patient relationships.

Project MATCH, a major evaluation study funded by the National Institute on Alcohol Abuse and Alcoholism at a cost of $27 million, required more than 8 years to conduct (Project MATCH Research Group, 1998). Using *DSM-IV* criteria for dependence (APA, 1994), 774 inpatients and 952 outpatients, mostly male, were randomly assigned to one of three individually administered treatments, **cognitive-behavioral coping** skills, Twelve-Step facilitation treatment (which involves aspects of AA), and **motivational enhancement therapy (MET)** as diagrammed in Figure 14.4.

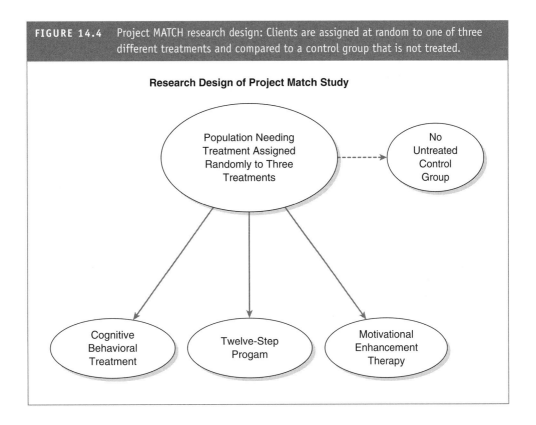

FIGURE 14.4   Project MATCH research design: Clients are assigned at random to one of three different treatments and compared to a control group that is not treated.

The cognitive-behavioral therapy program teaches alternative coping and problem-solving techniques for dealing with situations that represent high risk for drinking. Twelve weekly sessions were used to teach coping skills for dealing with intra- and interpersonal problems, including anger, depression, and anxiety. Active participation, accompanied by modeling and practice with positive corrective feedback, were essential aspects of the program.

The Twelve-Step facilitation program was a structured program based on the Twelve Steps of the well-known AA program. Indeed, patients were encouraged to also attend AA meetings. The emphasis of this program of 12 weekly sessions was on a view of alcoholism as a spiritual as well as a medical disease.

Finally, motivational enhancement therapy involved four sessions distributed over 12 weeks that used techniques for initiating immediate internally motivated changes. Two sessions were directed toward identification of present and future plans and toward instigating motivation for change. Two final sessions offered reinforcement from the therapist for progress and assessment with feedback to the client.

Demonstration of matching would refute extreme views about treatment that everything works about equally well or that one treatment is superior, two views that are probably myths (Miller, 1990). It was hypothesized that one type of treatment would work well for some alcoholics but another type of treatment would be better for others. For example, both cognitive-behavioral and Twelve-Step therapies were expected to work for patients with higher alcohol involvement because they needed the more extensive treatments. Motivational enhancement was hypothesized to be best for clients with high conceptual ability and low readiness to change.

Clients were evaluated at intake and every 3 months from the 3rd to the 15th month on drinking, psychological functioning, and consequences of drinking. Compliance of patients was extraordinarily high, and they all received substantial amounts of treatment. Although a high percentage of clients showed improvement in achieving abstinence (National Institute on Alcohol Abuse and Alcoholism, 1997), the overall success rates did not significantly differ across methods. Unfortunately, for the matching hypothesis, the predicted interactions between treatment method and type of alcoholic were not found. However, unexpectedly, psychiatric severity interacted with treatment. Thus, for low-psychiatric-severity outpatients, Twelve-Step facilitation treatment led to more abstinent days than did cognitive-behavioral therapy, but there were no differences between methods for outpatients with high psychiatric severity.

On the positive side, all groups showed improvements for most of the first year, suggesting that lack of differences between treatments might have reflected a ceiling effect in which there was little room for improvement. However, by the end of the year, a high percentage of patients relapsed according to the definition of using alcohol again. But when measured by the number of abstinent days, large increases occurred between the beginning and the end of the treatment.

Critique

A no-treatment control group was not included in the research design, but the researchers held that the improvement from baseline to follow-up points was so pronounced as to leave little doubt that all the treatments worked but equally well. Still, having a no-treatment control would have been worthwhile because some improvement may occur without formal treatment. All of the gains in the treated groups may not be attributable to specific treatments because some remission may occur over the duration of the treatment.

A key methodological procedure was the random assignment of patients to the type of treatment, a design feature that can be viewed as either a strength or a weakness of the study. Under typical procedures, different types of persons may be selectively attracted to different types of programs. However, under such conditions, rates of success cannot be clearly attributed to the nature of the program because the types of clients attending each type of program also would differ. The program with the highest success might just happen to have fewer severely impaired drinkers, and these drinkers might have done just as well even if they had received one of the other types of treatment.

Random assignment of patients to treatment method avoids this problem of interpretation of findings because it prevents self-selection into different treatment by patients. On the other hand, patients who might have strong preferences for one type of program but who are assigned to a different type may not do as well as they might do if they are allowed to receive their preferred type of treatment. Although randomized assignment is scientifically necessary and justifiable, in the real world patients are not randomly assigned to treatment. They often select methods in which they have faith and expect to have success. When treatments are randomly assigned, many alcoholics may not have confidence in the efficacy of the method to which they were assigned and consequently not do as well. The possibility that some self-selection occurred is consistent with findings of a secondary data analysis (Cutler & Fishbain, 2005) of 1,726 MATCH participants that compared improvement for participants who completed the 12-session program with that of participants who dropped out early. Surprisingly, a group that dropped out before receiving a single session showed improvement comparable to those who completed the entire program, and a group that dropped out after only one session had the worst outcome.

Although the Project MATCH participants were diverse, it cannot be claimed that the study included all types of alcoholics. It is conceivable that patients with different attributes and backgrounds may have responded differently to the treatments. For example, most of the patients were male, and different results may have occurred with female patients.

Despite the thoroughness and magnitude of the study, it compared only three treatment methods. It is conceivable that there might have been support for the matching hypothesis if other methods had been included or if other delivery systems had been used (e.g., group vs. individual or inpatient vs. outpatient). The outcomes were assessed after 1 year only; evaluation after a longer period might yet support the matching hypothesis. Over time, relapse rates, for example, might differ for different treatment methods and different types of alcoholics.

A review of studies on matching (Mattson, 1995; Mattson & Allen, 1991) concluded that the improvements in treatment outcomes were modest, typically around 10%, and that the best variables to use for matching are not yet known. In view of these findings, many treatment providers may not expend the added expense and time to provide more individualized treatment programs.

ALCOHOLICS WITH DUAL DIAGNOSES

When patients with alcohol use disorders also have psychiatric complaints, several different situations may be involved: alcohol-related symptoms, alcohol-induced psychiatric syndromes, and independent psychiatric disorders co-occurring with alcoholism. Alcohol abuse mimics psychiatric disorders by producing symptoms of depression, anxiety, psychosis, and antisocial behavior during intoxication and withdrawal that can persist for weeks following abstinence. Misdiagnoses that the patient has major depression, panic disorder, schizophrenia, or antisocial personality disorder can lead to failure to treat alcohol abuse or dependence.

Patients who present symptoms indicative of both psychiatric problems and substance use problems are observed regularly in acute mental health clinics. It is the task of the therapist to diagnose whether the patient has a major psychiatric problem that requires treatment or whether the substance abuse is the primary problem but one that contributes to his or her mood disorders.

Treatment Approaches

Whereas alcohol treatment facilities typically focus on alcohol abuse or dependence, they typically do not consider the appropriateness and effectiveness of these treatments for patients who also have a psychiatric disorder. Likewise, treatments for psychiatric disorders are not typically assessed in terms of their validity for patients who also have alcohol use disorders (Petrakis, Gonzales, Rosenheck, & Krystal, 2002).

Pharmacological Methods

Medication may be needed for alcohol dependents with a comorbid disorder. They may have difficulties with traditional alcoholism treatment and self-help groups because of discomfort in a group setting or with a treatment that involves confrontation. Moreover, patients with depression have thought disorders or slowed thinking that interferes with concentrating, learning, or completing treatment assignments.

Although medications may be beneficial for some comorbid patients, there are problems related to medication interactions and compliance issues. For example, disulfiram, which is used to block drinking, may precipitate several psychiatric symptoms, including delirium, depression, anxiety symptoms, mania, and psychosis (Larson, Olincy, Rummans, & Morse, 1992). Use of opioid antagonists such as naltrexone to treat patients with comorbid disorders may affect psychosis, affective or anxiety symptoms, or symptoms of posttraumatic stress disorder (PTSD).

Similar concerns exist in the use of pharmacological treatments for psychiatric problems when patients also have alcohol problems. Antidepressants such as the tricyclic antidepressants including desipramine and imipramine have been found effective in treating depression in alcoholics (Kranzler & Rounsaville, 1998), but it is unclear if they are effective in decreasing alcohol consumption. Selective serotonin reuptake inhibitors are effective in decreasing alcohol use as well as depressive symptoms (Cornelius et al., 1997) in patients with comorbid alcoholism and depression, but they may be effective only in certain subtypes of depressed alcoholics. Anxiety disorder treatment includes benzodiazepines, but they can become a source of addiction. In short, it is important to consider how alcohol may interact with the medication given for psychiatric problems.

Psychosocial Treatments

The recognition that pharmacotherapy alone may not adequately address all the treatment requirements of comorbid patients has led to specialized psychotherapy for dually diagnosed patients. Psychosocial treatments can help treat functional deficits in patients with chronic psychiatric disorders, patients with poor medication compliance, and patients for whom early abstinence may increase psychiatric symptoms, such as anxiety in patients with PTSD from the cessation of alcohol use.

A consensus (Petrakis et al., 2002) recommends that treatment for dual-diagnosis patients should occur in stages with immediate and short-term goals that may differ. Thus, although abstinence may be a long-term goal, patients with severe mental illness may not consider their substance abuse to be a problem. The immediate treatment goal here is the stabilization of the psychiatric illness, with subsequent work on their ambivalence about their alcohol use. Early abstinence from alcohol may lead to the emergence of symptoms of a psychiatric disorder, such as PTSD, which has been masked by previous alcohol use.

Psychosocial treatments for patients with dual diagnoses often require modification of standard treatment. For example, confrontation, a common and often effective technique in substance abuse treatment settings, may exacerbate psychotic thinking in patients with serious mental illness. They may see any lab testing for substance use as a sign of distrust.

Given the similarities and overlap among both mood or anxiety disorders and alcohol use disorders, treatment for comorbidity can be easier in some respects. Thus, cognitive behavioral therapy has been effective in treating anxiety disorders and alcohol dependence separately and should be easily integrated for patients with comorbid alcoholism and anxiety disorders.

On the other hand, Twelve-Step programs for the treatment of dually diagnosed patients may be less effective as those with severe mental illness may feel alienated, which will jeopardize regular attendance, regarded as essential for success from such programs.

OTHER DRUGS: TREATMENT OF ABUSE AND DEPENDENCY

Many of the issues related to the evaluation of alcoholism treatment apply to treatment of other drug dependencies. The first such large-scale study, the Drug Abuse Reporting Program (DARP), conducted in the early 1970s, included 44,000 clients in 52 federally funded treatment programs. Results showed that community-based drug abuse treatment reduced drug use and criminal behavior (Simpson, Chatham, & Brown, 1995).

In the late 1970s and 1980s, the Treatment Outcome Prospective Study provided longitudinal evidence up to 5 years on the effectiveness of federally funded treatment facilities (Ginsburg, 1978). This study involved 11,000 patients in 41 treatment programs in 10 cities. It expanded on the DARP by examining the relationship of patient characteristics, program environments, and available treatment services to outcomes. Results showed that treatment reduced use of heroin and other illicit drugs during as well as following treatment. The reduction in social costs related to predatory crime showed that the treatment was cost beneficial (Hubbard et al., 1989).

By the early 1980s, the "war on drugs" seemed to be winning, and drug abuse became a lower public and governmental concern. Around the same time, however, other drugs created new problems. Cocaine became cheaper, more widely available, and available in its more potent smokeable form, crack. Heroin use increased, and the use of needles for injections increased the risk of infection due to the rapidly rising HIV and AIDS epidemic (Fletcher, Tims, & Brown, 1997).

DATOS

The National Institute on Drug Abuse initiated a major study, the Drug Abuse Treatment Outcome Studies (DATOS), which tracked 10,010 drug abusers in nearly 100 treatment programs in 11 cities from 1991 to 1993 (Etheridge, Hubbard, Anderson, Craddock, & Flynn, 1997). Only about 75% of the original sample could be located after 1 year, and only about 70% of those were successfully interviewed.

The patients in different types of programs differed in their characteristics and drug use patterns. Most programs fell into one of four major types of drug abuse treatment: outpatient methadone treatment (OMT), outpatient drug-free (ODF) behavioral treatment, long-term residential (LTR) treatment, and short-term inpatient (STI) treatment, as indicated in Figure 14.5, which identifies the major methods for each type of facility. All four treatment modalities typically included supportive group therapy, urine monitoring during treatment, relapse prevention, and posttreatment involvement in self-help groups (Flynn, Craddock, Hubbard, Anderson, & Etheridge, 1997).

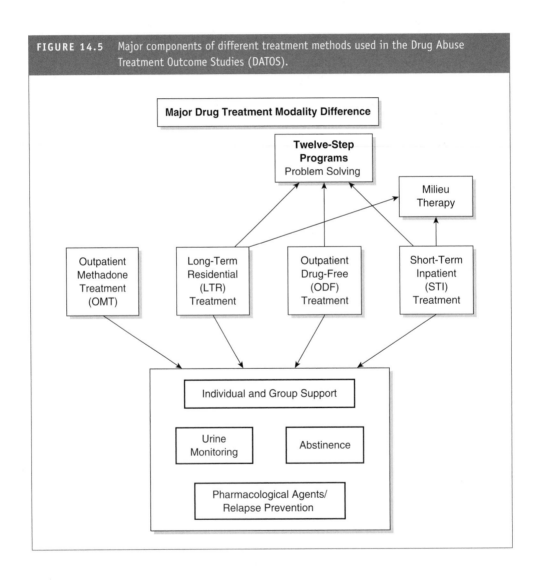

FIGURE 14.5   Major components of different treatment methods used in the Drug Abuse Treatment Outcome Studies (DATOS).

Overall, most patients were male (66%); 47% were African American, and 13% were Hispanic. Most of these patients were young but had been long-term drug users with the average age at first treatment being 29.5 years and many reporting having been addicted for 10–15 years on average before first entering treatment. The average age of a patient entering treatment was 32.6 years.

Although the treatments were similar in the percentage of male clients, they differed considerably on some other factors. OMT clients tended to be older and had longer treatment duration; LTR clients were least likely to be married or have health insurance. ODF clients were most likely to be referred by courts and to be African American or Hispanic. STI patients were most likely to be married and have health insurance and had the least likelihood of treatment lasting longer than 3 months.

Although patients were often described in terms of their primary drug problem, most of them were polydrug abusers; 97% had used alcohol, 95% had used cocaine, and 46% reported having used heroin before entering treatment. A random sample was selected for follow-up, and nearly 3,000 patients were interviewed a year later to assess drug use and behavioral functioning. Self-report was used widely, although urine testing also was employed so that gross distortions in reports of drug use could be detected.

All treatment programs were successful to some degree at a 1-year follow-up (Hubbard, Craddock, Flynn, Anderson, & Etheridge, 1997). Length of treatment was important because reductions in drug use were significantly greater for patients with moderate to severe problems if they were in treatment for 3 months or more (Simpson, Joe, Fletcher, Hubbard, & Anglin, 1999).

At the 1-year follow-up, there was reduced overall drug use. Methadone treatment reduced heroin use by 60%. In the follow-up year, only 27.8% of OMT patients reported weekly or more frequent heroin use, compared to 89.4% reporting heroin use prior to admission. Both LTR and ODF treatments resulted in more than 50% reductions in weekly or more frequent cocaine use at the 1-year follow-up with 1,648 cocaine-dependent patients. In addition, suicide attempts, predatory illegal activities, risky sexual behaviors, and other health-limiting behaviors declined while full-time employment occurred for most treatments.

The DATOS findings also showed that many drug abuse treatment patients received decreased health and social services (Etheridge et al., 1997). More than half of patients in all four types of treatment reported no aftercare services for medical, psychological, vocational, family, social, or legal problems. Thus, even as the need for these services increased, available services declined due to reduced funding.

The DATOS were an evaluation of treatment under naturalistic conditions rather than a controlled experiment. There was no untreated control condition, and the patients were not assigned randomly to treatment modality. Ethical and practical considerations precluded any use of randomized trials. Consequently, the results must be cautiously interpreted. Self-selection may have occurred, with the types of clients in the different treatments varying in some important way such as severity of dependency that could affect treatment outcome. Because there were no untreated controls, it is not possible to identify how much of the improvement was specific to the treatment components.

Drug Replacement Approaches

Programs to treat dependency on opiate drugs such as heroin include many components of programs used for alcohol dependency. In addition, a major strategy is to replace the drug under treatment with a less psychoactive drug. In the case of heroin, methadone is a component of many heroin treatment programs in which patients receive a standard dose of methadone on an outpatient basis. They also must undergo counseling, take routine urine tests, and refrain from use of any illegal drugs.

Properly administered, methadone has been effective in reducing use of heroin (Anglin & Hser, 1992), cutting down criminal activities related to heroin use (Hubbard et al., 1997), and improving health (Ginsburg, 1978). However, **methadone maintenance** has raised criticism because under this program, patients are still taking a psychoactive drug.

Other pharmacological approaches to countering the effects of heroin include the use of opioid antagonists such as naltrexone (ReVia®) and **LAAM** (levo-alpha-acetylmethadol), which works like methadone but requires lower doses. A random clinical trial (Anglin, Conner, Annon, & Longshore, 2007) compared 315 heroin users receiving LAAM versus methadone for a year. With LAAM there were fewer opiate-positive samples during clinic sessions. LAAM led to more abstinence during the last 24 weeks of treatment. LAAM participants were more likely to complete the program, and they were less likely to be discharged for arrest/incarceration. LAAM was more effective than methadone management in promoting retention and extended reduction in and abstinence from opiate use while in treatment.

SMOKING TREATMENTS

Quitting smoking is easy. I've done it many times.

—Mark Twain

Anyone can quit smoking for a short time. However, quitting for an extended period is much more difficult, and relapse into smoking is a common problem.

Measurement Issues

Comparing rates of quitting and evaluating smoking treatment success rates are difficult because of many measurement problems (Velicer, Prochaska, Rossi, & Snow, 1992). Estimates of rates of smoking cessation will depend in part on the temporal duration of the quitting. Shorter intervals should yield higher rates of success, but as the interval is increased, the success rate should diminish. The point prevalence rate refers to the level of quitting at a particular observation point that usually covers a brief interval. Quitters, using this criterion, would be a heterogeneous group because it would include smokers who have quit for a long period as well as those who have only quit recently.

Some quitters maintain continuous abstinence once an intervention starts. This abstinence covers a long period. Other quitters do not necessarily become abstinent when intervention starts but since then stop for a prolonged period. Because most studies of quitting do not make these distinctions about the duration of the cessation, comparisons across studies can be conflicting because different studies use different criteria of quitting. Not surprisingly, then, point prevalence rates of quitting are not highly related to health outcomes.

Treatment Approaches

Many techniques for smoking cessation are based on behavior modification principles such as fading or extinction. Other established behavioral methods involve conditioning procedures such as counterconditioning and aversive conditioning (Hajek, 1994). The treatments for smokers include diverse approaches such as acupuncture and hypnosis to reduce rapid smoking gradually and cue exposure.

Behavioral techniques based on operant conditioning theory involve sensitization and desensitization as well as contingency contracting. There is little evidence that any single form of behavior therapy is more effective than other forms (Hajek, 1996). In addition, nicotine replacement treatment can add substantially to the success of behavioral treatments; however, the addition of behavioral methods to nicotine replacement therapy is of little value.

Cognitive interventions help smokers identify reasons to quit and cues that trigger smoking, devise alternative coping skills, and provide social support for quitting. Minimal-contact approaches that emphasize self-help also have been developed (e.g., manuals or guides); they are inexpensive but of unknown effectiveness.

In addition to individual-level treatments, either in clinics or in self-help programs, there are community-oriented approaches. Unlike clinical approaches that deal with changing the smoking of individuals, community programs focus on reducing smoking by changing environments, media messages, and information campaigns.

Pharmacologic treatments (Haxby, 1995) such as nicotine chewing gum, lozenges, skin patches, and nasal sprays are effective, especially the nicotine skin patches and chewing gum. Nicotine replacement is acceptable in our society because tobacco is a legal drug that is widely used, whereas methadone is controversial because it is a replacement for an illegal drug, heroin. Nicotine still enters the body, but no smoke is involved. The harmful effects that nicotine produces should still occur. About 20%–25% of smokers receiving these adjuncts stop smoking at least for 6 months. However, given that about 10% of smokers are able to stop smoking without these aids, the net improvement is actually only 10%–15%.

Nicotine gum has an unpleasant taste that may deter its use. In addition, gum chewing is not always socially acceptable. Use of gum requires more effort and control by the smoker, whereas nicotine patches automatically release nicotine. Aside from remembering to apply the patches, the smoker needs to make little effort to receive the nicotine from patches.

The Food and Drug Administration approved bupropion hydrochloride (Wellbutrin®, Zyban®), a widely used antidepressant, for use in conjunction with nicotine gum and patches in 1997. In theory, it can help smokers deal with withdrawal by increasing dopamine neurotransmitter levels. A randomized, placebo-controlled clinical trial (McCarthy et al., 2008) compared four groups of adult daily smokers who received bupropion and counseling, bupropion only, counseling only, or none of these. Bupropion (in sustained-release pills) increased self-reported abstinence rates that were confirmed by physical measures at the end of treatment, relative to the placebo medication conditions. Medication effects on abstinence were more modest at 12 months. Counseling did not improve abstinence at any time point.

Different types of programs appeal to different individuals; what works for one person may not work for another, so care is needed in generalizing from overall success rates of different techniques. A match between the motivation level of the smoker for quitting and the type of intervention may be an important factor in success rates. Smokers who are willing to expend much time, effort, and money to quit may do better simply because they are more motivated to quit (Strecher, 1983).

Treatment of Smoking in Alcoholics

Among adult alcohol abusers, more than 85% also smoke at high levels (Abrams, Monti, Niaura, Rohsenow, & Colby, 1996). Furthermore, smokers dependent on nicotine have a higher likelihood of having alcohol use disorders (Breslau, Peterson, & Schultz, Andreski, & Chilcoat, 1996). Alcoholics who smoke are generally less successful in achieving and maintaining sobriety than are nonsmoking alcoholics (Hughes, 1993). Among alcoholics treated for both addictions, relapse to smoking is considered a risk factor for alcohol relapse. Similarly, nicotine dependence and the experience of nicotine withdrawal appear to be more severe in smokers with a history of alcohol dependence (Marks, Hill, Pomerleau, Mudd, & Blow, 1997). About half of nondrinking smokers (49%) succeeded in cessation, compared with only 7% of those who had been or were currently drinking (DiFranza & Guerrera, 1990).

In the past, treatment providers generally believed that smoking cessation was contra-indicated during alcoholism treatment. Attempts to require smoking cessation might jeopardize alcoholism treatment, either by increasing the clients' stress or by decreasing the effort that they could make toward achieving abstinence from alcohol. It was felt that smoking serves as an effective coping tool for dealing with alcohol cravings and with the stress associated with alcohol withdrawal or protracted abstinence.

On the other hand, given that relapse from one treated drug might be triggered by the use of nicotine or other drugs, it could be argued that treatment should try to treat all of a client's drug problems together. Smoking may trigger drinking (Shiffman & Balabanis, 1996). Thus, if only the alcoholism is treated, the smoking may increase the likelihood of relapse into drinking. In agreement with this argument, an analysis of Project MATCH data (Friend & Pagano, 2005) found that smokers whose cigarette consumption increased or remained unchanged were significantly more likely to relapse to alcohol use than those whose cigarette smoking decreased from baseline to the 15-month follow-up.

Combined treatment for both addictions may lead to better outcomes for addictions to both drugs (Hurt & Patten, 2003; Sullivan & Covey, 2002). On a neurobiological level, alcohol and nicotine act, at least in part, on the same brain pathways involved in reward and craving. Continued smoking or alcohol use may elicit or exacerbate craving for the other drug. Finally, treatments involving coping skill training may be more effective when the new skills are generalizable to both smoking and drinking.

Summary

A variety of treatment approaches have been developed for alcoholism. Treatment outcomes may not only depend on the treatment method and its setting but also vary with client variables such as drinking history, other forms of psychopathology, and demographic factors. Evaluation of treatment effectiveness in an objective and scientifically rigorous manner is difficult because random assignment to treatments and the use of no-treatment control groups are usually not feasible.

The issue of whether the treatment criterion should be abstinence or controlled drinking pits one of AA's central tenets about alcoholism against the scientific skepticism of the empirically oriented behavioral researchers who believe alcoholics could, in principle, learn to drink in moderation. This question, as it was posed, did not allow for a scientific answer, and the controversy has distracted researchers from more immediate concerns that can be evaluated empirically.

Some areas of overlap and agreement between rival conceptions of alcoholism may be overlooked because of differences in terminology. For example, the social learning focus on the acquisition of coping skills to reduce stress is not incompatible with AA, which urges alcoholics to make attitudinal and behavioral changes through its Twelve Steps, all of which can relieve stress.

The alcoholic family member's drinking disrupts family functioning and is harmful to the well-being of family members, but it is also possible that the family may often contribute to the alcoholic family member's drinking. Recognition of the reciprocal influence between the alcoholic and other members of the **family system** provides a fuller understanding of the complex interpersonal factors that must be addressed when treating alcoholism. Use of family therapy where the nonalcoholic family members undergo therapy with the alcoholic family member is growing and offers a promising approach.

Alcoholics vary in their psychological and sociological backgrounds, factors that may determine which treatment method, type of therapist, or amount of treatment will be most effective. However, attempts to match different types of alcoholics to the most appropriate treatment have not found much success. Most treatment methods seem to be effective for some alcoholics in comparison to no treatment, but overall, no single approach seems to be clearly superior to the others.

One view is that common features rather than specific aspects of treatment methods need further examination to determine how they may contribute to successful treatment. The working or therapeutic alliance between the patient and the therapist may play a key role in motivating the patient to be engaged in therapy. Processes that occur prior to actual treatment may play important roles in the patient's acceptance and participation of treatment, which, in turn, determine eventual likelihood of success.

Treatment for abuse of and dependency on other drugs such as heroin and cocaine can use similar principles and methods to those employed for alcoholism. The types of clientele at different drug treatment modalities vary along dimensions such as age, social background, type of drug, and severity of problem, so comparisons of their relative effectiveness can be misleading. In general, longer treatment is associated with better outcomes at a 1-year follow-up for all treatment modalities.

Smoking cessation success rates will depend in part on the temporal duration of the quitting; the shorter the interval being assessed, the higher the rates of success. Numerous smoking treatments exist ranging from pharmacological methods such as nicotine replacement to cognitive and behavioral approaches. No one method may be best, and a match between the type of treatment and the characteristics of the smoker may be an important determinant of success.

There are different views about the treatment of alcoholics who smoke. Some believe that smoking is the lesser problem and that alcoholics will be less successful in treatment if they have to stop smoking at the same time they are giving up drinking. Others believe that due to associations between the two behaviors, it is better to address the treatment of them concurrently. Alcoholics in treatment who continue to smoke will have cues from smoking that will trigger urges to drink.

Stimulus/Response

1. Behavioral approaches to alcoholism treatment seek to reinforce alternatives to the use of alcohol. What do you think would be some attractive alternatives, and how would you reinforce these other behaviors?

2. One method of cognitive behavior modification for treating drug problems is to change some of the cognitions that prompt drug use. What are some of these cognitions, and how do you think they might be changed?

3. Family therapy assumes that both the alcoholic and other family members are willing to work on the problem. What difficulties can you foresee in getting such participation, and how would you overcome them?

4. A 45-year-old intoxicated White woman seeks counseling because of her suicidal fantasies. Upon questioning her, you learn that about a week ago her longtime boyfriend left her. Prior to that event, she often worried that this relationship would not last. Do you think she is someone with a psychiatric mood disorder who has used alcohol as a form of self-medication or someone with an alcohol use disorder who is suffering from distorted ideation from her intoxication?

Later, her distraught boyfriend shows up, and you learn from him that he left her because she was drinking too much every day due to pressures at work. Does this new information alter your assessment?

Would your analysis be different if the patient was a 21-year-old male under similar circumstances (i.e., his long-term girlfriend has broken up with him)?

5. Paramedics bring to the emergency room a 31-year-old man who fell off his roof while making repairs. The ER physician smells alcohol on his breath and believes intoxication was a factor contributing to the accident. He wants to recommend that the patient undergo a blood alcohol test and possibly alcohol counseling, but he knows that some insurance companies will not cover treatment of injuries related to intoxication because the drinker was "at fault" for the accident. What would you do if you were the ER doctor?

6. Coerced drug treatment is rare for civilian populations, but it can be mandated for incarcerated populations. In fact, some research on the California prison system's drug treatment program claims some success. At one prison in San Diego, only 16% of its inmates who also completed an aftercare program came back into the system within 2 years of their release. In contrast, statewide, the recidivism rate is about 70%. Does this result mean that most of the treated inmates actually reduced their drinking or that they do not commit crimes (or do not get caught) at the levels of untreated inmates in other prisons? What follow-up study would you do to answer this question?

7. About 80% of the prisoners who are asked to attend drug treatment programs say they want nothing to do with them. But because the treatment program is involuntary, inmates who do not attend lose good-time credits and privileges. Do you feel the prisoners are justified in declining treatment, or do they not have the same rights as nonprisoners?

8. In a follow-up study of treatment programs for incarcerated felony offenders, 79% of participants were employed following their release. Only 35% were rearrested, compared with a national rearrest rate of 63%. Do you think that this evidence is *scientific* justification for mandatory treatment? Separate from your view on the scientific merit, what is your ethical view regarding coerced treatment of prisoners with drug addiction?

Relapse After Treatment of Alcohol and Other Drug Disorders

First the man takes a drink; then the drink takes a drink; then the drink takes the man.

—Japanese Proverb

One of the most frustrating and frequent obstacles to successful treatment and recovery is the high likelihood of relapse among individuals suffering from dependency on any drug. Estimated relapse rates within 6 months to a year following treatment for alcohol and smoking are discouraging as they have been found to be around 80% or higher (Brandon, Vidrine, & Litvin, 2007).

DEFINING RELAPSE

In part, the observed rates depend on how relapse is defined. For example, if relapse is identified as a return to any use following a period of remission, the rate will be higher than if the criterion is the first occurrence of an episode of heavy use. The rate will also be higher if a brief rather than a longer period of resumed use is required to qualify it as a relapse.

Widely different criteria for relapse make it difficult to make valid comparisons of results from different studies. For instance, a study (Maisto, Pollock, Cornelius, Lynch, & Martin, 2003) with adolescent alcoholics found that the relapse consequences varied with the way relapse was defined. Definitions based on whether "any" day of drinking occurred predicted the adolescents' current alcohol use disorder diagnosis. However, definitions that included "heavy drinking" (drinking any amount and having use-related problems) predicted higher average number of drinking days per month and more drinks per drinking day.

Lapse Versus Relapse

One useful distinction is between a **lapse** and a relapse (Brownell, Marlatt, Lichenstein, & Wilson, 1986). A lapse refers to a single or specific episode of a slip from sobriety. Implicit in the concept is the idea that individuals may experience a series of multiple lapses over a period of time. In contrast, a relapse is regarded by many as an all-or-none failure to abstain, rather than a process with intermediate degrees.

The line between lapse and relapse is not always clear or distinct. Each lapse could be viewed as a step further along the path toward the end of a cliff. Expectations of failure might occur after lapses that foster an attitude of futility. Following repeated lapses, future efforts to abstain may be abandoned. This linear view is a prevalent conception of relapse that inevitably culminates with a fall that could be regarded as the relapse.

A "positive" view of lapses considers that they can benefit patients by helping them identify what caused the slip and how it could be prevented in the future. If an episode of renewed use is seen as only a temporary setback, the individual can renew a commitment to overcome the undesired behavior so that eventual control may be achieved. Thus, relapse could be viewed as a process involving a series of periods of abstinence followed by lapses, renewed abstinence, and further lapses. This perspective allows for the hope that lapses could be informative and guide future attempts to maintain abstinence. Learning from one's mistakes helps prevent their recurrence.

A study (Marlatt, 1996) of a sample of lapses reported by alcoholics found that different types of lapses vary in their precipitating factors. The analysis suggested that situations involving high risk for lapse form a hierarchy, with the first level distinguishing between intrapersonal and interpersonal sources. A second level involved finer distinctions between five intrapersonal sources and three interpersonal sources. The intrapersonal type included coping with negative emotional states, coping with negative physical-psychological states, enhancement of positive emotional states, testing personal control, and giving in to temptations and urges while the interpersonal type included coping with interpersonal conflict, dealing with social pressure, and enhancing positive emotional states. At the third level of the hierarchy some of the second-level categories were broken down further such as the distinction between coping with frustration and/or anger and coping with other negative emotional states.

Gender differences were found in an analysis (Zywiak et al., 2006) of initial posttreatment relapses for a sample of alcoholics. Women were more likely to have negative affect relapses, and men were more likely to have social pressure relapses. Relapse conditions were also more consistent for men than for women.

CRAVING AND RELAPSE

One of the most commonly held beliefs about both lapses and relapse is that craving, or an uncontrollable urge, is a major precipitating factor for resumed use of alcohol and other drugs following abstinence. The mere sight or smell of alcohol and some other drugs as well as emotions, memories, and thoughts connected with their previous use might create urges, which then may trigger renewed use. There is no consensus on what craving involves, its role in relapse, or how to best measure it. In clinical and counseling settings craving is typically assessed with single-item questions as direct as "Do you experience craving?" Such indices are of unknown validity and unacceptable for research where multiple-item self-report measures with acceptable reliability and validity are essential. Craving can also be inferred from changes in behavioral performance and psychophysiological measures (e.g., blood pressure, salivation, respiration, or heart rate) during abstinence (Drobes & Thomas, 1999).

Craving, as defined by extremely uncomfortable physiological reactions to the absence of alcohol or other drugs, may occur during abstinence because prior prolonged use of alcohol and other drugs produces neuroadaptations in certain brain processes (Koob, 2006). Alcohol craving is associated with dopaminergic, glutamatergic, and opioidergic dysfunction in the brain reward system (ventral striatum including the nucleus accumbens). Alcohol-associated cues increased functional brain activation, which predicted an increased relapse risk, whereas high brain activity elicited by affectively positive stimuli was correlated with a decreased prospective relapse risk (Heinz, Beck, Grusser, Grace, & Wrase, 2008).

Craving also involves uncontrollable persistent thoughts about alcohol or other drugs, which resembles many aspects of obsessive-compulsive disorder, so it may be that both reflect some common neurophysiological mechanisms such as orbital frontal lobe function deficits, which limit impulse control (Anton, 1999). The maladaptive behaviors and high relapse rates of addicts may be "compulsive" due to dysfunction within inhibitory brain circuits in two frontal cortical regions (anterior cingulate and orbital frontal cortices; Lubman, Yucel, & Pantelis, 2004).

In contrast, a cognitive processing formulation (Tiffany, 1999) holds that craving is not always an automatic reaction but can involve the joint influence of expectations and automatic responses. Craving involves mental effort that may interfere with other activities. Thus, both an alcoholic trying to avoid alcohol and one seeking ways to obtain drinks may experience craving in which active cognitions are strong. In either case, these nonautomatic cognitive processes can strain cognitive capacity, especially if other life stresses are strong, and the alcoholic may resume or increase drinking.

A somewhat similar model of relapse based on self-control involves resource depletion (Muraven & Baumeister, 2000). It regards efforts to achieve self-control as analogous to exercising a muscle. These efforts can be very strenuous, especially when stress or negative affect is high, leading to fatigue that reduces the degree of self-control possible. Insofar as abstinence from drugs requires rigorous and exhausting self-control, increased lapses into drinking or other drug use may occur despite intentions to abstain.

A laboratory analogue of the model (Muraven, Collins, & Nienhaus, 2002) involved young male social drinkers who were told they would perform a beer taste test after which they would compete for a prize based on their performance on a driving test. First, on a random basis, they were assigned to work on either a 5-min arithmetic task or a 5-min thought suppression task (don't think about "white bears"). Since both groups expected to take a driving test after drinking beer (none actually did), they should have been motivated to minimize their beer intake to be able to perform well on the driving test. However, the thought suppression group consumed more beer and achieved a higher blood alcohol content than the control group that worked arithmetic problems. It was concluded that the mental effort of suppressing the thoughts of white bears "depleted" their ability to control the amount of beer they drank. Similar findings occurred in other experiments using different tasks (Ostafin, Marlatt, & Greenwald, 2008).

Evidence on Relationship of Craving to Relapse

Past studies have found only an overall modest correlation of craving with consumption of different drugs according to one review (Tiffany, 1990). The general assumption that subjective cravings are invariably associated with increased drug use was not upheld and implies that cravings are not necessary or sufficient for drug use (Singleton & Gorelick, 1998).

The role of conscious desire or craving was not a major self-reported cause of relapse among more than 1,600 patients with a variety of addictions, including alcohol, cocaine, and alcohol with a drug other than cocaine in a primary rehabilitation center (Miller & Gold, 1994). Relapse was not related to conscious craving, and it was rarely the primary reason given for relapse. These findings are consistent with the view that drug use is a highly ritualized and automatic behavior and thus relapse can occur without conscious thoughts or distinct craving states.

However, other research found that craving can contribute to relapse. In a prospective study (Bottlender & Soyka, 2004), 103 alcohol-dependent patients were interviewed at the start and end of outpatient treatment, as well as 12 months later. About a third of the patients relapsed during the treatment phase, and they had significantly higher craving as shown by a measure of obsessive-compulsive disorder completed at the start and at the end of treatment. They had higher scores on the subscales "obsessions" and "drinking control and consequences" compared to abstinent patients.

Craving was also found to predict relapse among 218 alcohol-dependent patients admitted to residential treatment (Gordon et al., 2006). The number of days of craving reported 1 week prior to discharge predicted the likelihood of a return to alcohol use at the 3-month follow-up.

Perhaps two types of relapses exist, those involving craving and those that do not. Furthermore, the likelihood that cravings are reported depends partly on the sensitivity or awareness of the individual as well as his or her own beliefs about the relationship between craving and relapse. Thus, self-fulfilling prophecies may occur for individuals with strong beliefs that craving increases relapse. The likelihood of craving being reported in conjunction with relapse may also depend on the specific situation. For example, when there are many competing background stimuli, craving may not be as readily noticed as in circumstances with less distraction.

Retrospective Evidence on Relapse

Interviews with alcoholics (Ludwig, 1986) reveal their phenomenological experiences about the nature of the Pavlovian "bells" that triggered their relapses. Only 11 of the 150 alcoholics could not identify any "bell," with 71% reporting one or two cues. Social situations and internal tensions were prominent. Also mentioned were external stressors, mealtimes, depression, music, and alcohol advertisements. In addition, individuals may have idiosyncratic cues such as reading in the bathtub or plowing the garden in the spring. Thus, alcoholics cite a wide variety of internal and external cues that trigger their renewed drinking. However, caution is necessary because some answers might be excuses made in attempting to justify their relapse (e.g., all the stress "made me do it").

Self-reported causes of relapse were identified in more than 300 individuals with a variety of addictions, including nonpharmacological problems (Cummings, Gordon, & Marlatt, 1980). Negative emotional states such as depression or anger were found in about 35% of cases (Marlatt & Gordon, 1985). This factor accounts for more than one third of the relapses not only among alcoholics but also among smokers, gamblers, and overeaters, as well as among a somewhat lower percentage of heroin addicts. Other major causes were interpersonal conflict (16%) and social pressure (20%). A small percentage of lapses involved drinkers testing their personal control or "willpower" by placing themselves in risky situations. This taxonomy treated categories as mutually exclusive, but there is evidence that multiple determinants, internal and external, rather than a single factor, precipitate relapse for both adults (Tate, Brown, Unrod, & Ramo, 2004) and adolescents (Ramo, Anderson, Tate, & Brown, 2005).

A taxonomy that allows for more than one precipitating factor was developed using information about the first relapse after treatment from 160 adults and 188 adolescents in substance abuse and psychiatric treatment who were followed after discharge for up to 18 months (Ramo & Brown, 2008).

Table 15.1 shows that adults were most likely to relapse in negative intrapersonal states (66.9%) with most involving (95%) frustration/anger or depression. For other intrapersonal states, adults were most likely to relapse when coping with urges to use in either the presence (55%) or the absence (26%) of cues. Similarly, negative intrapersonal (64.4%) and other intrapersonal (86.7%) states were frequent for adolescents. But for other intrapersonal states, adolescents were most likely to relapse when experiencing a *positive* emotional state (41%) and when tempted by cues (37.2%).

The primary differences that occurred were that adults were more likely than adolescents to relapse when experiencing a negative physiological state (25% vs. 9%), while adolescents were more likely to relapse when experiencing social pressure either directly or indirectly (70% vs. 46%). The findings supported expectations that adults would relapse more from negative physiological states than from social pressure because they might be more likely to be alone when they relapse. The opposite pattern was expected for adolescents where social pressure should be more likely, and although they experience negative physiological states, they may not view them as entailing high risk for relapse to the same extent adults do.

TABLE 15.1   Taxonomy of relapse characteristics for adults and adolescents in the 18 months after alcohol/other drug treatment.

Relapse Category	Adults ($n = 160$)	Adolescents ($n = 188$)
Negative intrapersonal state	**66.9**	**64.4**
Coping with frustration/anger	30.0	16.0
Coping with fear	2.5	0.5
Coping with depression	14.4	14.9
Coping with boredom	3.1	16.0
Concern about doing something (pressure, anxiety)	3.1	4.8
Anxiety	11.3	10.1
Concern for feeling like a failure	1.9	1.6
Other	0.6	0.5
Negative physiological state	**25.6**	**9.0**
Other intrapersonal state	**95.0**	**86.7**
Enhancing a positive emotional state	8.8	41.0
Test personal control	3.1	6.4
Given in to temptations in the presence of cues	55.0	37.2
Given in to temptations in the absence of cues	26.3	1.6
Other	1.9	0
Interpersonal	**30.0**	**36.2**
Coping with frustration/anger	15.6	17.0
Feeling criticized	0.6	3.2
Feeling rejected	2.5	2.7
Disappointment in a person	4.4	1.1
Tense around others	5.6	6.4
Nervous/uplight around the opposite sex	0.6	3.7
Other	0.6	2.1
Social pressure	**45.6**	**70.2**
Direct (e.g., an offer)	28.8	44.7
Indirect (e.g., cues but no offer)	16.9	25.5

Source: Based on "Classes of Substance Abuse Relapse Situations: A Comparison of Adolescents and Adults," by D. E. Ramo and S. A. Brown, 2008, *Psychology of Addictive Behaviors, 22*(3), pp. 372–379.

Note: Data for the five major relapse contexts are given in bold.

Limitations of Retrospective Self-Report

Evidence from retrospective self-report about the conditions and frequencies of resumed use following abstinence has problems, as memory is often inaccurate, even if unintentional. In addition, self-report can be distorted by attempts to avoid looking bad. That is, someone who has experienced a lapse might find that reporting stress and negative emotions as causes of lapses are acceptable as extenuating excuses. In contrast, the admission that the lapse stemmed from the discomfort from not drinking or using other drugs might be seen as a sign of weakness and hence be suppressed. Furthermore, these states may overlap, and alcoholics and other drug abusers may confuse them with each other.

Self-reports can also give an incomplete picture because they account for only episodes that involve conscious awareness. If, however, many lapses are of "variants of absentminded behavior" (Tiffany, 1990, p. 163) involving automatic or conditioned responses, self-reports will not detect them. One solution is the use of probe questions in an interview to increase recollection of subtle factors; however, the danger is that when asked, people may "invent" seemingly plausible accounts for why they lapsed. These reports may not be valid reflections of the actual processes.

Prospective Evidence on Relapse

Studies with a prospective orientation obtain measures of client behavior at varying points from the end of a treatment program up to the time of relapse. Factors that are correlated with relapse are identified. Prospective studies have problems with self-report that differ from those for retrospective studies. The act of thinking about experiences while they are occurring can be reactive and distort or disrupt ongoing processes and outcomes.

A review of studies (McKay, 1999) using prospective designs and near real-time measures found overall results were similar to those from retrospective methods regarding the factors involved with alcohol relapse. Major factors were negative affect, craving, lack of coping, and interpersonal problems. However, the two studies that made direct comparisons of retrospective data to either prospective or near real-time reports had mixed agreement.

The use of ecological momentary assessment (EMA) in which clients use beepers and palm-top computers to record near real-time information about the setting, urges, mood, and coping during or shortly after a lapse offers the advantage of avoiding reliance on retrospective memory (McKay, Franklin, Patapis, & Lynch, 2006). However, an important caveat is the effort involved in concurrent record-keeping might interfere with or distort naturally occurring behaviors.

EMA has been used to study smoking lapses. In one cessation program (Shiffman et al., 1997) smokers completed computer records of their lapses, which were later compared with retrospective accounts elicited 12 weeks after treatment. Recall of lapses was quite poor, and in comparison to the near real-time records, participants overestimated their negative affect and the number of cigarettes they had smoked during the lapse.

In another study (Shiffman et al., 2007) with 214 smokers in a cessation program, lapses were examined in relation to high-lapse-risk situations such as negative affect, arousal, socializing with others, the presence of others smoking, and consumption of coffee and alcohol. The results show wide individual differences in the situations where lapse occurred. Only negative affect predicted the first lapse but only when compared to EMA records and not when examined in relation to questionnaire responses.

One study (Catley & O'Connell, 2000) examined EMA reports made by 41 smokers who recorded data about their smoking as it occurred in daily life during the first 14 days of quitting. The analysis found that only 6% of the lapses could be considered "absent-minded lapses," and most participants were well aware of their desire to smoke and the difficulty of resisting urges. However, some smokers may have made attempts to justify absent-minded relapses because they knew they would have to later report their experiences.

MODELS OF RELAPSE

Different approaches for preventing relapse reflect different assumptions about the factors responsible for relapse. We will first examine conditioning models, which emphasize automatic or involuntary aspects of relapse and employ relatively passive methods for prevention such as cue extinction and pharmacological methods.

Classical Conditioning Models

According to the **classical conditioning** paradigm (Pavlov, 1927), stimuli that are originally neutral as cues for specific responses may come to acquire the power to elicit these responses. Thus, the well-known experiments of Pavlov with laboratory dogs showed that the presentation of stimuli such as a light or tone repeatedly in association with food powder came to elicit salivation. Such a light or tone was initially incapable of causing salivation, which is an unconditioned response (UCR) to the unconditioned stimulus (UCS) of food. But by pairing these stimuli that are unrelated to food frequently with the presentation of food, these stimuli became conditioned stimuli (CS) capable of eliciting salivation even in the absence of food, as shown in the top row of Figure 15.1. Because the salivation is in response to the CS rather than to the actual food, it is called the conditioned response (CR), whereas it is a UCR when it occurs in the presence of food.

In the case of alcohol (see the last three rows of Figure 15.1), certain physiological and psychological reactions occur as UCRs when alcohol (UCS) is consumed. If the taste, smell, or visual cues (CSs) associated with the drinking of alcohol occur alone later, there should be some partial activation of the responses (CRs) that alcohol produces. Thus, these cues (CSs) elicit craving, physiological arousal, and drug-seeking responses (CRs). The strength of the CR is in proportion to factors such as the length of prior drinking, the recency of past drinking, and the similarity between past drinking settings and the present one. Several models of relapse based on the classical conditioning paradigm have been proposed.

Positive Appetitional Model

One model based on classical conditioning (Stewart, deWit, & Eikelboom, 1984) emphasizes the positive incentive value of alcohol as a determinant of relapse. The **positive appetitional**

FIGURE 15.1   Role of classical conditioning in different models of alcohol relapse.

Comparison of Pavlov's Conditioning With Models of Alcohol Relapse

	INITIAL STAGE	MIDDLE STAGE	LATER STAGE
Pavlovian Classical Conditioning Model	CS tone → UCS (food) ↘ UCR (eat)	CS → CR (craving)	CS → CR (eat)
Positive Appetitional Model	CS cues → UCS (alcohol) ↘ UCR (drink)	CS → CR (craving)	CS → CR (lapse into drinking)
Compensatory Response Model	CS cues → UCS (alcohol) ↘ UCR (drink)	CS ↘ CR CR CR (weaker craving due to tolerance)	CS → CR (lapse into drinking)
Conditioned Withdrawal Model	CS cues → UCS (alcohol) ↘ UCR (drink)	CS → CR (withdrawal distress)	CS → CR (lapse into drinking)

model focuses on events that occur prior to when alcohol is consumed. Drinking alcohol produces a positive affective state, one that is conditioned to other stimuli such as the sight and smell associated with drinking that later have the capacity to trigger subjective desire or craving for alcohol and evoke the motivation to use the substance again. This model may apply more to early stages of drug use.

Compensatory Response Model

Although it is also based on the Pavlovian paradigm, the **compensatory response model** (Siegel, 1983) holds that conditioning involves responses that are opposite in direction from the original UCRs, presumably to restore homeostasis. Alcohol, for example, intensifies physiological arousal, so this reaction is followed by the attempt of the nervous system to suppress arousal. This process may be one explanation for the phenomenon of tolerance discussed in Chapter 5, whereby increasingly larger doses eventually are needed to produce an earlier level of arousal generated by a smaller amount. Because these conditioned cues act to reduce the effect of a drug, they could activate resumed use in an attempt to generate the arousal state associated with their drug. This model may be more applicable to experienced users who are not yet drug dependent.

Conditioned Withdrawal

One model, **conditioned withdrawal** (Wikler, 1973), focuses on negative interoceptive cues such as physiological reactions associated with the withdrawal reaction to the absence of alcohol. As with the preceding model, these internal cues are conditioned to external cues such as the room or physical setting where excessive drinking previously ended. Later, these cues can act as CSs to activate conditioned withdrawal reactions and experiences of craving. To reduce or eliminate these aversive withdrawal responses, one might relapse into drinking. This model deals with processes more likely to occur in drug-dependent individuals.

Neurophysiological Models

Two models that focus on changes in neurophysiological processes that occur with increased alcohol and other drug use were discussed earlier in Chapter 5. They are mentioned here briefly in reference to how the above conditioning models help explain relapse.

The opponent-process theory (Solomon, 1980) proposed that during initial use, a small amount of a drug produces a strong positive affect (state A), which leads to a relatively weak negative aftereffect (state B). Through conditioning processes, these affective states become associated with other stimuli that may later trigger drug use. In the early use of a drug, as proposed by the positive appetitional model, these stimuli arouse positive affective states for use. As drug use continues and increases, there is a reversal of the strength of the two states. Thus, after long-term use, CSs are associated with strong unpleasant feelings. During abstinence, these aversive stimuli, as postulated by the conditioned withdrawal model, may lead to relapse.

The incentive sensitization model (Berridge & Robinson, 1995; Robinson & Berridge, 1993) notes that among beginning users, both "wanting" and "liking" a drug tend to increase together. However, for users who are dependent on drugs, "wanting" stays strong with continued use, but "liking" (receiving pleasure from its use) actually decreases. Prolonged use of alcohol, for example, leads to neuroadaptations that create a hypersensitivity to it, as reflected by a strong "wanting" to drink, despite experiencing less "liking" when it is consumed. Through the process of classical conditioning, the heightened attention of a user becomes associated with stimuli previously associated with its use. These cues generate craving that increases the likelihood of relapse.

Treatment Methods Based on Conditioning Theories

Principles of classical conditioning methods such as **cue extinction** have been used to prevent relapse. This procedure is relatively passive insofar as the patient's role does not call for awareness or motivation. In cue extinction, the environmental stimuli that trigger cravings for alcohol and other drugs are weakened. The rationale behind this method is that exposure to alcohol or other drug cues in the absence of its actual consumption will eventually weaken drinking or other drug use urges as these associations lose their strength.

An example of a test of the clinical effectiveness of cue extinction treatment for alcohol dependence (Drummond & Glautier, 1994) used a controlled trial with 35 severely alcohol-dependent men who received either cue exposure or relaxation control following detoxification. Cue exposure involved 400 min of exposure to the sight and smell of preferred drinks provided over 10 days in a laboratory setting. The relaxation therapy control group spent the same amount of time in the laboratory but received only 20 min of exposure to alcohol cues. Results supported the extinction view as the cue exposure group had a more favorable outcome at a 6-month follow-up, with a delayed relapse to heavy drinking and less total alcohol consumption.

On the other hand, given that the sight and smell of an alcoholic drink are powerful cues that activate cravings among alcoholics, there is also the danger that cue exposure to alcohol could backfire and increase the likelihood of relapse. This risk is greater if negative mood is also present. In one study of 50 male alcoholic inpatients (Cooney, Litt, Morse, Bauer, & Gaupp, 1997), negative moods were induced with visual imagery before exposing participants either to their favorite alcoholic beverage or to spring water. The cues of the alcoholic beverage and negative affect imagery combined to produce the highest urges to drink. Stronger urges predicted shorter time to relapse after inpatient discharge.

It is crucial that clients receive careful explanations as to why they are being exposed to the sight of alcoholic beverages and strong cautions not to engage in such activities on their own, such as by visiting bars without supervision (Baker, Cooney, & Pomerleau, 1987).

Pharmacological Methods

The reduction of relapse for alcohol and some other drugs has been treated by pharmacological means. Naltrexone, an opiate antagonist, blocks the ability of opioids such as alcohol and morphine to stimulate brain receptors normally activated by these drugs. Prevention of the pleasurable responses in the brain ordinarily generated by alcohol's release of endogenous opioids may reduce alcohol consumption (Volpicelli, Clay, Watson, & Volpicelli, 1995).

Naltrexone was evaluated in a clinical trial with 70 male veterans who had been drinking for an average of 20 years (Volpicelli, Alterman, Hayashida, & O'Brian, 1992). Half of them received a 50-mg dose of naltrexone, and half received a placebo over a 12-week outpatient treatment. A double-blind procedure was used to minimize any bias. The men were also referred to Alcoholics Anonymous (AA) meetings, received alcoholism counseling, and were taught ways to prevent relapse.

Self-reports of alcohol drinking and craving were used. Relapse was defined in several ways: having five or more drinks on one occasion, consuming alcohol five or more times during the previous week, and having a blood alcohol concentration of 0.10% or greater when coming for treatment. Naltrexone-treated patients were approximately half as likely to relapse as the placebo patients. Craving for the placebo group was negligible, but the naltrexone group had a gradual decline in self-reported craving.

Patients received either a 50-mg dose of naltrexone or a placebo in a double-blind 12-week outpatient clinical trial (O'Malley et al., 1992). The 97 patients (72 men and

25 women), predominantly White and employed full-time, received one of two different types of therapy, coping skills or supportive therapy (nondirective).

Naltrexone reduced relapse rates by about half, as naltrexone patients reported drinking on 4.3% of the study days as compared to the 9.9% reported by placebo patients. Those who received naltrexone and supportive therapy were less likely to sample a drink for the first time after beginning treatment as compared to other treatment groups. Patients treated with naltrexone and coping skills therapy were as likely to lapse as the controls were, but they were less likely to relapse. Results suggest that naltrexone combined with coping skills therapy is an effective treatment approach to reducing craving and relapse.

Cognitive and Social Learning Theory

In contrast to the preceding models that attribute relapse to factors that may operate with low awareness or volition on the part of the drinker, the cognitive-behavioral approach is based on social learning theory (Bandura, 1977), which emphasizes factors such as the modeling of the behavior of others and the individual's cognitive appraisal of the factors affecting drug use. This approach employs active methods that involve decision making, coping skills, and problem-solving skills.

Relapse Prevention Model

The **relapse prevention model** is an influential cognitive-behavioral approach based on social learning (Marlatt & Gordon, 1985). First developed for relapse prevention, it is now also widely applied in treatment programs. This approach views alcoholism and other addictions as a set of strong learned responses with undesirable consequences that can be offset by the conscious decision to acquire a new set of habits.

The model challenges the value of AA's view that alcoholics must be completely abstinent, which, it argues, only *increases* the likelihood of relapse because AA holds that after a single slip or lapse from abstinence, a full-blown relapse will ensue (Marlatt & Gordon, 1985). The goal of abstinence offers no margin for error and is equivalent to "being out after only one strike." Such expectations may then become self-fulfilling prophecies for any unfortunate alcoholics who slip as it makes them more likely to engage in further drinking.

In the model, an abstaining drinker who resumes drinking experiences an **abstinence violation effect (AVE)** in which realization of the occurrence of a lapse creates conflict with the intended abstinence (Marlatt, 1978). AVEs may increase negative affect such as guilt, lower feelings of self-efficacy, and lower attributions of internal control. The magnitude of the AVE is assumed to be a function of factors such as the degree of prior commitment to abstinence, the duration of the abstinence period, the immediate subjective effect of the drug used, and the attributions for the lapse.

A study of social drinkers after they drank more than they intended examined factors affecting AVEs using handheld computers to record how much they drank and their cognitive and emotional reactions the next morning to their level of consumption (Muraven, Collins, Morsheimer, Shiffman, & Paty, 2005). Drinkers who had violated their self-imposed limits made on the previous day reported more guilt, even after controlling for acute negative symptoms of drinking and amount consumed. Greater distress over alcohol consumption was linked to more intake, intoxication, and more limit violations. Drinking beyond a self-imposed limit produced distress among social drinkers, and they responded to that distress by drinking more, validating the AVE concept.

Attributions

The attributions that clients make for their lapses may strongly influence how AVEs affect subsequent drinking (Connors, Longabaugh, & Miller, 1996). Several key dimensions on which these attributions fall are internal-external (e.g., self vs. other), stable-unstable (e.g., constant vs. variable), and global-specific (e.g., universal vs. unique). For example, an alcoholic explaining "what happened" when a lapse occurred might make some of the following attributions: "My drinking is due to my own weakness in self-control in refusing the offer" (internal), "I am always weak when offered a drink" (stable), and "I am weak in all situations when alcohol is offered" (global).

The dispositional attributions in this example will lead to more negative affect, including conflict and guilt, and increase likelihood of more lapses. In contrast, relapse is less likely for someone who makes attributions like "Everyone else was drinking" (external), "I usually can resist social pressure to drink" (unstable), and "I refuse offers of drinks in most situations" (unique).

Affective States

Negative mood seems to have a major role in precipitating relapses and crises among alcoholics. A relationship between negative bias and the extent of negative mood when tested was related to retrospective reports of relapses (Hodgins & Shimp, 1995). The most frequent precipitant of relapses and crises was negative emotional states, although minor relapses were more likely to be in response to social pressure. Females were more likely to report interpersonal and less likely to report intrapersonal determinants than males. Strong negative affect might have an indirect effect by lowering personal feelings of self-efficacy for dealing with a problem, which in turn might contribute to relapse in hopes that alcohol will reduce the negative affect. Positive expectations of disinhibitory effects of alcohol also might stimulate craving leading to drinking (Marlatt, 1985a, b).

Outcome Expectancies

If alcoholics believe that drinking has negative outcomes, they should be more likely to avoid relapse. In one study of 53 male alcoholics at a nonresidential alcohol dependence treatment facility (Jones & McMahon, 1994), alcohol expectancies were measured at admission to study their relationship to time to first drink following treatment. Expectancies were unrelated to relapse after 1 month. However, negative but not positive alcohol expectancies were related to less relapse at 3 months after treatment.

However, if expected outcomes of a drug are positive consequences including relief from pain and discomfort, relapse should be more likely. A study (Gwaltney, Shiffman, Balabanis, & Paty, 2005) of smokers in a cessation program used EMA to obtain near real-time data. The findings showed that increased positive expectancies made relapse more likely. In contrast, decreases in self-efficacy predicted relapse.

These effects of expected outcomes seem to occur even if the expectations involve implicit rather than explicit cognitions (Wiers et al., 2002). Current alcohol use and alcohol binge use after 1 year by 12- and 15-year-olds were better predicted by implicit associations with alcohol than by explicit alcohol expectancies (Thush & Wiers, 2007).

Motivation and Commitment

During the first stage in a relapse prevention program, developing motivation and commitment should be the primary goals (Brownell et al., 1986). Use of contracts involving contingencies of monetary rewards for sobriety have been tried widely but may work only for a self-selected sample because others may drop out or not even participate.

The cognitive-behavioral learning approach (Marlatt, 1985b) to relapse prevention teaches clients about the factors leading to relapse. They learn to recognize situations that represent high risk for them due to associations from their drug use and various internal (i.e., feelings, thoughts) and external (i.e., physical) surroundings and social contacts associated with alcohol and other drug use. As everyone is not affected by the same factors, each person has to learn his or her own danger cues. Behavioral methods such as modeling, role-playing, and feedback are used to teach these skills.

When alcoholics are at high risk for relapse situations, coping and self-efficacy are two important factors that affect the likelihood of relapse. In the model, coping contributes to the self-efficacy feelings that determine whether a lapse—and its ensuing AVE—will occur. Thus, if adequate coping skills are available to deal with the situation, a sense of self-efficacy will exist and reduce likelihood of relapse. On the other hand, poor coping skills reduce self-efficacy, which increases the chance of relapse.

The second stage, in which initial changes in behavior occur, has a low likelihood of relapse because the patient is still optimistic and motivated. Three important tasks are called for at this stage: decision making, cognitive restructuring, and coping skills (Brownell et al., 1986).

Decision Making

Decision making entails helping the patient identify the immediate as well as long-term positive and negative consequences of either controlled moderate drinking or abstinence versus relapse. Figure 15.2 illustrates a decision matrix in which the alcohol-dependent person identifies the positive and negative consequences, both short- and long-term, of being abstinent or continuing to drink.

Cognitive Restructuring

The goal of cognitive restructuring is to help develop rational interpretation of attitudes and feelings. For example, instead of blaming a lapse on their own lack of willpower or character, individuals may be helped to see that the situation they were in involved too much social pressure. They might be taught to think of craving as a normal part of recovery that can be treated rather than as a sign of hopelessness. The cognitive appraisal of the individual is a major factor in whether a slip or lapse inevitably leads to relapse. More relapse occurred among those persons who attributed their lapses to internal factors than among those who recognized the influences of external factors (Marlatt & Gordon, 1985).

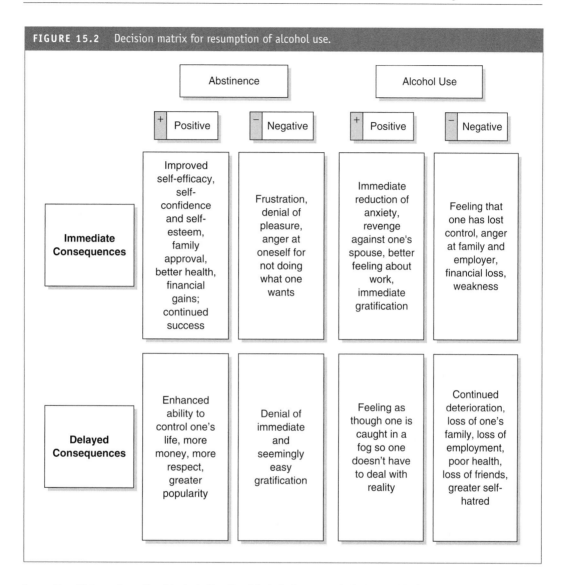

FIGURE 15.2   Decision matrix for resumption of alcohol use.

Source: From "Relapse Prevention," by L. A. Dimeff and G. A. Marlatt, 1995, in R. K. Hester and W. R. Miller (Eds.), *Handbook of Alcoholism Treatment Approaches: Effective Alternatives* (2nd ed., pp. 176–194), Needham Heights, MA: Allyn & Bacon. Copyright 1995 by Allyn & Bacon, Inc. Reproduced by permission of Pearson Education, Inc.

Coping

Coping skills are needed for dealing with stressful situations when alcoholics are at high risk for relapse. Cognitive forms of coping could entail distraction, thoughts involving delay, or thinking about the positive benefits of not drinking and the negative consequences of drinking. Behavioral forms of coping include eating, physical activity, escape, delay of action, and relaxation. Coping involves doing "something" as opposed to doing "nothing," but it need not involve complex reasoning or problem-solving skills (Shiffman, 1987).

Use of active and behavioral forms of coping was more effective than avoidance coping for 400 men and women receiving 6 months of alcoholism treatment (Maisto, Zywiak, & Connors, 2006). Active and behavioral coping led to a higher percentage of days abstinent, fewer drinks per drinking day, and a lower total number of drinks per month during the 6 months after treatment.

Self-Efficacy

Self-efficacy, one's perceived ability to deal effectively with problems in general as well as with problems in the use of alcohol and other drugs, is important for avoidance of relapse. The likelihood of a relapse can be related to one's feelings of self-efficacy in a high-risk-for-relapse situation. Individuals with a sense of control believe that they can overcome their dependence through their efforts (Bandura, 1999).

Increased self-efficacy of treated alcoholics randomly assigned to a cognitive-behavioral aftercare program was related to reduced drinking at a 6-month follow-up (Brown, Seraganian, Tremblay, & Annis, 2002). However, self-efficacy is not necessary for improvement, as a group of alcoholics randomly assigned to a Twelve-Step facilitation aftercare program also had reduced drinking if they followed the principles of the program.

A study (Moos & Moos, 2006) with 461 individuals compared those who obtained help with those who did not. The latter were less likely to achieve 3-year remission and were more likely to relapse. Those who had higher self-efficacy and less avoidance coping had less alcohol consumption and fewer drinking problems at 3 years, especially those showing remission without help. For those remitted at 3 years, lower self-efficacy and more avoidance coping were more likely to cause relapse by 16 years.

Maintaining Sobriety

Sobriety on a long-term basis is enhanced by continued monitoring, social support, and general lifestyle changes (Brownell et al., 1986). Monitoring may be done by the patient or by professionals, although in the latter instance, the line between the end of treatment and the beginning of maintenance becomes blurred. Counselors must be aware of their role in dealing with lapses by their clients (Daley, 1989). If they become angry or give up on the clients when lapses occur, counselors may unwittingly contribute to relapse.

Social support is helpful for most individuals, although the source of the support may be a critical factor in its effectiveness. Lifestyle changes that allow other forms of gratification to replace the addiction may be helpful. Alternatives such as exercise, meditation, and relaxation training can be used as aids against relapse (Brownell et al., 1986).

Evaluation of the Relapse Prevention Model

Hierarchy of Risk Situations. The Relapse Replication and Extension Project (RREP; Lowman, Allen, & Stout, 1996) evaluated the reliability and validity of Marlatt's relapse taxonomy (Marlatt & Gordon, 1985). Raters classified episodes of relapse in the 12 months following treatment for 563 clients receiving different methods of alcoholism treatment.

Both inpatients and outpatients had high rates (around 75%) of having at least one drink in this period. The findings raised doubts about the adequacy of the relapse hierarchy with regard to interrater reliability. It questioned the value of distinctions between intra- and interpersonal factors.

The RREP studies also failed to support Marlatt's relapse taxonomy (Marlatt & Gordon, 1985). However, the model is still influential and can be improved with changes in the classification categories and development of more structured assessment instruments (Kadden, 1996).

Role of Self-Efficacy and Coping. Although self-efficacy might be enhanced by the cognitive-behavioral training, the overall evidence showing that higher self-efficacy translates into less relapse is weak. People who learn coping skills and increase their self-efficacy are not necessarily less likely to relapse.

Although self-efficacy and coping may be related to relapse, does self-efficacy contribute to better coping, does better coping generate higher self-efficacy, or both? Another interpretation is that coping is the key to preventing relapse. Self-efficacy may only be an epiphenomenon, a feeling that accompanies good coping but does not itself do much to prevent relapse.

Similarly, some doubts exist about the role of coping skills in relapse prevention (Morgenstern & Longabaugh, 2000). A review of studies using cognitive-behavioral treatment showed no relationship between the assumed beneficial effects of copings skills and improvement. In one study (Litt, Kadden, Cooney, & Kabela, 2003), cognitive-behavioral treatment, which teaches coping skills, was compared with interactional/interpersonal therapy, which does not. Both methods produced comparably good outcomes in terms of abstinent days, heavy drinking days, and improved coping skills. The finding that acquiring specific coping skills through cognitive-behavioral training was not related to better outcomes raises doubts about their necessity for treating alcohol dependence.

Since relapse is less likely if drinkers expect negative outcomes (Jones & McMahon, 1996), some studies attempt to alter outcome expectancies on the assumption that they affect drinking. In a review of past studies of the relationship of positive and negative expectancies to drinking (Jones, Corbin, & Fromme, 2001), expectancies were found to be related to treatment outcome, but there was little evidence that modifying expectances during treatment would translate into changes in posttreatment alcohol consumption. Thus, among prevention programs, seven projects targeted positive expectancies, but only two examined if expectancy change was actually related to drinking changes, and in both cases it did not relate to subsequent consumption.

Role of Craving. The relapse prevention model has been criticized for insufficient recognition of the importance of craving in relapse. The model places more emphasis on "urges." The distinction is that craving is a subjective and sometimes subtle desire for an addictive drug, whereas urges are the conscious impulses or intentions to seek and consume it. The relapse prevention model holds that cognitive expectations can affect how CRs will influence coping responses, which in turn affect the likelihood of relapse. The treatment goal of reducing craving and urges assumes that they contribute to more drinking—a view, however, for which the evidence is not conclusive (Singleton & Gorelick, 1998).

Role of Social Factors. Another criticism of the model is its insufficient attention to the role of social factors that may affect relapse (Stanton, 2005). Thus, social or peer pressure to drink at social gatherings might lead to lapses by encouraging drinking in group settings. In contrast, if individuals' drinking leads to ostracism from friends and family members, they may be less likely to relapse (Peirce, Frone, Russell, Cooper, & Mudar, 2000).

Comparison to Other Treatments. Finally, although in comparison to receiving no treatment, cognitive behavioral training programs show improvements in abstinence rates, their outcomes are no better than those obtained with other forms of treatment (Longabaugh & Morgenstern, 1999). These conclusions are upheld for treated abusers of substances other than alcohol as well including opiates, cocaine, and nicotine (Carroll, 1996).

A DYNAMIC MODEL OF RELAPSE

One criticism of relapse prevention research is that it focuses on the examination of the factors involved in specific or isolated relapse episodes. An alternative conception to relapse as a discrete event is to think of it as an ongoing process entailing a series of inter-related episodes that may extend over months or even years.

A revision of the relapse prevention model (Witkiewitz & Marlatt, 2004) takes a dynamic view involving multiple factors that interact with each other to determine the likelihood of lapses. Figure 15.3 is complex, and only an overview will be described here. In high-risk situations, the likelihood of relapse is affected by *tonic processes* that involve distal factors including family history of substance abuse as well as by *phasic responses* that include immediate or current behavioral and cognitive processes related to substance use or nonuse. Thus, self-efficacy and coping responses, central factors in the earlier formulation, are still important, but there is greater recognition of the context of other influential factors. It is important to note that some of the arrows between different components are unidirectional (implying one direction of causality) and others are bidirectional (suggesting that the two components have reciprocal effects).

This dynamic model is better at accounting for sudden and unpredicted changes in drinking behavior. Relapse may be a phenomenon akin to the so-called "butterfly effect" (a butterfly flaps its wings in Tokyo and a tornado hits in Texas) analyzed by chaos theory (Lorenz, 1963) where seemingly small effects of one factor at the beginning of a process can influence events ever so slightly but may contribute to later sudden and unpredicted large outcomes. Use of techniques from catastrophe theory, a sophisticated mathematical modeling technique, yields a better fit between relapse predictors and drinking outcomes than does multiple regression, a statistical procedure widely used in psychological research.

Instead of viewing relapse as a linear process in which self-efficacy leads to coping, which in turn promotes abstinence, the revision postulates that multiple concurrent factors affect the likelihood of drinking. The dynamic interplay among these factors varies over time; on one occasion one factor may prevail and exert more influence whereas on another occasion a different factor may have more influence. The specific

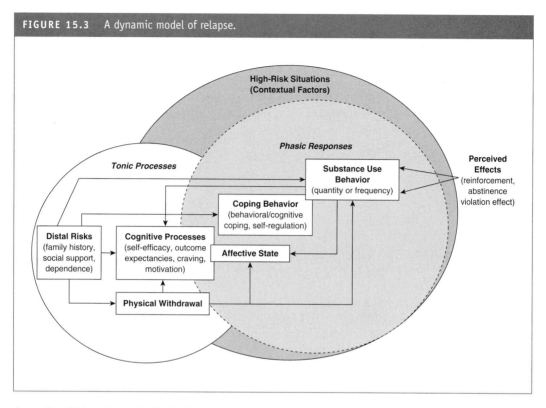

FIGURE 15.3 A dynamic model of relapse.

Source: From "Relapse Prevention for Alcohol and Drug Problems: That Was Zen, This Is Tao," by K. Witkiewitz and G. A. Marlatt, 2004, *American Psychologist, 59*(4), pp. 224–235.

factors determining drinking will differ for persons with different backgrounds such as family history of alcoholism, the social and environmental context, and demographic characteristics of the drinker.

Figure 15.4 provides a simple visualization of the dynamic interplay among the many factors affecting relapse. On the left side are several factors of varying magnitude that work to maintain sobriety while on the right side are several factors of varying magnitude that increase the likelihood of relapse. To keep the diagram simple, there are only three factors on each side, but in reality there can be more or fewer factors, and there can be more factors on one side than on the other. Furthermore, the sizes of each factor are continuously changing, and they can affect each other. The specific factors will vary for different individuals. The key determinant is the relative weight of all the factors on one side versus those on the other side. When they are equal, there should be no change. But when the negative factors outweigh the positive ones as in the top half of Figure 15.4., relapse should occur. When the positive factors exceed the negative ones as in the bottom half of Figure 15.4, abstinence or sobriety should be maintained.

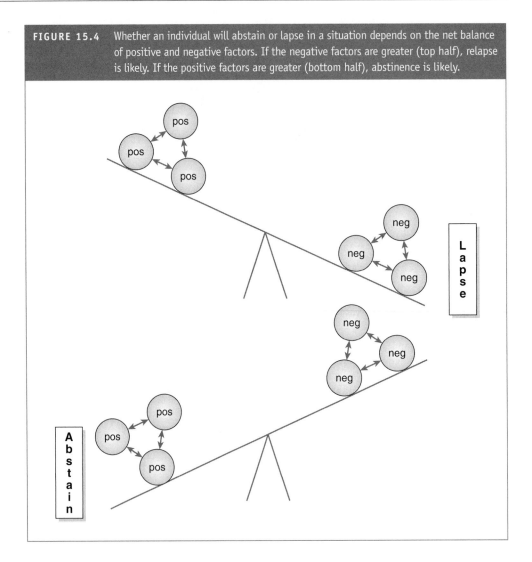

FIGURE 15.4 Whether an individual will abstain or lapse in a situation depends on the net balance of positive and negative factors. If the negative factors are greater (top half), relapse is likely. If the positive factors are greater (bottom half), abstinence is likely.

For example, the role of self-efficacy in preventing relapse among alcoholics given cognitive-behavioral treatment failed to be confirmed in the Matching Alcoholism Treatments to Client Heterogeneity study (Project MATCH Research Group, 1997). However, the failure may have stemmed from the complexity of the relapse process that could not be adequately measured by statistical methods typically used. A reanalysis (Witkiewitz, van der Maas, Hufford, & Marlatt, 2007) of relapse data for 952 outpatients from Project MATCH employed two advanced nonlinear statistical methodologies: catastrophe and growth mixture modeling, which are more appropriate for examining patterns where changes are considered discontinuous or abrupt rather than gradual and continuous.

The models estimated drinking consequence trajectories during the 12 months following treatment for each of the three Project MATCH treatment conditions. Both analyses found a dynamic relationship between self-efficacy and drinking outcomes. The growth mixture analyses supported the original matching hypothesis, specifically that cognitive behavior therapy would improve self-efficacy and hence reduce drinking, whereas motivational therapy would not benefit self-efficacy and hence not reduce drinking as much.

Another analysis of Project MATCH (Wu & Witkiewitz, 2008) showed that patients with high network support for drinking had, as predicted, the best outcomes immediately following treatment if they were assigned to Twelve-Step facilitation whereas in the original Project MATCH this matching effect occurred only at the 3-year follow-up.

SUCCESSFUL LAPSE RESISTANCE

Most of the evidence concerning relapse is based on clinical case histories and concentrates on *failures* to maintain abstinence. A complete analysis of treatment follow-up outcomes should also examine instances of successful resistance to urges. For example, while we know that many times cravings lead to relapse, how often are cravings successfully ignored, and how often do they fail to lead to relapse? What factors account for these opposite outcomes?

A "natural history" of relapse that also includes instances of successful resistance would be instructive for understanding the determinants of relapse by identifying factors leading to the failure to resist temptation. For instance, clinical observations (Ludwig, 1988) illustrate how alcoholics devise various ways of "self-talk" that help them succeed in avoiding relapse. Below are a few examples:

> Every time I get the urge to drink, I immediately think of being sick, vomiting, shakes, and being miserable. (Ludwig, 1988, p. 116)

> I'm a damn fool to take a drink, so I'm not going to take the chance. For the simple reason that I've got too much at stake. I've got a new home now, I've got a wife and family—three partners and a going concern—and one drink stands between me and all that. (Ludwig, 1988, p. 118)

> I can stay sober if I want to. It's my decision. A man has a responsibility, and he's got to face it. A man has some kind of control over everything. (Ludwig, 1988, p. 120)

> I'm really an alcoholic, and I can't handle it. One drink is all it takes. (Ludwig, 1988, p. 121)

> The wine on the grocery shelf said, Man you want me—you'd better buy me. You can really feel good on me. I prayed, God, I'm really miserable. You've got to get me though this. (Ludwig, 1988, p. 123)

Comparisons of coping differences between those who lapse and those who succeed in resisting temptation would be instructive, but the differences might reflect differences between lapsers and abstainers on other factors. This problem can be avoided by comparing lapses and successful resistance occasions within the same individuals.

One such study of smoking (Shiffman, Paty, Gnys, Kassel, & Hickcox, 1996) found that the outcome of a temptation, lapse or resistance, was related to individual as well as situational factors. Lapses, in comparison to resisted temptations or randomly scheduled assessments, were increased by negative affect and strong urges as well as by situational factors such as being in places where smoking was permitted, cigarettes were easily available, and others were smoking. Coping was used much more when temptation was successfully resisted than when lapses occurred. Cognitive coping (thoughts) was more effective than behavioral forms of coping (such as leaving a situation) for resisting temptation.

Analysis of smoking lapses among 130 participants that lapsed within 1 month of a self-initiated quit attempt in one study (Bliss, Garvey, & Ward, 1999) found there was more reported coping during resisted temptations than during lapses. Those who reported coping to resist urges were likely to use a combination of cognitive and behavioral forms, which was more likely to be successful in resisting temptation than the use of just one form of coping. Even during lapses, coping was used but ineffectively or to an insufficient degree. Perhaps, situational factors overwhelmed participants' coping efforts on those occasions.

Although the findings show a link between coping and resisting temptation, it is not clear if a causal relationship exists or how coping helps. Coping may delay smoking until the urge to smoke diminishes. Cognitive coping may help maintain a high level of confidence or motivation to quit while behavioral coping may work by removing individuals from environments that increase the urge to smoke.

Summary

The battle for recovery from alcohol and other drug dependencies does not end when a patient is discharged from a treatment program. As with other addictive behaviors, relapse occurs all too frequently.

Cravings for a drug often arise following abstinence or even reduced use. These insidious experiences involve often overpowering temptations to resume use of substances from which individuals have been abstinent for an extended period. Alcoholics, as well as those who cannot enjoy their own drinking if others are abstaining, rationalize that "just one little drink can't hurt." The inability to resist these urges that frequently challenge the sobriety of patients in remission jeopardizes their continued recovery.

Retrospective self-reports are the primary source of evidence about the factors precipitating relapse, but there are limitations such as accuracy of recall as well as deliberate distortions, lies, or excuses. Retrospective reports that relapses occurred because of crises and emotional distress may be overstated because they could be means of seeking sympathy or avoiding blame.

Prospective studies, including the use of near real-time methods such as ecological momentary assessment, avoid many of the limitations of retrospective self-reports but have their own problems such as reactivity, by which the measurement itself can distort the processes being studied.

The positive appetitional, compensatory response, and conditioned withdrawal models of relapse are based on concepts from classical conditioning theory in which originally neutral stimuli can become conditioned stimuli by association with an unconditioned stimulus. Thus, the sight, smell, or other cues (CS) that are paired with drugs (UCS) can come to elicit the reactions (UCR) that ordinarily occur in response to drugs. Thus, over time, cues (CS) associated with drug use might themselves trigger the urge or craving (CR) to use the drug.

The opponent process model focuses on affective and conditioned determinants underlying use. It explains how the cues at the early stages trigger alcohol and other drug use for positive affect whereas cues at later stages activate use to reduce negative affect. The incentive sensitization model takes a different approach by distinguishing between two processes: wanting and liking. With prolonged drug use, changes occur in the brain that serve to maintain or increase the "wanting" while reducing the "liking" of the drug. Conditioned stimuli also operate to affect these states.

Some methods for treating relapse are based on conditioning theory. One method used exposes alcoholics to alcohol-related cues, but drinking is not allowed. This technique delays the relapse of heavy drinking and leads to less total alcohol consumption. But there is also the danger that exposure to alcohol-related cues can backfire and increase the likelihood of relapse.

Pharmacological approaches to alcoholism treatment include the use of naltrexone, an antagonist of neurotransmitters ordinarily released by alcohol. By offsetting alcohol's effect on neurotransmission, naltrexone, combined with coping skills therapy, can be effective in reducing craving and relapse.

Social learning theory, with its emphasis on cognitive and behavioral coping, offers more opportunities for active involvement by the user. By learning how to identify high-risk situations for lapse, one may stay out of such situations. In such situations, resistance to temptation is greater if individuals have good coping skills and alternative behaviors. Social learning theory emphasizes the need for a sense of self-efficacy, the feeling that one can control outcomes, to deal effectively with the urges to drink. Resistance to temptation also may be strengthened further by the attitudes and behaviors of significant others who can provide social support and reinforcement to the recovering alcoholic.

Relapse involves the interplay of cognitive/affective, physiological, and behavioral factors. Environmental cues in conjunction with affective states, positive and negative, determine the arousal of urges to drink, physiological activation, and expectations about the effects of a drink. These effects can loop back and alter the initial affective states.

Individuals have different levels or types of cognitive and behavioral coping responses for dealing with situations with high risk for relapse. They also may make different attributions about the causes of their behavior and urges. These different factors influence each other. Thus, urges to drink can lower one's feelings of self-efficacy; conversely, strong feelings of self-efficacy may be associated with a reduction of urges. The availability of good coping skills for dealing with a situation where drinking urges are high can reduce those urges and physiological arousal, but the presence of compelling urges might weaken availability or benefits of these coping skills.

If the drinker concludes that the causes of the lapse are internal, stable, and global or the alcohol reduces negative affect, the chances of further deterioration are strong. Conversely, if the lapse is attributed to external, unstable, and specific factors or the drink has little influence on the affective state, the lapse may be an isolated event.

When an opportunity to drink arises, the outcome—lapse, normal use, or abstinence from alcohol—will depend on whether the coping responses and attributions or the urges to drink prevail.

Stimulus/Response

1. How can the adage "learn from your mistakes" be useful in helping prevent relapse for individuals who have stopped using alcohol and other drugs?

2. Once a small slip into resumed use of a drug occurs, a full relapse may follow. Do you think this outcome is due to a pharmacological or psychological reaction to making the slip? Design a study to test the relative influence of each factor.

3. Seemingly irrelevant decisions refer to behaviors that place the recovering individual at higher risk for relapse. For example, alcohol- or other-drug-dependent persons may suddenly find themselves in a drinking or other-drug-using situation even though there was no conscious intent to drink or use other drugs. Have you ever tried to reduce or stop using a drug and found yourself in this type of situation? How might alcoholism and other drug abuse counselors help prevent the occurrence of these predicaments?

4. If you know someone who is trying to quit using a drug, how might you and others unwittingly behave that might increase his or her risk of relapse? What are some things that you and others could do to help this person maintain abstinence?

Prevention of Alcohol
and Other Drug Problems

An ounce of prevention is worth a pound of cure.

—Benjamin Franklin

The misuse of alcohol and many other drugs inflicts a tremendous toll of pain and suffering on abusers and many around them. Alcohol and other drug dependency devastates the lives of many users and their family and friends who experience emotional, financial, and social damage. The types of problems associated with drugs differ in the extent to which harm occurs only to the user or also to innocent bystanders. Thus, physical health impairment caused by smoking or drinking mainly affects the user, whereas drinking and driving, interpersonal violence, and secondhand smoke threaten the physical and psychological well-being of others as well. Some problems such as impaired driving can be direct effects of drug use, but many other problems such as violence or depression may only be indirect consequences of drug use. In addition, even casual or "recreational" drug users can cause serious physical harm from accidents due to a single-use episode. Whether drinking leads to a "social problem" also must depend on social norms and definitions (e.g., the extent to which public drunkenness is tolerated varies in different societies). The concern of this chapter is with approaches to the prevention of alcohol- and other-drug-related problems.

In our society, people use licit drugs such as alcoholic beverages and, to a lesser extent, cigarettes privately in homes as well as in public places such as parks, stores, bars, and restaurants. Drinking is permissible in many public facilities such as parks, theaters, and stadiums. Distillers, wineries, breweries, and cigarette manufacturers spend vast sums of money to advertise in newspapers, in magazines, and on television with messages implying that life without these substances is incomplete. Images of good times, glamorous friends, and personal success are used to depict what people can expect to enjoy using alcoholic beverages and cigarettes.

Illegal drugs, on the other hand, are not as readily available as licit drugs are because their possession, sale, or use can lead to severe penalties, including incarceration. The locations where they can be obtained are less numerous, hidden, and often dangerous. The price of illicit drugs is also considerably higher than that of licit drugs. Nonetheless, those who want to acquire these drugs manage to find a way.

The tasks of prevention for licit and illicit drug use are quite different. With licit drugs, the influences of education, health, and legal and moral forces compete against the promotion and advertising of the alcohol and tobacco industries. Education about the health risks of cigarette smoking and alcohol consumption aims to reduce usage. Legal and economic disincentives include increased alcohol and cigarette taxes, zoning regulations for alcohol outlets, legal minimum drinking age for purchase and use, and restrictions on advertising. Although educational, health, and moral influences against use also exist for illicit drugs, the advertising, marketing promotions, and subsidies from the federal government for licit drugs are absent. Heavy reliance is placed on legal means to control availability of illicit drugs. Educational and informational campaigns against illicit drugs aim to reduce the desire or demand for illicit drugs. Nonetheless, illicit drugs hold high attraction to many users, and the profit motive for drug sellers is even greater than for those who market legal drugs.

Prevention is a difficult task, given the strong desires of many to consume alcohol and other drugs. In general, prevention efforts have failed to deal with the root of the problems. The focus is on creating barriers so that individuals cannot obtain or use the substances rather than identifying why people want to use them in the first place.

SOCIAL POLICY AND DRUGS

The goals and methods adopted by a society to deal with problems associated with alcohol and other drug use, abuse, and dependency are issues of intense controversy and heated debate. Social policy refers to the laws and programs that regulate the use of these substances. In the past, alcohol and other drug policy decisions have been based on many factors, including historical, philosophical, moral-religious, political, and economic considerations. Beliefs about fundamental issues of right and wrong, personal freedom, individual control, and social responsibility exert strong influences on how people feel about the proper place of alcohol and other drugs in our society. Firmly entrenched traditions are not easily changed. Politicians both play to and are controlled by their constituents. Lobbies for legal drugs have considerable political and economic power to fight for social policies and laws that favor their drugs and rule against illegal drugs. We will examine several divergent views about what our social policy about drugs should be.

All Drugs Should Be Banned

At one extreme is the zero-tolerance position that all psychoactive drugs are undesirable. All drugs are viewed as evil and should be banned because they serve hedonistic goals such as the experience of pleasure. A puritanical attitude and a longstanding American ideology that pleasure is selfish or incompatible with work have fostered a negative attitude toward all psychoactive drug use.

Any distinction between drug use and abuse is ignored because all drug use is seen as equivalent to abuse and addiction, sooner or later. The argument is that even if most abusers did not engage in any behaviors harmful to self or to others, they would eventually experience and suffer serious physical health hazards.

A common tactic is to arouse fear by creating the impression that the drug causes antisocial and criminal behavior among users. Usually the evidence is inconclusive but is portrayed as if it were not. Thus, the finding that criminals tend to use certain drugs does not prove that their drug use caused their criminal behavior. Alternatively, it may be that living a life of crime fosters drug use or some common third factor is responsible. Another tactic is to argue that use of one drug may cause the subsequent use of more dangerous drugs. This gateway or steppingstone theory is highly similar to the domino theory for international relations, in which a strategy of containment of evils such as communism in far-off lands is advocated to prevent these sinister forces from coming to our shores. Similarly, the association of certain drugs with immigrant populations such as opium with the Chinese, marijuana with Mexicans, and opiates with Italian immigrants is apt to increase support for bans against the drugs of disfavored immigrant groups.

All Drugs Should Be Available

An alternative perspective holds that individuals should have the choice to decide what course of action to take rather than be controlled by a paternalistic government. Individuals may be irrational in deceiving themselves as to the actual risk involved in using drugs, but they should be the ones to decide.

Some users do not seem to suffer harmful effects and feel it is their right to continue to enjoy their drugs. Some individuals may realize that potential dangers exist with use of drugs but feel they should be allowed to choose whether to take the tradeoff of possible future harm in return for immediate gratification. By outlawing any drug, society takes the choice away from the user.

Another argument in favor of allowing use of most psychoactive drugs is the fact that many drugs originated as medicines and have been used for such purposes over the course of their history, despite the fact that they also have been used for nonmedical purposes, often with harmful effects. Painkilling drugs such as ether, sedatives, morphine, opioids, and marijuana have been used for analgesic purposes in surgery. Stimulants such as cocaine have been offered as treatment for depression, melancholy, and weight control (amphetamines).

Some Drugs Should Be Banned; Others Should Not

A more temperate position is that some drugs are beneficial, on balance, and although their use should be controlled or limited, they should not be totally banned. Other drugs that, on balance, are harmful can more justifiably be controlled with sanctions for use or possession. Advocates regard legal drugs as those that most people can use without harm or risk of addiction. The minority of users of these drugs who unfortunately do become addicted are seen as suffering from a disease that medical treatment can remedy. Thus, they see no need to ban these substances because most of us do not have problems using them.

Politics Versus Science

Using scientific evidence on the impact of alcohol and other drugs on physical health, psychological well-being, and social problems, researchers have attempted to inform social policymakers and the public with objective data. Unfortunately, policymakers and voters often are less persuaded by scientific findings than by personal beliefs and emotional feelings, often powered by stereotypes and misconceptions about the causes and consequences of substance abuse.

In part, the failure of the scientific evidence to affect social policy has been because research is often too complicated for nonscientists to comprehend. In addition, the scientific evidence has not always yielded clear conclusions, either because of the complexity of the problem or because some scientific studies are flawed. Finally, science can only provide part of the input that determines effective social policy, which is also a political and economic decision.

A continuing debate exists over the effects of drugs. On one side is a tendency to demonize most, if not all, psychoactive drugs. Scare tactics and fear are used to intimidate; drugs are portrayed as the "bogeyman" who will get you, if you don't watch out. The message is that once you use an illicit drug, you will get "hooked," and you will experience all kinds of unpleasant consequences, social and physical.

On the other side, one argument is that not everyone who uses a drug gets "addicted" or experiences harm. It is believed that people can learn how to use a drug in a manner that is not harmful and that penalties against use are unjustified because drug use is a "victimless crime." Proponents of more liberal drug policies in the United States point to other nations such as the Netherlands where use of illicit drugs such as marijuana and heroin is tolerated without the widespread harm feared by drug opponents here (Nadelmann, 1997). At the same time, it must be cautioned that many other differences exist between the United States and other nations and that the societal effect of one drug will not necessarily be the same in different social settings. The eventual impact that a drug has in a society is affected by its beliefs and values, demographic characteristics, economic conditions, and political orientation.

Instead of assuming that all users will be affected in the same manner by drugs, a possibility is that the characteristics of the user and the setting in which the drug is used are important additional determinants of drug effects. In other words, the effects of drugs have a pharmacological basis, but the effects also depend on the social and psychological aspects of users such as their personalities, past experiences, social situation, and expectations.

THE PUBLIC HEALTH MODEL

A useful model for the analysis of public health problems considers the interactions of the *agent, host,* and *environment,* as shown in Figure 16.1. In the **public health model**, alcohol or another drug is the *agent* or "germ" that is the health threat. Prevention efforts directed toward the agent focus on restricting its availability by means such as pricing, limiting the hours when it can be sold or served publicly, and establishing minimum legal drinking age laws. The assumption is that less availability of the agent will lower its use and associated problems.

The *host* represents the potential or actual user who may eventually suffer harmful effects. Prevention efforts in this area might attempt to use education and persuasion to reduce the individual's desire or incentive to use the agent. In other words, if one can reduce the desire to use specific drugs, problems may be avoided, even if drugs are available. Finally, the *environment* includes both the physical and the social context in which the agent and host reside. A prevention focus on the environment might include the shaping of social attitudes and norms about alcohol and other drug use or the regulation of the physical environment in which these drugs might be consumed.

Successful prevention strategies may need to consider all of these components of the system of interrelated factors rather than focusing on only one. As Figure 16.1 indicates, each factor can influence the other factors, although the environment has more impact on the host than vice versa, as reflected by the dashed arrow leading from the host to the environment. The multiplicity of social and environmental forces, often beyond the control of individuals, that affect drug use must be recognized. In the case of alcohol, as Figure 16.2 indicates, laws and their enforcement, marketing and pricing, and media depictions are some of the environmental factors that must be considered in addition to any individual genetic or psychological factors when designing prevention strategies. We will take a closer look at these contextual factors in the following pages.

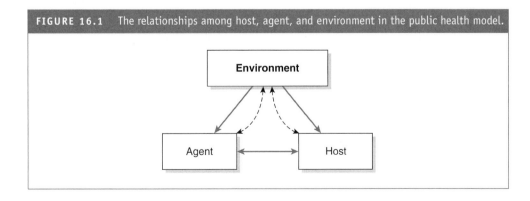

FIGURE 16.1   The relationships among host, agent, and environment in the public health model.

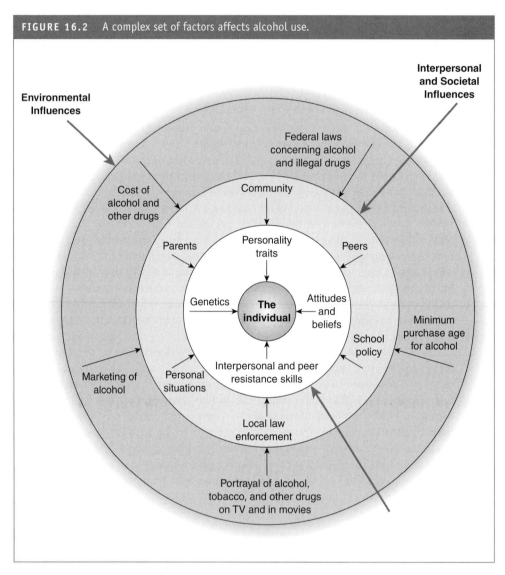

FIGURE 16.2   A complex set of factors affects alcohol use.

Source: From *Prevention Plus II: Tools for Creating and Sustaining Drug Free Communities* (DHHS publication No. ADM 89-1649), by the Office of Substance Abuse Prevention, 1989, Washington, DC: U.S. Government.

Control of Availability

Obviously, alcohol or any other drug must be physically available in the environment before it can cause problems. From this premise, many prevention efforts attempt to limit the physical availability of drugs (the agent). The assumption is that if drugs were less readily available in the environment, they would be consumed to a lesser extent and, it is hoped, with fewer related problems.

An underlying theoretical basis for this assumption is the **single distribution of consumption model** (Ledermann, 1956), which is based on comparisons of the relationship between per capita consumption of alcohol and rates of heavy drinking in many nations, as inferred from deaths due to liver cirrhosis. The frequency distribution of the amount of alcohol that different people drink is one in which most citizens drank at either low or moderate levels, with a small percentage consuming alcohol at the high end of the continuum. Advocates of this model—and similar ones—endorse social policies aimed at reducing alcohol availability based on the evidence that lower overall consumption of alcohol in a society is related to fewer alcohol problems.

However, social policymakers must consider other factors than the total consumption summed over all users in a society. A measure of total consumption does not distinguish between acute or short-term and chronic or long-term use. This distinction is important in setting social drug policies because the consequences of acute and chronic use levels are not the same. Whereas high levels of acute use can cause accidents, violence, and loss of productivity, chronic use also is more likely associated with harmful physical effects such as liver cirrhosis, even at low levels per drinking episode.

Aggregrate use levels cannot show how total use is distributed over the entire population (i.e., how many drinkers are heavy, moderate, and light drinkers and abstainers). The pattern of an individual's use may be more closely related to the extent of harm for that person. Also, the risks of harm may not have a linear or one-to-one relationship with consumption level, as noted earlier. If risks are exponentially related to consumption, for example, it is the heavy drinkers, even if they are a minority of the population, who contribute more to the overall or aggregate risk for society. The light drinkers, although they would represent a far larger percentage of the population, would have lower risks and contribute a smaller share of problems.

Aggregate measures of consumption such as per capita consumption, which reflect the overall amount of use in society, also may not predict risks of harm for individuals. Aggregate measures are convenient summaries, but they are not sensitive to individual variations in use. Regardless of the total use level in society as a whole, individual use levels are better predictors of each individual's risk level for a particular problem.

PRIMARY PREVENTION

Primary prevention attempts to stop problems related to alcohol and other drug use before they start. The benefits of primary prevention are often difficult to prove or require many years before they are evident. Consequently, this goal often has received a lower priority than the task of solving more immediate problems in which adverse consequences of drug abuse are more readily apparent. Diagnosing and identifying present drug abusers (secondary prevention) and treating persons already suffering from drug problems (tertiary prevention) usually demand priority over primary prevention of future problems.

Control of the availability of alcohol and other drugs is an important aspect of primary prevention and involves many different methods, but most can be classified as either **supply reduction** or **demand reduction**. Supply reduction methods, aimed at restricting or eliminating the physical presence of drugs, differ for licit and illicit drugs. For licit drugs, availability can be lowered by increased taxes and pricing as well as by regulations about conditions for sale and use. For illicit drugs, supply reduction involves destruction of existing sources, interdiction of supplies crossing national borders, and confiscation. Demand reduction methods for both licit and illicit drugs include education and persuasion attempts to reduce the attractiveness of drugs among potential users. In the case of illicit drugs, even though the demand or desire may be high, threats of incarceration and fines aim to suppress actual use. An overview of different methods of primary prevention is presented now.

Mass Media Influences

Mass media focus on promoting awareness and factual knowledge about the dangers of drugs. They aim to persuade audiences to avoid these substances, but they may have limited effectiveness. The indirect nature of mass media, as compared to the personal touch of in-person communication, may limit their impact. The advantage of mass media is that in theory they can reach large numbers of people rapidly, but in practice people may not attend to, remember, or even correctly interpret many messages in the presentations. Even if they learn the information, they may not modify their drinking behavior because many other factors help maintain its level.

A public service announcement (PSA) uses mass media to disseminate information on alcohol or other drugs aimed at dissuading their use. One study (Flynn et al., 2006) presented television and radio messages that promoted avoidance of alcohol to fourth and fifth graders in eight school districts. As a control comparison, children in the same grades in eight matched school districts were not exposed to these media. Follow-up surveys during the seventh and eighth grades showed the PSA interventions failed to affect alcohol use or its mediators. Unfortunately, at the same time the study occurred, community groups were implementing programs to reduce youth substance use in 10 of the 16 communities under study, which may have obscured any effect of the PSA intervention.

Excessively strong messages may backfire by creating reactance or increasing curiosity to experiment with drugs. This effect was shown in a study (Bensley & Wu, 1991) that presented college students with either a high- or a low-threat message against drinking. Later, they participated in a beer taste-rating task designed to unobtrusively measure consumption. Those who had received the high-threat message, especially among male heavy drinkers, consumed *more* beer than those who had received the low-threat message.

In contrast to the prevention goal of PSAs, the effect of mass media such as television program portrayal of characters using alcohol and other drugs may initiate and increase their use, especially among adolescents. Content analysis of a sample of television programs from 1976 to 1987 revealed that characters increased alcoholic beverage drinking to more than 10 acts per hour before the trend seemed to reverse (Wallack, Grube, Madden, & Breed, 1990). Another study (Mathios, Avery, Bisogni, & Shanahan, 1998) found alcoholic beverages were the most frequently portrayed food or drink in a sample of 276 programs on four major networks. A content analysis (DuRant et al., 1997) of 518 music videos shown at random times on television found that the lead performer was most often the one smoking or drinking, usually with a high degree of sexuality.

Whether exposure to such content actually has a causal influence on the level of alcohol use is conjectural. It is difficult to evaluate the effects of alcohol use portrayed in these programs because the types of individuals who view different types and amounts of programs are not equivalent. An alternative interpretation is that persons already favorably disposed toward alcohol and other drugs are more inclined to prefer media presentations that portray drinking and other drug use in a positive light than individuals with negative alcohol and drug attitudes.

As with most work in this area, the above studies measure the frequency of alcohol-drinking incidents, which is not the same as the percentage of characters who drink (Long, O'Connor, Gerbner, & Concato, 2002). When the prevalence rates of alcohol use among 1995–1996 prime-time TV characters were compared with rates of use in the U.S. population, the television rate was much lower not only for alcohol use (11.0% vs. 51.0%) but also for use of illicit drugs (0.8% vs. 6.1%) and for smoking tobacco (2.5% vs. 28.9%).

Nonetheless, some evidence suggests that more viewing of television leads young adolescents to begin use of alcohol. A prospective cohort study (Robinson, Chen, & Killen, 1998) with 1,533 ninth-grade students assessed the hours of television, music video, and videotape viewing; computer and video game use; and lifetime and past-30-day alcohol use at baseline and 18 months later. At the follow-up, 36.2% of baseline nondrinkers were drinking, and 50.7% of baseline drinkers continued to drink. For those who initiated drinking during this period, onset of drinking was significantly associated with baseline hours of television viewing, music video viewing, and videotape viewing controlling for age, sex, ethnicity, and other media use.

Impact of Advertising

Advertising and PSAs both use media to communicate about alcohol and other drugs. In contrast to PSA messages that emphasize health information, alcohol and tobacco advertising often relies on distorted and misleading glamorization about the benefits of the use of these drugs. The goal is to market sales of alcohol and tobacco products through the creation of images and fantasies associated with these products rather than to impart factual information.

Huge sums of money are spent to advertise alcoholic beverages in the United States. From 1998 to 2002, spending on televised beer ads increased by 45% to $972 million and increased by 530% to $18 million for liquor advertising. Although wine ads on television dropped by 22% to $48 million, it rose by 32% to $57 million for print ads (Center for Science in the Public Interest, 2003). One might assume that advertising is highly effective in encouraging alcohol consumption to justify such expenditures. However, correlational studies of the relationship between the amount of consumption and exposure to alcohol advertising do not allow for firm causal interpretations. Thus, people who like to drink also may enjoy watching alcoholic beverage ads more than lighter or nondrinkers do.

When ads for alcohol were banned in 17 developed nations from 1970 to 1983, per capita alcohol consumption was only 84% as high as in countries without such restrictions (Saffer, 1991). Moreover, alcohol abuse, as indexed by cirrhosis mortality and motor vehicle fatality rates, was lower in countries with alcohol advertising bans. The same conclusion was suggested by alcohol sales when a 58-year alcohol ad ban was removed (Makowsky & Whitehead, 1991) in Saskatchewan in 1983. Beer sales increased, sales of spirits decreased, and wine sales did not change following the return of alcohol advertising. However, alcohol ad bans on television are easily circumvented by increased use of other media such as magazines. A more effective strategy to reducing the alcohol consumption of teenagers and young adults might be counteradvertising as with PSAs (Saffer, 2002).

How children *interpret* advertising messages may have more impact than how often they are exposed to alcohol advertisements. A study (Austin, Chen, & Grube, 2006) with 652 boys and girls, aged 9–17 years, used computer-assisted interviews to assess their reactions to alcohol ads in television programs. Media alcohol portrayals influence children's drinking through a progressive decision-making process involving two processes, one logical and one affective. The logical process involves skepticism toward alcohol portrayals. However, a stronger affective response occurred to likeable characters in ads, which in turn made children want to imitate their attitudes and behaviors. In turn, these attitudes predicted expectancies and liking of or desire for beer toys and brands, which predicted later alcohol use.

Economic Controls

One assumption is that higher costs of a drug lead to reduced consumption because potential users may have less disposable income (Chaloupka, Grossman, & Saffer, 2002). Thus, higher alcohol excise taxes increase the purchase price of alcohol and should reduce aggregate alcohol consumption and its adverse consequences.

Alcohol Taxes

In support of this view, as noted earlier, increased liquor taxes between 1960 and 1975 in many states were associated with a decline in alcohol consumption (Cook, 1981). However, differences in the effectiveness of pricing on reducing consumption may exist for different beverage types. Beer is **price inelastic** (i.e., its consumption level does not vary much with the price), whereas consumption of distilled spirits and, to some extent, wine is **price elastic** and reduced by higher prices (Ornstein & Levy, 1983).

Although higher price may lead to less drinking for many light drinkers, it is less likely to be effective with highly addicted drinkers who might forego other needs to spend economic resources on alcohol. Aggregate comparisons do not allow us to identify which individuals are drinking less. As price goes up, does drinking decline evenly across the whole population or more so for some groups than for others? Higher prices may reduce alcohol use only for lighter drinkers and may not lower alcohol consumption of heavier drinkers for whom drugs are "price elastic" (Reuter & MacCoun, 1995).

A longitudinal study (Mohler-Kuo, Rehm, Heeb, & Gmel, 2004) evaluated how an alcohol tax *reduction* in Switzerland affected alcohol consumption. A randomly selected sample of 4,007 residents aged 15 years or older participated in the baseline survey conducted 3 months prior to the tax reform, and 73% of this sample participated in the follow-up survey done 28 months after the change. Alcohol-related problems were higher at follow-up, mainly mediated through increased alcohol consumption, particularly among younger age groups.

Price Effect on Consumption

A review of research (Leung & Phelps, 1993) found that higher prices are related to less consumption, after controlling for other factors such as income. This effect occurred for all types of alcoholic beverages, although beer had the least reduction in relation to price increases. An analysis (Gruenewald, Ponicki, Holder, & Romelsjo, 2006) of price effects on alcohol consumption from 1984 through 1994 for different beverage types in Sweden showed that consumers responded to price increases by reducing their total consumption and by switching their brand choices.

When alcoholic beverage prices increase, consumers tend to drink less and have fewer alcohol-related problems. Price is an important aspect of social policy about alcohol in view of the huge costs that alcohol abuse imposes on other people affected by such behavior (Cook & Moore, 2002).

A different situation may hold for illicit drugs. A major problem associated with the high price of illicit drugs is that heavy users may resort to various criminal activities to support their expensive drug habits. Price does not appear to deter the use of these drugs for those who are already dependent on them.

Educational Controls

School-based alcohol and other drug prevention programs have tried numerous curricula that usually involve several components aimed at different goals. Many of these programs focus on helping children resist peer influences by teaching coping skills and, through normative education, correcting the misperception that everyone is using drugs. Both objectives deal with factors that have been shown to have a strong relationship with alcohol use.

Resistance Skills Programs

Project DARE. A highly visible and promoted but also very controversial drug education program for elementary schools is the **Drug Abuse Resistance Education (DARE)** project. Initiated in 1983 in public schools by the Los Angeles Police Department, DARE was widely accepted throughout the nation and taught in more than half of all schools in the United States. The orientation of the curriculum was to teach **resistance skills** ("Just say no") to millions of schoolchildren using police officers from the community. Project DARE receives funding currently under the Safe and Drug-Free Schools and Communities Act of 1994, which provides more than $400 million annually for DARE and other programs.

Despite its popular appeal and support, independent evaluators found that the program did not do what it was supposed to do. Although DARE raised children's self-esteem, taught them skills to resist peer pressures to use drugs, and improved their attitudes toward police, it did not lower drug use (Ennett, Tobler, Ringwalt, & Flewelling, 1994). The critics charged that DARE became essentially a government-sanctioned monopoly, operating in 8,000 communities and more than half of the nation's schools, despite a lack of convincing evidence that it lowered drug use.

A follow-up study (Lynam et al., 1999) of 1,000 Midwestern participants in Project DARE was conducted 10 years after the students received the drug prevention curriculum in the sixth grade. The study compared pre-DARE levels of cigarette, alcohol, marijuana, and illicit drug use with levels at age 20. Pre- and postlevels of peer-pressure resistance and self-esteem were also compared. Although the DARE program had a few initial improvements in student attitudes toward drug use, the changes did not last. More important, there were no effects in actual initial drug use or during the follow-up period.

LifeSkills Training Program. This program assumes that resistance to alcohol use can be developed with experience just as inoculation can improve immunity to diseases. The LifeSkills Training program (Botvin, Baker, Dusenbury, Tortu, & Botvin, 1990; Botvin, Schinke, Epstein, Diaz, & Botvin, 1995) teaches general personal and social skills as well as drug resistance skills in a classroom setting. This 3-year curriculum, designed for middle school or junior high school students, uses a combination of techniques, including instruction, demonstration, feedback, reinforcement, behavioral rehearsal, and homework assignments. Students learn general as well as drug-specific problem-solving and decision-making skills, critical thinking skills for resisting peer and media influences, skills for increasing self-control and self-esteem, coping strategies for relieving stress and anxiety, and information about the drug use norms of their peers.

Different schools received either the prevention program with formal provider training and feedback, the prevention program with videotaped provider training and no feedback, or no treatment. Significant reductions ranging from 59% to 75% occurred for cigarette smoking, marijuana use, and immoderate alcohol use for those schools that received the prevention program in comparison to controls. Prevention effects also were found for normative expectations and knowledge concerning substance use, interpersonal skills, and communication skills. A follow-up 6 years later showed that the prevalence of cigarette smoking, alcohol use, and marijuana use for students in the LifeSkills Training program was 44% lower than for control students.

Normative Education

Many students believe that peers use drugs at higher levels than they actually do, a misperception that might encourage them to use drugs. To counter this tendency, about 3,600 fifth graders in 128 different classes in 45 different schools participated in the Adolescent Alcohol Prevention Trial (Hansen, Graham, Wolkenstein, & Rohrbach, 1991). Two types of programs, one involving resistance skills training and one providing **normative education** in which the students learned that many other students did not use drugs, were combined to create four conditions: normative education curriculum only, resistance training curriculum only, both curricula, and neither curriculum. The combination of normative education and resistance skills training was the most effective curriculum. In addition, the quality of program delivery, enthusiasm of the teachers, receptiveness of the students, and proper delivery of the program components, as judged by trainers, observers, and program specialists, contributed to the success of the students in acquiring resistance skills and perceived self-efficacy.

Data on cigarette and alcohol use from grade 7 to grade 11 in the Adolescent Alcohol Prevention Trial were examined to model changes in use and program efficacy over the

5-year period (Taylor, Graham, Cumsille, & Hansen, 2000). The normative education group as compared with the control group had lower average reported cigarette and alcohol use, lower rates of growth for reported cigarette and alcohol use, and less decline in reported rates of cigarette and alcohol use levels.

One method adopted by many colleges aimed at reducing alcohol use by all students is based on findings that social norms are among the best predictors of college student drinking. One study (Neighbors, Lee, Lewis, Fossos, & Larimer, 2007) assessed 818 first-year undergraduates (57.6% women) who reported at least one heavy-drinking episode in the previous month. Students who believed most students drank at higher levels tended to drink more than those who believed the social norm for drinking was lower. One conclusion is that thinking most other students drink heavily encourages higher drinking. However, the same findings may simply mean that those students who already drink heavily tend to think most other students do likewise.

Social norms marketing involves campuswide campaigns using cost-effective campus media (e.g., posters, newspaper advertisements) that contain a core message about student alcohol use norms. These messages "inform" students that most of their peers do not drink very much—for example, "When students party, most of them usually drink between 0 and 2 drinks" (the norm in the message varied for different colleges).

The rationale for the social norms approach is that most students hold a misconception that most other students drink large amounts (Carey, Borsari, Carey, & Maisto, 2006). The possibility that such beliefs encourage or pressure them to drink at higher levels is supported by findings that students with larger discrepancies between their own drinking and their perceptions of other student drinking increased their self-reported drinking a month later.

The social marketing approach holds that sending the message that the majority of students drink at lower levels will lead to lower student drinking. For example, an intensive social norms program conducted with student athletes at one private college found substantial benefits in lowering drinking (Perkins & Craig, 2006).

However, many social norms studies are inconclusive because they relied on self-reports of drinking measured before and after the campaign without comparisons to any control campuses that did not receive the messages. Some studies suggest that the campaigns do not decrease alcohol use and may, in fact, increase alcohol use. For example, a comparison of 37 colleges with 61 colleges without social norm programs (Wechsler et al., 2003) found no benefits of social norm campaigns.

The impact of social norms marketing was tested over a 3-year period at 18 colleges across the country that were randomly assigned to treatment and control groups (DeJong et al., 2006). Controlling for other predictors, students on campuses that had the social norms campaign had lower perceptions of student drinking levels as well as lower alcohol consumption 3 years later, as measured by several indices including a composite drinking scale and blood alcohol concentration for recent maximum consumption. In fact, on the control campuses, the mean level of drinking over 3 years actually increased. However, these findings involved cross-sectional or group comparisons of average changes. They cannot determine the extent to which individual students changed their own behavior over the 3 years. Other limitations were the reliance on self-report of alcohol use and a response rate of around 50% at baseline and just under 60% at the follow-up, allowing for the possibility that a self-selected rather than a representative sample of students participated in the study.

A longitudinal study (Neighbors, Dillard, Lewis, Bergstrom, & Neil, 2006) avoided some of these problems by measuring perceived norms and self-reported drinking frequency and weekly quantity twice within 2 months. About two thirds of the original sample of 70 men and 94 women college students completed the same measures at the follow-up. As expected by social norms theory, the initial perceived drinking norms predicted later drinking. In addition, initial weekly drinking quantity—but not frequency—predicted later perceived drinking norms, showing that the relationship between one's own drinking and one's beliefs about drinking norms is not as simple as assumed.

Community-Based Approach

A community-based approach to prevention holds that effective programs for students must also involve parental and community participation. A large-scale 3-year longitudinal study, the Midwestern Prevention Project (Johnson et al., 1990; Pentz, 1995), illustrates this model. Over 1,000 sixth and seventh graders in 24 intervention and 18 control schools in the Kansas City metropolitan area received a prevention curriculum of 10 sessions in the first year with five booster sessions in the second year. The curriculum included drink refusal skill training, homework involving role playing with parents and family, peer leader discussion of homework, and mass media programs about substance abuse,

Classes were randomly assigned to several different experimental treatment groups and one control group that was exposed to mass media and community organization. Students who began the program in junior high showed significantly less use of marijuana (approximately 30%), cigarettes (about 25%), and alcohol (about 20%) in their senior year than children in schools that did not offer the program. The most important factor affecting drug use among the students was increased perceptions of their friends' intolerance of drug use.

The project also included parent involvement and parenting skills training during the second year and added community-wide drug abuse prevention meetings aimed at improving community alcohol attitudes and promoting more restrictive drug ordinances to limit students' access to drugs in the community during the third year. Parental participation was negatively associated with adolescent use of alcohol and cigarettes (Rohrbach et al., 1994).

Another community prevention program, Project Northland, randomly assigned 2,350 sixth-grade children in 24 Minnesota rural and small-town school districts to a control and a treatment condition (Williams, Perry, Farbakhsh, & Veblen-Mortenson, 1999). Children were tracked for 3 years. By the eighth grade, children receiving the intervention who had been nonusers in the sixth grade had lower alcohol use as well as lower scores on Minnesota Multiphasic Personality Inventory-Adolescent scales that reflected adolescent school problems. However, no differences in cigarette smoking or marijuana use occurred.

The curriculum had five components: classroom curricula, peer leadership, youth extracurricular activities, parent involvement programs, and community activism. As with any multicomponent program, different aspects may vary in effectiveness, so each part must be evaluated (refer to Figure 14.3 for an example). Evaluation showed that the most effective parts of Project Northland were the planning of extracurricular activities and parent program components, whereas classroom curricula had only moderate benefits and community activism did not show any impact (Stigler, Perry, Komro, Cudeck, & Williams, 2006).

The Project Northland curriculum did not fare so well in a large urban community (Komro et al., 2008). The 5,812 students, primarily African American, Hispanic, and low income, in 61 Chicago public schools formed neighborhood study units that were assigned randomly to intervention or a "delayed program" control condition. Sixth-grade students received 3 years of intervention (curricula, family interventions, youth-led community service projects, community organizing). Annual classroom-based surveys measured their alcohol use and related risk and protective factors. Compared with a control condition receiving "prevention as usual," the intervention was *not* effective in reducing alcohol use, other drug use, or any hypothesized mediating variables (i.e., related risk and protective factors). The program that succeeded in rural Minnesota failed to have similar results in Chicago, showing that previously validated programs may not be successful for different settings or populations.

A 5-year community-level project with an environmental policy approach (Holder, 2000) attempted to reduce local alcohol-involved injuries and deaths in three communities with populations of approximately 100,000 each with racial and ethnic diversity that included a mix of urban, suburban, and rural settings. Outcomes for each community were compared to a control community that did not receive the prevention interventions.

The program design involved five mutually reinforcing components that aimed at developing community organization/support, setting standards for on-premises alcohol outlet servers to reduce serving intoxicated and/or underage customers, improving actual and perceived local drunk-driving enforcement efficiency, reducing retail availability of alcohol to minors, and zoning controls of outlet density to reduce availability of alcohol.

Overall, as compared to the control communities, the three communities where the program was implemented had reduced alcohol-involved crashes, lowered sales to minors, increased the responsible alcohol-serving practices of bars and restaurants, and increased community support and awareness of alcohol problems.

Legal Controls

Licit Drugs

Laws, in comparison to persuasion, education, or economics, are coercive means for controlling alcohol and other drug use. Prohibition of alcohol is the most extreme example of government policy directed at reducing availability of a drug. Although it was relatively effective in achieving its goals between 1919 and 1932 in the United States, it was abandoned eventually because its enforcement created other undesired problems such as bootlegging. Current laws involve restricting availability rather than total prohibition of alcohol through laws governing licensing and regulation of alcohol sales outlets, public intoxication, and driving under the influence of alcohol.

Alcohol Outlet Density. Licensing laws regulate where and when alcohol can be sold. Higher rates of assaults, crimes, and automobile accidents occur with greater density of alcohol outlets in an area. Analysis of 6 years from a database that linked information for alcohol outlets and crimes by ZIP code showed that areas with a higher density of licensed alcohol outlets such as bars and liquor stores tend to have more crime and violence (Gruenewald & Remer, 2006). Another analysis (Treno, Johnson, Remer, & Gruenewald, 2007) of the same data set showed that automobile accidents were positively associated with changes in numbers of licensed alcohol retail establishments, especially bars and off-premises outlets.

Server Training Laws. Servers in commercial alcohol outlets such as bars and restaurants are important regulators of alcohol availability. In many states, servers of alcohol must be licensed. Training programs to help promote server responsibility teach servers how to recognize when a patron has had too much to drink, provide the skills necessary to refuse service to intoxicated customers, and teach how to recognize fake driver's licenses and other forms of identification.

A multicommunity trial (Wagenaar, Toomey, & Erickson, 2005) in 20 Midwest cities examined how well a server training program in retail alcohol establishments and enforcement checks of alcohol sales to minors would reduce underage access to alcohol. Researchers attempted to purchase alcohol from on-premises and off-premises alcohol outlets without showing age identification. Effects of the training intervention were mixed. Specific deterrent effects were observed for enforcement checks, with an immediate 17% reduction in sales to minors, but these effects decayed entirely within 3 months in off-premises establishments and had only an 8.2% reduction in on-premises establishments.

Illicit Drugs

In the case of illicit drugs, the assumption is that laws against the sale and use of these drugs can keep the problem under control. Without these laws, the already substantial problems associated with illicit drug abuse might be even higher. Some might agree with the prediction but object to the methods used to enforce these laws, which often may infringe on civil liberties.

Although substantial funds are allocated to law enforcement, incarceration, and rehabilitation, the efforts have not appreciably reduced the demand for many illicit drugs. For fiscal year (FY) 2007 the federal budget for drug programs was $12.7 billion, an increase of $80.6 million over that for 2006. The proposed federal budget for FY 2009 continues the pattern of allocating much more for supply reduction than for demand reduction even though it has not proven effective (Carnevale Associates, 2008). The proposed FY 2009 budget for law enforcement and drug interdiction is about 57% greater than the FY 2002 amount. In contrast, prevention and treatment have a miniscule proposed budget increase of 2.7% for FY 2009 over the FY 2002 level.

About two thirds of the requested budget is for "disrupting the drug supply" with law enforcement, interdiction of supplies at borders, crop eradication, and substitution in other countries. Only about one third of the proposed budget is for demand reduction through education and intervention programs. However, the evidence on the effect of reduced supplies of illegal drugs on the demand for them is not convincing (Institute of Medicine, 1996).

In addition to legal methods of reducing supplies of illicit drugs, increased attempts have been made to reduce demand by arresting drug offenders (Zimring & Hawkins, 1992). Mandatory jail sentences for certain drug offenses exist in almost all states, leading to overcrowded jails, even though doubts have been raised about the cost-effectiveness of this approach in preventing use of illicit drugs such as cocaine (Caulkins, Rydell, Schwabe, & Chiesa, 1997).

About 1 in 4 jail inmates in 2002 had drug offenses, up from 22% in 1996. About 77% of convicted jail inmates were involved with alcohol or other drugs at the time of their current offense (James, 2004). In 2002, 2 in 5 inmates were dependent on alcohol or other drugs, while nearly 1 in 4 abused alcohol or drugs but were not dependent on them (Karberg & James, 2005).

But the question still remains: How effective are severe penalties for drug offenses as deterrents? For example, increased enforcement against illicit drugs might have an unintended and ironic effect (MacCoun & Caulkins, 1996). As more dealers get arrested, the cost of dealing drugs becomes higher. Consequently, the selling price of drugs rises to compensate surviving dealers for their higher risk. The lure of more sizable profits for dealers selling illicit drugs, coupled perhaps also by their underestimates of the objective risk of their arrest, could motivate more rather than less drug trafficking.

The impact of increased law enforcement on illicit drug consumers also seems to be limited as illicit drug use is still high. Whereas in 1985, 34% of all federal prisoners were incarcerated for drug violations, the rate increased to 60% by 1995 (Haney & Zimbardo, 1998). A slight drop in the *percentage* of all federal inmates who were incarcerated for drug violations, from 60% to 53%, occurred from 1995 to 2006 (Sabol, Couture, & Harrison, 2007). But that decline is not a sign of improvement because the *absolute* number of drug offenders in federal prisons had a large *increase* over the past decade. Thus, in 2006, 53% of a total of 176,268 inmates in federal prisons were drug offenders. By comparison, in 2000, 56% of 131,739 inmates were drug offenders, and in 1995, 60% of 88,658 inmates were drug offenders.

SECONDARY PREVENTION

If we cannot "prevent" alcohol and other drug problems from occurring due to the many factors in the environment that make use of these substances attractive, we can and must still develop countermeasures for the reduction and minimization of existing problems stemming from their excessive use. **Secondary prevention** refers to methods to reduce ongoing problems that alcohol and other drugs have created for society. How this task is achieved will be illustrated with three pervasive societal problems: underage drinking, driving under the influence, and drugs in the workplace.

Underage Drinking

The problems resulting from underage use of alcohol, tobacco, and other drugs are a major concern that has not received the attention it warrants. Underage drinking, for example, extracts a considerable price with an estimated social cost of $53 billion, with $19 billion from traffic crashes and $29 billion from violent crime (Bonnie & O'Connell, 2004). In addition, there are unmeasured losses in the form of impaired school and job performance that lead to lifetimes of future pain and suffering. Yet in FY 2000, the federal budget for preventing underage drinking was only $71.1 million as compared to $1.8 billion directed toward drug abuse prevention.

Underage drinking accounted for at least 16% of alcohol sales in 2001, leading to 3,170 deaths and $2.6 million in other harmful events. The estimated $61.9 billion costs included $5.4 billion in medical expenses, $14.9 billion in work loss and other resource costs, and $41.6 billion in lost quality of life (Miller, Levy, Spicer, & Taylor, 2006). In light of these high costs to society, youth drinking behaviors demand urgent attention.

Approaches to preventing underage drinking include efforts directed at the "host" or user through information provided in school curricula targeted at preventing alcohol, tobacco, or marijuana use. In addition, extracurricular activities involving social or life skills training or alternative activities and programs for adolescents' families have been used.

Attempts to reduce underage alcohol and other drug use also involve controlling the "agent" or drug and the environment. Laws and regulations set the minimum legal drinking age to 21, required age identification checks to minimize the commercial and social access of underage youth to alcohol, curtailed marketing of alcohol to minors, and reduced the availability of alcohol by increasing alcohol prices. The increased price of alcohol is more effective in lowering drinking than the other methods, which are often not strictly enforced and thus allow underage individuals to circumvent those obstacles (Komro & Toomey, 2002).

Because a large percentage of college students are under the minimum legal age for drinking, a prevention priority of colleges and universities involves targeting practices and policies affecting the availability and use of alcohol on campuses and in student housing facilities. Environmental strategies for reducing underage drinking among college students (and for general populations) are diverse, ranging from restricting alcohol at parties, prohibiting self-service, and checking age identification cards to creating alcohol-free residence halls and enforcement of alcohol regulations. A review (Toomey, Lenk, & Wagenaar, 2007) of studies that evaluated the effects of campus policies on prevention of underage drinking found mixed results for most methods, but campus policies were more effective when they were used in combination.

Driving Under the Influence

With the widespread availability and popularity of alcoholic beverages in our highly mobile society, it is inevitable that many drivers will operate motor vehicles with varying levels of alcohol in their body even though they may know it is illegal. They may realize that they have a good chance of not being detected because it is not possible for law enforcement personnel to apprehend every person driving under the influence of alcohol.

Secondary prevention deals with preventing recurrences of this type of behavior among those who are apprehended for **driving under the influence of alcohol (DUI)** or **driving while intoxicated (DWI)**. There is increasing recognition that many drivers are impaired when **driving under the influence of drugs (DUID)** or affected by both alcohol and other drugs.

General deterrence programs attempt to reduce DUI occurrences among those who have not engaged in such activity or at least have not yet been apprehended. A focus on deterrence uses the threat of license suspension or revocation, fines, higher insurance rates, and even jail sentences. Countermeasures based on education use didactic presentation of information coupled with some small-group interactions to increase awareness.

The preceding approaches focus on internal control by drivers, but other methods involve external or environmental factors. Roadside sobriety checkpoints and increased highway patrols, especially during holiday weekends, aim to deter DUI as well as apprehend any offenders. Ignition interlock devices that prevent vehicle operation unless the driver's breath alcohol content registers below the legal limit have also been used.

High-Risk and Repeat Offenders

Specific deterrence of DUI takes the form of punishing convicted offenders with fines, jail, and license revocation. Nonetheless, these actions are often ineffective as many drivers have repeat DUI convictions. Some of these DUI cases need treatment for alcohol abuse or dependency. The hope is that successful treatment for the substance problem will eliminate future DUI offenses by these cases. However, it is dangerous to overgeneralize and treat all DUI offenders as if they are alcohol abusers. While all DUI offenders should be sanctioned for their driving infractions, mandating those who are not abusers of alcohol to attend alcohol treatment programs may be inappropriate, unwarranted, and ineffective.

There may be personality differences between first and repeat offenders. In total, 358 first offenders and 141 multiple-DUI offenders were compared on personality traits, drinking behavior and problems, and driving records (McMillen, Adams, Wells Parker, Pang, & Anderson, 1992). Multiple offenders were higher in hostility, sensation seeking, psychopathic deviance, mania, and depression and had more nontraffic arrests, accidents, and traffic tickets than first offenders.

Shaffer et al. (2007) found that repeat DUI offenders had higher lifetime and 12-month prevalence of alcohol and other drug use disorders, conduct disorder, posttraumatic stress disorder, generalized anxiety disorder, and bipolar disorder compared with the general population. Almost half qualified for lifetime diagnoses of both addiction (i.e., alcohol, drug, nicotine, and/or gambling) and a psychiatric disorder. Lifetime and past-year comorbidity rates were higher among participants than in the general population.

Based on evidence of psychiatric and substance use disorders, it may be necessary to treat both problems in these cases if one expects to reduce repeat DUI offenses among this population. However, explanations relying on only one or two behavioral domains (e.g., driving characteristics, personality, demographics) to explain DUI relapse are insufficient for understanding all DUI offenders (Nochajski & Stasiewicz, 2006). Complex models are needed that examine how multiple factors—legal, social, and psychological—combine to contribute to repeat DUI offenses.

Alcohol and Other Drugs in the Workplace

The adverse effects of alcohol and other drug abuse and dependence often extend beyond the drinker's personal activities to the workplace, impairing performance and productivity. Absenteeism and tardiness, work productivity, workplace safety, and liability are major concerns related to the detrimental effects of drug use among employees in the workplace.

Prior to the temperance movements of the 19th century, alcohol use on the job was not always regarded as undesirable but was commonly accepted. As the hazards of drinking affecting work quality became recognized, management's solution was typically to discharge such personnel. In the 1940s, a movement arose to provide **employee assistance programs (EAPs)** in which supervisors were taught to use poor or deteriorating work performance as a sign of possible alcohol problems. Then attempts to counsel and refer the employee to alcoholism treatment would be made. The idea of EAPs was more humane than firing employees, but it was also hoped that the programs would be cost-effective by avoiding the expense of retraining, new hiring, work site accidents, poor productivity, and litigation. However, EAPs are often difficult to implement due to resistance from both employers and employees. It was not until the late 1980s that EAPs finally became widely accepted (Trice & Staudemeier, 1989), but research on their effectiveness has declined in the past decade (Blum & Roman, 1995).

At the same time that EAPs became more commonplace, the approach became more "broad-brush," extending beyond alcohol problems to include referral and treatment for illegal drug abuse as well as other psychological problems that might hamper work productivity, generate turnover and absenteeism, and cause workplace accidents. Currently, services are typically not provided at the work site but delivered through managed behavioral health care providers.

The potential of EAPs to motivate drug abusers and dependents to seek treatment rests in the fact that employers have one important leverage that family members and friends lack—namely, control over the employee's job. However, threats of dismissals and penalties are less effective than constructive confrontation (Trice & Sonnenstuhl, 1988) and peer referral in motivating help seeking.

In theory, EAPs promise a means of early intervention, but in practice, problems exist in their implementation such as threats to confidentiality, coerced treatment, and invasion of privacy. Although employers have a right to expect work performance to meet certain criteria, it is only when alcohol abuse interferes with these goals that employers can legitimately attempt to urge employees to accept alcoholism treatment. However, overzealous employers sometimes exceed these limits and monitor employee behaviors that employers and supervisors find unacceptable, even when they do not interfere with work performance (Fillmore & Kelso, 1987). In addition to these political concerns, the effectiveness of EAPs in modifying drinking problems is difficult to assess and thus has not been adequately evaluated. Self-selection may be involved since random assignment is not possible. Many studies lack control or appropriate comparison groups (Levy Merrick, Volpe-Vartanian, Horgan, & McCann, 2007).

Some studies show EAPs improved clinical and work outcomes. However, determining cost-related effects is difficult due to the lack of common performance measures. One review (Blum & Roman, 1995) of evaluation studies indicated that EAPs returned many employees with alcohol problems to effective performance, but none of these studies had comparisons with employees in settings without EAP services. There has been little well-designed research on the utility of EAPs and other mechanisms for addressing employee alcohol problems.

Workplace Drug Testing

The Federal Workplace Drug Testing Program created mandatory drug testing standards in 1988 with the most recent revision in 2004 (Bush, 2008). Drug testing is one objective approach that is aimed at preventing work impairment and accidents that may harm employees using drugs as well as create risks for coworkers. Several issues arise that complicate the use of drug-testing policies. Drug testing in broad EAPs is problematic because of issues of privacy and civil liberties (White, 2003). If employees choose to engage in drug use when they are not at work, should they be required to be tested for drugs if they perform their job duties competently when they are at work?

The implication under mandatory drug testing is that the employee is presumed guilty until proven innocent. That is, when drug tests are required, the burden of proof is on the employee. Given the potential safety problems created by employees under the influence of drugs in the workplace, it may be conceded that drug testing is defensible as a lesser evil in jobs where there is high risk for substantial harm from accidents or breach of security. However, this concession presumes that drug tests such as urinalysis are highly accurate, an assumption that is questioned (Hansen, 1993; Kapur, 1993; Zwerling, 1993).

HARM REDUCTION APPROACH

As noted earlier, one philosophy of alcohol and drug prevention efforts has involved supply reduction through strict legal enforcement, interdiction, and taxation to reduce the availability of drugs in the environment. A second approach, demand reduction, focuses on users through education and treatment to change their behaviors and motivations. Although these approaches, as shown in Figure 16.3, have different immediate goals and methods, both aim for the same long-term goal, reduced prevalence of users.

Harm reduction approaches started in the 1980s in the Netherlands and England, primarily in connection with the use of methadone maintenance to deal with the heroin epidemic. Proponents of this view hold that drug problems may never be "prevented" in any absolute manner (Marlatt, 1998). The harm reduction approach is less ambitious than the "war on drugs" campaigns waged by the federal government. It concedes that we cannot readily prevent drug abuse, but meanwhile we can at least try to minimize its harms. In some European cities such as Amsterdam, faced with widespread illicit drug problems, attempts were made to make the use of drugs less risky to users as well as nonusers. The rapid spread of HIV by heroin injectors prompted efforts to minimize the harm by clean needle exchange programs. The goal of this approach was not to condone or encourage heroin use but to contain or reduce the extent of health problems associated with its use.

For example, harm reduction advocates do not see methadone programs as an ideal solution for heroin addiction. Methadone is a longer-acting replacement for heroin that is taken orally so there is no risk for HIV exposure from using needles for injecting heroin. Its proponents see it as a drug of "lesser harm" than heroin and defend it on the grounds that methadone-treated heroin patients under medical supervision are less likely to experience cravings for heroin or commit crimes to gain drug money.

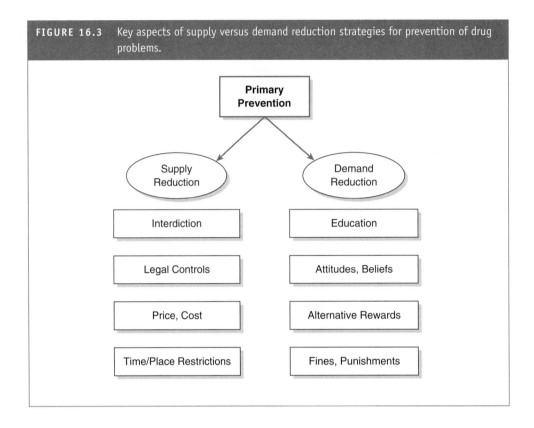

FIGURE 16.3   Key aspects of supply versus demand reduction strategies for prevention of drug problems.

Figure 16.4 shows that the **use reduction** approach is primarily aimed at reducing levels of use (arrow b), whereas the harm reduction approach focuses on reducing the "average harm" to both users and nonusers (MacCoun, 1998). In addition, it is important to note that there may be some unintended effects of each approach. Tradeoffs are involved when gains toward one goal may be offset by losses toward other goals. Use reduction efforts, when successful, might reduce the direct harm of a specific drug. However, drug use reduction also might unintentionally increase other forms of harm on average (dashed arrow c). Thus, increasing the price of a drug by making it illegal might lead users to criminal activities to obtain the drug. Similarly, the lack of clean needles for heroin users from a needle exchange program might not reduce use, yet it increases the risk of HIV infection.

Harm reduction, when successful at the individual level, might (arrow d) send "a wrong message" that a specific drug is not that dangerous. Consequently, at the societal level, there may be an increase in the overall use of a risky drug. For example, a clean needle exchange program might make intravenous drugs appear safer (less risky) than users previously thought, so they might end up engaging in more harmful use levels. By making clean needles available, the use of intravenous drugs is less risky, so the user might be less motivated to quit or to never start using heroin.

By lowering the actual or perceived risk of harm from a drug, there could be an unintended actual increase in use levels as a form of risk compensation by users (dashed arrow e).

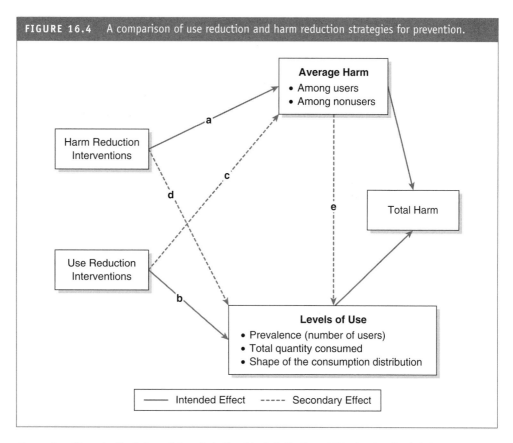

FIGURE 16.4   A comparison of use reduction and harm reduction strategies for prevention.

Source: From "Toward a Psychology of Harm Reduction," by R. J. MacCoun, 1998, *American Psychologist, 53*, pp. 1199–1208. Copyright 1998 by the American Psychological Association. Reprinted with permission.

Thus, putting filters on cigarettes to make them "safer" might encourage smokers to continue their use. Similarly, wearing a seatbelt may make drivers feel safer, so they may drive more recklessly. Giving condoms to adolescents could make them feel less risk in engaging in sexual intercourse. Hence, microlevel harm reduction among individuals ironically increases macrolevel harm for society as a whole.

Other factors must be considered in the development of acceptable and viable prevention strategies. Total harm, as shown in Figure 16.4, is a joint outcome of the average harm per use and the total use (total harm equals the number of users multiplied by the quantity each user consumes). Average harm per use includes harm to users (overdoses, AIDS) and harm to nonusers (crime victimization, HIV infection).

Quantity Reduction as a Middle Ground

Our national drug policy insists on making a sharp distinction between users and nonusers, and indices of drug problems are prevalence-oriented indices based on rates of use during a specific time period. However, harm stemming from drug use may be more closely linked to the total quantity of a drug consumed in society than to the total number of individual users. The smaller percentage of the population that engages in heavy use contributes more harm than the much more numerous light or infrequent users. Consequently, a focus on methods of **quantity reduction** for individual users may be a more fruitful strategy, one that falls between strategies of prevalence reduction and harm reduction. Exactly how to best achieve this goal is less clear. One could target the heaviest users and try to get them to reduce their consumption levels. An example with alcohol is "controlled drinking," a goal of heavy drinkers using alcohol at lower levels. The approach is not well accepted in the United States but widely embraced in England and in some European countries. Opponents object to this approach because they feel that abstinence is necessary for recovery.

Harm reduction has had some success, especially with needle exchange programs for heroin users. It would be more likely to gain acceptance if it not only reduced average harm but also caused no increase in overall drug use levels. Harm reduction goals aimed at total consumption might be more effective by aiming efforts at drinkers in the middle of the consumption distribution than by focusing on problem drinkers. Lowering consumption in this larger subpopulation may reduce the total social costs of alcohol more than concentrating on the smaller group at the high end of use.

Empirical studies have demonstrated that harm reduction approaches to alcohol problems are at least as effective as abstinence-oriented approaches to reducing alcohol consumption and alcohol-related consequences (Marlatt & Witkiewitz, 2002). Designing alcohol prevention and intervention programs that accommodate the preferences and needs of the targeted person or population is a goal. Harm reduction advocates seek to assist people in the direction of positive behavior change, whether that change involves abstinence, moderate drinking, or the reduction of alcohol use.

Opponents of harm reduction reject this philosophy as condoning drug use and "sending the wrong message." Uncompromising in its war on drugs, the absolute position calls for zero tolerance. However, unlike the situation for illicit drugs, the resistance to the harm reduction approach is much weaker when the drugs involved are legal. For drugs such as tobacco and alcohol, concern over public health seems to prevail over moralistic condemnation. Thus, no one seriously proposes prohibition of the production, sale, and consumption of alcoholic beverages or cigarettes. For legal drugs, it seems acceptable to tolerate use and try to keep use and harm under control by imposing high taxes, using warning labels, and placing restrictions on times and places of sale and consumption.

Harm reduction strategies have not been as widely acceptable as prevalence reduction plans. Most people believe they can control their own use of drugs, especially alcohol, so they find it difficult to think that others cannot do likewise. Attitudes about drug policy reflect core values. Many feel that drug abusers made their own bed, so they should be made to lie in it, even if they must suffer.

An assessment of the impact of harm reduction approaches was made from a review (Ritter & Cameron, 2006) of more than 650 harm reduction studies, mostly on illicit drugs, that had adequate control groups or pre-post comparisons. The harm reduction approach is backed by evidence on the efficacy, effectiveness, and economics of needle syringe exchange programs and outreach programs. There is less data so far regarding other harm reduction interventions such as noninjecting routes of administration, brief interventions, and supervised injecting facilities.

PROMOTING SOCIAL CHANGE

Social change with respect to licit and illicit drugs is impossible for individuals to achieve on their own because the tasks are overwhelming. Working together, however, well-organized groups of individuals have been effective in goading federal, state, and local governments to plan and implement acceptable and effective social policies to address problems related to use of alcohol and other drugs.

Community Activism

In the late 1970s, social activists formed grassroots nonprofit organizations such as Mothers Against Drunk Driving (MADD), Students Against Driving Drunk (SADD), and Remove Intoxicated Drivers (RID) to focus national attention and concern about the highway carnage created by alcohol- and other-drug-impaired drivers.

The most widely known and influential group, MADD, was started in 1980 by Candy Lightner after her 13-year-old daughter was killed by a repeat drunk driver. The initial mission of MADD was to provide support for family and friends of victims killed by drivers under the influence of alcohol or other drugs. Other groups modeled after MADD include a student organization, SADD, a peer-to-peer youth prevention organization founded in 1981 on the heels of MADD, with thousands of chapters in middle schools, high schools, and colleges. In 1997, SADD expanded its mission and name and now sponsors chapters called Students Against Destructive Decisions.

A Gallup Poll in 2005 found widespread belief that campaigns of MADD were largely responsible for major changes in American attitudes against drinking and driving (Fell & Voas, 2006). Statistics from the National Highway Traffic Safety Administration (NHTSA) show that alcohol-related traffic deaths in the United States declined by almost half from an estimated 30,000 in 1980 when MADD was founded to 16,694 in 2004. However, the number of traffic deaths that can be blamed on drinking drivers is not clear; nor is the amount of the reduction that is attributable to MADD because the NHTSA's Fatality Analysis Reporting System category of "alcohol-related deaths" includes *all* deaths on U.S. highways involving alcohol. But a high percentage of such deaths involved only a single car, and in most of those cases, the only death was the drunk driver. These incidents show the dangers of drinking drivers but are not cases where they killed innocent victims.

Improvements in highway design and vehicle safety as well as more negative public attitudes toward drunk driving since the 1980s may have also helped reduce all auto fatalities, not just alcohol-related deaths, since the early 1980s. These considerations in no way should deny the credit that MADD deserves for addressing the problems associated with drinking and driving.

MADD implemented its Victim Impact Panel program that involves regular meetings between convicted DUI offenders and victims or the relatives and friends of those killed by drunk drivers prior to sentencing. One assumption is that the emotional confrontation motivates offenders to curtail or stop drinking. An evaluation (Polacsek et al., 2001) of the impact of this program over a period of 2 years randomly assigned 813 (75% male) offenders in New Mexico to a DWI school or a DWI school plus a MADD Victim Impact Panel. The results found that the two groups did not differ in readiness for or actual reduced drinking or in recidivism.

MADD's successes led the organization to broaden its view of alcohol problems from drunken driving or road safety to public safety in general. It has lobbied for raising the minimum age for driving and lowering the legally allowable blood alcohol level for driving (McCarthy, 1999). In 1999, MADD tackled the problem of preventing underage drinking.

These organizations demonstrate that citizens can mobilize to deal with the societal inertia to confront the dangers created by drunk driving. These forces helped pressure the federal government to create the Presidential Commission on Drunk Driving in 1982, which has helped states and local communities take a tougher stance to enforce laws pertaining to drinking and driving. The withholding of federal highway funds from uncooperative states also served to motivate compliance.

Similarly, increased publicity, education, and awareness about the risks of fetal alcohol syndrome and other birth defects created by drinking among pregnant women illustrate how research can change public attitudes and concern about the health-related dangers of drinking. In some states, laws require establishments serving alcohol to post prominent signs warning patrons of other health risks of alcohol. Warning labels on alcoholic beverage containers also have been proposed as an effective method of reducing alcohol consumption (U.S. Department of Health and Human Services, 1987) by activist organizations such as the nonprofit Center for Science in the Public Interest.

Early prevention strategies for alcohol and drug problems centered on controlling the agent, alcohol, as illustrated by Prohibition (Langton, 1991). The focus then shifted to the host, or individual drinker, during the alcoholism movement of the 1970s. In the 1990s, the emphasis in prevention strategies again shifted, this time toward an emphasis on the environment. Programs to increase early detection and counseling can be seen as making the environment safer for others by reducing the chances that the drug user might harm others. For example, diversion programs for DUI and DUID offenders represent an early intervention to pressure individuals into alcoholism and other drug abuse counseling and treatment sooner than they would seek it on their own.

Similarly, as noted earlier in this chapter, many work organizations have recognized the impact of the work environment in creating drug problems. Historically, employers resisted the view that the workplace environment could itself be a factor contributing to alcohol problems among employees (Ames, 1989). Growing recognition that physical, social, or ideological working conditions may contribute to alcohol problems called for improvements in the work environment as well as early intervention to motivate the alcohol-dependent worker to seek treatment.

However, a negative feature of both DUI and DUID diversion programs and EAPs is the coercive nature of the interventions. Coerced treatment is problematic not only for those given the choice between treatment and going to jail or being fired (for alcohol- or other-drug-related work impairment) but also for the climate in alcoholism and drug treatment and recovery facilities. For example, traditionally, participants at self-help meetings such as Alcoholics Anonymous (AA) and Narcotics Anonymous were individuals who had reached "rock bottom" and were ready to admit they were powerless. However, with the large influx of coerced participants in AA and in public treatment facilities, many of whom are hostile and uncooperative, the situation is drastically altered in ways that may impair the effectiveness of these programs for voluntary participants (Weisner, 1987).

Furthermore, it is difficult to prove that individuals who are coerced into treatment benefit because it is not possible to include control groups of alcohol-dependent workers or DUI offenders who do not receive treatment (Weisner, 1990). The difficulty of proving that prevention is effective is also due to the lengthy interval needed before an intervention takes hold. When preventive measures are successful, they are not so readily acknowledged because nothing dreadful happened to alarm us. We do not realize that we have been saved because we did not observe the danger firsthand—"it is easy to count the numbers we have pulled out of the stream, but it is hard to count the numbers who would have fallen in if more effective control programs had not been adopted" (Cahalan, 1987, p. 124). Unfortunately, most people take action only after serious damage has occurred. An ounce of prevention may be worth the proverbial pound of cure, but most people apparently would rather not spend the ounce on the chance that no treatment will ever be required.

A TALE OF TWO DRUGS

These are most interesting times in the 21st century. Public attitudes about tobacco and marijuana have changed in almost opposite directions over the past generation. During the 1940s, cigarettes were widely accepted even though there was some suspicion of their health hazards. Since the U.S. Surgeon General's report of 1964 (U.S. Department of Health Education and Welfare), there has been increased public rejection of smoking as a desirable or healthy behavior. Although smoking tobacco may not become illegal, it certainly has become increasingly stigmatized.

The first medical report of tobacco's ill effects dates back to 1665. Samuel Pepys witnessed a Royal Society experiment in which a cat quickly expired after it was fed a drop of distilled oil of tobacco. However, the modern scientific evidence that tobacco causes disease did not progress until the 1940s. Epidemiological and experimental evidence that smoking causes cancer led to the "cancer scares" in the 1950s and, ultimately, to the 1964 Surgeon General's report on smoking and health, which concluded that smoking causes lung cancer.

Tobacco and Politics

Yet until the 1990s, the tobacco industry was largely successful in protecting itself through aggressive legal, public relations, and political strategies. A turning point occurred in 1994 when a scientist working at the Brown and Williamson (B&W) Tobacco Corporation, the second-largest private cigarette manufacturer in the world in 1992, became a whistleblower by releasing incriminating internal documents that revealed that the tobacco industry had deceived the public for at least 30 years. According to their own documents, B&W knew of nicotine's pharmacological (drug) impact. By the 1960s, the tobacco industry had proven in its own laboratories that cigarette tar causes cancer in animals. In addition, B&W's lawyers were acting on the assumption that nicotine is addictive as the documents revealed their strategies to minimize the industry's exposure to litigation liability and additional government regulation.

In the past, tobacco companies defended themselves on the grounds that there is no conclusive proof that smoking causes many diseases. They staunchly held that smoking is not addictive but involves free choice by smokers. By not promoting cigarettes as a drug for the medication of disease, the tobacco industry managed to avoid control and regulation by the Food and Drug Administration (FDA). However, rapidly changing attitudes about cigarettes that have occurred since the mid-1960s, with the growing evidence of the health risks and dangers of dependency from cigarettes, have brought tobacco under intense governmental and public scrutiny. During the 1980s, higher excise taxes and restrictions on advertising of cigarettes were imposed. Restrictions continued to expand and receive public acceptance during the 2000s.

What was previously seen as a perhaps dirty but harmless habit has increasingly come to be viewed negatively as new evidence of the health risks from smoking accrue. The above-mentioned revelations, leaked from within the industry that additives and higher doses of nicotine were deliberately designed by manufacturers to create stronger addictions, further damaged the credibility and acceptance of cigarettes.

In 1996, the FDA was able to successfully reclassify tobacco as a drug, depicting the cigarette as a highly efficient nicotine delivery mechanism. This development seemingly justified more restrictions on tobacco, although it fell far short of making it illegal (Kessler et al., 1997). At the end of 1999, however, the U.S. Supreme Court (Savage, 1999) decided not to support the argument that cigarettes are classifiable as drugs for medical purposes. Hence, the case for the FDA to make rulings affecting the sale and distribution of cigarettes is considerably weakened and in doubt.

Marijuana and Politics

In contrast, the trend for marijuana's image has been in the opposite direction from that of tobacco. Marijuana is still not a legalized drug, and the efforts to decriminalize it since the late 1960s have been far from successful. From the demonized depictions of marijuana as a source of "reefer madness" prevalent in the 1930s, marijuana became a hip drug popularized in the 1960s by hippies and college students. During the 1970s, there was considerable pressure to "decriminalize" marijuana use. If decriminalized, marijuana would still be illegal, but users would be treated more leniently if arrested for possession or use. The National Commission on Marihuana and Drug Abuse (1972), also known as the Shafer Commission, concluded that **decriminalization** was appropriate in view of the lack of evidence that marijuana is as dangerous as previously believed. However, President Nixon rejected the commission's report.

During the 1990s, marijuana was promoted for possible medical uses to alleviate pain. Although considerable controversy still rages, some research has shown it could have medical value for the terminally ill and for certain diseases. The White House Office of National Drug Control Policy (ONDCP) in 1997 commissioned a study by the Institute of Medicine to evaluate the potential medical uses of marijuana in response to mounting public pressure as evidenced by several state initiatives to allow medical uses of marijuana (Institute of Medicine, 1999). In the final report a cautious stance was taken:

> Marijuana is not a completely benign substance. It is a powerful drug with a variety of effects. However, except for the harm associated with smoking, the adverse effects of marijuana use are within the range tolerated for other medications. Thus, the safety issues associated with marijuana do not preclude some medical uses. (p. 126)

The commission maintained that a safer method than smoking was needed to deliver the active pharmacological ingredients of marijuana. The report recommended strict conditions for clinical trials of marijuana use for medical purposes, requiring they be limited to less than 6 months, be limited to patients with conditions for whom there is reasonable expectation of efficacy, and be reviewed by institutional review boards, as well as requiring data collected on efficacy.

It is instructive to see the parallels in the arguments used for and against the legalization or decriminalization of marijuana with those used for and against the criminalization of tobacco. In Table 16.1, it can be seen that essentially the same issues arise for both drugs. Proponents of each drug defend its use on grounds of free choice and individual rights whereas opponents of each drug cite health risks to condemn its use. Interestingly, for tobacco as well as for marijuana, both sides use economic consequences to support their

TABLE 16.1 Similarities in the pros and cons of legalizing a current illicit drug, marijuana, and the pros and cons of criminalizing a current legal drug, tobacco.

Legalize Marijuana		Criminalize Tobacco	
Pros	**Cons**	**Pros**	**Cons**
Increase Civil Liberties	Open Gateway to More Illicit Drugs	Close Gateway to Illicit Drugs	Restrict Civil Liberties
Jobs Created in Marijuana Industry	More Health Problems for Marijuana Users	Fewer Health Problems for Cigarette Users	Jobs Lost in Tobacco Industry
More Tax Revenues	More Treatment Costs	Fewer Treatment Costs	Less Tax Revenue
Fewer Legal and Police Costs	Increased Use of Marijuana	Decreased Use of Tobacco	More Legal and Police Costs
Less Crimes Related to Drug Gangs	Sends "Wrong Message" That Drugs Can Be Harmless	Sends "Right Message" That Drugs Can Be Harmful	More Crimes Related to Drug Gangs

opposing views. Tax revenues and employment motivate support for both drugs, but costs of treatment and loss of productivity generate opposition to both drugs.

One lesson to be learned from this comparison of the recent history of attitudes and social policy regarding tobacco and marijuana is that it is easier to prevent a legal drug from becoming illegal than it is to move an illegal drug to legal status. A legal drug is backed by a powerful industry with money and political influence, coupled with a larger constituency of addicted users to fight any legislative or economic regulations against the drug. In contrast, supporters of illegal drugs are afraid to show their support without risk of fines and imprisonment, and they have no large financial lobby to fight on the behalf of their drug of choice. The burden of proving that an illegal drug is benign is very difficult because a type of "Catch-22" is involved. Because it is illegal, it cannot be tested, and without tests, it cannot be vindicated. In contrast, substantial evidence that tobacco is very harmful seems insufficient to make much headway into making it illegal.

To Legalize or Not to Legalize

It is worth speculating what would happen if a currently illicit drug such as marijuana or cocaine were to become reclassified as legal or at least become decriminalized. How many law-abiding citizens who previously rejected these substances would then become users? And would the problems associated with use of these drugs when they were illegal, such as criminal activities to raise money to support these drug habits, be reduced once these drugs were legalized?

If large corporations could manufacture, advertise, and sell products from formerly illegal drugs in large volume for high profits, would the cost come down, thus leading to even greater use? And as tax revenues from sales of these now legal drugs pour into government coffers, would the sales and use of these drugs become more "acceptable" to society, as alcohol and tobacco are? It is not surprising, faced with the prospect that a change in legal status of drugs could have increase use, that opponents of currently illegal drugs want to draw a firm line in the sand between legal and illegal drugs.

In other words, are problems associated with illicit drugs due to their illegal status or to their pharmacological effects? Of course, changing the status of any drug from illegal to legal would not prevent physical problems associated with its use; certainly, the availability of alcohol has never been problem free. The issue here is not to decide which specific drugs should or should not be legal but to point out that the legal status of a drug itself has a major impact on the types and amounts of problems associated with its use.

Societal Roots of Drug Problems

Social class wars over legal and illegal drugs exist, with the middle class condemning illegal drugs that are often initially associated with the lower class. The middle and upper classes indulge in the use of currently legal drugs such as alcohol and tobacco, which are widely available even though they are harmful to individuals as well as to society.

Prejudices against some immigrant groups may have had more to do with instituting bans of drugs associated with these groups than clear evidence that these drugs are more dangerous than those accepted as legal in the United States such as alcohol and tobacco. In addition, manufacturers of products containing the "legal" drugs have defended their turf by attributing to the "illegal drugs" undesirable outcomes that could more readily stem from the marginalization in society faced by the users of these drugs that "forces" them into unrespectable forms of conduct.

Placing the blame on the drug or on the user overlooks how societal conditions foster and maintain a drug lifestyle among many disenfranchised members of society. To give one example, long-term changes in the economy have led to fewer manufacturing jobs and greater unemployment among those whose limited education and training prevent them from obtaining jobs requiring professional or technical skills. With nothing but time on their hands, doing drugs is a way of coping with lives with no hope. And with legitimate economic avenues closed, engaging in lucrative activities such as drug dealing becomes attractive. Consequently, it is hardly surprising that the war on drugs has led to an increasingly larger prison population from the inner cities, especially African Americans (Duster, 1997). Drugs, as well as those who abuse them, are only part of the problem. Until and unless social institutions can improve living conditions and provide economic opportunities for all, there will be no winners in the war on drugs, only losers.

THE FUTURE OF PREVENTION

Prevention of alcohol and other drug problems is a Herculean task. The powerful alcohol and tobacco industries, backed by their constituency of users, are formidable opponents to changes in social policies restricting the availability of these legal drugs (Mosher & Jernigan, 1989). Alcoholic beverage and tobacco companies have skillfully influenced legislators through financial donations and lobbyists, derogated industry critics, and formed powerful alliances with other groups that also face the threat of increased excise taxes. They have tried to create a favorable public image by providing research funds for scientific investigators and also improved public relations by funding public service campaigns such as warnings against drinking and driving, as well as product labels warning of health risks of smoking and drinking—and sponsoring sporting activities and cultural events.

Public recognition of or opposition to these industries has been blunted by the prevailing tendency to regard use problems as the fault of the individual while overlooking the sophisticated marketing practices of the alcohol and tobacco pitchmen that promote and encourage drinking and smoking. However, public health proponents can form coalitions at the state and federal levels to affect legislation and also organize local constituencies to combat alcohol and tobacco problems. Efforts to pass legislation to require warning labels, increase excise taxes, and obtain equal broadcast media time for counteradvertising are examples of campaigns involving the joint efforts and support of health, consumer advocate, educational, religious, and alcohol and tobacco treatment groups.

The public health model illustrates the complex interplay among several components—host, agent, and environment—that must be examined when planning prevention programs. Attempted restriction of alcohol availability to a zero level during Prohibition proved unworkable because it was too unpopular and impossible to enforce. Educational attempts have proved inadequate and often irrelevant to prevention because mere ignorance does not fully account for alcohol abuse.

Prevention is also a Sisyphean task, one in which any steps forward are followed by steps backward so that the journey is a never-ending task. Because most drinkers seem to experience the benefits of drinking without suffering any apparent harm, society appears willing to tolerate the price of having a certain number of alcohol-dependent individuals. As long as drinkers are viewed as not harming anyone but themselves, the public seems willing to allow them to pay the price for their excesses. But, as witnessed by the increased public reaction against drinking drivers, the line is drawn when the alcohol abuser begins to victimize the innocent. More awareness and concern about fetal alcohol syndrome may similarly arouse public attention to the dangers that a drinking mother may create for her unborn fetus. The message may be that instead of trying to motivate the drinker to control his or her drinking, we may be more successful in preventing problems if we can increase awareness of the dangers that alcoholics and alcohol abusers create for everyone. Once alerted to these dangers, people will be motivated to protect themselves and, indirectly, everyone else.

A clash between individual rights and the well-being and safety of the public occurs in many situations when government attempts to act on the public's behalf. There is often resistance when there is the perception that the government is meddling with individual freedoms to decide the personal lives of its citizens. Therefore, laws and social policies that restrict access to alcohol or tobacco to minimize the threat to others from excessive use of these drugs are opposed vigorously by those who want to preserve their rights to use alcohol and tobacco as they wish.

Society is "co-opted," however, because the legal drugs create thousands of jobs for workers in the drug and drug-related industries, with spillover to marketing, advertising, distribution, and sales of these drugs. A cynic would even note that alcoholism and smoking cessation treatment providers constitute large and profitable industries themselves. The profit motive sustains the growth and continuation of the sales and consumption of licit drugs.

The government also is co-opted because it gains tax revenues from the sales of the legal drugs. Of course, the tax revenues may have to be spent treating and rehabilitating people suffering from psychological and physical damage from these drugs. By increasing taxes in attempts to discourage licit drug consumption, the government could end up reducing its incoming revenues in the long run, if it is successful. Hence, the government may be reluctant or ambivalent in regulating licit drug availability too strictly.

As a society, we are in conflict over the proper use of drugs. Almost everyone wants freedom to pursue his or her own objectives. For some, these goals include the right to use the drugs of their choice. For others, these goals include opposite objectives to prevent others from using drugs they find objectionable. Exactly how all interests can be satisfied is a real dilemma. Somehow, society must achieve a balance—using legal, educational, economic, and moral controls—to regulate drug consumption so that those who benefit from such use do not create psychological and physical harm to either themselves or those around them.

Summary

The prevention of using alcohol and other drugs and the problems associated with their use involve a combination of educational, legal, and moral forces against the promotion, advertising, and sale of products from the alcohol and tobacco industries. A combined approach in which efforts are directed at the agent or drug, the host or user, and the environment or society is needed to make progress in preventing or at least reducing problems related to the use of alcohol. For illicit drugs, heavy reliance is placed on legal means to control their availability in addition to educational and informational campaigns against their use.

Primary prevention tries to stop problems related to use of alcohol and other drugs before they start. Diagnosing and identifying present drug abusers (secondary prevention) and treatment of persons already suffering from drug problems (tertiary prevention) usually take priority over primary prevention because they are such immediate problems.

One approach to prevention is to reduce the available supply of drugs. Creating conditions that raise costs of a legal drug due to pricing and taxes might reduce consumption, at least for lighter users. A different situation may exist with illicit drugs because heavy users may resort to criminal activities to support their expensive drug habits.

Another strategy involves demand reduction, as exemplified by school-based alcohol and other drug prevention programs that focus on teaching skills to children so they can cope without resorting to drugs. Normative education can help children resist peer influences to use drugs by correcting any misperception that most peers use drugs.

Drug testing is one objective approach used to reduce drug use that may lead to work impairment and accidents in the workplace. However, drug testing is not infallible and also may infringe on employees' privacy.

Another approach in alcohol and drug prevention efforts involves supply reduction through strict legal enforcement, interdiction, and taxation to reduce the availability of drugs. Use reduction efforts, when successful, might reduce the direct harm of a specific drug but also might unintentionally increase other forms of harm.

Harm reduction efforts, which concede that some drug use is unavoidable, try to minimize the harm created by use. Some success has been achieved, as with needle exchange programs for heroin users, which do not prevent heroin use but reduce the harm from infectious diseases conveyed by shared needles. Opponents of harm reduction reject this philosophy as condoning drug use and "sending the wrong message."

Society is compromised in its ability and desire to control alcohol and other drugs, however, because the legal drugs generate large excise tax revenues and create thousands of jobs in the drug industries, with spillover to marketing, advertising, distribution, and sales of these drugs. We also must acknowledge that our drug problem does not rest entirely on the characteristics of drugs or their users. Societal conditions may be among the root causes that contribute to drug abuse and dependency, and they also must be addressed if drug abuse and related problems are to be reduced in a just manner.

Stimulus/Response

1. In most high schools with a zero-tolerance drug policy, students caught drinking or using other drugs are usually suspended or banned from extracurricular activities. Do you think these responses are adequate or appropriate? Do you think these punishments will prevent drinking or other drug use? Some feel that these punishments only give offenders more free time to drink or use other drugs outside of school. An alternative policy is for school officials to talk to teens to determine if they have an alcohol or other drug problem and then refer such students to counselors and doctors. Do you think school officials should take this approach? How effective do you think it would be?

2. Experts feel that warning signs of substance abuse problems include changes in grades, more family fights, stealing, dropping friends, and lying. Do you agree that these are valid signs of substance abuse problems? Why or why not?

3. A study, released by the White House Office of National Drug Control Policy and the U.S. Department of Health and Human Services' Substance Abuse and Mental Health Services Administration, examined the most popular movie rentals and the most popular songs from 1996 and 1997. Illicit drugs appeared in 22% of the movies studied, and 27% of the songs had a clear reference to either alcohol or illicit drugs. Do you think the content is a cause or a reflection of attitudes and behavior? What studies need to be done to answer this question? What do you think the policy of the entertainment industry should be regarding alcohol and other drug depictions?

4. The consequences of substance use were depicted in about half of the movies in which they appeared and in about one fifth of the songs. In 26% of the movies, illicit drug use was shown in a humorous context. No report was given about what these consequences were and how they might have affected viewers. From your own experience, identify the major types of consequences you have seen in movies depicting drugs and speculate about the effects of such "messages" that viewers may have received.

5. Illicit drug use was associated with wealth or luxury in 20% of the songs in which drugs appeared, with sexual activity in 30%, and with crime or violence in 20%. What conclusions do you make from these statistics?
These results also mean that illicit drug use was not portrayed with wealth in 80% of the songs, not with sexual activity in 70%, and not with crime in 80%. Are the rates high or low?

6. Drug attitudes formed in 7th grade do not seem to affect use patterns in 12th grade. Do you think this evidence suggests that drug education is ineffective because it starts too soon, before most children are ready to think about drugs, or because it starts too late?

7. The U.S. Supreme Court ruled in 2002 that schools could conduct random drug tests on middle and senior high students engaged in extracurricular activities. What do you think are the pros and cons of this approach to reducing drug use among students?

8. Are the attitudes and values of our society related to alcohol and other drugs consistent with the information presented in school drug education curricula? If not, how does this disparity affect the success of school-based drug education?

9. How does marketing and advertising of alcohol and tobacco work against educational attempts to prevent alcohol and tobacco problems?

10. Controversy exists about the attempts of the alcohol and tobacco industries to increase drinking and smoking with advertising campaigns and promotions. A promotion by a brewery described a fictitious college course, Drinking 101, which featured drinking games and recipes. Critics said the catalog encouraged binge drinking and underage drinking (because most college students are under the legal drinking age). Do you think these marketing tactics would affect the drinking of college students? Why or why not?

11. Many college athletic programs receive support and funds from the alcohol industry. Should colleges continue or sever ties between their athletic programs and alcohol industry sponsors?

12. Should the alcohol and tobacco industries be allowed to sponsor ethnic community events, such as the popular annual Cinco de Mayo festivals in Latino communities?

13. The WorkSite Alcohol Study (Mangione et al., 1999), involving over 14,000 employees at seven major U.S. companies, found that casual drinkers had more incidents of absenteeism and tardiness than did alcohol-dependent persons. Casual drinkers were responsible for 59% of total alcohol-related productivity problems, compared to 41% for alcohol-dependent workers. Do the data allow for a fair comparison since there were three times as many casual drinkers as there were alcohol-dependent persons in these companies? Would these findings suggest to you that managers should direct more attention to the casual or social drinker than to those with alcohol dependency?

Glossary

Absolute alcohol: Pure ethanol, a type of alcohol, with no more than 1% water.

Abstainers: Nonusers of a drug; may be lifelong or only for a specified period.

Abstinence violation effect (AVE): A minor slip or lapse into use after a period of abstinence leads to a relapse.

Abuse: Continued alcohol or other drug use despite recurrent social, interpersonal, and legal problems associated with the use. See also *dependence*.

Acculturation: Process by which immigrants learn and adopt the customs of the host culture.

Acetaldehyde: A toxic byproduct of alcohol metabolism.

Acetate: A compound produced from the metabolism of acetaldehyde.

Acetylcholine (ACh): Neurotransmitter found in the parasympathetic nervous system.

Action potential: Electrical charges produced when a cell membrane is polarized and ion movement occurs through the cell.

Addiction: Commonly refers to dependency on drugs; term is not as widely used by researchers.

Addictive personality: View that certain individuals are prone to form addictions.

Adult Children of Alcoholics (ACOA): Self-help organization of individuals who feel dysfunctional from growing up in the home of alcoholic parent(s).

Age effect: When differences in alcohol and other drug effects are due to age differences per se.

Age of onset: Age when person starts using alcohol or other drugs; early- and late-onset drinkers differ.

Aggregate use: A total index summed over a whole group, as opposed to an index based on individuals.

Agonist: A substance that facilitates the effects of a psychoactive drug on receptor binding.

Al-Anon: Self-help organization modeled after Alcoholics Anonymous for the wives and families of alcoholics.

Alcohol abuse: A condition in which the user has many alcohol use-related problems, including work or school performance and social, financial, legal, physical, and mental health problems.

Alcohol dehydrogenase (ADH): An enzyme that breaks down or oxidizes alcohol, converting it to acetaldehyde. See also *cytochrome P450*.

Alcohol dependence syndrome (ADS): Alcoholism viewed as a continuum rather than a dichotomy of impairment. Problems related to alcohol use such as mental and physical health problems are viewed as a separate dimension. See also *dependence*.

Alcohol myopia: Term refers to alcohol's effect to restrict attention.

Alcohol-related birth defects (ARBD): Milder impairments in children in general populations attributed to mother's drinking during pregnancy that are more difficult to detect than fetal alcohol effects. See also *fetal alcohol syndrome*.

Alcohol Use Disorder and Associated Disabilities Interview Schedule (AUDADIS): A structured instrument used to assess *DSM-IV* disorders in epidemiological and clinic settings.

Alcoholics Anonymous (AA): A mutual support group for recovering alcoholics. It has served as the model for other recovery groups dealing with other addictive behaviors.

Alcoholism: Commonly used term for dependency, which is more often used by researchers.

Aldehyde dehydrogenase (ALDH2): An enzyme that converts acetaldehyde to acetate.

Alleles: One of two or more variants of a certain gene.

Allostasis: State involving a chronic deviation of reward set point due to changes in brain reward mechanisms produced by alcohol abuse.

Amphetamines: Stimulant drugs (called speed, if injected) originally used to increase alertness and work productivity but also widely abused.

Antabuse: Drug sometimes used in alcoholism treatment to deter drinking by creating adverse physical metabolic reactions if alcohol is consumed.

Antagonist: A substance that inhibits the effects of a psychoactive drug on receptor binding.

Anterograde amnesia: Memory loss in alcoholics of recent events after drinking. See also *Wernicke-Korsakoff syndrome*.

Antisocial personality disorder: Pathological condition involving hostility and aggression toward others.

Assortative mating: Mate selection based on similarity or matching of characteristics.

Attributions: Causal explanations for outcomes, as in accounts for relapse by persons following a period of abstinence.

Autonomic nervous system (ANS): Part of the nervous system that governs involuntary responses such as emotions and emergency responses.

Aversive conditioning: Treatment involving pairing of aversive outcomes such as pain or nausea with a drug so that future use may be stopped by thoughts of the aversive experiences.

Balanced placebo design: A four-group design to separate expectancy from the pharmacological effect of drugs. Participants in two groups are told to expect to receive alcohol, but only one group actually receives alcohol. Participants in two other groups are told to expect a nonalcoholic beverage, but one of the groups actually receives alcohol.

Barbiturates: Depressant drugs used for sedative effects such as in sleeping pills.

Bed nucleus of the stria terminalis (BNST): A descending pathway from the bed nucleus of the stria terminalis to nuclei within the hypothalamus and brainstem regulates stress and reward systems that are involved with affective responses to drugs of abuse.

Behavioral marital therapy: Treatment using cognitive-behavior modification with both partners involved in counseling.

Behavioral treatment: Approach based on learning theory; uses reinforcement, modeling, and role play to develop coping skills for high-risk situations for drug use.

Benzodiazepines: Prescription drugs used to reduce anxiety.

Beta-endorphins: Opioid peptide neurotransmitters in both the central and the peripheral nervous systems that suppress pain.

Binge drinking: Generally refers to drinking heavily over several days. Research studies use a more specific definition: five or more drinks on one occasion by men and four or more drinks on one occasion by women.

Biphasic effects: Opposite effects, stimulation and sedation, of alcohol and other drugs that occur from intake to elimination of a substance.

Blackout: Lack of memory for events that happened while drinking.

Blood alcohol level (BAL) or blood alcohol concentration (BAC): Measure of alcohol from blood or breath samples that is correlated with how much alcohol has been consumed in the past 1 to 2 hours.

Candidate genes: A gene in a chromosome region suspected of being involved in the expression of a trait such as alcoholism identified by linkage analysis to a region of the genome.

Case-control study: An epidemiologic method in which previously existing cases of a condition (alcoholism) are compared with controls with similar characteristics (e.g., gender, age, and alcohol use history) but who have not developed the condition of interest; the two groups are compared to determine which factors may account for the higher incidence of the condition in the case group.

Catalase: An enzyme that catalyzes the decomposition of hydrogen peroxide into water and oxygen.

Causal models: Quantitative analyses of patterns in data that are similar to theories in that both hypothesize which factors cause certain outcomes.

Central nervous system (CNS): Part of the nervous system involved with conscious and voluntary behaviors; includes brain and spinal cord.

Cerebellum: Part of the brain above the medulla that acts as a reflex center and controls coordination.

Child abuse: Physical or psychological harm to a child, nonsexual or sexual, caused by an adult.

Chromosome: A chromosome is a single piece of DNA found in cells that contains many genes, regulatory elements, and other nucleotide sequences.

Cirrhosis: Disease related to alcoholism that impairs the liver's ability to detoxify alcohol and other drugs.

Classical conditioning: Association of two otherwise unrelated stimuli enables one to elicit the other in the future; Pavlov's paradigm in which dogs are trained to salivate to a tone that precedes presentation of food powder is the model.

Cocaine: Central nervous system stimulant obtained from coca bush leaves.

Codependency: When someone close to the drug-dependent individual contributes to or abets that dependency.

Cognitive-behavioral coping: Techniques based on social learning theory, with emphasis on modeling and rehearsal of specific behaviors to obtain positive reinforcement.

Cohort effects: Differential results occur for different groups such as age groups.

Cohort study: An epidemiologic approach in which a group of people who share a common characteristic (e.g., everyone entering an alcoholism treatment program) is followed to determine how those who develop a certain condition (e.g., sobriety) differ from those who do not.

Comorbidity: Two or more disorders—abuse of two different drugs or abuse of a drug among those with a psychiatric disorder—occur together in same individuals.

Compensatory response model: A model of relapse focusing on cues associated with a drug's reduced effect or tolerance to prolonged use.

Conditioned withdrawal: A model of relapse focusing on cues associated with prior distress from lacking an accustomed drug to trigger relapse.

Controlled drinking: Belief that recovering alcoholics can drink in moderation without relapse.

Controlled observation: Data collected under conditions that allow for sound causal inferences such as in an experiment.

Controlled Substances Act: The federal law classifying drugs into five levels depending on their medical use and potential harm.

Convergence hypothesis: Idea that alcohol use, abuse, and dependency of men and women are becoming more similar.

Crack cocaine: Smokeable form of concentrated cocaine.

Craving: Intense desire to use a drug.

Cross tolerance: When tolerance developed for one drug carries over to a different drug, making it easier for the user to adapt to the second drug.

Cue extinction: Exposure of alcoholics to cues related to alcohol without letting them drink reduces likelihood of resumed drinking.

Cued recall: Stimuli previously associated with material to be recalled act as retrieval cues.

Cytochrome P450: A family of cytochromes, one of which (CYP2E1) can oxidize alcohol to form acetaldehyde; high alcohol levels stimulate CYP2E1 activity.

Decriminalization: Reducing enforcement of laws against the use of illegal drugs but maintaining their illegal status.

Delirium tremens (DTs): Part of the alcohol withdrawal syndrome that occurs during abstinence; involves agitation, shakes, tremors, and hallucinations.

Delta-9-THC: Delta-9-tetrahyrdocannabinol, the active ingredient in marijuana.

Demand reduction: Social policy to reduce desire for a drug in a population.

Dementia: Global deficit of intellectual function with impaired abstraction and judgment.

Denial: In psychodynamic theory, a failure to admit a problem or to accept treatment; often used in a circular manner so that anyone who has a problem but is not being treated is said to be in denial.

Deoxyribonucleic acid (DNA): Two long polymers of nucleic acids in all cells that contain the genetic instructions used in the development and functioning of all life.

Dependence: Condition in which users of a drug are unable to control its use. Synonymous with *alcoholism*.

Depolarization: Electrical potential of the cell membrane becomes more neutral as the message traverses through the neuron to the synapse.

Detoxification: Process of eliminating a drug from the body by the liver; also refers to medical intervention involved for heavy users.

Developmental trajectories: Patterns of changes in the course of use of a drug over time or age.

Diagnostic and Statistical Manual of Mental Disorders (DSM): A classification system of psychiatric disorders designed to provide more objective and standard diagnostic criteria. Last revised in 1990, the *DSM-IV* is the current version, and it is set for a revision by 2012.

Differential attrition: Dropout from treatment is selective, occurring more for some groups than for others.

Direct cause: Changes in personality such as depression or hostility that are attributed to the effects of alcohol and other drugs.

Disease conception of alcoholism: An influential medical model of alcoholism proposed by Jellinek (1960) and a cornerstone of Alcoholics Anonymous and many hospital treatment programs.

Dizygotic (DZ) twins: Twins (fraternal) from two separate eggs fertilized close in time by two separate sperms. See also *monozygotic (MZ) twins.*

Domestic violence: Physical or psychological harm inflicted between marital partners. Also called intimate partner violence (IPV).

Dopamine (DA): Neurotransmitter leading to reward states from most psychoactive drugs.

Dose, effective versus lethal: Quantity of a drug that will produce the intended effects versus quantity of a drug that may be sufficient to cause death.

Dose-response curve: The relationship between the amount of a drug and its effect on some behavior.

Downregulation: Process by which a cell decreases the quantity of a cellular component, such as RNA or protein, in response to an external variable to lower its responsiveness. The opposite process is called *upregulation.*

Drinking style: The pattern, physical and social context, and meaning of drinking.

Drug Abuse Resistance Education (DARE): A school-based program of drug education and prevention led by community police officers.

Dry family interaction: How the family interacts when the alcoholic is not drinking. See also *wet family interaction.*

DUI: Driving under the influence (DUI) refers to alcohol- or other-drug-impaired operation of a motor vehicle.

DUID: Driving under the influence of drugs (DUID) refers to operating a motor vehicle with levels of drugs in the body that are assumed to impair safety.

DWI: Driving while intoxicated (DWI) refers to alcohol- or other-drug-impaired operation of a motor vehicle.

Dyadic drinking: Drinking with another person. See also *solitary drinking.*

Ecstasy (MDMA): A popular but illegal amphetamine popularly used at rave parties.

Electroencephalogram (EEG): Pattern of electrical waves measured from the scalp with an electroencephalograph that reflects brain activity.

Employee assistance programs (EAPs): Provide guidance, information, counseling, and referral to employees with alcohol and other-drug-related problems.

Endogenous opiates: Pain-alleviating opiates generated in the body. See also *beta-endorphins.*

Endophenotypes: A genetic concept similar to phenotypes, endophenotypes are often more physiological. Not the underlying "genes" for a disorder, they govern processes related to it.

Enhanced reinforcement model: View that innate sensitivity increases the likelihood that alcohol and other drugs function as reinforcers by increasing positive affect or by reducing negative affect.

Enkephalins: Peptides involved with pain control.

Enzyme: A substance, usually a protein, that directs and accelerates chemical reactions in the body but does not itself undergo permanent change.

Epidemiology: Study of factors associated with the occurrence of different drug use patterns and consequences.

Epinephrine: Neurotransmitter found in the sympathetic nervous system.

Episodic drinking: Drinking on an unpredictable basis in amount or intervals, as opposed to steady or regular patterns of drinking.

Episodic memory: Storage of incidents or facts experienced by specific individuals. See also *semantic memory.*

Estrogen: Female sex hormone regulator of menstrual cycle and ovulation.

Ethanol: Scientific name for alcohol (ethyl alcohol).

Ethnography: Field research under natural rather than laboratory conditions.

Event-related potential (ERP): Electrical activity from a region of the brain in response to stimuli that is assumed to reflect attentional processes.

Expectancy: Belief about an outcome of the use of a drug.

Expectancy controls: Comparison groups that do not receive but think they are getting alcohol to drink; their behavior is compared with those who do receive alcohol to see if mere expectancy can produce similar effects to alcohol.

Explicit memory: Memories that the individual is highly aware of. See also *implicit memory.*

Facial flushing: A tendency for the face to blush when alcohol is consumed due to vasodilation; often accompanied by nausea, it is more prevalent among Asians and thought to protect against alcohol abuse.

Family history (FH): Index of how often a disorder occurs among close family members. If the disorder is common, the family history for that problem is termed positive.

Family interaction theory: Adolescents with affectionate parents, good attachment, and conventional values will experiment less with substance use and have fewer associations with alcohol- and drug-using peers.

Family system: Approach to understanding disorders that emphasizes the impact that each family member has on other members.

Fetal alcohol effects (FAE): Less apparent impairments than fetal alcohol syndrome found in children due to mother's drinking during pregnancy.

Fetal alcohol syndrome (FAS): A pattern of severe physical and psychological impairments found in children whose mothers drank excessively during pregnancy.

Free recall: Recall of material is tested without any cues provided.

Frontal lobe: Front area of both hemispheres of the cerebrum.

Frontal lobe hypothesis: View that alcoholism damages to the frontal lobe impair cognitive functions.

Functional magnetic resonance imaging (fMRI): Neuroimaging method widely used for brain mapping field due to its low invasiveness.

G protein: A molecule within a neuron that binds receptors to ion channels or enzymes.

Gamma-aminobutyric acid (GABA): The primary inhibitory neurotransmitter in the central nervous system.

Gateway drug: Notion that use of a gateway drug increases chances of taking other more harmful drugs.

Gene-environment interactions: When neither genetic nor environmental factors are the sole determinants of outcomes but the joint effects of both are involved.

Gene expression: The process by which the genetic information encoded in a gene's DNA sequence is converted into a functional protein.

General population survey: Survey that uses a random sample of the general population; also called a *household survey*.

Generalized/diffuse hypothesis: View that the amount of general brain damage determines amount of cognitive impairment in alcoholics.

Genetic marker: Physiological variable associated with a specific gene that is highly associated with a specific disease outcome.

Genotype: The complete genetic makeup of an organism determined by the particular combination of alleles for all genes.

Glutamate (NDMA): Amino acid that is the primary excitatory neurotransmitter in the central nervous system.

Half-life: Amount of time needed for a specific drug to be eliminated by half.

Hallucinogen: Drug capable of creating hallucinogenic altered states of consciousness.

Harm reduction: An approach to drug policy that falls between prohibition and legalization; tries to minimize harm that may occur for those who cannot be prevented from using drugs.

Harrison Narcotic Act: Major legislation in 1914 that made narcotics and many other drugs illegal.

Hashish: Psychoactive drug from resin from the cannabis plant.

Heavy drinking: Arbitrarily defined in survey research as having five or more drinks for men and four or more drinks for women several times a month.

Heritability: Proportion of genetic variability relative to environment variability as determined by comparing monozygotic and dizygotic twins in a specific study.

Heroin: Synthetic drug derived from morphine that is a more potent opiate.

Higher power: Alcoholics Anonymous concept that recovery requires that alcoholics acknowledge some factor more powerful than themselves.

Hippocampus: Brain region in the temporal lobe related to memory and learning.

Hyperexcitability: A state of heightened responsiveness to alcohol during withdrawal.

Hypothalamus: Small structure in limbic system that regulates many functions, including eating, drinking, and sexual behavior.

Impaired control: View that dependence involves a continuum of inability to refrain from using a drug, as opposed to an all-or-none loss of control.

Implicit cognitions: Cognitive processes that occur without the individual's conscious awareness.

Implicit memory: Memory without conscious awareness but which can affect behavior. See also *explicit memory*.

In vivo: Experiments conducted in an intact organism as opposed to in a test tube (in vitro).

Incentive-sensitization model: View that drug abuse produces neuroadaptations of brain reward systems that are hypersensitive so that drugs and drug-associated stimuli have incentive salience for addicts but no longer produce pleasurable or euphoric effects.

Incidence: The number or rate of new cases of some outcome in a given time period. See also *prevalence*.

Increased vulnerability hypothesis: View that older persons are cognitively impaired by alcohol more than younger persons.

Interactions (of drugs): The effect of a drug may vary with other drugs used or with different contexts of use.

International Classification of Diseases (ICD): A classification system developed by the World Health Organization for identifying major diseases, including disorders related to substance use.

Invulnerables: Term referring to children of alcoholics who do not develop alcohol abuse and dependency despite being at risk for these problems.

Ion: Electrically charged particles that enter and exit the neuron to send nerve impulses.

Ion channels: Areas on the neuron membrane that admit specific ions into the cell.

LAAM (levo-alpha-acetylmethadol): Synthetic narcotic similar to methadone but longer lasting and used to treat heroin addicts.

Lapse: Commonly called a slip, referring to a momentary return to drug use following a period of abstinence.

Latent growth curve models (multilevel models): Models of trends in alcohol and other drug use over three or more time points spanning several years identified with complex statistical techniques.

Linkage studies: Comparison of associations between an allele and a phenotype (e.g., alcohol abuse) in two groups of subjects (e.g., people with and without alcohol abuse).

Lipids: Fatty substances, including simple fats, their major components (i.e., fatty acids), and various fat-soluble substances (e.g., cholesterol).

Loss of control: View under the disease model of alcoholism that alcoholics experience an inability to stop drinking once they start.

Lysergic acid diethylamide (LSD): Hallucinogenic drug popularized during the 1960s.

Machismo: Latino/Hispanic concept of masculinity as a factor motivating drinking.

Macrophage: A type of immune cell that ingests foreign particles and microorganisms and synthesizes proteins and other substances important in inflammatory responses.

MAO inhibitors (monoamine oxidase inhibitors, or MAOIs): Drugs that block a specific enzyme, monoamine oxidase, so that antidepressant drugs can relieve depression.

Marijuana: Smoked drug from leaves of cannabis plant and most widely used illegal drug.

Marriage effect: Term refers to the finding that lower rates of alcohol problems occur with married than with single persons.

Matching: Assigning patients to treatments assumed to be more effective for them.

Mediator (mediator variable): Any personality variable or process that occurs or mediates between alcohol and other drug consumption and its effect on the user.

Medical model: Belief that addictions and dependency are physical diseases.

Metabolism: All chemical reactions occurring in a cell, an organ, or the body; more narrowly defined, it refers to the breakdown of a particular substance (e.g., alcohol) by specific enzymes.

Methadone: A synthetic opiate that is slower acting and taken by tablets used to treat heroin addicts.

Methadone maintenance: A program designed to help heroin addicts by giving them a replacement drug therapy, methadone, considered to be less addictive.

Methamphetamine (meth): Variant of amphetamine that is often easily made at home.

Minnesota model: The traditional 28-day hospital or clinic treatment program for addictions based on a disease model.

Mitochondria: Structures within cells that generate most of the cells' energy through the production of adenosine triphosphate (ATP).

Modeling: Process of learning skills and behaviors from observing a model performing these responses.

Moderator (moderator variable): Any variable such as a personality trait that moderates or is related to differences in the effect of alcohol and other drugs.

Molecular genetics: Study of the structure and function of genes at a molecular biology level.

Monitoring the Future (MTF) study: An annual national survey conducted by the University of Michigan to assess alcohol and other drug use of high school students.

Monoamines: Neurotransmitters involving only one amino group such as catecholamines (including dopamine, epinephrine, and norepinephrine) and the indoleamine serotonin. Excess and deficient amounts are thought to be a key factor in depression.

Monozygotic (MZ) twins: Twins (identical) from the fertilization of one egg by one sperm. See also *dizygotic (DZ) twins*.

Motivational enhancement therapy (MET): Treatment that emphasizes motivating the client to want to change and to assume responsibility for improvement.

Motivational interviewing: A method of structured nonconfrontational interviewing aimed at creating awareness and motivation in the alcohol or other drug abuser to reduce his or her substance abuse.

Multiple regulation model: View that smoking is determined by parallel or concurrent psychological and pharmacological mechanisms.

Multiple sex roles: Having several functions expected because of one's sex.

N-nitrosamines: Potent carcinogens present in smokeless tobacco, snuff, and tobacco smoke.

Naloxone: Analgesic used as antagonist for opioid overdoses

Naltrexone (ReVia®): An opiate antagonist that is believed to be useful to reduce craving in treating alcoholism.

Narcotic: Drug capable of producing sleep state and pain relief.

National Epidemiologic Survey on Alcohol and Related Conditions (NESARC): A national longitudinal survey started in 2001–2002 to assess alcohol and other drug use and its related consequences.

National Household Survey on Drug Abuse (NHSDA): An annual national survey to assess alcohol and other drug use in the general population.

National Survey on Drug Use and Health (NSDUH): The successor in 2002 to the annual National Household Survey on Drug Abuse.

Natural recovery: Recovery from addictions without formal treatment.

Negative affect model: Temperamental factors favoring depression or anxiety, combined with stressful life events and poor coping skills, produce negative affect that leads to alcohol and other drug abuse.

Neuron: A nerve cell; sensory neurons carry messages to and motor neurons carry messages from the central nervous system.

Neurotransmitter: Chemical released by neurons at the synapse that excite or inhibit adjacent neurons.

Nicotine: The active ingredient in tobacco cigarettes.

Nicotine regulation model: Theory that smokers try to maintain a desired level of nicotine from cigarettes.

Norepinephrine (NE): Neurotransmitter important for waking and appetite regulation.

Normative education: Approach for prevention in which children learn that there are not as many peers using drugs as they might think.

Nucleus accumbens: A nucleus in the midbrain related to positive reinforcement.

Odds ratio: Ratio of the odds of a condition (e.g., alcoholism) occurring in one group (e.g., men) versus the odds of it occurring in another group (e.g., women). An odds ratio <1.0 means the first group has a lower risk of the condition whereas an odds ratio >1.0 indicates that the first group has a higher risk of the condition.

Operant conditioning: Reinforcement procedures used to change behavior gradually; involves some trial-and-error active learning.

Opponent-process theory: Model of addictions focusing on the body's tendencies to produce an effect opposite to that of any drug. Over repeated use, a drug effect is weaker, but the opponent process becomes stronger, leading to more use to achieve the drug's earlier effects.

Oxidative stress: An imbalance between oxidants (e.g., free radicals) and antioxidants that can lead to excessive oxidation and cell damage.

P300 wave: A brain wave change occurring about 300 ms after attending to a signal; assumed to reflect the act of attending.

Pancreatitis: An acute or chronic inflammation of the pancreas.

Parasympathetic nervous system: Part of the autonomic nervous system that promotes a resting state.

Peer cluster theory: Adolescent peers are strong socializing influences on deviant behaviors such as alcohol and other drug use.

Peer selection theory: Adolescent alcohol and other drug users seek out or prefer the company of other adolescents who share their drug involvement.

Period effect: Results depend on the historical period when participants in a study lived.

Peripheral nervous system (PNS): Located outside the central nervous system, the PNS has two parts: the somatic nervous system, responsible for sensory and motor functions, and the autonomic nervous system, which has a sympathetic and a parasympathetic nervous system.

pH scale: A scale assessing the degree of alkalinity or acidity of chemicals.

Pharmacodynamics: The biochemical and physiological effects of drugs on the body and the mechanisms of drug action and the relationship between drug concentration and effect.

Pharmacokinetics: Examines how the body processes a drug including absorption and distribution, rate and duration of the effect, chemical changes of the substance in the body, and the effects and routes of excretion of the metabolites of the drug.

Placebo: A control condition in an experiment to assess psychological effects of drug taking. A substance is given that is not psychoactive to participants, who believe it is.

Polydrug abuse: Abuse of more than one psychoactive drug together or in quick succession.

Polymorphism: Existence of a gene in several allelic forms.

Positive appetitional model: A model in which relapse is in response to the presence of stimuli associated with the user's prior experiences of desired effects from a drug.

Positron emission tomography (PET): Neuroimaging tool produces three-dimensional images of functional processes in the body.

Power theory: Feeling of power from using alcohol is responsible for increased drinking.

Premature aging hypothesis: View that cognitive deficits in alcoholics are due to premature aging from chronic use of alcohol.

Prevalence: Number or rate of existing cases (old and new) of some outcome in some time period. See also *incidence*.

Price elastic: Price of alcohol and other drugs has large effects on consumption, e.g., raising price will reduce and lowering price will increase consumption.

Price inelastic: Price of alcohol and other drugs has little or no effect on consumption.

Primary prevention: Prevention aimed at stopping a problem before it even starts.

Proband: In genetic studies, term refers to the initial member of a family with a disorder being studied to determine any family patterns.

Project MATCH: A study that matched alcoholic clients to three different treatments, based on client characteristics, to see if matching them to more appropriate treatments would increase overall improvements.

Prospective study: Data are collected at several future points in time, starting with the present.

Proteins: Molecules composed of chains of amino acids linked together. Proteins help maintain the cell's structure and affect many biological functions, including the regulation of metabolic reactions.

Psychoanalytic approach: Based on views of Freud and his followers, drugs seen as involving unconscious unresolved conflicts.

Psychodynamic approach: Individual or group-structured therapy focusing on achieving insight.

Psychopathology: Commonly called abnormal behavior but includes psychiatric disorders, including personality disorder and affective or mood disorders.

Public health model: Approach emphasizing the need to consider the interrelationships of the user or host, the agent or drug, and the environment in which a user takes a drug.

Quantitative trait loci (QTL): A particular region of the genome containing a gene that is associated with the traits that are continuous variables determined by multiple, rather than single, genes (polymorphism).

Quantity-frequency index: Quantity and frequency of use are combined to provide a total use index.

Quantity reduction: Approach to social policy that emphasizes the need to lower the amount used per person to minimize harm.

Random assignment: Procedure of assigning participants to different treatments or procedures so each person has an equal chance to be in any treatment; essential for ruling out alternative explanations for experimental outcomes.

Random sample: A sample of participants for a study determined by methods that give an equal chance of being selected to all members of the population studied.

Rational emotive therapy (RET): Based on methods of Albert Ellis, this approach focuses on reasoning and logic for guiding behavior.

Rational Recovery® (RR): A for-profit organization emphasizing reason and personal responsibility for recovery from addictions.

Reactive oxygen species (ROS): Highly reactive oxygen-containing free radicals generated during oxidative metabolism. ROS can react with and damage lipids, proteins, and DNA in cells, causing oxidative stress.

Receptor: A protein on the surface of a cell that recognizes and binds to chemical messengers.

Recognition: A measure of memory where the original material is presented later, together with distracting alternatives, to an individual whose task is to identify the material presented earlier.

Redox state: Reduction-oxidation reactions, often used to describe the balance of NAD+ and NADH in a cell or an organ.

Relapse: Resumption of using a drug following a period of abstinence.

Relapse prevention model: Approach based on social and cognitive processes to teach self-awareness and -monitoring, as well as coping skills for managing high-risk situations for drug use.

Relative risk: The ratio of the frequency of a certain disorder (e.g., cancer) in groups exposed to a certain risk factor (e.g., heavy alcohol consumption) and in groups not exposed to the risk factor.

Remission: Recovery from abuse or dependency.

Resistance skills: Techniques for overcoming peer pressure to use drugs.

Retrieval: Output processes involved in finding information from memory. See also *storage*.

Retrospective study: Data collected at one point in time about behavior are linked to other data obtained at some earlier point in time. For example, do alcoholics who respond well in treatment start drinking later in life than those who do not?

Reuptake: Process of removing neurotransmitters from synapse and recycling for future use.

Risk factors: Variables that are predictive of a negative outcome such as drug abuse.

Rohypnol®: A club drug popular at all-night dances or raves; also called the "date-rape drug."

Schedule of drugs: Federal agency classification of controlled substances based on their medicinal value and risk of addiction.

Screening: Process of identifying at-risk individuals in greater need of intervention or treatment.

Secondary prevention: Treatment or intervention for individuals who have begun to develop alcohol and other drug problems.

Self-efficacy: Subjective feeling of competence to perform well.

Self-medication: Attempt to treat one's own health problems, often with excess use of drugs.

Self-report: A widely used method of obtaining information about alcohol and other drug use that is convenient but can be misleading, falsified, or inaccurate.

Self-selection: Individuals who enter a treatment or engage in some specific behavior are different in important ways from those who do not.

Semantic memory: Storage of commonly known information. See also *episodic memory*.

Sensitivity: Extent to which a measure accurately detects drug users, with few false negatives (users misclassified as not using).

Serotonin (5-hydroxytryptamine, or 5-HT): Neurotransmitter found in raphe nuclei that affects depression and mood states.

Sex role conflict: View that women feel conflict over traditional and modern views of their role.

Sex role deprivation: View that women were restricted to traditional sex roles and had no other opportunities.

Sex role theory: A set of views about how sex roles affect behavior.

Sexual dysfunction: Impaired sexual behavior or functioning, including impotence, lack of orgasm, infertility, and miscarriages.

Single distribution of consumption model: A theory that reducing alcohol availability would reduce alcohol-related problems because higher rates of alcohol consumption in a society are related to more alcohol-related problems.

Single-nucleotide polymorphisms (SNPs): Genetic variation that results from the exchange of only a single nucleotide.

SMART Recovery: A self-help organization emphasizing reason and personal responsibility for recovery from addictions.

Snowball sampling: A nonrandom method for obtaining participants for a study by using contacts referred by previous participants.

Social development model: Adolescents with poor family life situations might become nonconforming, rebellious, and alienated and use alcohol and other drugs to cope with family and parental conflict.

Social learning theory: Theory about how observation of models affects behavior.

Social norms marketing: Prevention strategy that assumes that young people erroneously think most peers drink more than they actually do; by publicizing lower social norms, it is assumed that young people will drink less.

Solitary drinking: Drinking alone. See also *dyadic drinking*.

Somatic nervous system (SNS): Part of the peripheral nervous system that governs voluntary control of striated muscles and receptor organs.

Specificity: Extent to which an index of drug use is accurate, with few false positives (nonusers misclassified as using).

Stages of alcoholism: Invariant progression through increasingly worse stages of alcoholism: prealcoholic, prodromal, crucial, and chronic.

Stages of change model: Model of recovery stages from dependency starting with precontemplation followed by contemplation, preparation, action, and maintenance.

State-dependent learning: Learning acquired in a specific situation that is forgotten is more likely to be recalled in the original context. See also *blackout*.

Storage: Input processes that place information into memory. See also *retrieval*.

Stress response dampening model: Alcohol acts to lessen the impact of stressors.

Structural equation modeling (SEM): Advanced statistical evaluation of the fit between patterns of relationships in the observed data with predictions derived from alternative models of causal relationships. See also *causal models*.

Structured Clinical Interview for *DSM-IV* (SCID): A semistructured interview for making major *DSM-IV* diagnoses; different versions for Axis-I and Axis-II disorders.

Subtypes of alcoholism: Jellinek's (1960) taxonomy of alcoholics based on use patterns and the physical reactions experienced such as tolerance and withdrawal.

Supply reduction: Drug policy approach focusing on reducing the available supply.

Surveillance indicators of use: Indirect measures of use based on records such as sales tax revenue, health statistics, and alcohol-related driving accidents.

Sympathetic nervous system: Part of the autonomic nervous system activated in emergency states.

Temperament: A general personality disposition, such as activity level, that is assumed to be biologically based or innate.

Temperance: Social movement to prevent alcohol use, often associated with religious groups. Originally intended to reduce alcohol consumption, it often demanded total abstinence.

Tolerance: A form of habituation to drugs in which repeated use leads to smaller effects.

Transmissibility: Influence of family history of alcoholism.

Triangulation: When two members of a family are in conflict, they may draw a third party into the conflict to take sides, adding to problems that family therapy must deal with.

Tridimensional Personality Questionnaire (TPQ): Personality instrument that measures three dimensions of Cloninger's temperament theory of alcoholism: novelty seeking, harm avoidance, and reward dependence.

Twelve Steps: A series of behaviors and attitudes that is the foundation for recovery in Alcoholics Anonymous.

Type 1 alcoholism (milieu-limited): Develops at a later age than Type 2, generally after age 25. Less severe than Type 2 and involves a greater influence of environmental factors. Involves dependence on alcohol along with guilt and fear (Cloninger, 1987).

Type 2 alcoholism (male-limited): More severe form than Type 1, typically developing before age 25 and found mostly among males (Cloninger, 1987). Greater role of heredity in this form than in Type 1.

Type A alcoholic: Later onset, fewer childhood risk factors, less severe dependence, fewer alcohol-related problems, and less psychopathological dysfunction compared to Type B (Babor et al., 1992).

Type B alcoholic: More childhood risk factors, familial alcoholism, early onset of alcohol-related problems, greater severity of dependence, more chronic treatment history (despite their younger age), greater psychopathological dysfunction, and more life stress compared to Type A (Babor et al., 1992).

Uncontrolled observations: Natural observations or correlations that may have several possible interpretations. See also *controlled observations*.

Use: A descriptive term to refer to any level of use of a substance.

Use reduction: A drug policy approach focusing on methods of reducing how much individuals use drugs.

Wernicke-Korsakoff syndrome: Cognitive deficits, including memory loss and confusion, attributed to brain damage from alcoholism. See also *anterograde amnesia*.

Wet family interaction: How the family interacts when the alcoholic is drinking. See also *dry family interaction*.

Withdrawal syndrome: Adverse reactions and discomfort experienced when alcohol and drug abusers and dependents do not have access to their drug.

Women for Sobriety: A self-help group for women focusing on recovery from addictions.

Working memory: Cognitive processes used for temporary storage and use of incoming information; similar to short-term memory.

World Health Organization (WHO): An international agency that deals with health issues and policy.

References

Aarons, G. A., Goldman, M. S., Greenbaum, P. E., & Coovert, M. D. (2003). Alcohol expectancies: Integrating cognitive science and psychometric approaches. *Addictive Behaviors, 28*(5), 947–961.

Abbey, A. (1991). Acquaintance rape and alcohol consumption on college campuses: How are they linked? *Journal of American College Health, 39,* 165–169.

Abbey, A., Ross, L. T., & McDuffie, D. (1994). Alcohol's role in sexual assault. In R. R. Watson (Ed.), *Drug and alcohol abuse reviews, Vol. 5: Addictive behaviors in women.* Totowa, NJ: Humana Press.

Abbey, A., Zawacki, T., Buck, P. O., Clinton, A. M., & McAuslan, P. (2001). Alcohol and sexual assault. *Alcohol Research and Health, 25*(1), 43–51.

Abbott, L. J. (1998). The use of alcohol by lesbians: A review and research agenda. *Substance Use and Misuse, 33*(13), 2647–2663.

Abel, E. L., & Sokol, R. J. (1987). Incidence of fetal alcohol syndrome and economic impact of FAS-related anomalies. *Drug and Alcohol Dependence, 19,* 51–70.

Ablon, J. (1984). Family research and alcoholism. In M. Galanter (Ed.), *Recent developments in alcoholism* (Vol. 2, pp. 383–395). New York: Plenum.

Abrams, D. B., Monti, P., Niaura, R., Rohsenow, D. J., & Colby, S. M. (1996). Interventions for alcoholics who smoke. *Alcohol Health and Research World, 20,* 111–117.

Academic ED SBIRT Research Collaborative. (2007). The impact of screening, brief intervention, and referral for treatment on emergency department patients' alcohol use. *Annals of Emergency Medicine, 50*(6), 699–710.

Ackerman, N. (1958). *The psychodynamics of family life.* New York: Basic Books.

Addicott, M. A., Marsh-Richard, D. M., Mathias, C. W., & Dougherty, D. M. (2007). The biphasic effects of alcohol: Comparisons of subjective and objective measures of stimulation, sedation, and physical activity. *Alcoholism: Clinical and Experimental Research, 31*(11), 1883–1890.

Adkisson, N. (c. 1860). Ruined by drink. Available from http://law.jrank.org/pages/4219/Alcohol-Temperance-Movement.html

Akutsu, P. D., Sue, S., Zane, N. W. S., & Nakamura, C. Y. (1989). Ethnic differences in alcohol consumption among Asians and Caucasians in the United States: An investigation of cultural and physiological factors. *Journal of Studies on Alcohol, 50,* 261–267.

Al-Anon. (1984). *Al-Anon family groups.* New York: Al-Anon Family Group Headquarters.

Al-Anon. (1986). *First steps: Al-Anon . . . 35 years of beginnings.* New York: Al-Anon Family Group Headquarters.

Alcoholics Anonymous. (1952). *Twelve steps and twelve traditions.* New York: Author.

Alcoholics Anonymous. (2005). *2004 membership survey* (fall ed.). New York: AA World Services.

Alcoholics Anonymous. (2008). *2007 membership survey.* New York: AA World Services.

Alcoholics Anonymous World Services. (1935). *Alcoholics Anonymous.* New York: Author.

Algan, O., Furedy, J. J., Demirgoeren, S., Vincent, A., & Poeguen, S. (1997). Effects of tobacco smoking and gender on interhemispheric cognitive function: Performance and confidence measures. *Behavioural Pharmacology, 8*(5), 416–428.

American Psychiatric Association. (1987). *Diagnostic and statistical manual of mental disorders* (3rd ed., revised). Washington, DC: Author.

American Psychiatric Association. (1994). *Diagnostic and statistical manual of mental disorders* (4th ed.). Washington, DC: Author.

American Psychiatric Association. (2000). *Diagnostic and statistical manual of mental disorders* (4th ed., text revision). Washington, DC: Author.

Ames, G. M. (1989). Alcohol-related movements and their effects on drinking policies in the American workplace: An historical review. *Journal of Drug Issues, 19,* 489–510.

Andreatini, R., Galduroz, J. C. F., Ferri, C. P., & Oliveira De Souza Formigioni, M. L. (1994). Alcohol dependence criteria in DSM-III-R: Presence of symptoms according to degree of severity. *Addiction, 89*(9), 1129–1134.

Anglin, M. D., Burke, C., Perrochet, B., Stamper, E., & Dawud-Noursi, S. (2000). History of the methamphetamine problem. *Journal of Psychoactive Drugs, 32*(2), 137–141.

Anglin, M. D., Conner, B. T., Annon, J., & Longshore, D. (2007). Levo-alpha-acetylmethadol (LAAM) versus methadone maintenance: 1-year treatment retention, outcomes and status. *Addiction, 102*(9), 1432–1442.

Anglin, M. D., & Hser, Y. (1992). Drug abuse treatment. In R. R. Watson (Ed.), *Drug and alcohol abuse reviews* (Vol. 4, pp. 1–36). Totowa, NJ: Humana Press.

Anglin, M. D., Hser, Y. I., & Booth, M. W. (1987). Sex differences in addict careers: 4. Treatment. *American Journal of Drug and Alcohol Abuse, 13,* 253–280.

Anthenelli, R. M., & Tabakoff, B. (1995). The search for biological markers. *Alcohol Health and Research World, 19*(3), 176–181.

Anthony, J. C., & Echeagaray-Wagner, F. (2000). Epidemiologic analysis of alcohol and tobacco use. *Alcohol Research and Health, 24*(4), 201–208.

Anthony, J. C., Warner, L. A., & Kessler, R. C. (1994). Comparative epidemiology of dependence on tobacco, alcohol, controlled substances, and inhalants: Basic findings from the National Comorbidity Survey. *Experimental Clinical Psychopharmacology, 2,* 244–268.

Anton, R. F. (1999). What is craving? Models and implications for treatment. *Alcohol Research and Health, 23*(3), 165–173.

Anton, R. F., O'Malley, S. S., Domenic A., Ciraulo, R. A., Cisler, D. C., Donovan, D. M., et al. (2006). Combined pharmacotherapies and behavioral interventions for alcohol dependence. The COMBINE study: A randomized controlled trial. *JAMA, 295,* 2003–2017.

Apte, M. V., Wilson, J. E., & Korsten, M. A. (1997). Alcohol-related pancreatic damage: Mechanisms and treatment. *Alcohol Health and Research World, 21*(1), 13–20.

Armeli, S., Todd, M., & Mohr, C. (2005). A daily process approach to individual differences in stress-related alcohol use. *Journal of Personality, 73*(6), 1657–1686.

Auerbach, K. J., & Collins, L. M. (2006). A multidimensional developmental model of alcohol use during emerging adulthood. *Journal of Studies on Alcohol, 67*(6), 917–925.

Austin, E. W., Chen, M. J., & Grube, J. W. (2006). How does alcohol advertising influence underage drinking? The role of desirability, identification and skepticism. *Journal of Adolescent Health, 38*(4), 376–384.

Babor, T. F., & Caetano, R. (2006). Subtypes of substance dependence and abuse: Implications for diagnostic classification and empirical research. *Addiction, 101*(Suppl. 1), 104–110.

Babor, T. F., Hofmann, M., DelBoca, F. K., Hesselbrock, V., Meyer, R. E., Dolinsky, Z. S., et al. (1992). Types of alcoholics: I. Evidence for an empirically derived typology based on indicators of vulnerability and severity. *Archives of General Psychiatry, 49*(8), 599–608.

Bacharach, S., Bamberger, P. A., Sonnenstuhl, W. J., & Vashdi, D. (2008). Aging and drinking problems among mature adults: The moderating effects of positive alcohol expectancies and workforce disengagement. *Journal of Studies on Alcohol and Drugs, 69*(1), 151–159.

Bachman, J. G., O'Malley, P. M., Schulenberg, J. E., Johnston, L. D., Bryant, A. L., & Merline, A. C. (Eds.). (2002). *The decline of substance use in young adulthood: Changes in social activities, roles, and beliefs*. Mahwah, NJ: Erlbaum.

Bachman, J. G., Wadswirth, K. N., O'Malley, P. M., Johnston, L. D., & Schulenberg, J. E. (1997). *Smoking, drinking, and drug use in young adulthood: The impacts of new freedoms and new responsibilities*. Mahwah, NJ: Erlbaum.

Baer, J. S., Barr, H. M., Bookstein, F. L., Sampson, P. D., & Streissguth, A. P. (1998). Prenatal alcohol exposure and family history of alcoholism in the etiology of adolescent alcohol problems. *Journal of Studies on Alcohol, 59,* 533–543.

Baer, J. S., Kivlahan, D. R., & Marlatt, G. A. (1995). High-risk drinking across the transition from high school to college. *Alcoholism: Clinical and Experimental Research, 19*(1), 54–61.

Baer, J. S., Sampson, P. D., Barr, H. M., Connor, P. D., & Streissguth, A. P. (2003). A 21-year longitudinal analysis of the effects of prenatal alcohol exposure on young adult drinking. *Archives of General Psychiatry, 60*(4), 377–385.

Bagnardi, V., Blangiardo, M., La Vecchia, C., & Corrao, G. (2001a). Alcohol consumption and the risk of cancer: A meta-analysis. *Alcohol Research and Health, 25*(4), 263–270.

Bagnardi, V., Blangiardo, M., La Vecchia, C., & Corrao, G. (2001b). A meta-analysis of alcohol drinking and cancer risk. *British Journal of Cancer, 85*(11), 1700–1705.

Baker, L. H., Cooney, N. L., & Pomerleau, O. F. (1987). Craving for alcohol: Theoretical processes and treatment procedures. In W. M. Cox (Ed.), *Treatment and prevention of alcohol problems: A resource manual* (pp. 184–202). Orlando, FL: Academic Press.

Ballard, H. S. (1997). The hematological complications of alcoholism. *Alcohol Health Research World, 21*(1), 42–52.

Bandura, A. (1977). *Social learning theory.* Englewood Cliffs, NJ: Prentice Hall.

Bandura, A. (1999). A sociocognitive analysis of substance abuse. *Psychological Science, 10,* 214–217.

Barnes, G. M., & Welte, J. W. (1990). Prediction of adults' drinking patterns from the drinking of their parents. *Journal of Studies on Alcohol, 51,* 523–527.

Baron, R. M., & Kenny, D. D. (1986). The moderator-mediator distinction in social psychological research: Conceptual, strategic and statistical considerations. *Journal of Personality and Social Psychology, 51,* 1173–1182.

Barrett, D. H., Anda, R. F., Croft, J. B., Serdula, M. K., & Lane, M. J. (1995). The association between alcohol use and health behaviors related to the risk of cardiovascular disease: The South Carolina Cardiovascular Disease Prevention Project. *Journal of Studies on Alcohol, 56*(1), 9–15.

Bartels, C., Kunert, H. J., Stawicki, S., Kroner-Herwig, B., Ehrenreich, H., & Krampe, H. (2007). Recovery of hippocampus-related functions in chronic alcoholics during monitored long-term abstinence. *Alcohol and Alcoholism, 42*(2), 92–102.

Baskin-Sommers, A., & Sommers, I. (2006). The co-occurrence of substance use and high-risk behaviors. *Journal of Adolescent Health, 38*(5), 609–611.

Bauman, K. E., Fisher, L. A., Bryan, E. S., & Chenoweth, R. L. (1985). Relationship between subjective expected utility and behavior: A longitudinal study of adolescent drinking behavior. *Journal of Studies on Alcohol, 40,* 272–282.

Beardslee, W. R., Son, L., & Vaillant, G. E. (1986). Exposure to parental alcoholism during childhood and outcome in adulthood: A prospective longitudinal study. *British Journal of Psychiatry, 149,* 584–591.

Beattie, M. (1987). *Codependent no more: How to stop controlling others and start caring for yourself.* New York: Harper/Hazelden.

Beatty, W. W., Tivis, R., Stott, H. D., Nixon, S. J., & Parsons, O. A. (2000). Neuropsychological deficits in sober alcoholics: Influences of chronicity and recent alcohol consumption. *Alcoholism: Clinical and Experimental Research, 24*(2), 149–154.

Beck, K. H., & Bargman, C. J. (1993). Investigating Hispanic adolescent involvement with alcohol: A focus group interview approach. *Health Education Research, 8*(2), 151–158.

Becker, H. (1963). *Outsiders: Studies in the sociology of deviance.* New York: Free Press.

Beckett, M., Burnam, A., Collins, R. L., Kanouse, D. E., & Beckman, R. (2003). Substance use and high-risk sex among people with HIV: A comparison across exposure groups. *AIDS Behavior, 7*(2), 209–219.

Beckman, L. J. (1980). An attributional analysis of Alcoholics Anonymous. *Journal of Studies on Alcohol, 41,* 714–726.

Beckman, L. J. (1993). Alcoholics Anonymous and gender issues. In B. S. McCrady & W. R. Miller (Eds.), *Research on Alcoholics Anonymous: Opportunities and alternatives* (pp. 233–250). Piscataway, NJ: Rutgers Center of Alcohol Studies.

Bell, R., Wechsler, H., & Johnston, L. D. (1997). Correlates of college student marijuana use: Results of a U.S. national survey. *Addiction, 92,* 571–581.

Bensley, L. S., Spieker, S. J., & McMahon, R. J. (1994). Parenting behavior of adolescent children of alcoholics. *Addiction, 89*(10), 1265–1276.

Bensley, L. S., Spieker, S. J., Van Eenwyk, J., & Schoder, J. (1999). Self-reported abuse history and adolescent problem behaviors II: Alcohol and drug use. *Journal of Adolescent Health, 24*(3), 173–180.

Bensley, L. S., & Wu, R. (1991). The role of psychological reactance on drinking following alcohol prevention messages. *Journal of Applied Social Psychology, 21,* 1111–1124.

Bergmark, A. (2008). On treatment mechanisms—what can we learn from the COMBINE study? *Addiction, 103,* 703–705.

Berman, M. O. (1990). Severe brain dysfunction. *Alcohol Health & Research World, 14,* 120–129.

Berridge, K. C., & Robinson, T. E. (1995). The mind of an addicted brain: Neural sensitization of wanting versus liking. *Current Directions in Psychological Science, 4,* 71–76.

Beseler, C. L., Aharonovich, E., Keyes, K. M., & Hasin, D. S. (2008). Adult transition from at-risk drinking to alcohol dependence: The relationship of family history and drinking motives. *Alcoholism: Clinical and Experimental Research, 32*(4), 607–616.

Biernacki, P. (1986). *Pathways from heroin addiction: Recovery without treatment.* Philadelphia: Temple University Press.

Bierut, L. J., Dinwiddie, S. H., Begleiter, H., Crowe, R. R., Hesselbrock, V., Nurnberger, J. I., et al. (1998). Familial transmission of substance dependence: Alcohol, marijuana, cocaine, and habitual smoking: A report from the Collaborative Study on the Genetics of Alcoholism. *Archives of General Psychiatry, 55,* 982–988.

Bierut, L. J., Saccone, N. L., Rice, J. P., Goate, A., Foroud, T., Edenberg, H., et al. (2002). Defining alcohol-related phenotypes in humans: The Collaborative Study on the Genetics of Alcoholism. *Alcohol Research and Health, 26*(3), 208–213.

Bijttebier, P., Goethals, E., & Ansoms, S. (2006). Parental drinking as a risk factor for children's maladjustment: The mediating role of family environment. *Psychology of Addictive Behaviors, 20*(2), 126–130.

Bischof, G., Rumpf, H.-J., Meyer, C., Hapke, U., & John, U. (2007). Stability of subtypes of natural recovery from alcohol dependence after two years. *Addiction, 102*(6), 904–908.

Bischof, G., Rumpf, H. J., Hapke, U., Meyer, C., & John, U. (2000). Gender differences in natural recovery from alcohol dependence. *Journal of Studies on Alcohol, 61*(6), 783–786.

Bischof, G., Rumpf, H. J., Hapke, U., Meyer, C., & John, U. (2003). Types of natural recovery from alcohol dependence: A cluster analytic approach. *Addiction, 98*(12), 1737–1746.

Black, C. (1981). *It will never happen to me.* Denver, CO: MAC.

Blane, H. T. (1977). Acculturation and drinking in an Italian American community. *Journal of Studies on Alcohol, 38,* 1324–1346.

Blane, H. T. (1988). Prevention issues with children of alcoholics. *British Journal of Addiction, 83,* 793–798.

Bliss, R. E., Garvey, A. J., & Ward, K. D. (1999). Resisting temptations to smoke: Results from within-subjects analyses. *Psychology of Addictive Behaviors, 13*(2), 143–151.

Blum, K., Sheridan, P. J., Wood, R. C., Braverman, E. R., Chen, T. J., & Comings, D. E. (1995). Dopamine D2 receptor gene variants: Association and linkage studies in impulsive-addictive-compulsive behaviour. *Pharmacogenetics, 5*(3), 121–141.

Blum, T. C., & Roman, P. M. (1995). *Cost-effectiveness and preventive implications of employee assistance programs* (Vol. Publication RP0907). Rockville, MD: Substance Abuse and Mental Health Services Administration.

Blume, A. W., Lostutter, T. W., Schmaling, K. B., & Marlatt, G. A. (2003). Beliefs about drinking behavior predict drinking consequences. *Journal of Psychoactive Drugs, 35*(3), 395–399.

Blume, S. B. (1994). Gender differences in alcohol-related disorders. *Harvard Review of Psychiatry, 2,* 7–14.

Bohman, M. (1978). Some genetic aspects of alcoholism and criminality: A population of adoptees. *Archives of General Psychiatry, 35,* 269–276.

Bohman, M., Sigvardsson, S., & Cloninger, C. R. (1981). Maternal inheritance of alcohol abuse: Cross fostering analysis of adopted women. *Archives of General Psychiatry, 38,* 965–969.

Bonnie, R. J., & O'Connell, M. E. (Eds.). (2004). *Reducing underage drinking: A collective responsibility.* Washington, DC: National Academy of Sciences.

Bookstein, F. L., Streissguth, A. P., Sampson, P. D., Connor, P. D., & Barr, H. M. (2002). Corpus callosum shape and neuropsychological deficits in adult males with heavy fetal alcohol exposure. *Neuroimage, 15*(1), 233–251.

Bottlender, M., & Soyka, M. (2004). Impact of craving on alcohol relapse during, and 12 months following, outpatient treatment. *Alcohol and Alcoholism, 39*(4), 357–361.

Botvin, G. J., Baker, E., Dusenbury, L., Tortu, S., & Botvin, E. M. (1990). Preventing adolescent drug abuse through a multimodal cognitive-behavioral approach: Results of a 3-year study. *Journal of Consulting and Clinical Psychology, 58,* 437–446.

Botvin, G. J., Schinke, S. P., Epstein, J. A., Diaz, T., & Botvin, E. M. (1995). Effectiveness of culturally focused and generic skills training approaches to alcohol and drug abuse prevention among minority adolescents: Two-year follow-up results. *Psychology of Addictive Behaviors, 9,* 183–194.

Bowen, M. (1974). Alcoholism as viewed through family systems theory and family psychotherapy. *Annals of the New York Academy of Sciences, 128,* 115–122.

Bowen, M. (1978). Alcoholism and the family. In M. Bowen (Ed.), *Family therapy in clinical practice* (pp. 259–268). New York: Jason Aronson.

Bowie, J. V., Ensminger, M. E., & Robertson, J. A. (2006). Alcohol-use problems in young Black adults: Effects of religiosity, social resources, and mental health. *Journal of Studies on Alcohol, 67*(1), 44–53.

Bradley, A. M. (1988). Keep coming back: The case for a valuation of Alcoholics Anonymous. *Alcohol Health and Research World, 12,* 192–201.

Bradley, K. A., Badrinath, S., Bush, K., Boyd-Wickizer, J., & Anawalt, B. (1998). Medical risks for women who drink alcohol. *Journal of General Internal Medicine, 13*(9), 627–639.

Brandon, T. H. (1994). Negative affect as motivation to smoke. *Current Directions in Psychological Science, 3,* 33–37.

Brandon, T. H., & Baker, T. B. (1991). The Smoking Consequences Questionnaire: The subjective expected utility of smoking college students. *Psychological Assessment, 3,* 484–491.

Brandon, T. H., Vidrine, J. I., & Litvin, E. B. (2007). Relapse and relapse prevention. *Annual Review of Clinical Psychology, 3,* 257–284.

Brandsma, J. M., Maultry, M. C., & Welsh, R. J. (1980). *Outpatient treatment of alcoholism: A review and comparative study.* Baltimore: University Park Press.

Brennan, P. L., & Moos, R. H. (1990). Life stressors, social resources, and late-life problem drinking. *Psychology and Aging, 5,* 491–501.

Brennan, P. L., & Moos, R. H. (1996a). Late-life drinking behavior: The influence of personal characteristics, life context, and treatment. *Alcohol Health & Research World, 20*(3), 197–204.

Brennan, P. L., & Moos, R. H. (1996b). Late-life problem drinking: Personal and environmental risk factors for 4-year functioning outcomes and treatment seeking. *Journal of Substance Abuse, 8,* 167–180.

Brennan, P. L., Moos, R. H., & Kim, J. Y. (1993). Gender differences in the individual characteristics and life contexts of late-middle-aged and older problem drinkers. *Addiction, 88,* 781–790.

Brennan, P. L., Moos, R. H., & Mertens, J. R. (1994). Personal and environmental risk factors as predictors of alcohol use, depression, and treatment-seeking: A longitudinal analysis of late-life problem drinkers. *Journal of Substance Abuse, 6,* 191–208.

Brennan, P. L., Schutte, K. K., & Moos, R. H. (1999). Reciprocal relations between stressors and drinking behavior: A three-wave panel study of late middle-aged and older women and men. *Addiction, 94,* 737–749.

Breslau, N., Kilbey, M., & Andreski, P. (1993). Nicotine dependence and major depression: New evidence from a prospective investigation. *Archives of General Psychiatry, 50,* 31–35.

Breslau, N., Peterson, E., Schultz, L, Andreski, P., & Chilcoat, H. (1996). Are smokers with alcohol disorders less likely to quit? *American Journal of Public Health. 86*(7), 985–990.

Breslow, R. A., Faden, V. B., & Smothers, B. (2003). Alcohol consumption by elderly Americans. *Journal of Studies on Alcohol, 64*(6), 884–892.

Breslow, R. A., & Graubard, B. I. (2008). Prospective study of alcohol consumption in the United States: Quantity, frequency, and cause-specific mortality. *Alcoholism: Clinical and Experimental Research, 32*(3), 513–521.

Breslow, R. A., & Smothers, B. (2004). Drinking patterns of older Americans: National Health Interview Surveys, 1997–2001. *Journal of Studies on Alcohol, 65*(2), 232–240.

Brewer, C. (1993). Recent developments in disulfiram treatment. *Alcohol and Alcoholism, 28*(4), 383–395.

Brice, C. F., & Smith, A. P. (2002). Effects of caffeine on mood and performance: A study of realistic consumption. *Psychopharmacology (Berl), 164*(2), 188–192.

Brick, J. B., Nathan, P. E., Westrick, E., & Frankenstein, W. (1986). Effect of menstrual cycle phase on behavioral and physiological responses to alcohol. *Journal of Studies on Alcohol, 47,* 472–477.

Brisbane, F. L., & Wells, R. C. (1989). Treatment and prevention of alcoholism among Blacks. In T. D. Watts & J. R. Wright (Eds.), *Alcoholism in minority populations* (pp. 33–52). Springfield, IL: C. C. Thomas.

Brook, J. S., Brook, D. W., Gordon, A. S., Whiteman, M., & Cohen, P. (1990). The psychosocial etiology of adolescent drug use: A family interactional approach. *Genetic, Social, and General Psychology Monographs, 116,* 111–267.

Brook, J. S., Cohen, P., & Jaeger, L. (1998). Developmental variations in factors related to initial and increased levels of adolescent drug involvement. *Journal of Genetic Psychology, 159*(2), 179–194.

Brown, S. A. (1993). Drug effect expectancies and addictive behavior change. *Experimental and Clinical Psychopharmacology, 1,* 55–67.

Brown, S. A., Goldman, M. S., Inn, A., & Anderson, L. R. (1980). Expectations of reinforcement from alcohol: Their domain and relation to drinking patterns. *Journal of Consulting and Clinical Psychology, 48,* 419–426.

Brown, T. G., Seraganian, P., Tremblay, J., & Annis, H. (2002). Process and outcome changes with relapse prevention versus 12-step aftercare programs for substance abusers. *Addiction, 97*(6), 677–689.

Brownell, K., Marlatt, G. A., Lichenstein, E., & Wilson, G. (1986). Understanding and preventing relapse. *American Psychologist, 41,* 765–782.

Bumpass, L. L. (2004). Social change and the American family. *Annals of New York Academy of Science, 1038,* 213–219.

Bureau of Justice Statistics. (1992). *Drugs, crime, and the justice system: A national report from the Bureau of Justice Statistics* (NCJ-133652). Washington, DC: U.S. Government Printing Office.

Bureau of Justice Statistics. (2005). *Substance dependence, abuse, and treatment of jail inmates, 2002* (No. NCJ 209588). Washington, DC: U.S. Department of Justice.

Burgard, S. A., Cochran, S. D., & Mays, V. M. (2005). Alcohol and tobacco use patterns among heterosexually and homosexually experienced California women. *Drug and Alcohol Dependence, 77*(1), 61–70.

Burk, J. P., & Sher, K. J. (1990). Labeling the child of an alcoholic: Negative stereotyping by mental health professionals and peers. *Journal of Studies on Alcohol, 51,* 156–163.

Burton, R., Johnson, R. J., Ritter, C., & Clayton, R. R. (1996). The effects of role socialization on the initial use: An event history analysis from adolescence into middle adulthood. *Journal of Health and Social Behavior, 37,* 75–90.

Bush, D. M. (2008). The U.S. Mandatory Guidelines for Federal Workplace Drug Testing Programs: Current status and future considerations. *Forensic Science International, 174*(2–3), 111–119.

Bushman, B. J., & Cooper, H. M. (1990). Effects of alcohol on human aggression: An integrative research review. *Psychological Bulletin, 107,* 341–354.

Buss, A. H. (1961). *The psychology of aggression.* New York: Wiley.

Bux, D. A., Jr. (1996). The epidemiology of problem drinking in gay men and lesbians: A critical review. *Clinical Psychology Review, 16*(4), 277–298.

Caces, M. F., Harford, T. C., Williams, G. D., & Hanna, E. Z. (1999). Alcohol consumption and divorce rates in the United States. *Journal of Studies on Alcohol, 60,* 647–652.

Cadoret, R. J., & Gath, A. (1978). Inheritance of alcoholism in adoptees. *British Journal of Psychiatry, 132,* 252–258.

Caetano, R. (1988). Drinking patterns and alcohol problems in a national sample of U.S. Hispanics. In National Institute on Alcohol Abuse and Alcoholism (Ed.), *Alcohol use among U.S. ethnic minorities* (Vol. Research Monograph No. 18. DHHS Pub. No. (ADM)87–1435). Washington, DC: U.S. Government Printing Office.

Caetano, R. (1990). Hispanic drinking in the U.S.: Thinking in new directions. *British Journal of Addiction, 85,* 1231–1235.

Caetano, R. (1993). Ethnic minority groups and Alcoholics Anonymous: A review. In B. S. McCrady & W. R. Miller (Eds.), *Research on Alcoholics Anonymous: Opportunities and alternatives* (pp. 209–232). Piscataway, NJ: Rutgers Center of Alcohol Studies.

Caetano, R., & Babor, T. F. (2006). Diagnosis of alcohol dependence in epidemiological surveys: An epidemic of youthful alcohol dependence or a case of measurement error? *Addiction, 101,* 111–114.

Caetano, R., Clark, C. L., & Tam, T. (1998). Alcohol consumption among racial/ethnic minorities: Theory and research. *Alcohol Health and Research World, 22*(4), 233–241.

Caetano, R., & Mora, M. E. (1988). Acculturation and drinking among people of Mexican descent in Mexico and the United States. *Journal of Studies on Alcohol, 49,* 462–471.

Caetano, R., Ramisetty-Mikler, S., & Field, C. A. (2005). Unidirectional and bidirectional intimate partner violence among White, Black, and Hispanic couples in the United States. *Violence and Victims, 20*(4), 393–406.

Caetano, R., Ramisetty-Mikler, S., & Rodriguez, L. A. (2008). The Hispanic Americans Baseline Alcohol Survey (HABLAS): Rates and predictors of alcohol abuse and dependence across Hispanic national groups. *Journal of Studies on Alcohol and Drugs, 69*(3), 441–448.

Caetano, R., Ramisetty-Mikler, S., & Rodriguez, L. A. (2009). The Hispanic Americans Baseline Alcohol Survey (HABLAS): The association between birthplace, acculturation and alcohol abuse and dependence across Hispanic national groups. *Drug Alcohol Dependence, 99*(1–3), 215–221.

Caetano, R., Ramisetty-Mikler, S., Wallisch, L. S., McGrath, C., & Spence, R. T. (2008). Acculturation, drinking, and alcohol abuse and dependence among Hispanics in the Texas-Mexico border. *Alcoholism: Clinical and Experimental Research, 32*(2), 314–321.

Cahalan, D. (1987). *Understanding America's drinking problem: How to combat the hazards of alcohol.* San Francisco: Jossey-Bass.

Caldwell, C. H., Sellers, R. M., Bernat, D. H., & Zimmerman, M. A. (2004). Racial identity, parental support, and alcohol use in a sample of academically at-risk African American high school students. *American Journal of Community Psychology, 34*(1–2), 71–82.

Caracci, G., & Miller, N. S. (1991). Alcohol and drug addiction in the elderly. In N. S. Miller (Ed.), *Comprehensive handbook of drug and alcohol addiction* (pp. 179–191). New York: Dekker.

Carey, K. B., Borsari, B., Carey, M. P., & Maisto, S. A. (2006). Patterns and importance of self-other differences in college drinking norms. *Psychology of Addictive Behaviors, 20,* 385–393.

Carnevale Associates. (2008). *Federal drug budget trend: Least effective programs being emphasized.* Gaithersburg, MD: Author.

Carpenter, K. M., Liu, X., & Hasin, D. S. (2006). The Type A–Type B classification in a community sample of problem drinkers: Structural and predictive validity. *Addictive Behaviors, 31*(1), 15–30.

Carroll, K. M. (1996). Relapse prevention as a psychosocial treatment: A review of controlled clinical trials. *Experimental and Clinical Psychopharmacology, 4,* 46–54.

Carroll, K. M., & Rounsaville, B. J. (2007). A vision of the next generation of behavioral therapies research in the addictions. *Addiction, 102*(6), 850–862.

Castillo Mezzich, A., Tarter, R. E., Giancola, P. R., Lu, S., Kirisci, L., & Parks, S. (1997). Substance use and risky sexual behavior in female adolescents. *Drug and Alcohol Dependence, 44*(2–3), 157–166.

Catalano, R. F., Morrison, D. M., Wells, E. A., Gillmore, M. R., Iritani, B., & Hawkins, J. D. (1992). Ethnic differences in family factors related to early drug initiation. *Journal of Studies on Alcohol, 53,* 208–217.

Catley, D., & O'Connell, K. A. (2000). Absentminded lapses during smoking cessation. *Psychology of Addictive Behaviors, 14*(1), 73–76.

Caulkins, J. P., Rydell, C. P., Schwabe, W., & Chiesa, J. (1997). *Mandatory minimum drug sentences: Throwing away the key or the taxpayers' money?* Santa Monica, CA: Rand Corporation.

Center for Science in the Public Interest. (2003). *Alcohol advertising expenditures, 1998–2002: Alcohol Policies Project fact sheet.* Washington, DC: Author. Available from http://cspinet.info/booze/iss_ads.htm

Centers for Disease Control and Prevention. (2008). *Youth Risk Behavior Surveillance—United States.* Atlanta, GA: U.S. Department of Health and Human Services.

Cermak, T. L. (1986). *Diagnosing and treating codependency: A guide for professionals.* Minneapolis, MN: Johnson Institute.

Cermak, T. L. (1989). Al-Anon and recovery. In M. Galanter (Ed.), *Recent developments in alcoholism: Emerging issues in treatment* (Vol. 7, pp. 91–104). New York: Plenum.

Cervantes, R. C., Gilbert, M. J., de Snyder, N. S., & Padilla, A. M. (1990–1991). Psychosocial and cognitive correlates of alcohol use in younger adult immigrant and U.S.-born Hispanics. *International Journal of the Addictions, 25,* 687–708.

Chait, L. D., & Perry, J. L. (1994). Acute and residual effects of alcohol and marijuana, alone and in combination, on mood and performance. *Psychopharmacology, 115*(3), 340–349.

Chalder, M., Elgar, F. J., & Bennett, P. (2006). Drinking and motivations to drink among adolescent children of parents with alcohol problems. *Alcohol and Alcoholism, 41*(1), 107–113.

Chaloupka, F. J., Grossman, M., & Saffer, H. (2002). The effects of price on alcohol consumption and alcohol-related problems. *Alcohol Research and Health, 26*(1), 22–34.

Chao, C. (2007). Associations between beer, wine, and liquor consumption and lung cancer risk: A meta-analysis. *Cancer Epidemiologic Biomarkers & Prevention, 16*(11), 2436–2447.

Chao, C., Slezak, J. M., Caan, B. J., & Quinn, V. P. (2008). Alcoholic beverage intake and risk of lung cancer: The California Men's Health Study. *Cancer Epidemiologic Biomarkers & Prevention, 17*(10), 2692–2699.

Charette, L., Tate, D. L., & Wilson, A. (1990). Alcohol consumption and menstrual distress in women at higher and lower risk for alcoholism. *Alcoholism: Clinical and Experimental Research, 14,* 152–157.

Charness, M. E. (1990). Alcohol and the brain. *Alcohol Health and Research World, 14*(2), 85–89.

Chasnoff, I. J. (1991). Cocaine and pregnancy: Clinical and methodologic issues. *Clinics in Perinatology, 18*(1), 113–123.

Chasnoff, I. J., Griffith, D. R., Freier, C., & Murray, J. (1992). Cocaine/polydrug use in pregnancy: Two-year follow-up [see comments]. *Pediatrics, 89*(2), 284–289.

Chassin, L., Curran, P. J., Hussong, A. M., & Colder, C. R. (1996). The relation of parent alcoholism to adolescent substance use: A longitudinal follow-up study. *Journal of Abnormal Psychology, 105,* 70–80.

Chassin, L., Fora, D. B., & King, K. M. (2004). Trajectories of alcohol and drug use and dependence from adolescence to adulthood: The effects of familial alcoholism and personality. *Journal of Abnormal Psychology, 113*(4), 483–498.

Chassin, L., Presson, C. C., Sherman, S. J., & Mulvenon, S. (1994). Family history of smoking and young adult smoking behavior. *Psychology of Addictive Behaviors, 8*(2), 102–110.

Chermack, S. T., & Giancola, P. R. (1997). The relation between alcohol and aggression: An integrated biopsychosocial conceptualization. *Clinical Psychology Review, 17*(6), 621–649.

Chermack, S. T., Stoltenberg, S. F., Fuller, B. E., & Blow, F. C. (2000). Gender differences in the development of substance-related problems: The impact of family history of alcoholism, family history of violence and childhood conduct problems. *Journal of Studies on Alcohol, 61*(6), 845–852.

Chermack, S. T., & Taylor, S. P. (1995). Alcohol and human physical aggression: Pharmacological versus expectancy effects. *Journal of Studies on Alcohol, 56*(4), 449–456.

Cheung, Y. W. (1993). Approaches to ethnicity: Clearing roadblocks in the study of ethnicity and substance abuse. *International Journal of the Addictions, 28,* 1209–1226.

Chi, I., Lubben, J., & Kitano, H. H. L. (1989). Differences in drinking behavior among three Asian-American groups. *Journal of Studies on Alcohol, 50,* 15–23.

Chiriboga, C. A. (1998). Neurological correlates of fetal cocaine exposure. *Annals of the New York Academy of Sciences, 846,* 109–125.

Cho, Y. I. (2004). Gender composition of occupation and industry and working women's alcohol consumption. *Journal of Studies on Alcohol, 65*(3), 345–352.

Churchill, W. (1996). Like sand in the wind: The making of an American Indian diaspora in the United States. In L. Foerstel (Ed.), *Creating surplus populations: The effects of military and corporate policies on indigenous people* (pp. 19–52). Washington, DC: Maisonneuve Press.

Clifford, P. R., Maisto, S. A., & Davis, C. M. (2007). Alcohol treatment research assessment exposure subject reactivity effects: Part I. Alcohol use and related consequences. *Journal of Studies on Alcohol and Drugs, 68*(4), 519–528.

Cloninger, C. R. (1987). Neurogenetic adaptive mechanisms in alcoholism. *Science, 236,* 410–416.

Cloninger, C. R., Bohman, M., & Sigvardsson, S. (1981). Inheritance of alcohol abuse: Cross fostering analysis of adopted men. *Archives of General Psychiatry, 38,* 861–868.

Cochran, S. D., Keenan, C., Schober, C., & Mays, V. M. (2000). Estimates of alcohol use and clinical treatment needs among homosexually active men and women in the U.S. population. *Journal of Consulting and Clinical Psychology, 68*(6), 1062–1071.

Cohen, J., Collins, R., Darkes, J., & Gwartney, D. (2007). A league of their own: Demographics, motivations and patterns of use of 1,955 male adult non-medical anabolic steroid users in the United States. *Journal of the International Society for Sports Nutrition, 4*(1), 12 [Epub ahead of print]. Available at http://www.jissn.com/content/4/1/12

Cohen, J. B., Dickow, A., Horner, K., Zweben, J. E., Balabis, J., Vandersloot, D., et al. (2003). Abuse and violence history of men and women in treatment for methamphetamine dependence. *American Journal of Addictions, 12*(5), 377–385.

Cohen, L. M., McCarthy, D. M., Brown, S. A., & Myers, M. G. (2002). Negative affect combines with smoking outcome expectancies to predict smoking behavior overtime. *Psychology of Addictive Behaviors, 16*(2), 91–97.

Cohen, S., & Shiffman, S. (1989). Debunking myths about self quitting. *American Psychologist, 44,* 1355–1365.

Collins, R. L., & McNair, L. D. (2002). Minority women and alcohol use. *Alcohol Research and Health, 26*(4), 251–256.

Connors, G. J., Longabaugh, R., & Miller, W. R. (1996). Looking forward and back to relapse: Implications for research and practice. *Addiction, 91*(12, Suppl. 1), S191–S196.

Conrod, P. J., Petersen, J. B., & Pihl, R. O. (1997). Disinhibited personality and sensitivity to alcohol reinforcement: Independent correlates of drinking behavior in sons of alcoholics. *Alcoholism: Clinical and Experimental Research, 21*(7), 1320–1332.

Conway, K. P., Swendsen, J. D., & Merikangas, K. R. (2003). Alcohol expectancies, alcohol consumption, and problem drinking: The moderating role of family history. *Addictive Behaviors, 28*(5), 823–836.

Cook, P. J. (1981). The effects of liquor taxes on drinking, cirrhosis and auto accidents. In M. H. Moore & D. R. Gerstein (Eds.), *Alcohol and alcohol policy: Beyond the shadow of prohibition* (pp. 255–285). Washington, DC: National Academy Press.

Cook, P. J., & Moore, M. J. (2002). The economics of alcohol abuse and alcohol-control policies. *Health Affairs, 21,* 120–133.

Cook, R. T. (1998). Alcohol abuse, alcoholism, and damage to the immune system: A review. *Alcoholism: Clinical and Experimental Research, 22,* 1927–1942.

Cooney, N. L., Litt, M. D., Morse, P. A., Bauer, L. O., & Gaupp, L. (1997). Alcohol cue reactivity, negative-mood reactivity, and relapse in treated alcoholic men. *Journal of Abnormal Psychology, 106*(2), 243–250.

Cooper, M. L., Frone, M. R., Russell, M., & Mudar, P. (1995). Drinking to regulate positive and negative emotions: A motivational model of alcohol use. *Journal of Personality and Social Psychology, 69*(5), 990–1005.

Cooper, M. L., Krull, J. L., Agocha, V. B., Flanagan, M. E., Orcutt, H. K., Grabe, S., et al. (2008). Motivational pathways to alcohol use and abuse among Black and White adolescents. *Journal of Abnormal Psychology, 117*(3), 485–501.

Cooper, M. L., Russell, M., Skinner, J. B., Frone, M. R., & Mudar, P. (1992). Stress and alcohol use: Moderating effects of gender, coping, and alcohol expectancies. *Journal of Abnormal Psychology, 101*(1), 139–152.

Copeland, A. L., Brandon, T. H., & Quinn, E. P. (1995). The Smoking Consequences Questionnaire–Adult: Measurement of smoking outcome expectancies of experienced smokers. *Psychological Assessment, 7,* 484–494.

Cornelius, J. R., Salloum, I. M., Ehlers, J. G., Jarrett P. J., Cornelius, M. D., Perel, J. M., et al. (1997). Fluoxetine in depressed alcoholics: A double-blind, placebo-controlled trial. *Archives of General Psychiatry, 54*(8), 700–705.

Costanzo, P. R., Malone, P. S., Belsky, D., Kertesz, S., Pletcher, M., & Sloan, F. A. (2007). Longitudinal differences in alcohol use in early adulthood. *Journal of Studies on Alcohol and Drugs, 68*(5), 727–737.

Cox, W. M. (1987). Personality theory and research. In H. T. Blane & K. E. Leonard (Eds.), *Psychological theories of drinking and alcoholism* (pp. 55–89). New York: Guilford.

Crabbe, J. C. (2002). Alcohol and genetics: New models. *American Journal of Medical Genetics, 114,* 969–974.

Crabbe, J. C., Phillips, T. J., Buck, K. J., Cunningham, C. L., & Belknap, J. K. (1999). Identifying genes for alcohol and drug sensitivity: Recent progress and future directions. *Trends in Neurosciences, 22*(4), 173–179.

Criqui, M. (1990). Comments on Shaper's "Alcohol and mortality: A review of prospective studies": The reduction of coronary heart disease with light to moderate alcohol consumption: Effect or artifact? *British Journal of Addiction, 85,* 854–857.

Crowe, L. C., & George, W. H. (1989). Alcohol and human sexuality: Review and integration. *Psychological Bulletin, 105,* 374–386.

Cummings, C., Gordon, J. R., & Marlatt, G. A. (1980). Relapse: Strategies of prevention and prediction. In W. R. Miller (Ed.), *The addictive behaviors: Treatment of alcohol, drug addiction, smoking and obesity* (pp. 291–321). New York: Permagon.

Curran, P. J., & Chassin, L. (1996). A longitudinal study of parenting as a protective factor for children of alcoholics. *Journal of Studies on Alcohol, 57*(3), 305–313.

Cutler, R. B., & Fishbain, D. A. (2005). Are alcoholism treatments effective? The Project MATCH data. *BMC Public Health, 5,* 75.

Daderman, A. M., Fredriksson, B., Kristiansson, M., Nilsson, L. H., & Lidberg, L. (2002). Violent behavior, impulsive decision-making, and anterograde amnesia while intoxicated with flunitrazepam and alcohol or other drugs: A case study in forensic psychiatric patients. *Journal of American Academy of Psychiatry Law, 30*(2), 238–251.

Daley, D. C. (1989). *Relapse prevention: Treatment alternatives and counseling aids.* Blue Ridge Summit, PA: Tab Books.

Darrow, S. L., Russell, M., Cooper, M. L., Midar, P., & Frone, M. R. (1992). Sociodemographic correlates of alcohol consumption among African-American and White women. *Women and Health, 18,* 35–51.

Davidson, E. S., & Schenk, S. (1994). Variability in subjective responses to marijuana: Initial experiences of college students. *Addictive Behaviors, 19*(5), 531–538.

Davies, D. L. (1962). Normal drinking in recovered alcohol addicts. *Journal of Studies on Alcohol, 23,* 94–104.

Davis, K. C., Hendershot, C. S., George, W. H., Norris, J., & Heiman, J. R. (2007). Alcohol's effects on sexual decision making: An integration of alcohol myopia and individual differences. *Journal of Studies on Alcohol and Drugs, 68*(6), 843–851.

Davis, L., Uezato, A., Newell, J. M., & Frazier, E. (2008). Major depression and comorbid substance use disorders. *Current Opinion in Psychiatry, 21*(1), 14–18.

Dawson, D. A. (1996). Gender differences in the probability of alcohol treatment. *Journal of Substance Abuse, 8*(2), 211–225.

Dawson, D. A. (2000a). Drinking as a risk factor for sustained smoking. *Drug and Alcohol Dependence, 59,* 235–249.

Dawson, D. A. (2000b). The link between family history and early onset alcoholism: Earlier initiation of drinking or more rapid development of dependence? *Journal of Studies on Alcohol, 61*(5), 637–646.

Dawson, D. A., Goldstein, R. B., Patricia Chou, S., June Ruan, W., & Grant, B. F. (2008). Age at first drink and the first incidence of adult-onset DSM-IV alcohol use disorders. *Alcoholism: Clinical and Experimental Research, 32*(12), 2149–2160.

Dawson, D. A., Grant, B. F., & Chou, P. S. (1995). Gender differences in alcohol intake. In W. A. Hunt & S. Zakhari (Eds.), *Stress, gender, and alcohol-seeking behavior* (pp. 3–21). Washington, DC: U.S. Government Printing Office.

Dawson, D. A., Grant, B. F., Chou, S. P., & Stinson, F. S. (2007). The impact of partner alcohol problems on women's physical and mental health. *Journal of Studies on Alcohol and Drugs, 68*(1), 66–75.

Dawson, D. A., Grant, B. F., & Harford, T. C. (1995). Variation in the association of alcohol consumption with five DSM-IV alcohol problem domains. *Alcoholism: Clinical and Experimental Research, 19*(1), 66–74.

Dawson, D. A., Grant, B. F., & Ruan, W. J. (2005). The association between stress and drinking: Modifying effects of gender and vulnerability. *Alcohol and Alcoholism, 40*(5), 453–460.

Dawson, D. A., Grant, B. F., Stinson, F. S., & Chou, P. S. (2006). Maturing out of alcohol dependence: The impact of transitional life events. *Journal of Studies on Alcohol, 67*(2), 195–203.

Dawson, D. A., Harford, T. C., & Grant, B. F. (1992). Family history as a predictor of alcohol dependence. *Alcoholism Clinical and Experimental Research, 16*(3), 572–575.

Day, N. L., Goldschmidt, L., Robles, N., Richardson, G., Cornelius, M., Taylor, P., et al. (1991). Prenatal alcohol exposure and offspring growth at 18 months of age: The predictive validity of two measures of drinking. *Alcoholism: Clinical and Experimental Research, 15,* 914–918.

Day, N. L., Leech, S. L., Richardson, G. A., Cornelius, M. D., Robles, N., & Larkby, C. (2002). Prenatal alcohol exposure predicts continued deficits in offspring size at 14 years of age. *Alcoholism: Clinical and Experimental Research, 26*(10), 1584–1591.

Day, N. L., & Richardson, G. A. (1991). Prenatal alcohol exposure: A continuum of effects. *Seminars in Perinatology, 15*(4), 271–279.

De Genna, N. M., Larkby, C., & Cornelius, M. D. (2007). Early and adverse experiences with sex and alcohol are associated with adolescent drinking before and during pregnancy. *Addictive Behaviors, 32*(12), 2799–2810.

De Leon, G. (1995). Residential therapeutic communities in the mainstream: Diversity and issues. *Journal of Psychoactive Drugs, 27*(1), 3–15.

deBlois, C. S., & Stewart, M. A. (1983). Marital histories of women whose first husbands were alcoholic or antisocial. *British Journal of Addictions, 78,* 205–213.

Deery, H. A., & Love, A. W. (1996). The Driving Expectancy Questionnaire: Development, psychometric assessment and predictive utility among young drink-drivers. *Journal of Studies on Alcohol, 57*(2), 193–202.

DeJong, W., Schneider, S. K., Towvim, L. G., Murphy, M. J., Doerr, E. E., Simonsen, N. R., et al. (2006). A multisite randomized trial of social norms marketing campaigns to reduce college student drinking. *Journal of Studies on Alcohol, 67,* 868–879.

Dennis, M. L., Foss, M. A., & Scott, C. K. (2007). An eight-year perspective on the relationship between the duration of abstinence and other aspects of recovery. *Evaluation Review, 31*(6), 585–612.

Dennis, M. L., Scott, C. K., Funk, R., & Foss, M. A. (2005). The duration and correlates of addiction and treatment careers. *Journal Substance Abuse Treatment, 28*(Suppl. 1), S51–62.

Denzin, N. (1987). *The alcoholic self.* Beverly Hills, CA: Sage.

Department of Health and Human Services. (1997). *National Household Survey on Drug Abuse: Population estimates 1996.* Rockville, MD: Substance Abuse and Mental Health Services Administration, Office of Applied Studies.

Department of Health and Human Services. (2003). *State of the science report on the effects of moderate drinking.* Washington, DC: Author.

Desiderato, L. L., & Crawford, H. J. (1995). Risky sexual behavior in college students: Relationships between number of sexual partners, disclosure of previous risky behavior, and alcohol use. *Journal of Youth and Adolescence, 24*(1), 55–68.

Devane, W. A., Hanus, L., Breuer, A., Pertwee, R. G., Stevenson, L. A., Griffin, G., et al. (1992). Isolation and structure of a brain constituent that binds to the cannabinoid receptor (comments). *Science, 258,* 1946–1949.

DiClemente, C. C. (1993). Alcoholics Anonymous and the structure of change. In B. S. McCrady & W. R. Miller (Eds.), *Research on Alcoholics Anonymous: Opportunities and alternatives* (pp. 79–98). Piscataway, NJ: Rutgers Center of Alcohol Studies.

DiClemente, C. C., Prochaska, J. O., Fairhurst, S. K., Velicer, W. F., Velasquez, M. M., & Rossi, J. (1991). The process of smoking cessation: An analysis of precontemplation, contemplation, and preparation stages of change. *Journal of Consulting and Clinical Psychology, 59,* 295–304.

DiFranza, J. R., & Guerrera, M. P. (1990). Alcoholism and smoking. *Journal of Studies on Alcohol, 51*(2), 130–135.

Dimeff, L. A., & Marlatt, G. A. (1995). Relapse prevention. In R. K. Hester & W. R. Miller (Eds.), *Handbook of alcoholism treatment approaches: Effective alternatives* (2nd ed., pp. 176–194). Needham Heights, MA: Allyn & Bacon.

Domenico, D., & Windle, M. (1993). Intrapersonal and interpersonal functioning among middle-aged female adult children of alcoholics. *Journal of Consulting and Clinical Psychology, 61,* 659–666.

Donovan, C., & McEwan, R. (1995). A review of the literature examining the relationship between alcohol use and HIV-related sexual risk-taking in young people. *Addiction, 90*(3), 319–328.

Donovan, D. M., Anton, R. F., Miller, W. R., Longabaugh, R., Hosking, J. D., & Youngblood, M. (2008). Combined pharmacotherapies and behavioral interventions for alcohol dependence (the COMBINE study): Examination of posttreatment drinking outcomes. *Journal of Studies on Alcohol and Drugs, 69*(1), 5–13.

Donovan, J., Jessor, R., & Jessor, L. (1983). Problem drinking in adolescence and young adulthood: A followup study. *Journal of Studies on Alcohol, 44,* 109–137.

Doran, N., Myers, M. G., Luczak, S. E., Carr, L. G., & Wall, T. L. (2007). Stability of heavy episodic drinking in Chinese- and Korean-American college students: Effects of ALDH2 gene status and behavioral undercontrol. *Journal of Studies on Alcohol and Drugs, 68*(6), 789–797.

Downs, W. R., Capshew, T., & Rindels, B. (2004). Relationships between adult women's alcohol problems and their childhood experiences of parental violence and psychological aggression. *Journal of Studies on Alcohol, 65*(3), 336–344.

Doyle, S. R., Donovan, D. M., & Kivlahan, D. R. (2007). The factor structure of the Alcohol Use Disorders Identification Test (AUDIT). *Journal of Studies on Alcohol and Drugs, 68*(3), 474–479.

Drabble, L., Midanik, L. T., & Trocki, K. (2005). Reports of alcohol consumption and alcohol-related problems among homosexual, bisexual and heterosexual respondents: Results from the 2000 National Alcohol Survey. *Journal of Studies on Alcohol, 66*(1), 111–120.

Driver, H. E., & Swann, P. F. (1987). Alcohol and human cancer (review). *Anticancer Research, 7,* 309–320.

Drobes, D. J., & Thomas, S. E. (1999). Assessing craving for alcohol. *Alcohol Research and Health, 23*(3), 179–186.

Drug Enforcement Administration. (1989). Controlled Substances Act. Washington, DC: U.S. Department of Justice.

Drummond, D. C., & Glautier, S. (1994). A controlled trial of cue exposure treatment in alcohol dependence. *Journal of Consulting and Clinical Psychology, 62*(4), 809–817.

Duka, T., Weissenborn, R., & Dienes, Z. (2001). State-dependent effects of alcohol on recollective experience, familiarity and awareness of memories. *Psychopharmacology (Berl), 153*(3), 295–306.

Duncan, S. C., Strycker, L. A., & Duncan, T. E. (1999). Exploring associations in developmental trends of adolescent substance use and risky sexual behavior in a high-risk population. *Journal of Behavioral Medicine, 22*(1), 21–34.

Dunn, M. G., Tarter, R. E., Mezzich, A. C., Vanyukov, M., Kirisci, L., & Kirillova, G. (2002). Origins and consequences of child neglect in substance abuse families. *Clinical Psychology Review, 22*(7), 1063–1090.

DuRant, R. H., Rome, E. S., Rich, M., Allred, E., Emans, S. J., & Woods, E. R. (1997). Tobacco and alcohol use behaviors portrayed in music videos: A content analysis. *American Journal of Public Health, 87*(7), 1131–1135.

Duster, T. S. (1997). Pattern, purpose, and race in the drug war: The crisis of credibility in criminal justice. In C. Reinarman & H. G. Levine (Eds.), *Crack in America: Demon drugs and social justice* (pp. 260–287). Berkeley: University of California Press.

Earleywine, M., & Newcomb, M. D. (1997). Concurrent versus simultaneous polydrug use: Prevalence, correlates, discriminant validity, and prospective effects on health outcomes. *Experimental and Clinical Psychopharmacology, 5*(4), 353–364.

Edenberg, H. J. (2002). The Collaborative Study on the Genetics of Alcoholism: An update. *Alcohol Research and Health, 26*(3), 214–217.

Edenberg, H. J., Dick, D. M., Xuei, X., Tian, H., Almasy, L., Bauer, L. O., et al. (2004). Variations in GABRA2, encoding the alpha 2 subunit of the GABA(A) receptor, are associated with alcohol dependence and with brain oscillations. *American Journal of Human Genetics, 74,* 705–714.

Edwards, E. P., Eiden, R. D., & Leonard, K. E. (2006). Behavior problems in 18- to 36-month-old children of alcoholic fathers: Secure mother-infant attachment as a protective factor. *Developmental Psychopathology, 18,* 395–407.

Edwards, G., & Gross, M. M. (1976). Alcohol dependence: Provisional descriptions of a clinical syndrome. *British Medical Journal, 1,* 1058–1061.

The effects of alcohol on physiological processes and biological development. (2004/2005). *Alcohol Research and Health, 28*(3), 125–129.

Eiden, R. D., Edwards, E. P., & Leonard, K. E. (2007). A conceptual model for the development of externalizing behavior problems among kindergarten children of alcoholic families: Role of parenting and children's self-regulation. *Developmental Psychology, 43*(5), 1187–1201.

Ekerdt, D. J., Labry, L. O., Glynn, R. J., & Davis, R. W. (1989). Change in drinking behaviors with retirement: Findings from the Normative Aging Study. *Journal of Studies on Alcohol, 50,* 347–353.

Elkins, R. L. (1991). An appraisal of chemical aversion (emetic therapy) approaches to alcoholism treatment. *Behaviour Research and Therapy, 29,* 387–418.

Ellis, A., McInerney, J. F., DiGuiseppe, R., & Yeager, R. J. (1988). *Rational-emotive therapy with alcoholics and substance abusers.* New York: Permagon.

Ellis, D. A., Zucker, R. A., & Fitzgerald, H. E. (1997). The role of family influences in development and risk. *Alcohol Health & Research World, 21*(3), 218–226.

Ellis, R. J., & Oscar-Berman, M. (1989). Alcoholism, aging, and functional cerebral asymmetries. *Psychological Bulletin, 106,* 128–147.

Emanuele, M. A., & Emanuele, N. V. (1998). Alcohol's effects on male reproduction. *Alcohol Health Research World, 22*(3), 195–201.

Emanuele, N., & Emanuele, M. A. (1997). The endocrine system: Alcohol alters critical hormonal balance. *Alcohol Health Research World, 21*(1), 53–64.

Emberson, J. R., Shaper, A. G., Wannamethee, S. G., Morris, R. W., & Whincup, P. H. (2005). Alcohol intake in middle age and risk of cardiovascular disease and mortality: Accounting for intake variation over time. *American Journal of Epidemiology, 161*(9), 856–863.

Emrick, C. (1987). Alcoholics Anonymous: Affiliation processes and effectiveness as treatment. *Alcoholism: Clinical and Experimental Research, 11,* 416–423.

Emrick, C. D. (1989). Alcoholics Anonymous: Membership characteristics and effectiveness of treatment. In M. Galanter (Ed.), *Recent developments in alcoholism: Emerging issues in treatment* (Vol. 7, pp. 37–53). New York: Plenum.

Engs, R. C. (1990). Family background of alcohol abuse and its relationship to alcohol consumption among college students: An unexpected finding. *Journal of Studies on Alcohol, 51*(6), 542–547.

Ennett, S. T., Tobler, N. S., Ringwalt, C. L., & Flewelling, R. L. (1994). How effective is drug abuse resistance education? A meta-analysis of Project DARE outcome evaluations. *American Journal of Public Health, 84,* 1394–1401.

Enoch, M., White, K. V., Harris, C. R., Rohrbaugh, J. W., & Goldman, D. (2001). Alcohol use disorders and anxiety disorders: Relation to the P300 ERP. *Alcoholism: Clinical and Experimental Research, 25,* 1293–1300.

Epstein, E. E., Fischer-Elber, K., & Al-Otaiba, Z. (2007). Women, aging, and alcohol use disorders. *Journal of Women Aging, 19*(1–2), 31–48.

Erblich, J., & Earleywine, M. (2003). Behavioral undercontrol and subjective stimulant and sedative effects of alcohol intoxication: Independent predictors of drinking habits? *Alcoholism: Clinical and Experimental Research, 27*(1), 44–50.

Erickson, P. G., Aldaf, E. M., Murray, G. F., & Smart, R. G. (1987). *The steel drug: Cocaine in perspective.* Lexington, MA: Lexington Books.

Etheridge, R. M., Hubbard, R. L., Anderson, J., Craddock, S. G., & Flynn, P. M. (1997). Treatment structure and program services in the Drug Abuse Treatment Outcome Study (DATOS). *Psychology of Addictive Behaviors, 11,* 222–260.

Evans, D. M., & Dunn, N. J. (1995). Alcohol expectancies, coping responses and self-efficacy judgments: A replication and extension of Cooper et al.'s 1988 study in a college sample. *Journal of Studies on Alcohol, 56*(2), 186–193.

Everitt, B. J., Dickinson, A., & Robbins, T. W. (2001). The neuropsychological basis of addictive behaviour. *Brain Research Review, 36,* 129–1381.

Evert, D. L., & Oscar-Berman, M. (1995). Alcohol-related cognitive impairments. *Alcohol Health & Research World, 19,* 89–96.

Falk, D. E., Yi, H. Y., & Hiller-Sturmhofel, S. (2006). An epidemiologic analysis of co-occurring alcohol and tobacco use and disorders: Findings from the National Epidemiologic Survey on Alcohol and Related Conditions. *Alcohol Research and Health, 29*(3), 162–171.

Fals-Stewart, W., Leonard, K. E., & Birchler, G. R. (2005). The occurrence of male-to-female intimate violence on days of men's drinking: The moderating effects of antisocial personality disorder. *Journal of Consulting and Clinical Psychology, 73*(2), 239–258.

Fein, G., & McGillivray, S. (2007). Cognitive performance in long-term abstinent elderly alcoholics. *Alcoholism: Clinical and Experimental Research, 31*(11), 1788–1799.

Fell, J. C., & Voas, R. B. (2006). Mothers Against Drunk Driving (MADD): The first 25 years. *Traffic Injury Prevention, 7*(3), 195–212.

Ferguson, F. N. (1968). Navajo drinking: Some tentative hypotheses. *Human Organizations, 27,* 159–167.

Fillmore, K. M. (1985). The social victims of drinking. *British Journal of Addiction, 80,* 307–314.

Fillmore, K. M. (1986). Issues in the changing drinking patterns among women in the last century. In *National Institute on Alcohol Abuse and Alcoholism, Women and alcohol: Health-related issues* (Research Monograph No. 16, DHHS Pub. No. (ADM)86–1139, pp. 69–77). Washington, DC: U.S. Government Printing Office.

Fillmore, K. M., & Kelso, D. (1987). Coercion into alcoholism treatment: Meanings for the disease concept of alcoholism. *Journal of Drug Issues, 17,* 301–319.

Fillmore, M. T., & Vogel Sprott, M. (1995). Expectancies about alcohol-induced motor impairment predict individual differences in responses to alcohol and placebo. *Journal of Studies on Alcohol, 56*(1), 90–98.

Finer, L. B. (2007). Trends in premarital sex in the United States, 1954–2003. *Public Health Reports, 122*(1), 73–78.

Fingarette, H. (1988). *Heavy drinking: The myth of alcoholism as a disease.* Berkeley: University of California Press.

Finlayson, R. E. (1995). Misuse of prescription drugs [Special issue: Drugs and the elderly: Use and misuse of drugs, medicines, alcohol, and tobacco]. *International Journal of the Addictions, 30*(13–14), 1871–1901.

Finn, P. R., & Pihl, R. O. (1987). Men at high risk for alcoholism: The effect of alcohol on cardiovascular reactivity and sensitivity to alcohol. *Journal of Abnormal Psychology, 96,* 230–236.

Finney, J. W., & Moos, R. H. (1984). Life stressors and problem drinking among older adults. In M. Galanter (Ed.), *Recent developments in alcoholism* (Vol. 2, pp. 267–288). New York: Plenum.

Finney, J. W., & Moos, R. H. (1991). The long-term course of treated alcoholism: I. Mortality, relapse and remission rates and comparisons with community controls. *Journal of Studies on Alcohol, 52,* 44–54.

Finney, J. W., & Moos, R. H. (1992). The long-term course of treated alcoholism: II. Predictors and correlates of 10-year functioning and mortality. *Journal of Studies on Alcohol, 53,* 142–153.

Finnigan, F., Hammersley, R., & Millar, K. (1995). The effects of expectancy and alcohol on cognitive-motor performance. *Addiction, 90*(5), 661–672.

First, M. B. (2002). *Structured Clinical Interview for DSM-IV-TR Axis I disorders, Research Version, Patient Edition, SCID-I/P.* New York: Biometrics Research, New York State Psychiatric Institute.

Fleming, J., Mullen, P. E., Sibthorpe, B., Attewell, R., & Bammer, G. (1998). The relationship between childhood sexual abuse and alcohol abuse in women—a case-control study. *Addiction, 93*(12), 1787–1798.

Fletcher, B. W., Tims, F. M., & Brown, B. S. (1997). The Drug Abuse Treatment Outcome Study (DATOS): Treatment evaluation research in the United States. *Psychology of Addictive Behaviors, 11,* 216–229.

Flynn, B. S., Worden, J. K., Bunn, J. Y., Dorwaldt, A. L., Dana, G. S., & Callas, P. W. (2006). Mass media and community interventions to reduce alcohol use by early adolescents. *Journal of Studies on Alcohol, 67*(1), 66–74.

Flynn, P. M., Craddock, S. G., Hubbard, R. L., Anderson, J., & Etheridge, R. (1997). Methodological overview and research design for the Drug Abuse Treatment Outcome Study (DATOS). *Psychology of Addictive Behaviors, 11,* 230–243.

Foran, H. M., & O'Leary, K. D. (2008). Alcohol and intimate partner violence: A meta-analytic review. *Clinical Psychology Review, 28*(7), 1222–1234.

Foroud, T., Edenberg, H. J., Goate, A., Rice, J., Flury, L., Koller, D. L., et al. (2000). Alcoholism susceptibility loci: Confirmation studies in a replicate sample and further mapping. *Alcoholism: Clinical and Experimental Research, 24,* 933–945.

Foy, D. W., Nunn, L. B., & Rychtarik, R. G. (1984). Broad-spectrum behavioral treatment for chronic alcoholics: Effect of training controlled drinking skills. *Journal of Consulting and Clinical Psychology, 52,* 218–230.

Freud, S. (1989). Three essays on the theory of sexuality. In P. Gay (Ed.), *Freud reader* (pp. 239–293). New York: Norton. (Original work published 1905)

Frezza, M., DiPadova, C., Pozzato, G., Terpin, M., Baraona, E., & Lieber, C. S. (1990). High blood alcohol levels in women: The role of decreased gastric alcohol dehydrogenase. *New England Journal of Medicine, 322*(2), 95–99.

Friedman, R. S., McCarthy, D. M., Bartholow, B. D., & Hicks, J. A. (2007). Interactive effects of alcohol outcome expectancies and alcohol cues on nonconsumptive behavior. *Experimental and Clinical Psychopharmacology, 15*(1), 102–114.

Friend, K. B., & Pagano, M. E. (2005). Changes in cigarette consumption and drinking outcomes: Findings from Project MATCH. *Journal of Substance Abuse Treatment, 29*(3), 221–229.

Fuller, B. E., Chermack, S. T., Cruise, K. A., Kirsch, E., Fitzgerald, H. E., & Zucker, R. A. (2003). Predictors of aggression across three generations among sons of alcoholics: Relationships involving grandparental and parental alcoholism, child aggression, marital aggression and parenting practices. *Journal of Studies on Alcohol, 64*(4), 472–483.

Gabrieli, W. F., Jr., Nagoshi, C. T., Rhea, S. A., & Wilson, J. R. (1991). Anticipated and subjective sensitivities to alcohol. *Journal of Studies on Alcohol, 52,* 205–214.

Gaines, A. D. (1985). Cultural conceptions and social behavior among urban Blacks. In L. A. Bennett & G. M. Ames (Eds.), *The American experience with alcohol: Contrasting cultural perspectives* (pp. 171–197). New York: Plenum Press.

Galvan, F. H., & Caetano, R. (2003). Alcohol use and related problems among ethnic minorities in the United States. *Alcohol Research and Health, 27*(1), 87–94.

Garland, M. A., Parsons, O. A., & Nixon, S. J. (1993). Visual-spatial learning in nonalcoholic young adults with and those without a family history of alcoholism. *Journal of Studies on Alcohol, 54*(2), 219–224.

Gebhard, P. H., Gagnon, J. H., Pomeroy, W. B., & Christianson, C. V. (1965). *Sex offenders.* New York: Harper and Row.

Gelernter, J., Liu, X., Hesselbrock, V., Page, G. P., Goddard, A., & Zhang, H. (2004). Results of a genomewide linkage scan: Support for chromosomes 9 and 11 loci increasing risk for cigarette smoking. *American Journal of Medical Genetics Part B: Neuropsychiatric Genetics, 128,* 94–101.

Genetics, pharmacokinetics, and neurobiology of adolescent alcohol use. (2004/2005). *Alcohol Research and Health, 28*(3), 133–142.

George, W. H., & Marlatt, G. A. (1986). The effects of alcohol and anger on interest in violence, erotica, and deviance. *Journal of Abnormal Psychology, 95,* 150–158.

George, W. H., & Norris, J. (1991). Alcohol, disinhibition, sexual arousal, and deviant sexual behavior [Special issue: Alcohol and sexuality]. *Alcohol Health and Research World, 15*(2), 133–138.

George, W. H., & Stoner, S. A. (2000). Understanding acute alcohol effects on sexual behavior. *Annual Review of Sex Research, 11,* 92–124.

Gfroerer, J., & Brodsky, M. (1992). The incidence of illicit drug use in the United States, 1962–1989. *British Journal of Addiction, 87*(9), 1345–1351.

Giancola, P. R. (2006). Influence of subjective intoxication, breath alcohol concentration, and expectancies on the alcohol-aggression relation. *Alcoholism: Clinical and Experimental Research, 30*(5), 844–850.

Giancola, P. R., & Corman, M. D. (2007). Alcohol and aggression: A test of the attention-allocation model. *Psychological Science, 18*(7), 649–655.

Giancola, P. R., & Zeichner, A. (1995). Alcohol-related aggression in males and females: Effects of blood alcohol concentration, subjective intoxication, personality, and provocation. *Alcoholism Clinical and Experimental Research, 19*(1), 130–134.

Giancola, P. R., & Zeichner, A. (1997). The biphasic effects of alcohol on human physical aggression. *Journal of Abnormal Psychology, 106,* 598–607.

Gilbert, D. G., McClernon, F. J., Rabinovich, N. E., Plath, L. C., Jensen, R. A., & Meliska, C. J. (1998). Effects of smoking abstinence on mood and craving in men: Influences of negative-affect-related personality traits, habitual nicotine intake and repeated measurements. *Personality and Individual Differences, 25*(3), 399–423.

Gilbert, M. J., & Cervantes, R. C. (1987). *Mexican Americans and alcohol.* Los Angeles: University of California.

Gill, J. (1997). Women, alcohol and the menstrual cycle. *Alcohol and Alcoholism, 32*(4), 435–441.

Ginsburg, H. M. (1978). Defensive research: The Treatment Outcome Prospective Study (TOPS). *Annals of the New York Academy of Sciences, 311,* 265–269.

Glantz, M. D. (1992). A developmental psychopathology model of drug abuse vulnerability. In M. D. Glantz & R. Pickens (Eds.), *Vulnerability to drug abuse* (pp. 389–418). Washington, DC: American Psychological Association.

Glaser, F., & Ogborne, A. C. (1982). Does A.A. really work? *British Journal of Addictions, 77,* 123–129.

Glass, T. A., Prigerson, H., Kasl, S. V., & Mendes-de-Leon, C. F. (1995). The effects of negative life events on alcohol consumption among older men and women. *Journals of Gerontology Series B: Psychological Sciences and Social Sciences, 50B*(4), S205–S216.

Glynn, S., Albanes, D., Pietinen, P., Brown, C. C., Rautalahti, M., Tangrea, J. A., et al. (1996). Alcohol consumption and risk of colorectal cancer in a cohort of Finnish men. *Cancer Causes and Control, 7,* 214–223.

Go, V. L., Gukovskaya, A., & Pandol, S. J. (2005). Alcohol and pancreatic cancer. *Alcohol, 35*(3), 205–211.

Goldman, M. S., Brown, S. A., & Christiansen, B. A. (1987). Expectancy theory: Thinking about drinking. In H. T. Blane & K. E. Leonard (Eds.), *Psychological theories of drinking and alcoholism* (pp. 181–226). New York: Guilford.

Goldstein, A. L., Barnett, N. P., Pedlow, C. T., & Murphy, J. G. (2007). Drinking in conjunction with sexual experiences among at-risk college student drinkers. *Journal of Studies on Alcohol and Drugs, 68*(5), 697–705.

Gomberg, E. (1994). Risk factors for drinking over a woman's life span. *Alcohol Health & Research World, 18,* 220–227.

Gomberg, E. L. (1993). Women and alcohol: Use and abuse. *Journal of Nervous and Mental Disease, 181*(4), 211–219.

Gomberg, E. S. L. (1984). *Femininity issues in women's alcohol use.* Presented at American Psychological Association Convention, Toronto, Ontario.

Gomberg, E. S. L. (1990). Drugs, alcohol, and aging. In L. Kozlowski, H. M. Annis, H. D. Cappell, F. B. Glaser, M. S. Goodstadt, Y. Isreal, H. Kalant, E. M. Sellers, & E. R. Vingilis (Eds.), *Recent advances in alcohol and drug problems* (Vol. 10, pp. 171–213). New York: Plenum.

Gomberg, E. S. L. (1995a). Health care provision for men and women. In M. V. Seeman (Ed.), *Gender and psychopathology* (pp. 359–376). Washington, DC: American Psychiatric Press.

Gomberg, E. S. L. (1995b). Older women and alcohol: Use and abuse. In M. Galanter (Ed.), *Recent developments in alcoholism: Women and alcohol* (Vol. 12, pp. 61–79). New York: Plenum.

Goodlett, C. R., & Horn, K. H. (2001). Mechanisms of alcohol-induced damage to the developing nervous system. *Alcohol Research and Health, 25*(3), 175–184.

Goodman, M. T., & Tung, K. H. (2003). Alcohol consumption and the risk of borderline and invasive ovarian cancer. *Obstetrics and Gynecology, 101*(6), 1221–1228.

Goodwin, D. W., Schulsinger, F., Hermansen, L., Guze, S. B., & Winokur, G. (1973). Alcohol problems in adoptees raised apart from biological parents. *Archives of General Psychiatry, 28,* 238–243.

Goodwin, D. W., Schulsinger, F., Moller, N., Hermansen, L., Winokur, G., & Guze, S. B. (1974). Drinking problems in adopted and nonadopted sons of alcoholics. *Archives of General Psychiatry, 31,* 164–169.

Goodwin, D. W., Schulsinger, F., Moller, N., Mednick, S., & Guze, S. B. (1977). Psychopathology in adopted and nonadopted daughters of alcoholics. *Archives of General Psychiatry, 34,* 1005–1009.

Gordon, J. R., & Barrett, K. (1993). The codependency movement: Issues of context and differentiation. In J. S. Baer, G. A. Marlatt, & R. J. McMahon (Eds.), *Addictive behaviors across the life span.* Newbury Park, CA: Sage.

Gordon, S. M., Sterling, R., Siatkowski, C., Raively, K., Weinstein, S., & Hill, P. C. (2006). Inpatient desire to drink as a predictor of relapse to alcohol use following treatment. *American Journal of Addictions, 15*(3), 242–245.

Gorman, J. M., & Rooney, J. F. (1979). The influence of Al-Anon on the coping behavior of wives of alcoholics. *Journal of Studies on Alcohol, 40,* 1030–1038.

Graham, K., Carver, V., & Brett, P. J. (1995). Alcohol and drug use by older women: Results of a national survey. *Canadian Journal of Aging, 14,* 769–791.

Graham, K., Wilsnack, R., Dawson, D., & Vogeltanz, N. (1998). Should alcohol consumption measures be adjusted for gender differences? *Addiction, 93*(8), 1137–1147.

Granfield, R., & Cloud, W. (1996). The elephant that no one sees: Natural recovery among middle-class addicts. *Journal of Drug Issues, 26,* 45–61.

Grant, B. F. (1996). Prevalence and correlates of drug use and DSM-IV drug dependence in the United States: Results of the National Longitudinal Alcohol Epidemiologic Survey. *Journal of Substance Abuse, 8,* 195–210.

Grant, B. F. (1997a). Barriers to alcoholism treatment: Reasons for not seeking treatment in a general population sample. *Journal of Studies on Alcohol, 58*(4), 365–371.

Grant, B. F. (1997b). Prevalence and correlates of alcohol use and *DSM-IV* alcohol dependence in the United States: Results of the National Longitudinal Alcohol Epidemiologic Survey. *Journal of Studies on Alcohol, 58*(5), 464–473.

Grant, B. F., Dawson, D. A., Stinson, F. S., Chou, S. P., Dufour, M. C., & Pickering, R. P. (2004). The 12-month prevalence and trends in DSM-IV alcohol abuse and dependence United States, 1991–1992 and 2001–2002. *Drug and Alcohol Dependence, 74*(3), 223–234.

Grant, B. F., Dawson, D. A., Stinson, F. S., Chou, P. S., Kay, W., & Pickering, R. (2003). The Alcohol Use Disorder and Associated Disabilities Interview Schedule-IV (AUDADIS-IV): Reliability of alcohol consumption, tobacco use, family history of depression and psychiatric diagnostic modules in a general population sample. *Drug and Alcohol Dependence, 71*(1), 7–16.

Grant, B. F., Harford, T. C., Chou, P., Pickering, R., Dawson, D. A., Stinson, F. S., et al. (1991). Prevalence of DSM-III-R alcohol abuse and dependence: United States, 1988. [Special Focus: Alcohol and Youth]. *Alcohol Health & Research World, 15,* (1), 91–96.

Grant, B. F., Harford, T. C., Dawson, D. A., Chou, P., DuFour, M., & Pickering, R. P. (1994). Prevalence of DSM-IV alcohol abuse and dependence: United States, 1992 [Special focus: Women and alcohol]. *Alcohol Health & Research World, 18*(3), 243–248.

Grant, B. F., Harford, T. C., Dawson, D. A., Chou, P. S., & Pickering, R. P. (1995). The Alcohol Use Disorder and Associated Disabilities Interview Schedule (AUDADIS): Reliability of alcohol and drug modules in a general population sample. *Drug and Alcohol Dependence, 39*(1), 37–44.

Grant, B. F., Harford, T. C., Hasin, D. S., Chou, P. S., & Pickering, R. (1992). *DSM-III-R* and the proposed *DSM-IV* alcohol use disorders, United States 1988: A nosological comparison. *Alcoholism: Clinical and Experimental Research, 16*(2), 215–221.

Grant, B. F., & Pickering, R. P. (1996). Comorbidity between DSM-IV alcohol and drug use disorders. *Alcohol Health & Research World, 20*(NIAAA Epidemiologic Bulletin No. 36), 67–72.

Grattan-Miscio, K. E., & Vogel-Sprott, M. (2005). Effects of alcohol and performance incentives on immediate working memory. *Psychopharmacology (Berl), 181*(1), 188–196.

Graves, K. L., & Leigh, B. C. (1995). The relationship of substance use to sexual activity among young adults in the United States. *Family Planning Perspectives, 27*(1), 18–22, 33.

Greeley, A., McCready, W. C., & Theisen, G. (1980). *Ethnic drinking subcultures.* New York: Praeger.

Green, C. A., & Polen, M. R. (2001). The health and health behaviors of people who do not drink alcohol. *American Journal of Preventive Medicine, 21,* 298–305.

Greenfield, T. K. (2000). Ways of measuring drinking patterns and the difference they make: Experience with graduated frequencies. *Journal of Substance Abuse, 12,* 33–50.

Greenfield, T. K., & Kerr, W. C. (2003). Tracking alcohol consumption over time. *Alcohol Research and Health, 27*(1), 30–38.

Greenfield, T. K., Midanik, L. T., & Rogers, J. D. (2000). A 10-year national trend study of alcohol consumption, 1984–1995: Is the period of declining drinking over? *American Journal of Public Health, 90,* 47–52.

Greenson, R. R. (1967). *The technique and practice of psychoanalysis.* New York: International Universities Press.

Grucza, R. A., & Bierut, L. J. (2006). Co-occurring risk factors for alcohol dependence and habitual smoking: Update on findings from the Collaborative Study on the Genetics of Alcoholism. *Alcohol Research and Health, 29*(3), 172–178.

Gruenewald, P. J., & Johnson, F. W. (2006). The stability and reliability of self-reported drinking measures. *Journal of Studies on Alcohol, 67,* 738–745.

Gruenewald, P. J., Ponicki, W. R., Holder, H. D., & Romelsjo, A. (2006). Alcohol prices, beverage quality, and the demand for alcohol: Quality substitutions and price elasticities. *Alcoholism: Clinical and Experimental Research, 30*(1), 96–105.

Gruenewald, P. J., Ponicki, W. R., & Mitchell, P. R. (1995). Suicide rates and alcohol consumption in the United States, 1970–89. *Addiction, 90*(8), 1063–1075.

Gruenewald, P. J., & Remer, L. (2006). Changes in outlet densities affect violence rates. *Alcoholism: Clinical and Experimental Research, 30*(7), 1184–1193.

Grunberg, N. E., Winders, S. E., & Wewers, M. E. (1991). Gender differences in tobacco use. *Health Psychology, 10*(2), 143–153.

Gurpegui, M., Jurado, D., Luna, J. D., Fernandez-Molina, C., Moreno-Abril, O., & Galvez, R. (2007). Personality traits associated with caffeine intake and smoking. *Progress in Neuropsychopharmacological Biological Psychiatry, 31*(5), 997–1005.

Gusfield, J. R. (1963). *Symbolic crusade: Status politics and the American temperance movement.* Urbana: University of Illinois Press.

Gutjah, E., Gmel, G., & Rehm, J. (2001). Relation between average alcohol consumption and disease: An overview. *European Addiction Research, 7,* 117–127.

Gwaltney, C. J., Shiffman, S., Balabanis, M. H., & Paty, J. A. (2005). Dynamic self-efficacy and outcome expectancies: Prediction of smoking lapse and relapse. *Journal of Abnormal Psychology, 114*(4), 661–675.

Haggard-Grann, U., Hallqvist, J., Langstrom, N., & Moller, J. (2006). The role of alcohol and drugs in triggering criminal violence: A case-crossover study. *Addiction, 101*(1), 100–108.

Hahm, H. C., Lahiff, M., & Guterman, N. B. (2003a). Acculturation and parental attachment in Asian-American adolescents' alcohol use. *Journal of Adolescent Health, 33*(2), 119–129.

Hahm, H. C., Lahiff, M., & Guterman, N. B. (2003b). Asian American adolescents' acculturation, binge drinking, and alcohol- and tobacco-using peers. *Journal of Community Psychology, 32*(3), 295–308.

Hajek, P. (1994). Treatments for smokers [Special issue: Comparing drugs of dependence]. *Addiction, 89*(11), 1543–1549.

Hajek, P. (1996). Current issues in behavioral and pharmacological approaches to smoking cessation. *Addictive Behaviors, 21*(6), 699–707.

Ham, H. P., & Parsons, O. A. (1997). Organization of psychological functions in alcoholics and non-alcoholics: A test of the compensatory hypothesis. *Journal of Studies on Alcohol, 58,* 67–74.

Haney, C., & Zimbardo, P. (1998). The past and future of U.S. prison policy: Twenty-five years after the Stanford Prison Experiment. *American Psychologist, 53*(7), 709–727.

Hanna, E. Z., Faden, V. B., & Harford, T. C. (1993). Marriage: Does it protect young women from alcoholism? *Journal of Substance Abuse, 5,* 1–14.

Hansen, W. B. (1993). School-based alcohol prevention programs. *Alcohol Health and Research World, 17*(1), 54–60.

Hansen, W. B., Graham, J. W., Wolkenstein, B. H., & Rohrbach, L. A. (1991). Program integrity as a moderator of prevention program effectiveness: Results for fifth-grade students in the Adolescent Alcohol Prevention Trial. *Journal of Studies on Alcohol, 52,* 568–579.

Harburg, E., DiFranceisco, W., Webster, D., Gleiberman, L., & Schork, A. (1990). Familial transmission of alcohol use: II. Imitation of and aversion to parent drinking (1960) by adult offspring (1977)—Tecumseh, Michigan. *Journal of Studies on Alcohol, 51,* 245–256.

Harford, T. C. (1993). Stability and prevalence of drinking among young adults. *Addiction, 88*(2), 273–277.

Harford, T. C., Hanna, E. Z., & Faden, V. B. (1994). The long- and short-term effects of marriage on drinking. *Journal of Substance Abuse, 6,* 209–217.

Harford, T. C., Yi, H. Y., & Hilton, M. E. (2006). Alcohol abuse and dependence in college and non-college samples: A ten-year prospective follow-up in a national survey. *Journal of Studies on Alcohol, 67*(6), 803–809.

Harris, R. A., & Buck, K. J. (1990). The processes of alcohol tolerance and dependence. *Alcohol Health & Research World, 14,* 105–110.

Hart, C. L., Ray, O., & Ksir, C. (2006). *Drugs, society, and human behavior* (12th ed.). New York: McGraw-Hill.

Hasin, D. (2003). Classification of alcohol use disorders. *Alcohol Research and Health, 27*(1), 5–17.

Hasin, D., Grant, B., Harford, T., Hilton, M. E., & Endicott, J. (1990). Multiple alcohol-related problems in the United States: On the rise? *Journal of Studies on Alcohol, 51*(6), 485–493.

Hasin, D., Schuckit, M. A., Martin, C. S., Grant, B. F., Bucholz, K. K., & Helzer, J. E. (2003). The validity of DSM-IV alcohol dependence: What do we know, what do we need to know? *Alcoholism: Clinical and Experimental Research, 27,* 244–252.

Hasin, D. S., Goodwin, R. D., Stinson, F. S., & Grant, B. F. (2005). Epidemiology of major depressive disorder: Results from the National Epidemiologic Survey on Alcoholism and Related Conditions. *Archives of General Psychiatry, 62*(10), 1097–1106.

Hasin, D. S., & Grant, B. F. (2004). The co-occurrence of DSM-IV alcohol abuse in DSM-IV alcohol dependence: Results of the National Epidemiologic Survey on Alcohol and Related Conditions on heterogeneity that differ by population subgroup. *Archives of General Psychiatry, 61*(9), 891–896.

Haskell, C. F., Kennedy, D. O., Wesnes, K. A., & Scholey, A. B. (2005/2006). Cognitive and mood improvements of caffeine in habitual consumers and habitual non-consumers of caffeine. *Psychopharmacology, 179*(4), 813–825.

Hatzenbuehler, M. L., Corbin, W. R., & Fromme, K. (2008). Trajectories and determinants of alcohol use among LGB young adults and their heterosexual peers: Results from a prospective study. *Developmental Psychology, 44*(1), 81–90.

Hawkins, J. D., Graham, J. W., Maguin, E., Abbott, R., Hill, K. G., & Catalano, R. F. (1997). Exploring the effects of age of alcohol use initiation and psychosocial risk factors on subsequent alcohol misuse. *Journal of Studies on Alcohol, 58*(3), 280–290.

Hawkins, J. D., & Weis, J. G. (1985). The social development model: An integrated approach to delinquency prevention. *Journal of Primary Prevention, 6,* 73–97.

Haxby, D. G. (1995). Treatment of nicotine dependence. *American Journal of Health System Pharmacology, 52*(3), 265–281.

Heath, A. C., Bucholz, K. K., Madden, P. A., Dinwiddie, S. H., Slutske, W. S., Bierut, L. J., et al. (1997). Genetic and environmental contributions to alcohol dependence risk in a national twin sample: Consistency of findings in women and men. *Psychological Medicine, 27*(6), 1381–1396.

Heath, A. C., Jardine, R., & Martin, N. G. (1989). Interactive effects of genotype and social environment on alcohol consumption in female twins. *Journal of Studies on Alcohol, 50,* 38–48.

Heath, D. B. (1988). American Indians and alcohol: Epidemiological and sociocultural relevance. In National Institute on Alcohol Abuse and Alcoholism (Ed.), *Alcohol use among U.S. ethnic minorities* (Vol. Research Monograph No. 18. DHHS Pub. No. (ADM)87–1435). Washington, DC: U.S. Government Printing Office.

Heinz, A., Beck, A., Grusser, S. M., Grace, A. A., & Wrase, J. (2008). Identifying the neural circuitry of alcohol craving and relapse vulnerability. *Addiction Biology, 14*(1), 108–118.

Heishman, S. J., Arasteh, K., & Stitzer, M. L. (1997). Comparative effects of alcohol and marijuana on mood, memory, and performance. *Pharmacology, Biochemistry, and Behavior, 58,* 93–101.

Helzer, J. E., & Pryzbeck, T. R. (1988). The co-occurrence of alcoholism with other psychiatric disorders in the general population and its impact on treatment. *Journal of Studies on Alcohol, 49,* 219–224.

Hendershot, C. S., Dillworth, T. M., Neighbors, C., & George, W. H. (2008). Differential effects of acculturation on drinking behavior in Chinese- and Korean-American college students. *Journal of Studies on Alcohol and Drugs, 69*(1), 121–128.

Herd, D. (1985). Ambiguity in Black drinking norms. In L. A. Bennett & G. M. Ames (Eds.), *The American experience with alcohol: Contrasting cultural perspectives* (pp. 149–170). New York: Plenum.

Herd, D. (1987). Rethinking Black drinking. *British Journal of Addiction, 82,* 219–223.

Herd, D. (1989). The epidemiology of drinking patterns and alcohol-related problems among U.S. Blacks. In National Institute on Alcohol Abuse and Alcoholism (Ed.), *Alcohol use among U.S. ethnic minorities* (Research Monograph No. 18., DHHS Pub. No. (ADM)89-1435, pp. 3–50). Washington, DC: U.S. Government Printing Office.

Herd, D. (1997). Sex ratios of drinking patterns and problems among Blacks and Whites: Results from a national survey. *Journal of Studies on Alcohol, 58*(1), 75–82.

Herd, D., & Grube, J. (1993). Drinking contexts and drinking problems among Black and White women. *Addiction, 88*(8), 1101–1110.

Herd, D., & Grube, J. (1996). Black identity and drinking in the US: A national study. *Addiction, 91*, 845–857.

Herd, D. A. (1994). The effects of parental influences and respondents' norms and attitudes on Black and White adult drinking patterns. *Journal of Substance Abuse, 6*(2), 137–154.

Hesselbrock, V. M., & Hesselbrock, M. N. (2006). Are there empirically supported and clinically useful subtypes of alcohol dependence? *Addiction, 101*(Suppl. 1), 97–103.

Hesselbrock, V. M., Hesselbrock, M. N., & Stabenau, J. R. (1985). Alcoholism in men patients subtyped by family history and antisocial personality. *Journal of Studies on Alcohol, 46*, 59–64.

Hewlett, P., & Smith, A. (2007). Effects of repeated doses of caffeine on performance and alertness: New data and secondary analyses. *Human Psychopharmacology, 22*(6), 339–350.

Hill, S. Y. (1995). Neurobiological and clinical markers for a severe form of alcoholism in women. *Alcohol Health and Research World, 19*(3), 249–256.

Hill, S. Y., Locke, J., & Steinhauer, S. R. (1999). Absence of visual and auditory P300 reduction in non-depressed male and female alcoholics. *Biological Psychiatry, 46*(7), 982–989.

Hilton, M. E. (1986). Abstention in the general population of the U.S.A. *British Journal of Addiction, 81*, 95–112.

Hilton, M. E. (1988). Trends in U.S. drinking patterns: Further evidence from the past 20 years. *British Journal of Addiction, 83*, 269–278.

Hingson, R. W., Heeren, T., & Edwards, E. M. (2008). Age at drinking onset, alcohol dependence, and their relation to drug use and dependence, driving under the influence of drugs, and motor-vehicle crash involvement because of drugs. *Journal of Studies on Alcohol and Drugs, 69*(2), 192–201.

Hinshaw, S. P. (1987). On the distinction between attention deficits/hyperactivity and conduct problems/aggression in child psychopathology. *Psychological Bulletin, 101*, 443–463.

Hodgins, D. C., & Shimp, L. (1995). Identifying adult children of alcoholics: Methodological review and a comparison of the CAST-6 with other methods. *Addiction, 90*(2), 255–267.

Hoffmann, D., & Hoffmann, I. (1997). The changing cigarette, 1950–1995. *Journal of Toxicology and Environmental Health, 50*(4), 307–364.

Holdcraft, L. C., & Iacono, W. G. (2002). Cohort effects on gender differences in alcohol dependence. *Addiction, 97*(8), 1025–1036.

Holder, H. D. (2000). Community prevention of alcohol problems. *Addictive Behaviors, 25*(6), 843–859.

Holdstock, L., King, A. C., & de Wit, H. (2000). Subjective and objective responses to ethanol in moderate/heavy and light social drinkers. *Alcoholism: Clinical and Experimental Research, 24*(6), 789–794.

Holloway, A. S., Watson, H. E., Arthur, A. J., Starr, G., McFadyen, A. K., & McIntosh, J. (2007). The effect of brief interventions on alcohol consumption among heavy drinkers in a general hospital setting. *Addiction, 102*(11), 1762–1770.

Holmila, M., & Raitasalo, K. (2005). Gender differences in drinking: Why do they still exist? *Addiction, 100*(1), 1763–1769.

Homish, G. G., & Leonard, K. E. (2005). Marital quality and congruent drinking. *Journal of Studies on Alcohol, 66*(4), 488–496.

Homish, G. G., & Leonard, K. E. (2007). The drinking partnership and marital satisfaction: The longitudinal influence of discrepant drinking. *Journal of Consulting and Clinical Psychology, 75*, 43–51.

Horwitz, A. V., White, H. R., & Howell-White, S. (1996). Becoming married and mental health: A longitudinal study of a cohort of young adults. *Journal of Marriage and Family, 58*, 895–907.

Hotaling, G. T., & Sugarman, D. B. (1986). An analysis of risk markers in husband to wife violence: The current state of knowledge. *Violence and Victimology, 1*, 101–124.

Hoyer, W. J., Semenec, S. C., & Buchler, N. E. (2007). Acute alcohol intoxication impairs controlled search across the visual field. *Journal of Studies on Alcohol and Drugs, 68*(5), 748–758.

Hser, Y. I., Anglin, M. D., & Booth, M. W. (1987). Sex differences in addict careers: 3. Addiction. *American Journal of Drug and Alcohol Abuse, 13,* 231–251.

Hubbard, R. L., Craddock, S. G., Flynn, P. M., Anderson, J., & Etheridge, R. M. (1997). Overview of 1-year followup in the Drug Abuse Treatment Outcome Study (DATOS). *Psychology of Addictive Behaviors, 11,* 261–278.

Hubbard, R. L., Marsden, M. E., Rachal, J. V., Harwood, H. J., Cavanaugh, E. R., & Ginzburg, H. M. (1989). *Drug abuse treatment: A national study of effectiveness.* Chapel Hill: University of North Carolina Press.

Hughes, J. R. (1992). Tobacco withdrawal in self-quitters. *Journal of Consulting and Clinical Psychology, 60*(5), 689–697.

Hughes, J. R. (1993). Treatment of smoking cessation in smokers with past alcohol/drug problems [Special issue: Towards a broader view of recovery: Integrating nicotine addiction and chemical dependency treatments]. *Journal of Substance Abuse Treatment, 10*(2), 181–187.

Hughes, T. L. (2003). Lesbians' drinking patterns: Beyond the data. *Substance Use and Misuse, 38*(11–13), 1739–1758.

Hughes, T. L., Wilsnack, S. C., Szalacha, L. A., Johnson, T., Bostwick, W. B., Seymour, R., et al. (2006). Age and racial/ethnic differences in drinking and drinking-related problems in a community sample of lesbians. *Journal of Studies on Alcohol, 67*(4), 579–590.

Hull, C. L. (1943). *Principles of behavior.* New York: Appleton-Century.

Hull, J. G., & Bond, C. F. (1986). Social and behavioral consequences of alcohol consumption and expectancy: A meta-analysis. *Psychological Bulletin, 99,* 347–360.

Humphreys, K. (2003). Alcoholics Anonymous and 12-step alcoholism treatment programs. In M. Galanter (Ed.), *Recent developments in alcoholism* (Vol. 16, pp. 149–164). New York: Plenum.

Hurlburt, G., Gade, G., & Fuqua, D. (1984). Personality differences between Alcoholics Anonymous members and nonmembers. *Journal of Studies on Alcohol, 45,* 170–171.

Hurt, R. D., & Patten, C. A. (2003). Treatment of tobacco dependence in alcoholics. In M. Galanter (Ed.), *Recent developments in alcoholism* (Vol. 16, pp. 335–359). New York: Plenum.

Husky, M. M., Mazure, C. M., Paliwal, P., & McKee, S. A. (2008). Gender differences in the comorbidity of smoking behavior and major depression. *Drug and Alcohol Dependence, 93*(1–2), 176–179.

Hussong, A., Bauer, D., & Chassin, L. (2008). Telescoped trajectories from alcohol initiation to disorder in children of alcoholic parents. *Journal of Abnormal Psychology, 117*(1), 63–78.

Hussong, A. M., & Chassin, L. (1997). Substance use initiation among adolescent children of alcoholics: Testing protective factors. *Journal of Studies on Alcohol, 58*(3), 272–279.

Hussong, A. M., Galloway, C. A., & Feagans, L. A. (2005). Coping motives as a moderator of daily mood-drinking covariation. *Journal of Studies on Alcohol, 66*(3), 344–353.

Hussong, A. M., Zucker, R. A., Wong, M. M., Fitzgerald, H. E., & Puttler, L. I. (2005). Social competence in children of alcoholic parents over time. *Developmental Psychology, 41,* 747–759.

Husten, C. G., McCarty, M. C., Giovino, G. A., Chrisman, J. H., & Zhu, B. P. (1998). Intermittent smokers: A descriptive analysis of persons who have never smoked daily. *American Journal of Public Health, 88*(1), 86–89.

Indian Health Service. (1982). *Analysis of fiscal year 1981 Indian Health Service and U.S. hospital discharge rates by age and primary diagnosis.* Rockville, MD: Author.

Institute of Medicine. (1990). Populations defined by structural characteristics. In *Broadening the base of treatment for alcohol problems* (pp. 356–380). Washington, DC: National Academy Press.

Institute of Medicine. (1996). *Pathways of addiction: Opportunities in drug abuse research.* Washington, DC: National Academy Press.

Institute of Medicine. (1999). *Marijuana and medicine: Assessing the science base.* Washington, DC: National Academy Press.

Iudice, A., Bonanni, E., Gelli, A., Frittelli, C., Iudice, G., Cignoni, F., et al. (2005). Effects of prolonged wakefulness combined with alcohol and hands-free cell phone divided attention tasks on simulated driving. *Human Psychopharmacology, 20*(2), 125–132.

Ja, D. Y., & Aoki, B. (1993). Substance abuse treatment: Cultural barriers in the Asian-American community. *Journal of Psychoactive Drugs, 25*(1), 61–71.

Jackson, J. K. (1954). The adjustment of the family to the crisis of alcoholism. *Quarterly Journal of Studies on Alcohol, 15,* 562–586.

Jackson, J. K. (1962). Alcoholism and the family. In J. Pittman & C. R. Snyder (Eds.), *Society, culture, and drinking patterns* (pp. 472–492). New York: Wiley.

Jacob, T., Haber, J. R., Leonard, K. E., & Rushe, R. (2000). Home interactions of high and low antisocial male alcoholics and their families. *Journal of Studies on Alcohol, 61*(1), 72–80.

Jacob, T., & Leonard, K. (1988). Alcoholic-spouse interaction as function of alcoholism subtype and alcohol consumption. *Journal of Abnormal Psychology, 97,* 231–237.

Jacob, T., & Leonard, K. (1992). Sequential analysis of marital interactions involving alcoholic, depressed, and nondistressed men. *Journal of Abnormal Psychology, 101,* 647–656.

Jaffe, A. J., & Glaros, A. G. (1986). Taste dimensions in cigarette discrimination: A multidimensional scaling approach. *Addictive Behaviors, 11*(4), 407–413.

James, D. J. (2004). Profile of jail inmates, 2002. In *Bureau of Justice Statistics special report.* Washington, DC: U.S. Department of Justice.

James, W. H. (1890). *The principles of psychology* (Vol. 1). New York: Henry Holt.

Jarvik, M. E. (1979). Biological influences on cigarette smoking. In N. A. Krasnegor (Ed.), *The behavioral aspects of smoking: National Institute on Drug Abuse Research Monograph* (Vol. 26, pp. 7–45). Washington, DC: U.S. Department of Health, Education, and Welfare.

Jellinek, E. M. (1943). Benjamin Rush's "An inquiry into the effects of ardent spirits upon the human body and mind, with an account of the means of preventing and of the remedies for curing them." *Quarterly Journal of Studies on Alcohol, 4,* 321–341.

Jellinek, E. M. (1952). Phases of alcohol addiction. *Quarterly Journal of Studies on Alcohol, 13,* 673–684.

Jellinek, E. M. (1960). *The disease conception of alcoholism.* New Brunswick, NJ: Hillhouse Press.

Jennison, K. M., & Johnson, K. A. (1998). Alcohol dependence in adult children of alcoholics: Longitudinal evidence of early risk. *Journal of Drug Education, 28*(1), 19–37.

Jeremy, R. J., & Hans, S. L. (1985). Behavior of neonates exposed in utero to methadone as assessed on the Brazelton scale. *Infant Behavior and Development, 8,* 323–336.

Jessor, R., & Jessor, S. (1977). *Problem behavior and psychosocial development: A longitudinal study.* New York: Academic Press.

Jessor, R., & Jessor, S. (1975). Adolescent development and the onset of drinking: A longitudinal study. *Journal of Studies on Alcohol, 36,* 27–51.

Johnson, C. A., Pentz, M. A., Weber, M. D., Dwyer, J. H., Baer, N., MacKinnon, D. P., et al. (1990). Relative effectiveness of comprehensive community programming for drug abuse prevention with high-risk and low-risk adolescents. *Journal of Consulting and Clinical Psychology, 58,* 447–456.

Johnson, F. W., Gruenewald, P. J., & Treno, A. J. (1998). Age-related differences in risks of drinking and driving in gender and ethnic groups. *Alcoholism: Clinical and Experimental Research, 22*(9), 2013–2022.

Johnson, J. L., Sher, K. J., & Rolf, J. E. (1991). Models of vulnerability to psychopathology in children of alcoholics: An overview [Special focus: Alcohol and youth]. *Alcohol Health and Research World, 15*(1), 33–42.

Johnson, P. B. (1982). Sex differences: Women's roles and alcohol use: Preliminary national data. *Journal of Social Issues, 39,* 93–116.

Johnson, P. B., Richter, L., Kleber, H. D., McLellan, A. T., & Carise, D. (2005). Telescoping of drinking-related behaviors: Gender, racial/ethnic, and age comparisons. *Substance Use & Misuse, 40*(8), 1139–1151.

Johnston, L. D., O'Malley, P. M., & Bachman, J. G. (1996). *National survey results on drug use from the Monitoring the Future Study, 1975–1995: Volume I. Secondary school students* (DHHS Pub. No. NIH 97–4139). Rockville, MD: National Institute on Drug Abuse.

Johnston, L. D., O'Malley, P. M., & Bachman, J. G. (1997). *Drug use among American high school seniors, college students and young adults, 1975–1995, Volume I: Secondary school students* (DHHS Pub. No. NIH 97–4139). Rockville, MD: National Institute of Drug Abuse.

Johnston, L. D., O'Malley, P. M., Bachman, J. G., & Schulenberg, J. E. (2007a). *Monitoring the Future national survey results on drug use, 1975–2006. Volume I: Secondary school students.* Bethesda, MD: National Institute on Drug Abuse.

Johnston, L. D., O'Malley, P. M., Bachman, J. G., & Schulenberg, J. E. (2007b). *Monitoring the Future national survey results on drug use, 1975–2006. Volume II: College students and adults ages 19–45.* Bethesda, MD: National Institute on Drug Abuse.

Johnston, L. D., O'Malley, P. M., Bachman, J. G., & Schulenberg, J. E. (2008). *Monitoring the Future national results on adolescent drug use: Overview of key findings, 2007.* Bethesda, MD: National Institute on Drug Abuse.

Johnston, L. D., Wadsworth, K. N., O'Malley, P. M., Bachman, J. G., & Schulenberg, J. E. (1997). *Smoking, drinking, and drug use in young adulthood: The impacts of new freedoms and new responsibilities.* Mahwah, NJ: Erlbaum.

Jones, A. S. (2007). Maternal alcohol abuse/dependence, children's behavior problems, and home environment: Estimates from the National Longitudinal Survey of Youth using propensity score matching. *Journal of Studies on Alcohol and Drugs, 68*(2), 266–275.

Jones, B. T., Corbin, W., & Fromme, K. (2001). A review of expectancy theory and alcohol consumption. *Addiction, 96*(1), 57–72.

Jones, B. T., & McMahon, J. (1994). Negative and positive alcohol expectancies as predictors of abstinence after discharge from a residential treatment program: A one-month and three-month follow-up study in men. *Journal of Studies on Alcohol, 55*(5), 543–548.

Jones, B. T., & McMahon, J. (1996). Changes in alcohol expectancies during treatment relate to subsequent abstinence survivorship. *British Journal of Clinical Psychology, 35*(Pt. 2), 221–234.

Jones, H. A., & Lejuez, C. W. (2005). Personality correlates of caffeine dependence: The role of sensation seeking, impulsivity, and risk taking. *Experimental and Clinical Psychopharmacology, 13*(3), 259–266.

Jones, K. L. (1986). Fetal alcohol syndrome. *Pediatrics in Review, 8,* 122–126.

Jones, K. L., Smith, D. W., Ulleland, C. N., & Streissguth, A. P. (1973). Pattern of malformation in offspring of chronic alcoholic mothers. *Lancet, 1,* 1267–1271.

Jones-Webb, R., Hsiao, C. Y., & Hannan, P. (1995). Relationships between socioeconomic status and drinking problems among Black and White men. *Alcoholism: Clinical and Experimental Research, 19*(3), 623–627.

Jones-Webb, R. (1998). Drinking patterns and problems among African-Americans: Recent findings. *Alcohol Health & Research World, 22*(4), 260–264.

Josephs, R. A., & Steele, C. M. (1990). The two faces of alcohol myopia: Attentional mediation of psychological stress. *Journal of Abnormal Psychology, 99,* 115–126.

Joutsenniemi, K., Martelin, T., Kestilä, L., Martikainen, P., Pirkola, S., & Koskinen, S. (2007). Living arrangements, heavy drinking and alcohol dependence. *Alcohol and Alcoholism, 42*(5), 480–491.

Kadden, R. M. (1996). Is Marlatt's relapse taxonomy reliable or valid? *Addiction, 91*(12, Suppl. 1), S139–S145.

Kalant, H. (1997). Opium revisited: A brief review of its nature, composition, non-medical use and relative risks. *Addiction, 92,* 267–277.

Kalant, H. (1998). Pharmacological interactions of aging and alcohol. In U. S. Department of Health and Human Services (Ed.), *Alcohol problems and aging* (pp. 99–116). Washington, DC: U.S. Government Printing Office.

Kandall, S. R. (1998a). Women and addiction in the United States—1850–1920. In C. L. Wetherington & A. B. Roman (Eds.), *Drug addiction research and the health of women* (pp. 33–52). Rockville, MD: National Institute on Drug Abuse.

Kandall, S. R. (1998b). Women and addiction in the United States—1920 to present. In C. L. Wetherington & A. B. Roman (Eds.), *Drug addiction research and the health of women* (pp. 53–80). Rockville, MD: National Institute on Drug Abuse.

Kandel, D. B., & Andrews, K. (1987). Processes of adolescent socialization by parents and peers. *International Journal of the Addictions, 22,* 319–342.

Kandel, D. B., Warner, L. A., & Kessler, R. C. (1998). The epidemiology of substance use and dependence among women. In C. L. Wetherington & A. B. Roman (Eds.), *Drug addiction research and the health of women* (pp. 105–130). Washington, DC: National Institute on Drug Abuse.

Kaprio, J., Koskenvuo, M., Langinvaino, H., Ramonov, K., Sarna, S., & Rose, R. J. (1987). Genetic influences on use and abuse of alcohol: A study of 5638 adult Finnish twin brothers. *Alcoholism: Clinical and Experimental Research, 11,* 349–356.

Kapur, B. M. (1993). Drug testing methods and clinical interpretations of results. *Bulletin of Narcotics, 45*(2), 115–154.

Karberg, J. C., & James, D. J. (2005). Substance dependence, abuse, and treatment of jail inmates, 2002. In *Bureau of Justice Statistics special report.* Washington, DC: U.S. Department of Justice.

Karlamangla, A., Zhou, K., Reuben, D., Greendale, G., & Moore, A. (2006). Longitudinal trajectories of heavy drinking in adults in the United States of America. *Addiction, 101*(1), 91–99.

Karno, M., Granholm, E., & Lin, A. (2000). Factor structure of the Alcohol Use Disorders Identification Test (AUDIT) in a mental health clinic sample. *Journal of Studies on Alcohol, 61*(5), 751–758.

Kaskutas, L. A. (1996). A road less traveled: Choosing the "Women for Sobriety" program. *Journal of Drug Issues, 26,* 77–94.

Kaskutas, L. A., Ammon, L., Delucchi, K., Room, R., Bond, J., & Weisner, C. (2005). Alcoholics Anonymous careers: Patterns of AA involvement five years after treatment entry. *Alcoholism: Clinical and Experimental Research, 29*(11), 1983–1990.

Kaslow, R. A., Blackwelder, W. C., Ostrow, D. C., Yerg, D., Palenicek, J., Coulson, A. H., et al. (1989). No evidence for a role of alcohol or other psychoactive drugs in accelerating immunodeficiency in HIV-1 positive individuals. *JAMA, 261,* 3424–3429.

Kassel, J. D. (1997). Smoking and attention: A review and reformulation of the stimulus-filter hypothesis. *Clinical Psychology Review, 17,* 451–478.

Kaufman, E. (1985). Family therapy in the treatment of alcoholism. In T. E. Bratter & G. G. Forrest (Eds.), *Alcoholism and substance abuse: Strategies for clinical intervention* (pp. 376–397). New York: Free Press.

Kelemen, W. L., & Kaighobadi, F. (2007). Expectancy and pharmacology influence the subjective effects of nicotine in a balanced-placebo design. *Experimental and Clinical Psychopharmacology, 15,* 93–101.

Keller, D. S. (1996). Exploration in the service of relapse prevention: A psychoanalytic contribution to substance abuse treatment. In F. Rotgers, D. S. Keller, & J. Morgenstern (Eds.), *Treating substance abuse: Theory and technique* (pp. 84–116). New York: Guilford.

Kendall, R. E. (1991). Relationship between the DSM-IV and the ICD-10. *Journal of Abnormal Psychology, 100,* 297–301.

Kendler, K. S., Heath, A. C., Neale, M. C., Kessler, R. C., & Eaves, L. J. (1992). A population-based twin study of alcoholism in women. *Journal of the American Medical Association, 268*(14), 1877–1882.

Kendler, K. S., Myers, J., & Prescott, C. A. (2007). Specificity of genetic and environmental risk factors for symptoms of cannabis, cocaine, alcohol, caffeine, and nicotine dependence. *Archives of General Psychiatry, 64*(11), 1313–1320.

Kendler, K. S., & Prescott, C. A. (2006). *Genes, environment, and psychopathology: Understanding the causes of psychiatric and substance use disorders.* New York: Guilford.

Kessler, D. A., Barnett, P. S., Witt, A., Zeller, M. R., Mande, J. R., & Schultz, W. B. (1997). The legal and scientific basis for FDA's assertion of jurisdiction over cigarettes and smokeless tobacco. *Journal of American Medical Association, 277*(5), 405–408.

Kessler, R. C., Chiu, W. T., Demler, O., Merikangas, K. R., & Walters, E. E. (2005). Prevalence, severity, and comorbidity of 12-month DSM-IV disorders in the National Comorbidity Survey Replication. *Archives of General Psychiatry, 62*(6), 617–627.

Kessler, R. C., McGonagle, K. A., Zhao, S., Nelson, C. B., Eshelman, S., Wittchen, H. U., et al. (1994). Lifetime and 12-month prevalence of DSM-III-R psychiatric disorders in the United States. *Archives of General Psychiatry, 51,* 8–19.

Kessler, R. C., Nelson, C. B., McGonagle, K. A., Edlund, M. J., Frank, R. G., & Leaf, P. J. (1996). The epidemiology of co-occurring mental disorders and substance use disorders in the National Comorbidity Study: Implications for prevention and service utilization. *American Journal of Orthopsychiatry, 66,* 17–31.

Kessler, R. C., & Ustun, T. B. (2004). The World Mental Health (WMH) Survey Initiative Version of the World Health Organization (WHO) Composite International Diagnostic Interview (CIDI). *International Journal of Methods Psychiatric Research, 13*(2), 93–121.

Keyes, K. M., Grant, B. F., & Hasin, D. S. (2008). Evidence for a closing gender gap in alcohol use, abuse, and dependence in the United States population. *Drug and Alcohol Dependence, 93*(1–2), 21–29.

Kilpatrick, D. G., Resnick, H. S., Saunders, B. E., & Best, C. L. (1998). Victimization, posttraumatic stress disorder, and substance use and abuse among women. In C. L. Wetherington & A. B. Roman (Eds.), *Drug addiction research and the health of women* (pp. 285–307). Rockville, MD: National Institute on Drug Abuse.

King, K. M., & Chassin, L. (2007). A prospective study of the effects of age of initiation of alcohol and drug use on young adult substance dependence. *Journal of Studies on Alcohol and Drugs, 68*(2), 256–265.

Kitano, H., & Chi, I. (1986–1987). Asian Americans and alcohol use. *Alcohol Health & Research World, 11*(2, Winter), 42–46.

Kitano, H., Chi, I., Rhee, S., Law, C. K., & Lubben, J. E. (1992). Norms and alcohol consumption: Japanese in Japan, Hawaii, and California. *Journal of Studies on Alcohol, 53,* 33–39.

Kitano, H., Hatanaka, H., Yeung, W., & Sue, S. (1985). Japanese-American drinking patterns. In L. A. Bennett & G. M. Ames (Eds.), *The American experience with alcohol: Contrasting cultural perspectives* (pp. 335–357). New York: Plenum.

Klassen, A. D., & Wilsnack, S. C. (1986). Sexual experiences and drinking among women in a U.S. national survey. *Archives of Sexual Behavior, 15,* 363–392.

Klatsky, A. L. (1999). Moderate drinking and reduced risk of heart disease. *Alcohol Research and Health, 23*(1), 15–23.

Klatsky, A. L. (2002). Alcohol and cardiovascular diseases. *Annals of New York Academy of Science, 957,* 7–15.

Klatsky, A. L., Armstrong, M. A., & Friedman, G. D. (1990). Risk of cardiovascular mortality in alcohol drinkers, ex-drinkers and nondrinkers. *American Journal of Cardiology, 66,* 1237–1242.

Klatsky, A. L., Friedman, G. D., & Siegelaub, A. B. (1979). Alcohol use, myocardial infarction, sudden cardiac death, and hypertension. *Alcoholism: Experimental and Clinical Research, 3,* 33–39.

Knupfer, G. (1972). Ex-problem drinkers. In M. Roff, L. Robins, & M. Pollack (Eds.), *Life history research in psychopathology* (Vol. II, pp. 256–280). Minneapolis: University of Minnesota Press.

Kolb, B., & Wishaw, I. Q. (1990). *Fundamentals of human neuropsychology* (3rd ed.) New York: Freeman.

Komro, K. A., Perry, C. L., Veblen-Mortenson, S., Farbakhsh, K., Toomey, T. L., Stigler, M. H., et al. (2008). Outcomes from a randomized controlled trial of a multi-component alcohol use preventive intervention for urban youth: Project northland Chicago. *Addiction, 103*(4), 606–618.

Komro, K. A., & Toomey, T. L. (2002). Strategies to prevent underage drinking. *Alcohol Research and Health, 26*(1), 5–14.

Koob, G. F. (1992). Neural mechanisms of drug reinforcement. *Annals of New York Academy of Sciences, 654,* 171–191.

Koob, G. F. (2006). The neurobiology of addiction: A neuroadaptational view relevant for diagnosis. *Addiction, 101,* 23–30.

Koob, G. F., & Le Moal, M. (1997). Drug abuse: Hedonic homeostatic dysregulation. *Science, 278*(5335), 52–58.

Koob, G. F., & Le Moal, M. (2001). Drug addiction, dysregulation of reward, and allostasis. *Neuropsychopharmacology, 24*(2), 97–129.

Koob, G. F., & Le Moal, M. (2005). Drug addiction and allostasis. In J. Schulkin (Ed.), *Allostasis, homeostasis, and the costs of physiological adaptation* (pp. 150–163). Cambridge, UK: Cambridge University Press.

Korhonen, T., Broms, U., Varjonen, J., Romanov, K., Koskenvuo, M., Kinnunen, T., et al. (2007). Smoking behaviour as a predictor of depression among Finnish men and women: A prospective cohort study of adult twins. *Psychological Medicine, 37*(5), 705–715.

Kozlowski, L. T., Pillitteri, J. L., & Sweeney, C. T. (1994). Misuse of "light" cigarettes by means of vent blocking. *Journal of Substance Abuse, 6*(3), 333–336.

Krank, M., Wall, A. M., Stewart, S. H., Wiers, R. W., & Goldman, M. S. (2005). Context effects on alcohol cognitions. *Alcoholism: Clinical and Experimental Research, 29*(2), 196–206.

Kranzler, H. R., & Li, T.-K. (2008). What is addiction? *Alcohol Health & Research, 31*(2), 93–95.

Kranzler, H. R., & Rounsaville, B. J. (Eds.). (1998). *Dual diagnosis and treatment.* New York: Marcel Dekker.

Kranzler, H. R., Tennen, H., Penta, C., & Bohn, M. J. (1997). Targeted naltrexone treatment of early problem drinkers. *Addictive Behaviors, 22,* 431–436.

Landrine, H., & Klonoff, E. A. (1998). *Culture change, tobacco and alcohol use among U.S. ethnic minorities: An operant model of acculturation.* Paper presented at the Conference on Acculturation: Advances in Theory, Measurement, and Applied Research, San Francisco.

Lang, C. H., Frost, R. A., Summer, A. D., & Vary, T. C. (2005). Molecular mechanisms responsible for alcohol-induced myopathy in skeletal muscle and heart. *International Journal of Biochemistry Cell Biology, 37*(10), 2180–2195.

Lange, L. G., & Kinnunen, P. M. (1987). Cardiovascular effects of alcohol. *Advances in Alcohol and Substance Abuse, 6,* 47–52.

Langeland, W., & Hartgers, C. (1998). Child sexual and physical abuse and alcoholism: A review. *Journal of Studies on Alcohol, 59,* 336–348.

Langenbucher, J. W., & Chung, T. (1995). Onset and staging of DSM-IV alcohol dependence using mean age and survival-hazard methods. *Journal of Abnormal Psychology, 104*(2), 346–354.

Langton, P. A. (1991). *Drug use and the alcohol dilemma.* Needham Heights, MA: Allyn & Bacon.

Lanza, S. T., & Collins, L. M. (2006). A mixture model of discontinuous development in heavy drinking from ages 18 to 30: The role of college enrollment. *Journal of Studies on Alcohol, 67*(4), 552–561.

Larkby, C., & Day, N. (1997). The effects of prenatal alcohol exposure. *Alcohol Health & Research World, 21*(3), 192–198.

Larson, E. W., Olincy, A., Rummans, T. A., & Morse, R. M. (1992). Disulfiram treatment of patients with both alcohol dependence and other psychiatric disorders: A review. *Alcoholism: Clinical and Experimental Research, 16*(1), 125–130.

Latvala, J., Parkkila, S., & Niemela, O. (2004). Excess alcohol consumption is common in patients with cytopenia: Studies in blood and bone marrow cells. *Alcoholism: Clinical and Experimental Research, 28*(4), 619–624.

Lau, M. A., Pihl, R. O., & Peterson, J. B. (1995). Provocation, acute alcohol intoxication, cognitive performance, and aggression. *Journal of Abnormal Psychology, 104*(1), 150–155.

Ledermann, S. (1956). *Alcool, alcoolisme, alcoolisation: Donnes cientifiques de caractere physiologique economique et social* [Alcohol, alcoholism, alcoholization: Scientific data of nature physiological, economic and social]. Paris: Presses Universitaires de France.

Lee, C. M., Neighbors, C., & Woods, B. A. (2007). Marijuana motives: Young adults' reasons for using marijuana. *Addictive Behaviors, 32*(7), 1384–1394.

Leeds, J., & Morgenstern, J. (1996). Psychoanalytic theories of substance abuse. In F. Rotgers, D. S. Keller, & J. Morgenstern (Eds.), *Treating substance abuse: Theory and technique* (pp. 68–83). New York: Guilford.

Legrand, L. N., Keyes, M., McGue, M., Iacono, W. G., & Krueger, R. F. (2008). Rural environments reduce the genetic influence on adolescent substance use and rule-breaking behavior. *Psychological Medicine, 38,* 1341–1350.

Leigh, B. C. (1987). Beliefs about the effects of alcohol on self and others. *Journal of Studies on Alcohol, 48*(5), 467–475.

Leigh, B. C., & Stacy, A. W. (2004). Alcohol expectancies and drinking in different age groups. *Addiction, 99*(2), 215–227.

Leigh, B. C., & Stall, R. (1993). Substance use and risky sexual behavior for exposure to HIV: Issues in methodology, interpretation, and prevention. *American Psychologist, 48*(10), 1035–1045.

Lemke, S., Schutte, K. K., Brennan, P. L., & Moos, R. H. (2008). Gender differences in social influences and stressors linked to increased drinking. *Journal of Studies on Alcohol and Drugs, 69,* 695–702.

Leonard, K. E. (1990). Summary: Family processes and alcoholism. In R. L. Collins, K. E. Leonard, & J. S. Searles (Eds.), *Alcohol and the family: Research and clinical perspectives* (pp. 272–281). New York: Guilford.

Leonard, K. E., & Das Eiden, R. (1999). Husband's and wife's drinking: Unilateral or bilateral influences among newlyweds in a general population sample. *Journal of Studies on Alcohol* (Suppl. 13), 130–138.

Leonard, K. E., & Eiden, R. D. (2007). Marital and family processes in the context of alcohol use and alcohol disorders. *Annual Review of Clinical Psychology, 3,* 285–310.

Leonard, K. E., & Roberts, L. J. (1998). Marital aggression, quality, and stability in the first year of marriage: Findings from the Buffalo Newlywed Study. In T. N. Bradbury (Ed.), *The developmental course of marital dysfunction* (pp. 44–73). New York: Cambridge University Press.

Leonard, K. E., & Senchak, M. (1996). The prospective prediction of marital aggression among newlywed couples. *Journal of Abnormal Psychology, 105,* 369–380.

Leung, S. F., & Phelps, C. E. (1993). My kingdom for a drink...? A review of estimates of the price sensitivity of demand for alcoholic beverages. In M. E. Hilton & G. Bloss (Eds.), *Economics and the prevention of alcohol-related problems* (NIAAA Research Monograph No. 25, NIH Pub. No. 93-3513, pp. 1–29). Bethesda, MD: National Institutes of Health, National Institute on Alcohol Abuse and Alcoholism.

Levenson, M. R., Aldwin, C. M., & Spiro, A. R. (1998). Age, cohort and period effects on alcohol consumption and problem drinking: Findings from the Normative Aging Study. *Journal of Studies on Alcohol, 59*(6), 712–722.

Leventhal, H., & McCleary, P. D. (1980). The smoking problem: A review of the research and theory in behavioral risk modification. *Psychological Bulletin, 88,* 370–405.

Levi-Strauss, C. (1966). *The savage mind.* Chicago: University of Chicago Press.

Levy Merrick, E. S., Volpe-Vartanian, J., Horgan, C. M., & McCann, B. (2007). Alcohol & drug abuse: Revisiting employee assistance programs and substance use problems in the workplace: Key issues and a research agenda. *Psychiatric Services, 58,* 1262–1264.

Lex, B. W. (1985). Alcohol problems in special populations. In J. H. Mendelsohn & N. K. Mello (Eds.), *The diagnosis and treatment of alcoholism* (2nd ed., pp. 89–187). New York: McGraw-Hill.

Lex, B. W. (1987). Review of alcohol problems in ethnic minority groups. *Journal of Consulting and Clinical Psychology, 55*(3), 293–300.

Lex, B. W. (1991). Some gender differences in alcohol and polysubstance users [Special issue: Gender and health]. *Health Psychology, 10*(2), 121–132.

Lex, B. W. (1994). Alcohol and other drug abuse among women [Special focus: Women and alcohol]. *Alcohol Health and Research World, 18*(3), 212–219.

Li, H. Z., & Rosenblood, L. (1994). Exploring factors influencing alcohol consumption patterns among Chinese and Caucasians. *Journal of Studies on Alcohol, 55,* 427–433.

Li, M. D. (2006). The genetics of nicotine dependence. *Current Psychiatry Reports, 8,* 158–164.

Li, M. D., Ma, J. Z., Cheng, R., Dupont, R. T., Williams, N. J., Crews, K. M., et al. (2003). A genome-wide scan to identify loci for smoking rate in the Framingham Heart Study population. *BMC Genetics, 4*(Suppl. 1), S103.

Li, T. K., Hewitt, B. G., & Grant, B. F. (2007). The alcohol dependence syndrome, 30 years later: A commentary. The 2006 H. David Archibald lecture. *Addiction, 102*(10), 1522–1530.

Lidberg, L., Tuck, J. R., Asberg, M., Scalia-Tomba, G. P., & Bertilsson, L. (1985). Homicide, suicide and CSF 5-HIAAA. *Acta Psychiatrica Scandinavica, 71,* 230–236.

Lieber, C. S. (1984). Alcohol and the liver: 1984 update. *Hepatology, 4,* 1243–1260.

Lieber, C. S. (1994). Susceptibility to alcohol-related liver injury. *Alcohol and Alcoholism* (Suppl. 2), 315–326.

Lieber, C. S., Garro, A. J., Leo, M. A., & Worner, T. M. (1986). Mechanisms for the interrelationship between alcohol and cancer. *Alcohol and Research World, 10,* 10–17.

Liguori, A., Gatto, C. P., & Robinson, J. H. (1998). Effects of marijuana on equilibrium, psychomotor performance, and simulated driving. *Behavioural Pharmacology, 9,* 599–609.

Liljestrand, P. (1993). Quality in college student drinking research: Conceptual and methodological issues. *Journal of Alcohol and Drug Education, 38,* 1–36.

Lipsey, M. W., Wilson, D. B., Cohen, M. A., & Derzon, J. H. (1997). Is there a causal relationship between alcohol use and violence? A synthesis of evidence. In M. Galanter (Ed.), *Recent developments in alcoholism* (Vol. 13, pp. 245–282). New York: Plenum.

Lipsky, S., Caetano, R., Field, C. A., & Larkin, G. L. (2005). Is there a relationship between victim and partner alcohol use during an intimate partner violence event? Findings from an urban emergency department study of abused women. *Journal of Studies on Alcohol, 66*(3), 407–412.

Liskow, B. I., & Goodwin, D. W. (1987). Pharmacological treatment of alcohol intoxication, withdrawal and dependence: A critical review. *Journal of Studies on Alcohol, 48,* 356–370.

Litt, M. D., Kadden, R. M., Cooney, N. L., & Kabela, E. (2003). Coping skills and treatment outcomes in cognitive-behavioral and interactional group therapy for alcoholism. *Journal of Consulting and Clinical Psychology, 71*(1), 118–128.

Litt, M. D., Kadden, R. M., Kabela-Cormier, E., & Petry, N. (2007). Changing network support for drinking: Initial findings from the network support project. *Journal of Consulting and Clinical Psychology, 75*(4), 542–555.

Littleton, J. (1998/Updated October 2000). Neurochemical mechanisms underlying alcohol withdrawal. *Alcohol Health & Research World, 22*(1), 13–24.

Liu, Y. C., & Fu, S. M. (2007). Changes in driving behavior and cognitive performance with different breath alcohol concentration levels. *Traffic Injury Prevention, 8*(2), 153–161.

Lloyd, H. M., & Rogers, P. J. (1997). Mood and cognitive performance improved by a small amount of alcohol given with a lunchtime meal. *Behavioural Pharmacology, 8*(2–3), 188–195.

Lohrenz, L. J., Connelly, J. C., Coyne, L., & Spare, K. E. (1978). Alcohol problems in several Midwestern homosexual communities. *Journal of Studies on Alcohol, 39,* 1959–1963.

Long, J. A., O'Connor, P. G., Gerbner, G., & Concato, J. (2002). Use of alcohol, illicit drugs, and tobacco among characters on prime-time television. *Substance Abuse, 23*(2), 95–103.

Longabaugh, R. (2007). The search for mechanisms of change in behavioral treatments for alcohol use disorders: A commentary. *Alcoholism: Clinical and Experimental Research, 31*(Suppl. 10), 21s–32s.

Longabaugh, R., & Morgenstern, J. (1999). Cognitive-behavioral coping-skills therapy for alcohol dependence: Current status and future directions. *Alcohol Research and Health, 23*(2), 78–85.

Longabaugh, R., Wirtz, P. W., Beattie, M. C., Noel, N., & Stout, R. (1995). Matching treatment focus to patient social investment and support: 18-month follow-up results. *Journal of Consulting and Clinical Psychology, 63*(2), 296–307.

Lorenz, E. N. (1963). Deterministic nonperiodic flow. *Journal of Atmospheric Sciences, 20,* 131–141.

Loukas, A., Zucker, R. A., Fitzgerald, H. E., & Krull, J. L. (2003). Developmental trajectories of disruptive behavior problems among sons of alcoholics: Effects of parent psychopathology, family conflict, and child undercontrol. *Journal of Abnormal Psychology, 112,* 119–131.

Lovibond, S., & Caddy, G. (1970). Discriminated aversive control in the moderation of alcoholics' drinking behaviour. *Behavior Therapy, 1,* 437–444.

Lowman, C., Allen, J., & Stout, R. L. (1996). Replication and extension of Marlatt's taxonomy of relapse precipitants: Overview of procedures and results. The Relapse Research Group. *Addiction, 91*(S12), S51–S71.

Lowry, R., Holtzman, D., Truman, B. I., Kann, L., Collins, J. L., & Kolbe, L. J. (1994). Substance use and HIV-related sexual behaviors among US high school students: Are they related? *American Journal of Public Health, 84*(7), 1116–1120.

Lubben, J., Chi, I., & Kitano, H. (1988a). Exploring Filipino-American drinking behavior. *Journal of Studies on Alcohol, 49,* 26–29.

Lubben, J., Chi, I., & Kitano, H. (1988b). The relative influence of selected social factors on Korean drinking behavior in Los Angeles. *Advances in Alcohol and Substance Abuse, 8,* 1–17.

Lubman, D. I., Yucel, M., & Pantelis, C. (2004). Addiction, a condition of compulsive behaviour? Neuroimaging and neuropsychological evidence of inhibitory dysregulation. *Addiction, 99*(12), 1491–1502.

Luczak, S. E., Wall, T. L., Shea, S. H., Byun, S. M., & Carr, L. G. (2001). Binge drinking in Chinese, Korean, and White college students: Genetic and ethnic group differences [Special issue: Understanding binge drinking]. *Psychology of Addictive Behavior, 15*(4), 306–309.

Ludwig, A. M. (1986). Pavlov's "bells" and alcohol craving. *Addictive Behaviors, 11,* 87–91.

Ludwig, A. M. (1988). *Understanding the alcoholic's mind: The nature of craving and how to control it.* New York: Oxford University Press.

Lynam, D. R., Milich, R., Zimmerman, R., Novak, S. P., Logan, T. K., Martin, C., et al. (1999). Project DARE: No effects at 10-year follow-up. *Journal of Consulting and Clinical Psychology, 67*(5), 590–593.

MacAndrew, C., & Edgerton, R. B. (1969). *Drunken comportment: A social explanation.* Chicago: Aldine.

MacCoun, R., & Caulkins, J. (1996). Examining the behavioral assumptions of the national drug control strategy. In W. K. Bickel & R. J. DeGrandpre (Eds.), *Drug policy and human nature: Psychological perspectives on the prevention, management, and treatment of illicit drug abuse* (pp. 177–197). New York: Plenum.

MacCoun, R. J. (1998). Toward a psychology of harm reduction. *American Psychologist, 53,* 1199–1208.

Macdonald, S., Erickson, P., Wells, S., Hathaway, A., & Pakula, B. (2008). Predicting violence among cocaine, cannabis, and alcohol treatment clients. *Addictive Behaviors, 33*(1), 201–205.

MacPherson, P. S., Stewart, S. H., & McWilliams, L. A. (2001). Parental problem drinking and anxiety disorder symptoms in adult offspring: Examining the mediating role of anxiety sensitivity components. *Addictive Behaviors, 26*(6), 917–934.

Maggs, J. L., & Schulenberg, J. E. (2004/2005). Trajectories of alcohol use during the transition to adulthood. *Alcohol Research and Health, 28,* 195–201.

Maher, J. J. (1997). Exploring alcohol's effects on liver function. *Alcohol and Health Research World, 21,* 5–12.

Maisto, S. A., & Carey, K. B. (1987). Treatment of alcohol abuse. In T. D. Nirenberg & S. A. Maisto (Eds.), *Developments in the assessment and treatment of addictive behaviors* (pp. 173–212). Norwood, NJ: Ablex.

Maisto, S. A., Carey, M. P., Carey, K. B., Gordon, C. M., & Schum, J. L. (2004). Effects of alcohol and expectancies on HIV-related risk perception and behavioral skills in heterosexual women. *Experimental and Clinical Psychopharmacology, 12*(4), 288–297.

Maisto, S. A., Clifford, P. R., & Davis, C. M. (2007). Alcohol treatment research assessment exposure subject reactivity effects: Part II. Treatment engagement and involvement. *Journal of Studies on Alcohol and Drugs, 68*(4), 529–533.

Maisto, S. A., Galizio, M., & Conners, G. J. (1995). *Drug use and misuse* (2nd ed.). New York: Holt, Rinehart, and Winston.

Maisto, S. A., Pollock, N. K., Cornelius, J. R., Lynch, K. G., & Martin, C. S. (2003). Alcohol relapse as a function of relapse definition in a clinical sample of adolescents. *Addictive Behaviors, 28*(3), 449–459.

Maisto, S. A., Zywiak, W. H., & Connors, G. J. (2006). Course of functioning 1 year following admission for treatment of alcohol use disorders. *Addictive Behaviors, 31*(1), 69–79.

Makimoto, K. (1998). Drinking patterns and drinking problems among Asian-Americans and Pacific Islanders. *Alcohol Health Research World, 22*(4), 270–275.

Makowsky, C. R., & Whitehead, P. C. (1991). Advertising and alcohol sales: A legal impact study. *Journal of Studies on Alcohol, 52*(6), 555–567.

Mangione, T. W., Howland, J., Amick, B., Cote, J., Lee, M., Bell, N., et al. (1999). Employee drinking practices and work performance. *Journal of Studies on Alcohol, 60*(2), 261–270.

Marks, J. L., Hill, E. M., Pomerleau, C. S., Mudd, S. A., & Blow, F. C. (1997). Nicotine dependence and withdrawal in alcoholic and nonalcoholic ever-smokers. *Journal of Substance Abuse Treatment, 14*(6), 521–527.

Marlatt, G. A. (1978). Craving for alcohol, loss of control, and relapse: A cognitive-behavioral analysis. In P. E. Nathan, G. A. Marlatt, & T. Loberg (Eds.), *Alcoholism: New directions in behavioral research and treatment* (pp. 271–314). New York: Plenum.

Marlatt, G. A. (1985a). Cognitive assessment and intervention procedures for relapse preventions. In G. A. Marlatt & J. R. Gordon (Eds.), *Relapse prevention: Maintenance strategies in the treatment of addictive behaviors* (1st ed., pp. 201–279). New York: Guilford.

Marlatt, G. A. (1985b). Relapse prevention: Theoretical rationale and overview of the model. In G. A. Marlatt & J. R. Gordon (Eds.), *Relapse prevention: Maintenance strategies in the treatment of addictive behaviors* (1st ed., pp. 3–70). New York: Guilford.

Marlatt, G. A. (1996). Taxonomy of high-risk situations for alcohol relapse: Evolution and development of a cognitive-behavioral model. *Addiction, 91*(Suppl.), S37–S49.

Marlatt, G. A. (Ed.). (1998). *Harm reduction: Pragmatic strategies for managing high-risk behaviors.* New York: Guilford.

Marlatt, G. A., Demming, B., & Reid, J. (1973). Loss of control drinking in alcoholics: An experimental analogue. *Journal of Abnormal Psychology, 81,* 233–241.

Marlatt, G. A., & Gordon, J. R. (Eds.). (1985). *Relapse prevention: Maintenance strategies in the treatment of addictive behaviors* (1st ed.). New York: Guilford,

Marlatt, G. A., & Rohsenow, D. J. (1980). Cognitive processes in alcohol use: Expectancy and the balanced placebo design. In N. K. Mello (Ed.), *Advances in substance abuse: Behavioral and biological research* (pp. 159–199). Greenwich, CT: JAI Press.

Marlatt, G. A., & Witkiewitz, K. (2002). Harm reduction approaches to alcohol use: Health promotion, prevention, and treatment. *Addictive Behaviors, 27*(6), 867–886.

Marshall, B. D., Fairbairn, N., Li, K., Wood, E., & Kerr, T. (2008). Physical violence among a prospective cohort of injection drug users: A gender-focused approach. *Drug and Alcohol Dependence, 97,* 237–246.

Martin, C. S., Earleywine, M., & Finn, P. (1990). Some boundary conditions for effective use of alcohol placebos. *Journal of Studies on Alcohol, 51,* 500–505.

Martin, C. S., Kaczynski, N. A., Maisto, S. A., & Tarter, R. E. (1996). Polydrug use in adolescent drinkers with and without DSM-IV alcohol abuse and dependence. *Alcoholism: Clinical Experimental Research, 20*(6), 1099–1108.

Martin, S. E., Bryant, K., & Fitzgerald, N. (2001). Self-reported alcohol use and abuse by arrestees in the 1998 Arrestee Drug Abuse Monitoring Program. *Alcohol Research and Health, 25*(1), 72–79.

Massak, A., & Graham, K. (2008). Is the smoking-depression relationship confounded by alcohol consumption? An analysis by gender. *Nicotine Tobacco Research, 10*(7), 1231–1243.

Masters, W. H., & Johnson, V. E. (1966). *Human sexual response.* Boston: Little, Brown.

Mathios, A., Avery, R., Bisogni, C., & Shanahan, J. (1998). Alcohol portrayal on prime-time television: Manifest and latent messages. *Journal of Studies on Alcohol, 59*(3), 305–310.

Mattson, M. E. (1995). Patient-treatment matching. *Alcohol Health and Research World, 18*(4), 287–295.

Mattson, M. E., & Allen, J. P. (1991). Research on matching alcoholic patients to treatments: Findings, issues, and implications. *Journal of Addictive Diseases, 11,* 33–49.

Mattson, S. N., & Riley, E. P. (1998). A review of the neurobehavioral deficits in children with fetal alcohol syndrome or prenatal exposure to alcohol. *Alcoholism: Clinical and Experimental Research, 22*(2), 279–294.

Mattson, S. N., Schoenfeld, A. M., & Riley, E. P. (2001). Teratogenic effects of alcohol on brain and behavior. *Alcohol Research and Health, 25*(3), 185–191.

Matzger, H., Delucchi, K., Weisner, C., & Ammon, L. (2004). Does marital status predict long-term drinking? Five-year observations of dependent and problem drinkers. *Journal on Studies of Alcohol and Drugs, 65*(2), 255–265.

May, P. A. (1996). Alcohol abuse and alcoholism among American Indians: An overview. In J. T. D. Watts & R. Wright (Ed.), *Alcoholism in minority populations* (pp. 95–119). Springfield, IL: C. C. Thomas.

Mayhew, K. P., Flay, B. R., & Mott, J. A. (2000). Stages in the development of adolescent smoking. *Drug and Alcohol Dependence, 59*(Suppl. 1), S61–S81.

McCarthy, D. E., Piasecki, T. M., Lawrence, D. L., Jorenby, D. E., Shiffman, S., Fiore, M. C., et al. (2008). A randomized controlled clinical trial of bupropion SR and individual smoking cessation counseling. *Nicotine Tobacco Research, 10*(4), 717–729.

McCarthy, J. D. (1999). Activists, authorities, and media framing of drunk driving. In E. Laraña, H. Johnston, & J. R. Gusfield (Eds.), *New social movements: From ideology to identity* (pp. 133–167). Philadelphia: Temple University Press.

McClelland, D. C., Davis, W. N., Kalin, R., & Wanner, E. (1972). *The drinking man.* New York: Free Press.

McCord, J. (1988). Identifying developmental paradigms leading to alcoholism. *Journal of Studies on Alcohol, 49,* 357–362.

McCord, W., & McCord, J. (1960). *Origins of alcoholism.* Stanford, CA: Stanford University Press.

McCrady, B. S. (1987). Implications of neuropsychological research findings for the treatment and rehabilitation of alcoholics. In O. A. Parsons, N. Butters, & P. E. Nathan (Eds.), *Neuropsychology of alcoholism: Implications for diagnosis and treatment* (pp. 381–391). New York: Guilford.

McCrady, B. S. (1989). Outcomes of family-involved alcoholism treatment. In M. Galanter (Ed.), *Recent developments in alcoholism* (Vol. 7, pp. 165–182). New York: Plenum.

McCrady, B. S. (1994). Alcoholics Anonymous and behavior therapy: Can habits be treated as diseases? Can diseases be treated as habits? [Special section: The nature and treatment of alcoholism]. *Journal of Consulting and Clinical Psychology, 62*(6), 1159–1166.

McCrady, B. S., & Delaney, S. I. (1995). Self-help groups. In R. K. Hester & W. R. Miller (Eds.), *Handbook of alcoholism treatment approaches: Effective alternatives* (2nd ed., pp. 160–175). Needham Heights, MA: Allyn & Bacon.

McCrady, B. S., & Epstein, E. E. (1995). Directions for research on alcoholic relationships: Marital- and individual-based models of heterogeneity. *Psychology of Addictive Behaviors, 9,* 157–166.

McCrady, B. S., & Miller, W. R. (1993). *Research on Alcoholics Anonymous: Opportunities and alternatives.* Piscataway, NJ: Rutgers Center of Alcohol Studies.

McCubbin, H. I., McCubbin, M. A., Thompson, A. I., & Han, S. Y. (1999). Contextualizing family risk factors for alcoholism and alcohol abuse. *Journal of Studies on Alcohol* (Suppl. 13), 75–78.

McGrath, C. E., Watson, A. L., & Chassin, L. (1999). Academic achievement in adolescent children of alcoholics. *Journal of Studies on Alcohol, 60*(1), 18–26.

McGue, M., Iacono, W. G., Legrand, L. N., Malone, S., & Elkins, I. (2001). Origins and consequences of age at first drink: I. Associations with substance-use disorders, disinhibitory behavior and psychopathology, and P3 amplitude. *Alcoholism: Clinical and Experimental Research, 25*(8), 1156–1165.

McGue, M., Sharma, A., & Benson, P. (1996). Parent and sibling influence on adolescent alcohol use and misuse: Evidence from a U.S. adoption cohort. *Journal of Studies on Alcohol, 57,* 8–18.

McKay, J. (1999). Studies of factors in relapse to alcohol, drug and nicotine use: A critical review of methodologies and findings. *Journal of Studies on Alcohol, 60*(4), 566–576.

McKay, J. R., Franklin, T. R., Patapis, N., & Lynch, K. G. (2006). Conceptual, methodological, and analytical issues in the study of relapse. *Clinical Psychology Review, 26*(2), 109–127.

McKee, S. A., Nhean, S., Hinson, R. E., & Mase, T. (2006). Smoking for weight control: Effect of priming for body image in female restrained eaters. *Addictive Behaviors, 31*(1), 2319–2323.

McKim, W. A. (2007). *Drugs and behavior: An introduction to behavioral pharmacology* (6th ed.). Upper Saddle River, NJ: Pearson Prentice Hall.

McMahon, J., & Jones, B. T. (1994). Social drinkers' negative alcohol expectancy relates to their satisfaction with current consumption: Measuring motivation for change with the NAEQ. *Alcohol and Alcoholism, 29*(6), 687–690.

McMillen, D. L., Adams, M. S., Wells Parker, E., Pang, M. G., & Anderson, B. J. (1992). Personality traits and behaviors of alcohol-impaired drivers: A comparison of first and multiple offenders. *Addictive Behaviors, 17*(5), 407–414.

Mechoulam, R., Hanus, L., & Martin, B. R. (1994). Search for endogenous ligands of the cannabinoid receptor. *Biochemical Pharmacology, 48,* 1537–1544.

Meilman, P. W. (1993). Alcohol-induced sexual behavior on campus. *Journal of American College Health, 42*(1), 27–31.

Meilman, P. W., Stone, J. E., Gaylor, M. S., & Turco, J. H. (1990). Alcohol consumption by college undergraduates: Current use and 10-year trends. *Journal of Studies on Alcohol, 51,* 389–395.

Mello, N. K., Mendelson, J. H., & Lex, B. W. (1990). Alcohol use and premenstrual symptoms in social drinkers. *Psychopharmacology, 101,* 448–455.

Mello, N. K., Mendelson, J. H., & Teoh, S. K. (1993). An overview of the effects of alcohol on neuroendocrine function in women. In S. Zakhari (Ed.), *Alcohol and the endocrine system* (Research Monograph No. 23, NIH Publication No. 93–3533, pp. 139–169). Bethesda, MD: National Institute on Alcohol Abuse and Alcoholism.

Melnick, G., De Leon, G., Hiller, M. L., & Knight, K. (2000). Therapeutic communities: Diversity in treatment elements. *Substance Use and Misuse, 35*(12–14), 1819–1847.

Merikangas, K. R., Stolar, M., Stevens, D. E., Goulet, J., Preisig, M. A., Fenton, B., et al. (1998). Familial transmission of substance use disorders. *Archives of General Psychiatry, 55,* 973–979.

Metten, P., & Crabbe, J. C. (1996). Dependence and withdrawal. In R. A. Deitrich & V. G. Ervin (Eds.), *Pharmacological effects of ethanol on the nervous system* (pp. 269–290). Boca Raton, FL: CRC Press.

Meyerhoff, D. J. (2001). Effects of alcohol and HIV infection on the central nervous system. *Alcohol Research and Health, 25*(4), 288–298.

Midanik, L., & Clark, W. B. (1994). The demographic distribution of US drinking patterns in 1990: Description and trends from 1984. *American Journal of Public Health, 84,* 1218–1122.

Midanik, L. T., Klatsky, A. L., & Armstrong, M. A. (1989). A comparison of 7-day recall with two summary measures of alcohol use. *Drug and Alcohol Dependence, 24,* 127–134.

Midanik, L. T., Tam, T. W., & Weisner, C. (2007). Concurrent and simultaneous drug and alcohol use: Results of the 2000 National Alcohol Survey. *Drug and Alcohol Dependence, 90,* 72–80.

Miller, B. A., & Downs, W. R. (1993). The impact of family violence on the use of alcohol by women [Special issue: Alcohol, aggression, and injury]. *Alcohol Health & Research World, 17*(2), 137–143.

Miller, B. A., Downs, W. R., & Gondoli, D. M. (1989). Spousal violence among alcoholic women as compared to a random household sample of women. *Journal of Studies on Alcohol, 50,* 533–540.

Miller, B. A., Downs, W. R., & Testa, M. (1993). Interrelationships between victimization experiences and women's alcohol use. *Journal of Studies on Alcohol* (Suppl. 11), 109–117.

Miller, B. A., Maguin, E., & Downs, W. R. (1997). Alcohol, drugs, and violence in children's lives. In M. Galanter (Ed.), *Recent developments in alcoholism* (Vol. 13, pp. 357–385). New York: Plenum.

Miller, B. A., Smyth, N. J., & Mudar, P. J. (1999). Mothers' alcohol and other drug problems and their punitiveness toward their children. *Journal of Studies on Alcohol, 60,* 632–642.

Miller, M. M. (1998). Traditional approaches to the treatment of addiction. In A. W. Graham & T. K. Schultz (Eds.), *Principles of addiction medicine* (2nd ed., pp. 315–326). Chevy Chase, MD: American Society of Addiction Medicine.

Miller, N. S., & Gold, M. S. (1994). Dissociation of conscious desire (craving) from and relapse in alcohol and cocaine dependence. *Annals of Clinical Psychiatry, 6,* 99–106.

Miller, P. M., Smith, G. T., & Goldman, M. S. (1990). Emergence of alcohol expectations in childhood: A possible critical period. *Journal of Studies on Alcohol, 51,* 343–349.

Miller, T. R., Levy, D. T., Spicer, R. S., & Taylor, D. M. (2006). Societal costs of underage drinking. *Journal of Studies on Alcohol, 67*(4), 519–528.

Miller, W. R. (1990). Alcohol treatment alternatives: What works? In H. B. Milkman & L. I. Sederer (Eds.), *Treatment choices for alcoholism and substance abuse* (pp. 253–264). Lexington, MA: Lexington Books.

Miller, W. R. (1996). Motivational interviewing: Research, practice, and puzzles. *Addictive Behaviors, 21*(6), 835–842.

Miller, W. R., Brown, J. M., Simpson, T. L., Handmaker, N. S., Bien, T. H., Luckie, L. F., et al. (1995). What works? A methodological analysis of the alcohol treatment outcome literature. In R. K. Hester & W. R. Miller (Eds.), *Handbook of alcoholism treatment approaches: Effective alternatives* (2nd ed., pp. 12–44). Needham Heights, MA: Allyn & Bacon.

Miller, W. R., & Hester, R. K. (1986). Matching problem drinkers with optimal treatments. In W. R. Miller & N. Heather (Eds.), *The addictive behaviors: Processes of change* (pp. 175–203). New York: Plenum.

Miller, W. R., Leckman, A. L., Delaney, H. D., & Tinkcom, M. (1992). Long-term follow-up of behavioral self-control training. *Journal of Studies on Alcohol, 53,* 249–261.

Miller, W. R., Zweben, D. S. W., DiClemente, C. C., & Rychtarik, R. G. (1995). *Motivational enhancement therapy manual* (Vol. 2). Rockville, MD: National Institute on Alcohol Abuse and Alcoholism.

Miller-Tutzauer, C., Leonard, K. E., & Windle, M. (1991). Marriage and alcohol use: A longitudinal study of "maturing out." *Journal of Studies on Alcohol, 52,* 434–440.

Mohler-Kuo, M., Rehm, J., Heeb, J. L., & Gmel, G. (2004). Decreased taxation, spirits consumption and alcohol-related problems in Switzerland. *Journal of Studies on Alcohol, 65*(2), 266–273.

Molina, B. S., Pelham, W. E., Gnagy, E. M., Thompson, A. L., & Marshal, M. P. (2007). Attention-deficit/hyperactivity disorder risk for heavy drinking and alcohol use disorder is age specific. *Alcoholism: Clinical and Experimental Research, 31*(4), 643–654.

Moncrieff, J., & Farmer, R. (1998). Sexual abuse and the subsequent development of alcohol problems. *Alcohol and Alcoholism, 33*(6), 592–601.

Monti, P. M., Rohsenow, D. J., Swift, R. M., Gulliver, S. B., Colby, S. M., Mueller, T. I., et al. (2001). Naltrexone and cue exposure with coping and communication skills training for alcoholics: Treatment process and 1-year outcomes. *Alcoholism: Clinical and Experimental Research, 25*(11), 1634–1647.

Moore, A. A., Gould, R., Reuben, D. B., Greendale, G. A., Carter, M. K., Zhou, K., et al. (2005). Longitudinal patterns and predictors of alcohol consumption in the United States. *American Journal of Public Health, 95*(3), 458–465.

Moore, K. L., & Persaud, T. V. N. (1993). The Developing Human (3rd ed.), Philadelphia: W. B. Saunders.

Moos, R., Brennan, P., & Schutte, K. (1998). Life context factors, treatment, and late-life drinking behavior. In Department of Health and Human Services (Ed.), *Alcohol problems and aging* (pp. 261–280). Washington, DC: U.S. Government Printing Office.

Moos, R. H., & Billings, A. G. (1982). Children of alcoholics during the recovery process: Alcoholic and matched control families. *Addictive Behaviors, 7*, 155–163.

Moos, R. H., Finney, J. W., & Chan, A. D. (1981). The process of recovery from alcoholism: I. Comparing alcoholic patients and matched community controls. *Journal of Studies on Alcohol, 42*, 383–402.

Moos, R. H., & Moos, B. S. (2005). Paths of entry into Alcoholics Anonymous: Consequences for participation and remission. *Alcoholism: Clinical and Experimental Research, 29*(10), 1858–1868.

Moos, R. H., & Moos, B. S. (2006). Rates and predictors of relapse after natural and treated remission from alcohol use disorders. *Addiction, 101*(2), 212–222.

Morgenstern, J., & Longabaugh, R. (2000). Cognitive-behavioral treatment for alcohol dependence: A review of evidence for its hypothesized mechanisms of action. *Addiction, 95*(10), 1475–1490.

Morgenstern, J., & McCrady, B. S. (1993). Cognitive processes and change in disease-model treatment. In B. S. McCrady & W. R. Miller (Eds.), *Research on Alcoholics Anonymous: Opportunities and alternatives* (pp. 153–166). Piscataway, NJ: Rutgers Center of Alcohol Studies.

Morgenstern, J., & McKay, J. R. (2007). Rethinking the paradigms that inform behavioral treatment research for substance use disorders. *Addiction, 102*(9), 1377–1389.

Morissette, S. B., Gulliver, S. B., Kamholz, B. W., Duade, J., Farchione, T., Devine, E., et al. (2008). Differences between daily smokers, chippers, and nonsmokers with co-occurring anxiety and alcohol-use disorders. *Addictive Behaviors, 33*(11), 1425–1431.

Moselhy, H. F., Georgiou, G., & Kahn, A. (2001). Frontal lobe changes in alcoholism: A review of the literature. *Alcohol and Alcoholism, 36*(5), 357–368.

Mosher, J. F., & Jernigan, D. H. (1989). New directions in alcohol policy. In L. Breslow, J. E. Fielding, & L. B. Lave (Eds.), *Annual review of public health* (Vol. 10, pp. 245–279). Palo Alto, CA: Annual Reviews.

Moskowitz, H., Burns, M. M., & Williams, A. F. (1985). Skills performance at low blood alcohol levels. *Journal of Studies on Alcohol, 46*, 482–485.

Moss, H. B., Chen, C. M., & Yi, H. Y. (2007). Subtypes of alcohol dependence in a nationally representative sample. *Drug and Alcohol Dependence, 91*(2–3), 149–158.

Moss, H. B., Chen, C. M., & Yi, H. Y. (2008). DSM-IV criteria endorsement patterns in alcohol dependence: Relationship to severity. *Alcoholism: Clinical and Experimental Research, 32*(2), 306–313.

Mudar, P., Leonard, K. E., & Soltysinski, K. (2001). Discrepant substance use and marital functioning in newlywed couples. *Journal of Consulting and Clinical Psychology, 69*, 130–134.

Mulia, N., Ye, Y., Zemore, S. E., & Greenfield, T. K. (2008). Social disadvantage, distress, and alcohol use among Black, Hispanic, and White Americans: Findings from the 2005 U.S. National Alcohol Survey. *Journal of Studies on Alcohol, 69*, 441–448.

Mumenthaler, M. S., Taylor, J. L., O'Hara, R., & Yesavage, J. A. (1999). Gender differences in moderate drinking effects. *Alcohol Research and Health, 23*(1), 55–64.

Mumola, C. J. (1999). Substance abuse and treatment, state and federal prisoners, 1997. In *Bureau of Justice Statistics special report* (p. 1). Washington, DC: U.S. Department of Justice.

Mumola, C. J., & Karberg, J. C. (2006). Substance abuse and treatment, state and federal prisoners, 2004. In *Bureau of Justice Statistics special report* (p. 1). Washington, DC: U.S. Department of Justice.

Muraven, M., & Baumeister, R. F. (2000). Self-regulation and depletion of limited resources: Does self-control resemble a muscle? *Psychological Bulletin, 126*(2), 247–259.

Muraven, M., Collins, R. L., Morsheimer, E. T., Shiffman, S., & Paty, J. A. (2005). The morning after: Limit violations and the self-regulation of alcohol consumption. *Psychology of Addictive Behaviors, 19*(3), 253–262.

Muraven, M., Collins, R. L., & Nienhaus, K. (2002). Self-control and alcohol restraint: An initial application of the self-control strength model. *Psychology of Addictive Behaviors, 16*(2), 113–120.

Murdoch, D., Pihl, R. O., & Ross, D. (1990). Alcohol and crimes of violence: Present issues. *International Journal of the Addictions, 25,* 1065–1081.

Murphy, C. M., & O'Farrell, T. J. (1994). Factors associated with marital aggression in male alcoholics. *Journal of Family Psychology, 8,* 321–335.

Murphy, C. M., & O'Farrell, T. J. (1996). Marital violence among alcoholics. *Current Directions in Psychological Science, 5,* 183–186.

Murphy, C. M., & O'Farrell, T. J. (1997). Couple communication patterns of maritally aggressive and nonaggressive male alcoholics. *Journal of Studies on Alcohol, 58,* 83–90.

Murray, A. L., & Lawrence, P. S. (1984). Sequelae to smoking cessation. *Clinical Psychology Review, 4,* 143–157.

Musto, D. F. (1987). *The American disease: Origins of narcotic control* (Expanded ed.). New York: Oxford University Press.

Nadelmann, E. A. (1997). Drug prohibition in the U.S.: Costs, consequences, and alternatives. In C. Reinarman & H. G. Levine (Eds.), *Crack in America: Demon drugs and social justice* (pp. 288–316). Berkeley: University of California Press.

Nagoshi, C. T., & Wilson, J. R. (1987). Influence of family alcoholism history on alcohol metabolism, sensitivity, and tolerance. *Alcoholism: Clinical and Experimental Research, 11,* 392–398.

Naimi, T. S., Brewer, R. D., Mokdad, A., Denny, C., Serdula, M. K., & Marks, J. S. (2003). Binge drinking among US adults. *JAMA, 289,* 70–75.

National Institute on Alcohol Abuse and Alcoholism. (1981). *Indian clients treated in NIAAA-funded programs.* Rockville, MD: Author.

National Institute on Alcohol Abuse and Alcoholism. (1990). *Seventh special report to U.S. Congress.* Washington, DC: U.S. Government Printing Office.

National Institute on Alcohol Abuse and Alcoholism. (1997). Matching alcoholism treatments to client heterogeneity: Project MATCH posttreatment drinking outcomes. *Journal of Studies on Alcohol, 58,* 7–29.

National Institute on Alcohol Abuse and Alcoholism. (1998). Drinking in the United States: Main findings from the 1992 National Longitudinal Alcohol Epidemiologic Survey (NLAES). In *U.S. alcohol epidemiologic data reference manual* (NIH Publication No. 99-3519, 1st ed., Vol. 6). Bethesda, MD: Author.

National Institute on Alcohol Abuse and Alcoholism. (2008). Parts of the brain involved in alcohol/nicotine dependence and psychiatric disorders. Rockville, MD. Available at http://www.niaaa.nih.gov/Resources/GraphicsGallery/Neuroscience/brain_psychiatricdisorders.htm

National Institute on Drug Abuse. (2006). *Methamphetamine: Abuse and addiction.* Bethesda, MD: Author.

Neff, J. A., Prihoda, T. J., & Hoppe, S. K. (1991). "Machismo," self-esteem, education and high maximum drinking among Anglo, Black and Mexican-American male drinkers. *Journal of Studies on Alcohol, 52*(5), 458–463.

Nehlig, A. (1999). Are we dependent upon coffee and caffeine? A review on human and animal data. *Neuroscience Biobehavioral Review, 23*(4), 563–576.

Neighbors, C., Dillard, A. J., Lewis, M. A., Bergstrom, R. L., & Neil, T. A. (2006). Normative misperceptions and temporal precedence of perceived norms and drinking. *Journal of Studies on Alcohol, 67*(2), 290–299.

Neighbors, C., Lee, C. M., Lewis, M. A., Fossos, N., & Larimer, M. E. (2007). Are social norms the best predictor of outcomes among heavy-drinking college students? *Journal of Studies on Alcohol and Drugs, 68*(4), 556–565.

Nephew, T. M., Williams, G. D., Yi, H.-Y., Hoy, A. K., Stinson, F. S., & Dufour, M. C. (2003). *Apparent per capita alcohol consumption: National, state, and regional trends, 1977–2000* (Surveillance Report No. 62). Rockville, MD: National Institute on Alcohol Abuse and Alcoholism.

Newlin, D. B., & Thomson, J. B. (1990). Alcohol challenge with sons of alcoholics: A critical review and analysis. *Psychological Bulletin, 108,* 383–402.

Newlin, D. B., & Thomson, J. B. (1991). Chronic tolerance and sensitization to alcohol in sons of alcoholics. *Alcoholism: Clinical and Experimental Research, 15*(3), 399–405.

Newlin, D. B., & Thomson, J. B. (1999). Chronic tolerance and sensitization to alcohol in sons of alcoholics: II. Replication and reanalysis. *Experimental and Clinical Psychopharmacology, 7*(3), 234–243.

NIDA/NIAAA. (1990). *National Drug and Alcoholism Treatment Unit Survey (NDATUS) 1989: Main findings report.* Rockville, MD: Author.

Nixon, S. J. (1995). Assessing cognitive impairment. *Alcohol Health & Research World, 19,* 97–103.

Nixon, S. J., Lawton-Craddock, A., Tivis, R., & Ceballos, N. (2007). Nicotine's effects on attentional efficiency in alcoholics. *Alcoholism: Clinical and Experimental Research, 31*(12), 2083–2091.

Nixon, S. J., & Parsons, O. A. (1991). Alcohol-related efficiency deficits using an ecologically valid test. *Alcoholism: Clinical and Experimental Research, 15,* 601–606.

Nixon, S. J., Tivis, R., & Parsons, O. A. (1995). Behavioral dysfunction and cognitive efficiency in male and female alcoholics. *Alcoholism Clinical and Experimental Research, 19*(3), 577–581.

Nochajski, T. H., & Stasiewicz, P. R. (2006). Relapse to driving under the influence (DUI): A review. *Clinical Psychology Review, 26*(2), 179–195.

Nolen-Hoeksema, S. (2004). Gender differences in risk factors and consequences for alcohol use and problems. *Clinical Psychology Review, 24,* 981–1010.

Norris, J., & Kerr, K. L. (1993). Alcohol and violent pornography: Responses to permissive and nonpermissive cues. *Journal of Studies on Alcohol* (Suppl. 11), 118–127.

Nurnberger, J. I., Jr., Wiegand, R., Bucholz, K., O'Connor, S., Meyer, E. T., Reich, T., et al. (2004). A family study of alcohol dependence: Coaggregation of multiple disorders in relatives of alcohol-dependent probands. *Archives of General Psychiatry, 61*(12), 1246–1256.

O'Connell, J. M., Novins, D. K., Beals, J., & Spicer, P. (2005). Disparities in patterns of alcohol use among reservation-based and geographically dispersed American Indian populations. *Alcoholism: Clinical and Experimental Research, 29*(1), 107–116.

O'Farrell, T., & Murphy, C. M. (1995). Marital violence before and after alcoholism treatment. *Journal of Consulting and Clinical Psychology, 63,* 256–262.

O'Farrell, T. J. (1995). Marital and family therapy. In R. K. Hester & W. R. Miller (Eds.), *Handbook of alcoholism treatment approaches: Effective alternatives.* (2nd ed., pp. 195–220). Needham Heights, MA: Allyn & Bacon.

O'Farrell, T. J., Choquette, K. A., Cutter, H. S., & Birchler, G. R. (1997). Sexual satisfaction and dysfunction in marriages of male alcoholics: Comparison with nonalcoholic maritally conflicted and nonconflicted couples. *Journal of Studies on Alcohol, 58*(1), 91–99.

O'Farrell, T. J., Van Hutton, V., & Murphy, C. M. (1999). Domestic violence before and after alcoholism treatment: A two-year longitudinal study. *Journal of Studies on Alcohol, 60*(3), 317–321.

O'Malley, P. M., & Johnston, L. D. (2002). Epidemiology of alcohol and other drug use among American college students. *Journal of Studies on Alcohol* (Suppl. 14), 23–39.

O'Malley, S. S., Jaffe, A. J., Chang, G., Schottenfeld, R. S., Meyer, R. E., & Rounsaville, B. (1992). Naltrexone and coping skills therapy for alcohol dependence: A controlled study. *Archives of General Psychiatry, 49,* 881–887.

Oetting, E. R., & Beauvais, F. (1987). Peer cluster theory, socialization characteristics, and adolescent drug use: A path analysis. *Journal of Counseling Psychology, 34,* 205–213.

Oetting, E. R., Deffenbacher, J. L., & Donnermeyer, J. F. (1998). Primary socialization theory: The role played by personal traits in the etiology of drug use and deviance. II. *Substance Use and Misuse, 33*(6), 1337–1366.

Oetting, E. R., & Donnermeyer, J. F. (1998). Primary socialization theory: The etiology of drug use and deviance. I. *Substance Use and Misuse, 33*(4), 995–1026.

Oetting, E. R., Donnermeyer, J. F., & Deffenbacher, J. L. (1998). Primary socialization theory: The influence of the community on drug use and deviance. III. *Substance Use and Misuse, 33*(8), 1629–1665.

Office of National Drug Control Policy. (2001). *The economic costs of drug abuse in the United States, 1992–1998* (Publication No. NCJ-190636). Washington, DC: Executive Office of the President.

Office of Substance Abuse Prevention. (1989). *Prevention plus II: Tools for creating and sustaining drug free communities* (DHHS Publication No. ADM 89-1649). Washington, DC: U.S. Government Printing Office.

Ogborne, A. C. (1993). Assessing the effectiveness of Alcoholics Anonymous in the community: Meeting the challenges. In B. S. McCrady & W. R. Miller (Eds.), *Research on Alcoholics Anonymous: Opportunities and alternatives* (pp. 339–356). Piscataway, NJ: Rutgers Center of Alcohol Studies.

Ogborne, A. C., & Glaser, F. (1981). Characteristics of affiliates of Alcoholics Anonymous. *Journal of Studies on Alcohol, 42,* 661–675.

Ohannessian, C. M., Hesselbrock, V. M., Kramer, J., Kuperman, S., Bucholz, K. K., Schuckit, M. A., et al. (2004). The relationship between parental alcoholism and adolescent psychopathology: A systematic examination of parental comorbid psychopathology. *Journal of Abnormal Child Psychology, 32*(5), 519–533.

Olenick, N. L., & Chalmers, D. K. (1991). Gender specific drinking styles in alcoholics and nonalcoholics. *Journal of Studies on Alcohol, 52,* 325–330.

Orford, J., & Edwards, G. (1977). *Alcoholism: A comparison of treatment and advice, with a study of the influence of marriage.* Oxford, England: Oxford University Press.

Orford, J., Hodgson, R., Copello, A., John, B., Smith, M., Black, R., et al. (2005). The clients' perspective on change during treatment for an alcohol problem: Qualitative analysis of follow-up interviews in the UK Alcohol Treatment Trial. *Addiction, 101,* 60–68.

Orford, J., & Velleman, R. (1991). The environmental intergenerational transmission of alcohol problems: A comparison of two hypotheses. *British Journal of Medical Psychology, 64*(2), 189–200.

Ornstein, S., & Levy, D. (1983). Price and income elasticities of demand for alcoholic beverages. In M. Galanter (Ed.), *Recent developments in alcoholism* (Vol. I, pp. 303–345). New York: Plenum.

Oscar-Berman, M. (2000). Neuropsychological vulnerabilities in chronic alcoholism. In A. Noronha, M. J. Eckardt, & K. Warren (Eds.), *Review of NIAAA's Neuroscience and Behavioral Research Portfolio* (Research Monograph No. 34, pp. 437–471). Bethesda, MD: National Institute on Alcohol Abuse and Alcoholism.

Oscar-Berman, M., & Marinlovic, K. (2003). Alcoholism and the brain: An overview. *Alcohol Research and Health, 27*(2), 125–133.

Ostafin, B. D., Marlatt, G. A., & Greenwald, A. G. (2008). Drinking without thinking: An implicit measure of alcohol motivation predicts failure to control alcohol use. *Behaviour Research and Therapy, 46,* 1210–1219.

Palfai, T. P., Monti, P. M., Colby, S. M., & Rohsenow, D. J. (1997). Effects of suppressing the urge to drink on the accessibility of alcohol outcome expectancies. *Behaviour Research and Therapy, 35,* 59–65.

Pandey, G. N., Fawcett, J., Gibbons, R., Clark, C. D., & Davis, J. M. (1988). Platelet monoamine oxidase in alcoholism. *Biological Psychiatry, 24,* 15–24.

Parker, D. A., & Harford, T. C. (1992). Gender-role attitudes, job competition and alcohol consumption among women and men. Meeting of the Research Society of Alcoholism: Life transitions and alcohol consumption: Work-related issues (1992, San Diego, California). *Alcoholism Clinical and Experimental Research, 16*(2), 159–165.

Parrott, A. C. (1995). Stress modulation over the day in cigarette smokers. *Addiction, 90*(2), 233–244.

Parrott, A. C., & Garnham, N. J. (1998). Comparative mood states and cognitive skills of cigarette smokers, deprived smokers and nonsmokers. *Human Psychopharmacology Clinical and Experimental, 13*(5), 367–376.

Parsons, O. A. (1993). Impaired neuropsychological cognitive functioning in sober alcoholics. In W. A. Hunt & S. J. Nixon (Eds.), *Alcohol-induced brain damage* (Research Monograph No. 22, NIH Pub. No. 93–3549, pp. 173–194). Bethesda, MD: National Institute on Alcohol Abuse and Alcoholism.

Parsons, O. A., & Nixon, S. J. (1998). Cognitive functioning in sober social drinkers: A review of the research since 1986. *Journal of Studies on Alcohol, 59*(2), 180–190.

Partanen, J., Bruun, K., & Markkaners, T. (1966). *Inheritance of drinking behavior: A study on intelligence, personality, and use of alcohol of adult twins.* Helsinki, Finland: Finnish Foundation for Alcohol.

Patterson, B. W., Williams, H. L., McLean, G. A., Smith, L. T., & Schaffer, K. W. (1987). Alcoholism and family history of alcoholism: Effects on visual and auditory event-related potentials. *Alcohol, 4,* 265–269.

Paul, J. P., Stall, R., & Bloomfield, K. A. (1991). Gay and alcoholic: Epidemiologic and clinical issues [Special issue: Alcohol and sexuality]. *Alcohol Health & Research World, 15*(2), 151–160.

Paul, J. P., Stall, R. D., Crosby, G. M., Barrett, D. C., & Midanik, L. (1994). Correlates of sexual risk-taking among gay male substance abusers. *Addiction, 89*(8), 971–983.

Pavlov, I. P. (1927). *Conditioned reflexes.* London: Oxford University Press.

Peele, S. (1989). *Diseasing of America: Addiction treatment out of control.* Lexington, MA: Lexington Books.

Peirce, R. S., Frone, M. R., Russell, M., Cooper, M. L., & Mudar, P. (2000). A longitudinal model of social contact, social support, depression, and alcohol use. *Health Psychology, 19*(1), 28–38.

Penick, E. C., Powell, B. J., Bingham, S. F., Liskow, B. I., Miller, N. S., & Read, M. R. (1987). A comparative study of familial alcoholism. *Journal of Studies on Alcohol, 48,* 136–146.

Pennings, E. J., Leccese, A. P., & Wolff, F. A. (2002). Effects of concurrent use of alcohol and cocaine. *Addiction, 97*(7), 773–783.

Pentz, M. A. (1995). Prevention research in multiethnic communities. In G. J. Botvin, S. Schinke, & M. A. Orlandi (Eds.), *Drug abuse prevention with multiethnic youth* (pp. 193–214). Thousand Oaks, CA: Sage.

Perkins, H. W., & Craig, D. W. (2006). A successful social norms campaign to reduce alcohol misuse among college student-athletes. *Journal of Studies on Alcohol, 67,* 880–889.

Perkins, K. A., Ciccocioppo, M., Conklin, C. A., Milanak, M. E., Grottenthaler, A., & Sayette, M. A. (2008). Mood influences on acute smoking responses are independent of nicotine intake and dose expectancy. *Journal of Abnormal Psychology, 117*(1), 79–93.

Perkins, K. A., Epstein, L. H., Sexton, J. E., Stiller, R. L., & Jacob, R. G. (1991). Effects of dose, gender, and level of physical activity on acute metabolic response to nicotine. *Pharmacology Biochemistry and Behavior, 40*(2), 203–208.

Pernanen, K. (1991). *Alcohol and human violence.* New York: Guilford.

Perrine, M. W. (1990). Who are the drinking drivers? The spectrum of drinking drivers revisited. *Alcohol Health & Research World, 14*(1), 26–35.

Pert, C., & Snyder, S. H. (1973). Opiate receptor: Demonstration in central nervous system tissue. *Science, 179,* 1011–1014.

Peterson, P. L., Hawkins, J. D., Abbott, R. D., & Catalano, R. F. (1994). Disentangling the effects of parental drinking, family management, and parental alcohol norms on current drinking by Black and White adolescents [Special issue: Preventing alcohol abuse among adolescents: Preintervention and intervention research]. *Journal of Research on Adolescence, 4*(2), 203–227.

Petrakis, I. L., Gonzales, G., Rosenheck, R., & Krystal, J. H. (2002). Comorbidity of alcoholism and psychiatric disorders: An overview. *Alcohol Research and Health, 26,* 81–89.

Petry, N. M., Martin, B., Cooney, J. L., & Kranzler, H. R. (2000). Give them prizes, and they will come: Contingency management for treatment of alcohol dependence. *Journal of Consulting and Clinical Psychology, 68*(2), 250–257.

Pettinati, H. M., O'Brien, C. P., Rabinowitz, A. R., Wortman, S. M., Oslin, D. W., Kampman, K. M., et al. (2006). The status of naltrexone in the treatment of alcohol dependence: Specific effects on heavy drinking. *Journal of Clinical Psychopharmacology, 26,* 610–625.

Pfefferbaum, A., Desmond, J. E., Galloway, C., Menon, V., Glover, G. H., & Sullivan, E. V. (2001). Reorganization of frontal systems used by alcoholics for spatial working memory: An fMRI study. *Neuroimage, 14*(1 Pt 1), 7–20.

Pfefferbaum, A., Rosenbloom, M., & Sullivan, E. V. (2002). Alcoholism and AIDS: Magnetic resonance imaging approaches for detecting interactive neuropathology. *Alcoholism: Clinical and Experimental Research, 26*(7), 1031–1046.

Pfefferbaum, A., & Rosenbloom, M. J. (1990). Brain-imaging tools for the study of alcoholism. *Alcohol Health and Research World, 14*(3), 219–231.

Phillips, S., Matusko, J., & Tomasovic, E. (2007). Reconsidering the relationship between alcohol and lethal violence. *Journal of Interpersonal Violence, 22*(1), 66–84.

Pickens, R. W., Svikis, D. S., McGue, M., Lykken, D. T., Heston, L. L., & Clayton, P. J. (1991). Heterogeneity in the inheritance of alcoholism: A study of male and female twins. *Archives of General Psychiatry, 48,* 19–28.

Pierce, J. P., Fiore, M. C., Novotny, T. E., Hatziandreu, E. J., & Davis, R. M. (1989). Trends in cigarette smoking in the United States: Projections to the year 2000. *JAMA, 261*(1), 61–65.

Pihl, R. O., Paylan, S. S., Gentes-Hawn, A., & Hoaken, P. N. S. (2003). Alcohol affects executive cognitive functioning differentially on the ascending versus descending limb of the blood alcohol concentration curve. *Alcoholism: Clinical and Experimental Research, 27*(5), 773–780.

Pihl, R. O., Peterson, J., & Finn, P. (1990a). An heuristic model for the inherited predisposition to alcoholism. *Psychology of Addictive Behaviors, 4,* 12–25.

Pihl, R. O., Peterson, J., & Finn, P. (1990b). Inherited predisposition to alcoholism: Characteristics of sons of male alcoholics. *Journal of Abnormal Psychology, 99,* 291–301.

Polacsek, M., Rogers, E. M., Woodall, W. G., Delaney, H., Wheeler, D., & Rao, N. (2001). MADD victim impact panels and stages-of-change in drunk-driving prevention. *Journal of Studies on Alcohol, 62*(3), 344–350.

Pomerleau, C. S., Cole, P. A., Lumley, M. A., Marks, J. L., & Pomerleau, O. F. (1994). Effects of menstrual phase on nicotine, alcohol, and caffeine intake in smokers. *Journal of Substance Abuse, 6*(2), 227–234.

Pomerleau, C. S., Pomerleau, O. F., & Garcia, A. W. (1991). Biobehavioral research on nicotine use in women [Special issue: Future directions in tobacco research]. *British Journal of Addiction, 86*(5), 527–531.

Pontieri, F. E., Tanda, G., Orzi, F., & Di Chiara, G. (1996). Effects of nicotine on the nucleus accumbens and similarity to those of addictive drugs [see comments]. *Nature, 382,* 255–257.

Porjesz, B., & Begleiter, H. (2003). Alcoholism and human electrophysiology. *Alcohol Research and Health, 27*(2), 153–160.

Porjesz, B., Begleiter, H., Reich, T., Van Eerdewegh, P., Edenberg, H. J., Foroud, T., et al. (1998). Amplitude of visual P3 event-related potential as a phenotypic marker for a predisposition to alcoholism: Preliminary results from the COGA project: Collaborative Study on the Genetics of Alcoholism. *Alcoholism: Clinical and Experimental Research, 22,* 1317–1323.

Power, C., Rodgers, B., & Hope, S. (1999). Heavy alcohol consumption and marital status: Disentangling the relationship in a national study of young adults. *Addiction, 94*(10), 1477–1487.

Prescott, C. A., Cross, R. J., Kuhn, J. W., Horn, J. L., & Kendler, K. S. (2004). Is risk for alcoholism mediated by individual differences in drinking motivations? *Alcoholism: Clinical and Experimental Research, 28*(1), 29–40.

Prescott, C. A., & Kendler, K. S. (1995). Twin study design. *Alcohol Health and Research World, 19,* 200–205.

Prest, L. A., Benson, M. J., & Protinsky, H. O. (1998). Family of origin and current relationship influences on codependency. *Family Process, 37*(4), 513–528.

Prochaska, J. O., DiClemente, C. C., & Norcross, J. C. (1992). In search of how people change: Applications to addictive behaviors. *American Psychologist, 47,* 1102–1114.

Project MATCH Research Group. (1997). Matching alcoholism treatments to client heterogeneity: Project MATCH posttreatment drinking outcomes. *Journal of Studies on Alcohol, 58*(1), 7–29.

Project MATCH Research Group. (1998). Matching alcoholism treatments to client heterogeneity: Treatment main effects and matching effects on drinking during treatment. *Journal of Studies on Alcohol, 59*(6), 631–639.

Rachman, S., & Teasdale, J. (1969). *Aversion therapy: Appraisal and status.* Coral Gables, FL: University of Miami Press.

Raffaelli, M., Stone, R. A. T., Iturbide, M. I., McGinley, M., Carlo, G., & Crockett, L. J. (2007). Acculturation, gender, and alcohol use among Mexican American college students. *Addictive Behaviors, 32,* 2187–2199.

Ramirez, R. A., & de la Cruz, G. P. (2002). *The Hispanic population in the United States: March current population reports.* Washington, DC: U.S. Census Bureau.

Ramo, D. E., Anderson, K. G., Tate, S. R., & Brown, S. A. (2005). Characteristics of relapse to substance use in comorbid adolescents. *Addictive Behaviors, 30*(9), 1811–1823.

Ramo, D. E., & Brown, S. A. (2008). Classes of substance abuse relapse situations: A comparison of adolescents and adults. *Psychology of Addictive Behaviors, 22*(3), 372–379.

Randall, C. L., Roberts, J. S., Del Boca, F. K., Carroll, K. M., Connors, G. J., & Mattson, M. E. (1999). Telescoping of landmark events associated with drinking: A gender comparison. *Journal of Studies on Alcohol, 60,* 252–260.

Randolph, W. M., Stroup-Benham, C., Black, S. A., & Markides, K. S. (1998). Alcohol use among Cuban-Americans, Mexican-Americans, and Puerto Ricans. *Alcohol Health & Research World, 22*(4), 265–269.

Rangarajan, S. (2008). Mediators and moderators of parental alcoholism effects on offspring self-esteem. *Alcohol and Alcoholism, 43*(4), 481–491.

Reed, M. B., Wang, R., Shillington, A. M., Clapp, J. D., & Lange, J. E. (2007). The relationship between alcohol use and cigarette smoking in a sample of undergraduate college students. *Addictive Behaviors, 32,* 449–464.

Reed, R. J., Grant, I., & Rourke, S. B. (1992). Long-term abstinent alcoholics have normal memory. *Alcoholism Clinical and Experimental Research, 16*(4), 677–683.

Regan, T. J. (1990). Alcohol and the cardiovascular system. *JAMA, 264,* 377–381.

Regier, D. A., Myers, J. K., Kramer, M., Robins, L. N., Blazer, D. G., Hough, R. L., et al. (1984). The NIMH Epidemiologic Catchment Area program: Historical context, major objectives, and study population characteristics. *Archives of General Psychiatry, 41,* 934–941.

Rehm, J. (2000). Alcohol intake assessment: The sober facts. *American Journal of Epidemiology, 151,* 436–438.

Rehm, J., Ashley, M. J., Room, R., Single, E., Bondy, S., Ferrence, R., et al. (1996). On the emerging paradigm of drinking patterns and their social and health consequences. *Addiction, 91,* 1615–1621.

Rehm, J., Gmel, G., Sempos, C. T., & Trevisan, M. (2003). Alcohol-related morbidity and mortality. *Alcohol Health Research World, 27,* 39–51.

Rehm, J., & Sempos, C. T. (1995). Alcohol consumption and all-cause mortality. *Addiction, 90*(4), 471–480.

Reich, T., Cloninger, C. R., Van Eerdewegh, P., Rice, J. P., & Mullaney, J. (1988). Secular trends in the familial transmission of alcoholism. *Alcoholism: Clinical and Experimental Research, 12,* 458–464.

Reich, T., Edenberg, H. J., Goate, A., Williams, J. T., Rice, J. P., VanEerdewegh, P., et al. (1998). A genome-wide search for genes affecting the risk for alcohol dependence. *American Journal of Medical Genetics, 81,* 207–215.

Reich, W., Earls, F., & Powell, J. (1988). A comparison of the home and social environments of children of alcoholic parents. *British Journal of Addiction, 83,* 831–839.

Reuter, P., & MacCoun, R. (1995). Assessing the legalization debate. In G. Estievenart (Ed.), *Policies and strategies to combat drugs in Europe* (pp. 39–49). Amsterdam, Netherlands: Kluwer.

Rickert, V. I., & Wiemann, C. M. (1998). Date rape among adolescents and young adults. *Journal of Pediatric and Adolescent Gynecology, 11*(4), 167–175.

Ritter, A., & Cameron, J. (2006). A review of the efficacy and effectiveness of harm reduction strategies for alcohol, tobacco and illicit drugs. *Drug Alcohol Review, 25*(6), 611–624.

Robbins, C. A. (1989). Sex differences in psychosocial consequences of alcohol and drug abuse. *Journal of Health and Social Behavior, 30,* 117–130.

Robinson, E. A., Cranford, J. A., Webb, J. R., & Brower, K. J. (2007). Six-month changes in spirituality, religiousness, and heavy drinking in a treatment-seeking sample. *Journal of Studies on Alcohol and Drugs, 68*(2), 282–290.

Robinson, T. E., & Berridge, K. C. (1993). The neural basis of drug craving: An incentive-sensitization theory of addiction. *Brain Research Review, 18,* 247–291.

Robinson, T. E., & Berridge, K. C. (2000). The psychology and neurobiology of addiction: An incentive-sensitization view. *Addiction, 95*(Suppl. 2), S91–S117.

Robinson, T. E., & Berridge, K. C. (2003). Addiction. In *Annual review of psychology* (pp. 25–53). Stanford, CA: Stanford University Press.

Robinson, T. N., Chen, H. L., & Killen, J. D. (1998). Television and music video exposure and risk of adolescent alcohol use. *Pediatrics, 102*(5), E54.

Rodés, J., Salaspuro, M., & Sorenson, T. I. A. (1999). Alcohol and liver disease. In I. MacDonald (Ed.), *Health issues related to alcohol consumption* (2nd ed., pp. 395–450): Oxford, England: Blackwell Science.

Rodriguez, M. (1994). Influence of sex and family history of alcoholism on cognitive functioning in heroin users. *European Journal of Psychiatry, 8*(1), 29–36.

Rogosch, F., Chassin, L., & Sher, K. J. (1990). Personality variables as mediators and moderators of family history for alcoholism: Conceptual and methodological issues. *Journal of Studies on Alcohol, 51,* 310–318.

Rohrbach, L. A., Hodgson, C. S., Broder, B. I., Montgomery, S. B., Flay, B. R., Hansen, W. B., et al. (1994). Parental participation in drug abuse prevention: Results from the Midwestern Prevention Project. *Journal of Research on Adolescence, 4*(2), 295–317.

Roizen, J. (1997). Epidemiological issues in alcohol-related violence. In M. Galanter (Ed.), *Recent developments in alcoholism* (Vol. 13, pp. 7–40). New York: Plenum.

Roizen, R. (1983). *Alcohol dependence symptoms in cross-cultural perspective: A report of findings from the World Health Organization study of community response to alcoholism.* Berkeley, CA: Alcohol Research Group.

Roosa, M. W., Sandler, I. N., Beals, J., & Short, J. L. (1988). Risk status of adolescent children of problem-drinking parents. *American Journal of Community Psychology, 16,* 225–239.

Rosenberg, H. (1995). The elderly and the use of illicit drugs: Sociological and epidemiological considerations [Special issue: Drugs and the elderly: Use and misuse of drugs, medicines, alcohol, and tobacco]. *International Journal of the Addictions, 30*(13–14), 1925–1951.

Rush, B. (1943). An inquiry into the effects of ardent spirits upon the human body and mind. *Quarterly Journal for the Study of Alcohol, 4,* 321–341. (Originally published in 1785)

Ruusa, J., Bergman, B., & Sundell, M. L. (1997). Sex hormones during alcohol withdrawal: A longitudinal study of 29 male alcoholics during detoxification. *Alcohol and Alcoholism, 32*(5), 591–597.

Ryan, C., & Butters, N. (1984). Alcohol consumption and premature aging: A critical review. In M. Galanter (Ed.), *Recent developments in alcoholism* (Vol. 2, pp. 223–250). New York: Plenum.

Ryan, C. M., Huggins, J., & Beatty, R. (1999). Substance use disorders and the risk of HIV infection in gay men. *Journal of Studies on Alcohol, 60*(1), 70–77.

Sabol, W. J., Couture, H., & Harrison, P. M. (2007). *Bureau of Justice statistics, prisoners in 2006.* Washington, DC: U.S. Department of Justice.

Saffer, H. (1991). Alcohol advertising and alcohol abuse. *Journal of Health Economics, 10,* 65–79.

Saffer, H. (2002). Alcohol advertising and youth. *Journal of Studies on Alcohol* (Suppl. 14), 173–181.

Saha, T. D., Stinson, F. S., & Grant, B. F. (2007). The role of alcohol consumption in future classifications of alcohol use disorders. *Drug and Alcohol Dependence, 89,* 82–92.

Samet, S., Waxman, R., Hatzenblehler, M., & Hasin, D. S. (2007). Assessing addiction: Concepts and instruments. *Addiction Science and Clinical Practice, 4*(1), 19–31.

Sampson, P. D., Bookstein, F. L., Barr, H. M., & Streissguth, A. P. (1994). Prenatal alcohol exposure: Birthweight, and measures of child size from birth to age 14 years. *American Journal of Public Health, 84*(9), 1421–1428.

Sampson, P. D., Streissguth, A. P., Bookstein, F. L., Little, R. E., Clarren, S. K., Dehaene, P., et al. (1997). Incidence of fetal alcohol syndrome and prevalence of alcohol-related neurodevelopmental disorder. *Teratology, 56*(5), 317–326.

Saules, K. K., Pomerleau, C. S., Snedecor, S. M., Mehringer, A. M., Shadle, M. B., Kurth, C., et al. (2004). Relationship of onset of cigarette smoking during college to alcohol use, dieting concerns, and depressed mood: Results from the Young Women's Health Survey. *Addictive Behaviors, 29*(5), 893–899.

Saults, J. S., Cowan, N., Sher, K. J., & Moreno, M. V. (2007). Differential effects of alcohol on working memory: Distinguishing multiple processes. *Experimental and Clinical Psychopharmacology, 15*(6), 576–587.

Savage, D. G. (1999, December 2). High court wary of classifying tobacco as drug. *Los Angeles Times,* p. 1.

Sayette, M. A. (1999). Does drinking reduce stress? *Alcohol Research and Health, 23*(4), 250–255.

Sayette, M. A., Breslin, F. C., Wilson, G. T., & Rosenblum, G. D. (1994). An evaluation of the balanced placebo design in alcohol administration research. *Addictive Behaviors, 19*(3), 333–342.

Sayette, M. A., Martin, C. S., Perrott, M. A., Wertz, J. M., & Hufford, M. R. (2001). A test of the appraisal-disruption model of alcohol and stress. *Journal of Studies on Alcohol, 62*(2), 247–256.

Sayette, M. A., & Wilson, G. T. (1991). Intoxication and exposure to stress: Effects of temporal patterning. *Journal of Abnormal Psychology, 100,* 56–62.

Schachter, S. (1977). Nicotine regulation in heavy and light smokers. *Journal of Experimental Psychology: General, 106,* 5–12.

Schachter, S. (1982). Recidivism and self-cure of smoking and obesity. *American Psychologist, 37,* 436–444.

Schafer, J., & Brown, S. A. (1991). Marijuana and cocaine effect expectancies and drug use patterns. *Journal of Consulting and Clinical Psychology, 59*(4), 558–565.

Schafer, J., Caetano, R., & Clark, C. L. (1998). Rates of intimate partner violence in the United States. *American Journal of Public Health, 88*(11), 1702–1704.

Scher, M. S., Richardson, G. A., Coble, P. A., Day, N. L., & Stoffer, D. S. (1988). The effects of prenatal alcohol and marijuana exposure: Disturbances in neonatal sleep cycling and arousal. *Pediatric Research, 24*(1), 101–105.

Schmidt, C., Klee, L., & Ames, G. (1990). Review and analysis of literature on indicators of women's drinking problems. *British Journal of Addiction, 85,* 179–192.

Schuckit, M. (1987). Biological vulnerability to alcoholism. *Journal of Consulting and Clinical Psychology, 55,* 301–309.

Schuckit, M. A., Anthenelli, R. M., Bucholz, K. K., Hesselbrock, V. M., & Tipp, J. (1995). The time course of development of alcohol-related problems in men and women. *Journal of Studies on Alcohol, 56*(2), 218–225.

Schuckit, M. A., Daeppen, J. B., Tipp, J. E., Hesselbrock, M., & Bucholz, K. K. (1998). The clinical course of alcohol-related problems in alcohol dependent and nonalcohol dependent drinking women and men. *Journal of Studies on Alcohol, 59*(5), 581–590.

Schuckit, M. A., Hesselbrock, V., Tipp, J., Anthenelli, R., Bucholz, K., Radziminski, S. (1994). A comparison of DSM-III-R, DSM-IV and ICD-10 substance use disorders diagnoses in 1922 men and women subjects in the COGA study. *Addiction, 89*(12), 1629–1638.

Schuckit, M. A., Klein, J. L., & Twitchell, G. R. (1995). The misclassification of family history status in studies of children of alcoholics. *Journal of Studies on Alcohol, 56*(1), 47–50.

Schuckit, M. A., & Smith, T. L. (2001). Correlates of unpredicted outcomes in sons of alcoholics and controls. *Journal of Studies on Alcohol, 62*(4), 477–485.

Schuckit, M. A., Smith, T. L., Kalmijn, J., & Danko, G. P. (2005). A cross-generational comparison of alcohol challenges at about age 20 in 40 father-offspring pairs. *Alcoholism: Clinical and Experimental Research, 29*(11), 1921–1927.

Schulenberg, J., O'Malley, P. M., Bachman, J. G., Wadsworth, K. N., & Johnston, L. D. (1996). Getting drunk and growing up: Trajectories of frequent binge drinking during the transition to young adulthood. *Journal of Studies on Alcohol, 57,* 289–304.

Schulenberg, J. E., Maggs, J. L., & O'Malley, P. M. (2003). How and why the understanding of developmental continuity and discontinuity is important: The sample case of long-term consequences of adolescent substance use. In J. T. Mortimer & M .J. Shanahan (Eds.), *Handbook of the life course* (pp. 413–436). New York: Plenum.

Schuler, G. D., Boguski, M. S., Stewart, E. A., Stein, L. D., Gyapay, G., Rice, K., et al. (1996). A gene map of the human genome. *Science, 274,* 540–546.

Schutte, K. K., Moos, R. H., & Brennan, P. L. (1995). Depression and drinking behavior among women and men: A three-wave longitudinal study of older adults. *Journal of Consulting and Clinical Psychology, 63*(5), 810–822.

Searles, J. S. (1988). The role of genetics in the pathogenesis of alcoholism. *Journal of Abnormal Psychology, 97,* 153–167.

Searles, J. S., Perrine, M. W., Mundt, J. C., & Helzer, J. E. (1995). Self-report of drinking using touch-tone telephone: Extending the limits of reliable daily contact. *Journal of Studies on Alcohol, 56*(4), 375–382.

Searles, J. S., & Windle, M. (1990). Introduction and overview: Salient issues in the children of alcoholics literature. In M. Windle & J. S. Searles (Eds.), *Children of alcoholics: Critical perspectives* (pp. 1–8). New York: Guilford.

Seitz, H. K., Gärtner, U., Egerer, G., & Simanowski, U. A. (1994). Ethanol metabolism in the gastrointestinal tract and its possible consequences. *Alcohol and Alcoholism* (Suppl. 2), 157–162.

Seitz, H. K., Maurer, B., & Stickel, F. (2005). Alcohol consumption and cancer of the gastrointestinal tract. *Digestive Diseases: Clinical Reviews, 23*(3–4), 297–303.

Seitz, H. K., Pöschl, G., & Simanowski, U. A. (1998). Alcohol and cancer. In M. Galanter (Ed.), *Recent developments in alcoholism*, (Vol.14, pp. 67–95). New York: Plenum.

Selzer, M. L. (1971). The Michigan Alcohol Screening Test: The quest for a new diagnostic instrument. *American Journal of Psychiatry, 127*(12), 1653–1658.

Sempos, C. T., Rehm, J., Wu, T., Crespo, C. J., & Trevisan, M. (2003). Average volume of alcohol consumption and all-cause mortality in African Americans: The NHEFS cohort. *Alcoholism: Clinical and Experimental Research, 27*(1), 88–92.

Senchak, M., Leonard, K. E., Greene, B. W., & Carroll, A. (1995). Comparisons of adult children of alcoholic, divorced, and control parents in four outcome domains. *Psychology of Addictive Behaviors, 9,* 147–156.

Shaffer, H. J., Nelson, S. E., LaPlante, D. A., LaBrie, R. A., Albanese, M., & Caro, G. (2007). The epidemiology of psychiatric disorders among repeat DUI offenders accepting a treatment-sentencing option. *Journal of Consulting and Clinical Psychology, 75*(5), 795–804.

Shaper, A. G. (1990). Alcohol and mortality: A review of prospective studies. *British Journal of Addiction, 85,* 837–847.

Shaper, A. G., & Wannamethee, S. G. (2000). Alcohol intake and mortality in middle aged men with diagnosed coronary heart disease. *Heart, 83*(4), 394–399.

Shaw, J., Hunt, I. M., Flynn, S., Amos, T., Meehan, J., Robinson, J., et al. (2006). The role of alcohol and drugs in homicides in England and Wales. *Addiction, 101*(8), 1117–1124.

Shedler, J., & Block, J. (1990). Adolescent drug use and psychological health. *American Psychologist, 45,* 612–630.

Sher, K. J. (1987). Stress response dampening. In H. T. Blane & K. E. Leonard (Eds.), *Psychological theories of drinking and alcoholism* (pp. 227–271). New York: Plenum.

Sher, K. J. (1997). Psychological characteristics of children of alcoholics. *Alcohol Health and Research World, 21,* 247–254.

Sher, K. J., Bartholow, B. D., Peuser, K., Erickson, D. J., & Wood, M. D. (2007). Stress-response-dampening effects of alcohol: Attention as a mediator and moderator. *Journal of Abnormal Psychology, 116*(2), 362–377.

Sher, K. J., & Trull, T. J. (1994). Personality and disinhibitory psychopathology: Alcoholism and antisocial personality disorder [Special issue: Personality and psychopathology]. *Journal of Abnormal Psychology, 103*(1), 92–102.

Sher, K. J., Walitzer, K. S., Wood, P. K., & Brent, E. E. (1991). Characteristics of children of alcoholics: Putative risk factors, substance use and abuse, and psychopathology. *Journal of Abnormal Psychology, 100*(4), 427–448.

Sherwood, N. (1993). Effects of nicotine on human psychomotor performance. *Human Psychopharmacology Clinical and Experimental, 8*(3), 155–184.

Sherwood, N. (1995). Effects of cigarette smoking on performance in a simulated driving task. *Neuropsychobiology, 32*(3), 161–165.

Shiffman, S. (1987). Maintenance and relapse: Coping with temptation. In T. D. Nirenberg & S. A. Maisto (Eds.), *Developments in the assessment and treatment of addictive behaviors* (pp. 353–385). Norwood, NJ: Ablex.

Shiffman, S., & Balabanis, M. (1996). Do drinking and smoking go together? *Alcohol Health & Research World, 20,* 107–110.

Shiffman, S., Balabanis, M. H., Gwaltney, C. J., Paty, J. A., Gnys, M., Kassel, J. D., et al. (2007). Prediction of lapse from associations between smoking and situational antecedents assessed by ecological momentary assessment. *Drug and Alcohol Dependence, 91*(2–3), 159–168.

Shiffman, S., Gwaltney, C. J., Balabanis, M. H., Liu, K. S., Paty, J. A., Kassel, J. D., et al. (2002). Immediate antecedents of cigarette smoking: An analysis from ecological momentary assessment. *Journal of Abnormal Psychology, 111*(4), 531–545.

Shiffman, S., Hufford, M., Hickcox, M., Paty, J. A., Gnys, M., & Kassel, J. D. (1997). Remember that? A comparison of real-time versus retrospective recall of smoking lapses. *Journal of Consulting and Clinical Psychology, 65*(2), 292–300.

Shiffman, S., Paty, J. A., Gnys, M., Kassel, J. A., & Hickcox, M. (1996). First lapses to smoking: Within-subjects analysis of real-time reports. *Journal of Consulting and Clinical Psychology, 64*(2), 366–379.

Shrier, L. A., Emans, S. J., Woods, E. R., & DuRant, R. H. (1997). The association of sexual risk behaviors and problem drug behaviors in high school students. *Journal of Adolescent Health, 20*(5), 377–383.

Siegel, S. (1983). Classical conditioning, drug tolerance, and drug dependence. In Y. Isreal, F. B. Glaser, H. Kalant, R. E. Popham, W. Schmidt, & R. G. Smart (Eds.), *Research advances in alcohol and drug problems* (pp. 207–246). New York: Plenum.

Sigvardsson, S., Bohman, M., & Cloninger, C. R. (1996). Replication of the Stockholm Adoption Study of alcoholism: Confirmatory cross-fostering analysis. *Archives of General Psychiatry, 53*(8), 681–687.

Simpson, D. D., Chatham, L. R., & Brown, B. (1995). The role of evaluation research in drug abuse policy. *Current Directions in Psychological Science, 4,* 123–126.

Simpson, D. D., Joe, G. W., Fletcher, B. W., Hubbard, R. L., & Anglin, M. D. (1999). A national evaluation of treatment outcomes for cocaine dependence. *Archives of General Psychiatry, 56,* 507–514.

Singer, M., Romero-Daza, N., Weeks, M., & Pelia, P. (1995). Ethnography and the evaluation of needle exchange in the prevention of HIV transmission. In E. Y. Lambert, R. S. Ashery, & R. H. Needle (Eds.), *Qualitative methods in drug abuse and HIV research* (Vol. 157, pp. 231–257). Washington, DC: U.S. Department of Health and Human Services.

Singleton, E. G., & Gorelick, D. A. (1998). Mechanisms of alcohol craving and their clinical implications. In M. Galanter (Ed.), *Recent developments in alcoholism* (Vol. 14, pp. 177–195). New York: Plenum.

Skinner, B. F. (1938). *The behavior of organisms.* New York: Appleton-Century-Crofts.

Slotkin, T. A. (1998). Fetal nicotine or cocaine exposure: Which one is worse? *Journal of Pharmacology and Experimental Therapeutics, 285,* 931–945.

Smith, B. D., Osborne, A., Mann, M., Jones, H., & White, T. (2004). Arousal and behavior: Biopsychological effects of caffeine. In A. Nehlig (Ed.), *Coffee, tea, chocolate, and the brain* (pp. 35–52). Boca Raton, FL: CRC Press.

Smith, G. T., Goldman, M. S., Greenbaum, P. E., & Christiansen, B. A. (1995). Expectancy for social facilitation from drinking: The divergent paths of high-expectancy and low-expectancy adolescents. *Journal of Abnormal Psychology, 104*(1), 32–40.

Smith-Warner, S. A., Spiegelman, D., Yaun, S. S., van den Brandt, P. A., Folsom, A. R., Goldbohm, R. A., et al. (1998). Alcohol and breast cancer in women: A pooled analysis of cohort studies. *JAMA, 279,* 535–540.

Snell, L. D., Glanz, J., & Tabakoff, B. (2002). Relationships between effects of smoking, gender, and alcohol dependence on platelet monoamine oxidase-B: Activity, affinity labeling, and protein measurements. *Alcoholism: Clinical and Experimental Research, 26*(7), 1105–1113.

Snodgrass, S. R. (1994). Cocaine babies: A result of multiple teratogenic influences. *Journal of Child Neurology, 9*(3), 227–233.

Sobell, L. C., Sobell, M. B., Leo, G. I., Agrawal, S., Johnson-Young, L., & Cunningham, J. A. (2002). Promoting self-change with alcohol abusers: A community-level mail intervention based on natural recovery studies. *Alcoholism: Clinical and Experimental Research, 26*(6), 936–948.

Sobell, L. C., Sobell, M. B., & Toneatto, T. (1991). Recovery from alcohol problems without treatment. In N. Heather, W. R. Miller, & J. Greeley (Eds.), *Self-control and addictive behaviors.* New York: Permagon.

Sobell, M. B., & Sobell, L. C. (1973). Individualized behavior therapy for alcoholics. *Behavior Therapy, 4,* 49–72.

Solomon, R. L. (1980). The opponent-process theory of acquired motivation: The costs and pleasure and the benefits of pain. *American Psychologist, 35,* 691–712.

Sonnenstuhl, W. J. (1996). *Working sober: The transformation of an occupational drinking culture.* Ithaca, NY: ILR Press Books.

Southwick, L., & Steele, C. (1987). Restrained drinking: Personality correlates of a control style. *Journal of Drug Issues, 17,* 349–358.

Spencer, G. (1989). Projections of the population of the United States, by age, sex, and race: 1988 to 2080. In *U.S. Bureau of the Census 1989 Current Population Reports Series P-25, No. 1018.* Washington, DC: U.S. Government Printing Office.

Spicer, P., Bezdek, M., Manson, S. M., & Beals, J. (2007). A program of research on spirituality and American Indian alcohol use. *Southern Medical Journal, 100*(4), 430–432.

Stafford, L. L. (2001). Is codependency a meaningful concept? *Issues in Mental Health Nursing, 22*(3), 273–286.

Stahre, M., Naimi, T., Brewer, R., & Holt, J. (2006). Measuring average alcohol consumption: The impact of including binge drinks in quantity-frequency calculations. *Addiction, 101*(1), 1711–1718.

Stanton, M. (2005). Relapse prevention needs more emphasis on interpersonal factors. *American Journal of Psychology, 60*(4), 340–341.

Steele, C. M., & Josephs, R. A. (1988). Drinking your troubles away II: An attention-allocation model of alcohol's effect on psychological stress. *Journal of Abnormal Psychology, 97,* 196–205.

Steele, C. M., & Southwick, L. (1985). Alcohol and social behavior I: The psychology of drunken excess. *Journal of Personality and Social Psychology, 48,* 18–34.

Steenrod, S., Brisson, A., McCarty, D., & Hodgkin, D. (2001). Effects of managed care on programs and practices for the treatment of alcohol and drug dependence. In M. Galanter (Ed.), *Recent developments in alcoholism* (Vol. 15, pp. 51–71). New York: Plenum.

Steinglass, P. (1981). The alcoholic family at home: Patterns of interaction in dry, wet, and transitional stages of alcoholism. *Archives of General Psychiatry, 38,* 578–584.

Steinglass, P., Bennett, L. A., Wolin, S. J., & Reiss, D. (1987). *The alcoholic family.* New York: Basic Books.

Sterling, R. C., Weinstein, S., Hill, P., Gottheil, E., Gordon, S. M., & Shorie, K. (2006). Levels of spirituality and treatment outcome: A preliminary examination. *Journal of Studies on Alcohol, 67,* 600–606.

Stewart, J., deWit, H., & Eikelboom, R. (1984). The role of unconditioned and conditioned drug effects in the self-administration of opiates and stimulants. *Psychological Review, 91,* 251–268.

Stewart, M. A., & deBlois, C. S. (1981). Wife abuse among families attending a child psychiatry clinic. *Journal of the American Academy of Child Psychiatry, 20,* 845–862.

Stigler, M. H., Perry, C. L., Komro, K. A., Cudeck, R., & Williams, C. L. (2006). Teasing apart a multiple component approach to adolescent alcohol prevention: What worked in Project Northland? *Prevention Science, 7*(3), 269–280.

Stitzer, M., & Petry, N. (2006). Contingency management for treatment of substance abuse. *Annual Review of Clinical Psychology, 2,* 411–434.

Stockdale, S. E., Tang, L., Zhang, L., Belin, T. R., & Wells, K. B. (2007). The effects of health sector market factors and vulnerable group membership on access to alcohol, drug, and mental health care. *Health Services Research, 42*(3, Part 1), 1020–1041.

Stoltenberg, S. F., Mudd, S. A., Blow, F. C., & Hill, E. M. (1998). Evaluating measures of family history of alcoholism: Density versus dichotomy. *Addiction, 93*(10), 1511–1520.

Stone, R. A., Whitbeck, L. B., Chen, X., Johnson, K., & Olson, D. M. (2006). Traditional practices, traditional spirituality, and alcohol cessation among American Indians. *Journal of Studies on Alcohol, 67*(2), 236–244.

Storgaard, H., Nielsen, S. D., & Gluud, C. (1994). The validity of the Michigan Alcoholism Screening Test (MAST). *Alcohol and Alcoholism, 29*(5), 493–502.

Stranges, S., Freudenheim, J. L., Muti, P., Farinaro, E., Russell, M., Nochajski, T. H., et al. (2004). Greater hepatic vulnerability after alcohol intake in African Americans compared with Caucasians: A population-based study. *Journal of the National Medical Association, 96*(9), 1185–1192.

Strecher, V. J. (1983). A minimal-contact smoking cessation program in a health care setting. *Public Health Reports, 98,* 497–502.

Streissguth, A. P., Bookstein, F. L., Barr, H. M., Sampson, P. D., O'Malley, K., & Young, J. K. (2004). Risk factors for adverse life outcomes in fetal alcohol syndrome and fetal alcohol effects. *Journal of Developmental and Behavioral Pediatrics, 25*(4), 228–238.

Streissguth, A. P., Clarren, S. K., & Jones, K. L. (1985). Natural history of the fetal alcohol syndrome: A 10-year follow-up of eleven patients. *Lancet, 2,* 85–91.

Streissguth, A. P., Herman, C. S., & Smith, D. W. (1978). Intelligence, behavior, and dysmorphogenesis in the fetal alcohol syndrome: A report on 20 patients. *Journal of Pediatrics, 92,* 363–367.

Streissguth, A. P., Martin, D. C., Martin, J. C., & Barr, H. M. (1981). The Seattle longitudinal prospective study on alcohol and pregnancy. *Neurobehavioral Toxicology and Teratology, 3,* 223–233.

Substance Abuse and Mental Health Services Administration. (2001). *Summary of findings from the 2000 National Household Survey on Drug Abuse.* Rockville, MD: Substance Abuse and Mental Health Services Administration, Office of Applied Studies.

Substance Abuse and Mental Health Services Administration. (2002). *Results from the 2001 National Household Survey on Drug Abuse* (Vol. II: Technical Appendices and Selected Data Tables). Rockville, MD: Substance Abuse and Mental Health Services Administration, Office of Applied Studies.

Substance Abuse and Mental Health Services Administration. (2007). *Results from the 2006 National Survey on Drug Use and Health (NSDUH): National findings.* Rockville, MD: Substance Abuse and Mental Health Services Administration, Office of Applied Studies.

Sue, S., Kitano, H. H. L., Hatanaka, H., & Yeung, W. (1985). Alcohol consumption among Chinese in the United States. In L. A. Bennett & G. M. Ames (Eds.), *The American experience with alcohol: Contrasting cultural perspectives* (pp. 359–371). New York: Plenum.

Sullivan, M. A., & Covey, L. S. (2002). Current perspectives on smoking cessation among substance abusers. *Current Psychiatry Reports, 4*(5), 388–396.

Sutocky, J. W., Shultz, J. M., & Kizer, K. W. (1993). Alcohol-related mortality in California, 1980 to 1989. *American Journal of Public Health, 83,* 817–823.

Svare, G. M , Miller, L. S., & Ames, G. (2004). Social climate and workplace drinking among women in a male-dominated occupation. *Addictive Behaviors, 29,* 1691–1698.

Swaim, R. C., Bates, S. C., & Chavez, E. L. (1998). Structural equation socialization model of substance use among Mexican-American and White non-Hispanic school dropouts. *Journal of Adolescent Health, 23*(3), 128–138.

Swanson, J. A., Lee, J. W., & Hopp, J. W. (1994). Caffeine and nicotine: A review of their joint use and possible interactive effects in tobacco withdrawal. *Addictive Behaviors, 19*(3), 229–256.

Szabo, G. (1997). Alcohol's contribution to compromised immunity. *Alcohol and Health Research World, 21,* 30–41.

Szasz, T. (1985). *Ceremonial chemistry: The ritual persecution of drugs, addicts, and pushers* (Revised ed.). Holmes Beach, FL: Learning Publications.

Szlemko, W. J., Wood, J. W., & Thurman, P. J. (2006). Native Americans and alcohol: Past, present, and future. *Journal of General Psychology, 133*(A), 435–451.

Tabakoff, B., & Hoffman, P. L. (1987). Biochemical pharmacology of alcohol. In H. Y. Meltzer (Ed.), *Psychopharmacology of alcohol: The third generation of progress* (pp. 1521–1526). New York: Raven Press.

Tabakoff, B., & Hoffman, P. L. (2000). Animal models in alcohol research. *Alcohol Research and Health, 24*(2), 77–84.

Tabakoff, B., Hoffman, P. L., & Petersen, R. C. (1990). Advances in neurochemistry: A leading edge of alcohol research. *Alcohol Health and Research World, 14,* 138–143.

Tarter, R. E. (1988). Are there inherited behavioral traits that predispose to alcohol abuse? *Journal of Consulting and Clinical Psychology, 56,* 189–196.

Tarter, R. E., Alterman, A. I., & Edwards, K. L. (1985). Vulnerability to alcoholism in men: A behavior-genetic perspective. *Journal of Studies on Alcohol, 46,* 329–356.

Tarter, R. E., Ammerman, R. T., & Ott, P. J. (Eds.). (1998). *Handbook of substance abuse: Neurobehavioral pharmacology.* New York: Plenum.

Tarter, R. E., & Edwards, K. (1988). Psychological factors associated with the risk for alcoholism. *Alcoholism Clinical and Experimental Research, 12,* 471–480.

Tarter, R. E., Moss, H., & Laird, S. B. (1990). Biological markers for vulnerability to alcoholism. In R. L. Collins, K. E. Leonard, & J. S. Searles (Eds.), *Alcohol and the family: Research and clinical perspectives* (pp. 79–106). New York: Guilford.

Tarter, R. E., Vanyukov, M., Kirisci, L., Reynolds, M., & Clark, D. B. (2006). Predictors of marijuana use in adolescents before and after licit drug use: Examination of the gateway hypothesis. *American Journal of Psychiatry, 163*(12), 2134–2140.

Tate, D. L., & Charette, L. (1991). Personality, alcohol consumption, and menstrual distress in young women. *Alcoholism Clinical and Experimental Research, 15*(4), 647–652.

Tate, S. R., Brown, S. A., Unrod, M., & Ramo, D. E. (2004). Context of relapse for substance-dependent adults with and without comorbid psychiatric disorders. *Addictive Behaviors, 29*(9), 1707–1724.

Taylor, B. J., Graham, J. W., Cumsille, P., & Hansen, W. B. (2000). Modeling prevention program effects on growth in substance use: Analysis of five years of data from the Adolescent Alcohol Prevention Trial. *Prevention Science, 1*(4), 183–197.

Taylor, S. P. (1967). Aggressive behavior and physiological arousal as a function of provocation and the tendency to inhibit aggression. *Journal of Personality, 35,* 297–310.

Taylor, S. P., & Chermack, S. T. (1993). Alcohol, drugs and human physical aggression. *Journal of Studies on Alcohol* (Suppl. 11), 78–88.

Temple, M. T., & Leigh, B. C. (1992). Alcohol consumption and unsafe sexual behavior in discrete events. *Journal of Sex Research, 29*(2), 207–219.

Temple, M. T., & Leino, V. (1989). Long-term outcomes of drinking: A 20-year longitudinal study of men. *British Journal of Addiction, 84,* 889–900.

Testa, M., Fillmore, M. T., Norris, J., Abbey, A., Curtin, J. J., Leonard, K. E., et al. (2006). Understanding alcohol expectancy effects: Revisiting the placebo condition. *Alcoholism: Clinical and Experimental Research, 30*(2), 339–348.

Thomas, D. B. (1995). Alcohol as a cause of cancer. *Environmental Health Perspectives, 103*(Suppl. 8), 153–160.

Thomas, J. C. (1989). An overview of marital and family treatments with substance abusing populations. *Alcoholism Treatment Quarterly, 6,* 91–102.

Thorndike, E. L. (1911). *Animal intelligence.* New York: Macmillan.

Thun, M. J., Peto, R., Lopez, A. D., Monaco, J. H., Henley, S. J., Heath, C. W., Jr., et al. (1997). Alcohol consumption and mortality among middle-aged and elderly US adults. *New England Journal of Medicine, 337,* 1705–1714.

Thush, C., & Wiers, R. W. (2007). Explicit and implicit alcohol-related cognitions and the prediction of future drinking in adolescents. *Addictive Behaviors, 32*(7), 1367–1383.

Tiffany, S. T. (1990). A cognitive model of drug urges and drug-use behavior: Role of automatic and nonautomatic processes. *Psychological Review, 97,* 147–168.

Tiffany, S. T. (1999). Cognitive concepts of craving. *Alcohol Research and Health, 23*(3), 215–224.

Timberlake, D. S., Hopfer, C. J., Rhee, S. H., Friedman, N. P., Haberstick, B. C., Lessem, J. M., et al. (2007). College attendance and its effect on drinking behaviors in a longitudinal study of adolescents. *Alcoholism: Clinical and Experimental Research, 31*(6), 1020–1030.

Tonigan, J. S., Connors, G. J., & Miller, W. R. (1998). Special populations in Alcoholics Anonymous. *Alcohol Health Research World, 22*(4), 281–285.

Tonigan, J. S., Miller, W. R., & Schermer, C. (2002). Atheists, agnostics and Alcoholics Anonymous. *Journal of Studies on Alcohol, 63*(5), 534–541.

Toomey, T. L., Lenk, K. M., & Wagenaar, A. C. (2007). Environmental policies to reduce college drinking: An update of research findings. *Journal of Studies on Alcohol and Drugs, 68*(2), 208–219.

Treno, A. J., Johnson, F. W., Remer, L. G., & Gruenewald, P. J. (2007). The impact of outlet densities on alcohol-related crashes: A spatial panel approach. *Accident Analysis and Prevention, 39*(5), 894–901.

Trice, H., & Sonnenstuhl, W. (1988). Constructive confrontation and other referral processes. In M. Galanter (Ed.), *Recent developments in alcoholism* (Vol. 6, pp. 159–170). New York: Plenum.

Trice, H. M., & Staudemeier, W. J. (1989). A sociocultural history of Alcoholics Anonymous. In M. Galanter (Ed.), *Recent developments in alcoholism: Emerging issues in treatment* (Vol. 7, pp. 11–35). New York: Plenum.

Trimble, J. E. (1991). Ethnic specification, validation prospects, and the future of drug use research. *International Journal of the Addictions, 25,* 149–170.

Trimpey, J. (1992). *The small book (Rational Recovery systems).* New York: Dell.

Tsuang, M. T., Lyons, M. J., Meyer, J. M., Doyle, T., Eisen, S. A., Goldberg, J., et al. (1998). Co-occurrence of abuse of different drugs in men: The role of drug-specific and shared vulnerabilities. *Archives of General Psychiatry, 55,* 967–972.

Tuchfield, B. S. (1981). Spontaneous remission in alcoholics: Empirical observations and theoretical implications. *Journal of Studies on Alcohol, 42,* 626–640.

Tulving, E. (1983). *Elements of episodic memory.* New York: Oxford University Press.

Turner, R. J., Lloyd, D. A., & Taylor, J. (2006). Stress burden, drug dependence and the nativity paradox among U.S. Hispanics. *Drug and Alcohol Dependence, 83*(1), 79–89.

Tweed, S. H., & Ryff, C. D. (1991). Adult children of alcoholics: Profiles of wellness. *Journal of Studies on Alcohol, 52,* 133–141.

Uekermann, J., & Daum, I. (2008). Social cognition in alcoholism: A link to prefrontal cortex dysfunction? *Addiction,103*(5), 726–735.

Uekermann, J., Daum, I., Schlebusch, P., & Trenckmann, U. (2005). Processing of affective stimuli in alcoholism. *Cortex, 41*(2), 189–194.

Urberg, K. A., Luo, Q., Pilgrim, C., & Degirmencioglu, S. M. (2003). A two-stage model of peer influence in adolescent substance use: Individual and relationship-specific differences in susceptibility to influence. *Addictive Behaviors, 28*(7), 1243–1256.

U.S. Bureau of the Census. (1992a). *1990 Census of population, general population characteristics, United States.* Washington, DC: U.S. Department of Commerce, Economics and Statistics Administration.

U.S. Bureau of the Census. (1992b). *Population projections of the United States, by age, sex, race, and Hispanic origin: 1992 to 2050.* Washington, DC: U.S. Government Printing Office.

U.S. Census Bureau. (2007). *Annual estimates of the population by sex, race, and Hispanic or Latino origin for the United States: April 1, 2000 to July 1, 2006* (NC-EST2006-03). Available from http://www.census.gov/popest/national/asrh/NC-EST2006-srh.html

U.S. Department of Commerce. (1978). Directive No. 15: Race and ethnic standards for federal statistics and administrative reporting. In *Statistical policy handbook* (pp. 37–38). Washington, DC: U.S. Department of Commerce, Office of Federal Statistical Policy and Standards.

U.S. Department of Health and Human Services. (1987). *Review of the research literature on the effects of health warning labels: A report to the U.S. Congress.* Rockville, MD: National Institute on Alcohol Abuse and Alcoholism.

U.S. Department of Health and Human Services. (1990). *Smoking and health: A national status report* (DHHS Publication No. (CDC) 87-8396). Rockville, MD: Centers for Disease Control.

U.S. Department of Health and Human Services. (2001). *Women and smoking: A report of the Surgeon General.* Washington, DC: U.S. Government Printing Office.

U.S. Department of Health Education and Welfare. (1964). *Smoking and health: Report of the Advisory Committee to the Surgeon General* (DHEW Publication No. (PHS) 1103). Washington, DC: U.S. Government Printing Office.

U.S. Surgeon General. (1998). *Tobacco use among U.S. racial/ethnic minority groups.* Washington, DC: U.S. Department of Health and Human Services.

Vachon, C. M., Cerhan, J. R., Vierkant, R. A., & Sellers, T. A. (2001). Investigation of an interaction of alcohol intake and family history on breast cancer risk in the Minnesota breast cancer family study. *Cancer, 92,* 240–248.

Van Hesselt, V. B., Morrison, R. L., & Bellack, A. S. (1985). Alcohol use in wife abusers and their spouses. *Addictive Behaviors, 10,* 127–135.

Van Thiel, D. H. (1983). Ethanol: Its adverse effects on the hypothalamic-pituitary-gonadal axis. *Journal of Laboratory Clinical Medicine, 101,* 21–33.

Vega, W. A., Alderete, E., Kolody, B., & Aguilar-Gaxiola, S. (1998). Illicit drug use among Mexicans and Mexican Americans in California: The effects of gender and acculturation. *Addiction, 93*(12), 1839–1850.

Velicer, W. F., Prochaska, J. O., Rossi, J. S., & Snow, M. G. (1992). Assessing outcome in smoking cessation studies. *Psychological Bulletin, 111,* 23–41.

Velleman, R. (1992a). A review of environmentally oriented studies concerning the relationship between parental alcohol problems and family disharmony in the genesis of alcohol and other problems: I. The intergenerational effects of alcohol problems. *International Journal of the Addictions, 27,* 253–280.

Velleman, R. (1992b). A review of environmentally oriented studies concerning the relationship between parental alcohol problems and family disharmony in the genesis of alcohol and other problems: II. The intergenerational effects of family disharmony. *International Journal of the Addictions, 27,* 367–389.

Velleman, R., & Orford, J. (1999). *Risk and resilience: Adults who were the children of problem drinkers.* Amsterdam, Netherlands: Harwood Academic Publishers.

Velleman, R., & Templeton, L. (2007). Understanding and modifying the impact of parents' substance misuse on children. *Advances in Psychiatric Treatment, 13,* 79–89.

Vogel-Sprott, M., & Barrett, B. (1984). Age, drinking habits and the effects of alcohol. *Journal of Studies on Alcohol, 45,* 517–521.

Volpicelli, J. R., Alterman, A. I., Hayashida, M., & O'Brian, C. P. (1992). Naltrexone in the treatment of alcohol dependence. *Archives of General Psychiatry, 49,* 876–880.

Volpicelli, J. R., Clay, K. L., Watson, N. T., & Volpicelli, L. A. (1995). Naltrexone and the treatment of alcohol dependence. *Alcohol Health & Research World, 18*(4), 272–278.

Von Knorring, A. L., Bohman, M., Von Knorring, L., & Oreland, L. (1985). Platelet MAO activity as a biological marker in subgroups of alcoholism. *Acta Scandinavica, 72,* 51–58.

Wagenaar, A. C., Toomey, T. L., & Erickson, D. J. (2005). Preventing youth access to alcohol: Outcomes from a multi-community time-series trial. *Addiction, 100*(3), 335–345.

Wagenknecht, L. E., Craven, T. E., Preisser, J. S., Manolio, T. A., Winders, S., & Hulley, S. B. (1998). Ten-year trends in cigarette smoking among young adults, 1986–1996: The CARDIA Study: Coronary Artery Risk Development in Young Adults. *Annals of Epidemiology, 8,* 301–307.

Waldorf, D., Reinarman, C., & Murphy, S. (1991). *Cocaine changes: The experience of using and quitting.* Philadelphia: Temple University Press.

Walitzer, K. S., & Dearing, R. L. (2006). Gender differences in alcohol and substance use relapse. *Clinical Psychology Review, 26*(2), 128–148.

Wall, A. M., McKee, S. A., & Hinson, R. E. (2000). Assessing variation in alcohol outcome expectancies across environmental context: An examination of the situational-specificity hypothesis. *Psychology of Addictive Behaviors, 14*(4), 367–375.

Wall, T. L., Thomasson, H. R., & Ehlers, C. L. (1996). Investigator-observed alcohol-induced flushing but not self-report of flushing is a valid predictor of ALDH2 genotype. *Journal of Studies on Alcohol, 57,* 267–272.

Wallace, J. (1985). Critical issues in alcoholism therapy. In S. Zimberg, J. Wallace, & S. B. Blume (Eds.), *Practical approaches to alcoholism psychotherapy* (pp. 23–36). New York: Plenum.

Wallace, J. (1996). Theory of 12-Step-oriented treatment. In F. Rotgers, D. S. Keller, & J. Morgenstern (Eds.), *Treating substance abuse: Theory and technique* (pp. 13–36). New York: Guilford.

Wallace, J. M., Jr., Bachman, J. G., O'Malley, P. M., Johnston, L. D., Schulenberg, J. E., & Cooper, S. M. (2002). Tobacco, alcohol, and illicit drug use: Racial and ethnic differences among U.S. high school seniors, 1976–2000. *Public Health Reports, 117*(Suppl. 1), S67–S75.

Wallace, J. M., Jr., Bachman, J. G., O'Malley, P. M., Schulenberg, J. E., Cooper, S. M., & Johnston, L. D. (2003). Gender and ethnic differences in smoking, drinking and illicit drug use among American 8th, 10th and 12th grade students, 1976–2000. *Addiction, 98*(2), 225–234.

Wallack, L., Grube, J. W., Madden, P. A., & Breed, W. (1990). Portrayals of alcohol on prime-time television. *Journal of Studies on Alcohol, 51*(5), 428–437.

Warburton, D. M. (1989). The neuropsychopharmacology of smoking. *Yakubutsu, Seishin, Kodo [Japanese Journal of Psychopharmacology], 9,* 245–256.

Warburton, D. M., Revell, A., & Thompson, D. H. (1991). Smokers of the future. *British Journal of Addiction, 86,* 621–625.

Warner, L. A., Valdez, A., Vega, W. A., De la Rosa, M., Turner, R. J., & Canino, G. (2006). Hispanic drug abuse in an evolving cultural context: An agenda for research. *Drug and Alcohol Dependence, 84*(Suppl. 1), S8–S16.

Warner, L. A., White, H. R., & Johnson, V. (2007). Alcohol initiation experiences and family history of alcoholism as predictors of problem-drinking trajectories. *Journal of Studies on Alcohol and Drugs, 68*(1), 56–65.

Weatherspoon, A. J., Danko, G. P., & Johnson, R. C. (1994). Alcohol consumption and use norms among Chinese Americans and Korean Americans. *Journal of Studies on Alcohol, 55,* 203–206.

Webster, D. W., Harburg, E., Gleiberman, L., Schork, A., & DiFrancesico, W. (1989). Familial transmission of alcohol use: I. Parent and adult offspring alcohol use over 17 years—Tecumseh, Michigan. *Journal of Studies on Alcohol, 50,* 557–566.

Wechsler, H., Dowdall, G. W., Davenport, A., & Castillo, S. (1995). Correlates of college student binge drinking. *American Journal of Public Health, 85*(7), 921–926.

Wechsler, H., Dowdall, G. W., Davenport, A., & Rimm, E. B. (1995). A gender-specific measure of binge drinking among college students. *American Journal of Public Health, 85*(7), 982–985.

Wechsler, H., Lee, J. E., Kuo, M., Seibring, M., Nelson, T. F., & Lee, H. (2002). Trends in college binge drinking during a period of increased prevention efforts: Findings from 4 Harvard School of Public Health College Alcohol Study Surveys: 1993–2001. *Journal of American College Health, 50*(5), 203–217.

Wechsler, H., & McFadden, M. (1979). Drinking among college students in New England. *Journal of Studies on Alcohol, 40,* 969–996.

Wechsler, H., Moeykens, B., Davenport, A., Castillo, S., & Hanson, J. (1995). The adverse impact of heavy episodic drinkers on other college students. *Journal of Studies on Alcohol, 56*(6), 628–634.

Wechsler, H., Nelson, T. E., Lee, J. E., Seibring, M., Lewis, C., & Keeling, R. P. (2003). Perception and reality: A national evaluation of social norms marketing interventions to reduce college students' heavy alcohol use. *Journal of Studies on Alcohol, 64*(4), 484–494.

Wegsheider, S. (1981). *Another chance: Hope and health for the alcoholic family.* Palo Alto, CA: Science and Behavior Books.

Weibel, J., & Weisner, T. (1980). *An ethnography of urban Indian drinking patterns in California.* Report presented to the California State Department of Alcohol and Drug Problems.

Weibel-Orlando, J. (1985). Indians, ethnicity, and alcohol: Contrasting perceptions of the ethnic self and alcohol use. In L. A. Bennett & G. M. Ames (Eds.), *The American experience with alcohol: Contrasting cultural perspectives* (pp. 201–226). New York: Plenum.

Weinhardt, L. S., & Carey, M. P. (2000). Does alcohol lead to sexual risk behavior? Findings from event-level research. *Annual Review of Sex Research, 11,* 125–158.

Weisner, C. M. (1987). The social ecology of alcohol treatment in the U.S. In M. Galanter (Ed.), *Recent developments in alcoholism* (Vol. 5, pp. 203–243). New York: Plenum.

Weisner, C. M. (1990). Coercion in alcohol treatment. In Institute of Medicine (Ed.), *Broadening the base of treatment for alcohol problems* (pp. 579–609). Washington, DC: National Academy Press.

Weissenborn, R., & Duka, T. (2003). Acute alcohol effects on cognitive function in social drinkers: Their relationship to drinking habits. *Psychopharmacology, 165,* 306–312.

Welte, J. W. (1998). Stress and elderly drinking. In U.S. Department of Health and Human Services (Ed.), *Alcohol problems & aging* (pp. 229–246). Washington, DC: U.S. Government Printing Office.

Welte, J. W., & Abel, E. L. (1989). Homicide: Drinking by the victim. *Journal of Studies on Alcohol, 50,* 197–201.

Welte, J. W., & Barnes, G. M. (1987). Alcohol use among adolescent minority groups. *Journal of Studies on Alcohol, 48,* 329–336.

Welte, J. W., & Mirand, A. L. (1995). Drinking, problem drinking and life stressors in the elderly general population. *Journal of Studies on Alcohol, 56*(1), 67–73.

Werler, M. M., Pober, B. R., & Holmes, L. B. (1985). Smoking and pregnancy. *Teratology, 32*(3), 473–481.

Werner, E. E. (1986). Resilient offspring of alcoholics: A longitudinal study from birth to age 18. *Journal of Studies on Alcohol, 47,* 34–40.

West, M. O., & Prinz, R. J. (1987). Parental alcoholism and childhood psychopathology. *Psychological Bulletin, 102,* 204–218.

Westermeyer, J. (1972). Chippewa and majority alcoholism in the Twin Cities: A comparison. *Journal of Nervous and Mental Disorders, 155,* 322–327.

White, F. J., & Kalivas, P. W. (1998). Neuroadaptations involved in amphetamine and cocaine addiction. *Drug and Alcohol Dependence, 51,* 141–153.

White, H. R., Brick, J., & Hansell, S. (1993). A longitudinal investigation of alcohol use and aggression in adolescence. *Journal of Studies on Alcohol* (Suppl. 11), 62–77.

White, H. R., Pandina, R. J., & Chen, P. H. (2002). Developmental trajectories of cigarette use from early adolescence into young adulthood. *Drug and Alcohol Dependence, 65*(2), 167–178.

White, T. (2003). Drug testing at work: Issues and perspectives. *Substance Use and Misuse, 38*(11–13), 1891–1902.

White, W. L. (1998). *Slaying the dragon: The history of addiction treatment and recovery in America.* Bloomington, IL: Chestnut Health System.

Whitfield, J. B., Pang, D., Bucholz, K. K., Madden, P. A., Heath, A. C., Statham, D. J., et al. (2000). Monoamine oxidase: Associations with alcohol dependence, smoking and other measures of psychopathology. *Psychological Medicine, 30*(2), 443–454.

WHO. (1978). *Mental disorders: Glossary and guide to their classification in accordance with the ninth revision of the International Classification of Diseases.* Geneva, Switzerland: Author.

WHO. (1990). *International classification of diseases, tenth revision (ICD-10).* Geneva, Switzerland: Author.

Widiger, T. A., Frances, A. J., Pincus, H. A., Davis, W. W., & First, M. B. (1991). Toward an empirical classification for the DSM-IV. *Journal of Abnormal Psychology, 100,* 280–288.

Widiger, T. A., & Samuel, D. B. (2005). Diagnostic categories or dimensions? A question for the Diagnostic and Statistical Manual of Mental Disorders—fifth edition. *Journal of Abnormal Psychology, 114*(4), 494–504.

Widom, C. S., & Hiller-Sturmhofel, S. (2001). Alcohol abuse as a risk factor for and consequence of child abuse. *Alcohol Research and Health, 25*(1), 52–57.

Widom, C. S., Ireland, T., & Glynn, P. J. (1995). Alcohol abuse in abused and neglected children followed-up: Are they at increased risk? *Journal of Studies on Alcohol, 56*(2), 207–217.

Widom, C. S., Schuck, A. M., & White, H. R. (2006). An examination of pathways from childhood victimization to violence: The role of early aggression and problematic alcohol use. *Violence and Victimology, 21*(6), 675–690.

Widom, C. S., White, H. R., Czaja, S. J., & Marmorstein, N. R. (2007). Long-term effects of child abuse and neglect on alcohol use and excessive drinking in middle adulthood. *Journal of Studies on Alcohol and Drugs, 68*(3), 317–326.

Wiers, R. W., & Stacy, A. W. (Eds.). (2006). *Handbook of implicit cognition and addiction.* Thousand Oaks, CA: Sage.

Wiers, R. W., Stacy, A. W., Ames, S. L., Noll, J. A., Sayette, M. A., Zack, M., et al. (2002). Implicit and explicit alcohol-related cognitions. *Alcoholism: Clinical and Experimental Research, 26*(1), 129–137.

Wikler, A. (1973). Dynamics of drug dependence. *Archives of General Psychiatry, 28,* 611–616.

Wilkie, H., & Stewart, S. H. (2005). Reinforcing mood effects of alcohol in coping and enhancement motivated drinkers. *Alcoholism: Clinical and Experimental Research, 29,* 829–836.

Willenbring, M. L. (2007). A broader view of change in drinking behavior. *Alcoholism: Clinical and Experimental Research, 31*(Suppl. 10), 84s–86s.

Willett, W. C., Green, A., Stampfer, M. J., Speizer, F. E., Colditz, G. A., Rosner, B., et al. (1987). Relative and absolute excess risks of coronary heart disease among women who smoke cigarettes. *New England Journal of Medicine, 317*(21), 1303–1309.

Williams, C. L., Perry, C. L., Farbakhsh, K., & Veblen-Mortenson, S. (1999). Project Northland: Comprehensive alcohol use prevention for young adolescents, their parents, schools, peers and communities. *Journal of Studies on Alcohol* (Suppl. 13), 112–124.

Williams, C. M., & Skinner, A. E. (1990). The cognitive effects of alcohol abuse: A controlled study. *British Journal of Addiction, 85,* 911–917.

Wilsnack, R. W., & Cheloha, R. (1987). Women's roles and problem drinking across the lifespan. *Social Problems, 34,* 231–248.

Wilsnack, R. W., Kristjanson, A. F., Wilsnack, S. C., & Crosby, R. D. (2006). Are U.S. women drinking less (or more)? Historical and aging trends, 1981–2001. *Journal of Studies on Alcohol, 67*(3), 341–348.

Wilsnack, R. W., Vogeltanz, N. D., Wilsnack, S. C., Harris, T. R., Ahlstrom, S., Bondy, S., et al. (2000). Gender differences in alcohol consumption and adverse drinking consequences: Cross-cultural patterns. *Addiction, 95*(2), 251–265.

Wilsnack, S. C. (1973). Sex role identity in female alcoholism. *Journal of Abnormal Psychology, 82,* 253–261.

Wilsnack, S. C. (1974). The effects of social drinking on women's fantasy. *Journal of Personality, 42,* 43–61.

Wilsnack, S. C. (1976). The impact of sex roles on women's alcohol use and abuse. In M. Greenblatt & M. A. Schuckit (Eds.), *Alcoholism problems in women and children* (pp. 37–63). New York: Grune & Stratton.

Wilsnack, S. C. (1984). Drinking, sexuality, and sexual dysfunction in women. In S. C. Wilsnack & L. J. Beckman (Eds.), *Alcohol problems in women: Antecedents, consequences, and intervention* (pp. 189–227). New York: Guilford.

Wilsnack, S. C. (1996). Patterns and trends in women's drinking: Recent findings and some implications for prevention. In J. M. Howard, S. E. Martin, P. D. Mail, M. E. Hilton, & E. D. Taylor (Eds.), *Women and alcohol: Issues for prevention research* (Research Monograph No. 32, pp. 19–63). Washington, DC: U.S. Government Printing Office.

Wilsnack, S. C., Hughes, T. L., Johnson, T. P., Bostwick, W. B., Szalacha, L. A., Benson, P., et al. (2008). Drinking and drinking-related problems among heterosexual and sexual minority women. *Journal of Studies on Alcohol and Drugs, 69*(1), 129–139.

Wilsnack, S. C., Klassen, A. D., Schur, B. E., & Wilsnack, R. W. (1991). Predicting onset and chronicity of women's problem drinking: A five-year longitudinal analysis. *American Journal of Public Health, 81,* 305–318.

Wilsnack, S. C., Klassen, A. D., & Wilsnack, R. W. (1984). Drinking and reproductive dysfunction among women in a 1981 national survey. *Alcoholism: Clinical and Experimental Research, 8,* 451–458.

Wilsnack, S. C., Vogeltanz-Holm, N. D., Klassen, A. D., & Harris, T. R. (1997). Childhood sexual abuse and women's substance abuse: National survey findings. *Journal of Studies on Alcohol, 58,* 264–271.

Wilsnack, S. C., & Wilsnack, R. W. (1978). Sex roles and drinking among adolescent girls. *Journal of Studies on Alcohol, 39,* 1855–1874.

Wilsnack, S. C., & Wilsnack, R. W. (1992). Women, work, and alcohol: Failures of simple theories. *Alcoholism: Clinical and Experimental Research, 16,* 172–179.

Wilsnack, S. C., Wilsnack, R. W., & Klassen, A. D. (1984). Women's drinking and drinking problems: Patterns from a 1981 national survey. *American Journal of Public Health, 74,* 1231–1238.

Wilson, G. T. (1987). Chemical aversion conditioning as a treatment for alcoholism: A re-analysis. *Behavior Research and Therapy, 25,* 503–515.

Wilson, G. T., & Lawson, D. M. (1978). Expectancies, alcohol, and sexual arousal in women. *Journal of Abnormal Psychology, 87,* 358–367.

Wilson, G. T., Lawson, D. M., & Abrams, D. B. (1978). Effects of alcohol on sexual arousal in male alcoholics. *Journal of Abnormal Psychology, 87*(6), 609–616.

Wilson, G. T., & Lawson, D. W. (1976a). The effects of alcohol on sexual arousal in women. *Journal of Abnormal Psychology, 85,* 489–497.

Wilson, G. T., & Lawson, D. W. (1976b). Expectancies, alcohol, and sexual arousal in male social drinkers. *Journal of Abnormal Psychology, 85,* 587–594.

Windle, M. (1997). Mate similarity, heavy substance use and family history of problem drinking among young adult women. *Journal of Studies on Alcohol, 58*(6), 573–580.

Windle, M., & Scheidt, D. M. (2004). Alcoholic subtypes: Are two sufficient? *Addiction, 99*(12), 1508–1519.

Windle, M., & Wiesner, M. (2004). Trajectories of marijuana use from adolescence to young adulthood: Predictors and outcomes. *Developmental Psychopathology, 16*(4), 1007–1027.

Windle, M., Windle, R. C., Scheidt, D. M., & Miller, G. B. (1995). Physical and sexual abuse and associated mental disorders among alcoholic inpatients. *American Journal of Psychiatry, 152*(9), 1322–1328.

Wing, G., Hofmann, F. G., & Woods, J. H. (2004). *A handbook on drug and alcohol abuse: The biomedical aspects* (4th ed.). New York: Oxford.

Winokur, G., Reich, T., Rimmer, J., & Pitts, F. N. (1970). Alcoholism III: Diagnosis and family psychiatric illness. *Archives of General Psychiatry, 23,* 104–111.

Wiseman, J. (1970). *Stations of the lost: The treatment of skid row alcoholics.* Englewood Cliffs, NJ: Prentice Hall.

Witkiewitz, K., & Marlatt, G. A. (2004). Relapse prevention for alcohol and drug problems: That was Zen, this is Tao. *American Psychologist, 59*(4), 224–235.

Witkiewitz, K., van der Maas, H. L., Hufford, M. R., & Marlatt, G. A. (2007). Nonnormality and divergence in posttreatment alcohol use: Reexamining the Project MATCH data "another way." *Journal of Abnormal Psychology, 116*(2), 378–394.

Wolchik, S. A., Braver, S. L., & Jensen, K. (1985). Volunteer bias in erotica research: Effects of intrusiveness of measure and sexual background. *Archives of Sexual Behavior, 14,* 93–107.

Wolff, P. (1972). Ethnic differences in alcohol sensitivity. *Science, 125,* 449–451.

The women's petition against coffee. (1674). London. Available from http://www.gopetition.com/famous-petitions-in-history/232/the-women-s-petition-against-coffee-1674.html

Wong, M. M., Klingle, R. S., & Price, R. K. (2004). Alcohol, tobacco, and other drug use among Asian American and Pacific Islander adolescents in California and Hawaii. *Addictive Behaviors, 29*(1), 127–141.

Wong, M. M., Nigg, J. T., Zucker, R. A., Puttler, L. I., Fitzgerald, H. E., Jester, J. M., et al. (2006). Behavioral control and resiliency in the onset of alcohol and illicit drug use: A prospective study from preschool to adolescence. *Child Development, 77*(4), 1016–1033.

Workman-Daniels, K. L., & Hesselbrock, V. M. (1987). Childhood problem behavior and neuropsychological functioning in persons at risk for alcoholism. *Journal of Studies on Alcohol, 48,* 187–193.

World Health Organization. (1978). *International classification of diseases, injuries, and causes of death* (9th rev.). Geneva, Switzerland: Author.

World Health Organization. (1990). *International classification of diseases and related health problems* (10th rev.). Geneva, Switzerland: Author.

Wright, D. M., & Heppner, P. P. (1991). Coping among nonclinical college-age children of alcoholics. *Journal of Counseling Psychology, 38,* 465–472.

Wright, D. M., & Heppner, P. P. (1993). Examining the well-being of nonclinical college students: Is knowledge of the presence of parental alcoholism useful? *Journal of Counseling Psychology, 40,* 324–334.

Wu, J., & Witkiewitz, K. (2008). Network support for drinking: An application of multiple groups growth mixture modeling to examine client-treatment matching. *Journal of Studies on Alcohol and Drugs, 69*(1), 21–29.

Yeomans, M. R., Ripley, T., Davies, L. H., Rusted, J. M., & Rogers, P. J. (2002). Effects of caffeine on performance and mood depend on the level of caffeine abstinence. *Psychopharmacology (Berl), 164*(3), 241–249.

York, J. L. (1995). Progression of alcohol consumption across the drinking career in alcoholics and social drinkers. *Journal of Studies on Alcohol, 56*(3), 328–336.

Yoshino, A., Kato, M., Takeuchi, M., Ono, Y., & Kitamura, T. (1994). Examination of the tridimensional personality hypothesis of alcoholism using empirically multivariate typology. *Alcoholism: Clinical and Experimental Research, 18*(5), 1121–1124.

Young, A., Grey, M., Abbey, A., Boyd, C. J., & McCabe, S. E. (2008). Alcohol-related sexual assault victimization among adolescents: Prevalence, characteristics, and correlates. *Journal of Studies on Alcohol and Drugs, 69*(1), 39–48.

Zakhari, S. (2006). Overview: How is alcohol metabolized by the body? *Alcohol Research and Health, 29*(4), 245–254.

Zamboanga, B. L., Raffaelli, M., & Horton, N. J. (2006). Acculturation status and heavy alcohol use among Mexican American college students: Investigating the moderating role of gender. *Addictive Behaviors, 31*(12), 2188–2198.

Zeiner, A., & Paredes, A. (1978). Differential biological sensitivity to ethanol as a predictor of alcohol abuse. In D. Smith (Ed.), *Multi-cultural view of drug abuse* (pp. 591–599). Cambridge, MA: Schenkman Publishing.

Zemore, S. E. (2007a). Acculturation and alcohol among Latino adults in the United States: A comprehensive review. *Alcoholism: Clinical and Experimental Research, 31*(12), 1968–1990.

Zemore, S. E. (2007b). A role for spiritual change in the benefits of 12-step involvement. *Alcoholism: Clinical and Experimental Research, 31*(Suppl. 10), 76s–79s.

Zhou, Q., King, K. M., & Chassin, L. (2006). The roles of familial alcoholism and adolescent family harmony in young adults' substance dependence disorders: Mediated and moderated relations. *Journal of Abnormal Psychology, 115*(2), 320–331.

Zimring, F. E., & Hawkins, G. (1992). *The search for rational drug control.* Cambridge, UK: Cambridge University Press.

Zucker, R. A. (1987). The four alcoholisms: A developmental account of the etiologic process. In P. C. Rivers (Ed.), *Alcohol and addictive behavior: Vol. 34. Nebraska Symposium on Motivation* (pp. 27–83). Lincoln: University of Nebraska Press.

Zucker, R. A., Donovan, J. E., Masten, A. S., Mattson, M. E., & Moss, H. B. (2008). Early developmental processes and the continuity of risk for underage drinking and problem drinking. *Pediatrics, 121*(Suppl. 4), S252–S272.

Zucker, R. A., & Ellis, D. A. (1996). The development of alcoholic subtypes: Risk variation among alcoholic families during the early childhood years. *Alcohol Health & Research World, 20*, 46–55.

Zumoff, B. (1997). Editorial: The critical role of alcohol consumption in determining the risk of breast cancer with postmenopausal estrogen administration. *Journal of Clinical Endocrinology & Metabolism, 82*(1656–1657).

Zwerling, C. (1993). Current practice and experience in drug and alcohol testing in the workplace. *Bulletin of Narcotics, 45*(2), 155–196.

Zywiak, W. H., Stout, R. L., Trefry, W. B., Glasser, I., Connors, G. J., Maisto, S. A., et al. (2006). Alcohol relapse repetition, gender, and predictive validity. *Journal of Substance Abuse Treatment, 30*(4), 349–353.

Author Index

Subject Index

About the Author

John Jung, a professor of psychology emeritus at California State University, Long Beach, received his PhD in experimental psychology from Northwestern University in 1962. He has authored several textbooks on memory, motivation, research methods, and ethical issues of psychological research with humans and has published numerous research articles on memory, social support, alcohol use, and health psychology. For 25 years, he directed the Career Opportunities in Research program for mentoring minority students to pursue doctoral training in psychology with a grant from the National Institute of Mental Health. He was faculty research coordinator for 10 years for the McNair Scholars Program funded by the U.S. Department of Education to increase representation of low-income first-generation college students in various majors pursuing doctoral degrees. He directed a program funded by the National Institute of Mental Health for 5 years to mentor young faculty researchers in obtaining research grants to study minority mental health disparities.

Supporting researchers for more than 40 years

Research methods have always been at the core of SAGE's publishing program. Founder Sara Miller McCune published SAGE's first methods book, *Public Policy Evaluation*, in 1970. Soon after, she launched the *Quantitative Applications in the Social Sciences* series—affectionately known as the "little green books."

Always at the forefront of developing and supporting new approaches in methods, SAGE published early groundbreaking texts and journals in the fields of qualitative methods and evaluation.

Today, more than 40 years and two million little green books later, SAGE continues to push the boundaries with a growing list of more than 1,200 research methods books, journals, and reference works across the social, behavioral, and health sciences. Its imprints—Pine Forge Press, home of innovative textbooks in sociology, and Corwin, publisher of PreK–12 resources for teachers and administrators—broaden SAGE's range of offerings in methods. SAGE further extended its impact in 2008 when it acquired CQ Press and its best-selling and highly respected political science research methods list.

From qualitative, quantitative, and mixed methods to evaluation, SAGE is the essential resource for academics and practitioners looking for the latest methods by leading scholars.

For more information, visit **www.sagepub.com**.